THE OXFORD HANDBOOK OF

RELIGION AND AMERICAN EDUCATION

THE OXFORD HANDBOOK OF

RELIGION AND AMERICAN EDUCATION

Edited by

MICHAEL D. WAGGONER

and

NATHAN C. WALKER

Foreword by

MARTIN E. MARTY

OXFORD

UNIVERSITY PRESS

OXFORD
UNIVERSITY PRESS

Oxford University Press is a department of the University of Oxford. It furthers
the University's objective of excellence in research, scholarship, and education
by publishing worldwide. Oxford is a registered trade mark of Oxford University
Press in the UK and certain other countries.

Published in the United States of America by Oxford University Press
198 Madison Avenue, New York, NY 10016, United States of America.

CIP data is on file at the Library of Congress
ISBN 978-0-19-938681-9

1 3 5 7 9 8 6 4 2

Printed by Sheridan Books, Inc., United States of America

www.ohrae.org

We dedicate this book to
Brendan W. Randall (b. 1966–d. 2017),
a scholar, colleague, and friend.

Contents

PART V RELIGION AND HIGHER EDUCATION

FOREWORD

....

MARTIN E. MARTY

ASTONISHMENT would likely characterize the response of Americans who are casual about religion if they come across a book as weighty as is this one, especially when they note that "religion and education" is the focus. Most of them are at least dimly aware that most local congregations of Protestants support Sunday Schools or other part-time educational institutions. If they are Catholics or know Catholicism, they will be aware of parochial schools as the main instrument for teaching children the essentials of Christian faith and practice through the high school years. Every Jewish center will employ a counterpart to these Christian institutions for education on the Sabbath. If readers should browse in a handbook like this, that astonishment would no doubt deepen. "Religion and Education" is a major and complex enterprise.

Awe would likely characterize the response of educators, teachers, tutors, and mentors among the less-casual participants in religious activities. They would read on after browsing to be directed at the end of each chapter to "future directions" and, more, to be referred to "references" that support the authors of chapters. They would also allow those in their acquaintance, especially those in professions responsible for such education, to become more aware, involved, informed, and inspired about the situations and resources, but also to take part in the enterprises of religious education.

Astonished and awed as we picture them becoming, we can also picture that several stereotypical or caricatured forms and expressions of religious education will have been challenged and replaced. For example, they will find full attention given to advanced academic endeavors. Among these are graduate schools of religion that are peers of those devoted to professions like law and medicine or to the liberal arts. To know that education on this level goes on is one thing, but knowing how to pursue such teaching, research, and learning in general demands specialized approaches, many of which are outlined on the pages that follow.

As awareness grows about opportunities and challenges at such levels, there will also be reason for the no-longer-casual observer or participant in religion-and-education to make new sense out of secondary education when it makes headlines or at least causes confusion and acrimony in immediate local communities. Citizens who place a high premium on religion and education bring intensity to the extremes of "pro" and "con" sides on the subject. Whoever doubts this is invited to visit school board meetings where holidays, greetings, and customs appeal to some elements of a community but are opposed by others. The records of the US Supreme Court decisions on "school prayer," "religious expressions in school ceremonies," and the presence of symbols such as the Christian cross give evidence of the need for light and the presence of heat in local controversies relating to any and all of these.

Controversy and bewilderment on the higher levels of education raise complex issues relating to the youngest students, because parents of various religious faiths or non-faiths care greatly about what is taught and practiced beginning at the kindergarten level. Here alternatives to public education or private religious education in complex communities abound, typically in homeschooling movements and expressions. This does not mean that religious education is something about which only parents disagree: religious professionals are puzzled, faith factions of diverse sorts differ from each other, and educators in public schools face problems related to personal identity.

Whether informed or not, sophisticated or otherwise, adult Americans find good reason to use the schools, public and religious alike, as arenas where valuable experiments will and should occur. This is true in no small measure because of the presence of pluralism with its many faces. The particularities of American life are infusers of the religious and spiritual elements in much education as well as the agents of religious indifference, hostility, or calculated passivity. Many ask, why not let public and charter and religious schools go about their business without interference by religious voices? Why not let the civic officials and the courts monitor what goes on in public and private schools alike?

Even in such situations, educators need assistance of the sort this handbook seeks to provide. Back up, some might say: let the often-invoked "Founding Fathers" of this nation and the major educators have the final word, and we will depend on their counsel. Not so fast, the veterans and experts will say. They will note that the attitudes people bring to religion in civil spheres are based in profound commitments to the teachings and practices of diverse, often competing, and sometimes warring sectors of the public. Rereading the writings of those Founders who tried to set the terms for living in a republic, not only in its religious dimensions, does not solve everything, as, again, the record of conflict in and during and over US Supreme Court records makes clear. One historian finally threw in the figurative towel with a judgment: the Founding Fathers solved the religious problem in the United States by *not* solving the religious problem.

Differences over education are complicated because beliefs and policies, as this book demonstrates, have many different sources and colorations. Regional differences count for much. The public understandings of and about religion find expression in, say, Utah, with its significant Latter-Day Saints populations, but vastly different ones in Boston or the Bronx, in Deep South Mobile, or counties in the Northeast where Jews are strongly represented. This handbook is written by educational veterans and experts who are aware of all this, but in most cases greet the situation as one of opportunity, not disaster.

From the first chapter on, one word or concept colors much of what follows: *choice.* In the previous centuries, where almost universally one religion was established by law, as it was in most countries that fed populations into the United States, the opportunity to choose approaches and concepts was both a luxury and a necessity. Fundamental to the issue of religious choice, as Jonathon Kahn makes clear, is the light or shadow thrown on religious education by the secular, secularization, and kin form of that verbal construct. Philosophers, politicians, and parents experience secularization in its many forms, all of which color choices about religious education. Recognizing the power of "the secular" or secularization is one thing; defining it is another, as many chapters in this book evidence.

The attempt to render education as being simply (simply?) a secular venture does not solve pedagogical policies or do justice to the presence and power of religious forces, which, the courts and citizenries agree, cannot be the only or even the main determiners of what goes on in the schools. Some of the authors here discuss the problem of providing moral bases in a republic if the secular voice is given the microphone and the secular approach given the yardstick. Sometimes the chapter authors put energy into the issue of character formation, which necessarily goes on in every school. How is this executed if religion, traditionally a major agent in character building, is absent?

Not only character is at issue. The student often has a question to deal with before speaking or acting, and not just "what shall I do?" but "who am I, and to what and whom do I belong?" For that reason, one of the key concepts that has to be addressed (and is, in this handbook) is *identity*. Benjamin Marcus treats this with a "Three Bs" framework: belief, behavior, and belonging. Religion and religions have much to say about all three, and they demand and deserve treatment of the sort they receive in this book.

As this foreword calls attention to pluralism and its dimensions in six "frameworks" chapters that we have regarded as providers of structure for many of the inquiries, the editors also remind us that many matters of "religion and American education" are not contained only in civic contexts. There is a larger and even more complex "out there" that deserves and, in this book, receives helpful treatment. The editors chose Sharon Daloz Parks to "begin at the beginning," by speaking of religious *faith* and, specifically, of "faith development," which has not been the assigned topic to the first six "frameworks" authors but inevitably grows as children grow in learning.

If the discussion of faith moves us readers beyond civic and structural issues, so it is with *morals* and moral education, which is needed but is always problematic, as Larry Nucci and Robyn Ilten-Gee regard it as they focus on the very young learners. They may be young, but much that belongs to religious education is very old and exists coded as "tradition." Mark A. Hicks reaches back into the traditions that haunt or inspire religious education. These traditions of faith and moral teaching are not confined to isolated religious communities. Eboo Patel and Noah J. Silverman carry the topic further by referring to "interfaith education," watching how this developed and how it faces change and provides innovative forms for reducing conflict and promoting understanding.

Most intimate among educational institutions, of course, are homes. "Homeschooling" has its historical roots in "oppositional" agencies whose leaders are often suspicious of inherited outside-the-home educational agencies. Another invention by and among those critical of conventional public school policies, particularly in funding, is the "charter school." Charter schools are not necessarily "oppositional," but they definitely are "alternative," and they raise issues of "church-and-state" combinations, which were explored in an earlier chapter. How did charter schools make their case, since they are not simply "public," though much of their funding is? All the chapters in this section illustrate how educational invention produces forms that challenge and, one hopes, may improve public education.

After visiting that intimate scene, the authors deal with the larger environment again, focusing on the legal-debate background to public funding of private religious schools by tracing the history and implications of a "no-funding rule," which is anything but settled and static. Public school issues, in this case as in others, come down to the debates over the law. John Witte, Jr. is the recognized expert on what all this means for law, which informs, is arbiter among, and polices mainly public school life. He and Brian Kaufman launch a sequence of historically detailed instances and problems.

The space given to introductions and forewords in books like this has to be limited, but they can also inspire readers and users of such a reference work to project directions. So our object from this point on is to point to what is ahead for them. "Religious Expression in Public Schools" by Kevin R. Pregent and Nathan C. Walker is another chapter whose subject produces debate about boundaries. What is ruled out and encouraged in here are issues with which, again, school boards must deal while unofficial individuals and groups want to, and do, express themselves, often creatively and sometimes obstructively. While much expression in public schools is ceremonial and symbolic, controversies over what to treat in respect to religion, and how to treat it, is most complex when a curriculum has to be developed. For instance, Walter Feinberg concentrates on the place of the Bible, given its role in American public and individual cases, but he also recognizes that "world religions" deserve and demand treatment. So powerful has the Bible been in American life that it cannot be avoided when educators aspire to help prepare students for experiences after they are awarded diplomas.

When I read these chapters for the first time my first impulse, in my "astonishment" and "awed" stages of response, was to say that the editors "thought of everything." That reaction was the response from someone whose personal religion-in-education can be a distant memory. One asks: "Now we've covered the subject?"

Then I turn the page and confront, in Charles J. Russo's chapter, what we picture most readers are highly aware of, coded as "extracurricular" activities and facilities. That topic only opens the door to other "worlds" in American education, a door that beckons not only educators but citizens of all sorts. It is not my assignment to present digests of these or argue with them. Who could resist arguing, as so many points of view are given a hearing or a reading?

But I began introducing this volume by speaking of being "astonished" and "awed," so I hope readers will also be astonished and awed as they are putting this handbook to work, and keeping it in play.

M.E.M.

Martin E. Marty, Fairfax M. Cone Distinguished Service
Professor Emeritus at the University of Chicago

Contributors

Daniel O. Aleshire served as the executive director of the Association of Theological Schools in the United States and Canada (ATS) from 1998 to 2017, having served on the staff of the Association since 1990. Previously, he was on the faculty of the Southern Baptist Theological Seminary and a research scientist at Search Institute in Minneapolis, Minnesota. An ordained minister, Aleshire holds a BS degree from Belmont University, the MDiv degree from the Southern Baptist Theological Seminary, and an MA and PhD in psychology from George Peabody College for Teachers (now Peabody College of Vanderbilt University). Aleshire has written on issues of ministry, theological education, Christian spirituality, and Christian education. He was part of a team of four researchers who conducted a three-year, in-depth ethnographic study of two theological schools, which was published as *Being There: Culture and Formation in Two Theological Seminaries* (Oxford University Press, 1997). It received the 1998 Distinguished Book Award from the Society for the Scientific Study of Religion. His most recent book, *Earthen Vessels: Hopeful Reflections on the Work and Future of Theological Schools*, was published in 2008 (Eerdmans Press). He has served on various boards or committees of organizations that oversee the nongovernmental recognition of accrediting agencies, most recently the Council on Higher Education Accreditation. He has also served as a member of the board of the Forum for Theological Exploration, the Advisory Committee for the Auburn Center for the Study of Theological Education, and advisory committees for various research projects related to theological education.

Janet Bordelon is the senior editor for the Institute of Curriculum Services in San Francisco, California. Her research focused on church-state issues in American history.

Mark A. Chancey is professor of Religious Studies in Dedman College of Humanities and Sciences at Southern Methodist University in Dallas, Texas. His most recent books are *Alexander to Constantine: Archaeology of the Land of the Bible* (Yale University Press, 2012), co-authored with Eric M. Meyers, and *The Bible in the Public Square: Its Enduring Influence in American Life* (SBL Press, 2014), co-edited with Carol Meyers and Eric M. Meyers. His four reports for the Austin-based watchdog group Texas Freedom Network and related journal articles have helped draw attention to academic, constitutional, and political aspects of Bible courses. He is a member of the editorial boards of *Religion & Education* and the Journal of the American Academy of Religion and chair of the Society of Biblical Literature's Educational Resources and Review Committee.

Susan L. Douglass is the education outreach coordinator for the Center for Contemporary Arab Studies at the School of Foreign Service at Georgetown University. She received her PhD in world history at George Mason University in 2016, and has an MA in Arab Studies from Georgetown University and a BA in History from the University of Rochester. Dr. Douglass has developed the education outreach program for the Alwaleed bin Talal Center for Muslim-Christian Understanding at Georgetown University in 2007, served as senior researcher for the United Nations Alliance of Civilizations, and managed several grant projects for the Ali Vurak Ak Center for Global Islamic Studies at George Mason University. She has contributed to curriculum projects such as *World History for Us All* and *Children and Youth in History*, and she has designed and developed online teaching resources such as *The Indian Ocean in World History* and *Our Shared Past in the Mediterranean*. Douglass' major publications include *World Eras: Rise and Spread of Islam, 622–1500* (Thompson/Gale, 2002), the children's book *Ramadan* (Carolrhoda Books, 2002), and the national study *Teaching About Religion in National and State Social Studies Standards* (Freedom Forum First Amendment Center and Council on Islamic Education, 2000).

Diana L. Eck is a professor of Comparative Religion and Indian Studies and the Frederic Wertham Professor of Law and Psychiatry in Society at Harvard University. Her academic work has a dual focus—India and America—and in both cases she is interested in the challenges of religious pluralism in a multireligious society. Her work on India includes the books *Banaras: City of Light, Darsan: Seeing the Divine Image in India*, and *India: A Sacred Geography*. Since 1991, she has headed the Pluralism Project, which now includes a network of some sixty affiliates exploring the religious dimensions of America's new immigration; the growth of Hindu, Buddhist, Sikh, Jain, and Zoroastrian communities in the United States; and the issues of religious pluralism and American civil society. Her works on religious diversity and interfaith include the books *A New Religious America: How A "Christian Country" Has Become the World's Most Religiously Diverse Nation* and *Encountering God: A Spiritual Journey from Bozeman to Banaras*. The later won the Grawemeyer Book Award in 1995. Prof. Eck received the National Humanities Medal from President Clinton and the National Endowment for the Humanities in 1996, the Montana Governor's Humanities Award in 2003, and the Melcher Lifetime Achievement Award from the Unitarian Universalist Association in 2003. At Harvard University, Prof. Eck has served as Chair of the Committee on the Study of Religion and of the Department of Sanskrit and Indian Studies as it made the transition to the Department of South Asian Studies. She is also a member of the faculty of Divinity. In 2012, Prof. Eck was named to a Harvard College Professorship in recognition of excellence in undergraduate teaching.

Walter Feinberg is professor emeritus of Education Policy, Organization and Leadership at the University of Illinois Urbana-Champaign. His research centers on the issue of education for democratic citizenship. Dr. Feinberg earned his PhD in Philosophy from Boston University. He served as the Charles Dun Hardie Professor of Educational Policy Studies at the University of Illinois and as director of the Program for the Study of Cultural Values and Ethics. A past president of the Philosophy of Education Society and the American Educational Studies Association, Feinberg's many books include *For Goodness Sake: Religious Schools and Education for Democratic Citizenry* (Routledge, 2006) and *Religious Education in Liberal Democratic Societies* (Oxford, 2003).

Milton Gaither is Professor of Education at Messiah College and founding member and co-director of the International Center for Home Education Research. He is the author of *History of American Education* (San Diego, CA: Bridgepoint Education, 2012); *Homeschool: An American History* (New York, NY: Palgrave MacMillan, 2008); and *American Educational History Revisited: A Critique of Progress* (New York, NY: Teachers College Press, 2003).

Eugene V. Gallagher is the Rosemary Park Professor of Religious Studies at Connecticut College. He regularly teaches courses on globalization and religion, the Western scriptural tradition, religions in the United States, new religious movements, and theories of religion. He is the author of *Divine Man or Magician? Celsus and Origen on Jesus, Expectation and Experience: Explaining Religious Conversion, Why Waco? Cults and the Battle for Religious Freedom in America* (with James D. Tabor), *The New Religious Movements Experience in America,* and *Reading and Writing Scripture in New Religious Movements: New Bibles and New Revelations,* and many essays on ancient Mediterranean religions and new religious movements. He has written essays on teaching for *Teaching Theology and Religion, Religion and Education, Spotlight on Teaching, To Improve the Academy,* and *Essays in Teaching Excellence.* He is currently co-General Editor of *Nova Religio: The Journal of Alternative and Emergent Religions* and Associate Editor of *Teaching Theology and Religion.*

Michael Galligan-Stierle, president of the Association of Catholic Colleges and Universities (ACCU), has over forty years of experience in higher education and various ministerial settings. The primary focus of his work has been in higher education and ministry with young adults as a campus minister, a religious studies professor, a seminary instructor, and a graduate ministry internship director. His 1996 book *The Gospel on Campus* is viewed as a standard for Catholic campus ministry in the United States. His book *Promising Practices: Collaboration Among Catholic Bishops and University Presidents* highlights proven ways that bishops, diocesan agencies, and Catholic colleges and universities collaborate. Michael holds a PhD in Sacred Scripture, an MA in Psychology, and an MA in Theology.

Steven K. Green is the Fred H. Paulus Professor of Law, affiliated professor of History, and director of the Center for Religion, Law and Democracy at Willamette University in Salem, Oregon. He is the author of *Inventing a Christian America* (Oxford University Press, 2015), *The Bible, the School, and the Constitution: The Clash that Shaped Modern Church-State Doctrine* (Oxford University Press, 2012), *The Second Disestablishment: Church and State in Nineteenth-Century America* (Oxford University Press, 2010), co-author of *Religious Freedom and the Supreme Court* (Baylor University Press, 2008), and author of more than forty book chapters and articles on church and state. He has also participated as co-counsel in three Supreme Court cases and filed more than twenty friend-of-the-court briefs at the high court.

Charles C. Haynes is founding director of the Religious Freedom Center of the Freedom Forum Institute, and a senior scholar at the First Amendment Center of the Freedom Forum Institute. He writes and speaks extensively on religious liberty and religion in American public life. Haynes is best known for his work on First Amendment issues in public schools. Over the past two decades, he has been the principal organizer and drafter of consensus guidelines on religious liberty in schools, endorsed by a broad range of religious and educational organizations. In January 2000, three of the guides were distributed by the US Department of Education to every public school in the nation ("A Parent's Guide to Religion in the Public Schools," "A Teacher's Guide to Religion in the Public Schools," and "Public Schools & Religious Communities"). Haynes is the author or co-author of six books, including *First Freedoms: A Documentary History of First Amendment Rights in America* and *Religion in American Public Life: Living with Our Deepest Differences*. His column, *Inside the First Amendment*, appears in newspapers nationwide. He is a founding board member of Character.org, and serves on the steering committee of the Campaign for the Civic Mission of Schools. He chairs the Committee on Religious Liberty, founded by the National Council of Churches. Widely quoted in news magazines and major newspapers, Haynes is also a frequent guest on television and radio. He has been profiled in *The Wall Street Journal* and on ABC's "Evening News." In 2008, he received the Virginia First Freedom Award from the Council for America's First Freedom. Haynes holds a master's degree from Harvard Divinity School and a doctorate from Emory University.

Mark A. Hicks is the Angus MacLean Professor of Religious Education at Meadville Lombard Theological School and director of the Fahs Collaborative, A Laboratory for Innovation in Faith Formation. He holds a doctorate in philosophy and education and a master's degree in higher and adult education, both from Teachers College, Columbia University, New York City. His scholarship and teaching have been recognized by peers for "Teaching Excellence" as well as making "contributions that stand the test of time" to the field of transformative teaching and research. His scholarship has appeared in journals such as *The Journal of Transformative Education, Multicultural Perspectives*, and *Educational Studies* and the first edition of *The Handbook of Research on the Social Foundations of Education*. As a curriculum developer, Dr. Hicks' work creates "aesthetic spaces" wherein participants can break through what John Dewey called "the crust of conventionalism" in order to find new ways of thinking and being. These ideas can be experienced in the Unitarian Universalist Association's *Tapestry of Faith* curriculum, *Building the World We Dream About*; the Fahs Collaborative Classroom's *Beloved Conversations: Meditations on Race and Ethnicity*; and the UU Ministry for Earth's ecojustice curriculum, *Our Place in the Web of Life*, with Pamela Sparr.

Robyn Ilten-Gee is a doctoral student in Human Development and Education at the University of California, Berkeley. She has worked as a journalism instructor and reporter with Youth Radio. Her current research is on adolescents' moral reasoning about adversity and conflict through multimodal storytelling. Her interests include exploring ways to use children's media and literature to facilitate moral development and critical discourse.

Douglas Jacobsen (PhD, University of Chicago) is distinguished professor of Church History and Theology at Messiah College in Grantham, Pennsylvania. His books include *Thinking in the Spirit: Theologies of the Early Pentecostal Movement* (2003), *Gracious Christianity* (2006), *The World's Christians* (2011), and *Global Gospel: An Introduction to Christianity on Five Continents* (2015).

Rhonda Hustedt Jacobsen (EdD, Temple University) is director of Faculty Development and Professor of Psychology at Messiah College in Grantham, Pennsylvania. Together, Jake and Rhonda co-direct the Religion in the Academy Project, a major research initiative examining the educational effects of religion and religious diversity. They have published three books with Oxford University Press: *Scholarship and Christian Faith: Enlarging the Conversation* (2004); *The American University in a Postsecular Age* (2008), winner of the Lilly Fellows Book Award; and *No Longer Invisible: Religion in University Education* (2012), winner of a Critics Choice Award from the American Educational Studies Association.

Jonathon S. Kahn is associate professor of Religion, and a member of American Studies, at Vassar College. He teaches in the areas of religion and modern philosophy, with a special interest in the intersection of religion, race, ethics, and politics. He was one of the co-founders of the workshop "Reconceiving the Secular Liberal Arts," sponsored by the Teagle Foundation. His writing about that workshop appears on the website "The Immanent Frame." He is the author of *Divine Discontent: The Religious Imagination of W. E. B. Du Bois* (Oxford University Press, 2009) and he is the co-editor of *Race and Secularism in America* (Columbia University Press, 2016).

Brian Kaufman is a civil rights lawyer practicing in Washington, DC. He joined the American Constitution Society for Law and Policy in September 2016 and currently serves as the Assistant Director of Lawyer Chapters. In this capacity, Brian works with over forty lawyer chapters across the country, supporting their growth and development in furtherance of actualizing ACS's mission of shaping law and policy to be instruments of social justice for all individuals and communities. Brian completed his undergraduate at degree at Boston College in 2006 with majors in International Studies and Theology. In 2007, Brian completed his Master of Arts in Theology, also at Boston College, with a focus on Catholic theological ethics and social justice. Prior to beginning his legal studies at Emory University School of Law in 2014, Brian studied, lived, and worked in Paris for four years. At Emory Law, Brian served as the vice president of External Affairs of Emory OUTLaw, an organization dedicated to diversity awareness, networking, and the legal issues affecting the LGBT community. During his third year of law school, Brian revived the ACS Emory Law Student Law Chapter and served as one of the co-presidents. Prior to joining ACS, Brian worked for the National Center for

Lesbian Rights as a Policy Law Fellow, focusing on NCLR's #BornPerfect Campaign, the campaign to protect LGBT youth from the dangerous and discredited practices of conversion therapy through legislation, litigation, and public education. Originally from the New York City area, Brian is passionate about spirituality, education, LGBT legal topics, and Baptiste yoga.

Emile Lester is an associate professor in the Department of Political Science and International Affairs at the University of Mary Washington. His book *Teaching Religions: A Democratic Approach for Public Schools* (University of Michigan Press, 2011) was based in part on his research report *Learning About World Religions in Public Schools* (First Amendment Center, 2006). The report and book have been featured in various media outlets, including *The New York Times, The Washington Post, USA Today,* National Public Radio, and C-SPAN, among other media outlets. The First Amendment Center and Wesley Theological Seminary hosted a special forum on the book at the Newseum in Washington, DC. In 2014, Prof. Lester's review of seven proposed textbooks for US Government Grade 12 courses in Texas entitled *A Triumph of Ideology Over Ideas* was published by the Texas Freedom Network. He testified before the Texas State Board of Education. The review received extensive media coverage, and led publishers to make significant revisions in textbooks that enhanced their historical accuracy and balance. His numerous articles on various topics in political science and related to religion and politics have appeared in a variety of scholarly journals, including *The Review of Politics, Polity, Journal of Church and State, Politics and Religion,* and *Public Affairs Quarterly.* He has also written for the prestigious public affairs journal *The American Interest* and the esteemed education magazine *Phi Delta Kappan.* Prof. Lester is working on a book examining political thought and American presidents, focusing on Franklin D. Roosevelt and John F. Kennedy.

Jennifer A. Lindholm is assistant vice provost in UCLA's division of undergraduate education. In that capacity, she is responsible for coordinating campus-wide initiatives associated with enhancing teaching and learning, addressing accreditation-related considerations, and facilitating student success. Before joining the division, she served from 2001 to 2006 as associate director of the Cooperative Institutional Research Program at UCLA's Higher Education Research Institute and as director of the institute's Triennial National Faculty Survey. During that period, Jennifer also held a joint appointment as visiting professor of higher education and organizational change in UCLA's Graduate School of Education & Information Studies. She also served as director and co-investigator for the decade-long (2001–2011) Spirituality in Higher Education project and co-authored *Cultivating the Spirit: How College Can Enhance Students' Inner Lives* (Jossey-Bass, 2011). Jennifer's most recent book is *The Quest for Meaning and Wholeness: Spiritual and Religious Connections in the Lives of College Faculty* (Jossey-Bass, 2014). Her other research and writing focuses on the structural and cultural dimensions of academic work; the career development, work experiences, and professional behavior of college and university faculty; issues related to institutional change; and undergraduate student development. Jennifer also works as a consultant to colleges and universities on topics related to her areas of research and administrative expertise.

Benjamin P. Marcus is the Religious Literacy Specialist with the Religious Freedom Center of the Freedom Forum Institute, where he examines the intersection of education, religious literacy, and identity formation in the United States. He has developed religious literacy programs for public schools, universities, U.S. government organizations, and private foundations, and he has delivered presentations on religion at universities and nonprofits in the U.S. and abroad. Marcus is a Fulbright Specialist, where he shares his expertise on religion and education with select host institutions abroad. Marcus chaired the writing group for the Religious Studies Companion Document to the C3 Framework, a nationally recognized set of guidelines used by state and school district curriculum experts for social studies standards and curriculum development. He earned an MTS with a concentration in Religion, Ethics, and Politics as a Presidential Scholar at Harvard Divinity School. He studied religion at the University of Cambridge and Brown University, where he graduated magna cum laude.

Martin E. Marty is the Fairfax M. Cone Distinguished Service Professor Emeritus of the History of Modern Christianity in the Divinity School where he taught for 35 years in the Divinity School, the Department of History, and the Committee on the History of Culture. He focused chiefly on late eighteenth and twentieth century American religious history in the context of "Atlantic Culture." His six-year "*Fundamentalism Project*" for the American Academy of Arts and Sciences (1988–1994) led him to enlarge his focus to global interreligious concerns. Author of over fifty books, Marty has written the three-volume *Modern American Religion* (University of Chicago Press). Other books are *The One and the Many: America's Search for the Common Good; Education, Religion and the Common Good and Politics, Religion and the Common Good; Dietrich Bonhoeffer's Letters and Papers from Prison: A Biography;* and his *Righteous Empire* won the National Book Award.

Paula Moore, associate vice president of the Association of Catholic Colleges and Universities, has overseen all communications for the association, including its marketing, publications, website, and media relations, since joining the staff in 2011. She had previously been at the American Council on Education for eleven years, serving most recently as its director of publishing. There, Moore oversaw the organization's publications and worked on promoting and branding the association. She directed its trademark and copyright program, instituting an intellectual property protection program. Prior to 2000, Moore worked as a magazine and trade press writer and editor for more than a decade. She was a finalist in 1996 for the Jesse H. Neal Awards, the most prestigious editorial honors in the field of specialized journalism.

Robert J. Nash has been a professor in the College of Education and Social Services, University of Vermont, Burlington, for forty-eight years. He specializes in philosophy of education, applied ethics, higher education administration, scholarly personal narrative writing, and religion, spirituality, and education. He has graduate degrees in English, Religious Studies, Applied Ethics and Liberal Studies, and Educational Philosophy. He holds a faculty appointment in the Department of Leadership and Developmental Sciences. He is the founder and director of the graduate degree in Interdisciplinary Studies in Education and the co-founder of the Higher Education and Student Affairs Program (HESA).

Adina C. Newman is a doctoral candidate in Educational Administration and Policy Studies at the George Washington University. Her research focuses on the implications of teaching about religion to upper elementary and middle school students in public education. She was nominated and selected to be a participant at the 2016 David L. Clark National Graduate Student Research Seminar in K-12 Educational Administration and Policy. Her experience spans over a decade in both the Jewish and secular education sectors as an administrator, consultant, content developer, and educator.

Larry Nucci is adjunct professor of Human Development and Education at the University of California, Berkeley, and professor emeritus of Educational Psychology at the University of Illinois at Chicago. He is the author/editor of seven books including *Education in the Moral Domain* (Cambridge, 2001), *Nice is Not Enough: Facilitating Moral Development* (Pearson, 2009), and the *Handbook of Moral and Character Education* (with Darcia Narvaez and Tobias Krettenauer; Routledge, 2014). He is the editor in chief of the journal *Human Development*.

Erik Owens is associate director of the Boisi Center and associate professor of the practice in theology and international studies at Boston College. His research explores a variety of intersections between religion and public life, with particular attention to the challenge of fostering the common good of a religiously diverse society. He is the co-editor of three books: *Gambling: Mapping the American Moral Landscape* (2009), *Religion and the Death Penalty: A Call for Reckoning* (2004), and *The Sacred and the Sovereign: Religion and International Politics* (2003), the last of which was called a "must read" by *Foreign Affairs* in 2009. At the American Academy of Religion, he chairs the Committee on the Public Understanding of Religion and leads its Public Scholars Project. He received his PhD in religious ethics from the University of Chicago, an MTS from Harvard Divinity School, and a BA from Duke University.

Julie J. Park is assistant professor of education at the University of Maryland, College Park. Her research addresses race, diversity, and equity in higher education, with a special focus on Asian-American college students. A recipient of the Promising Scholar/Early Career Award from the Association for the Study of Higher Education, she is the author of *When Diversity Drops: Race, Religion, and Affirmative Action in Higher Education* (Rutgers University Press, 2013), an examination of how a campus religious organization was affected by shifting demographic conditions following a state ban on affirmative action. Her work on religion examines the intersection between race and religion in campus communities, as well as the role of religion in shaping educational opportunity for communities of color. She sits on the editorial review board for the *Journal of Higher Education* and is also a research advisory board member for the National Commission on Asian American and Pacific Islander Research in Education and the Interfaith Diversity

Experiences and Attitudes Longitudinal Survey. Besides being widely published in academic journals, her writing has also been featured in venues such as the *Huffington Post, The Chronicle of Higher Education,* and *The Washington Post.* Dr. Park received her BA from Vanderbilt University and her PhD from the University of California, Los Angeles.

Sharon Daloz Parks, senior fellow at the Whidbey Institute and principal, *Leadership for the New Commons,* is a teacher, theorist, and author. Her undergraduate and master's degrees are from Whitworth University and Princeton Theological Seminary. Her doctorate from Harvard University focused on theology and human development. Subsequently, for sixteen years she held faculty and research positions at Harvard Divinity School, Harvard Business School, and Harvard's Kennedy School of Government. She has taught also at the Weston Jesuit School of Theology and Seattle University. Her publications include *Leadership Can Be Taught: A Bold Approach for a Complex World; Big Questions, Worthy Dreams: Mentoring Emerging Adults in Their Search for Meaning, Purpose and Faith;* and co-authored, *Common Fire: Leading Lives of Commitment in a Complex World.* She speaks and consults nationally. She is a member of the Religious Society of Friends (Quakers).

Eboo Patel is the founder and president of Interfaith Youth Core, a Chicago-based organization building the interfaith movement on college campuses. Author of the books *Acts of Faith* (2007), which won the Louisville Grawemeyer Award in Religion, *Sacred Ground* (2012), and *Interfaith Leadership: A Primer* (2006), Patel is a regular contributor to *The Washington Post, USA Today, Huffington Post,* National Public Radio, and CNN. He served on President Obama's inaugural Advisory Council of the White House Office of Faith-Based and Neighborhood Partnerships and holds a doctorate in the sociology of religion from Oxford University, where he studied on a Rhodes scholarship. He has taught courses on interfaith cooperation at many institutions, including the University of Chicago, Princeton Theological Seminary, Northwestern University, and Dominican University in Illinois, where he was the Lund-Gill Chair. Patel delivered the Greeley Lecture at Harvard University Divinity School and a series of lectures at Union Theological Seminary, where he served as a visiting distinguished guest lecturer during the 2012–2013 academic year.

Kevin R. Pregent, originally from central New York, is an instructor at the Religious Freedom Center of the Freedom Forum Institute in Washington, DC, where he previously served as a law and religion fellow. He received his BA from the University of Delaware and is in his final year of a JD degree program at Vanderbilt University Law School. He is a contributing author to *Religion in American Education: A Legal Encyclopedia* (Rowman & Littlefield).

Brendan W. Randall (b. 1966–d. 2017), to whom this book is dedicated, was a senior consultant for Interfaith Youth Core, a nonprofit organization devoted to working with higher education to promote interfaith cooperation as a social norm, and an advanced doctoral candidate at the Harvard Graduate School of Education, where his work focused on religious diversity and civic education. Mr. Randall was a former case study fellow and senior research associate for the Pluralism Project as well as a teaching fellow for Prof. Eck's case-study course on religious diversity in the United States. Mr. Randall had extensive experience researching, writing, and teaching case studies. One of his last publications included a co-authored chapter in the forthcoming book *Teaching Interreligious Encounters* entitled "The Case Study Method as a Means of Teaching About Pluralism" as well as an article in the *Journal of Inter-Religious Studies* entitled "Diana Eck's Concept of Pluralism as a Norm for Civic Education in a Religiously Diverse Democracy."

P. Jesse Rine is clinical associate professor and director of the M.S. program in higher education administration at Duquesne University. Previously he served as assistant provost at his alma mater, Grove City College (BA in Christian Thought), and directed the research programs of two national higher education associations in Washington, DC, the Council of Independent Colleges and the Council for Christian Colleges & Universities. Rine is a graduate of the Curry School of Education at the University of Virginia, where he earned his PhD in Higher Education with an emphasis in Social Foundations of Education. He also holds an MAT degree in Latin from Washington University in St. Louis. Rine is the recipient of the 2012 Outstanding Dissertation Award presented by the Religion & Education Special Interest Group of the American Educational Research Association.

Alyssa N. Rockenbach is a professor of higher education at North Carolina State University. Her research focuses on the impact of college on students, with particular attention to spiritual development, religious and worldview diversity in colleges and universities, campus climate, community service engagement, and gendered dimensions of the college student experience. Her current work includes a grant-funded initiative, the Interfaith Diversity Experiences and Attitudes Longitudinal Survey (IDEALS) in partnership with Dr. Matt Mayhew at Ohio State University and Interfaith Youth Core. In addition, she co-authored with colleagues the third volume of *How College Affects Students: 21st Century Evidence that Higher Education Works*. Dr. Rockenbach serves on the editorial boards of *Research in Higher Education* and *Journal of Higher Education*, and has been honored with national awards, including the American College Personnel Association Emerging Scholar Award, the Annuit Coeptis Emerging Professional Award, and the American Educational Research Association Religion & Education SIG Emerging Scholar Award. She teaches master's and doctoral courses related to research methods, quantitative analysis, and foundations of the higher education and student affairs profession. Dr. Rockenbach earned her PhD in Higher Education from the University of California, Los Angeles and her BA in Psychology from California State University, Long Beach.

Charles J. Russo, JD, EdD, is the Joseph Panzer Chair in Education in the School of Education and Health Services, director of its PhD Program, and adjunct professor in the School of Law at the University of Dayton. The 1998–99 President of the Education Law Association, and 2002 recipient of its McGhehey (Achievement) Award, he has authored or co-authored more than 260 articles in peer-reviewed journals and authored, co-authored, edited, or co-edited 57 books, and more than 950 publications.

Dr. Russo also speaks extensively on issues in Education Law in the United States and other nations. Along with having spoken in thirty-four states and twenty-six nations on all six inhabited continents, Russo taught summer courses in England, Spain, and Thailand. He has also served as a visiting professor at Queensland University of Technology in Brisbane and the University of Newcastle, Australia; the University of Sarajevo, Bosnia and Herzegovina; South East European University, Macedonia; the Potchefstroom Campus of Northwest University in Potchefstroom, South Africa; the University of Malaya in Kuala Lumpur, Malaysia; the University of Sao Paulo, Brazil; Yeditepe University in Istanbul, Turkey; Inner Mongolia University for the Nationalities in Tongliao, Inner Mongolia; and in both Peking University and Beijing Normal University in Beijing, China. He received a PhD Honoris Causa from Potchefstroom University, now the Potchefstroom Campus of Northwest University, in Potchefstroom, South Africa, in May 2004, for his contributions to the field of Education Law.

John A. Schmalzbauer teaches in the Department of Religious Studies at Missouri State University, where he holds the Blanche Gorman Strong Chair in Protestant Studies. He is the author of *People of Faith: Religious Conviction in American Journalism and Higher Education* (Cornell University Press, 2003). He served as co-investigator with Betty DeBerg on the National Study of Campus Ministries. Recent publications include chapters for *The New Evangelical Social Engagement* (Oxford, 2013) and *The Post-Secular in Question* (NYU Press, 2012).

Noah J. Silverman serves as senior director of learning and partnerships at Interfaith Youth Core (IFYC), a Chicago-based organization working to help build the interfaith movement on college campuses. He holds an MA in religious studies from New York University and has been involved in interfaith work for over fifteen years on three continents. Prior to rejoining IFYC in 2013, he served as the associate director of multifaith education at Auburn Theological Seminary in New York City, where he directed the international, interfaith teen-leadership program "Face to Face / Faith to Faith." He has worked for Religions for Peace at the United Nations, the Parliament of the World's Religions in Barcelona, the Interfaith Encounter Association and the Seeds of Peace Center for Coexistence in Jerusalem, and the Tony Blair Faith Foundation in London, in addition to consulting with Hillel, the JCC Association, and dozens of colleges and universities. Along with colleagues at IFYC, he has written numerous articles and chapters on the methodology of interfaith cooperation and the growing academic field of interfaith studies.

Kate E. Soules, is a curriculum specialist and instructor at the Religious Freedom Center of the Freedom Forum Institute. She is a PhD candidate, an educator, and researcher with a focus on teachers' religious literacy and preparation for religiously diverse schools. She is currently a doctoral student working on Curriculum and Instruction at the Lynch School of Education at Boston College. She has conducted original research with both pre-service and in-service teachers regarding their preparation to teach about religion.

Michael D. Waggoner, PhD, is professor of Education at the University of Northern Iowa, where he teaches in the Postsecondary Education: Student Affairs graduate program. His principal scholarly interests center on religion and spirituality in education. He is in his eighteenth year serving as editor for the peer-reviewed journal *Religion & Education*. He is also editor of the book series "Research in Religion and Education" for Routledge Books. He is a past chair of the Religion and Education Special Interest Group of the American Educational Research Association and is co-chair of the Religion in the Public Schools: International Perspectives Group of the American Academy of Religion. He is an invited member of the International Seminar on Religious Education and Values, an association of 240 scholars from thirty-six countries who study religion and education. His most recent books are *Sacred and Secular Tensions in Higher Education* (Routledge, 2011) and *Religion in the Public Schools: Negotiating the New Commons* (Rowman and Littlefield, 2013).

Nathan C. Walker is the executive director of 1791 Delegates, a consortium of constitutional and human rights experts who consult on issues of religion and public life. Walker is the author of *Cultivating Empathy: The Worth and Dignity of Every Person—Without Exception* (Skinner House Press, 2016) and *Exorcising Preaching: Crafting Intellectually Honest Worship* (Chalice Press, 2014). He is the co-editor with Edwin J. Greenlee of *Whose God Rules? Is the United States a Secular Nation or a Theolegal Democracy?* (Palgrave MacMillan, 2011). He is a contributing author to *The Oxford Encyclopedia of Politics and Religion*, edited by Paul Djupe (Oxford University Press, 2019); *Religion in American Education: A Legal Encyclopedia*, edited by Charles J. Russo (Rowman & Littlefield, 2019); and co-author with Lyal S. Sunga of *Promoting and Protecting the Universal Right to Freedom of Religion or Belief through Law* (International Development Law Organization, 2017). Formerly a resident fellow in law and religion at Harvard Divinity School, Walker received his doctorate in law, education, and religion from Columbia University, where he received his Master of Arts and Master of Education degrees. He received his Master of Divinity degree from Union Theological Seminary and is an ordained Unitarian Universalist minister. His website is www.ReligionAndPubliclife.com.

John Witte, Jr. (JD, Harvard; Dr. Theol. h.c., Heidelberg) is Robert W. Woodruff Professor of Law, McDonald Distinguished Professor, and director of the Center for the Study of Law and Religion at Emory University. A specialist in legal history, marriage law, and religious liberty, he has published over 250 articles, sixteen journal symposia, and thirty books. Prof. Witte's writings have appeared in fifteen languages, and he has delivered more than 350 public lectures throughout North America, Europe, Japan, Israel, Hong Kong, South Korea, Australia, and South Africa. With major funding from the Pew, Ford, Lilly, Luce, and McDonald foundations, he has directed fourteen major international projects on democracy, human rights, and religious liberty; on marriage, family, and children; and on law and Christianity. He edits "Emory University Studies in Law and Religion" (Eerdmans) and "Cambridge Law and Christianity Series" (Cambridge University Press), and co-edits *The Journal of Law and Religion*. He has been selected twelve times by the Emory law students as the most outstanding professor and has won dozens of other awards and prizes for his teaching and research.

INTRODUCTION

MICHAEL D. WAGGONER AND NATHAN C. WALKER

RELIGION has been inextricably entwined with education in the United States since the days of colonial British America. Beginning with mothers schooling their children at home from the Bible to the first establishment of Harvard College in 1636 with the principal mission to prepare clergy, the place of religion—and more to the point, whose religion and for what purpose—has been vigorously contested for nearly 400 years. This handbook aims to examine the current state of religion and American education from homeschooling to private religious schools to public schools to religious institutions and on through the range of public and private higher education. The book is organized into five sections: Frameworks; Lifespan Faith Development; Faith-Based K-12 education; Religion and Public Schools; and Religion and Higher Education. Within these sections forty leading scholars in the field of religion and education review these topics in thirty chapters.

PART I. FRAMEWORKS

The first unit is designed to expose readers from a variety of disciplines to frameworks that inform the study of religion and education: privatism, secularism, pluralism, religious literacy, religious liberty, and democracy. Rather than stereotypes of ideological perspectives, these chapters are designed to provide a sympathetic summary of schools of thought.

Privatism, as we understand it, was born over the great school battles over the nineteenth and twentieth centuries, resulting in the segregation of sectarian education. Historically, this has resulted in various political and legal issues associated with government funding and regulation of faith-based schooling, a term used to encompass both private religious institutions and homeschools. These themes are explored by Janet Bordelon in Chapter 1 on privatism. Secularism, on the other hand, is a conceptual frame often used to explain how privatism originated as a response to the policy agenda of "neutrality" in public schools, which Jonathon S. Kahn explores in chapter 2. Critics claim it is either an extension of a Protestant bias or a hostile state agenda to guarantee freedom *from* religion, but secularism need not be characterized as antireligious. Privatism and secularism have dominated many research agendas in the twentieth century, whereas the third framework, pluralism, is currently shaping the future direction of the field.

Pluralism advances the idea that freedom *of* religion is a constitutional guarantee and a fundamental human right. Unlike the self-selection process of privatism that can lead religious groups to segregate themselves from civil society, and unlike the legal agenda of secularism that can lead to government hostility toward private religious practices, pluralism argues that in one of the most religiously diverse countries in the world, the public square and public schools must serve as holding grounds for citizens to engage one another's differences. Pluralism is not simply a synonym for diversity; as Diana L. Eck and Brendan W. Randall note in Chapter 3, diversity is the evidence of difference, whereas pluralism is the engagement in that difference; pluralism is not religious relativism but an expression of individaul committments. One way to achieve this goal is for public schools to adopt the policy agenda that religious literacy is a compelling state interest, meaning that governments of pluralist democracies require graduates of public schools to demonstrate knowledge of religions and how religion manifests in people's lives. This is essential if students are to understand how various religious traditions use distinct sources of authority to govern their own communities and how individuals who affiliate with those religions may use those same sources differently to inform their own participation in a democracy. In this way, the state seeks not to banish religion from the public arena, but rather to treat the government as one arena in which citizens gain understanding about one another's differences, including religious ones. Understanding is neither endorsement, nor advancement, nor exclusion of religion. Aware that the United States is one of the most religiously diverse nations in the world, pluralists argue that the purpose of public schools is to strengthen democracy through increased knowledge of and engagement with one another, including citizens' religious diversity. Pluralism can be threatening to those with exclusive claims on religious truth, and offensive to those with secularist agendas. As a result, those who advance privatism often choose to support faith-based education and reject a state that can perpetuate "religious relativism". Likewise, secularists can be suspect of religion's inculcation in public schools and view pluralism as an incremental religious conversion of civil society, leading policymakers to ban religious expression from public schools. The consequence of both of these frameworks is segregated school systems—private religious schools in one sphere and public secular schools in another. Although imperfect, pluralism seeks to be a remedy for a bifurcated system that replicates inequity, arguing that we have more in common than what we may believe.

These three frameworks lay the landscape for the contributors and editors to explicitly problematize the stereotypes associated with these schools of thought. Moreover, these frameworks set the stage for a larger discussion about the role that education, and in particular the study of religion, can play in preparing students to be engaged and informed citizens in a pluralist democracy. In this context, we turn to Benjamin P. Marcus in Chapter 4 for an examination of the ways that American education can promote religious literacy as a fundamental civic competency. He examines what students need to know about religion and draws upon the writings of Diane L. Moore, who argues that there are three "central assertions about religions . . . (1) religions are internally diverse as opposed to uniform; (2) religions evolve and change over time as opposed to being ahistorical and static; (3) religious influences are embedded in all dimensions of culture as opposed to the assumption that religions function in discrete, isolated, 'private' contexts" (www.rlp.hds.harvard.edu). Marcus integrates this methodology into his examination of how people and communities engage in religious identity formation, with special attention to beliefs, behaviors, and acts of belonging.

In this context, Charles C. Haynes argues in Chapter 5 that religious literacy is a prerequisite for building and maintaining what leaders in the field refer to as "First Amendment schools," institutions that promote religious liberty for people of all religions and none. His chapter builds upon his previous collaborations with Warren Nord, where they affirmed schools that were "taking religion seriously across the curriculum." In Chapter 6, Emile Lester examines the framework of democracy, the idea that academic study *about* religion can serve as a democratic approach for public schools. Ideologically distinct from historical culture wars and religious infighting, the democratization of the study of religion offers American education the opportunity to advance a deeper understanding about one another's beliefs, aware that understanding need not imply agreement. To achieve this goal, students must develop religious literacy as a civic competency, as part of a public school's commitment to cultivating an informed democracy.

These implications, regardless of whether seen through the lens of privatism, secularism, and pluralism or whether by promoting religious literacy, religious liberty, or democratic education, have significant implications for civil society. American education is poised to address this crisis through systematic reforms in the public and private sectors, as demonstrated in the following units.

PART II. LIFESPAN FAITH DEVELOPMENT

Part II surveys the various ways that three institutions—the family, religion, and the state—can contribute to the moral, intellectual, and faith development of learners across their lifespans. Chapter 7, by Sharon Daloz Parks, and Chapter 8, by Larry Nucci and Robyn Ilten-Gee, review the state of interdisciplinary work on faith, moral, and character development. In Chapter 9, Mark A. Hicks surveys the various ways that faith communities are designing their lifespan religious education programs. The final chapter in this section, by Eboo Patel and Noah J. Silverman, explores the contemporary trend of religious communities to intentionally expose their adherents to neighboring faiths. As a formal extension of their own religious education, these interfaith programs are designed not only to advance the moral competency of self-differentiation, but also to deepen one's understanding of one's own religion's beliefs and practices. This unit sets the stage for an analysis in Part III of the purpose and nature of religiously affiliated schools in the United States, which are distinct from that of the purpose and nature of public schools (Part IV).

Part III. Faith-Based K-12 Education

This unit on faith-based education surveys the various pedagogical, political, and legal issues associated with homeschooling, private religious schools, and religiously affiliated charter schools.

In Chapter 11, Charles J. Russo, Kate E. Soules, Adina C. Newman, and Susan L. Douglass address sectarian education, focusing on the origins and effects of various types of private religious schools in the United States, with particular attention to Catholic, Protestant, Jewish, and Islamic schools. The chapter surveys the political and legal conflicts associated with the school choice movement at the state and federal levels and the pedagogical and democratic effects of faith-based schooling.

Milton Gaither, in Chapter 12 on homeschooling, illustrates how after becoming nearly extinct by the mid-twentieth century, parent-led home-based education has rebounded to serve over 2 million students in the United States today. The chapter surveys the motivations of proponents of faith-based homeschooling, such as claiming that "the public school is the functional equivalent of an established church," as well as the critiques of groups like the National Education Association that express concerns about the educational practices of religious fundamentalist families.

The final chapter in this unit, by Steven K. Green, focuses on the various legal battles that have derived from conflicts associated with public funding of private schools. Those issues include tuition vouchers and tax credits, transportation, textbooks, testing, and remedial services. These political landmines lay the foundation for a larger discussion about the intersection of religion and public schools in the subsequent unit, which is distinct from that of "religious education" in private settings.

Part IV. Religion and Public Schools

Public schools have proven to be the primary locus for the major church-versus-state battles in the United States. These legal issues can be classified into five areas in which the state tends to regulate religion in public schools: charter schools, religious expression, curricula, extracurricular activities, religious displays, and access to facilities. In

Chapter 14, Nathan C. Walker discusses religiously affiliated charter schools, examining the blurring of church-state and public-private funding of charter schools that affiliate themselves, either formally or informally, with particular religious groups. Beginning in Minnesota in 1991, the charter school movement originated from the tension found in parental dissatisfaction with public schools and the inability to afford private schools. This chapter examines the various ways that Catholic, Protestant, Jewish, and Islamic groups have used the charter school movement to institutionalize public-sponsored, faith-based education, leading to a series of constitutional challenges. In Chapter 15 John Witte, Jr. and Brian Kaufman review the overarching legal and political issues associated with religion in public schools. In Chapter 16, on religious expression, Kevin R. Pregent and Nathan C. Walker survey the legal issues associated with state-mandated Bible readings, prayers and moments of silence, and the recitation of the Pledge of Allegiance. Additional subjects include regulation of religious garb and insignia worn by students and teachers and accommodations given to religious students for religious expression, such as prayer rooms and excused attendance for observing religious holidays. Together, these chapters survey the legal issues around public schools featuring religious icons, imagery, or messages on school grounds, such as the Ten Commandments, the nativity scene, or religious symbols.

In Chapter 17 Walter Feinberg addresses curricular issues, making the legal distinction between teaching religion and teaching about religion, with focus on three academic disciplines: science, social studies, and physical education. A longstanding debate is whether science curricula should include teaching creationism or Intelligent Design instead of, or in parallel with, teaching evolution. Social studies curricula have become controversial when school boards have added explicit religious doctrine while eliminating terms like "separation between Church and state" and banning references to Thomas Jefferson, who introduced in 1802 the phrase now popular in the American lexicon. In regard to physical education curricula, a court recently determined that yoga may be taught in public schools even though critics express concerns about its Hindu origins. An overarching theme in these three debates is the difference between teaching religion and teaching about religion, the latter being a legitimate legal practice for the last fifty years. As a result, some school districts have approved elective courses about world religions and the Bible as literature. In Chapter 18, Mark A. Chancey reviews the place of the Bible in schools over the history of the United States. The primary question remains: How can public school teachers be adequately trained on how to teach such courses without falling into the political and legal pitfalls of entangling religion with public schools?

Charles J. Russo, in Chapter 19, examines the legal complications deriving from religious groups using public school facilities for worship. Specific attention is given to whether public schools engage in viewpoint discrimination by denying particular religious groups access to public facilities after school hours. A related topic is whether state universities are required to grant equal access to state funding of voluntary religious clubs, in particular if those clubs do not abide by the regent's general nondiscrimination policies.

In Chapter 20, Erik Owens covers the ways that a diversity of actors are working to achieve common ground in all the aforementioned subjects.

The primary purpose of this unit is to examine the main research areas associated with religion and K-12 public schools in the United States. This content sets the stage for the final unit, on religion and postsecondary education.

PART V. RELIGION AND HIGHER EDUCATION

Religious liberty and freedom of conscience contended with religious orthodoxy to shape higher education in colonial British America. Colleges proliferated on through the founding of the United States and into the national expansion of its first half-century. These institutions also began a differentiation and further expansion that would increase in pace through the industrial and scientific revolutions that swept the country over the ensuing century. Religion remained a central idea through this period, though its place in institutional norms and ethos varied as institutions reacted differently to theological, scientific, and social challenges.

This unit addresses the current state of American higher education as it has evolved from these beginnings, examining the place of religion within and across each of its sectors. The section is divided into two parts. The first part addresses institutional responses. Chapter 21, by Douglas and Rhonda Jacobsen, and Chapter 22, by P. Jesse Rine, focus on Protestant higher education as segmented along mainline and evangelical institutional lines. The Roman Catholic tradition interpreted its Christian mission in yet another manner and is treated by Michael Galligan-Stierle and Paula Moore in Chapter 23. In Chapter 24 Michael Waggoner turns the analysis to public colleges and universities, by far the largest sector of American higher education. These institutions are constrained by the US Constitution to maintain a neutral stance toward religion, yet a wide range of religious activity occurs on these campuses, ranging from formal instruction across disciplines to informal organizations at work in clubs and residence halls. In the final chapter of this first section Daniel O. Aleshire reviews the state of education in theological institutions, such as seminaries, divinity schools, and schools of theology. They derive from the earliest colleges, and part of the history of American higher education may be understood through their evolution.

The second part of this unit focuses on particular segments of the higher education enterprise that cut across institutional types. In Chapter 26, Alyssa Bryant Rockenbach and Julie J. Park address college students' stances toward religion and spirituality and what that may mean for teaching, learning, and attitudes toward civic life. College and university faculty and their attitudes and characteristics regarding religion and spirituality are the subject of Jennifer A. Lindholm's Chapter 27. The formal teaching of religious studies and theology is addressed in Chapter 28 by Eugene V. Gallagher, while in Chapter 29, Robert J. Nash discusses teaching about religion in the disciplines outside of religious studies. The book concludes with Chapter 30 by John A. Schmalzbauer on campus ministry as it exists in different forms from public to private higher education.

CONCLUSION

Religion in the public life of the United States continues to be a source of celebration and consternation. As the most religiously diverse country in the world, the United States offers successful examples of weaving a variety of religious and spiritual traditions into the warp and woof of a predominantly Christian democratic society. At the same time, a number of citizens feel threatened by religious difference: some fear displacement of what they feel is their rightful dominant heritage, while others feel that their viewpoints meet with discrimination from a majority religion, despite constitutional guarantees to their free expression and equal protection. The future of religion in American education depends upon a commitment by all citizens to learn about and to respect differences, including religion, recognizing them as a source of strength of our democracy. The *Oxford Handbook of Religion and American Education* aims to contribute toward that end.

PART I

FRAMEWORKS

CHAPTER 1

RELIGION, PRIVATIZATION, AND AMERICAN EDUCATIONAL POLICY

JANET BORDELON

INTRODUCTION

I attended my first school choice rally in 2012 at a Jewish Orthodox day school, the Robert M. Beren Academy in Houston, Texas. Houston boasts a growing Orthodox community thanks to a lower cost of living, coupled with the key ingredients necessary for Modern Orthodox Jewish living: day schools, Orthodox synagogues, *eruv* enclosures, kosher eateries, and *mikvah* ritual baths (Heiman 2012).

Hundreds of parents and students filled the auditorium for this rally in support of school choice. With a strong Brooklyn accent, the school's rabbi jumped onto the stage and fired up the crowd by asking: "Who's a proud American? Who's a proud Texan?!" The crowd cheered, and the rabbi continued: "We proud Americans like having choice . . . this is what democracy is all about. We choose our profession, how we lead our lives, what brand to buy at the supermarket, so why shouldn't we as Jews be able to choose our education and not decide between food or day school tuition?"

My evangelical father was with me and had never met an Orthodox Jew. He looked painfully confused and asked, "Are these people Jewish? They sound like Republicans to me."

Many of the people at the rally probably did hold Republican values, and I was not surprised by that. The more pressing question in my mind was this: Why would a Jewish school hold a school choice rally to advocate public funds going into their private religious entity? Wasn't this a blatant violation of the principle of separation of church and state, a principle that historically protected the American Jewish Congress from discrimination? Even more baffling was the fact that they were joined at this rally by not only Catholics but also evangelicals who have traditionally opposed government funds being used to support private schools. The main speaker was current Texas Lt. Governor Dan Patrick, who at that time was spearheading a campaign for tax credits as the chair of the Texas State Senate Educational Committee. Any student of US history would know that until fairly recently in our nation's history, this sort of collaboration would have been considered to be a rather "unholy alliance."

The purpose of this chapter is to explore how members of these religious groups came to support the use of government funds for religious schools and what ramifications this growing school choice lobby has on US educational policy.

Education Privatization: The Wave of the Future

Starting in the Reagan era, a neoliberal agenda began to influence the educational realm, dictating that the market is the ultimate arbiter of social worthiness. Cost efficiency and the cost/benefit ratio are considered to be the engines of both social and educational transformation. And according to Professor Michael Apple, this is happening on a broader scale:

> Democracy is no longer a political concept; rather, it is wholly an economic concept in which unattached individuals—supposedly making rational choices in an unfettered market—will ultimately lead to a better society . . . Not only does this fly in the face of a very long tradition of collective understandings of democracy in the United States, but it also has led to the destruction of many communities, jobs, health care, and so many other institutions. (Apple 2005, 209)

Various policy initiatives have emerged aimed at creating closer links between education and the economy or placing schools themselves into the market. High-stakes testing, public choice, and charter schools are some of the most significant and influential innovations thus far. Charter schools are public schools because they receive public funding but operate independently of the established public school system (see Chapter 14 in this volume). Growing in popularity and influence are school choice initiatives for private schools, particularly after Donald Trump became president and appointed school choice advocate Betsy DeVos as Secretary of Education. The current vehicles for transferring funds to private schools are vouchers and tax credits. Vouchers, also referred to as "opportunity scholarships," are state-funded scholarships that pay students to attend private school rather than public school. These can be low-income students who meet a specified income threshold, students attending chronically low-performing schools, students with disabilities, or students in military families or foster care. Fourteen states offer scholarship tax credit programs. These programs allow individuals and corporations to allocate a portion of the state taxes they owe to private, nonprofit, scholarship-granting organizations that issue scholarships to K-12 students. As a result of this credit, the state does not have to appropriate per-pupil education funding for students who receive scholarships.

According to the Friedman Foundation for Educational Choice, one of the leading lobbying groups for school choice initiatives for private schools, in 2014 roughly $1.233 billion was spent on tuition for approximately 337,000 students to attend private schools. Each student, on average, received approximately $3,660 in funding; however, funding levels differ from program to program and for different groups of students. Schools participating in 20 different voucher programs received approximately $716 million. Schools participating in 17 different tax-credit scholarship programs received approximately $505 million.

The money doesn't stop there. Funding for private religious schools can come from the following sources: security grants, reimbursement for government-imposed mandates, special education services, in-kind support (health care, textbooks, and technology), free transportation for all students, and energy efficiency rebates and grants. In states like New York, private schools receive millions each year through the following programs: Century Community Learning Centers, Learning Technology Grant Program, Mandated Services Aid, Comprehensive Attendance Policy, and the Academic Intervention for Nonpublic Schools.

The growing impact of the school choice lobby is evidenced by recent court decisions and legislation favoring a variety of forms of aid for religious schools (see *Arizona Christian School Tuition Organization v. Winn*, 131 S. Ct. 1436 (2011); *Zelman v. Simmons-Harris*, 536 U.S. 639 (2002); and *Mitchell v. Helms*, 530 U.S. 793 (2000)). Arguments favoring public support for private religious schooling are gaining intellectual force and weight in the realm of educational policy. The historical trends and shifting legal precedents surrounding these developments merit further study by educational policymakers and scholars.

All Those in Favor, Say "Pluralism"

The phrase "school choice" has been in use in some form since the 1960s. Simply put, school choice allows parents to choose where their child is educated, but this concept is more complex than it seems. There are many demands on the public sector to balance the prerogatives of parents and students with regard to education. Viewed in a historical, political, and sociological context, the debate over school choice is not really about choice but rather about control—over public money, group identity, and the role of religion in educational policy.

Proponents of using government funds for private schools root their arguments in two concepts: (1) parents have a right to educate their children and (2) state aid is a duty based on distributive justice and should not be limited to the economically privileged. They believe that private schools are essential for maintaining pluralism in American education. According to their reasoning, allowing for just public schools results in a monolithic, state-controlled unit that would fit all citizens into a single mold. While they recognize the legitimate role of the state in bringing about the common good of society, they believe that independent schools as well as state schools could meet the public purposes of compulsory education laws—for example, the development of young people to live and serve in a democracy. Proponents of government aid stress that equity requires governmental sharing of the private school's costs, since parents who send their children to private schools also, as taxpayers, help pay for tax-supported public schools. They also point out that private elementary and secondary schools provide legally required general subject curricula, which should be supported by taxpayer money (Kelman 1962).

Identity formation is also important to school choice advocates because the public schools are so secular. For some parents, forcing their children to learn about evolution or sex education in public schools violates their religious freedom. In fact, many of them argue that they are an embattled minority that needs protection from the majoritarian liberal secular order.

The Rise of the Catholic Parochial Aid Lobby

For much of our history as a country, the development of educational policy in America has reflected the religious and political interests of the white Anglo-Saxon Protestant (WASP) majority. Throughout the colonial period and until 1850, the vast majority of schools were created and operated by religious organizations and civil institutions and funded by a combination of tuition, gifts, and tax dollars. As support for public funds grew, public funds were withdrawn from all but Protestant schools. Following Horace Mann's campaign for common schools, Americans embraced the public school concept. This was in part due to the WASPish attitude toward Catholic and Jewish immigrants in the late 19th and 20th centuries. Students in these schools had to say Protestant prayers and read Protestant Bible verses. Nativists were able to compel most states to adopt Blaine amendments, which made it illegal for public money to go to nonpublic schools—Catholic schools in particular (Green 2012).

Private schools were allowed to coexist with public schools, but there were a few instances when states tried to require all children to attend public schools in order to assimilate immigrants into a WASPish American ideal. In *Pierce v. Society of Sisters*, the Supreme Court ruled that the US Constitution protected the right of parents to choose private education for their children. The *Pierce* decision became the "Magna Carta of private education" (Erickson 1978, 291). But parents had to pay for this privilege, and many parents began to resent being taxed for education they weren't using.

Moderate state support for private schools would come in the 20th century. According to the *Cochran v. Board of Education* decision (281 U.S. 370 (1930)), state support for textbooks at private schools represented a "child benefit," and thus the use of tax monies was justified because the children and the state, rather than the school itself, were the beneficiaries. This opened up the possibility of government funding of alternative educational options, which, in turn, helped to create a forceful Catholic lobby in the National Catholic Welfare Conference and the US Conference of Catholic Bishops.

THE RISE OF THE JEWISH LOBBY

Unlike Catholics, Jews flocked in numbers to the public schools in order to be accepted into mainstream society and went to supplementary schools for their religious education. As the community gained more economic clout and cultural status, they fought hard to rid public schools of their WASPish ways and make them religiously neutral (Schoenfeld 1999, 62). The American Jewish Congress emerged as the key player in this regard and other political issues (a distinct group from the AJC, American Jewish Committee). Leo Pfeffer was at the forefront of this battle; like many Jews, he was concerned about maintaining a high wall of separation between religion and politics in order to protect religious minorities (Windmueller 2001).

In 1945, in addition to working on de-Christianizing public schools, Pfeffer and the American Jewish Congress joined with educational groups in an attempt to persuade Congress to pass federal funding for education. By the early 20th century, there was a strong desire to have federal funding for education because state and local funding was so uneven across the nation: some states, like Mississippi, allocated less funding per pupil than other states, like Massachusetts. But such legislation wasn't passed until 1965 because of two issues. The first dealt with parochial aid; there was no federal Blaine amendment, so theoretically funds could go toward religious schools at the federal level. The other issue was race: Southern legislatures feared that accepting federal funds would require desegregation. Pfeffer and teachers' unions lobbied against any bill giving support to parochial schools.

The Clark bill, which would offer federal aid to public and nonpublic schools, was introduced in the Senate in 1961 and represented the first public pronouncement of Jewish support for parochial aid and the first domestic political issues to formally divide the Jewish community. The story made the front page of the *New York Times*. In his testimony Rabbi Moses Sherer, president of Agudath Israel, said:

> We deplore that an incorrect image has been foisted upon the American public of the Jewish position on this issue, and that, as a result, a false impression has arisen of the Jewish posture towards religious education . . . It is our view that to deny these tax-paying American citizens of Orthodox Jewish faith the benefit of their taxes in order to help defray the large expense of maintaining the Jewish parochial school system for their children is a discrimination which is not in accordance with basic American values. (Morris 1961, 1)

The option of looking to government to aid education represented a reversal of the well-entrenched separationist ideology. Pfeffer, the leading spokesman for separationism, was an Orthodox Jew, a member of Young Israel, and the parent of children in day schools (Novack 1974). Starting in 1960, more and more modern Orthodox abandoned their opposition to government aid in hopes of obtaining funding—particularly since the 1960s saw increased governmental assistance to education and other sectors of society, and private schools sought to reap the benefit of public aid.

The most pressing concern for Orthodox Jewish lobbying groups was their opposition to sending their children to mixed-gender schools. They wholeheartedly believed that their constitutional right to religious practice trumped Establishment Clause concerns. They argued that they needed government support in particular because the Jewish community, through communal funding agencies called federations, was not financially supporting these institutions. Despite the fact that Orthodoxy at the turn of the 20th century represented the largest group of Jewish Americans numerically, its influence was hardly felt in the American Jewish Congress at large, as it lacked the economic resources and political clout to exert influence until the mid-20th century, when they fought alongside more mainstream Jewish organizations to eradicate Sunday "blue laws."

Orthodox Jews became empowered by Jewish intellectuals like Will Herberg and Milton Himmelfarb. Because of their dissatisfaction with the social consequences of liberalism, Jewish intellectuals like Herberg and Himmelfarb called into question the liberal, separationist impulse and began to stress that First Amendment protections were concerned not just with mere tensions between a religion and the majority culture, but with legal restrictions and impositions on religious activity. Such restrictions, they argued, raised the potential for persecution that could weaken minority religious groups rather than strengthening them, particularly when it came to religious observance and practice (Herberg 1992). As Herberg wrote, "Minorities must not be oppressed, but majorities have their rights as well as minorities . . . Some balance must be struck somewhere, but such a balance obviously cannot be a matter of 'principle,' nor can it be fixed or frozen in a constitutional provision" (Herberg, "Religious Education and General Education," cited in Cohen 1992, 179).

They argued instead for greater Jewish involvement in American political life and abandonment of the Jewish separationist agenda in favor of a more pro-religion stance. Attacking the notion of separation of church and state, conservative and moderate Jewish thinkers began to suggest a more nuanced historical understanding of the First Amendment. Himmelfarb argued:

> Separationism is potentially tyrannical. It is harsh to those who prefer nonpublic schools for conscience' sake; and it stands in the way of a more important good (and more important safeguard of Jewish security), the best possible education for

all . . . All the evidence points to education, more than anything else, influencing adherence to democracy and egalitarianism. All the evidence points to Catholic parochial education having the same influence . . . Something that nurtures a humane, liberal democracy is rather more important than twenty-four-karat separationism. (Himmelfarb, cited in Dalin 1993, 4–5)

Over the next few decades, more and more influential legal scholars, jurists, and academics began to call for a reassessment of the Jewish support of a strict separation of church and state, particularly with respect to the role of religion in public life and governmental aid to religious entities and its implications for religionists, especially religious minorities. David Novack went so far as to claim that:

With few exceptions those Jews who have been in the forefront of de-Christianizing America were people of minimal Jewish commitment, minimal Jewish knowledge, who I am convinced, in their hearts were really threatened by the fact that a Christian American required that Jews be more Jewish. . . . The real Jewish fascination with secularism as a doctrine in and of itself is precisely that it offers a way out of Judaism. (Novack 1974, 65–66)

Orthodox Jews were ultimately fighting to keep Jews within the fold. To maintain Orthodox levels of Jewish practice and commitment, they created day schools. Between 1940 and 1965, the number of these day schools grew from 35 to 323 and enrollment from 7,700 to 63,500 (Waxman 2004). Advocates stressed they had to argue for government money in particular because the larger Jewish community refused to allocate money to them. During the early 1960s, Jewish federations supported only 30 of the 274 day schools in existence. In 1963 in New York City, Dr. Jospeh Kaminetsky of Torah Umesorah estimated that the Federation of Jewish Philanthropies allocated only $750,000 to the Jewish Education Committee, of which only $50,000 went to 179 day schools with 39,000 pupils that were struggling with budgets aggregating $11 million (Spiegel 1963, 24).

Orthodox Jews considered it insulting that the mainstream Jewish community refused to support their schools. In addition to this, Orthodox leaders were tired of being spoken for, particularly by groups like the American Jewish Congress, which tended to look down on their political outlooks and lifestyles. The Orthodox, who had large families, a lower standard of living, and a strict level of Jewish observance, did not match their liberal version of what an American Jew should be. They privileged Jewish education over secular education, and it bothered those in the mainstream that many students did not come out of the day schools prepared to join the modernizing American workforce. At one debate, a female American Jewish Congress member threw a subway token at Rabbi Sherer, remarking, "I guess you must need this for your ride home. That's all the aid you will get from the Jewish community. It isn't my responsibility to support your religious choices" (letter from Sherer to Maslow, 1968).

The Coffers Are Open, and the Battle Ensues

The battle came to a head once federal funding was passed. The Elementary and Secondary Education Act (ESEA) was the first federal funding for schools, and it opened up several possibilities for parochial aid. ESEA's purpose was to help schools in need, so it catered to schools with a significant population of students from impoverished families, although 90% of school districts were technically eligible. Title I funds provided services to students in parochial schools through funds granted to the public school districts for secular subject and special education. The public districts also hired teachers for the parochial school students. Under Title II, the law appropriated funds to build up library and textbook resources for public and private schools. President Lyndon Johnson managed to get the bill passed in under three months, with very little debate, and many compromises were made. (Most of the aid came from Title I funds.) Parochial school funding advocates could accept that some of their schools would receive indirect aid through their students, while aid opponents could claim that it was the needy students who benefited and not the school. The bill had the support of most Protestant churches, the Catholic Church, the National Education Association, the labor unions, and Jewish organizations except the American Jewish Congress.

The day after Johnson signed the ESEA into law, the American Jewish Congress, and eventually the Committee for Public Education and Religious Liberty (PEARL), initiated a series of judicial campaigns to minimize the amount of ESEA money that would make its way to private schools. One study looking at amicus brief participation found the American Jewish Congress to be the most active group in First Amendment cases, filing over 50 briefs from 1953 to 2005 (Oates 2010). In the late 1960s and 1970s Pfeffer focused his litigation efforts through PEARL, making it "the centralizing force in church-state litigation," along with the American Jewish Congress and the American Civil Liberties Union (ACLU; Ivers 1995, 185).

This prompted the Orthodox to found the National Jewish Commission on Law and Public Affairs in 1965. Established to counter Pfeffer, it comprised primarily young Orthodox attorneys in New York and Washington, DC (Schick 2012). The commission filed 27 amicus briefs over the course of its tenure (Oates 2010). Along with powerful Catholic lobbies, Jewish groups on both sides grew significantly, both exhibiting a bolder and more experimental approach that, scholar Greg Ivers wrote,

> placed law and litigation at the center of a more cohesive systematic campaign on the part of these organizations to assert without apology their constitutional rights . . . religious conservatives were much more effective in lobbying elected officials at the federal and state levels to include parochial schools in their public expenditures on elementary and secondary education . . . [and] religious lobbies representing accomodationist Protestants, Catholics, Jews and other religions began to enter

church-state litigation . . . with impressive regularity as both a direct sponsor and friend of the Court. (1992, 775)

The battle would take place both in legislatures and the courts across the country. After ESEA was enacted, almost every state legislature considered school choice measures in some form. Beyond the courts, interest groups drummed up support for legislative measures across the country since a number of states increased programs of auxiliary services or inaugurated new ones.

Two Key Cases

Two key cases, *Allen v. Board of Education* and *Flast v. Cohen*, set the stage for an epic culture war that would divide the populace and the court for decades, given their contradictory rulings. *Flast* was especially significant because it allowed widespread taxpayer challenges to federal and state funding of schools. Access to the federal courts was severely restricted during this time: not only did the Supreme Court not entertain taxpayer suits, but many lower federal courts didn't either. Before ESEA, Pfeffer expressed reservations about taxpayer suits for fear that it would open the floodgates for crackpot suits with inadequate lawyers stalling the court system. But when the legal tides turned in favor of public funding for parochial schools, Pfeffer used judicial review to initiate a war on it.

Flast v. Cohen was key for the American Jewish Congress's campaign against parochial aid. As Pfeffer said, "If we lose this case, it will spell the beginning of the end of the American public school system" (internal memo from Pfeffer to staff, 1966). The plaintiff was Florence Flast, a colleague and strong supporter of Pfeffer. The question posed to the court was whether Flast, by virtue of her status as a taxpayer, had standing to challenge a statute because it violated the First Amendment. The judge for the Southern District of New York, Robert Morgenthau, put the matter before federal Judge Marvin Frankel, an American Jewish Congress member. Bypassing both district courts and courts of appeals, he put the case before a special three-judge court. That court dismissed the case, allowing Marvin Frankel to appeal to the US Supreme Court (392 U.S. 83 (1968)). Following *Flast*, the American Jewish Congress, PEARL, and the ACLU filed at least 20 lawsuits challenging the constitutionality of state subsidies to parochial and private schools.

Also in 1968, in *Allen v. Board of Education* the US Supreme Court upheld the 1930 *Cochran* ruling and decided that it was constitutional to use money for secular textbooks in private schools (392 U.S. 236, 248). This decision set an important but confusing precedent. It distinguished between the secular and religious goals of parochial schools, saying that these goals could be isolated from each other, and that providing textbooks to meet secular goals served a public purpose. In so doing, it also admitted that private schools provided public benefits, which gave parochial aid advocates an "in" for the future. Once the state admitted that private schools do provide public benefits, it became possible to consider state financial assistance for the portion of education that provides secular public benefits.

With these two contradictory decisions, the stage was set for a judicial showdown in the 1970s and beyond.

HIGH TIDE OF SEPARATIONISM

During the 1970s and 1980s, the courts were on Pfeffer's side—with some interesting and frustrating exceptions. Pfeffer and his allies were able to convince the courts throughout the late 1960s and 1970s to declare that all but paltry sums of aid to private schools were unconstitutional. Pfeffer was able to get most ESEA funds intended for low-income students in parochial schools blocked.

Many didn't understand why the American Jewish Congress would oppose funds going to private schools to help educationally deprived children. For those who attended them, parochial schools were considered to be bastions of safety, discipline, and learning in the midst of urban public schools that were increasingly unsafe. Terence Cardinal Cooke of the US Catholic Conference (successor to the National Catholic Welfare Conference) reported that 87% of the parents of parochial school children in New York City earned less than $10,000 a year, and one-third earned less than $5,000. In fact, one in ten parochial school students lived below the poverty level. Plus, in Manhattan, more than 60% of elementary students attending parochial school were black or Hispanic, countering claims by opponents to parochial aid that parochial schools enrolled low levels of minorities. At parochial schools in inner cities across the country, he reported, 40% of students were black or Hispanic (Statement of Terence Cardinal Cooke 1972).

During this period, people of all races and creeds who lived in the inner cities felt ignored and isolated, and the policies of the liberal leaders were not helping them as racial tensions worsened. Orthodox Jews and inner-city Catholics felt especially slighted by these developments. Many people left the cities for the suburbs, leaving behind public schools that lacked funding and resources to educate students adequately. Between 1970 and 1975, New York City lost 15.3% of its total, intact, white families. Eighty-nine percent of all minorities were living in the metropolitan area (Vituelle-Martin 1978). This greatly skewed the city's tax base, and as a result the city almost went bankrupt in 1975.

In many cities, schools helped to stabilize the population and facilitated neighborhood integration (Vituelle-Martin 1978). William Ball, a Catholic lawyer who argued all of the landmark parochial school aid cases, wrote of the diversity of Catholic schools and the good work they did for religious minorities, in particular. He claimed that although the parochial schools were primarily for the education of Catholic children, non-Catholic children were admitted as a matter of universal policy. He wrote:

> The record of Catholic schools generally with respect to Negro and other nonwhite children has been distinctly creditable. These schools have for the most part not been located according to de facto zoning which divides neighborhoods racially or

economically. Thus, the Catholic school has been an invaluable training ground to prepare citizens for full participation in a pluralist society (Ball 1967, 695).

ENTER THE MORAL MAJORITY: THE REAGAN ERA AND EDUCATIONAL PRIVATIZATION

The 1980s marked a new direction for government financing of private schools. The election of Republican President Ronald Reagan brought a shift toward accomodationism in jurisprudence and the larger American mindset. Reagan campaigned on the issue of school choice and tax credits, in particular. A 1981 editorial in *Christianity Today* applauded the "radical reordering of economic policies being championed" by Reagan because it presented the "church with a fresh opportunity to recover its lost role and rebuild its shriveled muscle" in "its function of caring for physical needs within the community" ("Public Aid and the Churches' Duties," 1981, 1415). As Reagan's Education Secretary William Bennett suggested after Reagan left office, Reagan "transformed the nation's education agenda" by shifting the focus of the debate to "standards, excellence, values, parental involvement and choice" (McAndrews 2006, 131).

During this decade, important legal precedents would be set that helped to usher in the current school choice initiatives. Although national school choice initiatives would fail, a conservative jurisprudence began to emerge, ultimately making school choice politically viable. Martha Minow argues that this change of direction was accomplished because parochial aid advocates reframed the issue of aid to religious schools in terms of "the allegation of discriminatory treatment—government exclusion from otherwise available public aid for schools," which placed the spotlight on the treatment of religious students. Doctrinally, it was "switching the focus from the Establishment Clause to concerns about governmentally imposed viewpoint discrimination under freedom of speech" (Minow 2011, 830).

This tactic solidified in the case of *Bob Jones v. United States*. During the administration of President Jimmy Carter, many private schools were threatened with a loss of their tax-exempt status due to low minority enrollments. The government tried to make them establish racial quotas. For evangelicals like Ralph Reed, this Internal Revenue Service (IRS) policy was "nothing less than a declaration of war on their schools, their churches, and their children" (Brint and Schroedel 2009, 8).

As Randall Balmer observes, the *Bob Jones* case motivated evangelicals to consider getting involved in other political activities, which led them to adopt the abortion issue as their main cause even though *Roe v. Wade* had been decided almost 10 years earlier (Balmer 2010, 14, 17. *See also* Balmer, 2006). With the growing number of evangelical Protestant schools, a more powerful coalition was able to lobby state legislatures and Congress (Lupu 1999, 375). Evangelical parents decided they could no longer in good conscience pay taxes to public schools that they felt were devoid of moral values. Scholar Joseph Crespino argues that the Religious Right saw the battle over IRS regulation of private Christian academies as a "Kulturkampf," a struggle against attempts by secular authorities to control and suppress religious institutions that would eventually reconfigure American politics in the 1980s and 1990s. Former religious enemies became political allies as conservative Protestants, Catholics, and Orthodox and Conservative Jews worked together to help finance their religious school systems to counter what they believed was the imposition of secular humanism in the public schools. To this day, simply by declaring that a school is not discriminatory, the institution can retain its tax-exempt status, even if it refused admission to minorities.

In 1983, the Supreme Court in *Mueller v. Allen* held that a Minnesota statute allowing state taxpayers to deduct expenses toward public and private education was constitutional (463 U.S. 388 (1983)). In *Committee for Public Education and Religious Liberty v. Regan* (444 U.S. 646 (1980)) the US Supreme Court found a secular purpose in the statute—to improve educational outcomes for children. From *Mueller*, it was only a matter of time before the Supreme Court jurisprudence would come to support tax credits and vouchers.

Jewish neoconservatives and Orthodox thinkers sought common cause with the Republican Party and the Christian Right. The result was a range of well-heeled organizations that disliked government involvement in education and were working to put school choice initiatives into place. Among them were the Heritage Foundation, the Cato Institute, the American Federation for Children, and the Walton Family Foundation. This new alliance turned educational policy in a neoliberal direction, and the trend continues to grow. For the first time in at least 50 years, a majority of US public school students come from low-income families, according to a new analysis of 2013 federal data, a statistic that has profound implications for the nation (Layton 2015).

This trend is especially pronounced in poor Southern states like Mississippi. Private academies that allowed only white students grew in popularity following the 1970 order from the 5th US Circuit Court of Appeals to desegregate Mississippi's public schools. From 1968 to 1971, these private schools grew from educating just over 5,000 to 40,000 (Wolf 2014). Meanwhile, funding for public schools has been slashed. Most whites with means send their children to private religious schools, and many more parents who don't have the means might be able to do so as well, given recent attempts by the legislature to pass school choice initiatives. A new and powerful lobbying group, Empower Mississippi, is currently working on savings-account legislation for special-needs students, possibly opening the door for tax credits and vouchers. Our founding fathers believed in the power of education for sustaining democracy. Nationwide, minority students continue to be concentrated in high-poverty, low-achieving schools, while white students are more likely to attend high-achieving, more affluent schools. How to mitigate these economic and racial disparities while honoring religious differences will be the great test for educational policymakers moving forward.

CONCLUSION

Pfeffer resigned from the American Jewish Congress in the mid-1980s, stating that the group was becoming too close to the accommodationists when it came to church-state policies (to be fair, Pfeffer also suffered from health issues before he resigned). He lived until 1993, and I've often wondered what he would think of the Supreme Court's recent decisions. Would he be troubled? I think so. Pfeffer was a purist, but for good reason: he knew the dangers of anti-Semitism and racism, and he fought tirelessly to protect minorities throughout his career. He also deeply cared about the mission of public schools. Like the founding fathers, he understood how important education was for our constitutional enterprise to work. Putting unregulated funds into private entities would take away from the larger "project"—most notably exemplified through the writings of Horace Mann—behind the idea of public schools: civic education for the sake of a good citizenry.

Yet, here we are as a society at a huge impasse over religion and American educational policy. This is certainly true within the Jewish community in America. Jews historically supported public schools, yet on October 1, 2015, eJewish Philanthropy released "Strategic Directions for Jewish Life: A Call to Action," which included a platform plank supporting state tax policies that support Jewish schools. More and more American Jews feel the burden of what they refer to as "double taxation," meaning they pay taxes for public schools and tuition for private Jewish schools. Jews without means can't necessarily provide for a basic need (or not without great sacrifice): Jewish education for their children. Jews in Israel have better choices. Israel finances religious and secular schools with government funds, but there is also government oversight of the curriculum: schools must adhere to a common core curriculum in order to get funds, and schools that don't can't receive government funds. Perhaps we should look to other countries for more creative solutions that begin to accommodate religious differences without detracting from broader educational outcomes determined by educational policymakers. At the very least, it is good to start asking these broader questions, because we need to bridge the great religious divides that plague us now more than ever. I think we should start by asking what makes a good citizen and how we should adequately educate our young people to be productive and innovative. I think Pfeffer would agree that this would be a good start. His legacy should remind us that good arguments come from good data, evidence, and argumentation. If we adhere to that standard, we can better understand how to create sound and enduring educational policy that mitigates tensions surrounding religious differences.

FUTURE DIRECTIONS

1. How can American educational policy accommodate religious and cultural differences while still maintaining a broad civic educational program?
2. Should public funds going to private religious educational entities be regulated? If so, how and why?
3. How does American educational policy empower citizens to develop their own moral conscience/compass?

References

ARCHIVES AND MANUSCRIPT COLLECTIONS

American Jewish Historical Society (New York City)
American Jewish Congress records

BOOKS, ARTICLES, AND THESES

Apple, Michael W., Jane Kenway, and Michael Singh, eds. 2005. *Globalizing Education: Policies, Pedagogies & Politics*. New York: Peter Lang.

Ball, William. 1967. "Examination of the Church-State Issues in Federal Aid to Education." *Wilson Library Bulletin* 41 (March): 694–699.

Balmer, Randall. 2006. *Thy Kingdom Come: An Evangelical's Lament*. New York: Basic Books.

———. Spring 2010. "The World Turned Upside Down." *Critical Issues of Our Time* 3: 1–16.

Brint, Stephen, and Jean Reith Schroedel, eds. 2009. *Evangelicals and Democracy in America*. New York: Sage.

Cohen, Naomi. 1992. *Jews in Christian America: The Pursuit of Religious Equality*. Oxford: Oxford University Press.

Crespino, Joseph. 2009. *In Search of Another Country: Mississippi and the Conservative Counterrevolution*. Princeton, NJ: Princeton University Press.

Dalin, David, ed. 1993. *American Jews and the Separationist Faith: The New Debate on Religion and Public Life*. Lanham, MD: National Book Network.

Editorial, "Public Aid and the Churches' Duties." *Christianity Today* 25 (March 13): 1415.

Erickson, Donald. 1978. "The Supreme Court on Aid to Parochial Schools." *Theory and Practice* 17, no. 4: 291.

Green, Steven K. 2012. *The Bible, the School, and the Constitution: The Clash That Shaped Modern Church-State Doctrine*. New York: Oxford University Press.

Grossman, Lawrence. 2001. "Mainstream Orthodoxy and the Public Square." In *Jewish Polity and American Civil Society*, edited by Alan Mittleman, Jonathan D. Sarna, and Robert Light, 283–310. Lanham, MD: Rowman & Littlefield.

Heiman, Uriel. 2012. "Orthodox Union Has Found Solution to Orthodoxy's Problems: Houston." *Jewish Telegraphic Agency*, Feb. 2. Accessed Nov. 1, 2012 (http://www.jta.org/news/article/2012/02/02/3091491/orthodox-union-has-found-solution-to-orthodoxys-problems-houston).

Herberg, Will. 1979. *Judaism and Modern Man: An Interpretation of Jewish Religion*. New York: Atheneum.

Internal memo from Leo Pfeffer to staff, January 15, 1966, folder 19, box 259, American Jewish Congress records.

Ivers, Gregg. 1992. "Religious Organizations as Constitutional Litigants." *Polity* 25, no. 2: 243–266.

———. 1995. *To Build a Wall: American Jews and the Separation of Church and State*. Charlottesville: University Press of Virginia.

Kelman, Wolfe. 1962. "Religion: Federal Aid to Parochial Schools." *American Jewish Yearbook*. New York: American Jewish Committee.

Layton, Lynsdey. 2015. "Majority of U.S. Public School Students Are in Poverty." *Washington Post*, March 15. (http://www.washingtonpost.com/local/education/majority-of-us-public-school-students-are-in-poverty/2015/01/15/df7171d0-9ce9-11e4-a7ee-526210d665b4_story.html).

Letter from Sherer to Maslow, June 2, 1968, folder 1, box 255, American Jewish Congress records.

Lupu, Ira C. 1999. "The Increasingly Anachronistic Case Against School Vouchers." *Notre Dame Journal of Law, Ethics & Public Policy* 13, no. 375: 375–396.

McAndrews, Lawrence John. 2006. *The Era of Education: The Presidents and the Schools, 1965– 2001*. Urbana: University of Illinois Press, 2006.

Minow, Martha. 2011. "Confronting the Seduction of Choice: Law, Education, and American Pluralism." *Yale Law Journal* 120: 814–848.

Morris, John D. 1961. "New bill divides school-aid plans." *New York Times*, March 30, 1.

Novack, David. 1987. "Remarks at Jews in Unsecular America Conference" (Jan. 13–14, 1986), quoted in Paul T. Stallsworth, "The Story of an Encounter," in *Jews in Unsecular America*. Grand Rapids, MI: Eerdmans Pub Co.

Novack, Michael. 1974. *Choosing Presidents: Symbols of Political Leadership*. New Brunswick, NJ: Macmillan.

Oates, Kathryn Lindsay. 2010. "Group Efficacy: Religious Interests in the Court." Ph.D. Diss., University of Florida.

Schick, Marvin. January 2012. "The National Jewish Commission on Law and Public Affairs: An Analytical Report." Unpublished paper given to author.

Schoenfeld, Stuart. 1999. "Jewish Education and Jewish Continuity in the United States and Canada: A Political Culture Perspective." *Journal of Jewish Education* 65 (Spring-Summer), no. 1-2: 60–71.

Spiegel, Irving. 1963. "Jewish Schools Ask for Fiscal Help." *New York Times*, September, 19, 24.

Statement of Terence Cardinal Cooke of the USCC, Tax Credits for Nonpublic Education, Hearings Before Congress on H.R. 1972. 16141 and Other Pending Proposals. US Congress House Ways and Means Committee.

Vitulle-Martin, Thomas. 1978. "New York City's Interest in Reform of Tax Treatment of School Expenses: Rethinking the Middle Class in the City." *City Almanac* 13 (December), no. 4: 1–14.

Waxman, Chaim. May 2004. "American Modern Orthodoxy: Confronting Cultural Challenges." *Edah Journal* 4, no. 1: 1–13.

Windmueller, Steven. 2001. "Defenders: National Jewish Community Relations Agencies." In *Jewish Polity and American Civil Society*, edited by Alan Mittleman, Jonathan D. Sarna, and Robert Light, 13–66. Lanham, MD: Rowman & Littlefield.

Wolf, Anna. 2014. "Then and Now: When 'School Choice' Creates a Divide." *Jackson Free Press*, December 17.

Further Reading

Abrams, Eliot. 1997. *Faith or Fear: How Can Jews Survive in Christian America*. New York: Simon & Schuster.

Greely, Andrew, and P. H. Rossi. 1966. *The Education of Catholic Americans*. Chicago: Aldine Publishing Company.

Gurock, Jeffrey. 1952. "The Sectarian Conflict over Church and State." *Commentary* 14 (November): 450–462.

———. 2009. *Orthodox Jews in America*. Bloomington: Indiana University Press.

Herberg, Will. 1998. "The School Voucher Dispute." In *Vouchers for School Choice: Challenge or Opportunity: An American Jewish Reappraisal*, edited by Marshall J. Breger and David M. Gordis. Wilstein Institute for Jewish Policy Studies.

Himmelfarb, Milton. 1966. "Church and State: How High a Wall?" *Commentary* 42 (July): 23–29.

———. 1993. Cited in *American Jews and the Separationist Faith: The New Debate on Religion and Public Life*, edited by David Dalin, 4–5. Lanham, MD: National Book Network.

LaNoue, George R. 1968. "Church State Problems in New Jersey: The Implementation of Title I (ESEA) in Sixty Cities." *Rutgers Law Review* 22 (Winter), no. 2: 219–80.

Lewin, Nathan. "Judaism and American Public Life: A Symposium." *First Things*. 11: 16–36.

Pfeffer, Leo. 1958. *Creeds in Competition: A Creative Force in American Culture*. New York: Harper.

———. 1962. "Federal Funds for Parochial Schools? No." *Notre Dame Lawyer* 37 (March): 309–322.

———. 1967. *Church, State, and Freedom*. Boston: Beacon Press.

Schick, Marvin, ed. 1971. *Government Aid to Parochial Schools—How Far*. New York: COLPA.

———. October 2009. "A Census of Jewish Day Schools in the US 2008–2009." New York: Avi Chai Foundation.

CHAPTER 2

SECULARISM AND RELIGION IN AMERICAN EDUCATION

JONATHON S. KAHN

INTRODUCTION

AT the start of the twenty-first century, the nature and purpose of a liberal education—indeed, a secular education—in America is enormously encumbered. It is encumbered by an extremely turbid history of the mission of American education. It is encumbered by the roiling conditions of global capitalism, which at this moment is turning fissures and gaps in economic equality and the distribution of wealth into vast gulfs and chasms. And it is encumbered most crucially by the very idea of the secular. Over the last twenty years an array of new critics of the secular have radically ramified and revalued the secular's very meaning. Whatever might be possibly meant by a secular education today must take these scholars into account.

This chapter attempts a version of this. The two galvanizing questions of this chapter are "What is a secular education"? and "What might a secular education be in the twenty-first century?" The first section of this essay takes up a selection of the critics who have been rethinking and re-evaluating the very idea of the secular. In their hands, no longer is the secular flatly understood as a neutral or natural category denoting the absence of religion. They understand the secular as something more polymorphous, imbricated in and reliant on conceptions of religion and the forces of hegemony. Sometimes this version of the secular is called the "post-secular," but that term can be deceiving, implying that we have shrugged off our secular past. Instead, what might be called a "new secular" has emerged, one that embraces its history and the promises of its own instability.

Equipped with this fuller contemporary understanding of the secular, the second section of this essay re-evaluates historical narratives of the development of American higher education. The story I want to tell is indeed that of the emergence of American secular education, but it is not one that relies on the classic "secular subtraction" story where American common schools, colleges, and universities were once religious and then, as the nineteenth turned into the twentieth century, they became increasingly less so and thus more secular. Instead, the story of American secular education is better understood as a to-and-fro struggle with religious moods, dispositions, and perspectives that leaves them in a complicated, strained, and unacknowledged mutual clench.

The third and final section of this essay is devoted to imagining the new secular university of the twenty-first century when the strains of this clench are, at the very least, recognized and acknowledged, and perhaps reworked. A flurry of anxious writing post-9/11 and especially since the 2008 economic crisis has been devoted to rethinking the value and nature of a liberal education. I see these works—for example, by Andrew Delbanco and Michael Roth—as symptomatic of the struggle to envision education under a new secular dispensation. Perhaps unbeknownst to them, their efforts chime in interesting ways with efforts by theologically orthodox Christians—folks such as Stanley Hauerwas, George Marsden, and most crucially Alasdair MacIntyre—to reinvigorate education. Together these seemingly disparate sets of critics chart a possible path for the renewed intersection of knowledge and democratic practices.

THE NEW SECULAR

In 1968, when sociologist Peter Berger gave a lunchtime talk at the New School of Social Research, the secular seemed a known and stable good. Berger understood the secular as a distinct and separable realm from the religious. On this view, the secular was synonymous with modernity, progress, technology, and increasing industrialization. Berger spoke about religion as if it were an atavism, akin to an appendix, a useless remnant organ from our evolutionary past. At that lunchtime talk, the future for religion, as the *New York Times* reported, was "bleak" ("A Bleak Outlook," 1968). Berger claimed that short of a "third world war," religion would be confined to "small enclaves and pockets": "I think people will become so bored with what religious groups have to offer that they will look elsewhere" ("A Bleak Outlook," 1968, 3).

This was classic stuff of the period, a time when the "secularization thesis" reigned supreme. The secularization thesis had two main prongs: (1) public and political discourse would follow the rational lines of reason and (2) religion was in inexorable decline. The secular was, then, understood to be a confluence of the two: an epistemological presumption and a historical prediction that isolated and relegated religion to a small dustbin.

The secularization thesis did not hold. Mary Douglas, the esteemed anthropologist, announced its failure in the early 1980s (1982), and by the end of the twentieth century, scholars were rapidly unraveling its central tenets. First, a broad-based set of philosophers, philosophers of religion, theologians, and literary critics collectively made "the linguistic turn," coming to understand "reason" not as hooked up to universal foundations but as a form of discourse shaped by interests and historical contingencies.

So-called secular reason was not necessarily more neutral and cogent than forms of reason that found occasion to recur to God. Second, at the dawn of the twenty-first century, religion, both in America and around the world, clearly was not in inevitable retreat. As the century closed, Berger himself issues a famous apologia: "a whole body of literature written by historians and social scientists over the course of the 1950s and '60s, loosely labeled as 'secularization theory', was essentially mistaken." In one sweep he recants the secularization thesis whole cloth: "The world today . . . is as furiously religious as it ever was, and in some places more so than ever" (1999, 2).

Emphasis should be placed on the word "furious." At the start of the twenty-first century, fury—including but not limited to that of Christianity, Islam, Judaism, as well as nation-states and non-state actors—asserted itself in realms of human agency. The political and the religious reasserted their mutual relevance and it was increasingly difficult to figure out where one began and the other left off. It became increasingly untenable to carve the "religious" and the "secular" as distinct categories. This new century was going to require more sophisticated and variegated ways of understanding interactions between putatively religious and putatively nonreligious forces. From these pressures, new accounts of the secular emerged.

The explosion of writing on the secular since the beginning of the twenty-first century has been immense. For sociologists, anthropologists, philosophers, political theorists, gender studies scholars, race studies scholars, and scholars of religion, the secular has functioned as common coin, as a shared site of inquiry. In their hands, the meaning of the secular has ramified radically to the point where it is commonplace to talk about *varieties* of the secular and secularisms. Collectively, they make up a set of "new secular critics." The effect of their work has been to denaturalize the secular—to show the secular not as a neutral and timeless construct that denotes the clean absence of religion, but as deeply contingent and subject to hegemonic forces. It is commonplace to hear critics say things such as: "One of the virtues of Charles Taylor's work has been to show that we have become secular not *against* religion but *because* of religion." (Mendieta 2012, 307, emphasis original). The religious and the secular have become a mutually imbricated skein of modernity.

From this profusion, the "new secular" coalesces around two crucial rearticulations. Works by Charles Taylor and Jeffrey Stout, emerging out of a North American philosophical tradition, personify the first. The second is embodied by the work of Talal Asad and Saba Mahmood, which has its roots in the tradition of subaltern and postcolonial studies.

The revaluations of the secular by Stout and Taylor are of a similar nature, not in the least in their semantic play with the word "secular." Both Stout and Taylor reject the classic version of the secular, the version that involves a neutral notion of reason and subjects religion to special rules restricting it. In its stead, both propose alternative notions of the secular, what Stout calls "secularity" or "secularization" and what Taylor calls "secularity 3." For Taylor, "secularity 3" begins with an appraisal of modernity's pervasive pluralistic "conditions of belief": "Modern secularity must therefore be understood as this field of increasingly multiform contestation, in which every position is rendered uneasy and questionable because it can be challenged from many angles" (C. Taylor 2010, 306). For Stout secularity is marked not by "the tendency of the people participating in it to relinquish their religious beliefs or to refrain from employing them as reasons," but by "the fact that participants in a given discursive practice are not in a position to take for granted that their interlocutors are making the same religious assumptions they are" (2004, 97).

On Stout's terms, where *secularism* represents an ideological commitment to denying religious reasons public purchase, *secularity* or *secularization* is a discursive condition of exchange between religious and nonreligious citizens who are acutely aware that their own convictions are contestable. He likes to say that the secular are not secularists (Stout 2008). For Taylor, "secularity 3" similarly proffers a democratic ethics of dialogue: "I think what we badly need is a conversation between a host of different positions, religious, nonreligious, antireligious, humanistic, antihumanistic, and so on, in which we eschew mutual caricature and try to understand what 'fullness' means for the other" (C. Taylor 2010, 318). Taylor talks of the secular age as being one of "cross-pressures," where we necessarily find ourselves hearing, talking, and working with voices, religious and not, very different from our own (2004, Chapter 16). Thus, in Taylor's "secular age" or under Stout's "secularization," it is not only reasonable to be religious in public squares, but it is possible to be both secular and religious at once.

Talal Asad and Saba Mahmood certainly appreciate this version of the secular. For example, Asad speaks of an Egyptian "counter-public" that "gathers secular liberals and Islamists together . . . and provides a space of daily interaction and negotiation" (2012, 56). And Mahmood's radical subversion of the claim that "critique is secular" complements Stout and Taylor's disruption of "secular reason" and attempts to loosen the secular's fixation on religion as an exceptional discourse. Yet if Stout and Taylor focus on the philosophical incoherence of the secular, Asad and Mahmood are concerned with the way the secular functions to wield coercive power. The central insight that joins Asad and Mahmood is the claim that the secular has long masked its own theological project to pressure, discipline, and produce religion in privatized forms, what Asad calls "the secular formula for privatizing religion" (2003, 228). In order to do this, "nation-states have had to act as *de facto* theologians, rendering certain practices and beliefs as indifferent to religious doctrine precisely so that these practices can be brought under the domain of civil law" (Mahmood 2006, 326–327). Thus, secularism in practice is a form of nation-state power dedicated to "remaking certain kinds of religious subjectivities (even if this requires the use of violence) so as to render them compliant with liberal political rule" (Mahmood 2006, 328).

The implications of this insight are formidable. Their analysis suggests limits to the possibility of reconstructing the secular, for even if the secular concedes its exclusive focus on religious discourses and subjectivities, it remains the organizing language of the nation-state. In this, it retains its disposition toward power. Though Stout and Taylor may invite new voices and new concerns—even religious voices and religious concerns—into secular conversation, Asad and Mahmood have us understand that all conversations operate within rules, and who is to determine the deliberative rules of the new secular? Will not the state, or an authority akin to the state, even if reformed, necessarily be engaged in coercing logics and subjectivities? Even if the state gives up a secularism that is ideologically committed to the legal separation of religion and state, will it not in some way remain involved in the "rearticulation of religion in a manner commensurate with modern sensibilities and modes of governance"? (Mahmood 2008a, 448–449). The secular on this account always represents the governing language of power.

Yet, I think this is an unnecessarily defeatist reading of Asad and Mahmood. Never do they say that the critique of the secular ends with the elimination of the secular; never do they say that the end goal of their criticism is the evasion of power formation. Instead, I am more inclined to read them as cautioning against recreating secular myths that either hide or deny tendencies and possibilities of power formation. Asad and Mahmood are more constructively read as challenges to accounts of the new secular, asking not for the elimination of secular power but for a continued openness to critique on these terms. The new secular thus has multiple movements: it radically opens up the rules and practices of dialogue and engagement, and it attends as best it can to the way power dynamics continue to function in the very process.

Read in this complementary fashion, Stout, Taylor, Mahmood, and Asad collectively provide a set of helpful lenses on American education. They help us think retrospectively: they attune us to the way the secular as a mythic creation story—one that proclaims its own innocence and disavowal of power, particularly in regard to its suppression of religious discourses—was hotly at play in the emergence of secular education in America. They also help us think prospectively, offering models and caution in envisioning a new secular education that has wrestled more honestly and fully with its own formations. It is to these two stories that we turn in the next sections.

A Short History of
a Secular Education

Many professors and students at universities and colleges founded before the Civil War can easily replicate the exercise Julie Reuben (2010) runs with her classes at Harvard. Dig up a document that recounts the institution's earliest educational mission. Remark at the explicitness with which learning was tied to fostering the knowledge of Christianity and inculcating a Christian set of moral norms. And then note that not only are these concerns not the institution's current mission, but that today's mission in effect contravenes these earlier norms and goals.

It is possible to fit this story into a fairly standard narrative of secularization. American education, from its earliest forms in the public primary schools of the eighteenth and nineteenth centuries, emerged out of Protestant Christianities (see Beyerlein 2003 and McConnell 2012). As George Marsden writes in his masterful *The Soul of the American University*, "The American university system was built on a foundation of evangelical Protestant colleges" (1996, 4). Up to and even after the Civil War, the purpose of American education was to save individual Christian souls and shape Christian community according to agreed-upon standards.

However, at the dawn of the new century, conditions had changed radically. Freethinking scholars, emboldened by the progressive moods of technology, science, and experimentation, had embarked upon new modes of education, ones that emphasized individual originality and creativity over the "historic encumbrances" (Dewey 1962, 6) of religious authority and institutions. These secular energies thrived on neutral and objective inquiry, which resulted in enormous innovation and rapid scientific discovery. Above all, the emergence of secular education in the twentieth century represents a period in which the epistemologies of faith, belief, and authority were supplanted by what were understood to be superior epistemologies of fact, proof, and critical inquiry.

Christian Smith's work casts critical doubts on the coherence of this narrative. To be sure, parts of this story are not mistaken. By the start of the twentieth century, "Godtalk" had virtually disappeared from academic discourse and the production of knowledge: "By the 1890s, Christian higher education was being definitively supplanted by an education revolution championing a fundamentally secular model of higher education and inquiry, and relegating religion to chapel services and baccalaureate prayers" (C. Smith 2003a, 27). What Smith's account reveals, however, is that this process was not dictated simply by the neutral norms of objectivity and reason. He describes the ultimate supremacy of the research and scientific model of education over the religious not in terms of an "inherent logical warfare between faith and science," where science emerges as the natural victor. Instead, in ways that should remind us of Asad and Mahmood's analysis, Smith understands the battle as an ideological one about power, "a struggle for social status and institutional control by identifiable contending social groups" (C. Smith 2003a, 10). Smith recounts the emergence of a new intellectual elite in the beginning of the twentieth century—scientists, sociologists, historians, literary and philosophical scholars—who chaffed against traditional constraints on the access to political and intellectual prestige along with the material resources that went along with them: "What these secularizers were actually pursuing was not primarily a neutral public sphere, but a reconstituted moral order which would increase their own group status, autonomy, authority, and eventually income" (C. Smith 2003a, 37). Smith details the way emergence of new money—the enormous sums from the nation's industrialists, such as Ezra Cornell, Leland Stanford, Andrew Carnegie, John Rockefeller, and James Duke—shapes what counts as valuable and truthful knowledge. He explains how institutions such as Wesleyan, Brown, Rutgers, and Occidental "immediately severed their ties with their religious denominations in order to get a share of the Carnegie money" (C. Smith 2003a, 76). Throughout, Smith is not trying to invalidate secular knowledge. Instead, he is trying to disabuse those who would deny that the conditions of production of secular knowledge influence the function and value of that knowledge. Secularization, on this account, is properly understood not as a subtraction story in which unreliable forms of knowledge (read: religious) are progressively eliminated in favor of more accurate and objective forms (read: secular) forms of knowledge. In a wonderfully clear moment of summary, Smith describes secularization as a governing language of power:

> . . . the historical secularization of American higher education—and of American public life more generally—was not an abstract, natural, and inevitable by-product of some evolutionary modernization process. Rather, it is the achievement of intentional agents, influenced by particular ideologies and interests, seeking to enhance their own status and authority by actively displacing the competing status and authority of religious actors. (C. Smith 2003b, 105)

Equally significant is the way these new forms of knowledge began to resemble the very religious education they disdained. For example, Smith recounts the ways sociology's scientific pretenses were not just to study society but to transform society by ameliorating its ills. Of course, to do this, sociologists had to have a moral vision of what counted as transformation and what ills needed to be transformed. Marsden echoes this narrative in describing the way "Christianity could linger in the curriculum" of Johns Hopkins University as its faculty pursued science in the name of "general spiritual progress" (1996, 159). Anthony Kronman argues that the very norms of academic research have their roots in a tradition of Protestant German romanticism: "Drawing inspiration from an older tradition of Christian belief . . . it conferred a moral and spiritual legitimacy on the work of the academic researcher . . . an innerworldy path to salvation. The result was a spiritualization of the research ideal that persists to this day" (2007, 113).

Inevitably, the normative aspirations of secular education begin to mirror in content, and not just in form, a Christian worldview. Christian norms of decency, cleanliness, morality, and their social ramifications are smuggled into the science of society:

> . . . early American academic sociologists constructed sociology not simply as a valid scholarly enterprise, but in many ways as the functional equivalent of traditional Christianity. In a world full of human ills and evils, sociology would provide knowledge and guidance for a salvation and regeneration that would bring human life to fullness and perfections. (C. Smith 2003b, 126)

Asad and Mahmood would also remind us that this spiritualization needs to be seen as working in tandem with the power of the nation-state. Here their sensibilities intersect with the Christian critics of secularism like Hauerwas: "Now the university is expected to produce people educated to serve the bureaucracies of modernity in which it is assumed that the state is crucial for an ordered world" (2007, 179).

A similar story can be told about the role of the humanities over the course of the twentieth century. Marsden, Roberts, and Turner tell common stories about the emergence of the humanities. They recount the way university presidents, boards, and faculty accepted the dissolution of an explicit Protestant Christian common frame. Yet, this dissolution of an explicitly Christian common referent was not synonymous with utter moral fragmentation. Roberts and Turner frame the "triumph of the humanities" in terms of the ways in which humanistic study was able to provide higher education with distinct modes of moral, philosophical, aesthetic, and political coherence. The Protestant leaders and faculty invested the humanities with a set of moral and spiritual ideals—ideals of citizenship, character, civility, benevolence, and human sympathy as well as the larger "importance of developing a sense of the good, the true, and the beautiful" (Roberts and Turner 2000, 114). This mission was captured by the "great books" movement after the World War I at places like Columbia, Harvard, Chicago, and Yale. By injecting a Protestant sense of moral and political vision into humanistic studies— a vision that reinscribed dispositions to support the stability of the institutions themselves as well as the larger American nation—"the humanities helped to reassure many university leaders that the essence of the religious could survive the loss of an explicitly Christian framework of knowledge" (Roberts and Turner 2000, 108).

Critics like James K. A. Smith like to suggest that a modern secular liberal arts education has abandoned the work of "character formation," of training students in ways to think and be: "Even a 'secular' liberal arts college remains secular*ist* just to the extent it remains allergic to the notion of education as *formation*" (J. Smith 2010, emphasis original). Yet there is ample evidence that historically the aims of a secular education over the course of the twentieth century were deeply about character formation. Indeed, then and now, the mission statements of institutions of higher education bristle with hallmark phrases of liberal pluralism: "respect for diversity," "diversity of perspectives," "recognition of different types of knowledge," "a willingness to engage in ethical debate in a spirit of reasonable compromise," and "the achievement of balance between emotional engagement and intellectual detachment" are not value-neutral notions that are agnostic about the shape of human subjectivity. All of these notions affect and train participants in American educational systems—students and faculty alike—with a host of ethical standards and expectations. Even Hauerwas unhesitatingly acknowledges that "American higher education is an extraordinarily successful system of moral formation" (2007, 126).

Following the critics of the new secular, I have wanted to narrate this short history in ways that emphasize the mutual imbrication of the religious and the secular. They are neither identical nor discrete categories. They grasp each other in a mutual clench. That clench goes unrecognized when our understanding of American education refuses to acknowledge the variety of ways that the project of character formation has been translated into a secular vernacular. That clench goes equally unrecognized when our accounts of higher education insist on seeing the success of secular education flatly in terms of epistemological progress and not in terms of its abilities to aggregate resources and power for the benefits of its actors. The fairytale is not true: a secular education has never been about the neutral pursuit of knowledge and the radical freedom of individuals to shape themselves in any infinite form they see fit. It is only by acknowledging this ideology of the secular do we have any chance of loosening its hold on us and imagining new possibilities for education's secular future.

A New Secular Education

New secular critics have undermined the classic dogmas of secularism. They see philosophical bad faith in claims to epistemological privilege. They see democratic bad faith in *prima facie* restrictions on the sorts of vocabularies that are allowed to contribute to secular discourse. These new secular critics reckon deeply with how secularism historically masks and disavows institutional and political power and the resources that accrue from both. The result is that new secular critics imagine secular discourse as much more diverse and much more raucous than traditional accounts of secular life.

What does a secular education look like in this light? At the very least, new secular critics would insist that a secular education must foreground in very explicit and self-conscious ways the question: What is this education for? It is possible to answer the question by imagining an American secular education for the purposes of job training, technical knowledge, and economic efficiency that ultimately serve the purpose of national and global capitalism. We can include in this group certain enthusiasts of science, engineering, technology, and mathematics who value these fields for their virtuosity in producing new knowledge, innovative products and goods, and efficient solutions.

My point is not to denounce them; theirs is a viable account of modern education. But, as the entire history of American education shows, other powerful impulses persist within American life, impulses that demand education to speak to Du Bois's sentiment in the epigraph where "life [is] more than mean and the body more than raiment." For most new secular critics today, to ask, "what is education for?" is to ask what more is education for than the production of skillful efficiency and the accumulation of knowledge as capital. This is the crisis that Marc C. Taylor refers to in *Crisis on Campus* (2010). How can we connect the need to think broadly and liberally and holistically about what it is to exist when increasingly existence seems to demand highly specialized skills that necessarily shun the broad, the liberal, the holistic? Said slightly differently, life is precarious and often violent under the pressures of neoliberal globalization. On the one hand, one can sense that ameliorating those pressures is going to require immensely creative and liberal thinking that gathers and integrates fragmentary parts. On the other hand, one may be subject to the fear that one's own ability to survive these same pressures will require prowess in some particular fragment and thus require shunning integrative thinking. The anxieties of modern America have to do with the way the institutions of education are riven by these tensions—from today's regnant discourse on the importance of "high-quality" pre-K programs to the ubiquitous innovation of the STEM curriculum at all levels—and they cannot figure out ways to acknowledge or address them productively.

What is fascinating to note is that critics of remarkably different stripes speak in remarkably similar terms about these very problems in American education. Critics like Roth, Kronman, and Delbanco represent a coterie of ostensibly nonreligious voices who would find greater comfort in a tradition of American political liberalism associated with the humanism of Jefferson, Lincoln, and Emerson. Critics such as MacIntyre, Hauerwas, and Marsden speak from their explicit Christian traditions, and all are very clear that part of the problem of secular higher education is the way it has excluded Christ-shaped perspectives. Yet, as I say, their understandings of how education is faltering and how to fix it resonate with each other.

For example, Delbanco and Roth bemoan the fragmentation within higher education, its ethic of specialization, and its inability to place singular academic pursuits in broader contexts. Roth speaks of liberal education's difficulties in "counteracting the centripetal forces of modernization" (2014, 133). Delbanco talks of "invidious differentiation" (2012, 82) as the driving force of academic specialization. Their lament is that higher education not only refuses to provide students answers to questions like "how should we live our lives?" but it is unwilling "even to tell them what's worth thinking about" (Delbanco 2012, 85). What's also significant to see is that their motivating reasons for this type of moral and intellectual development are rooted in questions of community, human interrelation, and mutual acknowledgment: "Critical thinking is sterile without the capacity for empathy and comprehension that stretches the self" (Roth 2014, 184). Theirs are unabashed calls for higher education as character formation for the politics of this contested, "cross-pressured," and "fragilized" secular age.

MacIntyre, Hauerwas, and Marsden hit the same notes. Education has become too specialized, too fragmented, and too technical. MacIntyre points out that these factors have eliminated "the notion of a practice, of the narrative unity of life and of a tradition" (2002, 5) from American university education, and thus the only ways by which human character can be productively shaped have vanished. Hauerwas laments the lack in higher education of a "'hermeneutics of peoplehood'" (2007, 156) that puts community and other-regard as vital to the very nature of intellectual inquiry. In ways that his nonreligious colleagues surely would admire, MacIntyre envisions knowledge's telos— at all educational levels—in its capacity to "enable children to become reflective and independent members of their families and political communities and the inculcation of those virtues that are needed to direct us towards the achievement of our common and individual goods" (2002, 2).

There is something else crucial to note in this account. MacIntyre is Catholic and finds his feet in a Thomistic tradition of inquiry, but his call is not for universities to find a unitary religious foundation in order to do the formation work he envisions: "From a Catholic point of view the contemporary secular university is not at fault because it is not Catholic. It is at fault insofar as it is not a university" (2007). What he means by this is all universities need to present multiple and what he calls "rival traditions" of thought and belief. MacIntyre understands the primary role of universities as places where students confront in immediate and persistent ways "how fundamental disagreements about the human good arise" (2002, 12). This is not a practice in relativizing truths; the diversity of disagreement in this case is not a sop for letting a thousand flowers bloom. MacIntyre wants universities to be places of initiation for taking disagreement seriously, what he calls "constrained disagreement . . . imposed participation in conflict" (1990,

230). Multiple vocabularies are required, and this requires "ensur[ing] that rival voices [are] not illegitimately suppressed" (1990, 231).

The point of the secular university is the depth and vigor of its contestations. For these Christian critics, Christianity needs to be understood in the context of a secular university as a valid and vital strand of conversation, one that has been excluded to the detriment of the secular university itself. To be sure, it is possible to see these efforts as attempts to reassert the priority and power of Christian perspectives. The last thing universities needs is to cede ground to explicitly theological positions after a century of work to rid themselves of their dominance. In this vein, it is important to hear MacIntyre doubt whether Notre Dame is capable of substantial changes, so much is it in the thrall of the normative indicators of prestige and excellence that markets confer. In this sense these Christian critics mirror the work of secular critics by interrogating the political and social conditions of the production of all sites of knowledge.

This concern about the state of inquiry and disagreement in university life has its counterpart in Roth and Delbanco as well. Delbanco invokes an Emersonian ideal that "it is not instruction, but provocation, that I can receive another soul" (2012, 63) to make the case that if college professors are not unsettling their students' assumptions, then they are failing at their jobs. Of course, different students hold different assumptions, and the best professors will be able to unsettle many of them. To do this, professors will need to have the skills to present not only their own perspective but also the viability of perspectives not their own—which sounds exactly like the course of inquiry that MacIntyre describes. Roth, for his sake, ends his text by calling for a new understanding of the term "critical thinking." On his view, critical thinking, by focusing so intently on figuring out what is wrong with the other's position, often functions as an excuse for not opening oneself up to the possibility of being affected by sources from perspectives and traditions not one's own. Roth suggests that education has, in essence, lost the capacity to be surprised and moved by views other than those that already appeal to the vanity of its own self-assured pieties.

The coalescence of critics as different as Delbanco and MacIntyre is both suggestive and promising for a vision of a new secular education. Religious discourse and questions of character formation would be invited back into a secular education, but not for the sake of somehow civilizing that education with a type of moral code or formation that only religion can provide. Religion is necessary simply as a compelling and competing discourse, one that has thick traditions that can be used to give voice to perspectives that deeply question other regnant educational perspectives. Hauerwas, MacIntyre, and even Delbanco make the case that at this particular moment—when the logic of the state and its educational institutions work in service of the power of capital—religion can function as one among many counter-discourses to the logic of the market economy. These voices are reaching for ways of disrupting the ascendency within educational institutions of the logics and metrics of the state.

The new secular university comes with increased responsibilities. What seculariza-tion demands from its participants is that they think of their intellectual responsibilities in terms of learning a moral, religious, or historical language that is not their own. For under a secular moon, we always and forever will find ourselves compelled to enter into the discursive space of people unlike ourselves. Another way of phrasing this is that the responsibilities of the secular are dialogical responsibilities. We need to be charitable; we need to begin by thinking about the ways in which the person with whom we disagree might very well be entitled to the commitments with which we disagree. We need, also, to be evaluative—to actually evaluate and press and demand explanations from those with whom we disagree. On this view a liberal education is not a mannered affair; its mission is not to allay hostilities. Criticism stokes differences, though not by having people yell at each from across the room in their home languages, but by insisting that at least some of the conversation occurs in the language of those to whom they object. A secular education would provide the resources for participants to learn and take the terms of their interlocutor very seriously. It would note that the potential of learning to speak another language might redound back on one's own. The deep dialogical nature of speaking in another's tongue is its capacity for revealing what is wrong with ours.

Conclusion: Education as Liturgy

What this chapter has sought to reveal is how the construction of a secular education over the course of the twentieth century is rooted in the attempt to deny social and material power as central to the construction of knowledge. The research university's claims to pursue objective scientific truths partake in this denial. The humanities' desires to instill universal democratic norms to create good upstanding citizens partake as well. Today's new critics of the secular allow us to see these as self-justifying stories education tells about itself rather than unassailable accounts of disinterested inquiry. Once revealed, I have suggested that education must not simply embrace or recognize the ways in which power shapes knowledge. A new secular education has to be prepared to entertain alternative accounts of knowing. It has to realize that its role—its central job—is in teaching and training its students in how to understand, adjudicate, and live with these alternative forms. Modern secular educational institutions—from grade school on—need to understand themselves less as places that accumulate knowledge and more as places that *translate* knowledge—so that assumptions and underpinnings are revealed and then compared with other sorts of assumptions and underpinnings.

To do this, a new secular education would freely admit that character formation is fundamental to its work. It is already rife within the institution, from the disciplines and practices of the scientific lab to the small seminar table in the humanities. All of those spaces represent opportunities for students to experience the way different forms of inquiry give rise to different types of moral formation. As Patchen Markell writes,

> . . . if "ethics" at bottom refers to the formation of character . . . then college and university education would seem always to be implicated in ethics. . . . Classrooms are, after all, scenes of instruction, in which, if only by example,

we teach students the dispositions and habits that we take to be appropriate to various practices of inquiry and show them why these practices might be worth learning. (2010, 187)

A new secular education would be forthcoming about these stakes and introduce practices to reflect deeply on classroom pedagogy.

On these terms, a new secular education resembles nothing less than what James Smith describes as liturgy: "Our thickest practices—which are not necessarily linked to institutional religion—have a *liturgical* function insofar as they are a certain species of ritual practice that aims to do nothing less than shape our identity by shaping our desire for what we envision as the ideal of human flourishing" (2012, 167, emphasis original). Liturgy shapes desire through the body's performances and practices and not through the mind's epistemic capacities. By understanding contestation and disagreement as liturgical, we would do well to remember that dialogical contestation is not wholly about the pursuit of epistemological clarity and moral certainty. Seeing education as liturgy would remind us that the value of a secular education is in the way it is capable of creating conditions and situations in which all of its participants learn, as Hauerwas suggests, "to act wisely in a context of conflict, ambiguity, and change" (2007, 159). All of us need to be placed in contexts where we argue about matters of important concern simply to have the affective and bodily experience of being severely doubted by members of our community. The success of a secular education turns on how well we are able to attend to these experiences. And perhaps this form of a secular education will send its participants—students and faculty alike—into partnerships and projects based on realization of their mutual finitude.

FUTURE DIRECTIONS

1. What might new secular liturgies—practices, habits, activities—look like in American education?
2. How does the purpose or nature of education change if addressing income inequality is understood as crucial to the creation of a robustly secular education?
3. Is it the case that this understanding of a secular education is more easily addressed through the humanities and humanistic social sciences? In what ways do the humanities and social sciences need to improve or change their practices in order to embody this vision of a secular education more fully?
4. How can this vision of a secular education be translated and implemented for the STEM fields? Is there room for this sort of perspective when these fields are under stringent technical demands?
5. What further training might educators have to go through in order to thrive in this form of secular education?

References

"A Bleak Outlook is Seen for Religion." *New York Times*, February 25, 1968, 3.

Asad, Talal. 2003. *Formations of the Secular: Christianity, Islam Modernity*. Stanford: Stanford University Press.

———. 2012. "Thinking About Religious Belief and Politics." In *Cambridge Companion to Religious Studies*, edited by Robert Orsi, 36–57. New York: Cambridge University Press.

Berger, Peter. 1999. "The Desecularization of the World." In *The Desecularization of the World: Resurgent Religion and World Politics*, 1–18. Grand Rapids, MI: William B. Eerdmans.

Beyerlein, Kraig. 2003. "Educational Elites and the Movement to Secularize Public Education." In *The Secular Revolution: Power, Interests, and Conflict in the Secularization of American Public Life*, edited by Christian Smith, 160–196. Berkeley: University of California Press.

Delbanco, Andrew. 2012. *College: What It Was, Is, and Should Be*. Princeton, NJ: Princeton University Press.

Dewey, John. 1962. *A Common Faith*. New Haven, CT: Yale University Press.

Douglas, Mary. 1982. "The Effects of Modernization on Religious Change." *Daedalus* 111, no. 1: 1–19.

Hauerwas, Stanley. 2007. *The State of the University: Academic Knowledges and the Knowledge of God*. Malden, MA: Blackwell Publishing.

Kronman, Anthony. 2007. *Education's End: Why Our Colleges and Universities Have Given Up on the Meaning of Life*. New Haven, CT: Yale University Press.

MacIntyre, Alasdair. 1990. *Three Rival Versions of Moral Enquiry: Encyclopaedia, Genealogy, and Tradition*. Notre Dame, IN: University of Notre Dame Press.

———. 2002. "On Education." *Journal of the Philosophy of Education Society of Great Britain* 36, no. 1: 1–19.

———. "The End of Education: The Fragmentation of the American University." *Metanexus* (last modified March 20, 2007).

Mahmood, Saba. 2006. "Secularism, Hermeneutics, and Empire: The Politics of Islamic Reformation," *Public Culture* 18, no. 2: 326–328.

———. 2008a. "Is Critique Secular? A Symposium at UC Berkeley." *Public Culture* 20, no. (3): 447–452.

Markell, Patchen. 2010. "Education, Independence, and Acknowledgement." In *Debating Moral Education, Debating Moral Education: Rethinking the Role of the Modern University*, edited by Elizabeth Kiss and J. Peter Euben, 186–205. Durham, NC: Duke University Press.

———. 1996. *The Soul of the American University: From Protestant Establishment to Established Nonbelief*. New York: Oxford University Press.

McConnell, Michael. 2012. "Establishment at the Founding." In *No Establishment of Religion: America's Original Contribution to Religious Liberty*, edited by T. Jeremy Gunn and John Witte, 45–69. New York: Oxford University Press.

Mendieta, Eduardo. 2012. "Spiritual Politics and Post-Secular Authenticity." In *The Post-Secular in Question*, edited by Philip S. Gorski et al., 307–335. New York: New York University Press.

Reuben, Julie. 2010. "The Changing Contours of Moral Education in American Colleges and Universities." In *Debating Moral Education: Rethinking the Role of the Modern University*, edited by Elizabeth Kiss and J. Peter Euben, 27–54. Durham, NC: Duke University Press.

Roberts, Jon H., and James Turner. 2000. *The Sacred and the Secular University*. Princeton, NJ: Princeton University Press.

Roth, Michael S. 2014. *Beyond the University: Why Liberal Education Matters*. New Haven, CT: Yale University Press.

Smith, Christian. 2003a. "Introduction: Rethinking the Secularization of American Public Life." In *The Secular Revolution: Power, Interests, and Conflict in the Secularization of American Public Life*, edited by Christian Smith, 1–96. Berkeley: University of California Press.

———. 2003b. "Secularizing American Higher Education: The Case of Early American Sociology." In *The Secular Revolution: Power, Interests, and Conflict in the Secularization of American Public Life*, edited by Christian Smith, 97–159. Berkeley: University of California Press.

Smith, J. K. A. 2010. "Secular Liberal Arts Education? Or Still Secularist?" *Forsclavigera*, November 24, accessed June 12, 2015 (http://forsclavigera.blogspot.com/2010/11/secular-liberal-arts-education-or-still.html).

———. 2012. "Secular Liturgies and the Prospects for a 'Post-Secular' Sociology of Religion." In *The Post-Secular in Question: Religion in Contemporary Society*, edited by Philip S. Gorski et al., 159–184. New York: New York University Press.

Stout, Jeffrey. 2004. *Democracy and Tradition*. Princeton, NJ: Princeton University Press.

———. 2008. "The Folly of Secularism." *Journal of the American Academy of Religion* 76, no. 3: 533–544.

Taylor, Charles. 2004. *A Secular Age*. Cambridge: MA: Harvard University Press.

———. 2010. "Afterword: Apologia Pro Libro suo." In *Varieties of Secularism in a Secular Age*, edited by Michael Warner et al., 300–321. Cambridge, MA: Harvard University Press.

Taylor, Mark C. 2010. *Crisis on Campus: A Bold Plan for Reforming Our Colleges and Universities*. New York: Alfred A. Knopf.

Further Readings

Berry, Wendell. 1987. "The Loss of the University." In *Home Economics: Fourteen Essays*, 76–97. San Francisco: North Point Press.

Cady, Linell E., and Tracy Fessenden, eds. 2013. *Religion, the Secular, and the Politics of Sexual Difference*. New York: Columbia University Press.

Connolly, William. 1999. *Why I Am Not a Secularist*. Minneapolis: University of Minnesota Press.

Deresiewicz, William. 2014. *Excellent Sheep: The Miseducation of the American Elite and the Way to a Meaningful Life*. New York: Free Press.

Hollinger, David. 1996. *Science, Jews, and Secular Culture*. Princeton, NJ: Princeton University Press.

Jacobsen, Douglas, and Rhonda Jacobsen. 2008. *The American University in a Postsecular Age*. New York: Oxford University Press.

Jakobsen, Janet R., and Ann Pellegrini, eds. 2008. *Secularisms*. Durham, NC: Duke University Press.

Sommerville, C. John. 2009. *The Decline of the Secular University; Religious Ideas for the Secular University*. Grand Rapids, MI: William B. Eerdmans.

Sullivan, Winnifred Fallers. 2005. *The Impossibility of Religious Freedom*. Princeton, NJ: Princeton University Press.

Taylor, Charles. 2011. "Why We Need a Radical Redefinition of Secularism." In *The Power of Religion in the Public Sphere*, edited by Judith Butler et al., 34–59. New York: Columbia University Press.

Warner, Michael, et al., eds. 2010. *Varieties of Secularism in a Secular Age*. Cambridge, MA: Harvard University Press.

CHAPTER 3

....

PLURALISM IN RELIGION AND AMERICAN EDUCATION

....

DIANA L. ECK AND BRENDAN W. RANDALL

INTRODUCTION

....

IN terms of multiple traditions and beliefs, the United States is perhaps the most religiously diverse country in the world today. This diversity is not an entirely new phenomenon, but its degree and visibility have increased dramatically in the past fifty years following passage of the Immigration and Nationality Act of 1965. As with previous waves of immigration, the demographic transformation of America in the last half-century has raised a multitude of issues and challenges. Most importantly, this increased religious diversity has reignited debate over a fundamental civic question: What is the common identity that binds us together? Or, to use the language of the Constitution, who are the "We" in "We the People of the United States"?

Educational institutions are a critical site of encounter for the increased religious diversity that is a hallmark of modern America. Throughout US history, schools have served as a primary vehicle for inculcating civic identity and preparing individuals for membership in the broader society. How we respond to religious diversity in this context has enormous implications for our democratic society. To the extent that previous frameworks for dealing with difference, such as exclusion or assimilation, were ever desirable or effective, they no longer are. Increased religious diversity is an established fact and growing trend. The United States needs a more inclusive and robust civic framework for grappling with religious diversity in the twenty-first century, and educational institutions should promote this framework as a fundamental component of civic education. This is the framework of better understanding and engaging difference, the framework of pluralism.

RELIGIOUS DIVERSITY IN AMERICA

Religious diversity has always been an American reality. Even before the arrival of European settlers at the end of the fifteenth century, the indigenous peoples of the Americas had a great diversity of beliefs and life-ways. In the following three centuries, colonists representing a wide array of religious traditions crossed the Atlantic to form permanent communities in North America. Although the vast majority were Christian—Spanish and French Catholics, British Congregationalists, Anglicans, Quakers, and Methodists, Scottish Presbyterians, Dutch Reformed Christians, and German Lutherans and Anabaptists—colonial arrivals also included a small number of Sephardic Jews. Muslims also arrived during this period among captives brought to these shores from West Africa as part of the slave trade.

America's religious diversity continued to expand after the British North American colonies gained their independence. In the mid-nineteenth century, for example, Irish Catholics began to arrive in force, followed later by Italian Catholics. Similarly, German Jews began to arrive in the mid-nineteenth century, followed by Eastern European Jews in the late nineteenth century. Although still dominated by Europeans, immigration in the nineteenth century was by no means limited to those coming from Europe. Immigrants from East Asia included Chinese and Japanese who brought with them Buddhist, Taoist, and Confucian traditions. Similarly, Sikhs from South Asia as well as Christians and Muslims from the Middle East came in the nineteenth century, further diversifying the North American religious landscape.

Religious diversity may not be new to the United States, but its growth slowed substantially during the late nineteenth and early twentieth centuries as various restrictions on non-European immigration, beginning with the Chinese Exclusion Act of 1882, became more and more stringent over the decades. Following World War I, a general spirit of restriction brought about the enactment of the Emergency Quota Act of 1921 and the Johnson-Reed Act of 1924. Fueled by nativism, quota-based restrictions on immigration would remain in force until the Immigration and Nationality Act of 1965, which dramatically altered US immigration policy and opened the doors for far greater immigration from non-European countries. As President Lyndon Johnson (n.d./1966) put it in signing the act into law, "It corrects a cruel and enduring wrong in the conduct of the American Nation . . . it will make us truer to ourselves both as a country and as a people. It will strengthen us in a hundred unseen ways." Indeed, in the fifty years since that act was passed, immigrants have arrived in the United States from all over the world, further changing and transforming America's religious demographics. According to a recent report from the Pew Research Center (2015), for example, 96% of Hindus, 78% of Muslims, 64% of Orthodox Christians, 48% of Buddhists, and 43% of Catholics in the United States are either immigrants or the children of immigrants. These and other new immigrants have magnified the reality of America's religious diversity.

Along with increased diversity has come increased visibility. Many non-Christian communities founded what have become landmark religious centers (e.g., the Touro Synagogue in Newport, Rhode Island; the Mother Mosque of America in Cedar Rapids, Iowa; the Zenshuji Soto Mission in Los Angeles, California; and the Baha'i House of Worship in Wilmette, Illinois) well before the immigration reform of 1965. In the fifty years since then, however, the number and variety of religious centers have exploded. Non-Christian religious communities have constructed new architectural landmarks such as the Hsi Lai Temple in Hacienda Heights, California; the Hindu Temple Society of North America in Flushing, Queens; the Islamic Center of North America in Dearborn, Michigan; and the Gurdwara Sahib in Fremont, California.

These rapidly emerging immigrant communities also have discovered the leverage of religious organizations in American civil society and begun to create their own infrastructure. During the 1990s, for example, American Muslims developed multiple organizations aimed at facilitating their involvement in American society, including the Islamic Society of North America, the Muslim Public Affairs Council, and the Council on American Islamic Relations. Similarly, the Sikh community began to pursue organized advocacy in the 1990s, founding the predecessor to the Sikh American Legal Defense and Education Fund and the Sikh Council on Religion and Education. Later, following the harassment of Sikhs in the wake of the terrorist attacks of September 11, 2001, Sikh activists launched the Sikh Coalition. Hindus likewise formed the Hindu American Foundation in the early 2000s. These and other organizations have become influential representatives of their respective communities.

The impact of America's new religious reality also is evident in our educational institutions, especially as younger, more religiously diverse generations come to school. Although the majority of Americans still identify as Christian, the percentage has dramatically decreased, especially in recent years. According to the Pew Center (2015), the percentage of Americans adults who identified as Christian dropped to 70.6% in 2014, a nearly 8% decrease since 2007, while those who identified with non-Christian religious traditions grew to 5.9%, a 1.2% increase, and the unaffiliated grew to 22.8%, a 6.7% increase. This shift, moreover, is generational. Of those born between 1990 and 1996 (Younger Millennials), for example, just 56% identify as Christian and 8% identify with non-Christian religious traditions compared to 85% and 4% respectively of those born between 1928 and 1945 (Silent Generation).

Given the demographic shift in the population as a whole and youth in particular, cultural and religious diversity is now part of educational environments across the country, rural and urban, small and large. School districts in cities ranging from Moorhead, Minnesota, with about 6,000 students, to Dallas, Texas, with over 150,000 students, have had to respond to increasing religious diversity in their classrooms. Students in the Dallas Independent School District, for example, include Muslims, Jews, Hindus, Sikhs, Jains, Vietnamese and Laotian Buddhists, as well as numerous Christian denominations. Faced with this enormous religious diversity, the district formed what is essentially an interfaith group: a Religious Community Task Force to develop guidelines addressing a variety of issues ranging from cultural literacy to accommodation policies.

The changing religious demographics of the United States have raised significant questions for the practices of academic institutions ranging from elementary schools to colleges and universities. Does the Pledge of Allegiance, with the phrase "under God," unconstitutionally favor theists over non-theists, which include many Buddhists and Jains as well as atheists and Humanists? Does it force those students to choose between their religion and their citizenship? Are yoga classes actually a form of Hindu devotion, thereby raising establishment implications for public schools as well as the broader question of cultural appropriation? Does an assignment involving Islamic calligraphy or a field trip to a mosque inappropriately promote Islam? Should historically Christian spaces at colleges and universities be more accommodating to other traditions and beliefs? Must public institutions that close for Christian or Jewish holidays also close for Eid al-Fitr and Diwali? As these questions demonstrate, educational institutions are a critical site of encounter for religious diversity in the United States. How we respond to these and other issues, accordingly, has enormous implications for civil society.

TRADITIONAL RESPONSES TO DIVERSITY

Historically, one stance the United States has taken in the face of religious and cultural diversity has been to erect barriers of exclusion. Beginning with the Chinese Exclusion Act of 1882, for example, Asian exclusion legislation expanded with virtually every decade thereafter. The high-water mark of exclusion was in the late nineteenth and early twentieth centuries. Severe restrictions also were placed on citizenship, open to free white persons and excluding American Indians, slaves, free blacks, and Asians. In the 1923 case of *United States v. Bhagat Singh Thind* (261 U.S. 204), for example, the Supreme Court considered the claim of an Indian Sikh to US citizenship. Thind, a citizen who had served in the US Army in World War I, was subsequently stripped of his citizenship. Under federal law, naturalized citizenship was limited to "aliens being free white persons and aliens of African nativity and persons of African descent" (p. 207). Thind argued that as a "high-caste" (p. 210) Indian, he was ethnically Caucasian or Indo-European and thus racially white. The Supreme Court rejected this argument. Instead, it concluded that the statute's authors "intended to include only the type of man they knew as white" (p. 213), namely those of European descent.

Assimilation has traditionally been an alternative and more pervasive approach to diversity. This approach often is associated with Israel Zangwill's 1908 play *The Melting Pot*, about a Jewish immigrant forging a new life in the United States after fleeing a pogrom in Russia. In this vision, religious and ethnic differences disappear as immigrants from different cultures and countries are fused together to become Americans, an entirely new cultural identity. Although still a popular metaphor, various scholars have questioned the melting pot conception of assimilation as inaccurate or undesirable. Samuel Huntington (2004), for example, strongly rejects understanding immigrant assimilation as the formation of a composite American identity. Instead, Huntington argues that immigrants historically have assimilated by adopting various aspects of the dominant Anglo-Protestant culture. Rather than a melting pot fusing many identities, assimilation for Huntington, is a kind of Anglo-conformism. At the most, immigrants add spice and flavor to the preexisting Anglo-Protestant "tomato soup" (Huntington 2004, 128).

How have the metaphors of the "melting pot" or the "tomato soup" affected the schools as they deal with the new religious and cultural diversity? Although there are merits to both metaphors, tomato soup is probably the one more appropriate for describing the history of America's public schools, which have played a central role in assimilating newcomers. Beginning with the common schools of the nineteenth century, public schools have sought to promote a common civic identity, and religious practices were a pervasive element of this process. Prior to the Supreme Court's decisions in *Engel v. Vitale* (379 U.S. 421 (1962)) and *School District of Abington Township v. Schempp* (374 U.S. 203 (1963)), for example, prayer and Bible reading were common in public schools and continued to be in many areas for several years notwithstanding these court decisions. These practices, moreover, were overwhelmingly Protestant in nature. Although Horace Mann and other proponents of the common schools in the nineteenth century saw them as nonsectarian, in practice this merely meant that the schools did not favor one Protestant sect over another. Reading without comment from the King James Version of the Bible—a text favored by Protestants—was the norm, for example.

There were challenges to the Protestant domination of public education as the nation became more religiously diverse beginning in the mid-nineteenth century. Catholics in particular objected to reading the King James Bible without comment, and their resistance led to conflicts in many cities, including deadly riots in Philadelphia in 1844. Refusing to see this and other religious practices as nonsectarian, Catholics ultimately formed their own school systems, which in turn led to disputes over the public funding of education. As Catholics sought funding for their parochial schools, for example, many states passed constitutional amendments, known as Blaine amendments, barring public support for sectarian (i.e., Catholic) schools. The net result was that public education in the United States continued to reflect Protestant culture and beliefs well into the twentieth century, and still does so in several areas of the country today.

Calls for exclusion or assimilation in response to religious diversity are recurrent in America, however. In the wake of September 11, 2001, for example, various religious, intellectual, and political leaders have proposed restricting further Muslim immigration. Arguments supporting such proposals routinely include the narrative that Islam is fundamentally incompatible with democracy. This narrative, however, typically reflects either a profound ignorance or selective knowledge of Islam rather than a nuanced understanding of a complex and diverse tradition. The narrative, moreover, is disturbingly reminiscent of claims that Catholicism and the authority of the pope were incompatible with American democracy. Despite the fears of many prominent Protestant leaders, for example, the election of John F. Kennedy, the first Catholic president, did not initiate the downfall of American democracy. Today, Muslim political leaders and citizens are frequently called upon, as was JFK, to articulate that Islam is not incompatible with American democracy.

Even if the common narrative underlying calls for exclusion is flawed, what about assimilation? Huntington (2004), for example, argues that American democracy is rooted in a core "Anglo-Protestant" identity that Americans must adopt if we are to remain united as a nation. This Anglo-Protestant identity is the foundation of what Huntington calls the "American Creed" (2004, 340) of liberty, equality, democracy, civil rights, nondiscrimination, and the rule of law. According to Huntington,

> "the Creed is unlikely to retain its salience if Americans abandon the Anglo-Protestant culture in which it has been rooted. A multicultural America will, in time, become a multicreedal America, with groups with different cultures espousing distinctive political values and principles rooted in their particular cultures. (2004, 340)

Huntington's fear of diversity is overstated, however, and his reliance on the Anglo-conformist "tomato soup" model of assimilation is misplaced. It is true that diversity, including religious diversity, can pose a challenge for social cohesion. Religious disputes around the world are evidence of this. Robert Putnam (2007), moreover, has demonstrated that increased diversity is associated with reduced social capital as different groups turn inward for companionship and support. This loss of social capital, however, is not inevitable. Putnam also found that engaging diversity in a proactive and productive manner by developing robust cross-cutting relationships can build social capital. This kind of "bridging capital" is a hallmark of what we call "pluralism."

Finally, the Anglo-conformist model of assimilation articulated by Huntington also raises profound issues of privilege and power by giving those of Anglo-Protestant descent a unique insider status. This deep assimilation requires individuals to shed core aspects of their ethnic and religious identity to become members of American society. Practically speaking, this assimilation, moreover, becomes increasingly difficult as a society becomes more diverse and individual minority communities grow in size, and it contradicts the very premise of democracy. The American ethos insists that people have a right to their differences and need not shed them in order to become American. Today's demographic trends (discussed above) will only render Huntington's vision of assimilation more difficult if not impossible. America is, after all, an idea and a set of ideals, not an ethnicity. History has already demonstrated that Italians and Greeks, people of South Asian and East Asian origins, can simultaneously be themselves, participate in that ideal, and contribute to it.

A THIRD RESPONSE: PLURALISM

Exclusion and assimilation are not the only American stances in the face of the increased diversity associated with immigration over the last fifty years. More important is what we might call "pluralism"—that is, the engagement of our differences in the creation of a common society. As discussed above, defining the civic "we" amid increasing diversity is not a novel challenge in US history. Writing in 1915, for example, Horace Kallen advocated for "cultural pluralism" in response to the increased diversity associated with immigration in the nineteenth and early twentieth centuries. Rather than exclude immigrants or insist that they assimilate to "Anglo-Saxon" culture by shedding their differences, Kallen argued that immigrants could become part of the greater fabric of American society without abandoning their cultural distinctiveness.

For Kallen (1915a, 1915b), pluralism was not simply the best option in response to cultural diversity, it was the only feasible one. Assimilation would require draconian measures, including "the complete nationalization of education" (1915b, 219) associated with despotic regimes such as imperial Germany, but it was also a practical impossibility. Although people could change certain aspects of their identity, including their religious affiliation, they could not change their ancestry. As Kallen emphatically explained, "Jews or Poles or Anglo-Saxons, in order to cease being Jews or Poles or Anglo-Saxons, would have to cease to be" (1915b, 220).

The proper response to increased diversity for Kallen was to forge a common civic identity across difference that drew strength and vitality from cultural diversity. To illustrate his concept of cultural pluralism, Kallen offered the example of an orchestra:

> As in an orchestra, every type of instrument has its specific timbre and tonality, founded in its substance and form; as every type has its appropriate theme and melody in the whole symphony, so in society each ethnic group is the natural instrument, its spirit and culture are its theme and melody, and the harmony and dissonances and discords of them all make the symphony of civilization. (1915b, 220)

In Kallen's view, by bringing their many distinctive instruments, immigrants added depth to the American orchestra.

Kallen's orchestra is a persuasive metaphor for the dynamics of our religious diversity. Rather than mitigating difference through exclusion or assimilation, pluralism promotes civic cohesion across lines of difference. Pluralism in this context has four critical elements:

> First, pluralism is not diversity alone, but the *energetic engagement with diversity*. Diversity can and has meant the creation of religious ghettoes with little traffic between or among them. Today, religious diversity is a given, but pluralism is not a given; it is an achievement. Mere diversity without real encounter and relationship will yield increasing tensions in our societies.
>
> Second, pluralism is not just tolerance, but the *active seeking of understanding across lines of difference*. Tolerance is a necessary public virtue, but it does not require Christians and Muslims, Hindus, Jews, and ardent secularists to know anything about one another. Tolerance is too thin a foundation for a world of religious difference and proximity. It does nothing to remove our ignorance of one another, and leaves in place the stereotype, the half-truth, the fears that underlie old patterns

of division and violence. In the world in which we live today, our ignorance of one another will be increasingly costly.

Third, pluralism is not relativism, but the *encounter of commitments*. The new paradigm of pluralism does not require us to leave our identities and our commitments behind, for pluralism is the encounter of commitments. It means holding our deepest differences, even our religious differences, not in isolation, but in relationship to one another.

Fourth, pluralism is *based on dialogue*. The language of pluralism is that of dialogue and encounter, give and take, criticism and self-criticism. Dialogue means both speaking and listening, and that process reveals both common understandings and real differences. Dialogue does not mean everyone at the "table" will agree with one another. Pluralism involves the commitment to being at the table—with one's commitments. (Eck 2006)

The first element, *energetic encounter with diversity*, reminds us that pluralism is a dynamic rather than static phenomenon. Religious diversity is merely a descriptive term; it is the presence of people of differing religious (or nonreligious) beliefs living in close proximity to one another. By itself, diversity is neither inherently positive nor negative. Diversity can create a landscape of ghettos, people isolated from one another by the boundaries they created. Religious diversity can lead to conflict, such as polarized disputes over plans to remove the cross from Wren Chapel at William and Mary College or to broadcast the Islamic call to prayer from the chapel tower at Duke University. Religious diversity can also lead to cooperation and an engagement for positive ends, such as community service projects sponsored by interfaith organizations on college and university campuses across the country. Pluralism is a reflection of the latter.

The second element, the *active seeking of understanding across lines of difference*, emphasizes the fact that pluralism is active rather than passive. Tolerance alone does not necessarily require us to invest in the "bridging capital" that will enable us to communicate across our differences. We can exhibit tolerance by not discriminating against those with different religious beliefs while still conceiving of the relationship as "us" and "them" rather than "we." Developing a sense of shared identity requires a more proactive approach. People must be able to meet one another, connect with one another, and eventually develop the empathy that comes with knowledge and understanding. Mere tolerance does nothing to remove our ignorance of one another. Even in institutions of education and communities of learning, we know far too little of the various religious beliefs and practices that shape our daily lives. Basic connection and understanding facilitates deeper connection across difference and helps to transform "us" and "them" into "we."

The third element, the *encounter of commitments*, reminds us that religious pluralism has both civic and theological dimensions. Pluralism is not the erasure of commitment, but the robust encounter of commitments. In theological terms, scholars often categorize religious beliefs as exclusive, inclusive, or pluralistic. Theological exclusivists claim that their beliefs reflect the one truth to the exclusion of other religious or spiritual beliefs. For them, religious truth is fundamentally exclusive. Theological inclusivists also see their beliefs as solely true, but acknowledge that other traditions can reflect elements of that truth. Although their religious beliefs have pride of place, religious truth is not mutually exclusive. Finally, theological pluralists assert that religious traditions share much in common, such as love or compassion, but fundamentally the truth to which they point is transcendent and cannot be circumscribed by any one perspective or religion. Rather than being mutually exclusive, accordingly, religious traditions reflect different approaches to the transcendent truth.

John Hick, for example, has argued that different religious and spiritual traditions are merely culturally situated understandings of the same transcendent divine reality. According to Hick, "the great post-axial faiths constitute different ways of experiencing, conceiving and living in relation to the ultimate divine Reality which transcends all our varied versions of it" (204, 235–236). Drawing on Kant's distinction between the phenomenal and noumenal, Hick asserts that perceived differences between major religious traditions are merely "phenomenal manifestations of the Real occurring within the realm of religious experience" (2004, 243). For Hick, the true divine reality is transcendent and ineffable, and thus beyond ordinary human experience and description.

In the civic context, however, one's own religious stance, whether exclusivist, inclusivist, or pluralist, is essentially irrelevant. Here, we engage our differences around the common covenants of citizenship, the ideas and ideals of American constitutional democracy. Religious diversity is a natural product of the constitutional commitment to the free exercise of religion and the non-establishment of religion. People of different religions and people who profess no religious beliefs whatsoever are all equal stakeholders in American democracy. Our civic encounter of commitments does not privilege any particular religion or require a sense of the transcendent unity of religions. On the contrary, the *encounter of commitments* invites individuals to bring their religious and spiritual differences as well as commonalities to the table. Because it does not involve bracketing or harmonizing religious and spiritual differences, civic pluralism encompasses the entire spectrum of theological stances, from exclusivity to inclusivity to pluralism, but the "table" around which we discuss and engage is our common civic identity, the "we," of our citizenship and our constitutional commitments. It is here that "we" Protestants, Catholics, Jews, Muslims, or ardent secularists understand ourselves to be co-citizens in a common project.

Finally, pluralism is *based on dialogue*. It is a communal and interactive rather than an individual and solitary process. As "bridging discourse," pluralism is all about traffic, back and forth, even bumping into one another. Although one can learn much about other religious traditions and the experiences of others indirectly, such as through the study of comparative religions, it is not same as direct personal interaction. Religions are neither static nor are they monolithic. A textbook description of Hinduism may appear foreign to a self-identified Hindu, for example. Even the term "religion" does not sufficiently convey the wide variety of religious, spiritual, and nonreligious beliefs and worldviews. More importantly, the concept of pluralism ultimately is about developing the bridging infrastructure necessary for a common "we." This is not accomplished in isolation, but through common effort and engagement.

Pluralism and Education

As a prominent site of civic formation and religious encounter, educational institutions play a critical role in fostering the civic sense of "we" needed for a religiously diverse democracy such as the United States. The manner in which schools, colleges, and universities respond to the challenges noted above, for example, will signal their values and guide their students. Institutions that seek pluralistic solutions to these challenges will model for their students the attitudes and approaches needed to form a religiously inclusive society. Inculcation of pluralistic values, however, should not be limited to indirect means; instead, educational institutions should directly promote a pluralistic disposition as an essential component of civic education. To do so effectively, they must promote both cognitive and affective learning.

There has been a resurgence of interest in religious studies in recent years, fueled in no small part by the events of September 11, 2001. Much of this attention has focused on religious literacy. Scholars such as Diane Moore (2007) and Stephen Prothero (2007) make persuasive arguments about the need for far greater emphasis on religious literacy at all levels of education. In the domain of K-12 education, in particular, a variety of resources have emerged in the last fifteen years, especially for public schools. General guides include *Finding Common Ground: A First Amendment Guide to Religion and Public Schools* (Haynes, Thomas, and Ferguson 2007) and *Living with Our Deepest Differences: Religious Liberty in a Pluralistic Society* (McFall and Haynes 2009) as well as *Guidelines for Teaching About Religion in K-12 Public Schools in the United States* (AAR Religion in the Schools Task Force 2010). In addition, lesson plans and other resources for K-12 educators are available from various organizations such as the Religious Literacy Project, Teaching Tolerance, and the California 3Rs Project. Another useful resource is the online multimedia educational resource *On Common Ground: World Religions in America* (Pluralism Project 2016), which provides introductions to fifteen religious traditions through text, image, voice, and music.

Knowledge about various religious traditions and beliefs is an important element in promoting pluralism, but religious literacy alone is not sufficient: a pluralistic disposition involves affective as well as cognitive learning. Students need to develop a positive civic attitude toward religious diversity, not merely knowledge about different religious traditions. As discussed above, pluralism is dynamic, inclusive, and communal. Interactive pedagogies that involve activities such as discussion across difference and multiple perspective taking are essential to promoting a pluralistic orientation.

One pedagogy that we have found particularly effective for both cognitive and affective learning is the case-study method. Case studies have long been a staple of professional education in fields such as business, law, and education, where they are used to promote habits and skills as well as content knowledge. Inspired by her colleagues at the Harvard Business School, where the modern case-study method originated, Diana Eck pioneered the use of cases in the religious studies context. Along with researchers at the

Pluralism Project, Eck crafted a series of case studies addressing the civic challenges of religious diversity in America: a contentious dispute over the conversation of a Christian church to a Muslim mosque in suburban Chicago; the refusal of Muslim taxi drivers to carry passengers with alcohol in the Twin Cities; the request made to a Cambridge school superintendent to add the Muslim holiday Eid to the official school holiday calendar. Eck first used these and other case studies as part of a graduate seminar at Harvard University in 2007. She later developed a general education course for undergraduate as well as graduate students with Brendan Randall as one of her first teaching assistants.

The cases typically involve a protagonist who faces a specific dilemma or decision point. The cases are based on real-world events and contain rich detail, which enables nuanced analysis. In addition to the case, students read background material on the relevant religious traditions, communities, and issues. In class, Eck asks the students to inhabit multiple roles, including other actors as well as the protagonist. She also invites students to share their own religious (or nonreligious) perspectives and examine how such perspectives influence their reading, understanding, and analysis of the case. By discussing how to respond to real-world challenges involving religious diversity, students cultivate the attitudes and practice the skills needed to navigate such challenges successfully. They become not only scholars of religious diversity in the United States, but also leaders for a religiously diverse democracy.

Although originally designed for graduate studies, the case-study method can be used at all educational levels to promote a disposition of religious pluralism. Even young children can consider everyday questions arising from religious diversity and engage in multiple perspective taking. Educators simply need to use age-appropriate materials and techniques. By doing so, students of all ages can develop a greater understanding of and respect for different religion traditions, which is the basis of pluralism.

CONCLUSION

Today, the prominence and the visibility of religious diversity in the United States have given us a new and more complex America in which the issues of religious pluralism are more important than ever, especially as they relate to our constitutional democracy. This increased religious diversity in the United States is a reality that cannot be ignored. Despite partisan political rhetoric, neither exclusion nor assimilation is feasible today. Instead, if we are to fashion a national community—to form an *unum* from the *pluribus*—we must find a way to foster a sense of belonging and community while still respecting and embracing religious diversity. For those who welcome the new diversity, creating a workable pluralism will mean engaging people of different beliefs and cultures in the creation of a common society. It enables individuals to be members of the civic whole while still maintaining distinct religious identities. Pluralism is not a "given," however, but an achievement. Because schools play an essential role in preparing students to become citizens of a religiously diverse democracy, they are critical to this achievement.

FUTURE DIRECTIONS

1. How is increased religious diversity affecting education?
2. What are the most effective pedagogies for promoting pluralism?
3. What are the limits of pluralism in practice?

REFERENCES

AAR Religion in the Schools Task Force. 2010. *Guidelines for Teaching About Religion in K-12 Public Schools in the United States*. Atlanta, GA: American Academy of Religion.

Eck, Diana L. 2006. *What Is Pluralism?* Retrieved from http://pluralism.org/what-is-pluralism/

Haynes, C. C., O. Thomas, and J. Ferguson, eds. 2007. *Finding Common Ground: A First Amendment Guide to Religion and Public Schools*. Nashville, TN: First Amendment Center.

Hick, John. 2004. *An Interpretation of Religion: Human Responses to the Transcendent*, 2nd ed. New Haven, CT: Yale University Press.

Huntington, Samuel P. 2004. *Who Are We? The Challenges of America's National Identity*. New York: Simon & Schuster.

Johnson, Lyndon B. n.d. *LBJ on Immigration*. Retrieved from http://www.lbjlibrary.org/lyndon-baines-johnson/timeline/lbj-on-immigration (Reprinted from *Public Papers of the Presidents of the United States: Lyndon B. Johnson, 1965*, vol. II, 1037–1040. Washington, DC: Government Printing Office, 1966).

Kallen, Horace M. 1915a. "Democracy v. the Melting-pot: A Study of American Nationality (Part 1)." *The Nation* 100, no. 2590: 190–194.

———. 1915b. "Democracy v. the Melting-pot: A Study of American Nationality (Part 2)." *The Nation* 100, no. 2591: 217–220.

McFall, S., and C. C. Haynes, eds. 2009. *Living with Our Deepest Differences: Religious Liberty in a Pluralistic Society*. Nashville, TN: First Amendment Center.

Moore, Diana L. 2007. *Overcoming Religious Illiteracy: A Cultural Studies Approach to the Study of Religion in Secondary Education*. New York: Palgrave Macmillan.

Pew Research Center. 2015. *America's Changing Religious Landscape*. Washington, DC: Author.

Pluralism Project. 2016. *On Common Ground*. Retrieved from http://pluralism.org/ocg/.

Prothero, Stephen. 2007. *Religious Literacy: What Every American Needs to Know—and Doesn't*. New York: HarperOne.

Putnam, Robert D. 2007. "*E pluribus unum*: Diversity and Community in the Twenty-First Century." *Scandinavian Political Studies* 30, no. 2: 137–174.

Further Reading

Biondo, V. F., III, and A. Fiala, eds. 2014. *Civility, Religious Pluralism, and Education*. New York: Routledge.

Connolly, W. E. 2005. *Pluralism*. Durham, NC: Duke University Press.

Eck, Diana L. 2001. *A New Religious America: How a "Christian Country" Has Become the World's Most Religiously Diverse Nation*. New York: HarperCollins.

Hutchinson, W. R. 2003. *Religious Pluralism in America: The Contentious History of a Founding Ideal*. New Haven, CT: Yale University Press.

Jacobson, D., and R. H. Jacobson. 2012. *No Longer Invisible: Religion in University Education*. New York: Oxford University Press.

Jones, R. P. 2016. *The End of White Christian America*. New York: Simon & Schuster.

Wuthnow, R. 2005. *America and the Challenges of Religious Diversity*. Princeton, NJ: Princeton University Press.

CHAPTER 4

RELIGIOUS LITERACY IN AMERICAN EDUCATION

BENJAMIN P. MARCUS

INTRODUCTION

I grew up in an English-speaking family, in a town newly populated by Spanish-speaking immigrants from Latin America. In high school I enrolled in Spanish-language courses in order to break through the language barrier that prevented meaningful conversation with my neighbors. My teacher encouraged all students—native and non-native speakers alike—to test our fluency after five semesters by taking the National Spanish Exam. On the day of the test, I confidently answered oral and reading comprehension questions and filled in bubbles assessing my knowledge of formal grammar and obscure vocabulary words. I knew how to use the imperfect subjunctive, to choose between prepositions, and to interpret scholarly articles about obscure subjects. A few months later I found out that I received the highest score in my region. Yet the day after the exam, I was completely incapable of carrying on a fluent conversation with my classmates and friends who were native Spanish speakers.

What did the National Spanish Exam measure? I could read a certain type of literature and understand a certain form of spoken Spanish, but I could not carry on a casual conversation with my friends from Mexico, El Salvador, or Colombia who grew up speaking Spanish with their families. Nor could I make out the meaning of popular *reggaetón* lyrics, *telenovelas*, or colloquial expressions written on the signs of a local *carnicería*. I spoke a formulaic Spanish valued by academics and the elite, not the Spanish of my friends and neighbors.

The contrast between the practical fluency of native speakers and the merely formal understanding of language evaluated through tests analogizes the striking contrast between many Americans' ability to meaningfully express religiosity with co-religionists and their truncated understanding of others' religious identities. Using language as a metaphor for religion, I suggest that Americans read the world fluently using their own religious language, but many are incapable of understanding the language of the religious other in public life.

Religious literacy requires both a familiarity with the vocabulary of multiple religious languages and a deep linguistic understanding of the varieties of religious languages' grammar—the many ways individuals and communities construct their religious identities through belief, behavior, and the experience of belonging to a community. Effectively communicating with the religious other depends on utilizing a similar grammar—referencing shared aspects of religious identity—as much if not more so than using the same vocabulary. In other words, a religiously literate person must be a multilingual linguist.

I will, throughout this chapter, test the possibilities and limits of using language as a metaphor for religion in order to outline the content knowledge and skills needed to participate in the public sphere. I argue that each religion is like a language, with multitudes of dialects, each dialect relying on distinct vocabularies mediated by culture. Without turning this metaphor into a theory of religion, I explore how to teach people about religion in a way that enables them—whether religious or not—to read and interpret religious influence in public life.

THE STATUS QUO: RELIGIOUS LITERACY AS MULTILINGUALISM

Conventional approaches to religious literacy education attempt to make people into polyglots, capable of understanding multiple religious languages. However, many courses select a limited set of religious languages to provide focus for students, and they further delimit study by introducing a normative version of the vocabulary and grammar of belief. Within certain circles in the United States, the religious languages taught are limited to Judaism and Christianity—and only through the lens of the Bible. Mark Chancey describes the history of biblical literacy courses in the United States, using the case of North Carolina to show that many Bible-as-literature courses intentionally or unintentionally often cross over into confessional teaching about the Bible. Indeed, certain organizations such as the National Council on Bible Curriculum in Public Schools actively push teachers to use their materials, which promote a fundamentalist Protestant interpretation of the Bible and a Christian-centric reading of US history (Chancey 2007). Other more nuanced biblical literacy teaching materials created by Chancey and the Society of Biblical Literature seek to provide a non-confessional investigation of the Bible-as-literature while exploring its influence in contemporary public life (Chancey 2014). Despite the best intentions of the Society of Biblical Literature, these biblical literacy courses reinforce Judeo-Christian hegemony in the United States. Furthermore, whether inadvertently or not, biblical literacy courses suggest that the *de minimis* of religious literacy is knowledge of scripture and its role in society, insinuating that religious people construct and express their religiosity based on sacred texts—a thoroughly Protestant perspective.

Scholars like Huston Smith, Karen Armstrong, and Stephen Prothero attempt to develop readers' multilingual understanding of a larger number of religious languages by providing them with a more diverse set of facts, concepts, and terms to memorize—a content-based approach not dissimilar to language courses that focus primarily on vocabulary acquisition. Smith, one of the first to introduce systematically the major religions of the world to a wide audience, focuses self-consciously on a limited set of "ideas" found within each religion. He creates a neat narrative about those beliefs in each religion defined by him as "universal" and therefore distinct from the "local peculiarities" blamed on cultural context (Smith 1991, 3). Smith therefore implies that he has distilled the grammar and vocabulary of each religious language into its standard form, ignoring local dialects as impure derivatives.

Prothero also seeks to present specific facts and terms about different religions as well as a meta-narrative about the beliefs of each tradition, similar in certain respects to the meta-narratives provided by Smith. However, he differentiates his multilingual approach from that of Armstrong and Smith by focusing on the differences between each religion, not their similarities. In fact he specifically rejects the scholarship of Smith and that of Armstrong, which suggest that each religion offers a similar message (Prothero 2010, 334). Whereas Armstrong claims that each religion at its core teaches the golden rule, Prothero denounces this universalizing tendency and instead dedicates an entire book to the differences between the beliefs and resultant practices of different religions (Armstrong 2006; Prothero 2010).

In *Religious Literacy: What Every American Needs to Know—and Doesn't*, Prothero writes that religiously literate Americans should understand religious beliefs and practices as they are "employed in American public life" (Prothero 2007, 17). However, analysis of his fifteen-question "Religious Literacy Quiz" reveals two strong biases that underscore a focus on developing a limited multilingualism. First, Prothero is primarily concerned with the Judeo-Christian tradition: ten out of fifteen questions test knowledge about Judaism and Christianity, leaving only five questions to cover Islam, Hinduism, Buddhism, and even the US Constitution (Prothero 2007, 35–36). Second, as a metric of religious literacy, the content knowledge tested shows that Prothero defines religious literacy fundamentally, if not exclusively, as an understanding of narrative and doctrines that relate to scripture and theology. Of the fifteen questions in this quiz, four test knowledge about the composition or structure of scripture, three test knowledge of scriptural narrative, and five test knowledge of specific doctrines as they relate to scripture and theology. In fact, he concludes *Religious Literacy* with an extensive "Dictionary of Religious Literacy" that defines over two hundred terms largely related to scriptural narrative and doctrine, the twin cornerstones of his approach (Prothero 2007, 18).

Prothero's emphasis on Judeo-Christian scriptural narrative and doctrine extends into the nationally administered U.S. Religious Knowledge Survey, a research project for which Prothero served as a senior advisor. A number of scholars reference this study, conducted by the Pew Research Center, to point out that Americans are religiously illiterate: on average, Americans correctly answered only half of the questions testing their knowledge of certain facts about religion (Pew 2010). In fact black Protestants—the second most religious group in America according to the widely cited Faith Matters Survey—averaged a score of 42% (Pew 2010; Putnam and Campbell 2012, 23–24). Self-described atheists and agnostics scored highest of all, answering more questions correctly than Jews, white evangelicals, white mainline Protestants, black Protestants, Catholics, and other religious communities.

If we accept that religious individuals communicate fluently within their own religious communities, what exactly do atheists know about religion that religious people do not? What does it mean when scholars say that Americans are highly religious yet religiously illiterate (D. Moore 2006, 2007; Prothero 2007)? Some intellectuals, like R. Laurence Moore, even label Americans as hypocrites who "are stupefyingly dumb about what they are supposed to believe" (R. L. Moore 1994, 10). To respond to these questions and claims it is necessary to differentiate more precisely religious multilingualism from religious fluency by utilizing a linguistic mode of inquiry that focuses on religious identity.

A Re-evaluation: Religious Identity and Fluency

When I learned to speak Spanish, my teacher taught us the vocabulary and grammar of a highly formal, normative version of the language. As a non-native speaker, I considered this version the standard by which I could measure fluency. I arrogantly judged speakers who contravened the rules I learned, marginalizing local dialects as imperfect copies of true Spanish that were less capable of conveying meaning. This was foolish: two people who speak a Chilean dialect of Spanish can speak effectively and efficiently with one another through their shared dialect, perhaps more so than if they tried to speak with one another using a Castilian dialect. The Association of Spanish Language Academies and other elite organizations might take it upon themselves to evaluate the validity of these dialects, but linguists neutrally recognize each as a vehicle of meaning.

Proponents of religious literacy education frequently measure religious fluency against a normative understanding of religious traditions. Too often they do not recognize that religious individuals and communities express religion in myriad ways, and that co-religionists can often better evidence their religiosity to one another through their local "dialects." Theologians and other religious leaders within each religious tradition often assume responsibility for determining orthodoxy, thereby separating the formal, standard version of the language from heterodox, even blasphemous, expressions. It is entirely the prerogative of religious communities to develop methods for in-group and out-group boundary maintenance. However, non-confessional education in public schools has a constitutional responsibility to avoid religious normativity;

to analyze, not evaluate, the construction of each religious language; and to investigate how that language works—that is, how religious people communicate meaning through religion. While Prothero is correct that Judeo-Christian scriptural narrative and doctrine do appear in countless public conversations about religion in the United States, a more capacious definition of religious literacy would factor in the ability to understand the influence of religion in communities—including non-Judeo-Christian communities—that express religiosity without reference to scriptural narrative or doctrine.

Analyzing the types of questions posed by the Pew U.S. Religious Knowledge Survey, it is clear that this study demonstrates that Americans are not familiar with belief-centric, scriptural narrative, and doctrine-based vocabulary words—especially not for multiple languages. However, this is more of a measure of a limited multilingualism than religious fluency. Surely if the survey asked black Protestants about those aspects of religious identity most important to them—moving beyond a multilingual and belief-centric framework—then this highly religious group would have scored higher on the survey. As Thomas Lewis writes, "If those who are deeply 'religious' have so little 'religious' knowledge, then we ought to wonder whether 'religious' refers to the same thing in both halves of the sentence" (Lewis 2015, 121). Whereas the type of "religious" knowledge tested by Pew measures familiarity with a belief-based vocabulary in multiple religious languages, individuals and communities often describe themselves as "religious" when they can communicate meaning fluently with co-religionists. We should reject R. Laurence Moore's inflammatory accusation that religious Americans do not know what they are supposed to believe because it presupposes that religious fluency is measured by testing knowledge of a set of beliefs determined by elites.

Religious fluency requires far more than knowledge of beliefs because religious identities are not necessarily belief-based. Indeed, we must challenge many scholars' normative assumptions about what it means to be religious. Instead of unquestioningly accepting the post-Protestant Enlightenment characterization of religion as a system of doctrinal and theological beliefs that inspire specific behaviors, we should investigate the full complexity and variety of processes of religious identity formation within and between religions. In other words, instead of assuming that religious people care primarily about "basic facts" about belief related to scriptures, doctrines, and theology, we should always inquire anew how a religious individual or community assigns value to those "facts" about belief as well as rituals, social norms, religious communities, and personal religious experiences.

A more thorough linguistic analysis of religious identity will enable religious literacy advocates to develop richer definitions of religious literacy—especially if the goal of religious literacy is to allow individuals to read the role of religion in the world. Without denying that Americans lack a dictionary-length vocabulary for their own religion, much less the religions of others, we should not downplay the fact that Americans can speak fluently with their co-religionists using their own religious languages. Before we focus on building students' religious vocabulary, it is necessary to use a linguistic mode of inquiry to refine our own analysis of what it means to be fluent in these religious languages. Religious linguistics will reveal the structure that undergirds religious languages: the shared processes of religious identity formation that, in conjunction with a shared vocabulary, allow co-religionists to fluently communicate with one another.

RELIGIOUS FLUENCY BEYOND LANGUAGE

Though the metaphor of language and linguistics opens new possibilities for understanding the richness of lived religion, it is critical to remember that religious individuals and communities do not only communicate meaning or construct religious identities through writing or speech. Indeed, religious identity is constructed and reinforced through verbal communication and nonverbal experience. Citizens who have a deeper, more nuanced understanding of this complexity are better able to have meaningful conversations about the role of religion in society. This is not to suggest that profound religious literacy leads to agreement, but rather to propose that profoundly religiously literate citizens will engage with the religious other through the aspects of religion that are most important to each of them rather than engage in interreligious dialogue that follows a narrow script. Just as knowledge of the textbook vocabulary or formal grammar of a language does not ensure a fluent conversation, familiarity with certain religious concepts and terms does not necessarily signal an ability to understand religiosity or lived religious experience. A linguistic understanding of religious languages will allow people to recognize how religious individuals communicate within their community.

Some scholars describe this linguistic analysis as the development of an "insider perspective" about religion (Grelle 2013; Haynes and Nord 1998; Nord 2010). This approach requires an empathetic understanding of how religious languages operate, not a sympathetic show of support for religious expressions (Haynes and Nord 1998). An insider's perspective approach also assumes that religious literacy education, particularly in American public schools, should reflect lived religious experience and the role of religion in society instead of seeking to propose normative modes of religiosity (Lester 2013). That said, some scholars do propose that analyzing and developing an insider perspective of the construction of religious languages will better prepare students to safeguard religious liberty (Haynes and Nord 1998; Lester 2013; Nord 2010). Others see a deeper analysis of religious language as a means to "foster the skills, values, interest, and confidence in students to be able to participate as active moral agents in the conscious social reproduction of society in its most inclusive form" (D. Moore 2007, 24). Despite these differences, there is consensus that while education about religion should increase individuals' ability to participate fully and respectfully in civic life, it should not aim to change students' religious identity. It is critical, then, to understand the complexity of religious identity formation.

A New Approach: Religious Literacy as Multilingual Linguistics

I did not learn Spanish by studying vocabulary alone. I memorized lists of words and conjugation rules in order to formulate sentences. My teacher taught us that the noun generally precedes the adjective in Spanish, the opposite of English. We learned that Spanish speakers conjugate verbs differently according to their level of familiarity with an interlocutor, and some dialects in Central America completely omit the informal second-person-plural *vosotros*. Younger Spanish speakers de-gender nouns whenever possible, replacing the masculine *o* or feminine *a* with an *x* to include both women and men in plural nouns such as *Latinx*.

Many world religions courses seek to build students' knowledge about a number of religious languages, yet they often exclude the variations of vocabulary or grammar among religious dialects. By overlooking the range of processes of religious identity formation, these courses inadvertently essentialize religions, casting them as monoliths that students can easily compare and contrast. Diane L. Moore provides a corrective to this essentialist model of religious literacy education by advocating for a cultural studies approach (D. Moore 2006, 2007, 2010). According to Moore and her influential report published with the imprimatur of the American Academy of Religion, lessons grounded in a cultural studies approach will teach students three premises about religion: (1) "Religions are internally diverse, not homogeneous;" (2) "Religions are dynamic and changing, not static and fixed;" and (3) "Religions are embedded in cultures, not isolated from them. Religions influence and are influenced by culture" (D. Moore 2010, 12–15). Lessons that teach these three premises about religion will focus not only on teaching students a definition or definitions of the content of religious speech but on "the fundamental intersections of religion and social/political/cultural life through multiple lenses" (D. Moore 2006, 56). This requires both a familiarity with content knowledge about religion and a facility with the skills of critical inquiry, a dual focus in many ways similar to the citizenship education approach advocated by Bernard Crick in the United Kingdom (Crick 1998).

Moore's preferred mode of inquiry enables students to interrogate first and foremost the ways communities—religious, political, social, educational, and more—produce and reproduce power, often in oppressive ways (D. Moore 2006, 2007). If world religions courses teach a "standard" version of religious languages, Moore's three guidelines teach students to problematize these standards as hegemonic versions of each religious language that often obscure the processes of meaning making that create and maintain power (D. Moore 2007). While I believe she pursues a worthy civic endeavor, Moore's cultural studies approach focuses on power and powerlessness at the expense of a comprehensive method for analyzing the *why* or *how* of the three premises about religion.

In order to guide their inquiry about why and how religious languages are internally diverse, dynamic, and embedded in culture, students need a toolkit to analyze the grammatical differences between religious dialects. In a foreign-language classroom, a student might recognize that differences exist between two dialects, but she might have a hard time explaining those differences without the ability to differentiate between verbs, nouns, and adjectives. A student studying religion might similarly recognize that differences exist between religious dialects, but he must learn to identify and describe the relationship between the building blocks of religious language. This mode of analysis—religious linguistics—enables students to more profoundly understand the many ways religious individuals authoritatively communicate meaning with co-religionists.

3B Framework as Linguistic Analysis

I propose a specific "linguistic" mode of inquiry—the 3B Framework (Table 4.1)—that focuses on the complex processes of religious identity formation to provide explanations for the three facts about religion set out by Moore and the American Academy of Religion (see also Marcus 2016). If religious communities communicate meaning through different "languages," religious linguists interrogate the construction of those languages to more clearly see how individuals and communities communicate meaning. This linguistic framework is critical for understanding how religious communities express their religious language in internally diverse, dynamic ways within different cultures.

Religious linguists can understand the internal diversity of religious languages, akin to the dialects found within spoken languages, by analyzing how various religious communities value and combine each of the building blocks of religious language—in other words, how they construct their religious identities. Scholars disagree about how to label these components of religious identity, and the number of categories varies. For our purposes we will borrow from a framework used by many sociologists that focuses on belief, behavior, and belonging (Davie 1994; Haidt 2012; Putnam and Campbell 2012). This 3B model has variations, with one scholar adding a fourth category, bonding, and

Table 4.1 The 3B Framework

3B Framework	A: Transcendent	B: Mundane
1. Belief	theologies, doctrines, sacred narratives, and holy texts	social values and ethics
2. Behavior	holy rites and rituals	habits and daily practices
3. Belonging	trans-historical, trans-national community of co-religionists complete with a social structure	racial, ethnic, familial, gender, sexual, and other identities

others still translating the 3B or 4B frameworks into 3C or 4C schemes: most notably, creed, code, cult, and community structure (Saroglou 2011; Swidler and Mozjes 2000). Ninian Smart, a pioneer of the phenomenological approach to religion, uses seven categories—doctrinal, mythological, ethical, ritual, experiential, institutional, and material (Smart 1999). Whether three, four, or seven building blocks, the core idea remains: understanding the complexity of lived religion requires the ability to parse religious language and to analyze how individuals and communities value each component within their religious identities.

The scholars who developed these frameworks defined their building blocks differently and conceived of the relationship between these components in various ways. I have developed a definition of the 3Bs that breaks each component into two parts, one oriented toward a transcendent reality and the other connecting this with the mundane:

(1A) Beliefs refer to the theologies, doctrines, sacred narratives, and holy texts that religious people refer to when speaking about the divine or a transcendent reality.
(1B) Belief can also refer to the social values and ethics that guide daily life.
(2A) Behavior refers to holy rites and rituals as well as (2B) religiously inflected habits and practices associated with daily life outside of a strictly sacred setting.
(3A) Belonging refers to a trans-historical, trans-national community of co-religionists complete with a social structure and (3B) the racial, ethnic, familial, gender, sexual, and other identities that inform and are informed by the religious identities of individuals and communities.

Despite the apparent neatness of these six categories, it is critical to avoid a rigid differentiation between components that reinforces a false notion that any one aspect of religious identity remains unaffected by any other aspect. Research in sociology and psychology shows that belief, behavior, and belonging are mutually constitutive, overturning the post-Enlightenment idea that belief leads to behavior (Haidt 2012). Recognizing the interplay between all six components does not profane the sacred but rather—like the American Academy of Religion guidelines—affirms the exchange between religion and culture. Embodied human experience requires a clear-eyed analysis of how the mundane, including culture, affects and is affected by notions of the transcendent. An analysis of the exchange between the transcendent and mundane will, in turn, trouble attempts to cleanly differentiate between the religious and the secular: "religious" ideas about and experiences of the transcendent affect daily life just as mundane experience and "secular" ideas affect notions of the transcendent.

To gain a clearer understanding of the interaction between all six components of religious identity, it is critical to study the different ways that religious languages combine and value these components. The diversity of religious-language construction manifests both within and between religions. While some religious communities and individuals might communicate through a language that values belief above all else, others might privilege a sense of belonging and interpret beliefs through the lens of community experience. For example, in one study I conducted at a Catholic parish in Rhode Island, one respondent identified as Catholic because he felt that rites and celebrating holidays (i.e., behaviors) connect him with family (i.e., belonging), while another respondent identified as Catholic because of her belief in Jesus and the doctrine of transubstantiation. In analyzing religions it is critical to compare and contrast the construction of religious identity within and across the boundaries of religions, just as much if not more so than comparing and contrasting the religious vocabulary used by religious people to describe their religious identities. To use a different example, while vocabulary about salvation or nirvana may separate a progressive Christian language from a progressive Buddhist language, the grammatical constructions of those progressive religious languages may be more similar than the constructions of progressive and conservative Christian languages (see Haynes and Nord 1998, 174–175).

Yet too often Americans assume that they understand a religion when they learn about belief via doctrines and scriptural narrative. Defining religious identity solely according to belief would render unintelligible the experience of countless religious individuals and communities for whom behavior and belonging drive religious identity. Without a deep understanding of religious identity, how could you explain the fact that the majority of American Catholics support the use of contraception and the ordination of women except to label these Catholics ignorant or hypocritical (Lewis 2015; Pew 2015b)? If you believe that religious identity is predicated on belief, how could you explain the fact that half of all those who self-identify as Jewish are not completely confident that they believe in God (Putnam and Campbell 2012)? Or what of the statistical evidence that gender, age, race, ethnicity, and geographic region all affect religiosity in the United States (Putnam and Campbell 2012)? A religious linguist needs a firm grasp of the construction of religious identity through belief, behavior, and belonging in order to understand these and other examples of the complexity of lived religious experience.

With a deeper understanding of the internal diversity of religious languages, religious linguists can critically analyze the ways these dialects change over time and incorporate new vocabulary as "slang." Just as contemporary Spanish differs from that used by Cervantes in the seventeenth century, religious languages change over time, incorporating new words and transforming the meaning of old words according to ever-changing emphases on specific aspects of belief, behavior, and belonging. For example, Christian theologians like Augustine and Aquinas—divided by centuries, cultures, and the evolving status of the Roman Catholic Church in the world—define and refine definitions of sin. Even the same word within different dialects of a religious language can contain multiple meanings at one point in time. Whereas queer Christian theologians might define sin in relation to the HIV/AIDS epidemic, conservative Christian theologians might explain sin with reference to queer identities. And just as languages borrow from each other as they come into contact, creating new forms of language like Spanglish, religious languages can borrow terms and concepts from one another. Instead of critiquing Buddhists who use the word *sin* to describe Buddhist concepts, for example, a religious linguist will explore why and how the experience of belonging to an American Buddhist community within a majority Christian society affects grammar and the communication of meaning between Buddhist and non-Buddhist communities (Prothero 2010). The 3B Framework, then, grounds the mode of inquiry of religious linguistics and provides a means for understanding the processes of religious identity formation that account for the dialects, slang, and dynamism of religious languages.

Application: Interreligious Dialogue as Meaningful Conversation

Imagine trying to tell a friend about your childhood home using the following vocabulary list: apartment, city, kitchen, parents, and pet. For some readers, this vocabulary list may be perfect for the task: perhaps you grew up with a dog in a two-bedroom apartment in a large city, nurtured by your two parents, who cooked often and insisted everyone gather for meals around the kitchen table. For other readers, this vocabulary list is not only ill suited for the exercise, it actively inhibits the ability to clearly discuss the reality of your childhood home, forcing a definition by negation: perhaps you grew up in a house in the middle of cornfields, not in an apartment in the city; your father raised you alone, and given his long work hours preferred to eat at a local diner most days of the week; in fact, your strongest memories were of the family room, where you and your father watched reruns of *The Simpsons*. Now imagine translating this description of your childhood home into another language.

Meaningful dialogue cannot take place when two individuals discuss a subject in which neither has any vested interest—just as two people cannot substantively discuss the experience of growing up in their childhood homes by using the language of square footage. Yet interreligious dialogue often utilizes a predetermined vocabulary and grammar that overlooks the aspects of religious identity most important to the interlocutors. For example, "interfaith" dialogue that compares and contrasts beliefs might inadvertently preclude meaningful conversations by ignoring the religious identities of participants who value primarily experiences of behavior or belonging. This is especially important to keep in mind when designing interreligious dialogue opportunities for students (see Patel 2012). By not connecting with those aspects of religious life most important to young people, interreligious dialogue and engagement miss an opportunity to tap into those aspects of religion that might motivate or sustain them in daily life.

Meaningful interreligious dialogue engages the driving force behind participants' religious identity, whether belief, behavior, or belonging. Peter Ochs evocatively describes this as "hearth-to-hearth" dialogue that "emerges from places of maximal warmth, depth, and fire within each religious community and tradition that is engaged in the dialogue" (2015, 488). For Ochs, hearth-to-hearth dialogue flows from experience of the sacred. In a different context, Jonathan Haidt uses the phrase "follow the sacredness" to describe a similar model of dialogue that does not presuppose the importance of any specific concept to an interlocutor's identity or position on a given issue (2012, 364). While Ochs and Haidt might not agree on the definition of religion or the sacred, they both arrive at the conclusion that meaningful dialogue cannot begin with an imposed set of ideas about where meaning resides.

A method of interreligious dialogue deeply grounded in linguistics—especially through the belief, behavior, and belonging framework—encourages an individual both to look within to understand the construction of her own religious identity and to listen to how the other constructs his religious identity. An example: Mary might look within and realize that belief, especially theology, shapes her religious language. She might also recognize that behavior, in the form of rituals, is extremely important in her own life. Listening to Ali, she might learn that he constructs his religious language based on rituals and community life. Equipped with this knowledge, Mary is better able to speak with Ali about that aspect of religion about which they both care—ritual.

Despite the importance of identifying a linguistic marker of shared concern, interreligious dialogue should not disregard difference. Indeed, Mary and Ali might participate in extremely different rituals that affect and are affected by divergent beliefs within distinct communities. Meaningful conversations do not require agreement, nor do they require a religious relativism that values all religions equally. However, by focusing on an aspect of religious identity important to all speakers, linguistically informed dialogue increases the chances that individuals will eschew discussions about vocabulary words in favor of conversations about how they read the world around them according to their religious languages. Of course interlocutors will need a baseline multilingualism in order to avoid misunderstanding the religious language used by the other. But the content knowledge of multilingualism is in service to linguistically driven dialogue. Thus, we return with fresh eyes to the claim at the beginning of this chapter that religiously literate individuals—those equipped to engage in meaningful dialogue about the role of religion in private and public life—will be multilingual linguists.

CONCLUSION: OPPORTUNITIES TO STRENGTHEN RELIGIOUS LITERACY EDUCATION

In many ways the United States began a new chapter after September 11, but not everyone is on the same page. For the first time in its history, Protestants do not constitute a majority in the United States (Pew 2015a). Rather than celebrate this rich diversity, many Americans respond to the changing religious landscape with fear. Attacks on religious minorities are on the rise, and major political figures propose policies that undermine the religious freedom of marginalized communities (Criminal Justice Information Services Division 2014). American educational institutions must develop students' religious literacy so that they can engage in meaningful conversations about religion and its role in private and public life without relying on an essentialist understanding of various religions that perpetuates stereotypes.

I advocate for religious literacy education that utilizes the 3B Framework. Schools must enable students to interrogate how the complex process of religious identity formation creates religious dialects that permeate national and communal conversations. As multilingual linguists, students will have the ability to "read" both privileged and marginalized stories of religion in America by focusing on not only circumscribed belief-centric, scripturally driven manifestations of religion often favored by elites but also complex lived religious community experience. School lessons should nurture students' ability to utilize a linguistic mode of inquiry to study the construction of religious identity for different individuals and communities. A focus on linguistic analysis of primary and secondary sources—both written and nontextual—will facilitate the acquisition of content knowledge about religious vocabulary while also developing a civic competency: the ability to participate in meaningful dialogue about religion in public life.

Researchers have a number of exciting opportunities to contribute to the field of religious literacy education both by analyzing processes of religious identity formation across the nation and by testing pedagogical approaches to facilitate meaningful conversations. For example, pollsters can significantly contribute to the field by providing a deeper and broader understanding of the complexity of religious identity formation. A national survey that analyzes the varieties of religious identities within and between religious communities using the 3Bs would require a mixed-methods approach: in addition to questions that test religiosity by proxy such as "how strong is your belief in God" or "how important is religion in your daily life," these surveys could invite respondents to freely describe the aspects of religious identity that are most important in their lives (Putnam and Campbell 2012). A survey that combines the 3B Framework with the Faith Matters Survey would allow researchers to develop a deep understanding of religious identity while measuring the strength of individuals' religiosity. Analysts could map out the varieties of religious identities within religions—from almost exclusively belief-, behavior-, or belonging-focused to every possible combination of the three—and identify similarities between communities across traditions. The results would challenge the rigid distinction between religions by de-emphasizing the difference of vocabularies and underscoring the construction of religious identity.

Scholars and educators should also conduct research on religious literacy education in public schools to determine if current approaches favor belief, behavior, or belonging. Based on Prothero, Smith, and Armstrong's influential approaches to world religions—and given the widespread interchangeability of the word "religion" with "faith" in the United States—I suspect that most public school teachers who cover religion do so by presenting a limited set of beliefs in each tradition. I also hypothesize that students learn that beliefs cause behaviors and therefore overwhelmingly seek to explain behaviors by interrogating the beliefs of the actor, without reference to her or his community of belonging. A study of the 3Bs in religious literacy education might also explain the current state of "interfaith" dialogue in the United States, especially the emphasis on modes of interreligious engagement that focus primarily on conversations about theologies, doctrines, and scriptures (e.g., Ford and Pecknold 2006).

Perhaps most important for religious literacy scholar-activists, future research should assess the effect of a 3B religious literacy education on students' prejudices and stereotypes about the religious other, building on baseline research conducted over the last decade. One study supported by the European Commission found that students who learn about religion in school are more willing to talk about religions with students from different backgrounds, but this study included no specific recommendations for effective teaching frameworks (Weisse et al. 2009). Another famous study in Modesto, California, conducted by Emile Lester and Patrick Roberts measured the effects of a mandated world religions class on students' religiosity, prejudices, and willingness to stand up for the rights of the religious other (Lester and Roberts 2006). While the results of this test were encouraging—students maintained a consistent commitment to their own religions while exhibiting less prejudice toward the other—the Modesto world religions course applied an old model of religious literacy education that largely overlooked the complexity of religious identity formation and the internal diversity of traditions (Lester 2011, 2013; Lester and Roberts 2006). Researchers should measure whether a curriculum built around the 3B Framework is more or less effective in reducing stereotypes and prejudice. I hypothesize that a more nuanced religious literacy curriculum that enables and encourages students to participate in meaningful, "hearth-to-hearth" conversations with the religious other are more likely to reduce negative interactions between different religious individuals and communities. If true, this may have significant implications for policy proposals to prevent and reduce religion-related violence through education.

FUTURE DIRECTIONS

1. How can researchers design surveys that assess the relative importance of belief, behavior, and belonging for individuals' religious identities?
2. Do public conversations and school lessons about religion reference certain elements of religious identity more than others? Does this match the way Americans construct their own religious identities?
3. How will religious communities react to lessons about religion that treat belief, behavior, and belonging as mutually constitutive?
4. What are the most effective, constitutionally appropriate pedagogies for teaching about the various components of religious identity in a public school?

5. Are public school teachers able to facilitate meaningful conversations about religion in public life without inviting students to reflect deeply about the construction of their own religious identities?

6. Does a deeper understanding of the construction of religious identity lead to a reduction in prejudices and stereotypes about the religious other? Will it lead to new antagonisms between progressive and conservative individuals and groups within a religious community?

References

Armstrong, Karen. 2006. *The Great Transformation: The Beginning of Our Religious Traditions.* New York: Anchor Books.

Chancey, Mark A. 2007. "A Textbook Example of the Christian Right: The National Council on Bible Curriculum in Public Schools." *Journal of the American Academy of Religion* 75 (September), no. 3: 554–581.

———. 2014. "Public School Bible Courses in Historical Perspective: North Carolina as a Case Study." In *The Bible in the Public Square: Its Enduring Influence in American Life*, edited by Mark A. Chancey, Carol Meyers, and Eric M. Meyers, 193–214. Atlanta: Society of Biblical Literature Press.

Crick, Bernard, et al. 1998. *Education for Citizenship and the Teaching of Democracy in Schools.* Sudbury, Suffolk, UK: Qualifications and Curriculum Authority.

Criminal Justice Information Services Division. 2014. "2014 Hate Crime Statistics." Uniform Crime Reports. Washington, DC: Federal Bureau of Investigation. https://www.fbi.gov/about-us/cjis/ucr/hate-crime/2014.

Davie, Grace. 1994. *Religion in Britain Since 1945: Believing Without Belonging.* Oxford, UK: Wiley-Blackwell.

Ford, David F., and C. C. Pecknold, eds. 2006. *The Promise of Scriptural Reasoning.* Malden, MA: Blackwell Publishing.

Grelle, Bruce. 2013. "Promoting Civic and Religious Literacy in Public Schools: The California 3Rs Project." In *Religion in the Public Schools: Negotiating the New Commons*, edited by Michael D. Waggoner, 91–111. New York: Rowman and Littlefield Publishers.

Haidt, Jonathan. 2012. *The Righteous Mind: Why Good People Are Divided by Politics and Religion.* New York: Vintage Books.

Haynes, Charles C., and Warren A. Nord. 1998. *Taking Religion Seriously Across the Curriculum.* Nashville, TN: First Amendment Center.

Lester, Emile. 2011. *Teaching About Religions: A Democratic Approach for Public Schools.* Ann Arbor: University of Michigan Press, 2011.

———. 2013. "To Change Society or Reflect It?: Comparing the Cultural Studies and Community Consensus Approaches to Teaching about Religion." In *Religion in the Public Schools: Negotiating the New Commons*, edited by Michael D. Waggoner, 111–129. New York: Rowman and Littlefield Publishers.

Lester, Emile, and Patrick S. Roberts. 2006. *Learning About World Religions in Public Schools: The Impact on Student Attitudes and Community Acceptance in Modesto, Calif.* Nashville, TN: First Amendment Center.

Lewis, Thomas A. 2015. *Why Philosophy Matters for the Study of Religion—and Vice Versa*. New York: Oxford University Press.

Marcus, Benjamin. April 4, 2016. "Six Guidelines for Teaching About Religion." *Education Week* (http://blogs.edweek.org/edweek/global_learning/2016/04/six_guidelines_for_teaching_about_religion.html).

Moore, Diane L. November 2006. "Overcoming Religious Illiteracy: A Cultural Studies Approach." *World History Connected* 4, no. 1 (http://worldhistoryconnected.press.illinois.edu/4.1/moore.html).

———. 2007. *Overcoming Religious Illiteracy: A Cultural Studies Approach to the Study of Religion in Secondary Education*. New York: Palgrave MacMillan, 2007.

———. April 2010. "Guidelines for Teaching About Religion in K-12 Public Schools in the United States." American Academy of Religion (https://www.aarweb.org/sites/default/files/pdfs/Publications/epublications/AARK-12CurriculumGuidelines.pdf).

Moore, R. Laurence. 1994. *Selling God: American Religion in the Marketplace of Culture*. New York: Oxford University Press.

Nord, Warren A. 2010. *Does God Make a Difference?: Taking Religion Seriously in Our Schools and Universities*. New York: Oxford University Press.

Ochs, Peter. 2015. "The Possibilities and Limits of Inter-Religious Dialogue." In *The Oxford Handbook of Religion, Conflict, and Peacebuilding*, edited by Atalia Omer, R. Scott Appleby, and David Little, 488–515. New York: Oxford University Press.

Patel, Eboo. 2012. *Sacred Ground: Pluralism, Prejudice, and the Promise of America*. Boston: Beacon Press.

Pew Research Center. 2010. "U.S. Religious Knowledge Survey." Washington, DC: Pew Forum on Religion & Public Life (http://www.pewforum.org/files/2010/09/religious-knowledge-full-report.pdf).

———. 2015a. "America's Changing Religious Landscape." Washington, DC: Pew Forum on Religion & Public Life.

———. 2015b. "U.S. Catholics Open to Non-Traditional Families." Washington, DC: Pew Forum on Religion & Public Life.

Prothero, Stephen. 2007. *Religious Literacy: What Every American Needs to Know—and Doesn't*. New York: HarperOne, 2007.

———. 2010. *God Is Not One: The Eight Rival Religions That Run the World*. New York: HarperOne.

Putnam, Robert D., and David E. Campbell. 2012. *American Grace: How Religion Divides and Unites Us*. New York: Simon & Schuster.

Saroglou, Vassilis. November 2011. "Believing, Bonding, Behaving, and Belonging: The Big Four Religious Dimensions and Cultural Variation." *Journal of Cross-Cultural Psychology* 42, no. 8: 1320–1340.

Smart, Ninian. 1999. *Dimensions of the Sacred: An Anatomy of the World's Beliefs*. Berkeley: University of California Press.

Smith, Huston. 1991. *The World's Religions*. New York: HarperOne.

Swidler, Leonard, and Paul Mojzes. 2000. *The Study of Religion in an Age of Global Dialogue*. Philadelphia: Temple University Press.

Weisse, Wolfram, et al. May 2009. *Religion in Education: A Contribution to Dialogue or a Factor of Conflict in Transforming Societies of European Countries?* Hamburg: Universität Hamburg.

Further Reading

Chancey, Mark A., Carol Meyers, and Eric M. Meyers, eds. 2014. *The Bible in the Public Square: Its Enduring Influence in American Life*. Atlanta, GA: Society of Biblical Literature Press.

Eck, Diana L. 2001. *A New Religious America: How a "Christian Country" Has Become the World's Most Religiously Diverse Nation*. New York: HarperOne.

Moore, Diane L. 2007. *Overcoming Religious Illiteracy: A Cultural Studies Approach to the Study of Religion in Secondary Education*. New York: Palgrave MacMillan.

Peace, Jennifer Howe, Or N. Rose, and Gregory Mobley, eds. 2012. *My Neighbor's Faith: Stories of Interreligious Encounter, Growth, and Transformation*. Maryknoll, NY: Orbis Books.

Prothero, Stephen. 2007. *Religious Literacy: What Every American Needs to Know—and Doesn't*. New York: HarperOne.

Saroglou, Vassilis. November 2011. "Believing, Bonding, Behaving, and Belonging: The Big Four Religious Dimensions and Cultural Variation." *Journal of Cross-Cultural Psychology* 42, no. 8: 1320–1340.

Waggoner, Michael D., ed. 2013. *Religion in the Public Schools: Negotiating the New Commons*. New York: Rowman and Littlefield Publishers.

Wertheimer, Linda K. 2015. *Faith Ed.: Teaching About Religion in an Age of Intolerance*. Boston: Beacon Press.

CHAPTER 5

RELIGIOUS LIBERTY IN AMERICAN EDUCATION

CHARLES C. HAYNES

> One of America's continuing needs is to develop, out of our differences, a common vision for the common good. Today that common vision must embrace a shared understanding of the place of religion in public life and of the guiding principles by which people with deep religious differences can contend robustly but civilly with each other.
>
> Summary of Principles, The Williamsburg Charter

OVER the past two decades, broad coalitions of national religious, civil liberties, and educational groups have found agreement on many key issues concerning the constitutional role of religion in public schools under current law. Four major principles undergird this consensus:

1. As the US Supreme Court has made clear, the study of religion in public schools is constitutional.
2. The study of religion is tremendously important if students are to be educated about our history and culture and adequately prepared for global citizenship.
3. Public schools must teach *about* religions objectively or neutrally; their purpose must be education, not indoctrination.
4. Public schools must have sound policies that protect the religious liberty rights of all students under current law.

Unfortunately, consensus among national organizations has not ended confusion and conflict on the local level. Many people—indeed, many educators—are either unfamiliar with this consensus or remain reluctant to tackle issues that have historically divided Americans.

Despite frequent distribution of guidance by the US Department of Education and by religious, civil liberties, and educational groups informing educators and parents about current law governing the role of religion in public schools, school districts in many communities continue to largely avoid religion in the curriculum and, in some instances, unlawfully censor students' religious expression. In many other districts, particularly in Southern states, the majority religion continues to dominate the school culture in ways that often violate the First Amendment. Even in districts where individual teachers are attempting to do a good job of addressing religion in the classroom, there are few district-wide policies articulating how best to include study about religions and protect students' religious liberty rights.

Taking a proactive approach to religion-in-schools issues can be a risky business, especially at a time when litigation is often the first recourse rather than the last resort in the United States. But the greater risk is to ignore the distrust and discontent that have led many parents to conclude, fairly or unfairly, that public schools are either hostile to their religion and values or determined to promote the majority religion. In order to rebuild trust—and create school communities that are fair, just, and inclusive—local school boards and educators would be wise to take advantage of the constitutional and legal safe harbor provided by the national consensus about the role of religion in public schools.

The First Amendment School

Getting religion right in public education requires, first and foremost, taking religious liberty seriously throughout the culture of the school. The starting point for addressing religious issues in public schools is the First Amendment to the US Constitution, especially the opening sixteen words: "Congress shall make no law respecting the establishment of religion, or prohibiting the free exercise thereof." When properly understood and applied, the Religion Clauses constitute a civic framework within which public schools both protect the rights of all students and ensure appropriate study about religions across the curriculum.

At a time when extreme voices often dominate the debate in our culture wars, many educators and parents are understandably confused and conflicted about how best to interpret and apply the First Amendment in their schools. On one end of the spectrum are those who push for religion—their religion—to be privileged in school practices and policies. On the other end are those who insist that public schools must be religion-free zones. Caught in the middle, school boards and administrators are often reluctant to change the status quo, leaving in place practices that either promote one religion or ignore all religion.

In an effort to clear up this longstanding confusion—and to help school districts move from battleground to common ground—a coalition of twenty-one national organizations came together in the mid-1990s to articulate a shared vision of how to apply the First Amendment in public schools in a document entitled *Religious Liberty, Public*

Education, and the Future of American Democracy (1995). The core of the agreement is captured in Principle IV, which states:

> Public schools may not inculcate nor inhibit religion. They must be places where religion and religious conviction are treated with fairness and respect. Public schools uphold the First Amendment when they protect the religious liberty rights of students of all faiths or none. Schools demonstrate fairness when they ensure that the curriculum includes study *about* religion, where appropriate, as an important part of a complete education.

Endorsers include a broad range of advocacy groups, from the American Center for Law and Justice on the right to People for the American Way on the left. Leading educational organizations such as the National School Boards Association and the American Association of School Administrators signed on with the Anti-Defamation League, Christian Legal Society, Council on Islamic Education, American Jewish Committee, and others. In the years since that statement was first released, a series of additional consensus statements with specific guidance on religion in schools have been issued by coalitions of national organizations representing diverse religious and ideological perspectives. Drawing on these documents, the US Department of Education disseminated guidance in 2000 and 2003 that reflected, for the most part, the common ground reached by religious and educational groups.

Contrary to the rhetoric of the culture war, there is actually much common ground on how to address student religious expression and study about religions in public schools under current law.

STUDENT RELIGIOUS EXPRESSION

More than fifty years after the US Supreme Court's rulings on "prayer in schools," many Americans still hold the mistaken view that the Court prohibited students from expressing their faith during the school day. In reality, the Court never banned prayer from public schools; it barred *school-sponsored* religious practices. Writing for the majority in *Board of Education v. Mergens* (1990), Justice Sandra Day O'Connor underscored the "crucial difference between *government* speech endorsing religion, which the Establishment Clause forbids, and *private* speech endorsing religion, which the Free Speech and Free Exercise Clauses protect."

Under the First Amendment as interpreted by the Supreme Court, students *do* have the right to pray in public schools alone or in groups, as long as the activity does not disrupt the school or infringe on the rights of others. These activities must be truly voluntary and student-initiated. For example, students may gather around the flagpole for prayer before school begins, as long as the school does not sponsor the event and other students are not pressured to attend.

Students may also share their faith with others and read their scriptures during their free time. When it is relevant to the discussion and meets the academic requirements, students have the right to express personal religious views in class or as part of a written assignment or art activity. They may not, of course, harass or coerce others, disrupt the educational process, or force classmates to participate in a religious exercise.

Most legal experts agree that students have the right to distribute religious literature in public schools subject to reasonable restrictions imposed by school officials regarding time, place, and manner. This means that the school may specify when and where the distribution may occur. But the restrictions must be reasonable, and the schools must apply them evenly to all non-school student literature.

In secondary schools, the Equal Access Act of 1984 ensures that students may form religious clubs if the school allows other extracurricular clubs. The act is intended to protect student-initiated and student-led meetings. Outsiders may not "direct, conduct, control, or regularly attend student religious clubs, and faculty sponsors may be present at religious club meetings in a non-participatory capacity only." Schools must grant student religious clubs access to school facilities and media on the same basis as other extracurricular clubs.

Agreement on many issues involving student religious expression does not, of course, mean agreement on all issues. Conflicts remain, for example, about if and when school officials may draw the line on student religious expression before a captive audience at school events. At present, a patchwork of lower-court rulings and state laws provide different answers and the US Supreme Court has not yet fully resolved the matter.

The good news, however, is that considerable consensus has been achieved on students' religious liberty rights in public schools. This includes agreement on the need to accommodate, when reasonable and feasible to do so, the religious needs and requirements of our increasingly religiously diverse student population.

Religious Accommodation

In one of the most widely disseminated consensus statements, *A Teacher's Guide to Religion in the Public Schools* (First Amendment Center), twenty religious, religious liberty, and educational groups agree that "whenever possible, school officials should try to accommodate the requests of parents and students for excusal from classroom discussions or activities for religious reasons." If the request is focused on a specific discussion, assignment, or activity, it "should be routinely granted in order to strike a balance between the student's religious freedom and the school's interest in providing a well-rounded education."

This does not mean, however, school officials can or should accommodate all opt-out requests, especially when such requests are extensive. For example, schools cannot accommodate parents who want their child to be excused from the world history class every time religion is mentioned, because religion frequently comes up (or ought to) in the study of world civilizations. But when parents limit their requests to particular lessons or activities, schools should provide an alternative assignment for the student.

Schools are also increasingly asked to accommodate religious practices of students. Again, if honoring such requests is feasible without disrupting the school or involving school officials in endorsement of religion, they should be routinely granted. Providing a quiet space that is not being used so that Muslim students can pray at lunchtime, for example, raises no constitutional questions. But creating or designating a "prayer chapel" in the school would be a clear violation of the Establishment Clause.

Religious accommodation does not include placing school officials in the position of monitoring a student's compliance with religious requirements of the family's religious tradition. Enforcing religious obligations such as religious garb or dietary restrictions is the responsibility of the parents, not administrators or teachers.

Accommodating religious needs and requirements of students can be time-consuming, inconvenient, and often frustrating in a religiously diverse society. But religious accommodation in public schools serves the common good by upholding our commitment to religious freedom and building trust between schools and the communities they serve.

STUDY ABOUT RELIGIONS

Public schools that uphold the religious liberty rights of students should also ensure that the curriculum treats religion fairly and fully. Under US Supreme Court rulings, public schools are prohibited by the Establishment Clause from preferring one religion over another and from preferring religion over nonreligion. Writing for the majority in *Abington v. Schempp*, Justice Tom Clark described required religious exercises in public schools as a "breach of neutrality" barred by the First Amendment.

Justice Clark was careful, however, to make clear that government neutrality cannot result in hostility to religion. That is, government cannot prefer nonreligion over religion either. As he wrote, the government may not establish a "religion of secularism" by opposing or showing hostility to religion. Neither should neutrality be taken to mean that the curriculum must exclude religion. On the contrary, the study of religion is important. In the frequently quoted words of the Court's decision in *Abington v. Schempp*,

> [I]t might well be said that one's education is not complete without a study of comparative religion or the history of religion and its relationship to the advancement of civilization. It certainly may be said that the Bible is worthy of study for its literary and historic qualities. Nothing we have said here indicates that such study of the Bible or of religion, when presented objectively as part of a secular education, may not be effected consistently with the First Amendment.

Public schools clearly have permission to require that students learn about religion (leaving educators to determine where and how this should be done). In fact, if public schools may not inculcate nor inhibit religion, if they are to remain neutral concerning religion under the First Amendment, then the curriculum must include religious as well as secular ways of understanding the world.

In First Amendment Center's first consensus statement, *Religion in the Public School Curriculum*, released in 1989, seventeen religious and educational organizations— ranging from the National Association of Evangelicals to the National Education Association—described the necessity of teaching about religions this way:

> Because religion plays a significant role in history and society, study about religion is essential to understanding both the nation and the world. Omission of facts about religion can give students the false impression that the religious life of humankind is insignificant or unimportant. Failure to understand even the basic symbols, practices, and concepts of the various religions makes much of history, literature, art, and contemporary life unintelligible.

A public school curriculum that ignores religion marginalizes religion in our intellectual and cultural life, implicitly conveying the sense that religion is irrelevant in the search for truth in the various domains of the curriculum. On both civic and educational grounds, a fair and neutral curriculum would include considerable study of religion.

THE ROLE OF THE TEACHER

Fairness and neutrality in the public school curriculum are possible only when teachers have a clear understanding of their role under the First Amendment. Teachers in public schools are employees of the government (or, better, they are there to act on behalf of all citizens). In that capacity, they are subject to the Establishment Clause and thus required to be neutral concerning religion while carrying out their duties as teachers.

The neutrality required of teachers by the First Amendment is intended to prevent the government from imposing religious or antireligious views on students. True, in settings beyond the school, courts have let stand some traditional acknowledgments of religion in government settings (the Supreme Court itself opens with prayer). But when a captive audience of "impressionable young minds" is involved, the courts are stricter in applying the Establishment Clause.

This constitutional requirement of neutrality limits in some respects the academic freedom of the public school teacher. Teachers have the freedom, indeed the obligation, to expose students to the marketplace of ideas. They may not, however, either inculcate or denigrate religion. When teaching about religion, the teacher, like the curriculum, does not take sides concerning religion.

Does this mean a public school teacher may never mention personal religious views? What should happen when, for example, students ask the teacher to reveal his or her religion? Most religious liberty experts agree that teachers are free to answer the question but should consider the age of the students before doing so. Middle and high school students may be able to distinguish between a personal view and the official position of the school; very young children may not. In any case, the teacher may answer with a brief statement of personal belief but may not turn the question into an opportunity to proselytize for or against religion.

Teachers, like students, bring their religious identity through the schoolhouse door each morning. The Establishment Clause does not prohibit teachers from reading a religious book during noninstructional time, saying a quiet grace before meals, or wearing modest religious jewelry. If a group of teachers wishes to meet for prayer or scriptural study during the school day, there is no constitutional reason why they should not be permitted to do so as long as the activity is outside the presence of students and does not interfere with the rights of other teachers.

Constitutional violations occur when educators use their position as administrator, teacher, or coach to either promote or denigrate religion. Public school educators have a civic and professional duty to model First Amendment principles when carrying out their responsibilities during their contract day. A school culture that takes the First Amendment seriously is a place where administrators and teachers clearly understand how to apply religious liberty principles to protect the rights of students and address religion in the classroom.

TEACHER EDUCATION

Many parents who might accept the constitutional framework for teaching about religions in principle may also believe that in practice it is risky or dangerous to include religion in the curriculum because teachers, no matter how well intentioned, will inevitably display their ignorance and prejudices. Members of minority traditions may worry that in a predominantly Christian culture, alternatives to Christianity will not receive knowledgeable or fair treatment, and teachers may end up advocating Christianity, even if subtly or indirectly. Some Christians may be concerned that the Christianity is misrepresented or inadequately represented in the curriculum.

These are justifiable concerns. The great majority of teachers are not fully prepared to teach about religions. Many know little about religious traditions other than their own—if they have one. Having said that, many teachers—especially in the social studies—have been teaching more about religions in recent years, mostly without controversy. In some school districts, professional development opportunities have helped prepare teachers to teach unfamiliar material. In others, teachers have found ways to supplement their knowledge of religions with guest speakers, field trips, and creative use of primary sources.

Nonetheless, if study about religions is to be done well—and fully—in public schools, significant reforms in teacher and administrator preparation are needed:

- Schools of education must teach all prospective administrators and teachers the First Amendment framework for addressing religion in public schools. Educators must understand the civic and educational ground rules in order to protect the religious liberty rights of students and include study about religions in the curriculum in ways that are constitutionally and educationally sound.
- Public school teachers who deal with religiously contested matters in the curriculum should know something about the relationship of religion to their particular subjects and disciplines. Ideally, they should be required, as part of their certification, to take at least one course relating religion to their subject. Whether required or not, departments of religious studies should make such courses available as electives.
- To do the job well, teachers must have good textbooks and resource materials. To encourage the development of better teaching resources, state departments of education need to set standards that include more comprehensive treatment of religions at appropriate places in the curriculum.
- Universities and school districts should address topics related to teaching about religions in a variety of summer institutes and in-service workshops.
- Religious studies should become a certifiable field, requiring at least an undergraduate minor. Schools that offer electives in world religions or the Bible must have teachers competent to teach them.
- Local school boards must adopt religious liberty polices that outline the rights of students and make it clear that study about religions is an appropriate and important part of the curriculum. The development of these policies should include representatives of various constituencies, working together to establish guidelines consistent with the First Amendment and current law.

FINDING COMMON GROUND

The national guidelines agreed to by many religious, civil liberties, and educational groups provide an unprecedented opportunity for local school districts to find common ground on historically divisive issues concerning religion in public schools.

A good first step in districts without adequate policies on religion would be for the superintendent and school board to appoint a task force with educators, parents, students, and community leaders with diverse religious and political perspectives. The ground rules or civic framework for deliberations of the task force should be guided by the religious liberty principles that flow from the First Amendment. In the Williamsburg Charter, a vision of the First Amendment signed by nearly two hundred national leaders in 1988, these principles are described as the "3Rs" of religious liberty, as explained in

Finding Common Ground: The First Amendment Guide to Religion and Public Schools (2011, 18):

- *Rights.* Religious liberty, freedom of conscience, is a precious, fundamental and inalienable right.
- *Responsibilities.* Rights are best guarded and responsibilities best exercised when each person and group guards for all others those rights they wish guarded for themselves.
- *Respect.* Conflict and debate are vital to democracy. Yet if controversies about religion and politics are to reflect the highest wisdom on the First Amendment and advance the best interests of the disputants and the nation, then *how* we debate, and not only *what* we debate, is critical.

Since the signing of the charter and the adoption of national guidelines, the "rights, responsibilities, and respect" framework has enabled school districts in various regions of the country—from Wicomico County, Maryland, to Modesto, California—to reach common ground on comprehensive policies addressing religion in their local schools.

Conclusions

Civic agreement on First Amendment policies does not, of course, inoculate a school district from all conflict and controversy over religion. New culture war fights (e.g., how to address sexual orientation) or old culture war battles (e.g., teaching of creationism) will continue to spark debate and test the limits of "common ground." But school districts with policies that address core issues of religion and religious liberty in ways that enjoy broad public support enjoy a higher level of trust when conflicts do arise. When school officials have a track record of taking religious liberty seriously, people on all sides are more willing to engage in constructive dialogue and seek common ground.

In a democratic society, there are inevitably winners and losers in public policy disputes. But when school officials treat all sides with fairness and respect, then those who lose ground on a particular issue are more likely to remain engaged and to continue to support the school system. In fact, the issues surrounding religion in public schools allow for "winners" on all sides. There are ample opportunities for school districts to say "yes" to a role for religion, even as they must say "no" to school endorsement or promotion of religion.

For school leaders committed to fulfilling both the letter and the spirit of the First Amendment, acknowledgment of the constitutional place of religion in schools is not sufficient. Even adopting policies protecting religious liberty and encouraging study about religions does not go far enough. A school district that successfully navigates religious issues and concerns is one where policies and practices that touch on religion are implemented with broad involvement and support from parents, students, religious leaders, and other stakeholders in the school community. When agreement is reached, administrators and teachers must be adequately trained to carry out the policies. Only then is the school district adequately prepared to take religious liberty and religious literacy seriously.

After getting religion wrong in public schools for much of our history, we have an opportunity—indeed, a mandate—to get religion right in order to negotiate our religious and ideological divisions as we build one nation of many faiths and cultures. Using the civic framework provided by the First Amendment, Americans of all faiths and none are able to debate differences, understand one another, and work together to create school policies that protect the rights of every student and parent. If we are willing to take religious liberty and religious literacy seriously, a common vision for the common good may yet be possible in our schools—and in our nation—as we confront the challenges of living with our deepest differences in the twenty-first century.

FUTURE DIRECTIONS

1. How can public schools use the principles of rights, responsibilities, and respect to engage in civil dialogue and, where possible, find common ground on public policies that serve the common good?
2. How can public schools use the national consensus statements, which were endorsed by dozens of national religious and civil liberty organizations, to pre-emptively mediate conflicts about religion and American education? (They are downloadable at www.religiousfreedomcenter.org/resources.)
3. How can school districts and schools of education prepare teachers and administrators to be First Amendment specialists? How might First Amendment education be a core part of teacher education and principal-preparation programs throughout the country?
4. How can schools educate the public about the difference between the academic study of religion, designed to promote the civic competency of religious literacy, and devotional faith-based education?
5. How can American public schools become laboratories of democracy, modeling for the larger society how religious liberty and liberty of conscience is a fundamental constitutional and human right for people of all religions and none?

REFERENCES

First Amendment Center. 1995. "Religious Liberty, Public Education and the Future of American Democracy: A Statement of Principles." *Journal of Intergroup Relations* 22, no. 1: 34–36.

————. *Consensus Documents: A Teacher's Guide to Religion in Public Schools* and *Religion in the Public School Curriculum: Questions and Answers* (religiousfreedomcenter.org/resources).

Haynes, Charles C., and Oliver Thomas. 2011. *Finding Common Ground: A First Amendment Guide to Religion and Public Schools*. Nashville, TN: First Amendment Center.

FURTHER READING

al-Hibri, Azizah Y., Jean Bethke Elshtain, and Charles C. Haynes. 2001. *Religion in American Public Life: Living with Our Deepest Differences*. New York: W. W. Norton & Company.

American Jewish Congress, Christian Legal Society, and the First Amendment Center. *Public Schools & Religious Communities*. Nashville, TN: First Amendment Center.

American Jewish Committee and the Religious Freedom Education Project of the First Amendment Center. *Harassment, Bullying and Free Expression: Guidelines for Free and Safe Public Schools*.

Bible Literacy Project, Inc. and the First Amendment Center. *The Bible and Public Schools: A First Amendment Guide*.

Billings, Laura, and Terry Roberts. 2008. *A Discussion Guide to First Amendment Freedoms: A Documentary History of First Amendment Rights in America*. Oxford University Press and the First Amendment Center.

BridgeBuilders and the First Amendment Center. *Public Schools and Sexual Orientation: A First Amendment Framework for Finding Common Ground*.

"Religion and the Public Schools" (2001) *Social Studies Review* 40, no. 2., California Council for the Social Studies.

Carper, James C., and Thomas C. Hunt, eds. 2009. *The Praeger Handbook of Religion and Education in the United States*, 2 vols. Westport, CT: Praeger.

Center for Religion and Public Affairs, Wake Forest University School of Divinity. 2010. *Religious Expression in American Public Life: A Joint Statement of Current Law*.

Chancey, Mark, Carol Meyers, and Eric Meyers. 2014. *The Bible in the Public Square: Its Enduring Influence in American Life*. Atlanta, GA: Society of Biblical Literature Press.

Dart, John, and Jimmy Allen. 2000. *Bridging the Gap: Religion and the News Media*. Nashville, TN: First Amendment Center.

Douglass, Susan L. 2000. *Teaching About Religion in National and State Social Studies Standards*. Council on Islamic Education and the First Amendment Center.

First Amendment Center and Religious Freedom Center of the Newseum Institute. *Consensus Documents* (religiousfreedomcenter.org/resources): *What Is the Truth About American Muslims? Questions and Answers; Religious Liberty, Publication and the Future of American Democracy: A Statement of Principles; A Teacher's Guide to Religion in Public Schools; The Equal Access Act: Questions and Answers; Religion in the Public School Curriculum: Questions and Answers; Religious Holidays in the Public Schools: Questions and Answers; The Bible and Public Schools: A First Amendment Guide; Public Schools and Religious Communities: A First Amendment Guide; Public Schools and Sexual Orientation Guide; Harassment, Bullying and Free Expression: Guidelines for Free and Safe Public Schools*.

Greenawalt, Kent. 2007. *Does God Belong in Public Schools?* Princeton, NJ: Princeton University Press.

————. 2008/2009. *Religion and the Constitution: Volume I: Free Exercise and Religion and the Constitution: Volume II: Establishment and Fairness*. Princeton, NJ: Princeton University Press.

Guinness, Os. 2008. *The Case for Civility: And Why Our Future Depends on It*. New York: Harper One.

Haynes, Charles C. 1998. *Teaching About Religion in American Life: A First Amendment Guide*. New York: Oxford University Press and Nashville, TN: First Amendment Center.

————. 2008. *A Teacher's Guide to Religion in the Public Schools*. Nashville, TN: First Amendment Center.

Haynes, Charles C., Sam Chaltain, John E. Ferguson, Jr., David L. Hudson, Jr., and Oliver Thomas. 2003. *The First Amendment in Schools: A Guide from the First Amendment Center*. Nashville, TN: First Amendment Center and Alexandria, VA: Association for Supervision and Curriculum Development.

Haynes, Charles C., Sam Chaltain, and Susan M. Glisson. 2006. *First Freedoms: A Documentary History of First Amendment Rights in America*. New York: Oxford University Press and Nashville, TN: First Amendment Center.

Haynes, Charles C., and Warren A. Nord. 1998. *Taking Religion Seriously Across the Curriculum*. Alexandria, VA: ASCD.

Hudson, David L. Jr. 2003. *The Silencing of Student Voices: Preserving Free Speech in American' Schools*. Nashville, TN: First Amendment Center.

Hunter, James Davison, and Guinness, Os., eds. 1990. *Articles of Faith, Articles of Peace: The Religious Liberty Clauses and the American Public Philosophy*. Washington, DC: Brookings Institution.

Interfaith Alliance. 2013. *What is the Truth About American Muslims? Questions and Answers*. Interfaith Alliance and the Religious Freedom Education Project of the First Amendment Center. Washington, DC: Newseum Institute.

Kelley, Dean M. 2008/1997. *The Law of Church and State in America*. Nashville, TN: First Amendment Center.

Lester, Emile. 2011. *Teaching about Religions: A Democratic Approach for Public Schools*. Ann Arbor: University of Michigan Press.

Lester, Emile, and Patrick S. Roberts. 2006. *Learning about World Religions in Public Schools: The Impact on Student Attitudes and Community Acceptance in Modesto, Calif.* Nashville, TN: First Amendment Center.

Marus, Robert. 2006. *The Future of Religious Freedom in America*. A conference sponsored by the McCormick Tribune Freedom Museum in collaboration with the First Amendment Center, Chicago, October 10–11, 2005.

McFall, Shaun, and Charles C. Haynes, eds. 2007. *Living with Our Deepest Differences: Religious Liberty in a Pluralistic Society*, new ed. rev. Nashville, TN: First Amendment Center.

Moore, Diane L. 2007. *Overcoming Religious Illiteracy: A Cultural Studies Approach to the Study of Religion in Secondary Education*. New York: Palgrave Macmillan.

————, ed. 2010. *American Academy of Religion Guidelines for Teaching About Religion in K–12 Public Schools in the United States*.

National PTA and the First Amendment Center. *A Parent's Guide to Religion in the Public Schools*. Nashville, TN: First Amendment Center.

Nord, Warren A. 1995. *Religion and American Education: Rethinking a National Dilemma*. Chapel Hill: University of North Carolina Press.

————. 2010. *Does God Make a Difference?: Taking Religion Seriously in Our Schools and Universities*. New York: Oxford University Press.

Nord, Warren A., and Charles C. Haynes. 1998. *Taking Religion Seriously Across the Curriculum*. Nashville, TN: First Amendment Center.

Paige, Rod. 2003. *Guidance on Constitutionally Protected Prayer in Public and Elementary Schools*. Washington, DC: US Department of Education.

Prothero, Stephen. 2007. *Religious Literacy: What Every American Needs to Know—and Doesn't*. New York: HarperOne.

Rogers, Melissa, and Charles C. Haynes, eds. 2002. *Religious Liberty in American Life: Preparing Religious Leaders for Civic Engagement in the 21st Century: A Working Document*. Pew Forum on Religion & Public Life and the First Amendment Center.

Teaching About Religion in Public Schools: Where Do We Go From Here? 2003. A conference sponsored by the Pew Forum on Religion & Public Life and the First Amendment Center, Washington DC.

Wachlin, Marie, and Byron R. Johnson. 2006. *Bible Literacy Report II: What University Professors Say Incoming Students Should Know*. Front Royal, VA: Bible Literacy Project, Inc.

Waggoner, Michael D., ed. 2013. *Religion in the Public Schools: Negotiating the New Commons*. Lanham, MD: Rowman & Littlefield.

CHAPTER 6

··

DEMOCRACY, RELIGION, AND AMERICAN EDUCATION

··

EMILE LESTER

OVER the last half-century, two democratic movements have mounted profound challenges to the handling of religion in US public schools. In the early 1960s, the Supreme Court responded to appeals from secularists, religious minorities, and the nonreligious by banning sectarian prayers and Bible reading in public schools. Confusion over the extent of the Court's rulings caused many administrators to curtail constitutionally permissible treatments of religion in the classroom. These changes coincided with a renewed commitment to political activism among evangelical Protestants in the early 1970s. Often joined by other conservative Christians, many evangelicals protested against what they perceived as the secularization of, and even hostility toward, religion in public schools. They supported either restoring the previous status quo favoring Christian beliefs and practices, or implementing what they argued was a balanced curriculum that allowed Christian beliefs to coexist alongside beliefs that conflicted with their religious views.

Both of these movements were inspired by the promises that modern democracies make to their citizens. Protesters against sectarian practices and beliefs acted on the guarantee that modern democracies make to protect the fundamental rights of all equally and especially those of vulnerable minorities threatened by the power and sentiment of the majority. Evangelicals took seriously the requirement that public institutions in a democracy ought to reflect the views and allow for the robust participation of ordinary citizens instead of being dominated by political and administrative elites (Hunter 1991). The continuing and profound tension between these movements must cause us to wonder if something precious to democracy must be sacrificed when US public schools today deal with religion.

Both of these promises of democracy figure prominently in the work of perhaps the seminal theorist of modern democracy, Jean-Jacques Rousseau. Rousseau's *The Social Contract* is the first work on democracy to confess that the inherent tension in modern democratic ideals might not be capable of resolution. This chapter's first section considers the democratic movements that have impacted teaching about religion in US public schools through the prism of Rousseau's thought, and presents Rousseau's views on what treatment of religion might resolve the tension between democracy's conflicting goods. The chapter's middle section shows how Modesto, a midsized city in California's Central Valley, fashioned a required world religions course that succeeded in large part in accommodating the democratic demands of religious minorities and of conservative Christians, including evangelicals, in ways that Rousseau might not have anticipated.

The third section, though, cautions that the success of this course may have come at the expense of other vital democratic goals recognized not only by Rousseau, but by other significant democratic theorists like Jurgen Habermas and Benjamin Barber as well as by notable authorities on religion and education, including Warren Nord and Diane Moore. If a more inclusive understanding of democracy is to be honored, the conclusion suggests, school districts aspiring to follow in Modesto's footsteps might need to take risks in the classroom that Modesto consciously sought to avoid.

DEMOCRACY IN OUR CULTURE WARS

Following the publication of Rousseau's *Social Contract*, democracy could and never would be thought of in the same way. The direct democracy Rousseau cherished was no historical novelty, but the way that Rousseau justified it was radically new. When Pericles memorialized direct democracy in his funeral oration, he celebrated the advantages of wealth and power this form of government had accrued for Athens. It was left to Rousseau to argue that only a government in which all had the equal right to participate and equal power to determine laws could be legitimate. Representative government for Rousseau was merely a pale imitation of true democracy. Representatives often err in taking the pulse of their constituents, or come to hold that they know better what is good for their constituents than constituents themselves do. Only direct democracy was faithful to the inalienable right of all to have their actual wills reflected in the policies that governed them (Rousseau 1987).

The direct democracy that Rousseau envisioned has remained an ideal as even he realized it must. Yet the failure to fulfill the ideal does not acquit democracies of the obligations to approximate it. The spirit of Rousseau's emphasis on robust participation has reverberated across American history. From the anti-Federalists in the late eighteenth century to the Populists in the late nineteenth century to the Progressives of the early twentieth century and to the civil rights and student movements of the later twentieth century, American democracy has been challenged and recharged by movements calling for an enhanced voice for ordinary citizens who feel ignored or forgotten.

One of the latest American entries into the Rousseauian ranks marching in support of participatory democracy is among the most surprising because it involves a group normally thought of not as radical, but traditionalist and conservative. Beginning in the early 1970s, many evangelical Christians began objecting more vociferously to what they perceived as the growing secularization of public institutions and the increasing vulgarization of American culture. Evangelicals had long objected to these trends, but after *Roe v. Wade* evangelicals began to respond to them with greater political activism instead of an emphasis on enhanced inward piety. Interest groups like the Moral Majority and Christian Coalition organized a previously prevailing opinion into a potent political force (Smith 1998).

The rise of the Religious Right, as with previous participation-based movements, posed a challenge of inclusion for American democracy, but it also revealed a tension in the ideal of democracy in Rousseau's theory and American practice. Concern among evangelicals about exclusion from fair representation in positions of power such as political parties, public schools, and the mainstream media is sincere and more than occasionally well founded. Yet the responses and reforms favored by many evangelicals are often equally, if not more, exclusionary. Banning abortion and refusing to extend full citizenship rights to homosexuals, for instance, is viewed as oppressive by the many Americans whose views on moral freedom and family and marriage are more permissive and pluralistic. Even if the proportion of evangelicals in the nation as a whole is not sufficient to impose these policies on a national level, their political strength is adequate enough to lead to their enactment in some states and many localities. A successful democracy is defined not only by robust participation, but by the protection of minority rights. Inclusion of the will of evangelicals would be a hollow victory if it came at the expense of the exclusion of religious minorities and others who disagreed with them.

In the *Social Contract*, Rousseau is aware of and concerned with the possibility of majority tyranny in a robust participatory democracy. His efforts to preempt this possibility gave birth to the concept of the general will, his most famous contribution to political thought. The general will prevails, according to Rousseau, when citizens share a visceral identification with the welfare of others that would efface feelings of exclusion. To this end, Rousseau believed that democracy would function best in small, homogeneous nations where similar circumstances and backgrounds would give all citizens shared interests. Rousseau's willingness to take stringent measures to bring about the general will and uniformity of sentiment is also manifest in his treatment of religion in the *Social Contract* (Rousseau 1987). For his ideal democracy, he prescribes the universal adoption of a largely nonsectarian, civil religion consisting of simple precepts such as belief in a beneficent God who rewards the virtuous and punishes the vicious. Allegiance to the social compact must trump the pursuit of conscience when they conflict, for "it is impossible to live in peace with those one believes to be damned" (Rousseau 1987, 220).

The diversity of our ethnic and racial heritages and the extent of our territory, though, make the United States a particularly unsuitable patient for the general will that Rousseau prescribes. While the multitude of Protestant denominations and the policy of disestablishment made our nation's religious pluralism impressive from the outset, the United States has only grown more religiously varied with the arrival of non-Christian minorities from outside our borders, and the rise of atheism and spiritualism within (Eck 2002). When Will Herberg wrote in the late 1950s of the emerging consensus and tolerance among Protestants, Catholics, and Jews, a civil religion still seemed remotely within reach (Bellah 1980). It is difficult to fathom, though, even the most basic precepts of civil religion that could be shared by, say, hard-shell Baptists, Hindus, and humanists in the United States today. The belief in the inviolable right to and the sanctity of the individual's religious conscience nurtured by the thought of Roger Williams and James Madison has only further mitigated attempts to use religion as a source of social cohesion. The ideas of this tradition and the fact of diversity are at odds with the notion of a common religious interest that Rousseau's civil religion presumes.

The debate over religion in public schools raised by the increased political activism of evangelical Christians reflects the tension in Rousseau's democratic theory and American practice. Our almost unimaginable diversity demands that public schools play a central and critical role in solidifying social cohesion and promoting tolerance. Public schools' performance of this role is especially critical because it is increasingly rare for Americans of different moral and political beliefs to, among other things, live in the same neighborhoods or receive news from the same media outlets (Bishop 2008). At the same time, the right to pass along our cultural values is precious, and establishes a presumption against schools interfering in unwanted ways with the ability of parents to transmit their religious beliefs to their children. When schools disparage or ignore religion or particular forms of religion, they imperil this delicate process of transmission. If it is too much to ask in a democracy like ours that all citizens feel that major public institutions belong *to* them, it is imperative that all citizens at least feel that they belong *in* them. Since the early 1960s, many evangelical Christians have expressed that neither they nor their views are fully welcome in public schools.

Several prominent studies of public school textbooks suggest that evangelical Christians may have legitimate cause for concern. Paul Vitz's 1986 review of elementary school textbooks in California and Texas found endorsement of liberal perspectives on issues related to the family and culture, but neglect of traditional moral approaches often espoused by conservative Christians and Jews. The same pattern in public school textbooks was apparent on theological issues as well according to Warren Nord's survey of North Carolina history texts in 1989 and 1992. These texts' description of early Judaism and Christianity, for instance, "downplay or completely ignore sin, salvation, damnation, the millennium, cosmology, and faith" (Nord 1995, 140). Nord's subsequent study of textbooks suggested that the role and relation of religion altogether in various disciplines was either ignored or minimized. One American history text, for instance, devoted more discussion to railroads in the nineteenth century than to the role of religion in the twentieth century (Nord 2010).

While evangelical Christians may be right to call attention to the neglect of their beliefs, the responses many politically active evangelicals favor have led to an exaggeration of their views. For instance, a Texas State Board of Education dominated by conservative Christians in 2010 relied heavily on the advice of controversial Christian Right historian David Barton in drafting their social studies standards (Blake 2010). Several scholarly studies have pointed out that the adopted standards contain numerous inaccuracies relating to the influence of the Bible on the Founders and the Constitution, and misleading statements about the history and legal tradition surrounding the First Amendment's separation of church and state (Chancey 2014; Green 1999). State school boards controlled by a majority of conservative Christians elsewhere around the nation have endorsed Intelligent Design as a scientific alternative to evolution and accepted Bible elective courses that favor a sectarian, literalist interpretation of the Bible and the political agenda of the Religious Right.

Not only do these outcomes conflict with best educational practices, but the processes by which they were reached reflect a distortion of the participatory democracy Rousseau celebrated. Evangelical Christian interest groups frequently focus attention on local and state school board elections because such elections are often plagued by low voter turnout. The results of these elections may thus give a disproportionately large voice to evangelical Christians compared to their numbers in the electorate at large. Indeed, these election results may not even be adequately representative of evangelical Christian views overall. Surveys of evangelicals by Christian Smith (2000) and Alan Wolfe (2003), for instance, indicate that a majority of evangelicals, while concerned about the exclusion of their views from the mainstream, are welcoming of expanding diversity and do not wish to use government to impose their views on non-evangelicals. Sectarian policies enacted by school boards may express the views of politically active evangelicals most likely to vote in school board elections and be elected to school boards rather than the sentiments of evangelical Christians in general.

Those who have paid attention to these controversies may be tempted to conclude that religion in public schools simply lies at the intersection of incommensurable democratic goals. Democracies are organic ecosystems whose complex parts develop and shift over time. As desirable as elegant solutions to our thorniest political problems might be, it may be the case that the democratic demand of robust participation for evangelicals may simply not fit with the democratic requirement of respect for the inviolable individual rights of all. The status quo treatment of religion in most public schools may weaken social cohesion by alienating evangelicals, but implementing alternatives may undermine cohesion by alienating the nonreligious and religious minorities even more. If the goods of democracy cannot be all balanced at once, our society must simply choose the lesser of all evils. Before reaching this conclusion, though, an experiment in educating about religion in one California public school district is worth a look.

DESCRIBING DIVERSITY

The required world religions course that the Modesto, California, public high schools first implemented in 2000 does not focus on evangelical Protestantism. The course includes no discussion, for instance, of Intelligent Design, or of the distinctive views on marriage, family, and abortion that conservative evangelicals share. Instead, the course covers seven major religious traditions over nine weeks, which means it has little time to linger over the details or the complexity of each religious tradition and confines itself to relating the most accessible and undisputed aspects of each religious tradition.

Yet much about the way the course approaches teaching about religion is a palimpsest that reveals its roots in a dispute spotlighting Modesto's considerable evangelical community. The dispute centered on the promotion of respect for the rights of gay students. When superintendent James Enochs became concerned about the harassment of gay students in his district, he adopted a vigorous antidiscrimination policy. Modesto, a city of just under 200,000, in 2000 was home to five Protestant megachurches, and the Central Valley in which it lies is known to state residents as the California Bible Belt. Three members of the Modesto school board at the time of the dispute had run on platforms sympathetic to conservative Christian concerns about public schools. Many evangelicals grew concerned that the schools were overstepping their authority not only by legislating morality, but by interfering with the religious rights of parents to teach their children what behaviors were and were not sinful. Like evangelicals elsewhere, Modesto's evangelicals feared that their city's public schools no longer represented or cared to represent the sentiment of a large segment of the Modesto community (Lester 2011).

Enochs called in Charles Haynes from the First Amendment Center to mediate a resolution to the dispute between the various stakeholders in Modesto's schools. Seemingly against the odds, the meetings produced consensus about a "safe schools policy" intended to guarantee respect for each student's safety while refraining from interference with the rights to religious conscience of students and their parents. The required world religions course was the policy's central pillar because without civility about religion, the entire structure of the agreement threatened to collapse. Not only had conservative Christian anxieties been the source of this most recent acrimony, but Modesto was also home to a remarkable diversity of religions stemming from recent immigration. Migration from South Asia swelled the ranks of Hindus, Sikhs, Buddhists, and Hmongs, from the Middle East led to the establishment of a Muslim community, and from Latin America buttressed the membership of Catholic churches. With its long- and well-established evangelical churches, and expanding numbers of non-Christians, religious composition and change in Modesto paralleled provocatively that of the United States as a whole.

To accommodate this mélange, Modesto administrators hewed to two simple rules in their pedagogical approach to teaching about religion—respect for diversity and description of faiths. The emphasis on diversity sprang from a democratic desire to protect minority rights. The course administrators designed began with a two-week primer of US traditions of disestablishment and religious freedom highlighting the efforts of their pioneers such as Roger Williams. Having fostered an atmosphere of respect, the course then devoted an equal time of one week each to examining seven major world religions. Prior to the course's implementation, administrators solicited participation in a religious advisory panel from a wide range of Modesto's religious communities to review the curriculum. The panel ended up consisting of Protestant, Catholic, Islamic, Sikh, Jewish, and Greek Orthodox clerics.

The course focused on describing basic facts about each religion's history, beliefs, and rituals while reserving judgment about their truth and merit. The district encouraged teachers to stick as closely to the curriculum as possible, and discouraged them from fostering debates comparing and contrasting religious traditions that might either disparage the merits of one religion at the expense of another or foster a perception that all religious views were equally valid. While social studies and humanities courses usually aim to make substantial room for critical thinking, Modesto's world religions course barely cracked the door open for it, if at all.

The manifest purpose of this "just the facts" approach was to preempt controversy and community complaint. This goal fits with Rousseau's emphasis on maintaining social cohesion even as it eschews any possibility of bringing about the consensus on civil religion that Rousseau hoped would bring about this cohesion. If constitutional requirements precluded, and Modesto's profound diversity prevented, discussion of even the thinnest of civil religions, then Modesto's stakeholders could at least agree to *avoid discussion* of the religious controversies that did and could divide them. Modesto's course was based on a consensus that the community could find no consensus about religion.

Modesto's descriptive approach, though, also happened to address in a nuanced way long-held anxieties about religion in schools voiced by evangelical and conservative Christians. The main lamentation of these groups has been that removing devotional practices and restricting teaching about religion in the curriculum implied to students that religion was not important and perhaps even signaled the hostility of schools and government to religion. Even if this claim is sometimes exaggerated, having schools discuss religion in an independent required course did much to reverse conservative Christian perceptions about public schools in Modesto's community. Father Joseph Illo of St. Joseph's Catholic Church recalled that when the course was presented to the religious advisory council, "all [the members] congratulated the schools on actually talking about religion because that's usually a pariah in schools and academia" (Lester 2011, 147).

If evangelicals and conservative Christians want their children to appreciate the importance of and respect of schools and society for religion in general, though, they are also eager to convey that *their* religion is true. Evangelicals and conservative Christians are more likely than other believers to hold that their beliefs present a correct and exclusive path to truth and salvation (Stolzenberg 1993). Teaching about different religious traditions alongside each other could encourage impressionable minds to measure the value and truth of their faith against those of others in ways that distance them from the beliefs they have at the course's start. Yet this is not the only way that teaching about religion could interfere with evangelical and conservative Christian beliefs. To those who believe that salvation only comes through Christ's atonement, coming to believe that other faiths provide an equally valuable path to heaven is as damning as apostasy. Learning about other religions carries the risk that conservative Christian students may lose sight of what makes their beliefs unique and uniquely true.

Having schools describe different faiths while cordoning them off from critical thought comparisons offers a solution to this conundrum. It affirms the value of religion while insulating the religious consciences of conservative Christian students from undue interference. Rousseau might not have appreciated the course's end result of enabling evangelicals to maintain their exclusive religious beliefs, but the taking account of the long-neglected demands of a substantial and vocal constituency in the debate over religion and public schools is at home with his views on participatory democracy. Modesto's course may not have been the destination in the religion-in-schools debate that most evangelicals dreamed of, but it offered a welcome harbor for a group that previously felt cast adrift.

The course's acceptance by previously warring elements of Modesto's religious community validated its careful construction. Divided by earlier controversies at the intersection of culture and religion, members of Modesto's school board expressed unanimous support for the course. Parents have the right to opt their children out of the required course, but few have chosen to exercise this right. The course has not been subject to a single legal challenge or organized protest from any of Modesto's many religious and political factions since its implementation fifteen years ago. While interviews with a wide range of clerics in Modesto indicated that acceptance of the course was at times grudging, the more common reaction to the course was enthusiastic. One pastor of a large evangelical megachurch told me in an interview that he was "thrilled" his daughter was taking the course and appreciated the course's recognition of religion's importance. A liberal pastor approved of the way that students in his congregation were able to use "the course to incorporate different religions into their perspectives" (Lester 2011, 147).

A written survey of over three hundred students both before and after taking the course, and personal interviews with twenty-three students that I conducted with Patrick Roberts, suggested the course's success in the classroom as well as the community. The course satisfied democratic demands for equal treatment by enhancing students' respect for the rights of religious minorities. Students emerged from the course significantly more likely to agree that "people of all religions should be able to put religious displays outside of their homes" and "students of all religions should be able to wear religious symbols outside of their clothing in public schools." Enhanced respect for abstract principles of religious liberty was accompanied by a greater willingness to extend four basic civil rights to a concrete "least-liked group" they were asked to select. A Russian Orthodox student told us about a change of mind regarding a Hindu family across the street. Prior to the course he thought that the family's practice of "praying to a statue" was "just plain dumb. But I notice now they had a pretty good reason to" (Lester 2011, 115–118).

As encouraging as this shift in views was, the reasoning behind it might be a cause for democratic concern. If students were becoming more respectful of other religions because they were embracing the truth or value of other religions, it would upset the delicate equilibrium between extending respect to non-Christian minorities while protecting conservative beliefs from encroachment.

Fortunately, the course's emphasis on description, like its emphasis on diversity, had its intended effect. Several teachers did encourage students to consider that the religions they studied held similar moral values through exercises like providing a handout with versions of the Golden Rule from the sacred text of each religion studied. A significantly greater number of students did emerge from the course believing that "all religions share the same basic moral values." Yet the percentage of students agreeing "that one religion is definitely right, and all others" did not change significantly after taking the course. Five of the students we interviewed even told us that taking the course had strengthened their commitment to their religion (Lester 2011, 125–130).

Modesto administrators took a calculated risk that students were mature enough to realize that the sharing of several basic moral similarities between faiths did not mean that faiths were similar in other crucial respects, or that the choice between faiths was trivial or frivolous. Not only do the surveys and interviews attest to the wisdom of this risk, but even prominent Modesto evangelicals acknowledged the course's successful balancing act. Thus, an associate pastor at a Baptist megachurch expressed satisfaction to us that students who take the course emerge with "a clearer understanding of the distinctives" between Christianity and other religions (Lester 2011, 148).

Modesto's course, in effect, conveyed a view that functioned like Rousseau's civil religion in providing a basis for social cohesion among students and community members while avoiding the violation of conscience that Rousseau's civil religion entails. This approach substituted agreement about shared moral principles for agreement in Rousseau's civil religion about articles of faith. *Contra* Rousseau, the course's success suggests that it may indeed be possible to live peacefully with those one believes is damned.

DENIAL OF DELIBERATION

Modesto's course seems to have resolved crucial dilemmas of democracy Rousseau identified in unanticipated ways. Yet Rousseau and other important democratic thinkers might still refrain from celebrating it as a cure-all for democracy. Rousseau's concept of the general will reflects a conviction that democracy is special not only because it respects where we begin from but because it helps to shape where we end. One need not share Rousseau's obsession with uniformity of opinion or sacrificing of private interests for the state's welfare and the use of coercive means to achieve this to find value in the impulse behind them. Democratic thinkers of more recent vintage following in Rousseau's footsteps have modified his views on the general will through their call to recognize deliberation as an essential element of democracy.

Jurgen Habermas (1998, 2001) has argued persuasively that increased deliberation improves the quality of the political and social institutions that touch our lives. Acrimony and resentment stem not only from the prevalence of selfish motivations for voting and political activism, but the failure to understand our opponents' circumstances and the reasons behind their political choices. Robust deliberation, debate, and discussion can help to render the barriers dividing us from each other more permeable and porous. Deliberation may at times reveal shared reasoning and resolutions to disputes that opponents were not aware of, and yield greater social cohesion. Yet even when delibera-tion does not produce such results, it can demonstrate that disagreements are not as dire as previously thought, reduce the bitterness felt by temporary losers in policy debates, and remind citizens of the obligations and comforts of the shared social enterprise of which they are part. Just because it is unrealistic to expect that citizens in democracies such as the United States will come to treat each other as members of an extended family does not mean that we are condemned to treating each other politically as enemies or perfect strangers. Instead of democratic decision-making being akin to having isolated diners ordering their food alone, deliberation can enable citizens to view each other as frequent dinner companions whose conversations enlighten each other's tastes and make shared meals more enjoyable.

Benjamin Barber's concept of strong democracy has emphasized that deliberation can aid not only in the pursuit for social excellence but in the quest for individual self-awareness. We can only realize the full value of the robust opportunities for freedom of speech and expression democracies offer us, Barber (1984) contends, when we use this freedom to explore the many possible perspectives we can inhabit. Only mean-ingful encounters with those who hold their views sincerely and strongly can challenge the boundaries of who we are and enable us to locate the multitudes within. When confronted with the onslaught of others' views, we have no choice but to change and move ourselves to new frontiers, or better define and defend the ground of identity we stand on. Either way, we emerge more conscious of how we choose the views we hold, and what is gained and lost in this choice. Deliberation not only provokes us from our political selfishness, but awakens us from the rut of solipsism.

Amy Gutmann has drawn on these insights as well as her own pioneering work on democracy and deliberation to argue that public schools can and ought to play a cru-cial role in facilitating deliberation. After all, no other public institution in our de-mocracy brings us into contact so regularly with those from different backgrounds. Gutmann (1999, 42, 44, 49) urges that public schools take advantage of this diversity to enable students to engage in the "conscious reproduction of society." A deliberative public school would not only expose students to the many different ways their fellow citizens pursue meaning, but provide students with frequent opportunities to partici-pate in robust discussions and decision-making with teachers, school administrators, and classmates. When exercising their authority fairly and prudently, teachers can find acceptance among their students as respected referees establishing ground rules of reciprocity that allow all voices to participate equally and share in mutually accepted outcomes.

Scholars writing on religion and education have also taken account of these features of deliberation in creative and provocative ways. Championing a cultural studies approach that like Habermas's and Gutmann's approach sees deliberation as a tool for social transformation, Diane Moore (2007) urges schools to recognize that teaching about religion offers an opportunity to reassess the justice and legitimacy of domi-nant social practices. As well as being sources of comfort and truth, Moore reminds us that religions have at times played a regrettable role in reinforcing political and social oppression. Appreciating how controversial cultural assumptions shaped the historical development of world religions can spur criticism of the effect of these beliefs in our own society today. Discourse in the democratic classroom, Moore stresses, can be a potent weapon in the struggle for righteous and occasionally radical reform.

Appreciative like Barber of the connection between democracy and self-discovery, Warren Nord and Nel Noddings each urge in their own unique ways that teaching about religion ought to open new mental vistas to students. Religions, for Nord (2010), offer distinct perspectives that enrich and expand our understanding of core intellectual disciplines ranging from science to history to literature as well as suggesting how these disciplines can be integrated. Immersing ourselves in the conversations within and between religions "from the inside" broadens and deepens our intellectual ability to engage in an examined life. Noddings (1993) calls our attention to the value of cultivating wonder about the questions and phenomena that most perplex us. No account of the questions that most cause us to wonder could be close to complete without examining religious approaches to them, and religions would cease to be what they are without maintaining a sense of wonder about the sublime at their core. No discussions of religion in the classroom could be true to the religions being examined if they failed to inspire the sense of wonder that often distinguishes religious approaches to the world from other intellectual endeavors. While Nord's approach focuses slightly more on the answers religions provide, Noddings's is more concerned with the questions religions ask.

Modesto's administrators, though, aimed to meticulously circumscribe the challenge that the world religions course would pose to the worldviews students begin with. For fear of provoking controversy, teachers were encouraged to stick to the facts of religion. The curriculum skimmed the surface of religious beliefs, but did not plumb the depths of the justification for religions and the moral views associated with them. While the course did not intentionally aim to suppress wonder or prevent students from using the material to challenge their views of self and society, it is also true that the course did not do much to encourage these pursuits. In theory, the course was careful not to celebrate the contributions that religions in general or particular have made to civilization, and was even more wary of hinting that religions may have at times impeded civilization's progress. In effect, though, the very discussion of religion free of criticism provoked Modesto Rabbi Paul Gordon to object that the course took a "warm and fuzzy" approach to religion (Lester 2011, 139). Gordon was not only lamenting that the course might make students from nonreligious or minority religious backgrounds feel discomfort, but that the course might have been killing the religions taught with kindness by failing to subject their tenets to critical scrutiny.

Our survey suggests that this "warm and fuzzy" approach and lack of opportunities for deliberation may have limited the course's ability to enable students in the present and future to address injustice and work for reform in their community. The percentage of students willing to "defend a student whose religious beliefs were insulted by another student" increased significantly after the course. Yet when asked if they were willing to write a letter to a newspaper or even to sign a petition to protest religious discrimination in their community, students' views after the course were the same as when they began the course. A sentiment against the evil of intolerance might mean little if citizens do not have the skills or motivation to make their voices heard (Lester 2011). The causes of political apathy in the United States today are numerous, and it would be unreasonable to hold public schools accountable for not eliminating it. Modesto's course, though, might have done more to help combat apathy than it did. Civic education research suggests that narratives about the experience of others can play a crucial role in motivating students to see their citizenship obligations in concrete terms (Conover and Searing 2000). Concerned about offending religious communities in Modesto by suggesting that various religions' records of tolerance might be less than flawless, the course offered no narratives from victims of religious discrimination.

The irony of the lack of deliberation inside of Modesto's classroom is that the Modesto course itself was the product of an admirable and successful exercise in democratic deliberation. Modesto's various religious and cultural factions were willing to suspend the aggressive assertion of their interests and identities to participate in a more civil form of discourse. With assistance from Charles Haynes's mediation, the stakeholders in Modesto's schools reached a resolution and achieved a level of consensus that exceeded their expectations. Even Haynes was surprised, telling us that the district "took what I said and made the leap" even though "I didn't think they were going to do it" (Lester 2011, 111).

Moreover, the discussions did not cause stakeholders to feel as if they had sacrificed or departed from their religious identities. Secularists did not convert to conservative Christianity, and evangelicals did not cease to hold that homosexuality was sinful. Yet they did make their views vulnerable to challenge and reflection in a way that enabled them to consider others' and their own views from a new perspective. The lesson of their choice and its rewards is that achieving robust democracy requires not just restraint toward and respect for minority rights or majority sentiment, but the willingness to risk individual identity and social peace and cohesion. Democratic deliberation is not for the faint of heart, and carries the risk of reversal. The mediation of Modesto's factions could well have backfired and caused even more enmity, but without this risk the fruits of Modesto's course could not have been realized.

When Modesto's course was initiated, the spirit of caution about classroom discussion was understandable. Simply introducing a required world religions course intended for all students into a divided community that had so recently been the site of controversy was already bold; fully embracing deliberation in the classroom would have been foolhardy. Yet making an official policy with almost no room for deliberation and debate perhaps played it too safe. Proponents of democratic schooling and teaching about religion wishing to learn from Modesto's mistakes as well as its abundant accomplishments would do well to look to the process Modesto used as well as the product. If the conversations that led to the course's creation improved the outlook of parents and the community as a whole, perhaps borrowing something of this spirit of deliberation might work similar wonders for students.

FUTURE DIRECTIONS

1. Can required courses on religion include open-ended and stimulating discussions comparing religious traditions without offending the religious sensibilities of a significant number of students?
2. Can required world religions courses like that in Modesto find acceptance from evangelical and other conservative Christians in communities throughout the nation as was the case in Modesto?
3. Should public schools in a democracy do more than they currently do to welcome input from religious communities about how religion is taught in public schools, or should the content of courses about religion be determined solely by academic experts?
4. Is it necessary or inappropriate for public schools in a democracy to examine the ways that religions throughout history or currently justify repressive social norms and practices?
5. Should the primary goal of public schools in a democracy be to protect or to challenge the religious beliefs that students have upon entering schools? Or is it better if public schools simply ignore religion for the most part?
6. Is the descriptive approach to teaching about religion used in Modesto's course the best or only appropriate approach for a required religion course in public schools? Might a different approach to teaching about religion in public schools be warranted in elective courses about religion?

REFERENCES

Barber, Benjamin. 1984. *Strong Democracy*. Berkeley: University of California.

Bellah, Robert. 1980. *Varieties of Civil Religion*. New York: Harper and Row.

Bishop, Bill. 2008. *The Big Sort: Why The Clustering of Like-Minded Americans Is Tearing Us Apart*. New York: Houghton Mifflin.

Blake, Mariah. 2010. "Revisionaries." *Washington Monthly* (January/February), 13–18.

Chancey, Mark. 2014. "Rewriting History for a Christian America: Religion and the Texas Social Studies Controversy of 2009–2010." *Journal of Religion* 94, no. 3: 325–353.

Conover, Pamela, and Donald Searing. 2000. "A Political Socialization Perspective." In *Rediscovering the Democratic Purposes of Education*, edited by Lorraine McDonnell, 91–126. Lawrence: University of Kansas.

Eck, Diana. 2002. *A New Religious America*. San Francisco: HarperCollins.

Green, Steven K. 1999. "The Fount of Everything Just and Right? The Ten Commandments as a Source of American Law." *Journal of Law and Religion* 14: 525–558.

Gutmann, Amy. 1999. *Democratic Education*, Princeton, NJ: Princeton University.

Habermas, Jurgen. 1998. *Between Facts and Norms*. Cambridge, MA: MIT Press.

———. 2001. *Moral Consciousness and Communicative Action*. Cambridge, MA: MIT Press.

Hunter, James Davidson. 1991. *Culture Wars: The Struggle to Define America.* New York: Basic Books.

Lester, Emile. 2011. *Teaching About Religions: A Democratic Approach for Public Schools.* Ann Arbor: University of Michigan.

Moore, Diane. 2007. *Overcoming Religious Illiteracy.* New York: Palgrave MacMillan.

Noddings, Nel. 1993. *Educating for Intelligent Belief and Unbelief.* New York: Teachers College.

Nord, Warren. 1995. *Religion and American Education: Rethinking a National Dilemma.* Chapel Hill: University of North Carolina.

———. 2010. *Does God Make a Difference?* Oxford: Oxford University.

Rousseau, Jean-Jacques. 1987. *The Basic Political Writings.* Indianapolis: Hackett.

Smith, Christian. 1998. *American Evangelicalism: Embattled and Thriving.* Chicago: University of Chicago.

———. 2000. *Christian America: What Evangelicals Really Want.* Berkeley: University of California.

Stolzenberg, Nomi. 1993. "'He Drew A Circle That Shut Me Out.'" *Harvard Law Review* 106: 581–667.

Vitz, Paul C. 1986. "Religion and Traditional Values in Public School Textbooks." *National Affairs: The Public Interest* 34: 79–90.

Wolfe, Alan. 2003. *The Transformation of American Religion.* New York: Free Press.

FURTHER READING

Feinberg, Walter, and Richard Layton. 2014. *The Liberal Case for Teaching Religion in the Public Schools.* Ann Arbor: University of Michigan Press.

Greenawalt, Kent. 2005. *Does God Belong in the Public Schools?* Princeton, NJ: Princeton University Press.

Nord, Warren, and Charles Haynes. 1998. *Taking Religion Seriously Across the Curriculum.* Nashville, TN: First Amendment Center.

Prothero, Stephen. 2007. *Religious Literacy: What Every American Needs to Know—And Doesn't.* San Francisco: HarperCollins.

Wertheimer, Linda. 2015. *Faith Ed: Teaching about Religion in an Age of Intolerance.* New York: Beacon.

PART II

LIFESPAN FAITH
DEVELOPMENT

CHAPTER 7

···

FAITH DEVELOPMENT

···

SHARON DALOZ PARKS

INTRODUCTION

MAEVE, barely five years old, is sitting at the kitchen counter exploring "something special" that we have brought to her. It is something we found—dead but still beautiful—in our driveway. When she removes the cover of the ordinary refrigerator dish, she exclaims, "a luna moth"! Then, not taking her eyes away from the six-inch, sea-foam-green wingspan, in a voice filled with wonder and reverence, she simply says, "Wow!" There is a pause, and then she turns to her grandfather and says, "They only live a week, you know." (No, we don't know and are amazed that she does. Later, we learn that only two evenings prior, visiting another home, she had seen a cluster of moths around the porch light and was captivated by the size of the luna moth. Returning home, her parents had helped her learn more about it online.)

Now, entirely of her own volition, she hops off the stool and opens a kitchen drawer in a successful search for a larger, better-fitting container. After carefully placing the luna moth inside and ensuring that the lid is snug, she goes to the ragbag, finds an old dishtowel, and after some experimentation, wraps her luna moth container in it. We then follow her into the playroom, where she places the wrapped container in her empty Lego box, fitting the lid tight. She moves to the dress-up box and brings forth a large red scarf. I remark, "Oh, that's a good idea to wrap it in a scarf." She responds imperiously, "It's not a scarf. It's a colorful cloth." I consider myself informed. After securing the colorful cloth around the Lego-boxed, dishtowel-wrapped refrigerator dish, she picks it up, and (circular floor plan) she walks—or processes?—arms outstretched, throughout the first floor of her home, ending in the living room where she sets her treasure in the center of the coffee table. Then, without a word, she departs upstairs to prepare for bed. And we have just observed a moment of meaning-making and the birthing of religion in her young life.

Gregg Levoy (2014, 8) observes:

> The reasons why children's enthusiasm for learning and discovery and their spirit of wonder often devolve into a sense of passionless duty to achieve and comply are

complicated. Some reasons are social and bureaucratic, some personal and parental. But none of them are developmental. The passion for learning doesn't naturally wane as we get older. Something gets in the way.

In Maeve we see a child's capacity for wonder, fascination, curiosity, learning—and at her core, a capacity also for reverence, care, and the seeds of sacred ritual. The experience of wonder is a primary gateway into a recognition of the Mystery of life itself—a Mystery that we apprehend and can never fully comprehend. Suffering is another primary gateway, and it is unlikely that Maeve will be able to avoid it. Throughout her life, Maeve will be developing her capacity to learn and to become a woman of conscience and competence in the face of the wonder and suffering of our world—unless something gets in the way (Parks 2005).

What might that be? In a society of demands and distractions, her aliveness could become routinized and numb. But more specifically, her capacity for wonder and inquiry could become captive to imposed beliefs, and her capacity for composing a creative, fitting response to her sense of the sacred could become cramped within ill-fitting images-symbols and narratives. Or, she could simply find herself too much alone in the sometimes hard work of meaning-making—sorting out reality, truth, and trustworthiness, and the desire to have an effect, to belong, to love and be loved. That is, she could suffer the absence of a community grounded and alive in the daily, ongoing work of discerning the fitting connections among things and a worthy narrative to live by, within the ultimate Mystery that we all share.

Today's generations are particularly vulnerable to something present or absent getting in the way. Our generations are asked to live at one of those great hinge points in history—a cusp time—when at the hand of our travel, communication, biological, nuclear, and artificial intelligence technologies, human cultures are being profoundly reordered. We know this *personally* as our lifestyles shift and the human lifespan has been significantly extended for many; *ecologically* as we are learning that we are an integral part of a vast tissue of life in which everything is connected to everything else; *economically* as we are all cast into a complex global economy; and *ecumenically* as the whole inhabited world is meeting and colliding in ways both perilous and promising. All of our cultural covenants are under review (including our educational institutions and religious traditions), as we all stand on unprecedented, morally ambiguous, and ethically challenging frontiers. As a consequence, we live in a time when the old forms rattle, and the new forms wait to be born.

THE EMERGENCE OF FAITH DEVELOPMENT THEORY

We should not be surprised that in this milieu, we are necessarily undergoing a reconsideration of "faith" and what it means to be "faithful." This is the context within which a young Christian minister-professor-scholar-theologian-ethicist, James W. Fowler, after listening to people's stories of their journeys of faith, was prompted to seek out more adequate patterns of interpretation. The consequence of his interdisciplinary inquiry over four decades was the emergence of a theory of "faith development." This theoretical lens is composed of four primary, interdependent facets comprising a vital perspective for the reconsideration of the nature of faith and belief, religion and spirituality, and their potential transformations across the lifespan. The four facets are (1) a more dynamic and spacious understanding of "faith"; (2) emergent insights from the study of biological and cognitive development (constructive-developmental psychology); (3) the role of images, symbols, narratives, and rituals; and (4) the power of the social field in the formation of faith.

A Dynamic and Spacious Understanding of Faith

Drawing on the work of Wilfred Cantwell Smith, a scholar of world religions, Fowler distinguished "faith" from "belief." While in its root usage "belief" conveyed a sense of "to hold dear" or "to prize," for many today "belief" has come to signify assent to a fixed proposition or abstract dogma, or a merely personal opinion, increasingly often belonging to someone else, and even connoting doubt.

The word "faith" when equated with "belief" is now, therefore, used primarily as a noun. "Faith," however, may be understood also as a verb—something that not only religious folk have, but rather something that all human beings do. Smith directs us to remember that in earlier times "faith" meant "allegiance, loyalty, integrity, love, commitment, trust and entrusting, and the capacity to perceive and to respond to transcendent qualities in oneself and one's environment" (Smith 1977, 69). As Fowler (1981, 11) summarizes,

> Smith gives a persuasive demonstration that the language dealing with faith in the classical writings of the major religious traditions never speaks of it in ways that can be translated by the modern meanings of belief or believing. Rather, faith involves an alignment of the heart or will, a commitment of loyalty and trust. His treatment of the Hindu term for faith, *sraddha*, perhaps puts it best: "It means, almost without equivocation, *to set one's heart on.*" To set one's heart on someone or something requires that one has "seen" or "sees the point of" that to which one is loyal. . . . It is a mode of knowing, of *acknowledgment.*

This setting of the heart does not occur once and for all; rather, it is an ongoing activity—a process of "faithing"—in the midst of the daily human experience of a dialogue between trust and fear, power and powerlessness, alienation and belonging, suffering and wonder. This meaning-making dialogue orients one's thought and actions—moral choice and ethics—as human beings continually compose and recompose what is ultimately true and trustworthy and act in alignment with that "reality."

This liberation of "faith" from "belief" is resonant with theologians Paul Tillich and H. Richard Niebuhr, who uncover faith as a broad phenomenon, a universal human concern—a capacity at the core of human life to have a felt sense of a transcendent dimension that Niebuhr speaks of as an "ultimate environment" within which the whole of life is oriented and held. Thus Fowler (1981, 5), building on their collective insight, writes:

> Prior to our being religious or irreligious, before we come to think of ourselves as Catholics, Protestants, Jews or Muslims, we are already engaged with issues of faith. Whether we become nonbelievers, agnostics, or atheists, we are concerned with how to put our lives together and with what will make life worth living. Moreover, we look for something to love that loves us, something to value that gives us value, something to honor and respect that has the power to sustain our being.

It is from this perspective that we can recognize Maeve's response to the luna moth as her making meaning of an experience evoking wonder and worthy of honor and respect—yielding values that orient her life.

Evolving Patterns of Biological and Cognitive Development

The underlying recognition here is the fact of the composing mind. A human mind is not a dependable transmitter, but it is a powerful composer and transformer. Thus Fowler recognized that the discipline of constructive-developmental psychology, revealing predictable, deep structural patterns underlying the activity of the composing mind, held significant implications for "faithing."

The two grandfathers of developmental psychology are Erik Erikson and Jean Piaget. Early on, Fowler turned to Erikson to interpret common patterns across individual narratives of faith. Rooted in the psychoanalytic tradition, Erikson was attentive to the changes in human experience and perception grounded in biological maturation that we move through, "ready or not." Each of his eight life stages is defined by biological development and a corresponding task that is continually reworked in the succeeding stages, beginning in infancy with the establishment of "Basic Trust vs. Basic Mistrust," moving into "Autonomy vs. Shame and Doubt," and so on (Erikson 1963).

While teaching at Harvard Divinity School, Fowler was encouraged to be in dialogue also with Lawrence Kohlberg and his work in moral development at Harvard's Graduate School of Education. Fowler was thereby introduced to the work of Piaget, a genetic epistemologist who, fascinated by the consistency of the "wrong answers" that children gave on IQ tests, subsequently posited the development of underlying structures of logic, or "stages." His stages evolve through time from infancy at least through adolescence. This schema begins with a Sensorimotor stage, moving into Pre-operational or

Intuitive, then Concrete Operational, and Formal Operational stages—each structure a more refined system of differentiation in the relationship of subject and object, self and other, and able to hold greater complexity (Piaget 1976).

The Role of Image, Symbol, Narrative, Ritual

Fowler saw that a broad understanding of the development of faith perceived solely as meaning-making activity evolving through underlying cognitive *structures* had powerful implications for education and religion, but was insufficient to account for the development of a worthy faith. The *content* that structures or stages hold also has formative power. That is, naming is an integral dimension of meaning-making and "faithing" and is a manifestation of the human imagination—our capacity to give form to our experience.

Samuel Taylor Coleridge (1969) identified *imagination* as the highest power of the human mind. In contrast to mere fantasy, imagination is the means by which we compose, hold, and express "reality." An image (whether word, sound, gesture, symbol, metaphor, story, poetry, or policy) lends an outward form to an inner experience. Imagination is the process by which we form and re-form our knowing. Faith as "faithing" may be understood, therefore, as the place of experience and the imagination—experience and the meaning we make of it, the form we give to it (Lynch 1973). We can begin to see how images hold insight and become symbols and narratives when they serve as keys to whole patterns of meaning, and thus they play a vital part in the composing and recomposing of faith. Moreover, images function differentially according to the capacity of the underlying structures in which they are held.

Fowler (1981) traced the development of the role of symbols within the emerging story of biological, cognitive, and faith development, discerning the outlines of a predictable developmental sequence. In the evolution of the capacity to receive and employ images, since every image is finite in its capacity to grasp the transcendent Mystery of life, we may need to shed prior images—even those that held the sacred—and search out yet more adequate images, symbols, narratives, and rituals. Or we may need to allow images to accrue new layers of meaning in the service of a more viable faith.

When perceived through this lens, we can understand religion as a distillation of images and narratives that function as metaphors, powerful enough to reveal and hold the meaning-making of individuals and their communities through time. Maeve created a rudimentary veneration and ritual in response to the wonder of the luna moth—her imagination creating a fitting form to honor the integrity of her experience of reality. Though her memory of that moment may not be sustained because as a five-year-old her intuitive holding of that moment is limited (i.e. "episodic"), we adults who had the privilege and pleasure of observing her are unlikely now to see a luna moth without our own enhanced sense of wonder and reverence. In the cog-wheeling of the generations, we come to faith in the faith—the imaginations—of others.

The Power of Relationship and the Social Field

We begin to see, therefore, how in the process of "faithing" we are dependent upon the character and adequacy of our social field—its capacity to provide developmental prompts and viable images. As we consider the trajectory of Maeve's meaning-making and how it might evolve across her lifespan as she composes and recomposes self, world, and "God," it is notable that Fowler (1981, 132) writes: "Our research convinces me that education at this age—in the home, in synagogues and churches, in nursery schools and kindergartens—has a tremendous responsibility for the quality of images and stories we provide as gifts and guides for our children's fertile imaginations."

Indeed, development in Piaget's view is dependent upon more than the biological-cognitive unfolding of the individual alone. It requires an interaction between self and other that promotes the discovery of the inadequacy of the current, underlying structure of knowing. Development is dependent upon the relationship between the self and one's surroundings. Dwelling within a world including luna moths, parents who love her and nurture her curiosity, grandparents who arrive with an offering, and access to resources and institutions that nourish her creativity, Maeve is continually prompted to revise and enlarge her meaning-making. Thus we are remiss if we perceive faith as a wholly personal, individual matter. The development of self and the development of faith is a psycho-*social* phenomenon. "Faithing" becomes a matter, in part, of the company we keep—the ways we are met or abandoned within our social surroundings.

Fowler (1981, 33), drawing in part on Niebuhr, insists that

> . . . faith is everywhere a relational matter. The *patterns* of faith that make selfhood possible and sustain our *identities* are *covenantal in form*. Our relations of trust in and loyalty to our companions in community are deepened and sanctioned by our trust in and loyalty to shared transcendent centers of value and power.

Such covenants are often tacit, invisible, and revealed as much by their betrayal as by the times in which we are mutually loyal in a practice of "good faith." (And note that not only religious traditions but political, economic, or other ideologies may be similarly held as transcendent centers of value and power or "ultimate," and thus function "religiously"—that is, as a way of interpreting not merely a feature of life but the whole of life.)

Fowler's work significantly deepened our understanding of human beings as meaning-makers, seeking pattern, order, and coherence in the force field of our lives. We tend to reserve the word "faith" for meaning-making in its most comprehensive dimensions, embracing all that is most ultimate and intimate. If "faithing" potentially develops in ways that can take more into account, we begin to see what it asks and costs (both individually and collectively) to compose and recompose a sense of one's "ultimate environment"—that is, to grapple again and again with the big questions: What ultimately matters—anything? What is ultimately real, true, trustworthy? How do we know? Who and what are we? What is required of us? How do we learn and make worthy meaning at the crossroads of suffering and wonder?

STAGES OF FAITH

Thus, placing a broad phenomenological understanding of faith alongside the insights of developmental psychology, and incorporating the significance of the roles of symbols and the social field, Fowler began to explore and describe the necessarily dynamic, developmental, imaginal, and social character of faith. Working at the edges of an emerging interdisciplinary and illuminating discourse, Fowler initiated a process of further inquiry, initially involving more than four hundred qualitative interviews.

After a decade of work (published in several preliminary forms), in 1981 Fowler published *Stages of Faith: The Psychology of Human Development and the Quest for Meaning*. Against a rich and robust theoretical backdrop, he traced six stages of faith:

Infancy (Undifferentiated Faith)
Early Childhood (Intuitive-Projective Faith)
Childhood (Mythic-Literal Faith)
Adolescence (Synthetic-Conventional Faith)
Young Adulthood (Individuative-Reflective Faith)
Adulthood (Conjunctive Faith)

Each of these stages takes into account successive transformations in the form of logic, perspective-taking, form of moral judgment, bounds of social awareness, locus of authority, form of world coherence, and symbolic function (Fowler 1981).

Though others had begun to make connections among models of human development, learning, and faith, Fowler's work coalesced a new horizon of understanding and practice, an attractor that intuitively and substantively opened into a new conversation between religion and education—both within religious communities and beyond. Most notably, religious educators among mainline Christians (both Protestant and Roman Catholic) and Jews actively pursued the implications for practices of "faithing" within homes, Sunday Schools, and youth groups. Over time faith development theory also found audiences focused on pastoral care, spiritual direction, preaching, and congregational life—especially among those hungry for more spacious ways of interpreting the variances of faith expressions and more adequately conceived ways of designing curriculum in response to questions of readiness and potential. As faith development theory also provided avenues into "secular" educational institutions and disciplines, Fowler's seminal work, along with other neo-Piagetian perspectives, joined a wave of both critique and elaboration.

Critique

A primary critique of early models, including Fowler's, was their linear and hierarchical character and the consequent vulnerability to both distortion of human experience (not so linear) and elite inference (higher is better). Ronald Marstin eloquently addressed the latter, contending that, for example, in the development of a capacity for adjudicating justice, higher *is* better precisely "because it can take more into account" (Marstin 1979, 34, 37). The more lockstep linear (ladder) features of the earliest models quickly gave way to more fluid spirals, as the dynamic and complex relationships among evolving structures, content, lifespan phases, and the social field were increasingly accommodated. Moreover, thoughtful educators recognized that the appropriate use of identifying stages or eras of human development is not to diagnose or categorize another person (or group) from some "superior" perspective, but rather to ask the deeper question: *Taking into account how each of us is making meaning at this moment in time, what do we now mean to each other?*

The Motion of Life Itself

In this ferment, while Fowler was at work at Harvard's Divinity School, Robert Kegan, at the Harvard Graduate School of Education, along with others inspired by Kohlberg's work, was exploring similar terrain. Kegan (1980, 407) wrote in a seminal article: "There is a common paradigm . . . which informs the work of many of the American theorists and practitioners. . . . I call this paradigm "constructive-developmental" because it attends to the *development* of our *construing* or meaning-making throughout life." Further, he acknowledged that it was fair to say that the work of Piagetians ("neo" or otherwise) could be characterized as about "*cognition,* to the neglect of *emotion;* the *individual,* to the neglect of the *social;* the *concept,* to the neglect of *being; stages,* to the neglect of *process;* and *what is new and changed* in a person, to the neglect of *the person who persists through time*" (Kegan 1980, 406). That said, Kegan then made a philosophical-theological move. He saw that the paradigm was truncated if it was reduced to development as a succession of stages (subject/object, self/other differentiations), even though it is one of the most robust and universal phenomena to be found in nature and formed the "deep structure" in constructive-developmental stage theories. He wrote (1980, 407):

> But the relation of self to other goes on in a context . . . which is prior to the self-other relation, a context which actually gives rise *to* it. I call this context "meaning-constitutive evolutionary activity," by which I mean to refer to something that is more than biology, philosophy, psychology, sociology, or theology, but is that which all of these, in their different ways, have studied. I am referring to the restless creative motion of life itself, which is not first of all "individual" *or* "world," "organism" *or* "environment," but is the source of each.

Thus so perceived, persons are not their stages of development; rather, stages of development reveal relative truces in the person's participation in *the motion of life itself.* From this stance, Kegan invited the recognition that claiming a religious or spiritual dimension to this developmental paradigm does not attach something onto the frame-work or speak from its periphery; rather, it speaks from its heart:

> The same reality said to be philosophically real, biologically real, psychologically real and socially real, is also "religiously" real, that it partakes of the numinous ("a white light still and moving"), the graceful ("a grace of sense"), the holy, the tran-scendent . . . and the oneness of all life. This underlying motion, especially as it is seen in its spiritual reality, is, I believe what James Fowler refers to when he speaks. . . of an "ultimate environment." (Kegan 1980, 409–410)

In pointing to this prior motion of life itself, manifested in human beings as meaning-constitutive evolutionary activity, it is not too much to say that in relation to develop-mental models, Kegan laid down the track that everyone else's developmental train rides on.

Fowler had already taken into account some of the limitations of the neo-Piagetian models that Kegan identified, most notably addressing the overly "cognitive" character of the model by insisting that faith in its transformations is both rational and "passional" (Fowler and Keen 1978, 37). But it was Carol Gilligan who not only brought a missing, vital voice into the story of constructive-developmental theory, but in so doing revealed its robust capacity to serve as an aperture into new realms of insight.

In a Different Voice

The reader may note that all of the theorists informing Fowler's early work were male. Coinciding with second-wave feminism, Carol Gilligan, another theorist in the Kohlberg wheelhouse, in 1982 published *In a Different Voice: Psychological Theory and Women's Development*. It was followed in 1986 by *Women's Ways of Knowing*, written by Mary Field Belekny, Blythe McVicker Clinchy, Nancy Rule Goldberger, and Jill Mattuck Tarule. These, along with others who listened with particular attention to the experi-ence of women and the development of moral reasoning, heard another, different voice articulating the value of belonging as well as differentiation, inclusion along with in-dividuation, love as well as justice, acts of care as well as restraints on aggression, and home as well as journey—the recognition that human life is formed in the alchemy of both venturing and abiding (Parks 1989).

Gilligan, for example, uncovered different modes of moral understanding and thinking about conflict and choice. She heard how Jake diffuses a potentially explo-sive interpersonal conflict by casting it as an impersonal conflict of claims in a logic of fairness—an objective way to decide who will win. But the hierarchical ordering with its winning and losing still holds a potential for violence. In Amy's construction, a web of relationships—a network of connection sustained by communication—shifts the moral problem from one of unfair domination to one of unnecessary exclusion. Jeffrey thinks about who goes first and Karen thinks about who is left out. Whether thinking about responsibility to self or to others, Amy tends to respond contextually and Jake tends to respond with an appeal to rules (Gilligan 1982). Neither of these two ways of making meaning in relationship to moral dilemmas is necessarily exclusive to one gender or the other, and both nature and nurture appear to play a role in shaping whichever polar preference may take form within a particular person or community.

Stage and Phase

We may be suspicious also that the early models of developmental stages seem to coincide with assumed phases of life—whether we are looking at Erikson's eight or Fowler's six stages. Indeed, as our societies become more complex and the lifespan is significantly extended for some populations, the need for further inquiry is obvious. Notably, as the human lifespan is stretched, two decades are particularly feeling the pain: broadly speaking, people in their twenties and people in their sixties are receiving double messages. Twenty-somethings are told that they are going to live "forever" and they have plenty of time to explore their options as vast new fields of learning are emerging, and there is no guaranteed, straight path to a meaningful and economically viable life trajectory. At the same time, another, urgent message insists that they had better "get theirs" in a world prepared to pass them by. Sixty-somethings, who in an earlier time could assume they have landed on the threshold of an imminent retirement with the hope of a few good "sunset" years, now face the specter of living another two decades or more, vulnerable to outliving their friends, finances, and brains. This later phase of life (as *phase*) is largely uncharted territory from the perspective of the constructive-developmental nature of faith, but it is beginning to draw the attention of theorists studying spiritual and faith formation.

The Twenty-Something Years

Informed by Fowler, Kegan, Gilligan, and especially William G. Perry (1999), whose seminal work on the intellectual and ethical development of college students has had broad influence in higher education, I posited a structural "stage" of human development in a place Kohlberg, Kegan, Fowler, and others have cast as simply "transitional" or as a "moratorium." This typically twenty-something era is marked by its own structure and tasks. The threshold of this era from a constructive-developmental point of view is marked by the capacity for critical, systemic thought (the capacity to step outside of one's one thinking and ask, "Why do I think that way?" and also the capacity to recognize not only interpersonal but also systemic relationships—a vital feature of becoming a full adult within a diverse society harboring democratic aspirations). This development is characteristic of Fowler's and Kegan's stage four, but it is distinctive in that the locus of authority remains outside the self but is not the conventionally "assumed Authority" of stage three. Rather, Authority is now more consciously "chosen" by the young or emerging adult because the particular source of Authority (now a more mentoring presence) makes sense in terms of the meaning-making of the emerging adult.

In alignment with the constructivist model, biological maturation is a necessary but insufficient condition for this era in development. Indeed, some "adults" may live all of their lives within a conventional "adolescent" (stage three) form of knowing that, irrespective of its apparent sophistication, is ultimately dependent upon an assumed source of Authority outside the self, and is thus vulnerable to the exploitations of demagoguery in its manifold forms (Parks 1986, 2011). Jeffrey Jensen Arnett, a social psychologist, and his colleagues have similarly taken on the work of illuminating what might be described as an underrecognized phase and stage in the human lifespan (Arnett 2004).

Emerging adulthood harbors a pivotal juncture in the formation of faith, because for the first time "faith" as meaning-making at the level of ultimacy becomes conscious of its own composing activity (everyone is making it up!), and thus the possibility of a stark unqualified meaninglessness comes into view. Faith becomes adult when it can have a doubt of itself. This new capacity for existential doubt relativizes and reorients all of the big questions that constitute the composing of a responsible adult life.

The challenge to the social field is to recognize, support, challenge, inspire, and be accountable to the promise of young, emerging adult development—especially in the dimension of faith. Thus, in terms of the question, "What do we now mean to each other?" this stage of young, emerging adulthood and the task of achieving critical, systemic thought distinctively calls for mentors and mentoring environments—within educational institutions and throughout the wider culture.

Faith Development and the Public Square

As useful and influential as faith development theory may have become in disclosing more adequate ways in which to perceive and respond to the evolution of the meaning-making in children, adolescents, and emerging adults, the primary promise of faith development as coalesced by Fowler and elaborated by others has not yet been realized. It is significant that though Fowler carried on a rich dialogue with religious educators, seminarians, pastors, and religious scholars, his primary attention in the later years of his work was given to the implications of faith development for the life of the public square (Fowler 1991).

Though developmental perspectives have broad ramifications for our reconsideration of the key domains of education, politics and governance, economics, the environment, public media, and religion, public discourse in American society does not yet reflect even a rudimentary grasp of constructive-developmental insight, especially in terms of its implications for responsible adult citizenship in an increasingly complex world. Specifically, the development of faith understood as meaning-making in its most comprehensive dimensions undergirds—by intention or default—the formation of responsible citizenship manifested through individual persons, organizations, and institutions across sectors. Yet for many people, belief, religion, faith, and spirituality are presumed to be at best a personal matter and, therefore, optional and problematic—divisive and even dangerous—in the public square. At the same time, however, there has never been a greater need for consciousness, conscience, and competence grounded in the development of mature adult meaning-making.

George Rupp, former dean of Harvard Divinity School and former president of both Rice and Columbia universities, observes that the narrative of individualism in the West that connects persons to the larger society through markets, bureaucracies, or media is resisted by other cultures on the grounds that it too often ignores the networks of intermediate institutions that narrate and animate traditional communities and cultures. Human beings need networks of belonging, and communities of religious faith notably serve to confirm the crucial, covenantal role of the social field in mediating the triadic relationship of the self to our lived relationship with Mystery and with each other. Such communities, however, often foster fortified tribal, parochial boundaries and varying forms of violence when the modal, normative structures of faith are inadequate (i.e., not yet sufficiently mature) and unable to take into account the complex, systemic, and often daunting realities of the wider social field.

In this hinge time, as cultures meet and collide in unprecedented ways, the challenge for communities everywhere, as Rupp suggests, is to nurture particular values and practices that yield coherence and meaning, while at the same time practicing a self-critical consciousness that welcomes and listens to the outsider and affirms an inclusiveness that is open to all. Rupp (2012, 44) concludes with the recognition that "to pursue this new communitarianism will require sustained commitment over generations. But this aspiration will also come to be a pragmatic necessity in the crowded, tension-filled world of the 21st century."

Integral to Rupp's analysis is a call for religious communities that dependably support the development of a mature, post-critical faith as the modal norm for adult development—a capacity for "faithing" that can hold value commitments with both conviction and a provisional humility and can practice curiosity and compassion while tolerating paradox and ambiguity. In other words, the promise embedded in recognizing the constructive-developmental and imaginal features of the life of faith is that in our religiously variegated world, we can learn to recognize the faiths of others (whether religious per se or ideologies religiously held) and our own faith as essential personal and collective manifestations of the meaning-constitutive activity at the core of human life. Sacred symbols and narratives may be held and engaged as powerful, revelatory, and yet finite attempts to apprehend though we can never fully comprehend the Mystery we all share. Faith development theory invites us to more artfully create learning communities that both honor each stage in the development of faith and provide "developmental lures" into its ongoing evolution. Specifically, we can cultivate norms of adult faith that are expressive of the capacity to think critically, systemically, and compassionately in relationship both to others and to one's self. To do so is to cultivate what Ken Wilbur (2000, 95), in his efforts to both integrate and elaborate developmental perspectives and render them more accessible to non-academic audiences, describes as "spiritual intelligence."

If Maeve, her generation, and the generations to follow are to be educated for the capacity for aliveness, a robust "faith-full-ness," and a grounded and creative citizenship in response to the wonder and suffering of their world, then faith development theory provides an essential perspective for the formation of post-conventional faith and practice of religion. The question becomes not whether in our globalized world we become Muslims, Jews, Buddhists, Taoists, Confucianists, or Christians, as significant as that question is. The vital question is this: Will there be *faith* on Earth, and will it be *good* faith—faith sufficiently inclusive so as to challenge and transcend the destructive idolatries of national, ethnic, racial, and religious identities and to draw us together as a human community in covenants of trust and loyalty to each other?

Faith development theory invites us into the "new secular," meaning that rather than banishing "faith" from the public square in the quest for civility, every faith is brought into public dialogue without privileging one over another. Rather, each participates in an ongoing interdependent practice of submitting its best offering to the ongoing test of lived, communal experience, maintaining a posture of curiosity, discernment, and an expectation of learning—working the question: What do we now mean to each other? This is the great work of religion and education in today's world, learning to discover how and by what faith and faiths we all may dwell together within the small planet home we share.

FUTURE DIRECTIONS

1. What is the relationship between the modal moral valence of a social field and the development of faith and conscience within an individual?
2. How does faith development theory inform the conditions for intercultural and interreligious dialogue, discernment, respect, and compassion?
3. What will be the contributions of neuroscience to theories of faith development?

REFERENCES

Arnett, Jeffrey. 2004. *Emerging Adulthood: The Winding Road from the Late Teens Through the Twenties*. New York: Oxford University Press.

Coleridge, Samuel Taylor. 1969. *The Collected Works of Samuel Taylor Coleridge*. Vol. 6. *Lay Sermons*, "The Statesman's Manual," ed. R. White. Princeton, NJ: Princeton University Press.

Erikson, Erik H. 1963. *Childhood and Society*, 2nd ed. New York: Norton.

Fowler, James W. 1981. *Stages of Faith: The Psychology of Human Development and the Quest for Meaning*. San Francisco: Harper and Row.

———. 1991. *Weaving the New Creation: Stages of Faith and the Public Church*. San Francisco: Harper Collins.

Fowler, Jim, and Sam Keen. 1978. *Life Maps: Conversations on the Journey of Faith*. Jerome Berryman (Ed.). Waco, TX: Word, Incorporated.

Gilligan, Carol. 1982. *In a Different Voice: Psychological Theory and Women's Development*. Cambridge, MA: Harvard University Press.

Kegan, Robert. 1980. "There the Dance Is: Religious Dimensions of a Developmental Framework." In *Toward Moral and Religious Maturity*, edited by J.W. Fowler and A. Vergote. 403–440. Morristown, NJ: Silver Burdett.

Levoy, Greg. 2014. *Vital Signs: The Nature and Nurture of Passion*. New York: Jeremy P. Tarcher/Penguin.

Lynch, William F. 1973. *Images of Faith: An Exploration of the Ironic Imagination*. Notre Dame, IN: Notre Dame Press.

Marstin, Ronald. 1979. *Beyond Our Tribal Gods: The Maturing of Faith*. Maryknoll, NY: Orbis.

Parks, Sharon. 1986. *The Critical Years: The Young Adult Search for a Faith to Live By*. San Francisco: Harper & Row Publishers.

Parks, Sharon Daloz. 1989. "Home and Pilgrimage: Companion Metaphors for Personal and Social Transformation." *Soundings* 72, no. 2–3: 297–315.

———. 2003. "To Venture and to Abide: The Tidal Rhythm of Our Becoming." Chap. 3 in *Developing a Public Faith: New Directions in Practical Theology*, edited by Richard R. Osmer and Fredrich L. Schweitzer. St. Louis: Chalice Press.

———. 2005. "How Then Shall We Live? Suffering and Wonder in the New Commons." In *Living the Questions*, edited by Sam M. Intrator, 298–307. San Francisco: Jossey-Bass.

———. 2011. *Big Questions, Worthy Dreams: Mentoring Emerging Adults in Their Search for Meaning, Purpose, and Faith*. 10th anniv. ed. San Francisco: Jossey-Bass.

Perry, William G. 1999. *Forms of Intellectual and Ethical Development in the College Years: A Scheme*. San Francisco: Jossey-Bass Publishers.

Piaget, Jean. 1976. *The Child & Reality: Problems of Genetic Psychology*, translated by Arnold Rosin. New York: Penguin Books.

Rupp, George. 2012. "Dreams, Dreads, and the New Global Community." *Reflections: Yale Divinity School* 99 (Fall), no. 2: 38–44.

Smith, Wilfred Cantwell. 1981. *Belief and History*. Charlottesville: University of Virginia.

Wilbur, Ken. 2000. *A Theory of Everything: An Integral Vision for Business, Politics, Science, and Spirituality*. Boston: Shambhala Publications.

FURTHER READING

Daloz, Laurent A. Parks, Cheryl H. Keen, James P. Keen, and Sharon Daloz Parks. 1996. *Common Fire: Leading Lives of Commitment in a Complex World*. Boston: Beacon Press.

Dykstra, Craig, and Sharon Parks, eds. 1986. *Faith Development and Fowler*. Birmingham, AL: Religious Education Press.

Osmer, Richard R., and Friedrich L. Schweitzer, eds. 2003. *Developing a Public Faith: New Directions in Practical Theology*. St. Louis: Chalice Press.

Rupp, George. 2015. *Beyond Individualism: The Challenge of Inclusive Communities*. New York: Columbia University Press.

CHAPTER 8

MORAL EDUCATION

LARRY NUCCI AND ROBYN ILTEN-GEE

Introduction

MORALITY is a core component of all major religious systems, and because of that moral education has often been conflated or equated with religious socialization. This was certainly the case in the early history of public education in the United States (Arthur 2013). This view of moral education raises problematic issues, however, associated with constitutional provisions for the separation of church and state, and throughout American history there have been efforts to differentiate the teaching of morality from religious instruction. For example, in the late nineteenth century a group calling itself the Ethical Union emerged for the specific purpose of rooting morality in nonreligious arguments, and separating it from the values of the church. In 1886 the Ethical Union formed the Moral Instruction League, which set out to replace the religious curriculum in American schools with a secular moral curriculum of its own (Arthur 2013). Such moves toward secularization have been met with cyclical periods of Christian evangelism (Fogel 2002) that have found expression through social conservative political movements calling for a return to prayer in schools, the posting of the Ten Commandments on school walls, and opportunities for students to engage in Bible study. There have also been efforts to reconcile these competing interests by differentiating teaching *about* religion from efforts to engage in religious socialization (Haynes and Thomas 2007).

The goal of this chapter is to situate moral education within a space that is concordant with the moral component of religion, and yet does not equate morality with the particularistic norms of any given religion. Our discussion will push the role of moral education a bit further to address the more troublesome possibility that some societal and religious standards may in fact be in conflict with morality. The challenge that this poses for moral education, and that we address in this chapter, is how to educate youth so that they will act in ways that are consistent with morality and will be able to contribute to the moral growth of the social world they inherit. We will begin with an overview of the research from developmental psychology that will help us to identify the domain of morality, and how it is differentiated from matters of convention and personal preference (Smetana, Jambon, and Ball 2014; Turiel 2002). This discussion of the psychological underpinnings of our approach to moral education will include a review of studies that have examined these questions directly with devoutly religious children and adolescents. We will also address the recent work of researchers (Haidt 2001; Jensen 2011) who have proposed that religious values form a distinctive type of morality that can be differentiated from the universalistic perspective that has been identified by developmental psychology. With this grounding in moral psychology, we will shift the focus of the chapter to the specifics of moral education. Our discussion of moral education will begin with the groundwork that takes place in early childhood and elementary education to foster growth in young children's moral intuitions of fairness and harm and emerging understandings of social rules, along with skills for emotion recognition and capacities for self-control. In other places we have referred to these basic practices as educating for "nice" people (Nucci 2009). We will then move to consideration of educational practices for the development of more mature moral capacities that would allow for participation in furtherance of the morality of society, and the lifelong growth of the individual as a moral being.

DEVELOPMENT IN THE MORAL DOMAIN: FOUNDATION FOR MORAL EDUCATION

The proposals for moral education presented here stem from work in developmental psychology that has differentiated a domain of morality from the emergence in early childhood of understandings of social right and wrong defined by the conventions of society (Smetana et al. 2014). *Morality* as outlined in this research has to do with our judgments about interpersonal actions such as hitting or sharing that impact the welfare or rights of persons. Because these assessments are based upon the effects of actions, judgments of right and wrong are not contingent upon the presence or absence of a governing social rule. Moreover, when individuals make judgments about moral actions they view their assessments of right and wrong as universally binding because of the perceived objective nature of the interpersonal effects of the action (e.g., unprovoked hitting would hurt whether it occurred in one culture or another). Moral judgments are structured by the person's underlying conceptions of fairness and harm (Turiel 2002).

In contrast with morality, *conventions* are the consensually determined social standards that regulate or coordinate the actions of a particular social group within settings defined by the governing conventions. Conventions are understood to be local and alterable, and the right or wrong of actions is contingent upon the existence of a governing conventional norm. As discussed by Searle (1969) conventions are constituent components of social systems. They define how the "game" is to be played within a particular social framework. Developmental research has found that understandings about convention reflect underlying concepts of social organization, with an adult-like understanding of conventions not emerging until middle adolescence (Midgette, Noh, Lee, and Nucci 2016; Turiel 2002).

Morality and convention are further differentiated from a personal domain of privacy and individual choice (Nucci 2014). Maintaining control over personal decisions such as choice of friends, aspects of personal appearance, and privacy in areas such as a personal diary are central to the construction of a personal autonomy and identity. The construction of a personal domain is central to children's and adolescents' development of moral concepts of rights as "basic freedoms" (Nucci 2014). Although a personal domain appears to be ubiquitous, the balance between the personal and cultural or religious standards of interpersonal obligation vary, and that variation accounts for much of what appears to be cultural differences in morality (Miller and Bland 2014).

Although many of our social decisions require the application of knowledge from only one of these social cognitive domains, deciding upon a course of action in many social contexts requires weighing or coordinating personal, conventional, and moral considerations. For example, deciding how to respond to a party invitation from someone you find boring may entail weighing the conventions of polite discourse, moral concerns for not hurting the feelings of the person offering the invitation, and personal considerations of how to spend your own leisure time. Moral development is a combination of changes in the ways that individuals reason about fairness, welfare, and rights, and how they weigh and apply those assessments in such multifaceted contexts (Turiel 2002).

MORALITY AND RELIGIOUS NORMS

These distinctions among morality, convention, and the personal have been sustained in numerous studies conducted in a wide range of cultural contexts over the past forty years (Smetana et al. 2014; Turiel 2002). The basic distinction between morality and convention is maintained even by children who have been diagnosed with autism (Blair 2005; Leslie, Mallon, and DiCorcia 2006). Of direct relevance to our discussion of moral education in the context of this volume are studies that have also examined whether the distinction between morality and convention extends to reasoning about religious norms (Nucci 1985; Nucci and Turiel 1993). In those studies, Christian and Jewish children were asked whether actions considered wrong within their religious traditions would be alright if scripture had not included information that God had an objection to the act. Findings from this research revealed that nearly all of the children and adolescents interviewed felt religious restrictions that are similar to secular conventions would be alright if there were no religious rules or biblical injunctions regulating the acts. These actions included such things as working on the Sabbath, a woman leading worship services, Catholic priests marrying, or not wearing head coverings during worship. On the other hand, at least 80% of participants maintained that moral acts such as stealing from another person, unprovoked hitting, slander, or damaging another's property would continue to be wrong even if God or scripture had been silent about the act.

More recently, Kuyel and Cesur (2013) found similar results with Turkish Muslim undergraduate students of varying degrees of religious affiliation, indicating that these findings are not limited to Judeo-Christian children and adolescents. These results with Muslims indicate that religiously devout children and adults reason about morality within the context of their religious normative systems in much the same way as people the world over reason about morality in nonreligious contexts (see Nucci 2001 for a more complete discussion). This is not to say that there are no variations in the ways that members of various religions approach particular issues, as we will discuss below. What these findings do indicate is that the moral component of religiously based social values stems from the same set of core considerations for human welfare and fairness.

Is There a Separate Morality of "Divinity"?

Some researchers take issue with this set of conclusions about religious moral thinking. Following the work of Richard Shweder (1990), Lene Jensen (2011) and Jonathan Haidt (2012) have argued that what is captured within social domain theory is but one form of morality, which they refer to as the morality of *autonomy*. The morality of autonomy, they argue, is an outgrowth of Western Enlightenment philosophy and represents a particular emphasis on reasoning and efforts to locate moral decisions around issues of fairness and rights (Shweder 1990). In their view, there are at least two additional other types of moral thinking: community and divinity. From their cultural psychology perspective, each of these three ethics may be emphasized to a greater or lesser degree as a function of cultural priorities (Jensen 2011; Shweder 1990). An example of the prioritization of a morality of *divinity* within the framework of American culture would be religiously based objections to homosexuality and same-sex marriage.

While this depiction offered by the cultural psychology perspective may serve to validate some religiously driven cultural practices, it also implies that all acts committed in the name of religion have just as much embedded moral validity to them as acts committed out of a sense of fairness or protection of others. If the ethic of divinity is a morality in itself, we have no way of discriminating between religious laws that tell us not to kill our neighbor and those that tell us *to* kill. For example, if the ethic of divinity and the ethic of autonomy are interchangeably supreme, we cannot condemn religiously based "honor" killings of female family members (Wikan 2002), or religiously based acts of terrorism, like shooting of the fifteen-year-old Afghani Nobel Peace Prize winner, Malala Yousafzai, for advocating that girls receive an education. Within the framework of the Three Ethics perspective these acts of violence are to be understood as moral because of their concordance with this supposed ethic of the divine. The problem posed by the moral relativism inherent in this equation of religiously based cultural norms with morality has not been lost on Richard Shweder. Shweder, who is not a relativist, has noted that it exposes cultural psychology to criticisms of being merely an "account of the despotism of tradition" (Shweder 2011, p. 310). From an educational perspective, this is not an idle concern: for moral education to be "moral," the processes and outcomes of that education must themselves be defensible on moral grounds (Kohlberg 1971).

From the perspective of social cognitive domain theory, issues like homosexuality are understood in terms of underlying sets of factual assumptions about what is "natural" in conjunction with beliefs about what is presumed to be required by supernatural entities such as the Abrahamic God (Turiel 2002). Judgments of the morality of any action, including homosexuality, reflect coordination by the religious person of moral concerns like fairness with these other nonmoral considerations. Included within these attempts by monotheistic believers to coordinate morality with religious considerations is whether a particular religious prescription is actually in keeping with God's true moral nature defined in terms of justice, love, and mercy (Nucci 2001). We simply note here that there is considerable resistance to the violent practices depicted above being waged by religiously devout members (such as Malala Yousafzai) within these same cultures (Turiel 2002; Wikan 2002) whose own reading of the "divine" precludes any dissociation of divinity from a morality rooted in concerns with fairness, human welfare, and rights. We also note that much of the progressive change that has occurred in human history has been spearheaded by such individuals with deep religious convictions employing morality as we have defined it.

THE PRACTICE OF MORAL EDUCATION

Our discussion of the practice of moral education is made with a full realization that the research base for this field is far from complete (Nucci and Turiel 2007). Despite the claims of a "new synthesis in moral psychology" (Haidt 2007) trumpeted in the *New York Times*, much of what goes on in classrooms in the name of moral education is continuous with longstanding cultural practices of children's socialization. These practices form the "basics" of moral education in that they emphasize attention to the child's emotional capacities for empathy and pro-social behavior. Also, generally underplayed in the discussions of the supposed new "moral psychology" is the critical role that cognition plays in our emotional lives. Researchers who study the development of emotion have noted that cognitions constructed in the context of our emotional experiences alter or enter into the regulation of affect and the final appraisal of social situations (Pizarro and Bloom 2003). As we will outline below, the focus of educational attention to children's social and emotional development is directed precisely at these cognitive areas of emotion recognition, emotion regulation, and self-control.

Our relatively brief discussion of these "basics" will be informed by the research that differentiates morality from societal convention and that emphasizes the role of developmental factors in children's moral growth. As we noted in our introduction, however, defining moral education solely in terms of these basics is an insufficient goal for moral education in that it does not address the students' capacities to employ moral *reasoning* to challenge the moral status quo, and thus contribute to the moral advancement of society, and the lifelong project of moral growth of the individual. A considerable part of what is "incomplete" in our picture of moral development is how to characterize the development of moral judgment and how one would go about measuring moral growth. The standard picture of moral development as moving through a well-defined stage sequence (Kohlberg 1984) has been largely abandoned (Nucci and Turiel 2007). Our educational approach builds from more recent work that has defined moral development in terms of the intersection between the development of moral understandings with the coordination of morality with nonmoral considerations (Nucci and Turiel 2007; Turiel 2002). From this perspective children and adolescents may apply morality to evaluate social norms and personal goals from a moral point of view at any point in development. Although it is not until early adolescence that students are able to apply morality to evaluate social *systems*, they are capable of engaging in a moral critique of their own and their peers' behavior, as well as the surrounding social norms, throughout their educational experience.

The Basics

Building Social and Emotional Competencies: Classrooms Based on Care and Trust

One of the recent advances in the study of moral development has been the discovery that the precursors to morality emerge in infancy (Hamlin 2013), and that by the third year of life children are able to make basic moral judgments (Smetana et al. 2014). Research on the emotional correlates of morality (Arsenio and Lover 1995) and recent findings on the brain regions associated with moral functioning (Blair 2003) sustain basic claims of the importance of attention to affective experiences for moral development. In particular this work points to the centrality of establishing caring classroom environments (Noddings 2002) that foster the child's construction of a worldview based on "goodwill" (Arsenio and Lover 1995), characterized by the presumption that social life operates for the most part according to basic moral principles of fairness and mutual respect. Watson has argued that classrooms combining the affective connections of care regulated by moral reciprocity and continuity form communities that establish relationships among students and teachers based upon trust (Watson and Ecken 2003). Trust is basic to the construction of an overall sense of school or classroom community, which in turn is one of the primary predictors of pro-social conduct in schools (Battistich 2008).

Even within the context of these caring environments, however, many children require additional support in developing their skills at emotion recognition and emotion regulation. These competencies are the focus of an area of education known as Social and Emotional Learning (SEL) (Elias, Kranzler, Parker, Kash, and Weissberg 2014). Although SEL emerged initially from research on how to educate students with behavioral problems and difficulties with self-control, it has moved into the mainstream of American education and is part of the broader fabric of skill-building that supports students' moral functioning (Elias et al. 2014). More recently, SEL has begun to incorporate practices drawn from Eastern contemplative traditions to build what is referred to as "mindfulness" as a component of students' awareness of the feelings and needs of themselves and others around them. Several school-based studies have provided evidence that engagement in mindfulness activities contributes to students' moral decision-making and behavior (Roeser et al. 2014).

Developmental Discipline and Domain-Appropriate Responses to Student Transgressions

Within the context of this basic framework of care and trust and support for building students' basic social and emotional skills, schools and classrooms contribute to students' moral and social development through their approach to school rules and discipline. Proponents of developmental discipline (Watson and Ecken 2003) claim that minimizing top-down directives and having students help create class rules are positive ways of maintaining a climate of trust between students and teachers. Engaging students, particularly in elementary school, in resolving their own interpersonal conflicts, rather than imposing adult solutions, helps to build children's sense of autonomy and fair reciprocity (Nucci 2001).

When teachers do use directives or respond to a breach of classroom rules, those messages are most effective when they are aligned with the domain of the transgression. (Killen, Breton, Ferguson, and Handler 1994; Nucci 2001). For example, if a student gets up to sharpen her pencil without raising her hand, the teacher might say, "Joy, doing that does not help our class function smoothly and it disrupts the lesson." In this response, the teacher is treating the action as a violation of a classroom norm. Or, the teacher could say, "Joy, sharpening your pencil like that is wrong and harmful to others," instead of treating the action as a moral transgression. The domain-concordant response is the first option, since rules about when to sharpen pencils are simply conventions to help the classroom function smoothly. Studies show that teachers who respond to transgressions in domain-concordant ways are more respected and appear more knowledgeable to students (Nucci and Powers 2014).

Students' moral growth is supported by consequences that are educative rather than punitive, and that allow for the transgressor to remain part of the classroom and school community (Nucci 2001). Zero-tolerance policies and the use of disciplinary suspensions have been shown to be far less effective in altering students' attitudes and behavior than approaches that employ restorative justice, in which the wrongdoer is encouraged to take full responsibility for the transgression and to take steps to ameliorate or undo the harm or damage caused by the misconduct. However, as mentioned earlier, the teacher might consider the domain of the transgression before deciding whether to initiate a restorative justice circle, which might be more effective for moral transgressions versus conventional ones.

Finally, a developmental approach to establishing and enforcing school rules would acknowledge the links between student behavior and shifts in students' understandings of morality and societal convention. This becomes particularly relevant in early adolescence. With respect to social convention, young adolescents enter a phase in which they question the conventions they upheld during middle childhood (Nucci, Creane, and Powers 2015; Turiel 1983). The support for conventions of maintaining basic order (e.g., to keep kids from running in the hallways) evaporates as young people reconsider the arbitrariness of conventional regulation and conclude that they are "simply the arbitrary dictates of authority." Thus, there is a greater tendency for students at this point in development to violate school conventions.

Coincident with these developmental shifts in concepts of convention are basic changes in the ways that adolescents draw boundaries between convention and matters of personal prerogative and privacy (Smetana 2011). Areas where conventions and norms of family and school touch upon personal expression (dress, hairstyle), personal associations (friendships), personal communication (phone, email), access to information (internet), and personal safety (substance use, sexuality) become zones of dispute wherein adolescents lay increasing claims to autonomy and control. The combined developmental phase of negation of convention with the extension of what is considered personal renders the period of early adolescence a difficult transition.

Understandably, schools often respond by emphasizing greater teacher control and discipline. An alternative approach recommended by Eccles, Wigfield, and Schiefele (1998) is that schools include more opportunities for students to have input into the norms governing classroom practices. More specifically, the research would suggest that the focus of such student input and discourse should be around matters of social convention and personal prerogative. Other work exploring the impact of developmental discourse around issues of convention has demonstrated that such discussion can effectively contribute to students' levels of understanding about the social functions of such norms (Nucci et al. 2015).

While the majority of adolescent misconduct concerns issues of convention, some of the efforts to establish autonomy and identity entail risk-taking and moral transgressions. For example, shoplifting tends to peak between the ages of twelve and fourteen years (Nucci 2001). This corresponds to the transitional period in early adolescent moral reasoning uncovered in our research (Nucci and Turiel 2007). The Swiss developmentalists Fritz Oser and Roland Reichenbach (2005) have argued that educators should view such moral misconduct as an essential component for moral growth and seize upon moral transgressions as an opportunity for what they refer to as "realistic discourse." Oser and Reichenbach's position is that "negative morality," just as in mistakes in math class, represents the basis from which a genuine moral epistemology and moral orientation arise. This approach to moral misconduct in adolescence is to make it the subject of moral discourse in which students must confront one another's actual misdeeds, interpretations of their motives, and the consequences of their actions.

Employing the Academic Curriculum
to Develop Moral Reasoners

Up to this point we have discussed the elements of school culture and educational practices that contribute to students' development of an appreciation for the function of society's conventions, and the basic social and emotional tools for interacting with others with a sense of fairness and compassion. However, attaining the larger educational goals of building the capacity for lifelong moral growth, and enabling students to contribute to the morality of society, requires going beyond these basics. The key element for empowering students to engage the world as moral agents is to develop their capacities for critical moral reflection and moral reasoning. Within American public schools there is no separate curricular space for moral education. Thus, the approach that we take is to embed moral education within the teaching of regular academic subjects (Nucci 2009). Schools are specialized institutions designed to bring students beyond their own direct encounters with the world, and the regular academic curriculum is rife with issues of morality. Within the context of language arts and history, students encounter a broad range of events, personal struggles, social customs, and cultural patterns that allow them to engage their notions of fairness, social justice, and norms of behavior against a backdrop of human experience. Moreover, there is mounting evidence from our own work and that of others that attention to social and moral development may also enhance academic engagement and performance (Berkowitz, Battistich, and Bier 2008). In our most recent project, the participating urban middle school history teachers and their district coordinators were sufficiently pleased with the impact of the integration of moral education on student learning of world and American history that we have been asked to extend this approach to the entire district (Nucci et al. 2015).

There are five keys to employing the curriculum to stimulate students' moral development:

1. Domain concordance—the topics or issues that are the focus of lessons are matched with the domain of the focus of the discussion.
2. Developmental appropriateness—the topics and structure of discussion are matched with the students' levels of development.
3. Transactive discourse—the discussions engage students in producing transactive statements.

4. Engaged deliberation—the discussion entails respectful attempts to incorporate the views expressed to arrive at a shared position.
5. Academic relevance—the discussion should contribute to the academic goals of the lesson and include an academic product. This last key is self-evident and won't be discussed further.

Domain Concordance and Developmental Appropriateness

The principle of domain concordance means that the topics selected for a moral discussion would involve issues of fairness, human welfare, and rights, and the discussion would be on those issues rather than on social rules or the social order. A moral discussion around slavery, for example, would center on the basic issues of fairness and human welfare and not around the social organizational functions of the norms that established slavery as an accepted social practice. Conversely, a lesson exploring West African family roles would be an excellent context for a discussion of societal conventions and their function in organizing social institutions such as the family. A study examining whether attention to domain mattered for socio-moral development found that domain-concordant discourse raised students' developmental levels in both the moral and conventional domains, while domain-discordant discourse (treating issues of morality as matters of convention and vice versa) had no impact on students' development (Nucci and Weber 1993). This study also reported that domain-concordant teaching increased the tendencies of students to spontaneously coordinate moral and conventional elements when discussing or writing about multifaceted issues such as customary practices that provide different opportunities for men and women.

In addition to domain concordance, the selection of topics and the structure of lessons also need to match the conceptual level of the students within domains. This seemingly self-evident principle is often overlooked in both traditional approaches to moral socialization and well-intentioned efforts to engage children in so-called social justice curricula. Students often fail to grasp the intended moral messages in readings intended to present them with moral exemplars precisely because their own understandings of morality are often so far apart from the presumed theme of the text (Narvaez 2002). Similarly, attempts to enlist early elementary school children in moral outrage toward structural social injustice may make the adults feel good but are largely a waste of time given that the majority of students prior to middle school have no conception of societies as systems.

Finally, although there are productive ways to use the academic curriculum to engage younger students in moral discussion based upon the academic curriculum, it would seem to be unproductive to do so with students prior to third grade who are still mastering basic literacy, and unnecessary given the great amount of basic moral and social knowledge to be gained from their direct social experience.

Transactive Discourse

If there is a "magic bullet" for stimulating conceptual development, it is the engagement of students in transactive forms of discussion (Berkowitz and Gibbs 1983; Sionti, Ai, Rosé, and Resnick 2011). Transactive discourse is a conversation in which the statements offered by participants build upon the logical arguments already expressed. A discussion is considered transactive if the argument or perspective being tossed back and forth between speakers morphs over the course of the discussion. There are two broad categories of transacts:

> *Representational statements* are lower-order transacts that reiterate the information that is already on the table, or request more information. Examples of representational transacts are requesting information, requesting clarification, paraphrasing a statement, asking for justification, and making a concession to the opposite viewpoint while reaffirming one's own position.
> *Operational transacts* are higher-order transacts that entail acting upon or transforming the information included in prior statements. Examples of operational transacts are identifying a contradiction in the another person's position, refining one's position, extending the logic of one's position, and offering an integration of one's position and the position maintained by others in the discourse.

Research examining the impact of transactive discourse on moral development has indicated that the ratio of operational to representational transacts within a dialogue is associated with conceptual development. In our own work we have found positive associations between these ratios of operational to representational transacts in the development of understandings of convention and moral reasoning, as well as the spontaneous tendencies of middle school students to coordinate moral and conventional elements of complex social issues (Nucci et al. 2015). Our work indicates that students from fifth grade and above are capable of engaging meaningfully in these kinds of discussions.

Engaged Deliberation

The final critical element for productive moral discourse is that it be centered around what the political philosopher Anthony Laden (2012) refers to as "engaged deliberation." It is this crucial element that integrates the "basics" of moral education described above with the furtherance of education toward mature moral development and civic engagement. During an engaged deliberation the discussants enter the discourse with differing, perhaps even competing, positions. In contrast with an attempt to dominate the discussion or to "win" as in a debate, the goal of engaged deliberation is to leave the discourse with a shared position that reflects the rationally agreed-upon perspectives of all members of the discourse. This process of deliberation is one form of what Laden refers to as *reasoning*. Laden contrasts this view of reasoning with what he refers to as the "standard picture." In the standard picture reasoning takes place inside the head of an individual and follows the rules of logic. This standard picture of reasoning has been at the center of most developmental approaches to moral education, with "logic" replaced by structures of moral judgment (Nucci, Narvaez, and Krettenauer 2014). Laden argues that while this standard picture captures the structure of thought—a component of reasoning—it misses the essentially social nature of what it is that we do when we engage in reasoning. Reasoning entails participating in discourse with another person with the purpose of establishing shared meanings and jointly accepted positions. It is through "reasoning" in this social sense that we collectively evaluate and restructure our social and moral positions and their underlying justifications. Thus, reasoning requires a level of trust and mutual respect that is in line with the formal discourse ethics offered by Habermas (1990), and in interesting ways is reminiscent of Piaget's (1965 [1932]) account of mature morality based upon reciprocity and mutual respect.

In the context of reasoning all assumptions are on the table, and all arguments are open to critique and modification. In the context of a moral discourse, appeals to authority, religious or otherwise, are subject to scrutiny for their factual accuracy and coherence with moral criteria. All participants in the discourse are accorded respect and their positions taken seriously. Reasoning as a social activity thus requires a level of trust and community that conjoins the integration of reasoning as an educational practice with the "basics" of moral education described above. Incorporating reasoning as an educational practice in this social sense also shifts the goals of developmentally based moral education from a sole focus upon stimulating the development of students' conceptual structures of understanding of social convention and morality, what Saxe (2014) refers to as the ontogenetic line of development, to include students' capacity to participate as members of democratic civil society and in the moral growth of the culture, what Saxe refers to as the socio-genetic line of development.

EDUCATION FOR PURPOSE

The process of moral development and moral education as we have described it entails shifts in the student's understandings of the social world, and orientations toward morality. These are not simply superficial adjustments in a moral calculus. As students develop emotionally and morally, they are changing components of themselves as moral beings. In the process of constructing social and emotional skills, capacities for moral reasoning, and their relationship to the socio-moral world, students construct a fundamental part of who they are (Lapsley and Narvaez 2004; Nucci 2004). One of the tasks of adolescence and young adulthood is to position the self with respect to that social world. The final consideration for moral education is to appeal to this search by youth to help them define themselves in ways that will direct their efforts toward goals that are concordant with moral development. William Damon (2009) has recently referred to this process in youth as a search for "purpose."

In pursuing a purpose, children have an opportunity to refine their moral ideas. However, it is not the actual content of a purpose that matters, nor is it the achievement of having one that is important. Rather, it is the presence of a supportive and motivating context in the lives of adolescents—one that helps them search for a purpose—that facilitates their moral development. The context for constructing this sense of purpose can be secular as the student pursues career goals in medicine or the arts through school and community service. For others, that context is the church or the mosque. A religious context can foster the development of a purpose greater than oneself, and provide structure in one's life that leads to an effort at self-improvement consistent with moral development. In the nascent days of the United States, John Adams said, "There are only two creatures of value on the face of the earth: those with the commitment, and those who require the commitment of others" (Kashatus 1990, 113). Unlike Adams, it is not our intention to divide the world into people with purpose and those without, as it is not our claim that one needs to have some ultimate purpose in life to be moral. Purpose is a tool that children and adolescents can use to help them make decisions throughout their lives (Damon 2009). In this respect religion can play a positive role in moral development by giving young people purpose and teaching them to make commitments, as long as it is also coupled with humility and an understanding that morality is an ongoing process of reflection and updating grounded in the underlying moral principles of justice and welfare.

Conclusion

Moral education is often misunderstood as a process of socialization combined with fostering particular virtues or character strengths. From that perspective moral education is sometimes conflated with the adoption of particular religious values and commitment to a particular religion. We have argued that existing evidence supports a developmental approach to moral education in which foundational capacities of social and emotional development, linked with stimulation of fundamental moral cognition around issues of fairness and human welfare, form the basics of educational practices that are concordant with secular and religious morality. We have also argued that although these basics are sufficient for the education of fundamentally good "nice" people, they do not provide a sufficient educational approach for the stimulation of mature morality. Nor do these basics contribute to the capacities of individuals to participate in moral discourse that would lead to mature morality and the capacity to contribute toward the moral "updating" of society and its conventions. Moral education contributes to the development of these mature moral capabilities by engaging students in active processes of "reasoning" (Laden 2012) around complex issues entailing overlaps among morality, societal and religious convention, and empirical beliefs (Nucci and Turiel

2007). Engaging students in such processes of reasoning from a critical moral perspective poses a distinct challenge to educators. As John Dewey once put it, "Anyone who has begun to think places some part of the world in jeopardy." Throughout history and continuing through the present, people have died challenging institutional orthodoxy in order to update society and its institutions to make them commensurate with morality. From our perspective, it is precisely this sort of commitment to moral growth that is at the heart of moral education.

FUTURE DIRECTIONS

1. How do we prepare future teachers to engage in moral education that makes use of the research from developmental psychology?
2. How do we efficiently assess moral and social growth based upon recent findings from developmental research?
3. How do we make use of emerging technologies to assess responsive engagement and transactive classroom moral discourse in real time?
4. How can we address moral education among students whose families and communities hold values that are antithetical to social change?

REFERENCES

Arsenio, W., and A. Lover. 1995. "Children's Conceptions of Sociomoral Affect: Happy Victimizers, Mixed Emotions, and Other Expectancies." In *Cambridge Studies in Social and Emotional Development. Morality in Everyday Life: Developmental Perspectives*, edited by M. Killen and D. Hart, 87–128. New York: Cambridge University Press.

Arthur, J. 2013. *Citizens of Character: New Directions in Character and Values Education.* Luton: Andrews UK Limited.

Battistich, V. A. 2008. "The Child Development Project: Creating Caring School Communities." In *Handbook of Moral and Character Education*, edited by L. Nucci and D. Narvaez, 328–351. Mahwah, NJ: Erlbaum.

Berkowitz, M. W., V. A. Battistich, and M. C. Bier. 2008. "What Works in Character Education: What Is Known and What Needs to Be Known." In *Handbook of Moral and Character Education*, edited by L. Nucci and D. Narvaez, 1st ed., 414–430. New York: Routledge.

Berkowitz, M. W., and J. C. Gibbs. 1983. "Measuring the Developmental Features of Moral Discussion." *Merrill-Palmer Quarterly* 29, no. 4: 399–410.

Blair, R. J. R. 2003. "Neurobiological Basis of Psychopathy." *British Journal of Psychiatry* 182: 5–7.
———. 2005. "Responding to the Emotions of Others: Dissociating Forms of Empathy Through the Study of Typical and Psychiatric Populations." *Consciousness and Cognition* 14: 698–718.

Damon, W. 2009. *The Path to Purpose: How Young People Find Their Calling in Life.* New York: Simon and Schuster.

Eccles, J. S., A. Wigfield, and U. Schiefele. 1998. "Motivation to Succeed." In *Handbook of Child Psychology*, 5th ed., Vol. 3: N. Eisenberg (Ed.), *Social, Emotional, and Personality Development* W. Damon (Ed.) 1017–1095. New York: Wiley.

Elias, M., A. Kranzler, S. Parker, V. M. Kash, and R. Weissberg. 2014. "The Complementary Perspectives of Social and Emotional Learning, Moral Education, and Character Education." In *Handbook of Moral and Character Education*, edited by L. Nucci, D. Narvaez, and T. Krettenauer, 2nd ed., 271–289. New York: Routledge.

Fogel, R. W. 2002. *The Fourth Great Awakening and the Future of Egalitarianism.* Chicago: University of Chicago Press.

Habermas, J. 1990. *Discourse Ethics: Notes on a Program of Philosophical Justification.* Cambridge, UK: Polity Press.

Haidt, J. 2007. "The New Synthesis in Moral Psychology." *Science* 316, no. 5827: 998–1002.

———. 2012. *The Righteous Mind: Why Good People Are Divided by Politics and Religion.* New York: Vintage.

Hamlin, J. K. 2013. "Moral Judgment and Action in Preverbal Infants and Toddlers: Evidence for an Innate Moral Core." *Current Directions in Psychological Science* 22, no. 3: 186–193.

Haynes, C., and Oliver Thomas. 2007. *Finding Common Ground: A Guide to Religious Liberty in Public Schools.* Nashville, TN: First Amendment Center.

Jensen, L. A., ed. 2011. *Bridging Cultural and Developmental Approaches to Psychology: New Syntheses in Theory, Research, and Policy.* New York: Oxford University Press.

Kashatus, W. C. 1990. "Forging a Link with Our Past: The Responsibility of Teaching American History." *History Teacher* 24, 113–119.

Killen, M., S. Breton, H. Ferguson, and K. Handler. 1994. "Preschoolers' Evaluations of Teacher Methods of Intervention in Social Transgressions." *Merrill-Palmer Quarterly* 40, 399–415.

Kohlberg, L. 1971. "From Is to Ought: How to Commit the Naturalistic Fallacy and Get Away with It in the Study of Moral Development. In *Cognitive Development and Psychology*, edited by T. Mischel, 151–235. New York: Academic Press.

Kohlberg, L. 1984. *The Psychology of Moral Development: The Nature and Validity of Moral Stages.* New York: Harper & Row.

Kuyel, N., and Cesur, S. May 2013. *The Connection Between Religious Rules and the Moral Judgments of the Less Religious and More Religious Turkish Muslims.* Paper presented at the meeting of the Jean Piaget Society, Chicago.

Laden, A. 2012. *Reasoning: A Social Picture.* New York: Oxford University Press.

Lapsley, D., and D. Narvaez, eds. 2004. *Moral Development, Self, and Identity.* Mahwah, NJ: Lawrence Erlbaum Associates.

Leslie, A. M., R. Mallon, and J. A. DiCorcia. 2006. "Transgressors, Victims, and Crybabies: Is Basic Moral Judgment Spared in Autism." *Social Neuroscience* 1, no. 3-4: 270–283.

Midgette, A., J. Y. Noh, I. J. Lee, and L. Nucci. 2016. "The Development of Korean Children's and Adolescents' Concepts of Social Convention." *Journal of Cross Cultural Psychology* 47: 903–917.

Miller, J. G., and C. Bland. 2014. "A Cultural Psychology Perspective on Moral Development." In *Handbook of Moral Development*, edited by M. Killen and J. Smetana, 2nd ed, 299–314. New York: Psychology Press.

Narvaez, D. 2002. "Does Reading Moral Stories Build Moral Character?" *Educational Psychology Review* 14: 155–171.

Noddings, N. 2002. *Educating Moral People: A Caring Alternative to Character Education.* Williston, VT: Teachers College Press.

Nucci, L. P. 1985. "Children's Conceptions of Morality, Societal Convention, and Religious Prescription." In *Moral Dilemmas: Philosophical and Psychological Issues in the Development of Moral Reasoning*, edited by Carol Gibb Harding, 137–174. Chicago, IL: Precedent Publishing, Inc.

———. 2001. *Education in the Moral Domain*. Cambridge, UK: Cambridge University Press.

———. 2004. "The Promise and Limitations of the Moral Self-Construct." In *Changing Conceptions of Self and Mind*, edited by M. Chandler, C. Lightfoot, and C. Lalonde, 49–72. Mahwah, NJ: Erlbaum.

———. 2009. *Nice Is Not Enough: Facilitating Moral Development*. Upper Saddle River, NJ: Merrill/Prentice Hall.

———. 2014. "The Personal and the Moral." In *Handbook of Moral Development*, edited by M. Killen and J. Smetana, 2nd ed., 538–558. New York: Psychology Press.

Nucci, L., M. Creane, and D. W. Powers. 2015. "Integrating Moral and Social Development Within Middle School Social Studies: A Social Cognitive Domain Approach." *Journal of Moral Education* 44, 479–496.

Nucci, L. P., D. Narvaez, and T. Krettenauer. (Eds.). 2014. *Handbook of Moral and Character Education*, 2nd ed. New York: Routledge.

Nucci, L. and Powers, D. W. 2014. "Social cognitive domain theory and moral education." In *Handbook on moral and character education*, edited by L. Nucci, D. Narvaez, and T. Krettenauer, 2nd ed., 121–139. Oxford, UK: Routledge.

Nucci, L., and E. Turiel. 1993. "God's Word, Religious Rules, and Their Relation to Christian and Jewish Children's Concepts of Morality." *Child Development* 64, no. 5: 1475–1491.

Nucci, L., and E. Turiel. 2007. *Development in the Moral Domain: The Role of Conflict and Relationships in Children's and Adolescents' Welfare and Harm Judgments*. Paper presented as part of the symposium "Moral Development Within Domain and Within Context" at the biennial meeting of the Society for Research in Child Development, Boston, MA.

Nucci, L., and E. K. Weber. 1993. Research on classroom applications of the domain approach to values education. In *Handbook of Moral Behavior and Development*, Vol. 3: W. Kurtines and J. Gewirtz (Eds.), 251–265. New York: Lawrence Erlbaum & Associates.

Oser, F. K., and R. Reichenbach. 2005. "Moral Resilience—The Unhappy Moralist." *Advances in Psychology* 137: 203–224.

Piaget, J. 1965 (1932). *The Moral Judgment of the Child*. New York: Free Press.

Pizarro, D. A., and P. Bloom. 2003. The intelligence of the moral intuitions: A comment on Haidt (2001). *Psychological Review*, 110, 193–196.

Roeser, R. W., D. R. Vago, C. Pinela, L. S. Morris, C. Taylor, and J. Harrison. 2014. "Contemplative Education." In *Handbook of Moral and Character Education*, L. Nucci, D. Narvaez, and T. Krettenauer (Eds.), 223–247. New York: Routledge

Saxe, G. B. 2014. *Culture and Cognitive Development: Studies in Mathematical Understanding*. Mahwah, NJ: Lawrence Erlbaum Associates, Inc.

Searle, J. R. 1969. *Speech Acts: An Essay in the Philosophy of Language*. Cambridge, UK: Cambridge University Press.

Shweder, R. A. 1990. "In Defense of Moral Realism: Reply to Gabennesch." *Child Development* 61, no. 6: 2060–2067.

———. 2011. "Commentary: Ontogenetic Cultural Psychology." In *Bridging cultural and developmental approaches to psychology: New synthesis in theory, research and policy*, L. Jensen (Ed.), 303–310. New York, NY: Oxford University Press.

Sionti, M., H. Ai, C. P. Rosé, and L. Resnick. 2011. "A Framework for Analyzing Development of Argumentation Through Classroom Discussions." In Niels Pinkwart and Bruce M. McLaren, eds., *Educational Technologies for Teaching Argumentation Skills*, 28–55. Berlin, Germany: Bentham eBooks Ebsco Information Services.

Smetana, J. G. 2011. "Adolescents' Social Reasoning and Relationships with Parents: Conflicts and Coordinations Within and Across Domains." In *Adolescent Vulnerabilities and Opportunities: Constructivist and Developmental Perspectives,* E. Amsel and J. G. Smetana (Eds.). 139–158. Cambridge, UK: Cambridge University Press.

Smetana, J., M. Jambon, and C. Ball. 2014. "The Social Domain Approach to Children's Moral and Social Judgments." In *Handbook of Moral Development*, edited by M. Killen and J. Smetana, 2nd ed., 23–45. New York: Psychology Press.

Turiel, E. 1983. *The Development of Social Knowledge: Morality and Convention.* Cambridge, UK: Cambridge University Press.

———. 2002. *The Culture of Morality: Social Development, Context, and Conflict.* Cambridge, UK: Cambridge University Press.

Watson, M., and L. Ecken. 2003. *Learning to Trust: Transforming Difficult Elementary Classrooms Through Developmental Discipline.* Indianapolis, IN: Jossey-Bass.

Wikan, U. 2002. *Generous Betrayal: Politics of Culture in the New Europe.* Chicago: University of Chicago Press.

CHAPTER 9

RELIGIOUS EDUCATION IN
THE TRADITIONS

MARK A. HICKS

INTRODUCTION

RELIGIOUS education teaches people how to practice a religious way of life and informs their beliefs, behaviors, and acts of belonging (See Marcus, Chapter 4 in this volume and Saroglou 2011). Religious education is an act of learning by which children, youth, and adults are moved toward living the ultimate values of a community of faith. While the nature of that journey varies widely depending on the aims of a particular religious group, religious education is primarily rooted in the hope that the learner can transcend a particular human socialization in order to achieve an aim that is important to their religious tradition.

As an academic discipline, the *process* of education, what some refer to as "schooling," focuses on pedagogy—that is, technique, procedures, and skills that lead to a specific learning outcome. In that way, religious and secular education share similar characteristics in that both compel the learner to think and act in ways that show intellectual literacy with ideas. Likewise, every religion believes its historical evolution signals an important insight into the human condition that must be shared across generations. Thus, religious education, like secular education, is often shaped by the utilitarian impulse to inspire its followers to take the aspirations, commitments, and visions of their historical community into future living.

Still, there are important differences between religious and secular education. We know that every act of teaching carries a moral dimension nested in a particular worldview (Sizer and Sizer 2000). Yet, mastery of content alone is insufficient for the project of living a flourishing, values-based life. A *religious* education implies the ability to move beyond first-order facility of the matter so as to discern deeper meaning and value. Thus, to teach religiously is to orient learning programs toward exploring the moral, spiritual, and social dimensions of human experience, using the aims of imaginative inquiry to discover and open doors that fuel a sense of possibility into human life (Harris 1991).

This dance of explorative meaning-making is not culturally bound and cuts across religious traditions.

History of American Religious Education

The roots of American religious education are remarkably parallel to the evolution of American schooling. The ancient traditions of Protestant, Catholic, Jewish, and Muslim religions, for example, concerned themselves with transmitting their great stories of wisdom from one generation to the next. As each of these religious groups landed on the shores of North America, a new sense of urgency shaped their thinking and practice about the relevance and role of religious instruction in the lives of the faithful. According to Blumenfeld (2012), education in the early days of New England had to be religion-based; everyone had to be able to read the Bible. Nelson (2006) writes that in 1790, Benjamin Rush founded a nonsectarian First Day School, or Sunday School. The schools were not religious, per se, but used religious books as their primary texts. She writes, "The First Day School was an enormous success and was followed by the establishment of several others like it, designed to promote literacy and public virtue through education. The schools were soon duplicated in New York, Rhode Island, Massachusetts, New Hampshire, Maine and Delaware" (Nelson 2006, 6–7). The format was widely praised as a model for religious instruction aimed at literacy, upright living, and citizenship, thus providing future generations with a cultural and religious foundation that would preserve and advance Christian civilization.

Education, however, was not simply an exercise in cultural and religious literacy as its lessons were a vehicle for indoctrinating cultural—*moral*—values into the citizenry. Haidt (2015) argues that a core set of tensions have always framed the moral (i.e., visions of "the good") discourse in American life (see Chapter 8 in this volume). They include care/harm, fairness/cheating, loyalty/betrayal, authority/subversion, sanctity/degradation, and liberty/oppression. Haidt's paradoxical framing provides useful insight into the decisions and strategies chosen by educational practitioners over time. First, it signifies how societal aims and questions about the moral good are historically linked with curriculum choices. Religious and secular educators, as well as state and federal government, have a long, compelling interest in supporting democratic ideals, preserving American culture, addressing social problems, and bringing new generations of learning into American cultural and economic systems (Oaks and Lipton 2003). Second, it signals the paradoxical nature of discerning human experience (Jarvis 2012). The educator—especially the religious educator—is called to sit in the intersection of such paradox with an eye toward creating educational experiences that spark the leaner's curiosity (Dewey 1997a, 1997b). This learning also includes considerations about moral and ethical aims that run counter to cultural meta-narratives.

For example, the Native American's experience of "religious education" is wrapped in the legacy of colonialization by European settlers. Weaver (1997) argues that when Americans thought about Native people, it was from the perspective of "subjects of missionalization rather than as living beings" (432). Boyer (1994) argues that the Western tradition of Enlightenment is a complete anathema to Native People, as they do not conceive of themselves as being isolated from nature or their experience of their lives. For this reason, Western approaches to religious education for Native people failed miserably (Forbes 1993).

This failure, in part, was a result of popular teaching practices of the era. Prior to 1830, catechisms—memorizing and reciting specific answers to Bible questions—was the pedagogy of choice. This "systematic statement of doctrine" (Marthaler 1990, 101) was popular across traditions. In tenth-century Islam, the *kuttab* (a place of writing) and later the *madrasa* (a place of study) included studies such as "memorization and recitation of the Qur'an, reading, writing, spelling, voweling letters, arithmetic, and some basic religious duties like the rules of ablutions and prayer" (Kadid 2007a, 7). While such practices worked in Muslim education, the rigidity of canonical instruction came under criticism in the Western world. Boys (2001) argues this seminal shift was articulated in 1870 in Channing's *Discourse Pronounced Before the Sunday School*. Channing, the Unitarian theologian stated, "the great end in religious instruction, whether in the Sunday school or the family, is, not to stamp *our* minds irresistibly on the young, but to stir up their own, not to make them see with our eyes, but to look inquiringly and steadily with their own." The impulse to respond to the demands of secular life through a religious lens is a symbolic tension that remains tight. Religious educators—both historically and at present—have been called to grapple with how to impart the important thoughts and values of a tradition in ways that affirm religiosity while operating in a larger sociocultural context.

We see this tension in the homeschooling movement, whose roots reach back to seventeenth-century America (Gaither 2008). Learning in the home—ranging from housekeeping to literacy and vocational instruction—was viewed as a natural and appropriate location for teaching values and morally sanctioned behavior. When Colonial legislatures noticed children were not getting adequate instruction in the home, laws were created to alter such practice. For example, the infamous "Old Deluder Satan" bill of 1647 (see Chapter 11 in this volume) "required towns in Massachusetts with fifty or more students to have a school [but] the evidence suggests that most people did not comply" (Massachusetts Bay Company and Gaither 1853, 19). Gaither notes that most towns and families opted to pay fines rather than start schools because families feared losing control over family life if they enrolled their children in what we would now call public school. By the 1970s, approximately 15,000 families were enrolled in homeschooling, most of which were conservative Protestants. The US Department of Education (2016) registered 1.8 million homeschooled children in 2012, representing 3.4% of the total student population in the United States.

Despite the diversity of competing cultural, pedagogical, and political values, the origins of the religious education discipline, across the board, are marked by the challenges and rewards of creating vibrant and relevant programs of religious learning while reconciling those lessons in an ever-changing world.

Transformation of Legal and Social Norms

Secular education, writ large, always had an uneasy relationship with religious education. This suspicion morphed into resistance when practices associated with religiosity manifested as a universal good for all students, regardless of the child and family's religious tradition. Those who believed these offenses were an outright violation of separation between church and state pushed their objections through the American legal system. Over decades, these challenges—adjudicated through school boards and state legislatures—ultimately resulted in landmark court cases decided by the US Supreme Court (see Chapters 13 and 15 in this volume). These cases removed the assumption of sameness in the practice of how religious thinking and teaching can be implemented in a pluralistic society. Ripples from these decisions are still strongly felt today and are flashpoints across the religious and political landscape. Some of the most salient cases are as follows:

West Virginia State Board of Education v. Barnette (1943), which declared no child could be compelled to pledge allegiance to the flag;

Everson v. Board of Education (1947), which permitted public funds to reimburse parents for transportation, regardless of whether they enrolled their children in private or public schools; and

Abington v. Schempp (1963), which rejected state statutes that required students enrolled in public schools to participate in religious exercises.

The Supreme Court decisions of the 1960s and 1970s signaled simultaneously a threat to *and* a celebration of religious freedom. Critics blasted the decisions as the moment when "the courts kicked God out of school" (Ahlstrom 1972, 17) while others appreciated the freedom not to have children coerced with state-mandated devotional activities. Thematically, however, these decisions aligned with sweeping shifts in social and demographic realities that fundamentally challenged the assumption of a singular American culture. Some of these major shifts included the following:

1. Challenges to time-honored theological constructs;
2. The social, political, and intellectual liberation of people of color, women, and sexual minorities;
3. Substantial growth in immigration and the swelling influence of those communities on American culture;
4. Generational shifts in ways of knowing and acting; and
5. The ontological and behavioral revolution brought about by technology.

SEISMIC SHIFT IN THEOLOGY AND RELIGIOUS EDUCATION

Prothero's *God Is Not One* (2011) is one among many voices that dismantle the notion of a monocultural God, arguing that "differences in doctrine, ritual, mythology, experience and law" (p. 2) point us toward very real distinctions and understandings of who God is and how God operates. Theological commitments are the foundation upon which religious educators build pedagogy. Thus, religious practices and theological assumptions are linked in a circular fashion. Little (1995) posits that theology is a way to "mount the 'watchtower' [as a way to observe] faith and life in all directions, in order to detect the presence of blindness, unbelief, unfaithfulness, and sin, and give warning before it is too late" (p. 15). Watching from the tower thus allows the educator to notice what is happening on the ground, turning observations into data points for shaping practice.

Most keen observers concur that the countercultural shifts that began in the 1950s marked a disruption of long-held theological worldviews, namely, for this discussion, multiculturalism (Steffer 1990) and postmodernism (Magnus 1996). As a pair, they exploded notions of orthodoxy, assumptions about cultural certainty, and a monocultural view of how life is experienced (Wilkerson 1997). While some theologians and religious educators trivialized these shifts as a threat to social and theological order, others embraced these new perspectives as an opportunity to discern how cultural and theological differences shape a journey of faith (Horell 2003).

SEISMIC SHIFT FROM VOICES AT THE SOCIAL MARGIN

Similar to underrepresented religious voices who believed the dominant culture created systems that curtailed human choice, racial and ethnic minorities, women, the poor, working-class people, and sexual minorities moved to claim their intellectual and social identities as being as equal and relevant as those in the dominant culture (Jenkins and Kratt 1997).

From a curricular point of view, religious educators found it necessary to explore the theological framework of multiculturalism. Karl Rahner, a Catholic theologian, noted "we may not understand . . . 'people of God' as one homogeneous mass, whose 'sense of faith' takes place in some ideal place. Instead the people of God is a collection of many *peoples*, each with different experiences, histories, and cultures" (in Beaudoin 2003, 64). Such compelling arguments affirmed those who believed that marginalized intellectual and cultural voices also needed space to name their particular experience on life's journey (Wilkerson 1997). The emergence of formerly silenced ethnic groups demanded a rethinking of values and norms, especially within religious traditions thought to be culturally monocultural. No longer could the educator assume, for example, that all Baptists were alike; one had to take into account the nuances of a Korean Baptist, who had a different standpoint from a black Baptist or a Spanish-speaking Baptist (Emerson 2008). On face value, these intellectual and social shifts required being attentive to how a broader range of life experiences shape religious teaching and learning.

SEISMIC SHIFTS IN IMMIGRATION

Likewise, immigration patterns further diversified the patterns of religious education. The Pew Research Center (2015) reported that the nation's foreign-born population swelled from 10 million in 1965 to a record 45 million in 2015. By 2065, the United States will have a projected 78 million immigrants. People of color (including Latino/a people) make up a significant percentage of that group. At the same time, traditional standard-bearers—Catholics, evangelical and historically black Protestants, Jews, Mormons, and Orthodox Christians—show a marked decline within the age group of "under 29," suggesting that the traditional worldviews of the existing religious majority no longer hold a central position of cultural and religious dominance. Thus, religious education today, more than ever before, not only consider its place as a transmitter of moral and cultural values, but do so in a way that reflects a globalized worldview. This shift forecasts that educational programs cannot be practiced as if the world were an ivory tower, but must reflect the real lives and cultural orientation of a living people.

Such recognition is especially important for religious traditions whose membership is open to those who share strong geographic, familial, or cultural ties. Jewish day schools, for example, are charged with "preventing attrition from Jewish communities, ensuring Jewish continuity and strengthening Jewish identity" (Cohen and Kelner 2007, 80–100). There is alarm within the liberal Jewish community that children and youth are Jewishly illiterate and alienated from Jewish culture (Bekerman and Rosenfeld 2011). Similar concerns are voiced within Muslim communities (Kadi 2007a, 2007b). Scholars argue that practitioners must be attentive to the fluid complexity of geopolitical, cultural, and individual identity dispositions in order to speak coherently to educational programs within such groups (Charme and Zelkowicz 2011).

SEISMIC SHIFT IN TECHNOLOGY AND RELIGIOUS INSTRUCTION

The emergence of technology into virtually every aspect of American life provides yet another example of how matters of social transformation impact the work of the religious educator. By every possible measure, the modernization of our world via technology has resulted in an unprecedented shift in how humans interact. Amkraut (2011) posits that a person "can connect interactively with unlimited points of access in the virtual universe, constantly defining and redefining the terms of his or her association with other individuals and institutions to suit his or her unique needs" (p. 597). In the ground-breaking report *Thirteen Trends and Forces Affecting the Future of Faith Formation in a Changing Church and World*, Roberto (2009) discusses how American children, youth, and adults are using the power of the internet to source and answer their questions, as well as to form relationships that previously could only be accomplished within brick-and-mortal religious settings. Indeed, the internet has created a "public religious education" that, like the ebb and flow of a river, guides itself where it needs to go. Entrepreneurial religious educators respond by experimenting with new forms of learning, using the power of the internet to forge connections for children, youth, and families. Daily (2013), for example, speaks of innovations that "push" (i.e., insert) religious learning and experiences directly into the flow of family life through electronic devices like smartphones. Such ideas carry pedagogical capitol among practitioners. Instead of devoting hours staffing religious education classrooms with volunteer teachers, educators use technology to transform ordinary experiences of life into sacred moments of reflection (e.g., soccer games, meals, the death of a family pet) (Bellavance-Grace 2013). Instead of a day of rest and churchgoing, Sunday has become monopolized by children's sporting events, family outings, playdates, or part-time jobs for older youth. Parents, too, find that Sundays represent a rare day off with the potential to relax and enjoy family life, which might include not attending church at all. Some educators who find denominational teaching materials outdated or inappropriate for their audiences use technology to fashion themselves as "educational curators," working in the tradition of museum curators who search through available content for the best and most relevant materials for their particular context (Oddone 2015). Other educators are using technology to provide access to religious seekers who cannot participate traditionally in religious communities because of geographical isolation, psychological introversion, physical impairment that prohibits mobility, long-term illness, or, perhaps, a narrowly focused identity affiliation that is best served in more private settings (e.g., suicide support groups, transgender youth, people with body image issues, or victims of physical abuse) (Riley 2015). And, finally, the internet makes the publishing of ideas no longer reliant on national, centralized headquarters, making learning materials more accessible and less expensive to produce.

Educational researchers have certainly noticed the marked increase of technology in religious life and, like secular educators, worry about the long-term impact of such practices, especially in a context where meaning-making and building relationships are primary learning goals. New, emerging fields of study, such as "social scholarship," seek to understand how new social media practices shape student learning (Greenhow and Gleason 2014). Daily (2013) explores how mobile technology can respond to the age-old challenge of providing religious instruction (i.e., information about religion) to the general public in the tradition of public education. Hammer and Kellner (2000) document how to use multimedia as a strategy for bringing the experiences of marginal and oppressed people to the mainstream in compelling ways. Innovative educators frequently apply "open source" technologies that encourage practitioners to be as pedagogically creative as their minds allow. Examples such as video conferencing, PowerPoint, digital cameras, and social media (e.g., Facebook, Instagram) build learning communities where, in synchronous fashion, all participants are present at the same time at a location of their choice. Such strategies speak to the realities of busy lives and, at the same time, show the potential to create meaningful dialogue among participants.

And, yet, there are concerns. As a relatively new tool for religious learning, religious educators encounter young students as "digital natives," so many learners are more technologically savvy than their teachers. Likewise, there is a tendency to view technology as a clash of dualisms—the true believer who sees technology as improving teaching and learning versus the cynic who doubts its value (Hook 2005). Mercer and Simpson (2015, 5) warn that "education is lost and becomes only a cacophony of misunderstood shibboleths" when learning is disconnect from meaning-making. Thus, religious educators are called to engage with new strategies of learning while staying committed to the core task of meaning-making.

Seismic Shift: Demographics and Generational Ways of Knowing

Religious observer Phyllis Tickle (2012) argues that we are currently in an era she calls the "Great Emergence," noting that every five hundred years or so the institutionalized church undergoes a radical transformation that remakes the religion. The popular press regularly chronicles sweeping changes in family, social, and institutional life, all of which forces the church, writ large, to re-evaluate its learning programs on a regular basis. Empirical studies about the state of the brick-and-mortar congregational meeting house bear out these ideas (Alshire and Graham 2015; Pew 2015). Pandika (2015) cites data from the Barma Research Group that Sunday School programs were dropped by "tens of thousands" of congregations between 1997 and 2004. From 2004 to 2010, Sunday School attendance dropped nearly 40% among evangelical Lutheran churches in America and almost 8% among Southern Baptist churches.

These changes are accompanied by the emergence of young people, many of whom have vastly different values and expectations about social life. Taylor (2014) describes what he calls "The Next America," which will feature more racial/ethnic diversity, wider understanding of gender norms, different family structures, greater variations of religious affiliation, and the use of technology. Waddle (2015, 6) describes as current trends in congregational life "more ethnic diversity, greater acceptance of gays and lesbians, increasingly informal worship styles, declining size, and declining denominational affiliation."

In summary, changes in thought, culture, and social context have historically shaped the role and practice of religious teaching and learning. Religious educators, by design, are required to understand the context in which they work and offer practical solutions that ground the learner religiously for conscious participation in the world.

PRACTICES FOR LIVING RELIGIOUSLY

Religious educators are always curious about how people become religious (see Chapter 4 in this volume). Saroglou (2011, 1320) suggests that people become religious through four psychologically framed events: "Believing, Bonding, Behaving and Belonging." Saroglou proposes that religiosity can be conceptualized by observing seekers as they search their lived experiences for meaning and the truth; act on their desire to explore the self-transcendent nature of their emotions; find ways to exert self-control in order to behave according to a moral standard that has personal value; and, finally, express a need to belong to a trans-historical group that enhances collective self-esteem and identification with a group.

Saroglou's typology helps us understand the decisions religious educators make as they create meaningful learning experiences, especially given the current diversity of cultural and generational contexts. Roberto (2015), for example, builds upon the notion of "faith formation" (see Chapter 7 in this volume), which has historical roots in the academic tradition of cognitive and social developmental growth models. Here, educators seat problems of how and why religious learning occurs in an "ecosystem" of interrelated learning tools. In such a system, the educator and the learner are jointly invested in finding ways to live a spiritually rich life. In 1952, Sophia Fahs noted the power of an experiential learning guided by native curiosity (Hunter 1976). Fahs called for religious professionals to stop fearing uncertainty and reorient themselves as "fellow searcher[s]" exploring and collaborating in the service of learning (Hunter 1976, 244).

Given the diversity of learning needs, how does the deepening of faith occur? Rituals—or symbolic actions—allow religious communities to signify what matters, and convey beyond words emotions like love, fidelity, and compassion (White 1990). The symbolic, reflective action embedded in each ritual provides the opportunity to make meaning of a life encounter. Thus, rituals, conceived broadly, are the tools that make believing, bonding, behaving, and belonging a moment of powerful learning. Tables 9.1 and 9.2 provide examples of symbolic learning practices that, over time, ground seekers in faith.

Even as religious rituals differ broadly, they share the principle of how to explore and affirm the mysterious and sacred nature of life. At the risk of not citing examples from every religious tradition, Table 9.3 is an object lesson that models how theological commitments of a religious tradition can translate into educational practices that teach faithful living. It is expected that the representative traditions teach for outcomes broader than those listed, and, likewise, that many other religious traditions teach for similar aims.

Table 9.1 Formal Rituals that Promote a Religious Identity

- Church School/Sunday School (children, youth, and adult education)
- Corporate gatherings of the faithful (Sunday worship, Mass, Shabbat, Jumu'ah, etc.)
- Small-group ministry/covenant groups (gender-based groups, singles ministry, youth/elder groups, bereavement groups, racial/ethnic caucuses, addiction groups, etc.)
- Lay/professional ministry (pastoral care, hospitality, ushers, teacher, blogger, etc.)
- Lay leadership roles (pastor/priest, shaman, elder, deacon, acolyte, trustee, choir director, etc.)
- Eucharist/Lord's Supper, Seder, High Holy Days, etc.

Mission Work

- Mission trips (domestic and abroad)
- Pilgrimages (Hajj, travel to Holy Land, birthplace of religious group)
- Evangelism (sharing stories of faith and about God's love)
- Social justice action (response to natural disasters, large-scale human tragedy such as gun violence or racial injustice, etc.)

Rites of Passage

- Puberty (coming of age, rites of passage, writing credos, Bar/Bat Mitzvah)
- Adult baptism (statements of confession, conversion, etc.)
- Marriage ceremonies sanctioned by a sacred being
- Death (wakes, funerals, sitting Shiva)
- Confirmation classes (membership classes, etc.)

Rituals

- Religious holidays (e.g., Christmas, Ramadan, Pentecost, Passover, Solstice)
- Baby dedication, baptism
- Retreats (dedicated time for focused introspection, networking, skill development)
- Summer camps for children, families, affinity groups
- Sports teams, music, and theater groups

Table 9.2 Informal Rituals

- Prayer, meditation
- Contemplation of sacred texts (Bible, Qur'an, Torah)
- Family worship, centering, saying grace
- Singing, visual arts, yoga, exercise
- Fasting
- Personal retreats
- Contemplative practices (breathing, walking, chanting)

Table 9.3 Correlation of Instructional Aims to Teaching Practices

A tradition educating for:	Area of teaching focus:
Ethics *Sample communities of practice:* Humanists, atheists	• Use of compassionate reason to address social responsibility • Nurture relationships of care for all living beings • Foster creative, joyful living for self and others • Affirm life and the sense of possibility • Promote a free and open society that shares equitably the bounties of life • Encourage the use of reason—not emotion alone—to make decisions about the quality and practices of living.
Religious identity *Sample communities of practice:* Jews, Muslims, Mormons	• Teach the importance of the tradition's story and why it must continue • Encourage individual connections to the power of the large-group story • Foster robust relationships within the group • Prevent attrition among believers within the kinship circle
Salvation/Evangelism *Sample communities of practice:* Christian evangelicals, black churches	• Transform people for God's reign in the world • Arouse interest and invite newcomers into the religion • Tell the sacred story through teaching/preaching • Explore dimensions of faith in response to sacred texts • Translate stories of faith into individual lives and social action
Social Justice *Sample communities of practice:* Unitarian Universalists, United Church of Christ, Jesuits	• Participate in public dialogue that serves the common good • Make better persons for a better world while making the world better for humane living • Provide ethical roots that lead to social reform • Connect spiritual depth to social action • Prepare learners for social action, advocacy, mobilization, critical reflection-in-action
Empowerment *Sample communities of practice:* Black churches/churches of color, LGBT congregations	• Eradicate structural oppression in order to foster human flourishing • Pronounce important intellectual, social, and spiritual contributions of marginalized people and perspectives • Provide hopeful scaffolding that helps the oppressed heal from the wounds of victimization, marginalization, powerlessness, violence, and internalized oppression
Integration & Mindfulness *Sample communities of practice:* Native American spirituality, Buddhism	• Living life "is" living religion • Living in harmony and balance with the world around you • Awareness of suffering and our role in perpetuating and ending it • Awareness of interdependence with the world

CONCLUSION

The work of educating people about religion—whether from a devotional perspective within the content of a religious tradition (as discussed here) or from an academic perspective in the context of public schooling (as discussed in Chapter 5 in this volume)—has been a valiant and often hotly contested enterprise for religious educators, families, religious communities, government, and the general public. Religious education, as the handmaiden of theology, is charged with making the promise of a particular religious tradition real in the hearts and minds of the seeker. To achieve that aim, the religious educator has to be a critical optimist, taking into account emerging trends, conflicting ideas, and the always evolving disposition of human beings.

Andrew Revkin (2008) notes that "there are a billion teenagers on planet earth right now. A hundred thirty years ago there were only a billion people altogether. . . . Now there are a billion teenagers and they could just as easily become child soldiers and drug dealers as innovators and the owners of small companies. . . ." While these numbers are startling in their own right, religious educators have, across time and context, been aware of this precariously tender and important call in shaping the sacred trajectory of life. The work of religious education, by its nature, is work that understands the givens of the human condition, yet, still, points children, youth, and adults to the difficult, rewarding, and life-giving task of making meaning out of life.

FUTURE DIRECTIONS

1. How do the instructional aims of a particular religious community align with the curricular focus of that community's educational program? What theological and ethical assumptions drive those decisions?

2. Compare and contrast the religious education objectives of communities that educate with the intent to help individuals and families form a strong religious identity as compared to communities that educate for empowerment. What are the different sources of authority that are used within the curriculum? To whom are these communities accountable? What role does tradition play over one's direct experience?

3. Choose three different religious traditions and compare and contrast how religious educators in those traditions emphasize what Vassilis Saroglou describes as the four religious dimensions of religious identify formation: believing, bonding, behaving, and belonging.

4. Consider the different approaches taken by religious communities when teaching about the religious other. How are other religions represented by one another? How do notions of superiority or inferiority form when religious communities, in seeking to differentiate themselves, speak about the other religious traditions? How does this differ if the community holds exclusive as compared to inclusive theological positions?

5. After reflecting on the nature of religious education within religious traditions, compare and contrast this to the academic study of religion. What is the difference? Why is this distinction important when it comes to public education?

References

Ahlstrom, Sidney. 1972. *A Religious History of the American People*. New Haven, CT: Yale University Press.

Alshire, Daniel O., and Stephen Graham. September 2015. "ATS 2015 State of the Industry Webinar." Pittsburgh, PA.

Amkraut, Brian. 2011. "Technology: The Digital Revolution That Is Shaping Twenty-First-Century Jewish Education—a Fleeting Snapshot from the First Decade." In *International Handbooks on Jewish Education*, edited by Helena Miler, Lisa D. Grant, and Alex Pomson, 597–614. Basel, Switzerland: Springer International Publishing.

Beaudoin, Tom. 2003. "'Virtual' Catechesis: Religious Formation the Post-Vatican II Generations." In *Horizons & Hopes: The Future of Religious Education*, edited by Thomas H. Groome and Harold Daly Horell, 63–80. Mahwah, NJ: Paulist Press.

Bekerman, Zvi, and Sue Rosenfeld. 2011. "Culture: Restoring Culture to Jewish Cultural Education." In *International Handbooks on Jewish Education*, edited by Helena Miler, Lisa D. Grant, and Alex Pomson, 47–62. Basel, Switzerland: Springer International Publishing.

Bellavance-Grace, Karen. 2013. "Full Week Faith." *Rethinking Religious Education and Faith Formation Ministries for Twenty-First Century Unitarian Universalists*. Fahs Fellowship Papers. Chicago, IL: Meadville Theological Seminary.

Blumenfeld, Sam. 2012. "Religion in Early American Education." *The New American: That Freedom Shall Not Perish*, October 18, 2012. Accessed at www.thenewamerican.com/reviews/opinion/item/13262-religion-in-early-american-education.

Boyer, Paul. Fall 1994. "Living Spiritually." *Tribal College: Journal of American Indian Higher Education* 6, no. 2.

Boys, Mary C. 2001. *Educating in Faith*. Lima, OH: Academic Renewal Press.

Charme, Stuart, and Tali Zelkowicz. 2011. "Jewish Identities: Educating for Multiple and Moving Targets." In *International Handbooks on Jewish Education*, edited by Helena Miler, Lisa D. Grant, and Alex Pomson, 163–181. Basel, Switzerland: Springer International Publishing.

Cohen, Steven M., and Laurence Kotler-Berkowitz. July 2004. *The Impact of Childhood Jewish Education on Adults' Jewish Identity: Schooling, Israel Travel, Camping and Youth Groups*. New York: United Jewish Communities.

Daily, Eileen M. 2013. "The Promise of Mobile Technology for Public Religious Education." *Religious Education* 108, no. 2: 112–28.

Dewey, John. 1997a. *Democracy and Education*, later printing ed. New York: Free Press.

———. 1997b. *Experience and Education*, reprint ed. New York: Free Press.

Emerson, Michael O. 2008. *People of the Dream: Multiracial Congregations in the United States*. Princeton, NJ: Princeton University Press.

Forbes, Jack D. 1993. *Africans and Native Americans: The Language of Race and the Evolution of Red-Black Peoples*, 2nd ed. Champaign, IL: University of Illinois Press.

Gaither, Milton. 2008. *Homeschool: An American History*, 1st ed. New York: Palgrave Macmillan.

Greenhow, Christine, and Benjamin Gleason. 2014. "Social Scholarship: Reconsidering Scholarly Practices in the Age of Social Media." *British Journal of Educational Technology* 45, no. 3: 392–402.

Haidt, Jonathan. 2015. "Moral Foundations." Moral Foundations.org.

Hammer, Rhonda, and Douglas Kellner. 2000. "Multimedia Pedagogy and Multicultural Education for the New Millennium." *Religious Education* 95, no. 4: 474–89.

Harris, Maria. 1991. *Teaching and Religious Imagination: An Essay in the Theology of Teaching.* San Francisco: Harper San Francisco.

Hook, William J. 2005. "Implications of a Digital Age for Theological Education." *Theological Education* 41, no. 1: 57–62.

Horell, Harold Daly. 2003. "Cultural Postmodernity and Christian Faith Formation." In *Horizons and Hopes: The Future of Religious Education*, edited by Thomas H. Groome, and Harold Daly Horell, 135. Mahwah, NJ: Paulist Press.

Hunter, Edith F. 1976. *Sophia Lyon Fahs: A Biography*, 2nd ed. Boston: Beacon Press.

Jarvis, Peter. 2012. *Paradoxes of Learning: On Becoming an Individual in Society*, 1st ed. New York, NY: Routledge.

Jenkins, Carol A., and Dale Kratt. 2007. "Sociological Foundations of Religious Education." In *Multicultural Religious Education*, Wilkerson, B. (Ed.), 432. Birmingham, AL: Religion Education Press.

Kadi, Wadad. 2007. "Education in Islam." In *Islam and Education: Myths and Truths*, edited by Wadad Kadi and Victor Billeh, 5–18. Chicago: University of Chicago Press.

Little, Sara. 1995. "Reformed Theology and Religious Education." In *Theologies of Religious Education*, Miller, R. C. (Ed.), 11–34. Birmingham, AL: Religion Education Press.

Magnus, Mernard. 1996. "Postmodernism." *The Cambridge Dictionary of Philosophy.* London: Cambridge University Press.

Marcus, Benjamin P. 2018. "Religious Literacy in American Education," in Michael D. Waggoner and Nathan C. Walker, eds., *The Oxford Handbook of Religion and American Education.* New York, NY: Oxford University Press.

Marthaler, B. L. 1990. "Catechism." *Harper's Encyclopedia of Religious Education.* New York, NY: Harper and Row.

Massachusetts Bay Company and Nathaniel Shurtleff. 1853. *Records of the Governor and Company of the Massachusetts Bay in New England*, vol. 2: 1642–1649. Sheffield, England: William White.

Mercer, Ron, and Mark Simpson. 2015. "What Would Kant Tweet? The Utilization of Online Technology in Course Involving Formation, Meaning and Value." *Theological Education*, 49, no. 2: 1–18.

National Center for Education Statistics. 2016. *Homeschooling in the United States: 2012.* U.S. Department of Education, NCES 2016–096.REV.

Nelson, Roberta. 2006. *Claiming the Past, Shaping the Future: Four Eras in Liberal Religious Education.* Boston, MA: Liberal Religious Educators Association.

Oaks, Jeannie, and Martin Lipton. 2003. *Teaching to Change the World*, 2nd ed. Boston: McGraw-Hill Companies.

Oddone, Kay. 2015. "Learning the Art of Digital Curation." November 10, 2015. Accessed at http://www.linkinglearning.com.au/learning-the-art-of-digital-content-curation-2/.

Pandika, Melissa. 2015. "Has the Sun Set on Sunday School?" *USA Today*, March 22.

Pew Research Center. 2015. *Pew: Religious Landscape Study.* Washington, DC: Pew Research Center.

Prothero, Stephen. 2011. *God Is Not One: The Eight Rival Religions That Run the World*, reprint ed. New York, NY: HarperOne.

Revkin, Andrew. 2008. "Climate Change is Not the Story of Our Time." *The New York Times*, Dec. 1, 2008.

Riley, Meg. 2015. "Church of the Larger Fellowship." http://www.questformeaning.org/clfuu/.

Roberto, John. 2009. *Thirteen Trends and Forces Affecting the Future of Faith Formation in a Changing Church and World: Faith Formation 2020*, Summer 2009. Naugatuck, CT: LifeLong Faith Associates.

———. 2015. *Reimagining Faith Formation for the 21st Century*. Naugatuck, CT: LifeLong Faith Associates.

Saroglou, Vassilis. 2011. "Believing, Bonding, Behaving, and Belonging: The Big Four Religious Dimensions and Cultural Variation." *Journal of Cross-Cultural Psychology* 42, no. 8: 1320–1340.

Sizer, Theodore, and Nancy Sizer. 2000. *The Students Are Watching: Schools and the Moral Contract*. Boston: Beacon Press.

Steffer, R. W. 1990. "Multicultural Education." *Harper's Encyclopedia of Religious Education*. San Francisco: Harper and Row.

Taylor, Paul. 2014. *The Next America*. http://www.21stcenturyfaithformation.com/challenges.html.

Tickle, Phyllis. 2012. *The Great Emergence: How Christianity Is Changing and Why*. Ada, MI: Baker Books.

US Department of Education. 2008. "Issue Brief: 1.5 Million Homeschooled Students in the United States in 2007." NCES-2009-030.

Waddle, Ray. 2015. "Faith Futures: An Interview with Mark Chaves." Yale University.

Weaver, Jace. 1997. "Native Americans and Religious Education." In *Multicultural Religious Education*, Wilkerson, B. (Ed.). Birmingham, AL: Religion Education Press.

White, J. S. 1990. "Sacraments." In *Harper's Encyclopedia of Religious Education*. New York, NY: Harper and Row.

Wilkerson, Barbara. 1997. *Multicultural Religious Education*, 2nd ed. Birmingham, AL: Religious Education Press.

CHAPTER 10

RELIGIOUS EDUCATION BETWEEN THE TRADITIONS

EBOO PATEL AND NOAH J. SILVERMAN

INTRODUCTION

AT the outset of his career, the great twentieth-century scholar of comparative religion, Wilfred Cantwell Smith, had an experience that illustrates many of the key themes in religious education between traditions (what we later term "interfaith education"). While teaching among religiously diverse faculty at a Christian college in the 1940s in Lahore, in what is now Pakistan, he suddenly had a startling realization about the obvious: most of his colleagues and students at the missionary college were not Christian; they were Sikhs, Muslims, and Hindus. "The Christians among us," he writes, "were attempting to illustrate and practice our faith; our colleagues of other communities, often reverent men, were willing to work with us towards constructing and maintaining a community—a community religiously diverse" (W. C. Smith 1962, 4).

Had he been asked before he arrived in South Asia what a Christian ought to do when confronted with someone of a different religion, he might well have answered that the Christian ought to convert him or her. He was, after all, a Presbyterian minister at a missionary college. When he found himself, however, in a situation where he had grown to respect people of other religions as colleagues and, especially, living in an unfamiliar country, had come to rely on them as friends, other thoughts arose as well. How were he and his non-Christian colleagues, together, going to most effectively teach their students? What could they do about the increasing religious violence in the subcontinent? What did their religiously diverse community have to say about the colonial regime in place at the time?

Cantwell Smith was beginning to ask questions about what it meant to be a Christian in a religiously diverse environment where conversion was not the primary goal. This question is foundational to an interfaith understanding of identity, which is to say that his relationships with the religiously diverse people around him had deeply influenced his relationship with his own Christian tradition. This is, after all, what is meant by the term "interfaith":

Inter—how people relate to the diversity around them

Faith—people's orientation around the key symbols and tenets of their tradition and/ or worldview

Interfaith—how people's orientation around their religious or philosophical tradition impacts the relationship they have with the diversity around them, and how their relationships with the diversity around them shape the way they orient around their religious or philosophical traditions.

Cantwell Smith records his insights about this experience in the introduction to his then controversial but now classic 1962 book called *The Faith of Other Men* (later republished as *Patterns of Faith Around the World*): "The problem is for us all to learn to live together with our seriously different traditions not only in peace but in some sort of mutual trust and mutual loyalty," to arrive at a point where "we can appreciate other men's values without losing allegiance to our own." And he noted, as if peering into the future, "The religious life of mankind from now on, if it is to be lived at all, will be lived in a context of religious pluralism" (94–96).

Over a half-century later, it is clear how prescient these words were. As the sociologist Robert Putnam writes, "The most certain prediction that we can make about almost any modern society is that it will be more diverse a generation from now than it is today. This is true from Sweden to the United States and from New Zealand to Ireland" (137). This raises profound questions about everything from the continuity of religious identities and communities to the social cohesion of diverse societies. If, as Cantwell Smith predicted, religious education must be "lived in a context of religious pluralism," how should religious educators respond to this context to ensure the continuity of their tradition? How can the uniqueness—and, in some cases, exclusive truth claims—of a given tradition be promoted without jeopardizing social cohesion in a diverse society such as the United States? This chapter argues that religious education can be effective at achieving both continuity for religious communities and social cohesion within a diverse society by proactively engaging religious diversity through *interfaith* education, a concept defined and explored below.

The chapter begins with an examination of the changing social reality of religious identity in the late twentieth and early twenty-first centuries, including some of the theoretical frameworks that help contextualize this shifting landscape, and continues to articulate a taxonomy of potential religious responses to the presence of increased religious diversity. The second section advocates for the superiority of one of those responses—namely, the proactive engagement of religious diversity through interfaith education—and identifies the mechanisms by which religious and philosophical communities can pursue it. Finally, the chapter suggests seminary education as a prime site for inculcating interfaith education, and thus disseminating it across the lifespan of religious education.

The Social Landscape of Religious
Identity Amidst Diversity

In his landmark 1979 book *The Heretical Imperative*, the sociologist of religion Peter Berger makes a central theoretical insight into the social condition of modernity: "modernity pluralizes both the institutions and plausibility structures" (17). He argues that this is the signature characteristic of the modern era. Where there were once only a few institutions—the family, the Church, and the state, all closely aligned—there are now myriad, and they are often at cross-purposes. Communications technology, immigration policy, and air travel, among other factors, have contributed to a world in which people from different backgrounds are interacting with greater frequency than ever before. This is inescapable, Berger argues, and it is significantly different from the world our ancestors experienced.

Furthermore, just as modernity pluralizes, pluralism relativizes. The consequence of the intense and frequent interaction with dissimilar people and ideas is that institutions and traditions lose their taken-for-granted status. The multiplicity of ways of being human is now manifestly apparent to everyone, and the idea that one must follow a preordained path loses its saliency as a result. Today most people in the Global North lead lives characterized by choice—which, Berger points out, is at the root of the word "heresy"—and interaction with different types of people on a regular basis is an unavoidable feature of modern life. The social theorist Anthony Giddens (1991) emphasizes that this dynamic makes the modern world challenging to negotiate. When you encounter a person with a pattern of life different than your own—someone who doesn't go to church on Sunday in a town of Christians, someone who eats pork in a town of Jews—you start to ask yourself a series of questions that most human beings through most of human history, raised as they were in monocultures, never had to deal with: If they don't go to church on Sunday, why do I? If I have been taught that my way is the only way, what do I now think of their other way? Giddens observes that these questions lead to the development of the *reflexive self*, wherein self-identity is actively shaped, reflected on, self-monitored, and, ultimately, self-constructed. Since historical traditions no longer maintain a monopoly on authority, that authority has moved from within familial, religious, and political structures to within the self. Consequently, identity—and for our purposes religious identity—has moved from fate to choice.

This shift has significantly affected traditional religious identity and the continuity of religious communities. It can be summarized in one word: decline. Numerous empirical studies have charted the now well-worn fact of the decay of traditional religious association, particularly among mainline Protestant, Catholic, and Jewish communities in Europe and the United States. Gallup and Pew data suggest that in the sixty-year period from 1954 until 2014, Protestant Christians have gone from 71% to 37% of the US population. Former Catholics, if imagined as a denomination unto themselves, now constitute the second largest religious community in the United States. The percentage of US adults who say they are Jewish when asked about their religion has dropped by about half since the late 1950s. Taken together, these trends contribute to the growth of the so-called religious "nones": a full one-fifth of the general US public are religiously unaffiliated, and that number rises to one-third among adults under the age of thirty.

These trends present serious challenges to those tasked with ensuring the continuity of religious traditions, an enterprise that is often achieved through religious education. In the modern context, where the lifelong religious identity of young people can no longer be presumed, religious educators are increasingly encouraged to think of themselves as offering a product that is in direct competition with the product of their peers of different traditions and the secular culture around them. Due to its inherent relativistic posture, such an economic metaphor often fails to appreciate the cultural and theological nuance of religious identity and communal continuity. For some communities, the very idea of such a "religious marketplace" is anathema to the very core and particular beliefs that they are striving to impart to the next generation, and it remains a tricky business even for those who have adopted such a mindset. The sociologists Christian Smith and Melina Lundquist Denton (2005) have observed how, in an attempt to remain accessible and civil amid growing religious diversity, many Christian communities are sending the "wrong messages that historical faith traditions do not matter, that all religious beliefs are basically alike, that no faith tradition possesses anything that anybody particularly needs" (63). The authors suggest that while such a "bland oatmeal approach to faith" does not entice US teens, "obnoxious, offensive talk . . . merely turns people off" as well. Smith and Denton write, "We suspect that there is plenty of room for faith traditions to claim and emphasize confidently their own particularities and distinctions without risking religious division or conflict." This may be the proverbial case of "easier said than done." How, then, are religious communities—and, more precisely, religious educators—meant to maintain their particularities in the midst of the twin forces of modernity: pluralization and relativization?

Broadly speaking, if religious communities seek to eschew relativism, maintain their distinct religious identity, and ensure their continuity, there are four basic directions that they can take in a world where religious identity has moved from fate to choice: they can build "bunkers," "barriers," "bludgeons," or "bridges."

Bunkers

One possible response to religious diversity is to build bunkers of isolation. Such a response is characterized by the idea that, as a religious community, everyone should do as much as they can to remove themselves from interaction with people who are different from them. Essentially, in the face of the increased religious diversity of modernity, this mentality rejects modernity altogether. In the United States, ultra-Orthodox Jews and the Amish often showcase this response to modernity and diversity. Like most religious communities, these groups believe that their way of life embodies righteousness and holiness, but, unlike others, they have concluded that the best way to preserve it is to seal themselves off from the perceived moral vacancy of modernity. While bunkering reflects a commitment to core principles of a belief system, it also shields us from each other. The continuity of the tradition is often maintained—and at a higher rate than many other communities—but at the price of engagement with new ideas from outside the community. It thus obviates the imperative to respond to religious difference by minimizing the saliency of diversity in all aspects of life. In Berger's framework, it is a retreat from modernity and its attendant diversity altogether.

Barriers

The second response to religious diversity can be understood as building barriers. Religious communities that build barriers share with those who build bunkers an emphasis on the fact that religious traditions have different doctrines, goals, and, ultimately, understandings of truth. But communities that adopt this response do engage in modernity precisely to highlight these divisions and assert their worldview's superiority, often in ways that are intentionally demeaning to others. Thus, while they do not withdraw entirely from modern society, they are most intent on making clear their differences from other groups and rarely seek positive engagement with others. Diversity is engaged solely to be rejected. The quintessential example of a barrier-building religious community is the Westboro Baptist Church. Westboro Church members are famous for their provocative and almost absurdist protests against LGBT people, Jews, women, and almost any other group outside their small assembly based in Topeka, Kansas. Their main form of protest is to literally form barriers outside of cultural events, funerals, and speeches of people and groups with whom they disagree. Actively denouncing interaction is their response to the religious diversity surrounding them.

Bludgeons

In its most extreme form, the barrier outlook crosses the line from uncivil speech to violent action and becomes bludgeoning. Unfortunately, the international news provides us with all too many ready examples of this response to religious diversity. From the barbarity of the Islamic State in Iraq and Syria to Hindu mob violence in Gujarat, examples of religiously motivated violence abound and hardly need exposition. What is worth noting, however, is that this mentality requires as much careful nurturing and inculcation as any other. In her seminal study of religiously motivated violence, *Terror in the Name of God* (2004), Jessica Stern makes clear that religious violence is rarely a spontaneous eruption of religious passions. On the contrary, it is the product of well-organized, well-funded, well-led, and well-*taught* training programs. "The most important aspect of training," she writes, "is mental training and religious indoctrination. . . . The story that recruits must learn is about identity—it is about who *we* are as distinct from *them*" (261). The us/them dichotomy that underpins this mentality also finds expression in

Western scholarship. The late political scientist Samuel Huntington famously argued in *The Clash of Civilizations* that "the central axis of world politics in the future is likely to be" (29) ". . . the conflict between 'the West and the Rest'" (183–206). Lest anyone be confused about how such borders are drawn, Huntington clarified, "civilizations are differentiated from each other by history, language, culture, tradition and, most important, religion."

Bridges

Beginning in the early 1990s, a new movement swept through education extolling the endless virtues of diversity in everything from classroom makeup to curricula to educators. Diana Eck (2001), a scholar of South Asian religions at Harvard, pointed out that diversity, in and of itself, is neither a positive nor a negative situation; it is simply a descriptive and ever-more-present sociological fact. It says nothing of the nature of the interactions or relationships between the diverse constituents; indeed, some of the most violent places in the world are also some of the most diverse. Eck (2006) argues that what diversity proponents really are advocating for is what she terms "pluralism." Pluralism goes beyond the mere fact of people from different backgrounds living in close proximity to an "energetic engagement with diversity" through "the active seeking of understanding across lines of difference." In Eck's postulation, such seeking results not in relativism but in "the encounter of commitments," requiring participants to hold their "deepest differences . . . not in isolation, but in relationship to one another." Religious pluralism can be defined as a form of proactive cooperation between people who orient around religion differently that affirms the identity of individuals and communities, while emphasizing that the well-being of each depends on the health of the whole. It is characterized by three components: (1) respect for particular identities (religious and other); (2) positive relationships between diverse communities; and (3) active partnerships that promote a commitment to the common good. Such a response constitutes a fourth religious response to modernity: teaching adherents to proactively build bridges of cooperation with other religious communities.

INTERFAITH EDUCATION: PROMOTING SOCIAL COHESION AND THE CONTINUITY OF RELIGIOUS COMMUNITIES THROUGH THE "BRIDGE" OF PLURALISM

In a world too often characterized by barriers and bludgeons, this chapter makes two arguments. The first, and perhaps better understood, argument is that in a diverse democracy such as the United States, Eck's notion of active pluralism represents the best response to modernity and religious diversity. At the outset, it is the only engaged response to diversity that does not involve either acquiescing to relativism or devolving into one community's attempts to outshout or silence others. The political philosopher Michael Walzer argues in *What It Means to Be an American* that the challenge of a diverse society is to "embrace difference and maintain a common life" (1996, 17).

Eck's and Walzer's theoretical framework has been substantiated through empirical research. Robert Putnam and Lewis Feldstein demonstrated in *Better Together* (2003, 1–10) that the benefits to society of what they termed *bridged social capital*—the type of social capital that reaches over potential barriers between communities—are far more impactful than those of what they deemed *bonded social capital*, the type that stays within one community. Putnam further demonstrated, in collaboration with David Campbell (2010), that building relationships across lines of difference has an exponential effect on reducing overall prejudice in a society. Their research into the *Pal Al phenomenon* indicated strong statistical evidence that people's regard for entire religious groups improves through a positive, meaningful relationship with even one member of that group, often formed through a common activity. Furthermore, they write, "We have reasonably firm evidence that as people build more religious bridges they become warmer toward people of many different religions, not just those religions represented within their social network" (533). More than reduce prejudice, an empirical study in India by the social scientist Ashutosh Varshney (2002) showed that the primary difference between cities in India that experienced interreligious violence and others that remained calm in similar circumstances was, effectively, bridged social capital.

So, why is pluralism important for diverse democracies? Because it strengthens bridged social capital, reduces prejudice, and prevents identity-based violence. This is all fairly intuitive, but it is also all substantiated by social science research.

The second argument of this chapter is perhaps more counterintuitive. Not only is it good for social cohesion, but when pursued through interfaith education, religious pluralism is also the best option for achieving the continuity of religious identities and communities. Before presenting the theory and analysis to support this argument, it may be useful to introduce in this chapter an illustrative real-world story from one of the co-authors:

When Eboo Patel's son, Zayd, was three, he attended the birthday party of one of his Jewish friends. After observing his friend's family for a bit, Zayd asked Patel what "mazel tov" meant and why people kept saying it to the birthday boy. Patel responded that it meant "congratulations." Zayd persisted, inquiring why they do not just say "congratulations." Patel explained that Zayd's friend and his family were Jewish, and that "mazel tov" was how Jews said congratulations in their language on special occasions. After contemplating this notion, Zayd, who had previously expressed various degrees of disinterest in the Muslim education classes to which his parents had dutifully taken him, asked Patel what people would say on Zayd's birthday. Patel stopped himself before he gave the obvious answer—"happy birthday"—when he realized that that was not the answer Zayd wanted. Zayd wanted to know if they, as Muslims, had their own language to mark special occasions. Zayd wanted the version of "mazel tov" that was his. Patel proudly told his son that he would say "mubaraki" (the Urdu derivation of the Arabic word "mabrook," which means "congratulations") on Zayd's birthday. When Zayd's birthday came, something else noteworthy happened. Zayd opened a present to discover a copy of a book about the prophet Muhammad. Although Zayd quickly moved on to other packages, Patel noticed that Zayd's Hindu friend, Karthik, had given him the book. Upon learning this, Zayd's interest blossomed and he took it and opened the pages. "Karthik knows about the Prophet Muhammad?" Zayd asked. "He sure does," Patel replied.

This anecdote reveals something both profound and sensible: encounters with other people's religious language, practice, and stories actually make one's own tradition more relevant and attractive. It is understandable why parents and religious communities, even those sympathetic to the "pluralism is good for society" argument, may feel that they need to teach their children "their own tradition first" before engaging in interfaith programming. But in the modern context of intense and frequent interaction with religious diversity, teaching children what it means to follow their tradition in an imagined vacuum, devoid of the jazz and war of the religious diversity that surrounds them, falls somewhere between naively nostalgic and dangerously retrograde. The question is, rather, how do parents and religious communities make the existence of religious diversity an asset in faith formation instead of an obstacle? As this anecdote illustrates, Zayd better understands himself as a Muslim when others show interest in this aspect of his identity and, critically, when he knows how Islam can exist in positive relationship with non-Muslims.

The purpose of religious education within and between religious traditions ought to be largely about promoting an understanding of how that tradition positively relates to others. This is what is meant by *interfaith* education, which can be defined as education that promotes engaged religious pluralism. But not only does interfaith education contribute to social cohesion by fostering religious pluralism on a societal level, crucially it also supports the continuity of religious communities by making particular religious identities both salient and attractive in a world of religious diversity.

As discussed, a useful metaphor for thinking about promoting religious pluralism is that of building "bridges" of cooperation with other religious communities. If extended, the bridge metaphor is also useful for thinking about the ways in which religious and philosophical communities can effectively employ interfaith education. Physical bridges exist to connect two otherwise disconnected places, a "here" and a "there," and they must be made of a substantive material. To effectively build bridges—to engage in interfaith education—religious and philosophical communities must enact each part of this triad:

1. Developing and teaching a "theology or ethic of interfaith cooperation" that grounds their own identity in relation to others (establishing the "here")
2. Nurturing and teaching appreciative knowledge of and shared values between diverse religious and philosophical traditions (recognizing and seeking the "there")

3. Engaging in relationship-building activities that promote the common good with other communities (building bridges made of substance).

Developing a Theology or Ethic of Interfaith Cooperation

People often think about interfaith education as being entirely focused on teaching about other religious and nonreligious groups, but there is some truth to the notion that one must know something about one's own tradition to effectively engage with others. Or, in other words, before any community seeks out a "there," they must first establish their "here": the identity of each community or individual and his/her/their understanding of what makes their orientation around religion discrete. This is not to fall into any of the common pitfalls of interfaith work by excluding the nonreligious or the multireligious, or being blind to intra-faith complexity. It is rather to acknowledge and affirm the distinctiveness of individual and communal religious identity over and above both relativism and syncretism. The world's myriad religious and ethical traditions, while manifested in literally millions of ways, are not, in fact, all the same, nor are they merely just different versions of the same basic message. The scholar of religion Stephen Prothero makes this argument eloquently in his book *God Is Not One* (2010).

In the context of interfaith education, this process must also include the development of "a theology or ethic of interfaith cooperation" (Patel & Meyer, 2015, 479). More than a generalized understanding of one's own tradition, this consists of a specific exploration and synthesis of the texts, histories, stories, heroes, literature, and so forth within that tradition that speak to positive relationships with the religious other. A theology or ethic of interfaith cooperation makes those pieces salient, interprets and applies them to the contemporary dynamic of religious diversity, and strings them together in a coherent narrative. For some traditions, such an ethic or theology has a long and salient history, like the Muslim understanding of Jews or Christians as the "people of the Book." For other traditions, the line of thinking is there but has not always found a clear voice. Teaching interfaith education allows students to discover through, for example, thinkers like Paul Knitter (Roman Catholicism; 2002), Jonathan Sacks (Judaism; 2002), Miroslav Volf (evangelical Christianity), Chris Stedman (Secular Humanism; 2012), Feisal Abdul Rauf (Islam; 2004), and the Dalai Lama (Buddhism; 2010), that the impulse to interfaith cooperation is not just a twenty-first-century innovation but finds authentic and legitimate expression within diverse traditions.

Nurturing Appreciative Knowledge of Shared Values Between Diverse Traditions

Once both a distinct identity and an understanding of how that identity promotes relationships with others are delineated, interfaith education moves toward establishing the "there" of religious pluralism: the recognition that while not unified, the world's myriad religious and ethical traditions are not so diverse, so disparate, and so mutually unintelligible that there are not and cannot be any points of commonality between them. Put differently, interfaith education teaches individuals and communities to appreciate that others have their own, distinctive "here," and then makes a genuine effort to connect with it.

Most often, people's views toward other religious traditions and communities have everything to do with the particular and limited knowledge they have about them. The Dalai Lama addresses this point in his book *Toward a True Kinship of Faiths: How the World's Religions Can Come Together* (2010). He recounts that, during the early 2000s, he began to be disturbed by the news reports of violence he saw being committed in the name of Islam. At the same time, he did not think he could merely dismiss a religion of 1.6 billion people as inherently violent and destructive. Realizing that his personal knowledge of Islam was not that deep, he began to study: reading the Qur'an more closely and engaging in interfaith dialogue with Muslims, uncovering stories of mercy and justice, and all the while looking for themes of compassion in Islam. His Holiness had an incomplete and largely negative understanding of Islam, so he sought to gain what could be called "an appreciative knowledge" of the tradition that more fully represented its complexity and beauty.

Appreciative knowledge is the stories, heroes, poetry, scripture, and art from another tradition that one admires. At its core, appreciative knowledge is having accurate and positive knowledge about other traditions. But while a standard religious literacy might begin with the basic texts and practice of major religious traditions, interfaith education seeks to promote those texts, practices, leaders, and stories that speak toward widely shared values and a sense of the common good. In other words, the knowledge people most often appreciate in other traditions connects with the values in their own.

This is apparent in some well-known interfaith relationships. As a young seminarian, Martin Luther King, Jr. was so taken by Gandhi's writings about *satyagraha* (nonviolence, or, literally, "love force") precisely because it resonated with his own Christian theology of love (Gandhi 2013). The converse was also true; as a young man in South Africa, Gandhi studied the Bible and found in Jesus' Sermon on the Mount a clear statement about his own ideas around love, equality, and active but peaceful resistance to repressive authority. In Jesus, Gandhi found resonance with his Hindu beliefs. In Gandhi, King found resonance with his Christian beliefs. Consequently, King developed an appreciation of Hinduism in large part because Gandhi's articulation of nonviolence resonated with the deep significance King felt as a Christian with Jesus' command to "turn the other cheek" (King 1960). Similarly, when the Dalai Lama began studying Islam, he was looking for the value that he most cherished in Buddhism: compassion.

Appreciative knowledge is almost always built upon these "shared values" that exist across multiple traditions. Shared values are simply articulations of common concerns that people of all religious and nonreligious traditions tend to share. Teaching interfaith education is the often painstaking work of identifying these shared values and learning how they are articulated in distinct and divergent ways in disparate traditions, often with profoundly different implications. A shallow reading of shared values might cause one to see such an approach as diminishing the differences between traditions, but in fact the opposite should be the case, as Fasching and deChant (2001) explored in their analysis of the shared value of nonviolence in diverse traditions. Shared values do not imply uniformity, but rather looking at the particular theologies, stories, and practices that connect to these values uncovers the real differences in how diverse communities understand and embody them: what Christianity has to say about compassion, embodied in God's love for humanity on the cross, is simply not the same thing as what Islam says in naming God "the most compassionate, the most merciful." At the same time, naming compassion as a shared value identifies the common ground from which interfaith engagement can begin.

Engaging in Relationship-Building Activities that Promote the Common Good

The bridge metaphor is useful to make a third and final theoretical point. Physical bridges must be solid enough to cross and withstand the weight of their traversers. So, too, interfaith relationships must be made of substantive material. Mere tolerance is not enough. For interfaith education to move beyond a cerebral exercise, individuals must first identify and then *act* together on issues of common concern. Pluralism, on an individual and a societal level, is imprinted through actions. There are innumerable areas of overlap in the religious and philosophical commitments of disparate communities and individuals, often oriented around the aforementioned shared values. Part of what makes shared values so central to interfaith education is that not only are they deeply held and widely shared, they can also be acted on together. Interfaith education must move beyond the classroom to devising projects that enable diverse people to work together to enact their respective commitments.

Admittedly, the religious diversity described here is not yet apparent in every corner of the United States, and the challenge to engage other communities in communal service projects may seem a bridge too far, if you will, for some. Fortunately, the same forces that are contributing to rapid diversification—travel, immigration policy, and, most notably, communications technology—can also help overcome situations where it is not as yet present. A rural Sunday School class unable to pragmatically engage face to face with the closest synagogue, mosque, or temple forty miles away need look no further than a computer to nonetheless participate in dialogue and various long-distance service projects, such as fundraising for disaster relief, fighting disease in impoverished areas, or collaboratively engaging the political process around common concerns.

Another pedagogical resource available to religious educators seeking to help their students move from a cognitive to an embodied understanding of religious pluralism is the case-study method. Popularized by Harvard Business School, the case-study method allows students to inhabit real-world situations by forcing them to wrestle with the issues at hand, not as an outside analyst, but as the protagonist themselves. Adopting and adapting this approach to questions of religious diversity, the Pluralism Project at

Harvard University, founded by Diana Eck, has developed dozens of case studies about actual situations of interreligious engagement and tension. Other interfaith organizations, including Interfaith Youth Core (where both co-authors work), have followed suit. These case studies provide an invaluable resource to interfaith educators seeking to challenge their students to grapple with and internalize the opportunities and challenges presented by religious diversity today.

SEMINARIES AS A PRIME SITE FOR INTERFAITH EDUCATION

For interfaith education to deliver on its potential to achieve social cohesion and to foster the continuity of individual and communal religious identity, clearly it needs to be adopted across the lifespan of religious education, from secondary through undergraduate to graduate and seminary education. Recently, considerable efforts have taken hold in North American undergraduate education under the umbrella of an emerging academic (sub)field of "interfaith and interreligious studies." It is worth noting, however, that seminaries are uniquely situated to play an outsized role in this process. Through their faculty, seminaries tend to have an association and collaboration with higher education more broadly by way of professional associations such as the American Academy of Religion (which since 2012 has had an "Interfaith and Interreligious Studies" working group) and the Society of Biblical Literature. Through their administration and their students, many seminaries are associated with denominational bodies, and their very purpose is to form religious leaders for the future guidance and maintenance of communities and the denomination as a whole.

Fortunately, many seminaries have already begun responding to the challenge of interfaith education. Indeed, recently there has been a dramatic growth in the number of seminaries offering courses and programs in interfaith education, due in no small part to a project undertaken by the Association of Theological Schools from 2010 to 2012. Under the leadership of Stephen Graham (2012), ATS engaged in the "Christian Hospitality and Pastoral Practices Project," which sought educational changes in its 273 member schools that prepare the majority of professional religious leaders in the United States and Canada. The aim of the project was to analyze existing curricula and effect curricular and co-curricular change within member schools "to enhance the abilities of graduates to function effectively in pastoral contexts in a multifaith society" (1). In addition to documenting the current state of the field, the project also led to a new accreditation standard concerning interfaith education for all member schools.

Even before it became a requirement, a handful of vanguard institutions had already begun to take on interfaith education proactively. Laying the groundwork for the ATS project, in 2009 Auburn Theological Seminary embarked on a survey of 150 Christian,

Jewish, Muslim, Buddhist, and multireligious institutions in the United States that train religious leaders, a first-of-its-kind study of how seminaries across the United States were dealing with the challenge to educate religious leaders for a religiously diverse world. The final report, *Beyond World Religions: The State of Multifaith Education in American Theological Schools* (Mosher and Baird 2009), identified twenty vanguard institutions that had made substantial institutional commitments to the enterprise of interfaith education. Interestingly, the list spanned religious, denominational, and political persuasions, including institutions such as Catholic Theological Union (the largest Roman Catholic graduate school of theology and ministry in North America), Fuller Theological Seminary, and the joint programs of Hebrew College and Andover-Newton Theological Seminary. Union Theological Seminary, long a front-runner in this area, recently approved a fifth field of inquiry; alongside the centuries-old foursome of Bible, Systematic Theology, Ethics, and Practical Theology, they have added a new concentration in Interreligious Engagement.

Graduates of these programs are, not surprisingly, already beginning to impact religious education across the lifespan of faith formation. In Philadelphia, the Rev. Nicole Diroff helps lead the stellar community-based "Walking the Walk" program, which annually engages over two dozen local congregational youth groups in a service- and dialogue-oriented yearlong interfaith curriculum. Elizabethtown College in Pennsylvania recently approved the first undergraduate major in interfaith studies, an effort spearheaded by the Rev. Tracy Sadd. Indeed, more often than not, the most innovative interfaith education programs for any age today are led by clergy and scholars who were theologically formed in seminaries with a long track record of engaging interfaith education.

CONCLUSION

While the conditions that contribute to the urgent need for interfaith education are distinctly modern, the central idea is nothing new. A half-century ago, the great Orthodox rabbi, scholar, civil rights leader, and Holocaust survivor Abraham Joshua Heschel gave a lecture at the Union Theological Seminary entitled "No Religion Is an Island":

> The religions of the world are no more self-sufficient, no more independent, no more isolated than individuals or nations. Energies, experiences, and ideas that come to life outside the boundaries of a particular religion or all religions continue to challenge and to affect every religion. . . . No religion is an island. We are all involved with one another. Spiritual betrayal on the part of one of us affects the faith of all of us. Views adopted in one community have an impact on other communities. Today religious isolationism is a myth. For all the profound differences in perspective and substance, Judaism is sooner or later affected by the intellectual, moral, and spiritual events within the Christian society, and vice versa. (1991, 1)

Heschel, who was a descendent of a long lineage of Eastern European Hasidic rabbis and had escaped the trains to Auschwitz by mere weeks, was articulating a concept that he knew was both central to the centuries-old tradition of Judaism and its future survival: there is no "us" without "you." Those who have embarked on the project of developing a theology or ethic of interfaith cooperation are often surprised to discover how deep and old the narrative of cooperation runs in their tradition. What is unique to the modern age is not the fact of encounter and exchange between different religious traditions, it is that the future survival of those traditions depends on those encounters becoming mutually beneficial and enriching. This is the promise and peril contained in religious pluralism: that through their interdependence religious communities are able to not only endure but thrive, and that without it they face either atrophy or internecine destruction. It is therefore critical for both the future of the American idea that "from many, we can be one" and the continuity of religious communities that we continue to see a flourishing of interfaith education across the lifespan of faith formation in this country.

FUTURE DIRECTIONS

1. To date, little longitudinal research has been done to track the correlation between intentional interfaith education and long-term religious identity. Such a longitudinal study would be invaluable in validating (or refuting) the claims made here.
2. As a nascent field, standards and benchmarks are still being established for what excellence looks like in interfaith education. Future work in this area should more clearly delineate the borders and standards of excellence.
3. Some have critiqued interfaith education for overlooking justice issues that may be present in communities of other traditions. Of course, every tradition's notion of justice is slightly distinct. How can interfaith education both acknowledge social issues in which different religious communities often diverge (e.g., LGBT rights, women's rights, abortion, the future of Israel/Palestine) while still building and maintaining authentic relationships across these lines of difference?

REFERENCES

Berger, Peter L. 1979. *The Heretical Imperative: Contemporary Possibilities of Religious Affirmation*. Garden City, NY: Anchor Books.

Eck, Diana L. 2006. *What is Pluralism?* The Harvard University Pluralism Project, accessed on January 22, 2018, www.pluralism.org/what-is-pluralism/.

Eck, Diana L. 2001. *A New Religious America: How a "Christian Country" Has Become the World's Most Religiously Diverse Nation*. New York: HarperOne.

Fasching, Darrel J., and Dell deChant. 2001. *Comparative Religious Ethics: A Narrative Approach*. Oxford: Blackwell Publishers, Ltd.

Gandhi, Mahatma. 2016. *My Experiments with Truth*. New Delhi: Rajpal & Sons.

Giddens, Anthony. 1991. *Modernity and Self-Identity: Self and Society in the Late Modern Age*. Redwood City, CA: Stanford University Press.

Graham, Stephen R. 2012. "Christian Hospitality and Pastoral Practices in a Multifaith Society: An ATS Project, 2010–2012." *Theological Education* 47, no. 1: 1–10.

Heschel, Abraham Joshua. 1991. "No Religion is an Island." In *No Religion is an Island: Abraham Joshua Heschel and Interreligious Dialogue*, edited by Harold Kasimow and Byron L. Sherwin, 3–22. Maryknoll, NY: Orbis Books.

King, Martin Luther. 1986. "The World House." In *A Testament to Hope*, edited by James M. Washington, 617–633. San Francisco: Harper Collins.

King, Martin Luther. 1960. "Pilgrimage to Nonviolence," *Christian Century*, April 13, 1960. In *The Papers of Martin Luther King, Jr., Volume V: Threshold of a New Decade, January 1959–December 1960,* Clayborne Carson, Tenisha Armstrong, Susan Carson, Adrienne Clay, and Kerry Taylor, (Eds.). Berkeley: University of California Press, 2005.

Knitter, Paul F. 2002. *Introducing Theologies of Religions*. Maryknoll, NY: Orbis Books.

Lama, The Dalai. 2010. *Toward a True Kinship of Faiths: How the World's Religions Can Come Together*. New York: Three Rivers Press.

Mosher, Lucinda, and Justus Baird. December 14, 1009. *Beyond World Religions: The State of Multifaith Education in American Theological Schools*. New York: Center for Multifaith Education, Auburn Theological Seminary.

Patel, Eboo and Cassie Meyer. 2015. "Youth and Interfaith Conflict Transformation," In *The Oxford Handbook of Religion, Conflict, and Peacebuilding*, Atalia Omer, R. Scott Appleby, and David Little, (Eds.), 479. New York: Oxford.

Prothero, Steven. 2010. *God Is Not One: The Eight Rival Religions That Run the World*. New York: HarperOne.

Putnam, Robert, and David Campbell. 2010. *American Grace: How Religion Divides and Unites Us*. New York: Simon and Schuster.

Putnam, Robert, and Lewis M. Feldstein. 2003. *Better Together: Restoring the American Community*. New York: Simon & Schuster.

Rauf, Feisal Abdul. 2004. *What's Right with Islam Is What's Right with America*. New York: HarperCollins.

Sacks, Jonathan. 2002. *The Dignity of Difference: How to Avoid the Clash of Civilizations*. New York: Continuum.

Smith, Christian, with Melinda Lundquist Denton. 2005. *Soul Searching: The Religious and Spiritual Lives of American Teenagers*. New York: Oxford University Press.

Smith, Wilfred Cantwell. 1962. *The Faith of Other Men*. New York: New American Library.

Stedman, Chris. 2012. *Faitheist: How an Atheist Found Common Ground with the Religious*. Boston: Beacon Press.

Stern, Jessica. 2004. *Terror in the Name of God: Why Religious Militants Kill*. New York, NY: Harper Perennial.

Varshney, Ashutosh. 2002. *Ethnic Conflict and Civic Life: Hindus and Muslims in India*. New Haven, CT: Yale University Press.

Volf, Miroslav. 2011. *A Public Faith: How Followers of Christ Should Serve the Common Good*. Grand Rapids, Michigan: Brazos Press.

Walzer, Michael. 1996. *What It Means to Be an American*. New York: Marsilio Publishers.

Further Reading

Baird, Justus. 2013. "Multifaith Education in American Theological Schools: Looking Back, Looking Ahead." *Teaching Theology & Religion* 16, no. 4: 309–321.

Berling, Judith. 2004. *Understanding Other Religious Worlds: A Guide for Interreligious Education*. Maryknoll, NY: Orbis Books.

Boys, Mary C., and Sara S. Lee. 2006. *Christians & Jews in Dialogue: Learning in the Presence of the Other*. Woodstock, VT: Skylight Paths.

Cornille, Catherine, ed. 2013. *The Wiley-Blackwell Companion to Inter-Religious Dialogue (Wiley-Blackwell Companions to Religion)*. Malden, MA: John Wiley & Sons, Ltd.

Cunningham, David, ed. Forthcoming. *Hearing Vocation Differently*. Oxford: Oxford University Press.

Davis, Adam, eds. 2009. *Hearing the Call Across Traditions: Readings on Faith and Service*. Woodstock, VT: Skylight Paths Press.

Eck, Diana L. 1993. *Encountering God: A Spiritual Journey from Bozeman to Banaras*. Boston: Beacon Press.

Heckman, Bud, and Rori Picker Neiss, eds. 2008. *Interactive Faith: The Essential Interreligious Community Building Handbook*. Woodstock, VT: Skylight Paths Publishing.

Jacobsen, Douglas, and Rhonda Hustedt Jacobsen. 2012. *No Longer Invisible: Religion in University Education*. Oxford: Oxford University Press.

Marty, Martin E. 1997. *The One and the Many: America's Struggle for the Common Good*. Cambridge, MA: Harvard University Press.

Mays, Rebecca Kratz, ed. 2008. *Interfaith Dialogue at the Grass Roots*. Philadelphia: Ecumenical Press.

McCarthy, Kate. 2007. *Interfaith Encounters in America*. New Brunswick, NJ: Rutgers University Press.

Moore, Diane. 2007. *Overcoming Religious Illiteracy: A Cultural Studies Approach to the Study of Religion in Secondary Education*. New York: Palgrave.

Nash, Robert, et al. 2008. *How To Talk About Hot Topics on Campus: From Polarization to Moral Conversation*. San Francisco: Jossey-Bass.

Niebuhr, Gustav. 2008. *Beyond Tolerance: Searching for Interfaith Understanding in America*. New York: Viking Penguin.

Patel, Eboo. 2007. *Acts of Faith: The Story of an American Muslim, the Struggle for the Soul of a Generation*. Boston: Beacon Press.

———. 2012. *Sacred Ground: Pluralism, Prejudice, and the Promise of America*. Boston: Beacon Press.

———. 2016. *Interfaith Leadership: A Primer*. Boston: Beacon Press.

Patel, Eboo, and Patrice Brodeur. 2006. *Building the Interfaith Youth Movement: Beyond Dialogue to Action*. Lanham, Boulder, New York, Toronto, and Oxford: Rowman & Littlefield Publishers, Inc.

Patel, Eboo, and Cassie Meyer. 2010. "Defining Religious Pluralism." *Journal of College and Character* 11, no. 2.

———. 2011. "The Civic Relevance of Interfaith Cooperation for Colleges and Universities." *Journal of College and Character* 12, no. 1.

———. 2011. "Teaching Interfaith Literacy." *Journal of College and Character* 12, no. 4.

Patel, Eboo, Jennifer Howe Peace and Noah J. Silverman, eds. Forthcoming. Interreligious/ Interfaith Studies: Defining a New Field Boston: Beacon Press.

Peace, Jennifer, Or Rose and Gregory Mobley, eds. 2012. *My Neighbor's Faith: Stories of Interreligious Encounter, Growth and Transformation*. New York: Orbis Books.

Prothero, Steven. 2007. Religious *Literacy: What Every American Needs to Know—and Doesn't*. New York: HarperOne.

Putnam, Robert D. 2007. "*E Pluribus Unum*: Diversity and Community in the Twenty-first Century. The 2006 Johan Skytte Prize Lecture." *Scandinavian Political Studies* 30, no. 2: 137–174.

Roozen, David A., and Heidi Hadsell. 2009. *Changing the Way Seminaries Teach: Pedagogies for Interfaith Dialogue*. Hartford, CT: Hartford Seminary.

Wuthnow, Robert. 2005. *America and the Challenges of Religious Diversity*. Princeton, NJ: Princeton University Press.

PART III

FAITH-BASED K-12 EDUCATION

CHAPTER 11

PRIVATE RELIGIOUS SCHOOLS

CHARLES J. RUSSO, KATE E. SOULES,
ADINA C. NEWMAN, AND SUSAN L. DOUGLASS

INTRODUCTION

ONE of the greatest strengths of the American educational system is the rich diversity of choices it offers parents in the form of public and nonpublic elementary and secondary schools, along with the wide array of options available in public schools, when selecting where they wish to have their children educated. The Supreme Court protected parents' right to choose where their children are to be educated in its 1925 opinion in *Pierce v. Society of Sisters* (1925). *Pierce* is often referred to as the Magna Carta of American nonpublic schools, including those that are faith-based (sometimes also referred to as private or parochial), because it upheld the rights of these institutions to educate young Americans in the religious traditions their parents requested.

Acknowledging parents' right to direct the upbringing of their children in *Pierce*, a unanimous Supreme Court ruled that Oregon's compulsory attendance law, which essentially forbade parents from sending their children to nonpublic schools, was unconstitutional. Protecting the rights of parents to choose where their children would be educated, the Justices eloquently reasoned that "[t]he child is not the mere creature of the state; those who nurture him and direct his destiny have the right, coupled with the high duty, to recognize and prepare him for additional obligations" (*Pierce* 1925, 535).

Against this background, and in light of the long, fruitful history of faith-based nonpublic schools, this chapter provides an overview of the rich history and development of nonpublic schools in the United States. The chapter reviews the history of faith-based nonpublic schools in essentially an historical sequence, demonstrating how the educational system opened its doors in welcoming the diversity central to burgeoning religious and cultural communities. We start by reviewing the history of Protestant elementary and secondary schools before examining developments in Roman Catholic, Jewish, and Islamic schools, and we end with questions for further study challenging readers to make up their own minds about the future direction of faith-based nonpublic schools.

PROTESTANT SCHOOLS

The American education system has its roots in Protestant schooling from the earliest European settlers in British North America. Early colonists in Massachusetts adopted the "Ye old deluder Satan Act" in 1647, requiring towns of a specified sizes to provide for the education of their children (Fraser 1999). The "ye old deluder" statute, so called because it was created to combat Satan's desire to delude people into ignorance of scriptures in order to lead them to damnation, required all towns with more than fifty households to establish and maintain schools. Further, the act imposed fines on officials who did not follow the law. Retaining its original spelling, the statute declares:

> It being one chiefe project of ye ould deluder, Satan, to keepe men from the knowledge of ye Scriputures,. . . . [i]t is therefore ordred, yt evry towneship . . . [with fifty households shall] forthwith appoint one . . . to teach all such children . . . to write & reade [and] whose wages shall be paid eithr by ye parents or mastrs of such children, or by ye inhabitants in genrall" (Commager 1965, 29).

This act, and similar laws in other colonies, aimed to ensure that children were literate by having direct access to scripture. Protestant values, imagery, and doctrine infused early schools and education in the British colonies. The *New England Primer*, one of the most commonly used schoolbooks in the colonies and the early United States, is a prime example of the pervasiveness of Protestantism in education, as it teaches literacy and numeracy through rhymes, parables, prayers, and lessons derived directly from scripture and Puritan theology (Nord 1995).

As the new nation began to take shape in the nineteenth century, the Protestant influence on education continued. The common schools, championed by Horace Mann and an early iteration of public education, were officially nonsectarian, but in reality they were still deeply Protestant in character, using the Protestant King James translation of the Bible and Protestant versions of prayers—although this Protestantism was often conflated with civic virtues (Macedo 2000; Nord 1995).

At the time, many Protestants embraced the ecumenical Protestant Christianity, stripped of denominational particularities, of the common schools in support of creating a common national identity and promoting the assimilation of new immigrants (Macedo 2000; Nord 1995). Even so, other Christian groups opposed the nonsectarian nature of the common schools. While Catholic opposition to the common schools

received considerable attention in the second half of the nineteenth century, earlier opposition to common schools came from Protestant denominations.

German Lutheran immigrants to Pennsylvania established their own schools. These
schools preserved Lutheran orthodoxy but also helped to maintain the minority language and culture of the communities (Glenn 1988). By the 1870s, the Missouri Synod
supported over 400 schools serving over 26,000 students (Glenn 1988). Orthodox
Presbyterians also sought to maintain a separate identity and began to create their own
network of schools (Fraser 1999; Glenn 1988). However, the Presbyterian school system
was short-lived—as the public school movement grew and became more successful,
Presbyterians did not want to be viewed as separate from the American public
(Fraser 1999).

The Protestant schools in the nineteenth century that were able to maintain their
own identities outside of the common school system were often those connected to
communities with unique linguistic or ethnic identities. Attempts of other mainline
denominations to create their own school systems in the mid-nineteenth century rarely
gained traction. As Catholics began to push for a share of the public school funding for
their own schools, many Protestants put aside denominational differences to support a
public school system that was still firmly grounded in Protestant practices and values
(Glenn 1988).

Over the course of the nineteenth century and the early/mid-twentieth century,
the common schools gradually become more secular and morphed into the present public school system. Protestant private schools that remained were generally closely tied to particular denominations. As a series of Supreme Court cases
removed remaining religious practices, such as daily Bible reading and school-
sponsored prayers, from public schools (*Engel v. Vitale* 1962; *Abington Township
v. Schempp* 1963), private schools became a refuge from public schools that some conservative evangelicals saw as morally inadequate or hostile to spiritual values (Laats
2012). The number of private Protestant schools grew dramatically starting in the
mid-1960s, and 90% of the Protestant schools in operation today were founded after
that time (Cardus 2011).

As of 2012, approximately 12,800 Protestant schools served over 1.3 million students
(Broughman and Swaim 2013). Protestant schools make up 42% of private schools and
61% of all religiously affiliated private schools. Approximately 4,500 of the schools
are identified as conservative Christian schools, although another large portion
of schools do not affiliate with a particular denomination (Broughman and Swaim
2013). Over a third of non-Catholic religious schools simply identify as "Christian
(unspecified)" (Broughman and Swaim 2013, 7). Baptist schools make up another 15%.
While many denominations have only a small number of schools, denominations
with notable numbers of schools (making up more than 5% of all Protestant schools)
include Seventh-day Adventists, Amish, Mennonites, and Missouri Synod Lutherans
(Broughman and Swaim 2013).

The diffuse nature of Protestantism and the lack of comprehensive governing bodies
make it challenging to get a detailed picture of the landscape of Protestant schools.

A handful of associations, such as the Council for American Private Education, the American Association of Christian Schools, and the Association of Christian Schools International, regularly gather data on the schools as well as provide resources, advocacy, and networking to member schools. While some schools emphasize the doctrine of a particular denomination, others play down denominational differences in favor of advocating Christian teachings and lifestyle more generally.

The motivations for families to send their children to these schools can vary widely. Some families view the public school system as hostile to their moral and spiritual values and seek schools that will nurture those values (Sikkink 1999). A thread of anti-public school rhetoric within conservative Protestant Christianity promotes private education and homeschooling as the only moral alternative to public schools that are painted as failing, both academically and spiritually. For other families, Protestant schools simply offer more intimate educational settings aligned with their religious values. Despite the great variation among Protestant schools, they generally prioritize the religious development of their students and place a high value on the role of family, church, school, and community to support this development (Uecker 2008).

As with all private schools, Protestant schools must compete for students in a crowded educational marketplace. Protestant schools tend to be relatively small, averaging about 100 to 150 students (Broughman and Swaim 2013). They must balance being affordable for families while being able to offer quality education and opportunities to attract families that might otherwise choose public schools.

The average yearly tuition for Protestant schools can range from $8,000 to over $16,000, putting private education out of reach for many families, although in some states tuition vouchers may help to offset some of those costs ("Private School Facts," 2016). When private Protestant schools are financially out of reach, other families may choose to homeschool their children or to explore the idea of "missionary schooling," sending Christian students to public schools to serve as witnesses or missionaries for their faith.

Protestant schools represent a broad set of Christian social and theological beliefs. Some conservative Christian schools face criticism for curricula that promote a creationist view of science or conservative perspectives on sexual health education and gender roles. One of the challenges for Protestant schools as they continue to evolve into the twenty-first century will be finding ways to balance their theological values and identities with changing social norms and helping students to negotiate the tensions that may arise, especially for more socially and theologically conservative schools. Schools will need to navigate tensions between their beliefs and doctrine with laws on discrimination based on sexual orientation and gender identity and insurance requirements for funding contraceptives. As the United States becomes increasingly religiously diverse and as secularism becomes more a part of public discourse, Protestant schools will be tasked with maintaining their unique identity while preparing their students for an increasingly complex society.

Protestant schools are far from being a unified group. With roots in the earliest schools in the country, they are an important part of the fabric of American education.

As they continue to respond to the needs of Protestant families and students, these schools will continue to offer a wide range of educational options while espousing many different perspectives on both faith and schooling.

ROMAN CATHOLIC SCHOOLS

Roman Catholic elementary and secondary education has long been a major force for the common good in American elementary and secondary education (Bryk, Lee, and Holland 1993). As with many kinds of institutions, though, there is ebb and flow as closures in cities such as Buffalo ("10 Catholic Elementary Schools to Close," 2014), home to some of the oldest Catholic schools in the nation, have been common over the past fifty years. Yet, growth is on the horizon as new Roman Catholic elementary and secondary schools continue to open in such ethnically diverse locations as various parts of Florida (Matus 2013).

Enrollment in Roman Catholic schools peaked during the 1965–66 school year, when there were more than 5.4 million students in almost 13,000 schools across the nation (Mahr 1984, xi). However, the 1970s and 1980s witnessed a steep decline in the number of both Catholic schools and their students. Despite this steady decline, Catholic schools, as a single denomination, as opposed to amorphously identified Christian schools encompassing a variety of religious traditions, remain the largest nonpublic school "system" in the United States insofar as they account for 19.9% of children enrolled in faith-based nonpublic schools (US Department of Education 2016, 6).

In reality, though, using the language of organizational theory, Catholic schools are not so much a system as a loosely coupled collection of independent schools sharing a common belief system: many of them act independently of strict diocesan requirements and controls. Even as the number of Catholic schools and their share of the student population have declined over the past half-century, they continue to offer an array of options for children from a variety of socioeconomic and ethnic backgrounds throughout the United States.

History

Amid a growing tide of anti-Catholic sentiment, American Catholic bishops gathered at the Third Plenary Council of Baltimore in 1884 and issued a declaration that has had a dramatic impact in shaping the face of education in the United States. The Council issued a statement, to the effect, that there will be a parish school near every Catholic church, and were one does not yet exist, one will be erected and maintained by the Church in perpetuity (McCloskey 1964, 94). The Council added that "all Catholic parents are bound to send their children to the parish school, unless it is evident that a sufficient training in religion is given either in their own home, or in other Catholic schools" (McCloskey 1964, 94).

Following the Council's dictate, Catholic education embarked on a period of remarkable growth as the rapidly increasing Catholic immigrant population was augmented by a seemingly endless supply of priests, brothers, and nuns to staff the schools. In fact, combined with the rapidly growing immigrant population that was largely unwelcome in many public schools, by the turn of the century, the 200 Catholic schools in operation in 1860 grew to about 5,000 a decade after the council (Mahr 1987). During this same time, the number of Catholics in the United States rose from 7,855,000 in 1890 to an incredible 17,735,553 in 1920 (Buetow 1970, 167, citing the *Official Catholic Directory*).

In conjunction with this growth spurt, Catholic and other nonpublic schools received a major boost from the unanimous 1925 ruling of the US Supreme Court in *Pierce*. *Pierce* was filed by Roman Catholic nuns and officials from the Hill Military Academy in a challenge to Oregon's compulsory attendance law, which essentially would have required all parents, other than those who today would be categorized as in need of special education, to attend only public schools.

Relying of the Fourteenth Amendment rather than the Religion Clauses of the First Amendment to the Constitution, the *Pierce* Court invalidated Oregon's compulsory attendance law, with its animus toward nonpublic schools, particularly Roman Catholic ones, as unconstitutional. The Court struck the law down because it would have deprived the operators of the schools of their property interests without providing them with their Fourteenth Amendment rights to due process. Moreover, the *Pierce* Court noted that while state officials may oversee such important features as health, safety, and teacher qualifications relating to the operation of nonpublic schools, they could not do so to a greater extent than they do for public schools.

The law largely would have prevented most parents from sending their children to the nonpublic schools of their choice. Limiting parents' rights in such a manner, the Supreme Court pointed out, was unconstitutional because it "unreasonably interfere[d] with the liberty of parents and guardians to direct the upbringing and education of children under their control" (*Pierce* 1925, 534–535). *Pierce* thus protected the right of parents to have their children educated in the nonpublic schools of their choice.

Enrollment Development and Challenges

The growth of Catholic education in the United States peaked in 1965, at which time there were 5,481,300 children enrolled in Catholic schools (Mahr 1984, xi). Catholic schools entered a period of steady decline little more than a decade later: in 1979–80, this figure declined more than 2 million to 3,269,800 students. As of the 2015–16 school year, the 6,525 Catholic schools in the United States (5,325 elementary and 1,200 secondary) enrolled 1,915,836 students, 1,337,630 in elementary/middle schools and 578,206 in secondary schools (McDonald and Schultz 2017). At the start of the academic year, 14 new schools opened, 86 schools consolidated or closed, and 1,795 schools have waiting lists for admission (McDonald and Schultz 2017).

In an effort to stem these enrollment declines, Roman Catholic schools attracted more diverse student bodies. At the start of the 2015–16 school year, 20.3% of students in Roman Catholic elementary and secondary schools were racial minorities; 16.1% were Hispanic/Latino and 6.5% were reported as unknown in the racial data collection. Non-Catholic enrollment in the schools stood at 333,679, or 17.4% of total enrollments.

Enrollment declines in Roman Catholic schools can be attributed to a variety of overlapping factors, including the following:

1. The birth rate has sharply diminished, in general as well as for Catholics.
2. Catholic families have moved out of large urban areas such as Boston, Chicago, and New York to locations where Catholic schools were unavailable. This trend is starting to be overcome in states such as Florida.
3. Costs of tuition and fees at Catholic schools have increased.
4. Catholic parents have shown greater acceptance of the public schools insofar as Catholics were more easily able to enter the mainstream (particularly after John F. Kennedy became the first, and to date only, member of the Roman Catholic Church to become president) by eschewing Catholic schools.
5. Social attitudes have changed.

A closely related factor was the dramatic decline in the number of women and men who entered the religious life. Because of this precipitous drop, a greater percentage of lay faculty and administrators were hired in Catholic schools. In 1920, 92% of teachers in Catholic schools were members of religious orders; in 1940, there were 91.2%; in 1950, there were 90.1% (McDonald and Schultz 2014, 3). Dramatic change was in the offing: the percentage of lay teachers rose to 26.2% in 1960, 51.6% in 1970, 71.0% in 1980, 85.4% in 1990, 93.0% in 2001, and 96.3% in 2010 (McDonald & Schultz 2014, 3). As of the 2016–17 school year, the percentage of lay teachers in Catholic schools was 97.2% (74.7% are women and 22.5% are men); only 2.8% are members of religious communities or clergy (1.8% are sisters, 0.5% are brothers, and 0.5% are priests) (McDonald and Schultz 2017). This change had a major impact on American Catholic education, both financially and in presenting a challenge to the ability of individual schools to maintain their Catholic identities.

From the time of its inception in the United States until the late 1960s, education was the all-but-exclusive mission of members of religious orders in the Roman Catholic Church for two closely related reasons. First, education was a traditional mission of Catholic religious communities of women and men. Teaching orders migrated from Europe to the United States in the nineteenth century to staff the burgeoning number of Catholic schools. A growing number of religious communities established in the United States focused on teaching as their primary work. The second reason was a financial one: given the rapid growth of Catholic education, it would have been all but impossible to have provided appropriate compensation for lay staff. Not surprisingly, the economic necessity presented little alternative but for the religious to continue to staff and operate Catholic schools. This problem was exacerbated because Catholic schools continued to charge minimal tuition, did not devise long-term plans for their financial well-being, and did not adjust their plans for such costs until the steady, virtually irreversible, decline was well under way.

Amid a variety of social changes sweeping across the United States, until the mid-twentieth century, a steady supply of American Roman Catholics entered the religious life. This seemingly endless supply of vocations to the religious life actually began to run dry at the end of World War II. Catholic historian Harold Buetow (1970) reported that the post-1945 decline in the number of people who entered the religious life can be attributed to the low birth rate during the Great Depression coupled with the toll taken by World War II on religious staff in Catholic schools.

Given the amount of time and education needed to meet the upgraded standards of teacher education in the post-World War II United States and world, there was an unavoidable lapse of time before the declining ranks of properly prepared religious teachers could join the faculties of Catholic schools. Concomitantly, as members of religious orders received greater freedom to pursue opportunities of their own interest within the religious life, as opposed to obediently accepting assignments to teach, fewer and fewer turned to education, preferring to work in a variety of other fields involving the social sciences.

Four major challenges, the first three of which are closely intertwined, confront Catholic education today. First, Catholic school leaders must deal with the steady decline in enrollments since the mid-1960s. To date, educational leaders have taken tentative steps to resolving the enrollment crisis by seeking to attract increasing numbers of students from diverse economic, cultural, religious, ethnic, and racial backgrounds, including the disabled.

A second issue is to define the Catholic character of these schools so as to maintain their unique identity at a time when increasing numbers of their students are not active members of the Catholic Church. This is an especially challenging task for the many Catholic schools located in inner-city neighborhoods where populations are largely not Roman Catholic.

Third, Catholic schools must find a way to remain a financially viable option for parents at a time of rising costs associated with operating schools. During the 2013–14 school year the average tuition in Catholic elementary schools was $3,880, with actual costs of $5,847; the mean first-year tuition in Catholic secondary schools was $9,622, with actual costs of $11,790 (McDonald and Schultz 2014, 18). The differences between tuition charged and actual per-pupil costs are typically covered by contributions from the parishes, religious orders, and dioceses sponsoring the schools. These tuition charges are undoubtedly daunting for many families because Catholic schools maintain a commitment to serving the poor, many of whom cannot afford to pay tuition. Yet even at these tuition rates, insofar as staff members in Roman Catholic schools seek to earn living wages, educational leaders must find ways of acquiring sufficient funds without driving the cost so high that even more families leave these schools.

In light of the persistent lack of religious personnel, a fourth challenge for Catholic school leaders is continuing to identify and prepare new generations of lay staff for their schools. As salaries remain low and the hours relatively long, leaders must find ways of ensuring a steady supply of qualified and dedicated educators who can work in the Catholic schools.

Despite their many past successes, American Catholic schools face a less than clearly charted course for the future. However, even as Catholic schools address uncertainty, they will likely continue to make meaningful contributions to American education for many years into the future.

JEWISH SCHOOLS

According to the 2013–14 census conducted by the Avi Chai Foundation, a private foundation endowed to encourage commitment to Judaism and mutual understanding among all of Jewish traditions, there were 255,000 students age four through twelfth grade enrolled in 861 Jewish day schools in thirty-seven states and the District of Columbia, an increase of 70,000 students since the first census of its kind in 1998–99 (Wertheimer 2008). Most of this growth is attributed to surges in New York and New Jersey, which account for three-quarters of all day school students, while day school enrollment elsewhere remained relatively stable over the same fifteen-year period.

The number of students enrolled in Jewish day schools is projected to reach 300,000 by the next census in 2018–19 (Schick 2014). A salient feature of these day schools is their small size: 40% of them serve fewer than 100 students and another 20% serve between 101 and 200 students. Yet, although in the aggregate American Jewish day schools are on the rise, the future of these schools differs vastly according to their religious affiliation, and this has varying implications for American Jewish education in the twenty-first century.

The origins of Jewish education in the United States can be traced to the birth of the nation, although private Jewish day schools were not a staple of Jewish education until well into the twentieth century. During the colonial and early national periods, Jewish education focusing on lessons for liturgical purposes, including basic knowledge in Hebrew reading and Torah, was provided primarily by tutors in private homes and was not considered a communal responsibility. Congregation Shearith Israel in New York City ran a day school sporadically in the decades immediately prior to and after the American Revolution, but it eventually evolved into a charity school to offer the poor both a secular and Jewish education until 1825, when the state ceased funding of all religiously sponsored charity schools (Graff 2008; Sarna 1998).

A common thread binding each educational model throughout the history of American Jewish education is the desire to balance acculturation into the American mainstream while simultaneously maintaining Jewish identity; how to achieve the latter effectively has served as a prominent source of debate for two centuries. With nondenominational public schools beginning to proliferate in the early nineteenth century, many Jews, including recent emigrants from German-speaking lands, viewed public education as a conduit to the American way of life.

The increase in formally organized Jewish congregations precipitated the creation of Jewish Sunday schools that instilled students with knowledge about God, stories from the Hebrew Bible, and basic Hebrew reading skills to participate in a synagogue prayer service (Graff 2008). The arrival of Sunday schools highlighted the preeminence of public schools in their charge to inculcate American values within Jewish youth, while also providing a modicum of Jewish education and a defensive measure against Christian missionary attempts.

The influx of German Jewish immigrants, though, also elicited the emergence of private Jewish day schools during the mid-nineteenth century. For reasons that included uncertainty about public school educational outcomes, apprehension about what some perceived as the Protestant domination of American public schools (Sarna 1998), and the lack of time necessary to deliver an adequate Jewish education on a part-time basis, these immigrants founded more than two dozen private Jewish day schools dedicated to both secular and Judaic studies as well as the German language to maintain their cultural roots (Graff 2008). Nevertheless, as public schools became the sole recipients of state funding and garnered a reputation of success, by 1875 all Jewish day schools had closed and were replaced by various supplementary options, such as Jewish Sunday schools, Sabbath schools, and other afternoon options.

Beginning in the late nineteenth century and lasting to World War I, the third wave of immigration brought around 2 million Jews to the United States along with their supplementary educational options, including so-called Talmud Torahs and *hadarim*, which both offered varying degrees of religious instruction in Yiddish. Secular Yiddish schools with socialist proclivities to instill *Yiddishkeit* (Yiddish culture) among their students as an alternative to American public schools were also founded. Programs committed to modern Hebrew language immersion and cultural Zionism also became popular during this period, and instruction in Hebrew language became a staple of synagogue-based schools—Hebrew schools—that still pervades congregational schools and Zionist-leaning day schools into the present.

Although private Jewish day schools began to reopen, they were not a popular option in the early decades of the twentieth century insofar as they were mostly under the auspices of Orthodox Judaism. By 1939, all but three of the thirty day schools in the United States were in New York. These schools included modern Orthodox coeducational schools, such as the Ramaz School in New York City and the Maimonides School just outside of Boston, that integrated both Jewish and secular education for its students and still exist today (Graff 2008).

The impact of World War II was the major catalyst for private Jewish day school education in the United States. With the Holocaust generating the need to sustain the Jewish people and the establishment of the state of Israel eliciting pride in Jewish identity, Jewish education had a new purpose and direction beginning in the mid-twentieth century. Refugees immediately prior to and after the war included ultra-Orthodox groups that created their own networks of day schools. Torah Umesorah, the network for several Orthodox schools, grew from 14,000 students in 1946 to 260,000 students under its auspices today.

Non-Orthodox Jewish networks were also founded in the decades after World War II to unite their respective Jewish day schools: the Conservative Solomon Schechter Day School Association, the Reform Progressive Association of Reform Day Schools, and RAVSAK for community day schools, which all lasted until 2016, when there was a shift for collaboration among non-Orthodox school networks. There may be wide discrepancies in affiliation and practice—both religious and educational—within these school networks; for instance, Torah Umesorah includes a wide spectrum from modern Orthodox schools that integrate the secular and religious to yeshivas and Chassidic schools dedicated to more Judaic and religious instruction. However, such networks provide support for school sustainability, professional development, and other educational resources to promote day school success.

In the twenty-first century, Jewish day schools can be divided into two main categories: Orthodox and non-Orthodox. The Orthodox category, which includes Chassidic, Yeshiva World, Chabad, Centrist Orthodox, Modern Orthodox, and Immigrant/Outreach, constitute 87% of students, with the former two groups alone representing 60% of the day school population. In contrast, Reform and Conservative day schools experienced a sharp decline in the twenty-first century, with these schools enrolling only 5% of Jewish day school students compared to 12% just fifteen years prior. Much of this decrease can be attributed to sharp drops in enrollment from elementary to middle school and then from middle to high school, as parents believe they have given their children sufficient Jewish education in their earlier years and must consider college by saving tuition money and sending their children to secondary schools with perceived higher academic prestige (Schick 2014). Paralleling the migration of Jews since the 1960s from metropolitan areas to smaller communities, nondenominational, self-determining, and pluralistic community day schools also fall under the banner of non-Orthodox and have remained stable at 8% of day school students over the same period.

The future trajectories and challenges for Orthodox and non-Orthodox Jewish day schools are not comparable. With continued growth for Orthodox Jewish day schools, especially those that are the most religious on the spectrum due to the high fertility rates among the population, issues relate to finding sufficient facility space, trained teachers, and resources to meet the high demand. In contrast, non-Orthodox Jewish day schools face a steep uphill battle. Three major challenges frame this future. First, the cost of private Jewish day school education can be exorbitant, in many cases rivaling that of college tuition. Providing both a Jewish and secular education is expensive and requires large endowments achieved through fundraising and philanthropic efforts.

Initiatives to provide affordability and sustainability among Jewish day schools are vital for their future as well as the future of American Jewry. With more than half of Jews intermarrying (the rate is 71% among non-Orthodox Jews) (Lugo et al. 2013) and with enrollment in supplementary schools ostensibly on the decline (Wertheimer 2008), Jewish day schools are perceived as a beacon of hope, with graduates less likely to date outside the religion and more likely to be involved in Jewish activities and leadership at the college level (Chertok et al. 2007).

A second challenge for Jewish day schools is proving their value over other options in the educational marketplace. Jewish day schools must compete not only against free public school options, including the recent onset of Hebrew charter schools (see chapter 14 in this volume), but also against other private schools that may be perceived as better equipped to prepare students for postsecondary education. Other concerns about Jewish day schools include the lack of diversity and resources for students with special learning needs.

Because Jewish day schools are disproportionately smaller, they may offer fewer academic and extracurricular opportunities, and this may be undesirable to families. Yet, according to research conducted by Brandeis University, alumni of non-Orthodox Jewish high schools felt prepared academically on par with graduates from independent private high schools in history, writing, and study skills; exhibited the highest level of academic confidence; felt the greatest support from their teachers; were involved in college life and Jewish activities; and displayed a strong sense of civic responsibility (Chertok et al. 2007). Non-Orthodox Jewish day schools need to track and market their achievements to recruit not only students but also donors.

Finally, the landscape of non-Orthodox Jewish day schools is likely to continue its shift away from denominational affiliation. With only a handful of Reform day schools and Conservative day schools continuing to close *en masse*, Jewish community day schools are ostensibly the future of non-Orthodox private Jewish day school education. The recent disbandment of non-Orthodox school networks and organizations dedicated to Jewish day school sustainability and educational leadership to form Prizmah: Center for Jewish Day Schools as the "one-stop shopping" for individualized and holistic guidance and reform highlights the trend to move beyond denominational affiliation to maintain and strengthen the non-Orthodox Jewish day school movement. Educational stakeholders will need to continue collaborating toward a pluralistic vision, while also tackling the issues previously discussed, in order for non-Orthodox Jewish day schools to remain a viable option in the United States.

ISLAMIC SCHOOLS

Educational institutions were the first organizations that Muslims developed as a community in the United States, often as a program within mosques (Islamic houses of worship). Schools developed first among African-American Muslims, and mostly from the 1970s among immigrant Muslims. The most widespread form of Islamic education takes place in weekend schools attached to mosques and Islamic centers, while full-time Islamic schools serve a smaller percentage of Muslim children. There are limited data on various types of schooling, but several studies have produced a reliably accurate overview, and institutional means for updating this information have been established.

Weekend Schools

Mosques (in Arabic, *masjid*, or place of bowing in prayer) are the primary Islamic institutions established by American Muslims. They range from prayer rooms to architecturally significant structures raised by local communities. A national survey conducted by Ihsan Bagby in 1994 counted 962 mosques, another 2001 study counted 1,209, and the third, in 2011, identified 2,106 mosques. The first two studies found that 71% hosted education programs for children and youth and 46% provided adult education (Bagby 2012, 4; Bagby, Perl, and Froehle 2001, 13).

Attendance figures from the 2001 study yielded estimates that 29,500 adults and 79,600 children and teens attended mosque education programs. These data were not part of the 2011 study, but average Friday attendance of 353 people at each mosque found in the 2011 study yielded an estimated 200,000 adults and children in such programs (Bagby 2012, 4–7).

Weekend schools teach children who attend public or private schools basic knowledge about Islamic beliefs, worship practices such as the Five Pillars, and the values that undergird them. Recitation and memorization of the Qur'an and Arabic instruction supports these basic objectives. Apart from the Arabic Qur'an itself, weekend schools generally use English-language instructional materials published in the United States (Khan, Husain, and Masood 2005). Weekend schools are an essential link to religious knowledge, cultural heritage, and social integration among a highly diverse Muslim population.

Homeschooling

A small but significant number of Muslim parents, like their Christian counterparts, choose homeschooling as an alternative to public or private education. In the early 1990s, Cynthia Sulaiman established the Muslim Home School Network and Resource (MHSNR), which provided legal advice, links to homeschooling associations, and recommended resources. Priscilla Martinez (2009) documented the rationales and varieties of Muslim practice in homeschooling and their connections to multidenominational American homeschool organizations.

Ikhlas Homeschool is a website with information for Muslim families that also publishes the *Muslim Home School in America* journal. There are many local and regional Muslim homeschooling networks and cooperative organizations, some of which collaborate across confessional lines. Muslim homeschooling experiences range from providing basic education in a close-to-home environment for only younger children, to adventurous K-12 programs linked to local enrichment programs in parks, science centers, astronomy clubs, museums, and theaters, as well as cooperative learning in which homeschooling families share their professional expertise to offer specialized courses at the secondary level.

Full-Time Islamic Schools

Clara Muhammad Schools were the first formal Muslim schools developed in North America, founded in 1932 by the wife of Nation of Islam (NOI) founder Elijah Muhammad. These primary and secondary schools aimed to implement NOI's values, knowledge, and self-help model (Rashid and Muhammad 1992). By 1975, there were forty-one University of Islam schools, the largest of which were well equipped, served K-12 students, and had certified teachers and bus fleets. In 1975 Elijah Muhammad's son W. D. Muhammad led most of the NOI community into mainstream Sunni Islam, and the schools underwent a corresponding transition in training, leadership, and curriculum, especially in Islamic studies and the social studies curriculum; conferences were held during the 1980s for this purpose (Skerry 2005).

From a high of forty-one schools in the 1970s, the Clara Muhammad Schools declined to about thirty in the early 1990s. The Mohammed Schools Consortium of the U.S. and Bermuda currently lists twenty-four schools of various types. The Mohammed School of Atlanta is described as "the only private African-American Muslim school accredited by the Georgia Accrediting Commission (GAC), the Commission on International and Trans-Regional Accreditation (CITA), and Southern Association of Colleges and Schools (SACS)." Cities listed with full-time schools are Detroit; Atlanta; Corona, New York; Baltimore; Oakland; Los Angeles; Brooklyn; New Medina, Mississippi; Philadelphia; Little Rock; Milwaukee; Stockton, California; Dallas; and St. Louis. Hartford, Memphis, Richmond, and Kansas City are listed as having weekend schools in the Consortium. (The website states that the list of schools is not exhaustive.)

Establishment of full-time Muslim or Islamic schools among immigrant and mixed communities in the United States parallels the history of mosque growth, but at a much slower pace. The earliest full-time schools were the Islamic School of Seattle (1980), the Orange Crescent School in Garden Grove, California (1983), the Al-Ghazaly School in Jersey City (1984), the New Horizon School in Pasadena, California (1984), the Muslim Community School in Potomac, Maryland (1985), and the Islamic Saudi Academy in Virginia (1985). The latter operated under the auspices of the Embassy of Saudi Arabia and closed in 2016. Development continued in the 1990s with the Universal School in Chicago (1991), the Universal Academy in Tampa (1992), and the Darul Arqam Schools of Greater Houston (1992).

The Islamic Society of North America established the Council of Islamic Schools of North America (CISNA) in 1991 to assist the schools. CISNA is not a governing body for the schools, but it has brought indigenous American Muslims and immigrants together for curriculum and teacher training projects, and assisted schools in achieving accreditation (CISNA 2015).

Since Islamic school growth has taken place in autonomous local communities, accurate data are difficult to obtain. According to the 1994 Mosque Study, 17% of mosques reported running a full-time school; the 2011 study found that 21% supported schools, or reported schools in the local area. After September 11, 2001, media reports trained a spotlight on Muslim schools, and some speculated that there were as many as four hundred Islamic schools in the United States.

The first systematic survey of schools was undertaken by Karen Keyworth, Founding Director of the Islamic Schools League of America (ISLA). ISLA established a Muslim educators' listserv in the late 1990s, incorporated ISLA in 1998, and set up an online registration process in 2004 that yielded detailed data on 106 schools. The Institute for Social Policy and Understanding (ISPU), a Muslim think tank, supported Keyworth's work, publishing the most reliable and rich source of data on the schools to date. Information was gleaned from self-reporting databases, membership rosters, mail surveys, and telephone interviews.

Keyworth's study built upon baseline data from Bagby's mosque study and Pew's demographic surveys (Pew Forum on Religion & Public Life, Mapping the Global Muslim Population 2009). The 2011 ISPU report yielded a figure of 235 schools as the "definitive number of Islamic schools in the United States," extrapolating Muslim school enrollment at between 26,00 and 35,500 students (Keyworth 2011, 13). The study revealed that 21% of the schools were governed by mosque administration, and "fully 45% are completely independent entities . . . Almost 75% of schools indicate that they are operating either independently or autonomously" (Keyworth 2011, 18–19).

Keyworth estimated that at most 3.5% of Muslim students attended full-time Islamic schools, compared with about 10% of American children in private schools overall. Out of an estimated 850,000 school-age Muslim children in the United States, probably about 32,000 are enrolled in a full-time Islamic school (Keyworth 2011 p. 15). Keyworth reported that 93% of Islamic full-time schools enroll 300 or fewer students, and 85% were founded a decade ago or less (Keyworth 2011, 15). Few schools occupy new, purpose-built structures, with more than half housed in buildings ten years or older. Slightly less than half are in newer buildings, either mosques or separate schools. Gender separation is not uniform in the schools, since classes are often small and separation requires additional rooms and teachers. Some separate girls and boys after middle elementary or higher, and many schools do not go beyond the eighth grade in any case. A few schools deliberately have gender-mixed classrooms to promote interaction among boys and girls.

Keyworth found that 10% of Muslim schools reported employing only certified teachers; 36% of schools reported that all academic teachers were certified. Only 13% of schools reported no certified teachers, but 49% of schools employed uncertified Arabic and/or Islamic studies teachers, because the path to state certification is not straightforward for these school subjects. By comparison, US private schools regularly hire as many as 48% uncertified teachers (Keyworth 2011, 17). Uncertified teachers may hold bachelor's, master's, and even doctoral degrees. As for the religious composition of Islamic school faculty, about 50% of schools reported hiring between 10% and 30% non-Muslim teachers, likely due to a shortage of certified Muslim educators. Only 28% of the schools reported a commitment to hire Muslim faculty exclusively (Keyworth 2011, 17–18).

The number of Islamic schools accredited with associations such the National Association of Independent Schools, the Southern Association of Colleges and Schools, and the Middle States Association of Colleges and Schools is uncertain. Accreditation is an expensive and lengthy process that only well-established schools can achieve and maintain. Non-accredited schools are still subject to zoning laws, local occupancy permits, and compliance with fire and safety inspections. Keyworth's report noted that a growing number of Islamic schools are accredited or seeking accreditation as a stamp of official approval that makes them attractive to donors and parents.

Curriculum development is among the most important challenges for Islamic schools. Rather than following the tradition of American independent schools' progressive, innovative curricula, most Islamic schools have followed a pattern of adherence to local public school academic programs and even state testing regimens, adding Islamic studies and Arabic instruction. A few integrated curriculum projects such as Dawud Tauhidi's Tarbiya Project combined creative cross-curricular learning and service learning, and increasingly, Islamic Montessori programs are implemented in preschool or primary grades.

Efforts toward curricular innovation are stymied by parents', funders', and board members' lack of educational expertise and their fear that children will not be adequately prepared for college, especially in the coveted STEM fields. Funding, expertise, and curriculum development time are challenging barriers to innovation for many schools, whose communities want excellent mainstream education, but may prefer to emphasize Islamic schools as safe havens from the risk that public schools pose to their children's Islamic identity formation. Despite these challenges, however, there has been steady improvement and growth: some schools have won mainstream awards for excellence, while many have become well-established institutions with generations of successful graduates.

CONCLUSION

As something of a work in progress, the educational system in the United States has historically expanded its reach by welcoming the rich diversity found in various religious and ethnic communities as well as their schools. One can only hope that the nation will continue to foster an attitude of openness welcoming religious diversity so that parents can ensure that their children are educated as they wish, keeping in mind that students are not the mere creatures of the state.

FUTURE DIRECTIONS

1. Given the range of educational options, socioeconomic conditions, religious beliefs, and other family circumstances, how do families choose to send their children to private Protestant schools? What are the critical motivators for families to choose private Protestant education over other options?

2. Because there is no unifying organization for Protestant schools, it can be challenging to develop a complete picture of these schools, particularly in terms of ideological diversity. What is the landscape of ideologies and theologies in American Protestant schools, and how is that diversity distributed?

3. Given the increasing cost of Roman Catholic schooling, can these schools remain viable?

4. Does the fact that the vast majority of administrators, teachers, and staff in Roman Catholic schools are now lay, rather than religious, have these schools preserved their unique identities as Catholic?

5. Should vouchers and other forms of governmental assistance be made available to help parents send their children to faith-based schools (see Chapter 13 in this volume)?

6. With the marked decline in non-Orthodox Jewish day schools over the course of the twenty-first century, what are the most effective strategies to foster day school enrollment?

7. What roles can technology play in Jewish day schools to promote sustainability, especially in smaller schools with limited endowments, teachers, and resources (see Chapter 9 in this volume)?

8. How does the growth of full-time Islamic schools—despite the small proportion of Muslim children who attend them—reflect the social integration of the Muslim community, and what programs and curricular trends in such schools indicate their desire to integrate students into participatory citizenship in the countries where they live?

9. What proportion of Muslim students from various ethnic and educational backgrounds attend college and pursue advanced degrees, and what trends in Muslim students' choice of fields of study can be measured (e.g., STEM fields vs. humanities and social sciences)?

10. How will increased collaboration among organizations of Muslim educators and Muslims' participation in mainstream professional educational organizations affect the future of curriculum development and accreditation of Islamic full-time schools?

References

Bagby, Ihsan. 2012. *The American Mosque 2011: Basic Characteristics of the American Mosque: Attitudes of Mosque Leaders.* Report Number 1 from the US Mosque Study 2011. Washington, DC: Council on American-Islamic Relations.

Bagby, Ihsan, Paul M. Perl, and Bryan T. Froehle. 2001. *The Mosque in America: A National Portrait. A Report from the Mosque Study Project,* April 26. Washington, DC: Council on American-Islamic Relations.

Broughman, S. P., and N. L. Swaim. 2013. *Characteristics of Private Schools in the United States: Results from the 2011–12 Private School Universe Survey.* Washington, DC: National Center for Education Statistics.

Bryk, A. S., N. E. Lee, and P. B. Holland. 1993. *Catholic Schools and the Common Good.* Cambridge, MA: Harvard University Press.

Buetow, Harold A. 1970. *Of Singular Benefit: The Story of Catholic Education in the United States.* New York: Macmillan.

Cardus Education Survey. 2011. *Do the Motivations for Private Religious Catholic and Protestant Schooling in North America Align with Graduate Outcomes?* Hamilton, Ontario. Retrieved from https://www.cardus.ca/research/education/publications/surveys/.

Chertok, Fern, Leonard Saxe, Charles Kadushin, Graham Wright, Aron Klein, and Annette Koren. 2007. "What Difference Does Day School Make? The Impact of Day School: A Comparative Analysis of Jewish College Students." Brandeis Institutional Repository, accessed on January 22, 2018, http://hdl.handle.net/10192/22974.

Commager, Henry Steele, ed. 1965. *Documents of American History, vol. I: to 1898,* 7th ed. New York: Appleton-Century-Crofts.

Council of Islamic Schools in North America. Available at http://www.cisnaonline.info/.

Fraser, James W. 1999. *Between Church and State: Religion and Public Education in a Multicultural America.* New York: St. Martin's Press.

Glenn, Charles Leslie. 1988. *The Myth of the Common School.* Amherst: University of Massachusetts Press.

Graff, Gil. 2008. *And You Shall Teach Them Diligently: A Concise History of Jewish Education in the United States 1776–2000.* New York: Jewish Theological Seminary of America.

Keyworth, Karen. 2011. *ISPU Report: Islamic Schools of the United States: Data-Based Profiles.* Institute for Social Policy and Understanding. Available at https://www.ispu.org/islamic-schools-of-the-united-states-data-based-profiles/.

Khan, Shaza, Wajahat Husain, and Sehar Masood. 2005. "Situating Weekend Islamic Schools in the American Muslim Context." Paper delivered at the ISNA Education Forum, March 10. Available at http://www.docstoc.com/docs/26374575/Situating-Weekend-Islamic-Schools.

Laats, Adam. 2012. "Our Schools, Our Country: American Evangelicals, Public Schools, and the Supreme Court Decisions of 1962 and 1963." *Journal of Religious History* 36, no. 3: 319–334.

Lugo, Luis, Alan Cooperman, Gregory A. Smith, Conrad Hackett, Cary Funk, Neha Sahgal Phillip Connor, Jessica Hamar Martinez, et al. 2013. *A Portrait of Jewish Americans: Findings from a Pew Research Center Survey of US Jews.* Pew Research Institute.

Macedo, Stephen. 2000. *Diversity and Distrust: Civic Education in a Multicultural Democracy.* Cambridge, MA: Harvard University Press.

Mahr, M., ed. 1984. *NCEA/Ganley's Catholic Schools in America.* Montrose, CO: Fisher Publishing Co.

———, ed. 1987. *NCEA/Ganley's Catholic Schools in America.* Montrose, CO: Fisher Publishing Co.

Martinez, Priscilla. 2009. "Muslim Homeschooling." In *Educating the Muslims of America,* edited by Yvonne Haddad, Farid Senzai, and Jane I. Smith, 109–121. Oxford/New York: Oxford University Press.

Matus, Ron. 2013. "10 Myths about Faith-Based Schools." *RedefinED,* November 1.

Neil Gerald McCluskey, ed. 1964. *Catholic Education in America: A Documentary History.* New York: Teacher's College.

McDonald, Dale, and Margaret Schultz. 2014. *United States Catholic Elementary and Secondary Schools 2013–2014: The Annual Statistical Report on Schools, Enrollment and Staffing.* Arlington, VA: National Catholic Education Association.

McDonald, Dale, and Margaret Schultz. 2017. *United States Catholic Elementary and Secondary Schools 2016–2017: The Annual Statistical Report on Schools, Enrollment, and Staffing.* Arlington, VA: National Catholic Educational Association.

Mohammed Schools Consortium of U.S. and Bermuda. Available at http://mohammedschools.tripod.com/id4.html.

Nord, Warren A. 1995. *Religion and American Education: Rethinking a National Dilemma.* Chapel Hill: University of North Carolina Press.

"Pew Forum on Religion and Public Life, Mapping the Global Muslim Population." 2009. Available at http://www.pewforum.org/Mapping-the-Global-Muslim-Population.aspx.

"Private School Facts." 2016. Retrieved from http://www.capenet.org/facts.html

Rashid, Hakim M., and Zakiyyah Muhammad. 1992. "The Sister Clara Muhammad Schools: Pioneers in the Development of Islamic Education in America." *Journal of Negro Education* 61 (April 1), no. 2: 179.

Sarna, Jonathan D. 1998. "American Jewish Education in Historical Perspective." *Journal of Jewish Education* 64, no. 1-2: 8–21.

Schick, Marvin. 2014. *A Census of Jewish Day Schools in the United States, 2013–2014.* Jerusalem: Avi Chai Foundation.

Sikkink, D. 1999. "The Social Sources of Alienation from Public Schools." *Social Forces* 78, no. 1: 51–86.

Skerry, Peter. 2005. "America's Other Muslims." *Wilson Quarterly* 29 (Autumn), no. 4: 16–27.

"10 Catholic elementary schools to close." 2014. *Buffalo (NY) News*, January 15.

Uecker, Jeremy E. 2008. "Alternative Schooling Strategies and the Religious Lives of American Adolescents." *Journal for the Scientific Study of Religion* 47, no. 4: 563–584.

US Department of Education. 2016. "Characteristics of Private Schools in the United States: Results from the 2013–14 Private School Universe Survey: First Look. Table 1," p. 6. Washington, DC: U.S. Department of Education. Available at http://nces.ed.gov/pubs2016/2016243.pdf.

Wertheimer, Jack. 2008. *A Census of Jewish Supplementary Schools in the United States, 2006–2007.* New York, NY: Avi Chai Foundation.

FURTHER READING

American Broadcasting Corporation. *Page 2: Muslim Home Schooling on the Rise—ABC News.* Available at http://abcnews.go.com/Health/story?id=117997&page=2#.UBMMcqOEEUM.

An-Na'im, Abdullahi Ahmed. *Religion and Culture: Meeting the Challenge of Pluralism, a Ford Foundation Project.* Available at http://religionandpluralism.org/LouCristillo.htm#Resources.

Bagby, Ihsan. *Masjid Study Project.* Available at http://higginsctc.org/terrorism/Masjid_Study_Project_2000_Report.pdf.

Bagby, Ihsan. *The American Mosque 2011.* Available at http://faithcommunitiestoday.org/sites/faithcommunitiestoday.org/files/The%20American%20Mosque%202011%20web.pdf.

Bergen, Peter, and Swati Pandey. 2005. "The Madrassa Myth." *New York Times*, June 14. Available at http://www.nytimes.com/2005/06/14/opinion/14bergen.html.

Cooper, Bruce S., and Marc N. Kramer. 2002. "The New Jewish Community, New Jewish Schools: Trends and Promises." *Journal of Catholic Education* 5, no. 4: 488–501.

Haddad, Yvonne Y., and Jane I. Smith, eds. 2014. *The Oxford Handbook of American Islam*, 1st ed. New York: Oxford University Press.

Haddad, Yvonne Yazbeck, Farid Senzai, and Jane I. Smith, eds. 2009. *Educating the Muslims of America*. Oxford/New York: Oxford University Press.

Horan, Deborah. 2002. "Put Off by Public Schools, More Muslims Home-teach." *Chicago Tribune*, December 16. Available at http://articles.chicagotribune.com/2002-12-16/news/0212160217_1_home-school-muslims-pupils.

Ikhlas Homeschool. "Muslim Homeschool Resources | Ikhlas Homeschool." Available at http://www.freewebs.com/ikhlashomeschool/allabouthomeschool.htm.

Institute for Social Policy and Understanding. *Islamic Education in America*. Available at http://ispu.org/GetReports/35/1897/Publications.aspx.

———. *Georgetown Report*. Available at http://ispu.org/pdfs/georgetown%20report%20(si).pdf.

———. *Educating the Muslims of America*. Available at http://ispu.org/Getbooks/33/1822/Publications.aspx.

Islamic Schools League of North America. *Islamic Schools as Change Agents*. Available at http://www.theisla.org/filemgmt_data/admin_files/IslamicSchoolsAsChangeAgents.pdf.

Keyworth, Karen. *Institute for Social Policy and Understanding Report on Islamic Schools*. Available at http://ispu.org/pdfs/609_ISPU%20Report_Islamic%20Schools_Keyworth_WEB.pdf.

Krasner, Jonathan B. 2012. *The Benderly Boys and American Jewish Education*. Lebanon, NH: Brandeis University Press.

Mohammed Schools of Atlanta. Available at http://mohammedschools.org/.

Sulaiman, Cynthia. "Outside, In: From Public School to Home-school." Available at http://www.muslimhomeschool.net/hsa/outsidein.html.

Woocher, Jonathan. 2012. "Reinventing Jewish Education for the 21st Century." *Journal of Jewish Education* 78, no. 3: 182–226.

Zaman, Mujadad, and Nadeem A. Memon, eds. 2016. *Philosophies of Islamic Education: Historical Perspectives and Emerging Discourses*. New York: Routledge.

Zaytuna Institute. "Kinza Academy: Homeschooling, Traditional Education, Hamza Yusuf." Available at http://www.kinzaacademy.com/.

CHAPTER 12

RELIGION AND HOMESCHOOLING

MILTON GAITHER

AMERICANS have been using their homes as educational space since colonial times, yet there is a key difference between the domestic education of past centuries and the home-schooling movement that emerged in the 1970s and has grown steadily ever since. The home-based education of the past was nearly always done for pragmatic rather than ideological reasons. Sparse population and limited resources meant that formal schools were impracticable for many in colonial America or on the western frontiers of the nineteenth century. Laws criminalizing schooling for slaves drove many African Americans to clandestine learning in private quarters. Women and lower-class men who could not gain admittance to colleges enrolled in correspondence programs by the millions. Missionaries, diplomats, and world travelers with children relied on mail-ordered curricula to keep their children up to par while they were in the field. These are but a few examples of the many ways the home was called upon, and in some cases still is, to fill in for formal schools when necessary. But this is not homeschooling in the modern sense of the term (Gaither 2008).

Homeschooling emerged as a self-consciously political act in the 1970s for a variety of reasons, first among left-leaning members of the counterculture and then among a much larger group of conservative Christians. At first these disparate types of homeschoolers worked together to secure a more amenable political and legal climate. Once that work had been done, however, religious conservatives quickly came to dominate the movement, especially its public relations and communications channels. Though the internet has ended the conservative Christian monopoly on information, Christian organizations continue to shape and define the movement at the local, state, and national levels, and they are increasingly being joined by Americans of other faiths. In this chapter we will examine how and why highly religious Americans have been and remain the primary homeschooling demographic.

WHY HOMESCHOOLING HAPPENED

Several broad social trends of the second half of the twentieth century converged to make the homeschooling movement possible. Here I would like to discuss four: suburbanization, feminism, political radicalism and privatization, and the increasing bureaucratization and secularization of the public school system. Together these broad social changes explain why religious conservatives, who historically had been some of the strongest supporters of public education, turned in large numbers in the 1980s and thereafter to homeschooling.

Suburbanization

The migration of Americans from farms and cities to the suburbs is one of the major contextual factors in explaining the homeschooling movement. In the decades leading up to the explosion of homeschooling in the late 1970s and 1980s tens of millions of Americans left rural farm life and moved to the suburbs. By 1980 over 40% of the population, more than 100 million people, lived in suburbia, a geographic space sequestered from the civic-mindedness and public outlook that historically characterized both urban and small-town American life (Hayden 2003; Jackson 1985).

Suburban homes have grown ever bigger and more comfortable since the 1950s. According to the National Association of Home Builders, the average house size increased 15% in the 1970s and another 21% in the 1980s. The median size of a new home in 2002 was 20% larger than in 1987, and after a slight dip during the recession of 2008 new homes have continued to grow in size (Sarkar 2011). As people have invested more and more in the interior space that situates their private lives, it has seemed natural to shift energy away from public space. Suburbia has provided a comfortable material space for homeschooling, and the privatized, anti-government outlook it encourages has contributed to homeschooling's growing popularity.

Feminism

The mass movement to suburbia impacted American women in many ways. While Betty Friedan's *Feminine Mystique*, first published in 1963, had argued that suburban life isolated and infantilized women, recent scholarship has found that postwar suburban women on the whole were far more engaged civically than the stereotype would allow. The suburban home was often the springboard for aggressive political involvement, especially among religious conservatives. Women organized locally to fight pornography, to promote or resist integration, to defeat communism, to change zoning laws, and much else. They were particularly motivated by school-related issues and often described their activism in anti-statist terms (Nickerson 2012; Self 2012).

Women's roles changed as well. Women's employment outside the home had been increasing slowly in the decades before World War II. Each decade between 1940 and 1990 saw a 10% increase in the percentage of married women in the workforce. By 1985, 50% of women with children under six were working outside the home. Such shifts correlated with ever-increasing levels of education among American women. By 1960 one-third of all higher education degrees in the United States were awarded to women, by 1980 almost half were, and by 2012 women were earning about 60% of university degrees (Bailey 2004; National Center for Education Statistics 2012; US National Center for Education Statistics 2008).

The homeschooling movement cannot be understood apart from the dramatic rise in female education and political participation that the feminist movement has secured. Though most homeschooling mothers would utterly reject the term "feminist" as a self-designation, most homeschoolers' roles transcend those of the 1950s-era housewife and mother (McDannell 2005). Homeschooling has become a means for women whose religious beliefs compel them to stay at home to nevertheless put their educational experience and talents to good use. Home has become workplace, the mother an educational professional. Women form "the backbone of the homeschool movement's impressive organizational system" (Stevens 2001, 15–16), crafting lives of powerful dissent from established norms even as they seek to convince others that homeschooling is not abnormal (Lois 2013).

Political Radicalism and Privatization

Since the 1980s commentators have been much exercised over the division of the country into warring camps on most social issues. But what is often missed in such an analysis is the underlying symmetry of vision both sides possess. Recent scholarship has emphasized how both the cultural left and right in the decades that saw the beginnings of homeschooling largely gave up on earlier notions of collective identity and social cohesion, turning instead to patterns of thought that stressed individual identity, choice, and desire (Farber 2003; Rodgers 2012; Schulman 2001).

Given this pan-ideological commitment to local, authentic, private life and contempt for establishment liberalism, it is not surprising that members of both the countercultural right and the countercultural left began to practice and advocate for homeschooling. On the left, disillusionment with the pace of social change prompted many to drop out of mainstream America. Many turned to communal living or homesteading. Family and childbearing were big parts of the earthy orientation, and natural childbirth was often associated with permissive parenting and education. Many on the left saw formal schools as symbols of everything wrong and destructive in modern life and kept their kids at home. They found a champion and organizer in the person of John Holt, a leading school critic of the 1960s who by the mid-1970s had given up on schools entirely and was urging parents to liberate their children from them. Holt's magazine *Growing Without Schooling* became the first national homeschooling periodical when it debuted in August 1977, and his celebrity advocacy and frequent appearances on *The Phil Donahue Show* and other venues brought homeschooling into the national limelight for the first time (Gaither 2008; Schulman 2001).

On the right, profound changes were happening to American Protestants. The old denominational distinctions were fading, replaced by a sharp binary between "conservative" churches that embraced a fierce biblical literalism wedded to moral traditionalism even as their worship became more free and casual, and "liberal" churches that, even if they still worshipped in a manner consonant with earlier centuries, tended to shy away from the more miraculous and exclusive claims of Christianity. American Protestants realigned themselves according to this divide, and the results were good news for conservatives and bad news for liberals. Dramatic growth in the conservative, separatist sector spawned a host of alternative cultural institutions that mimicked even as they condemned the cultural mainstream: Christian bookstores, romance fiction, radio and television stations, rock concerts and festivals, music awards, theme parks, summer camps. A parallel Christian culture was emerging that allowed Christian kids to participate in the trappings of mainstream youth culture but still maintain their theological distinctiveness (Luhr 2009; Stowe 2011).

One important facet of this new Christian counterculture was its political activism. Early in the 1960s studies of voting patterns consistently found that religiously conservative people were the least likely Americans to be involved in politics. But the ensuing decades saw an infusion of countercultural sensibility into the most conservative segments of the population. Shocked and outraged by social change, conservatives adopted the techniques of the left to forward their own agenda (Williams 2012). While earlier conservative political movements like Prohibition or the anti-obscenity Comstock Laws had used government to accomplish their aims, for conservatives of the late 1960s and 1970s government itself was the problem, suffused as it was, as many conservatives believed, with communists and moral libertines. Groups like the John Birch Society and later the Moral Majority organized millions of Americans to fight government initiatives. Their bases of operations were tens of thousands of living rooms across the country, and their membership was largely female. Homemakers and mothers did much of the grassroots organizing and not a little of the actual teaching at conservative meetings. These were not Betty Friedan's etiolated domestics: they were empowered, articulate, and unabashedly conventional. In the name of the home these women were coming out of the living room into the public square (Dochuk 2010; Rymph 2006; Schreiber 2008).

Bureaucratic and Secular Public Schools

After World War II disenchantment with public education grew on both the political left and right until by the 1970s it had become pervasive. Schools were attacked from the right for being insufficiently intellectual in titles like *Educational Wastelands*, *American Education: A National Failure*, and *The Literacy Hoax*. Left-leaning books, indicting the authoritarianism of public education, were even more merciless, bearing titles like *Growing Up Absurd, Free the Children*, and *Crisis in the Classroom* (Cremin 1989). Parents looked on as fights between teachers and administration got nasty. They worried about the records schools kept on their children and would not let them see. Some parents protested against schoolbooks that mentioned witchcraft, evolution, world government, pacifism, and other cultural flashpoints. Sex education, life adjustment, and progressive pedagogies like the "new math" and whole language reading instruction came under fire (Luker 2007; McClellan 1999). Court-ordered busing to racially integrate public schools was for many the last straw, leading parents in many parts of the country to bitterly oppose public education (Baugh 2011).

This growing animus against government schools, however, coincided with ever-increasing reliance on them by most American families. By the 1970s public education had become a massive, nearly universal experience for Americans. Despite pronounced population growth and increases in school enrollments, the number of school districts contracted profoundly (from 117,000 districts in 1939 to 16,000 in 1980), meaning that more and more children were going to bigger and bigger schools further and further away from their neighborhoods. Such schools increasingly came to resemble one another, as textbook publishing, state and national testing programs, and national reports exerted a homogenizing effect (Cremin 1988).

By the late 1970s Americans of various political persuasions were looking for an alternative. The left, led by John Holt, was first to put homeschooling on the national agenda. Homeschooling was not at first considered by many conservatives because in the 1960s and 1970s most of them were still trying to keep public school values consistent with their own. But while activism gained them victories in some locales, conservatives rightly discerned that they were losing the battle over control of the nation's public schools. The 1962 and 1963 Supreme Court decisions outlawing organized school prayer and school-sponsored Bible reading shocked and devastated many conservatives, and over the ensuing decades many of them began pulling their children out of public schools and placing them in upstart Protestant day schools (see Chapter 11 in this volume; DelFattore 2004; Dierenfield 2007; Nickerson 2012). In 1967 the three leading Christian school umbrella organizations had a combined membership of 102 schools, but in the late 1970s and 1980s new schools blossomed across the country: by 1990, over 3,000 Christian schools were on the rolls (Carper and Hunt 2007, 203–204).

For some conservative Christians, however, private schools were not the answer. Reasons for dissatisfaction with private schooling varied: some families couldn't afford the tuition; some disagreed with the theology the school espoused; some had negative experiences with principals or teachers; some, especially those with children with special needs, felt that the school couldn't address their child's individual circumstances; some believed that the Bible gave responsibility for education to parents only; and some, especially mothers, simply wanted to spend more time with their children (Lois 2013; Vigilant, Trefethren, and Anderson 2013). In the early 1980s Christian psychologist and radio show host James Dobson repeatedly featured Seventh-Day Adventist educators Raymond and Dorothy Moore on his program *Focus on the Family*. The Moores, who had for some time been arguing that children should not go to school until age ten to twelve at the earliest, delivered a message that resonated with thousands of disaffected evangelicals and fundamentalists, and the Christian homeschooling movement was born. As we have seen, circumstances were right. By the late 1970s many conservatives lived in comfortable suburban homes that could easily accommodate a homeschool. Many Christian housewives were well educated and committed both to their children and to staying at home. Housewives formed the backbone of most pro-family movements. If such women as these could protest, organize voters, conduct study groups, and lead Bible studies and women's clubs at their churches, could they not teach their own children how to read, write, and cipher? Many decided they could (Filene 1998; Gaither 2008; Lytle 2006).

THE MOVEMENT: SUCCESS AND SCHISM

Homeschoolers in the late 1970s and early 1980s organized themselves into support groups all over the country. They were led by John Holt and Raymond Moore, both of whom traveled the country constantly speaking at group meetings and advocating for homeschooling in legislatures and courts. In the early years these groups usually accepted all comers regardless of religious affiliation or pedagogical philosophy. Homeschoolers in those days were in a precarious position—misunderstood and held in suspicion by neighbors and family members, distrusted and occasionally persecuted by authorities, confused about what was legal and how to do what they were trying to do. Support groups were a lifeline for many struggling homeschooling mothers, providing sympathetic ears, advice for the daily grind of teaching, and especially expertise regarding how to navigate the educational and legal system. And since homeschooling's fundamental ideals made intuitive sense to many Americans, the movement was quite successful at convincing the nation, especially its courts, legislatures, and media, that this was a harmless and perhaps even noble phenomenon. At first exposure, many Americans recoiled against the notion of children being kept out of school, but as they listened to Holt describing how schools destroy the native curiosity of children or to Moore citing scores of studies purportedly showing that early institutionalization damages children, and as they saw that many homeschooled children were excelling academically, attitudes and laws shifted (Gaither 2008).

Though it is frequently claimed that homeschooling was illegal in most of the country before the 1980s, in actuality the homeschoolers of the 1970s and 1980s faced a complex and often vague tangle of state compulsory education statutes. These varied widely concerning the legality of teaching children at home. At the dawn of the movement in the late 1970s, fourteen state statutes said nothing at all about education at home but usually mentioned the acceptability of children being taught in a private school. Fifteen explicitly mentioned home instruction in one way or another. The remaining twenty-one contained phrases like "equivalent instruction elsewhere" or "instruction by a private tutor" that could be read to imply recognition of home education as a legitimate option. The thirty-six states with either explicit or implied provisions for home instruction differed markedly over the specificity of their rules governing nonpublic school instruction and over establishing who was in charge of it all. Some were very vague. Some empowered local school boards to govern such matters. Some statutes established robust requirements. Six even required that any teacher of children regardless of venue be certified by the same standards the state used to certify public school teachers (Stocklin-Enright 1982; Tobak and Zirkel 1982).

As the homeschooling movement grew, much energy was devoted to clarifying and in many cases changing the legal codes. Two basic lines of attack were adopted. Some homeschoolers sought to define home-based instruction as a fundamental constitutional right, grounded either in the First Amendment's Free Exercise Clause or the Fourteenth Amendment's Due Process Clause. With rare exception such arguments failed at the state level, and to date no case with these principles at stake has made it to the Supreme Court. The second, and much more successful, strategy was to secure state court decisions that interpreted state statutory language in a manner favorable to homeschooling or, barring that, to change the state statutes themselves to make homeschooling clearly legal and less cumbersome. In some states, homeschoolers secured favorable court decisions that found homeschools to be private schools. In others, courts agreed that the state statutes were unconstitutionally vague, forcing the legislatures to compose new homeschooling legislation that was nearly always more permissive than public school personnel wanted. Finally, states with explicit requirements that homeschoolers found onerous were put under tremendous pressure, often involving massive demonstrations, to relax their laws. By 1993 every state in the union had done so, and homeschooling had become clearly legal nationwide even for parents without teacher certification. To this day differences remain in the level of state scrutiny of homeschoolers, and minor skirmishes flare up any time an ambitious legislator seeks to increase regulations on homeschooling. But those who wish to regulate homeschooling have never been able to match the political energy and organizational aptitude of these highly motivated parents (Gaither 2008).

Yet even as the homeschooling movement was moving from victory to victory in the legislative and legal arena during the 1980s, internal matters were growing tense. 1985 is a seminal date for the homeschooling movement, for it marked both the death of John Holt, by far the most visible national advocate, and the emergence of the Home School Legal Defense Association (HSLDA) on the national scene. In hindsight, a schism looks inevitable. In the early 1970s there were perhaps 10,000 to 15,000 homeschooled children in the United States. By the mid-1980s the best scholarly estimates place the number at somewhere between 120,000 and 240,000, and most of these new recruits, perhaps as many as 85% or 90% of them, were conservative Protestants (Murphy 2012). These new homeschoolers chafed against a national leadership headed by Holt, an atheist and advocate for child rights and world government, and the Moores, Seventh-day Adventists with a very low view of formal pedagogy. From within their own ranks emerged a younger generation of conservative leaders who quickly coordinated their efforts and wrested control of the movement. Support groups around the country that had been open to many different religious and pedagogical orientations split into rival groups, one (usually much larger and better organized) for conservative Protestants only and another for everyone else. Statewide organizations and their annual conventions split along the same lines. Suddenly homeschoolers who could not sign Protestant statements of faith were not allowed to join, speak at, or advertise their products at conventions across the nation. Veterans of the Holt and Moore years broadcasted their frustration as much as they could, but they were such a small minority within the movement that their anger and criticisms of HSLDA and other conservative leaders made little impact on the movement (Gaither 2008).

HSLDA's membership figures best illustrate where the movement's momentum lay. When it was founded in 1983 HSLDA had about 200 members. In 1985, its breakout year, it grew from 1,200 to 2,000. By 1987 it had 3,600 members. Throughout the 1980s membership figures doubled every thirteen months. By 1994 38,000 members were served by thirty-eight full-time employees. By 1999 HSLDA employed sixty people full-time and membership topped 60,000 for the first time. At the same time, the organizations founded by Holt, Moore, and other leaders not connected to the conservative Protestant culture either stagnated or declined.

Why was there such one-sided growth? Homeschooling is nearly impossible without at least one full-time houseparent, and the conservative Protestant celebration of the stay-at-home mom gave it a far larger population of possible recruits than more liberal orientations, which tend to sanction public roles for women. Furthermore, it was a deep suspicion of secular people and ideas that had led conservative Protestants to homeschooling in the first place, and they were not about to flee from secular liberalism in one venue only to embrace it in another. As a result, by the 1990s homeschooling had become associated in the minds of most Americans with separatist, far-right fundamentalist Christianity. But since the late 1990s that public perception has been changing (Seelhoff 2000; Stevens 2001).

THE NEW HOMESCHOOLING

Homeschooling has been around long enough that it does not draw the same level of press attention or public comment today as it did in the 1990s. Occasionally something homeschool-related will make the news, as when a homeschooled child wins a major national competition, when it becomes known that a celebrity had been homeschooled, when a case of horrific child abuse comes to light, or when a major law or court case changes the status quo (Clemmit 2014). But in general it can be said that homeschooling has become an accepted and normal part of the educational options on offer in the United States.

As homeschooling has become less controversial and more familiar, more and more people, all kinds of people, are turning to it as an option for their children. Most people who use their homes to teach their children still do so as a form of protest against public education. They are still "homeschoolers." But more and more people are choosing this path not out of frustration with secularism or numbing bureaucracy or inflexible curriculum or age segregation but simply because it makes sense for the time being given their family circumstances. They are the new domestic educators, returning to the historical practice of using the home to educate for pragmatic rather than ideological reasons. In this final section we will briefly examine a few examples of this broad and amorphous trend (Dunn and Serthick 2008).

Recent survey research has revealed a considerably more heterogeneous population of homeschoolers than earlier and more limited studies had found. Polling data from the National Center for Education Statistics have found far higher rates of minority homeschooling than previously believed: around 23% in both 2003 and 2007, and 32% in 2011 (Noel, Stark, and Redford 2013; Planty et al. 2009). African-American homeschooling has received the lion's share of media attention, but the trend extends as well to Latinos, Native Americans, Orthodox Jews, conservative Catholics, Mormons, and Muslims, as well as more fringe elements like far-left neo-pagans and far-right white supremacists. Many of these people are turning to homeschooling for some of the same ideological reasons that Protestants did so in the 1980s and 1990s, and support groups and resources, especially online, have multiplied to meet their needs (Gaither 2009).

Homeschooling has begun to make sense to some Americans for very different reasons, however. Many families with children in time-consuming activities such as music or dance programs, sports, acting, or modeling have turned to homeschooling for its flexible scheduling. Parents with special needs children of all sorts, from those with autism spectrum disorder to peanut allergies, are finding home-based education a more convenient and comfortable approach for their children (Bollinger et al. 2006; Hurlbutt 2012; Schetter and Lighthall 2009). Some "creative class" families are turning to homeschooling as a way to integrate education into the telecommuting, globe-trotting lives they lead (Conlin 2006; L. Miller 2012). Home-based tutoring is experiencing such rapid growth that tutoring agencies cannot meet the demand. With increasing frequency the popular press reports on the latest celebrity to have grown up homeschooled or to be choosing this option for her or his own child (Clemmit 2014). Homeschoolers such as these make it clear that what was at one point a fringe movement of hippies and fundamentalists is now quite fashionable.

The look of homeschooling has become nearly as diverse as its practitioners. New hybrid forms have made it increasingly difficult to distinguish between homeschooling and plain old schooling. For years now, homeschoolers, especially those with older children, have created co-ops, sports teams, bands, clubs, resource centers, and the like, often meeting in area churches or community centers, that look quite a bit like traditional schools. More recently, public schools, having lost the fight to suppress homeschooling, have begun to court homeschoolers and the tax dollars their patronage represents. Some districts have opened satellite campuses that offer free enrichment courses to homeschoolers. Others are experimenting with dual enrollment programs that allow students to attend public schools part time and stay home for the rest of the day. Homeschoolers are increasingly participating in after-school activities like sports. Some districts have opened to homeschooled teens their programs that pay for college classes for high schoolers. Most dramatically, and most controversially, many states now allow children to receive a complete public school education in their homes for free through cyberschools (Gaither 2009).

My summary here of the increasing diversity of children being taught at home and of the institutional configurations being used to do so should not obscure the fact that most who homeschool still choose this option out of frustration with or protest against formal, institutional schooling and seek to offer an alternative, usually conservative Christian, worldview to their children by teaching them at home. Yet even here changes are detectable, of which two are especially notable. First, in terms of curriculum there has been a widespread movement away from the fundamentalist "school in a box" format that dominated in the 1980s and 1990s toward a wider range of options (Laats 2010). Perhaps the most popular of the newer models is the "classical" education approach that seeks to embody an educational philosophy first articulated by British author and intellectual Dorothy Sayers in 1947 (Leithart 2008). Classical homeschooling is phenomenally popular among Christian homeschoolers even though it emphasizes nonreligious texts to a far greater degree than such mainstays as Accelerated Christian Education, ABeka, or Bob Jones Complete (Anthony and Burroughs 2012; Hahn 2012). Second, a small but growing body of research on young adults who were homeschooled in conservative Christian contexts is finding that these children frequently move away from their parents' conservative religious and political convictions despite their parents' best efforts (Hoelzle 2013; Kunzman 2009; Pennings et al. 2011).

The pedagogical and ideological diversification that can be seen even among conservative Christian homeschoolers reinforces the observation that increasing numbers of homeschoolers choose it as an accessory, hybrid, temporary stopgap measure, or out of necessity given their circumstances. This new form of domestic education is challenging the historic dichotomies between public and private, between school and home, and between formal and informal that have played such an important role in American education policy for the past 170 years. Trends toward accommodation, adaptation, and hybridization, such as we have discussed here, will likely increase as US education policy seeks to catch up to the sweeping demographic, technological, and economic changes that characterize our society today. Ironically, a movement born in opposition to public schools might offer public education one of its most plausible reform paradigms for the twenty-first century's post-industrial, virtual, destabilized global soul.

FUTURE DIRECTIONS

1. With the notable exception of a recent and excellent biography of Rousas Rushdoony, the major and minor figures associated with the homeschooling

movement have yet to receive serious scholarly biographical attention. We need good biographies of John Holt, Raymond and Dorothy Moore, Mary Pride, John W. Whitehead, Bill Gothard, Gregg Harris, Michael Farris, Linda Dobson, and many other leaders.

2. Since education policy in the United States is largely a state affair, each state has its own distinct history. A few states (Georgia, Texas, Hawaii, the Carolinas, and Indiana are standouts) have received sensitive treatment, but for most states very little of their unique story is known.

3. With rare exception very little has been written about many of the curricula and pedagogical approaches that have been and in many cases continue to be influential in the homeschooling world.

4. While much has been written about conservative Protestant homeschoolers and African-American homeschoolers, far less scholarship has been devoted to other groups. Particularly needed are studies of the history of homeschooling among Roman Catholics, Mormons, Jews, and other minority religious groups.

REFERENCES

Anthony, K. V., and S. Burroughs. 2012. "Day to Day Operations of Home School Families: Selecting from a Menu of Educational Choices to Meet Students' Individual Instructional Needs." *International Educational Studies* 5: 1–17.

Bailey, B. 2004. "She Can 'Bring Home the Bacon': Negotiating Gender in Seventies America." In *America in the Seventies*, edited by Beth Bailey and David Farber, 107–128. Lawrence: University Press of Kansas.

Baugh, J. 2011. *The Detroit School Busing Case: Milliken v. Bradley and the Controversy over Desegregation*. Lawrence: University Press of Kansas.

Bollinger, M., et al. 2006. "The Impact of Food Allergy on the Daily Activities of Children and their Families." *Annals of Allergy, Asthma, and Immunology* 96: 415–421.

Carper, J., and T. Hunt, eds. 2007. *The Dissenting Tradition in American Education*. New York: Peter Lang.

Clemmit, Marcia. 2014. "Homeschooling: Do Parents Give their Children a Good Education?" *CQ Researcher* 24 (March 7): 217–240.

Conlin, M. 2006. "Meet My Teachers: Mom and Dad." *Business Week*, 80–81.

Cremin, L. 1988. *American Education: The Metropolitan Experience, 1876–1980*. New York: Harper and Row.

———. 1989. *Popular Education and its Discontents*. New York: Harper and Row.

DelFattore, J. 2004. *The Fourth R: Conflicts over Religion in America's Public Schools*. New Haven, CT: Yale University Press.

Dierenfield, B. 2007. *The Battle over School Prayer: How Engel v. Vitale Changed America*. Lawrence: University Press of Kansas.

Dochuk, D. 2010. *From Bible Belt to Sunbelt: Plain-Folk Religion, Grassroots Politics, and the Rise of Evangelical Conservativism*. New York: Norton.

Dunn, J., and M. Serthick. 2008. "Home Schoolers Strike Back: California Case Centers on Parents' Rights." *Education Next* 8: 11.

Farber, D. 2003. "Democratic Subjects in the American Sixties: National Politics, Cultural Authenticity, and Community Interest." In *The Conservative Sixties*, edited by David Farber and Jeff Roche. New York: Peter Lang.

Filene, P. 1998. *Him/her/self: Gender Identities in Modern America*. Baltimore: Johns Hopkins.

Gaither, M. 2008. *Homeschool: An American History*. New York: Palgrave MacMillan.

———. 2009. "Home Schooling Goes Mainstream." *Education Next* 9: 11–18.

Hahn, C. 2012. "Latin in the Homeschooling Community." *Teaching Classical Languages* 4: 26–51.

Hayden, D., ed. 2003. *Building Suburbia: Green Fields and Urban Growth, 1820–2000*. New York: Pantheon.

Hoelzle, B. R. 2013. "The Transmission of Values and the Transition into Adulthood Within the Context of Home Education." *Journal of Research on Christian Education* 22: 244–263.

Hurlbutt, K. S. 2012. "Experiences of Parents Who Homeschool Their Children with Autism Spectrum Disorders." *Developmental Disabilities* 26: 239–249.

Jackson, Kenneth T., ed. 1985. *Crabgrass Frontier: The Suburbanization of the United States*. New York: Oxford.

Kunzman, R. 2009. *Write These Laws on Your Children: Inside the World of Conservative Christian Homeschooling*. Boston: Beacon Press.

Laats, A. 2010. "Forging a Fundamentalist 'One Best System': Struggles over Curriculum and Educational Philosophy for Christian Day Schools, 1970–1989." *History of Education Quarterly* 50: 55–83.

Leithart, P. J. 2008. "The New Classical Schooling." *Intercollegiate Review* 43: 3–12.

Lois, J. 2013. *Home Is Where the School Is: The Logic of Homeschooling and the Emotional Language of Motherhood*. New York: New York University Press.

Luhr, E. 2009. *Witnessing Suburbia: Conservatives and Christian Youth Culture*. Berkeley: University of California Press.

Luker, K. 2007. *When Sex Goes to School: Warring Views on Sex—and Sex Education—Since the Sixties*. New York: Norton.

Lytle, M. 2006. *America's Uncivil Wars: The Sixties Era from Elvis to the Fall of President Nixon*. New York: Oxford.

McClellan, G. 1999. *Moral Education in America: Schools and the Shaping of Character from Colonial Times to the Present*. New York: Teachers College Press.

McDannell, C. 2005. "Creating the Christian Home: Home Schooling in Contemporary America." In *American Sacred Space*, edited by D. Chidester and E. Linenthal, 187–219. Bloomington: Indiana University Press.

Miller, L. 2012. "Homeschooling, City-Style." *New York Magazine*, October 22. Retrieved from http://nymag.com/guides/everything/urban-homeschooling-2012-10/.

Murphy, J. 2012. *Homeschooling in America: Capturing and Assessing the Movement*. Thousand Oaks, CA: Corwin.

National Center for Education Statistics. 2012. *Digest of Education Statistics*, Table 220. Available at http://nces.ed.gov/programs/digest/d12/tables/dt12_220.asp.

Nickerson, M. 2012. *Mothers of Conservatism: Women and the Postwar Right*. Princeton, NJ: Princeton University Press.

Noel, A., P. Stark, and J. Redford. 2013. *Parent and Family Involvement in Education*. From the National Household Education Surveys Program of 2012 (NCES 2013-028), National Center for Education Statistics, Institute of Education Sciences, US Department of Education, Washington, DC. Retrieved from http://nces.ed.gov/pubsearch.

Pennings, R., et al. 2011. *Cardus Education Survey*. Hamilton, ON: Cardus.

Planty, M., et al. 2009. *The Condition of Education 2009*. National Center for Education Statistics, Institute of Education Sciences, US Department of Education, Washington, DC.

Rodgers, D. 2012. *Age of Fracture*. Cambridge, MA: Belknap Press.

Rymph, C. 2006. *Republican Women: Feminism and Conservatism from Suffrage Through the Rise of the New Right*. Chapel Hill: University of North Carolina Press.

Sarkar, M. 2011. *How American Homes Vary by the Year They Were Built*. Retrieved from U.S. Census Bureau website: http://www.census.gov/hhes/www/housing/housing_patterns/pdf/Housing%20by%20Year%20Built.pdf.

Schetter, P., and K. Lighthall. 2009. *Homeschooling the Child with Autism Spectrum Disorder: Answers to the Top Questions Parents and Professionals Ask*. San Francisco: Jossey-Bass.

Schreiber, R. 2008. *Righting Feminism: Conservative Women and American Politics*. New York: Oxford University Press.

Schulman, B. 2001. *The Seventies: The Great Shift in American Culture, Society, and Politics*. New York: Free Press.

Seelhoff, C. 2000. "A Homeschooler's History, Part I." *Gentle Spirit Magazine* 6: 32–44.

Self, R. 2012. *All in the Family: The Realignment of American Democracy*. New York: Hill and Wang.

Stevens, M. 2001. *Kingdom of Children: Culture and Controversy in the Homeschooling Movement*. Princeton, NJ: Princeton University Press.

Stocklin-Enright, B. 1982. "The Constitutionality of Home Instruction: The Role of Parents, State, and Child." *Willamette Law Review* 18: 563–612.

Stowe, D. 2011. *No Sympathy for the Devil: Christian Pop Music and the Transformation of American Evangelicalism*. Chapel Hill: University of North Carolina Press.

Tobak, J., and P. Zirkel. 1982. "Home Instruction: An Analysis of the Statutes and Case Law." *University of Dayton Law Review* 8: 1–60.

US National Center For Education Statistics. 2008. *Digest of Education Statistics*. Available at http://www.census.gov/compendia/statab/tables/08s0292.pdf (accessed October 10, 2008).

Vigilant, L., L. Trefethren, and T. Anderson. 2013. "'You Can't Rely on Somebody Else to Teach Them Something They Don't Believe': Impressions of Legitimation Crisis and Socialization Control in the Narratives of Christian Homeschooling Fathers." *Humanity & Society* 37, no. 3: 201–224.

Williams, D. K. 2012. *God's Own Party: The Making of the Christian Right*. New York: Oxford University Press.

FURTHER READING

Carper, J. 2007. "Homeschooling Redivivus: Accommodating the Anabaptists of American Education." *The Dissenting Tradition in American Education*, edited by J. Carper and T. Hunt, 239–264. New York, NY: Peter Lang.

Hunter, J. 1991. *Culture Wars: The Struggle to Define America*. New York, NY: Basic Books.

Isserman, M., and M. Kazin. 2000. *America Divided: The Civil War of the 1960s*. New York, NY: Oxford University Press.

Kaestle, C. 1991. *Literacy in the United States: Readers and Reading Since 1880*. New Haven, CT: Yale University Press.

Kunzman, Robert, and Milton Gaither. 2013. "Homeschooling: A Comprehensive Survey of the Research." *Other Education* 2, no.1: 4–59.

Flipse, S. 2003. "Below-the-Belt Politics: Protestant Evangelicals, Abortion, and the Foundation of the New Religious Right, 1960–1975." In *The Conservative Sixties*, edited by David Farber and Jeff Roche. New York, NY: Peter Lang.

Lynn, S. 1994. "Gender and Progressive Politics: A Bridge to Social Activism of the 1960s." In *Not June Cleaver: Women and Gender in Postwar America, 1945–1960*, edited by J. Meyerowitz, 103–127. Philadelphia, PA: Temple University Press.

Meyerowitz, J. 1996. "Women, Cheesecake, and Borderline Material: Responses to Girlie Pictures in the Mid-Twentieth Century U.S." *Journal of Women's History* 8: 9–36.

Miller, T. 1999. *The Sixties Communes: Hippies and Beyond*. Syracuse, NY: Syracuse University Press.

Murray, S. 2003. *The Progressive Housewife: Community Activism in Suburban Queens, 1945–1965*. Philadelphia, PA: University of Pennsylvania Press.

Schoenwald, J. 2003. "We Are an Action Group: The John Birch Society and the Conservative Movement in the 1960s." In *The Conservative Sixties*, edited by David Farber and Jeff Roche, 21–36. New York, NY: Peter Lang.

Steigerwald, D. 1995. *The Sixties and the End of Modern America*. New York, NY: St. Martin's.

CHAPTER 13

···

PUBLIC FUNDING OF PRIVATE RELIGIOUS SCHOOLS

···

STEVEN K. GREEN

INTRODUCTION

···

FOR the first fifty-five years of adjudicating church-state controversies by the modern Supreme Court (1947–2002), no issue directed the Court's jurisprudence more than that of religion and education. That general issue had two components, seemingly distinct but interrelated both synergistically and historically: (1) religious activity in the public schools and (2) the public funding of private religious education. Of the two, religious activity in public schools—prayer and Bible reading, invocations at athletic events and graduation ceremonies, the distribution of religious literature, student "Bible clubs," and the teaching of religious alternatives to evolution, to name the most prominent controversies—has always been the more highly charged issue, at least in modern times. The public outcry over the Court's seminal decisions outlawing prayer and Bible reading in 1962 and 1963 led to failed efforts to amend the US Constitution to permit such practices (*Engel v. Vitale; Abington Township v. Schempp*). Few legal holdings have generated more opprobrium against the Court, the abortion decisions notwithstanding.

Yet the public funding of private, religious education has been more significant for the development of modern church-state jurisprudence. It was on this subject that the Court first asserted national jurisdiction over Establishment Clause matters in the states. It was in that case (*Everson v. Board of Education* 1947) that the Court endorsed a rigorous separationist approach to church-state matters. The "non-establishment of religion" principle meant, in the words of the Justices, that neither the federal nor state governments could "pass laws which aid one religion, aid all religions, or prefer one religion over another." The clause "was intended to erect 'a wall of separation between Church and State.'" And it was out of the issue of public funding of religion that the Court announced its analytical "test" or standard to govern the entire realm of church-state jurisprudence (the infamous three-part "*Lemon* test"). Thus, while "prayer and Bible reading" controversies have garnered more notoriety in the press and the public imagination, the issue of public funding of religion—of religious schools in particular—was the one that laid the foundation for a half-century of church-state jurisprudence.

The controversy over the public funding of private schools, the vast majority (85%) of which are religiously related, has involved four distinct, intersecting issues that have at times been at tension with each other: (1) the nation's moral and financial commitment to free, universal public education; (2) the longstanding tradition of religious education among some religious communities (see Chapter 11 in this volume); (3) the constitutional (and generally public) aversion to government funding of religious instruction and indoctrination; and (4) the educational needs of schoolchildren. At times, these competing values have seemed irreconcilable in the Court's decisions. On one hand, the Court has recognized the constitutional right of parents to send their children to religious schools, and the Justices and Congress (through supportive legislation) have commended the value of religious education and its contribution to society. On the other hand, the Court has reaffirmed a constitutional norm of "no-aid separationism" that favors public education over religious education, while at times Justices have implied ignoble motives on the part of religious school officials and their lobbyists in their efforts to secure public financial support.

This inconsistency, in part, reflects the long history of this controversy, one that frequently was cloaked in religious and ethnic conflict and suspicion. This ambivalence among Justices, policymakers, and liberal academics over whether the public funding of religious education is consistent with American constitutional and political values has continued to the present day, though since the 1980s a visible attitudinal shift has taken place toward favoring greater public assistance for private religious education. Today, laws provide many forms of in-kind and indirect assistance directed at students rather than to religious educational institutions (e.g., special education services, tax credits, vouchers), programs that courts have generally upheld. Only aid that is fungible and goes directly to the religious schools (e.g., teacher salary supplements, unrestricted grants), or that involves the government in supporting religious instruction, is prohibited by the courts.

Yet, while recent Court decisions have moderated the "no-aid" rule, it remains a constitutional principle. The United States is an anomaly among many Western democracies in distinguishing between public and private religious schools when it comes to the funding of education. That policy can only be understood by examining the nation's history.

HISTORICAL BACKGROUND OF
THE NO-FUNDING RULE

The Court's initial no-funding decisions (1947–1980) revealed several implicit historical assumptions: (1) that when it came to elementary and secondary education, a clear distinction had always existed between public and private schooling; (2) that the character of public schooling had always been nonsectarian and religiously inclusive, while religious private schooling was sectarian in orientation; (3) that there was no tradition of public funding of religious schooling, at least one that had received legal sanction; and (4) that the principle of church-state separation had remained relatively static throughout our nation's history. Those assumptions are not necessarily borne out in the nation's history, however.

Other chapters in this book address the history of American public education in more detail, so that will not be attempted here. However, some background may be helpful. Before the American Revolution, "public schooling"—at least in the sense of free schooling available to all children and under the control of public officials—was all but nonexistent. Educational opportunities for children turned chiefly on the basis of income or class standing. Children from wealthy families or the merchant class received training though tutors or in small academies. Only in New England was there a loose system of town or "district" schools open to most children, though those schools were frequently not free as parents often paid a "rate" for their children's education. In addition, most early schools and academies involved cooperation among local officials, private individuals, and religious figures (local clergy). In New England towns, for instance, the local Congregational minister—supported through public tax assessments— often served as the schoolteacher. Modern distinctions between public and private schooling were blurred and generally did not exist. Finally, most education, if not all schooling, had a strong religious component in which religious values were taught using texts, such as the *New England Primer*, that were steeped in Protestant doctrine. No one, not even early education reformers such as Benjamin Rush, envisioned education divorced from teaching religious values, which were deemed essential for instilling moral virtue and character traits in children (Green 2012).

The impulse for "public" education arose out of several events following the American Revolution. First, leading Founders advocated for a system of publicly funded schools to expand educational opportunities in the new republic. Part of that impulse was to enable people to participate in the new experiment in self-governance. John Adams, for one, encouraged states to provide for a "liberal education of youth, especially of the lower class of people" (Adams 1776, 28). Education was "essential to the continuance of republican governments," echoed Noah Webster, as it "gives every citizen an opportunity for acquiring knowledge and fitting him for places of trust" (Webster 1790, 65– 66). Closely related was the belief that virtue and self-discipline needed to be instilled in the future generations if the nation was going to prosper and succeed. These goals required not only an educated populace, but one that was schooled in common, republican values. This belief in a close connection between an educated people, civic virtue (including those characteristics of industry and self-discipline), and American republicanism would hold sway into the nineteenth century. And some believed that a common education with an emphasis on moral character would have a sobering effect on the potentially unruly lower classes. Summing up these strains, one journal would write in the mid-nineteenth century that "education and intelligence not only insure order, quiet and peace, but add immeasurably to the material wealth, civilization, and well-being of the community." Based on this impulse, several states wrote provisions into their new constitutions encouraging the establishment and public support of common schools (Cremin 1951 107–121; Kaestle 1983, 112–113).

Despite this commitment to establishing common schools in the short or long term, officials in some locations chose to fund existing schools, which, as noted, often operated through public-private-religious arrangements. In several eastern cities, the initial recipients of funding were denominationally run "charity" schools, which served children from the poorer and working classes. In other instances, as the nation expanded geographically and new towns were created, public officials provided funds for existing denominational schools—Presbyterian, Congregational, Methodist, Lutheran, or Catholic—in lieu of creating separate public schools. This latter pattern was most common in communities that were religiously homogeneous or that had been established by one religious group. (In some rural communities, the practice of designating local religious schools as "public" schools continued into the twentieth century.) Thus, at least initially, neither the idea nor practice of public funding of education excluded the financial support of private, religious schooling (Jorgenson 1987).

The policy, and then constitutional rule, against funding of private religious schooling arose in the early decades of the nineteenth century. In several eastern cities, education reformers established "nonsectarian" charity schools to serve children of various religious faiths. Officials in these schools—such as the New York City Free School Society— deemphasized religious instruction in their curriculum while they touted the broader appeal of their programs. Rather than teaching contested religious doctrines, educators taught religious (i.e., Protestant) values they believed were universal among Christians. These schools grew in size and number, and over time gained an increasing share of city and state school funds. Shortly, free school officials objected to the public funding of the competing denominational schools. In the 1820s, the New York Free School Society was able to block city funding of Baptist and Methodist schools on the basis that only Society schools provided a "common" education as envisioned by early reformers. In contrast to its curriculum designed to appeal to children of all faiths, the Society argued, the object of the denominational schools was "to inculcate the particular doctrines and opinions of the sect having the management of them" (Bourne 1870, 129). At the same time, the Society raised early arguments that funding denominational schools violated church-state principles: (1) that providing public funds to denominational schools "impose[d] a direct tax on our citizens for the support of religion" in violation of rights of conscience; (2) that funding of religious schools would cause competition and rivalry among faiths; and (3) that the school fund was "purely of a civil character," not to be under the control of a religious institution. "[T]he proposition that such a fund should never go into the hands of an ecclesiastical body or religious society, is presumed to be incontrovertible upon any political principle approved or established in this country. . . . that church and state shall not be united" (Bourne 1870, 88).

In 1825, the New York City Common Council agreed with the Society and voted to cease funding denominational charity schools. The City declared that the school fund was "purely of a civil character, designed for a civil purpose," intimating that education in a religious school would not satisfy that purpose, despite such schools providing a civil purpose for thirty years. Besides asserting that funding religious education failed a public purpose, the City also described the prohibition in quasi-constitutional terms, asking rhetorically whether entrusting the fund "to religious or ecclesiastical bodies is not a violation of an elementary principle in the politics of the State and country" (Bourne 1870, 67). After 1825, only those schools of the Society and the handful of non-denominational charity schools remained eligible to receive public school funds. Within a decade, the Free School Society had reincorporated as the "Public School Society" in order to secure its position as the city's "public" school (Bourne 1870, 52–67, 88, 142–145; Pratt 1967, 158–168).

The initial conflicts over public funding of denominational schools were significant in the development of the no-funding rule in two respects. At least initially, the prohibition was religiously generic: in New York public officials applied the rule to Protestant schools, emphasizing the denominational control ("religious or ecclesiastical bodies") and the sectarian content of the curriculum. This focus provided a pass to the Protestant-oriented "nonsectarian" curriculum that was arising in common schools. Second, the prohibition was cast not only in terms of universality and public control, but also in con-stitutional terms: the public funding of religious instruction was "a violation of the con-stitutional rights and conscientious scruples of the people" (Bourne, 1870, 140).

The rule against funding religious schooling—based in part on nascent ideas of church-state separation—arose before the significant influx of Catholic immigrants be-ginning in the mid-1830s. That influx caused a strain on the emergent common schools as Irish and then German Catholic children swelled the school ranks. Before long, conflict arose between public school officials—many with backgrounds as Protestant clergy—and Catholic leaders over the curriculum and Protestant orientation of the common schools. Catholic officials objected not only to the Protestant-oriented reli-gious exercises—prayer, readings from the Protestant King James Bible, hymn singing—but also to textbooks that frequently equated Protestantism with republican values while associating Catholicism with autocracy. School officials and Protestant leaders reacted defensively to the Catholic complaints, particularly to Catholic criticisms of the King James Bible, and often refused to compromise. The conflict then fueled a rise in anti-Catholic nativism (Green 2012).

In response to the perceived hostility of public schools, Catholic bishops in the 1830s and 1840s issued calls for a system of Catholic parochial schools. As those schools were established, Catholic officials made appeals to state legislatures and public school boards for a share of the state school funds. In most instances, public officials rejected Catholic requests to divide the school fund. One of the earlier and more notable episodes in-volved an 1840 petition by New York Bishop John Hughes to the New York Common Council to fund the city's burgeoning parochial schools. In a closely watched hearing that lasted two days, Hughes debated Public School Society lawyers and Protestant min-isters over the value of religious education and the meaning of church-state separation. After failing to secure funds from the city, Hughes took his campaign to the state capital, threatening to exert his political influence among rank-and-file Catholics. Hughes' tactic raised the ire of Protestants and nativists, though he almost succeeded in having the Democratic-controlled Assembly enact a bill authorizing a division of the school fund between public and Catholic schools. In the end, Hughes' efforts backfired, and the New York legislature enacted a law that prohibited granting public funds to any school in which "any religious sectarian doctrine or tenet shall be taught, inculcated, or practiced," thereby incorporating the no-funding principle into law.

The New York episode and resulting law served as a bellwether for the future of religious school funding in other states: between 1835 and the Civil War, at least seven states enacted laws or constitutional provisions prohibiting the application of public monies for the benefit of any religious school or society (Green 2012).

Despite laws and constitutional provisions prohibiting the public funding of religious schooling—and fierce opposition to such funding among public school officials and Protestant leaders—the no-funding rule was often stricter in theory than in practice. In communities with large immigrant populations (e.g., Irish and German), local public officials often acceded to requests by Catholic and Lutheran school leaders to authorize funding from alternative sources (e.g., discretionary funds, local taxes). In addition, public officials sometimes interpreted the no-funding rule to apply only to education taking place in religious schools so as not to bar funding of other religious institutions. Before long, a distinction arose between the public funding of religious schools and religiously affiliated charities, such as orphanages. Because the latter were not chiefly engaged in religious education and instruction—and technically not covered by the language of many no-funding laws—local public officials responded favorably to funding requests for charitable enterprises. (This was at a time when cities and states provided few charitable services themselves.)

This distinction between schools and charities created an anomaly in the law: in one case, a New York court held that the Roman Catholic Orphan Asylum of Brooklyn was ineligible to receive state school funds for its educational program. A different New York court held, however, that another Catholic orphanage could receive funding for the education and care of its wards—provided the funds came from local tax revenues rather than the school fund. Thus the rigor of the no-funding rule often turned on the primary character of the religious institution (charity v. school) and the source of public funding, rather than on whether public monies subsidized religious education. By the 1870s, religious charitable institutions—chiefly Catholic—were receiving hundreds of thousands of dollars in public financial assistance, usually administered by local officials who were attuned to the political strength of the large, immigrant religious communities (Green 2012).

In the 1870s a national controversy arose over public funding of religious institutions, schools and charities alike. The funding crisis was precipitated by a series of exposés revealing the close collaboration between Democratic officials in New York City and other eastern cities and Church leaders over the funding of Catholic charities. An 1872 report by the New York Council of Political Reform indicated that the Tammany Hall-controlled government was disproportionately funding Catholic charities over

Protestant and Jewish charities, often at a rate of four or five to one, with little oversight on how the funds were being spent. In some instances, funds went directly to Catholic schools. At the same time, Catholic leaders announced their intentions to establish more parochial schools and seek additional public financial support.

Protestant leaders and Protestant-leaning newspapers reacted vehemently to these revelations, and before long, the crisis caught the attention of national political figures. Republican leaders, with their evangelical Protestant base, raised calls for a political solution to finally resolve the "School Question." In the fall of 1875, President Ulysses S. Grant, hoping to resurrect his political career, issued a call to "[e]ncourage free schools, and resolve that no one dollar, appropriated for their support, shall be appropriated to the support of any sectarian schools. . . . Keep the Church and State forever separate" (Green 2012, 187). In a later address to Congress, Grant proposed a constitutional amendment to prohibit the "granting of any school funds or taxes . . . for the benefit of or in aid, directly or indirectly, of any religious sect or denomination" (Green 2012, 193). Shortly thereafter, Representative James Blaine, the front-runner for the 1876 Republican nomination for president, introduced into Congress a proposed amendment to that effect (commonly called the Blaine Amendment). Democrats, with their large Catholic constituency, generally opposed the measure, and the School Question quickly became a leading issue in the ensuing election; as the *New York Times* opined, an "appeal to religious passions was worth twenty five thousand votes to the Republicans" (Green 2012, 188). A Democratic-controlled House of Representatives enacted a watered-down version of the Blaine Amendment, but the Senate resurrected a more rigorous version of it that, by a partisan vote, fell just short of the two-thirds majority necessary for a constitutional amendment.

Although the Blaine Amendment failed to be incorporated into the federal constitution, it served as a model for the later adoption of no-funding provisions in the constitutions of several states. In the fifty years following the Blaine Amendment, twenty-one states adopted express no-funding provisions in their constitutions. Even though the Blaine Amendment no doubt provided inspiration for many state provisions, it and the state counterparts were merely affirming a principle against funding religious schooling that had been developing since the 1820s (Green 2012).

THE MODERN CONTROVERSY OVER RELIGIOUS SCHOOL FUNDING

By the beginning of the twentieth century, the distinction between public and private religious schooling was firmly established in America (despite hybrid public-religious-schools operating in a few locales). In addition, the general rule against providing public funds for religious education was also well established in law and practice. Catholic educational officials, however, never surrendered their goal of obtaining public support for their parochial schools. In a few instances, they succeeded in securing minor forms of public aid, usually of a supplemental nature, such as loans of textbooks and reimbursements for children's transportation costs. In 1930, the US Supreme Court upheld a Louisiana law that provided free textbooks to children attending religious schools on the ground that the assistance served a public purpose by benefitting children, not the religious schools. In so holding, the Court did not directly address the church-state question of public funding of religious education. By the mid-1930s, supplemental assistance was becoming more common; one report indicated that in 1937, 370 Catholic schools nationwide benefited from such appropriations. That report was precipitated by a challenge to a 1936 New York law that authorized reimbursements for transportation to and from parochial schools. After the New York Court of Appeals struck down the law in 1938 on the basis of the state's no-funding constitutional provision, voters enacted a constitutional amendment authorizing the legislature to fund transportation costs of children "to and from any school or institution of learning," the state's no-funding rule notwithstanding. Still, at this stage, public funding for religious schooling was relatively modest (Pratt 1967).

The precedent created by such arrangements was difficult to contain, as it suggested that other forms of public assistance for religious education might follow. The implications of this trend were not lost on opponents of religious school funding, so in 1943 litigants challenged a recently enacted New Jersey law authorizing reimbursements for transporting children to and from any school, including religious schools. After the New Jersey Court of Errors and Appeals upheld the reimbursement law, the plaintiffs appealed the issue to the US Supreme Court. The plaintiffs argued that even though the financial aid in question was relatively insignificant, there was "no logical stopping point" to the type of funding available under either a "public purpose" or "child benefit" theory (Green, 2012, 245). As an *amicus* for the plaintiffs wrote in a brief, if those theories were carried to their logical conclusion, it "would enable any one leading sect to control the schools" (Green 2012, 245; Fair 1997, 1–21).

The case of *Everson v. Board of Education* (1947) was not litigated in a vacuum, however; the case coincided with a postwar movement to improve America's educational system. As part of that impetus, in 1947 members of Congress proposed providing federal assistance to primary and secondary schools. Fueling this movement was the belief that, in light of the threats of Nazism and communism, education served as "the most effective bulwark of democracy against totalitarianism" (Kiezer 1970, 84). To ensure this goal, legislators proposed a permanent program of federal grants to states to equalize educational opportunities. Under some versions of the legislation, parochial schools were to be included as recipients of the federal monies. Both issues—federal involvement in education in the states, and then the funding of religious schooling—were highly controversial, with Southern segregationists opposing any federal involvement in state schooling and liberals and Protestant leaders opposing the funding of religious schools. Although educational funding legislation remained stalled in Congress for years, the specter of federal funding of education in the states, both public and private schooling, loomed over the Court's early forays into the constitutionality of public assistance to religious schooling. As Justice Wiley Rutledge would remark sardonically in his *Everson* dissent, the lawsuit was "not therefore just a little case over bus fares" (*Everson* 1947, 57; Kizer 1970).

With that backdrop, the Court's erratic holding in *Everson* becomes more understandable. The Court initially embraced a rigorous notion of church-state separation, one that affirmed the no-aid principle: "No tax in any amount, large or small, can be levied to support any religious activities or institutions, whatever they may be called, or whatever form they may adopt to teach or practice religion." The purpose of the Establishment Clause of the US Constitution, Justice Hugo Black wrote, was "to erect 'a wall of separation between Church and State'" (*Everson* 1947, 16). Yet, despite that rhetoric, a five-Justice majority upheld the New Jersey reimbursement law on the ground that it was "part of a general program under which it pays the fares of pupils attending public and other schools." The law was neutral with respect to religion and nonreligion, Justice Black wrote. In addition, Black noted, because the reimbursement went to parents of the schoolchildren, the "State contributes no money to the [religious] schools." The law "does no more than provide a general program to help parents get their children, regardless of their religion, safely and expeditiously to and from accredited schools" (*Everson* 1947, 17–18). The decision thus sent an inconsistent message to legislators and policymakers: public financial aid to religious schools was unconstitutional, though some forms of assistance that indirectly benefited religious schools were permissible, provided the program was religiously neutral.

To be expected, few people were satisfied with Black's decision. Catholic educators objected to the Court's embrace of no-aid separationism while Protestants, liberals, and public educators worried that the exception to the general rule would invite other forms of assistance for religious education. People from the latter group formed Protestants and Other Americans United for Separation of Church and State (POAU) to lobby against all forms of "parochiaid," while POAU joined with ACLU and Jewish groups to challenge state appropriations benefiting religious schools. In 1968, the Supreme Court extended its *Everson* ruling by upholding a New York law that provided free textbooks for children attending public and private schools (*Board of Education v. Allen*). Though acknowledging that religious schools ultimately benefited from the program, the Court emphasized that "no funds or books [were] furnished to parochial schools, and the financial benefit [was] to parents and children, not to schools," despite the program making "it more likely that some children choose to attend a sectarian school" (*Allen* 1968, 243–244). Justice Black, the author of *Everson*, dissented, distinguishing textbooks from bus fares, arguing that "[w]ith respect to the latter, state financial support actively and directly assists the teaching and propagation of sectarian religious viewpoints in clear conflict with the First Amendment's establishment bar" (*Allen* 1968, 253).

In its early holdings, the high court had distinguished between financial aid that went directly to the religious schools and minor forms of assistance from which the schools benefited indirectly. A major break in the psychological barrier to government funding of religious education came with the enactment of Title I of the Elementary and Secondary Education Act of 1965 (ESEA), which represented the first substantial federal law to provide financial assistance to education nationwide. Responding to disparities in education funding among the states and seeking to address the unmet educational needs of disadvantaged children, ESEA granted "financial assistance . . . to local educational agencies serving areas with concentrations of children from low-income families to expand and improve their educational programs . . . which contribute particularly to meeting the special educational needs of educationally deprived children." Recognizing the scope of the problem, Congress mandated that ESEA apply not only to public schools, but also to "educationally deprived children . . . enrolled in private elementary and secondary schools," including religious schools (Kelley 1966, 417–418). Initially, ESEA provided funds for remedial education and counseling, supplemental services and equipment, audiovisual devices, and mobile teaching units. Yet neither the law nor the accompanying regulations expressly limited the types of eligible services, provided they were "secular, neutral, and nonideological" and supplemented "and in no case supplant[ed] the level of services" already provided by the private, religious schools (Kelley 1966, 417–418). In a related decision in 1974, the Supreme Court held that the mere inclusion of religious schools under the provisions of ESEA did not violate the Establishment Clause (*Wheeler v. Barrera* 1974).

Title I of ESEA firmly established the legitimacy of private, religious education and the public interest in serving children attending those schools. It provided an impetus for states to experiment with other forms of financial assistance for private, religious education. Many of those initial efforts involved more direct forms of assistance, such as tuition reimbursements and supplements for the salaries of religious school teachers. That legislation met a firewall at the Supreme Court during the 1970s and early 1980s, however, a period in which the high court reviewed over a dozen cases involving government funding of religious schools and colleges. The tension in the *Everson* and *Allen* holdings forced the Court to articulate a more consistent analytical standard for reviewing challenges to public funding programs. What emerged was the "*Lemon* test," named after a 1971 case, which held that funding laws must (1) have a secular purpose, (2) not have the primary effect of advancing or inhibiting religion, and (3) not result in excessive entanglement between government and religious institutions (*Lemon v. Kurtzman*). Based on that somewhat rigorous standard, the Court invalidated a host of state programs designed to assist private religious schools, including tuition reimbursements, teacher salary supplements, tax credits, building maintenance and repair grants, and educational materials and equipment, all on the ground that the programs directly subsidized the activities of "sectarian educational institutions." The decisions were based on the theory that most private religious schools were "pervasively sectarian" in their operation:

> The very purpose of many [parochial] schools is to provide an integrated and secular and religious education; the teaching process is, to a large extent, devoted to the inculcation of religious values and belief. Substantial aid to the educational function of such schools, accordingly, necessarily results in aid to the sectarian school enterprise as a whole (Meek, 1975, 366).

Such language appeared to offer little leeway for anything more than the most supplemental and indirect forms of government assistance for religious education. But the distinctions the Court had articulated in its early decisions—child benefit and indirect aid—regained their significance as a more conservative majority arose on the high court in the 1980s. Even in its more separationist holdings the decade before, the Justices had not declared that children attending religious schools were ineligible to receive public assistance, provided the aid was discrete, supplemental, and not divertible for religious purposes.

Building on those principles, two trends emerged in the 1980s and 1990s that broke down the seemingly intractable rule of no-aid separationism. The first was an expansion on the idea of indirect aid to religion, here in the form of tax deductions/credits and scholarships to students that could be applied toward religious education. So, in 1983 and 1986 respectively, the Court upheld a state tax deduction for expenses associated with private schooling, including tuition costs, and a disability-based scholarship for a student to attend a religious college (*Mueller v. Allen* 1983; *Witters v. Washington* 1986). The idea was that the assistance benefited individuals who then exercised their "independent private choice" of whether to apply their government benefit toward religious education. The religious schools, the Justices noted, were indirect beneficiaries of the government funding.

With that precedent set, during the 1990s, legislatures in various states, including Wisconsin, Florida, Illinois, Ohio, and Puerto Rico, enacted tax credit and voucher programs for private and religious schooling. Opponents argued that because the programs reimbursed tuition costs, chiefly at religious schools, and were not restricted to discrete and identifiably secular items, the vouchers and credits provided substantial aid toward religious education. State supreme courts struck down the majority of programs, but the Ohio program finally made its way to the Supreme Court in 2002 (*Zelman v. Simmons-Harris* 2002). There, in a highly watched decision, the Court upheld the Ohio tuition voucher program. Writing for the five-Justice majority, Chief Justice William Rehnquist held that

> where a government aid program is neutral with respect to religion, and provides assistance directly to a broad class of citizens who, in turn, direct government aid to religious schools wholly as a result of their own genuine an independent private choice, the program is not readily subject to challenge under the Establishment Clause (*Zelman* 2002, 652).

Under this theory of neutral "private choice," the Court was not concerned about the amount of the voucher assistance or whether it could be applied toward religious instruction. The "incidental advancement of a religious mission" through the voucher funds, Rehnquist noted, "is reasonably attributable to the individual recipient, not to the government."

In contrast, the dissenters argued that the cumulative amount of the voucher aid for many religious schools resulted in substantial financial assistance for religious education. With this decision in *Zelman*, a significant bar to public financial assistance to religious schooling was lifted.

The second trend was the Court's reconsideration of the ban on many forms of direct financial aid to religious schools. In a 1997 case dealing with ESEA Title I programs, the Court held that local education agencies no longer had to provide their services in "neutral" sites but could conduct remedial education and counseling on the campus of religious schools. The Court would no longer presume any impermissible advancement of religion or a "symbolic link" between religion and government under such programs. Three years later, in *Mitchell v. Helms* (2000), the high court relaxed the no-funding ban even further by holding that *direct* forms of government aid, such as instructional and educational equipment, were constitutional. Where the form of assistance was religiously neutral and distributed equally among public, private, and religious schools, the Court would not presume that the aid would be diverted for religious uses. In so ruling, a plurality of the Justices expressly refuted the "pervasively sectarian" doctrine, noting that "the religious nature of a recipient should not matter to the constitutional analysis, so long as the recipient adequately furthers the government's secular purpose." After the *Zelman* and *Mitchell* holdings, the only form of prohibited government financial assistance to religious schools appears to be aid that is not religiously neutral (i.e., is fungible and/or can be used for religious worship or indoctrination) or that involves the government in supporting religious indoctrination.

Conclusion

Considering the changes to Supreme Court jurisprudence in the 1990s and 2000s, the rule regarding public funding of private, religious schooling has undergone a dramatic transformation, not only since the nineteenth century, but since the 1970s. Old assumptions, and hopefully prejudices, about the role and contribution of private religious education to American society have been laid to rest. Still, as interpreted by the Supreme Court, the Constitution continues to bar the complete financing of private religious education, providing that government funds cannot be used subsidize religious instruction, worship, or indoctrination.

Future Directions

1. Based on the development in the law, will the Supreme Court likely maintain its current distinction between direct and indirect funding of private, religious education?

2. Do the developments in the law regarding public funding for private religious schooling invite a re-evaluation of role of private schooling in the United States and suggest an affirmative obligation to fully fund such schooling?

3. Does the public funding of private, religious schooling continue to raise concerns about government support of religious indoctrination?

4. Have attitudes among the general public toward religious-based education changed over the previous generation, including its eligibility for public funding, or do concerns remain about the propriety of government support for private schooling?

REFERENCES

Adams, John. 1776. *Thoughts on Government*. Philadelphia: John Dunlap.

Bourne, William Oland. 1870. *History of the Public School Society of the City of New York*. New York: William Wood & Co.

Cremin, Lawrence A. 1951. *The American Common School: A Historic Conception*. New York: Teachers College, Columbia University.

Fair, Daryl R. 1997. "The Everson Case in the Context of New Jersey Politics." In *Everson Revisited*, edited by Jo Renee Formicola and Hubert Morken, 1–21. Lanham, MD: Rowan & Littlefield.

Green, Steven K. 2012. *The Bible, the School, and the Constitution: The Clash that Shaped Modern Church–State Doctrine*. New York: Oxford University Press.

Hamburger, Phillip. 2002. *Separation of Church and State*. Cambridge, MA: Harvard University Press.

Holscher, Kathleen. 2012. *Religious Lessons: Catholic Sisters and the Captured School Crisis in New Mexico*. New York: Oxford University Press.

Jorgenson, Lloyd P. 1987. *The State and the Non-Public School*. Columbia, MO: University of Missouri Press.

Kaestle, Carl. 1983. *Pillars of the Republic: Common Schools and American Society*. New York: Hill & Wang.

Kelley, Dean M. 1966. "State Regulations of the Participation of Pupils of Private Schools in Title I of the Federal Aid to Education Act of 1965." *Journal of Church and State* 8: 415–429.

Kizer, George A. 1970. "Federal Aid to Education: 1945–1963." *History of Education Quarterly* 1:84–102.

1941. Note, "Catholic Schools and Public Money." *Yale Law Journal* 50: 917–927.

Pratt, John Webb. 1967. *Religion, Politics, and Diversity: The Church–State Theme in New York History*. Ithaca, NY: Cornell University Press.

Sorauf, Frank J. 1971. *The Wall of Separation: The Constitutional Politics of Church and State*. Princeton, NJ: Princeton University Press.

Webster, Noah. 1790. "On Education of Youth in America." In *Essays on Education in the Early Republic*, edited by Frederick Rudolph. Cambridge: Belknap Press.

Winer, Laurence H., and Nina J. Crim. 2015. *God, Schools, and Government Funding*. Farnham, England: Ashgate.

REFERENCED CASES

Abington Township v. Schempp, 374 U.S. 203 (1963).
Agostini v. Felton, 521 U.S. 203 (1997).
Board of Education v. Allen, 392 U.S. 236 (1968).
Engel v. Vitale, 370 U.S. 421 (1962).
Everson v. Board of Education, 330 U.S. 1 (1947).
Lemon v. Kurtzman, 403 U.S. 602 (1971).
Meek v. Pittenger, 421 U.S. 349 (1975).
Mitchell v. Helms, 530 U.S. 793 (2000).
Mueller v. Allen, 463 U.S. 388 (1983).
Wheeler v. Barrera, 417 U.S. 402 (1974).
Witters v. Washington Department of Services for the Blind, 474 U.S. 481 (1986).
Zelman v. Simmons-Harris, 536 U.S. 639 (2002).

PART IV

··

RELIGION AND
PUBLIC SCHOOLS

··

CHAPTER 14

RELIGIOUSLY AFFILIATED CHARTER SCHOOLS

NATHAN C. WALKER

CHARTER schools have grown significantly since 1991, when Minnesota became the first state to enact charter school legislation. By the 2013–14 school year, the country's charter schools educated more than 2.2 million students. According to the US Department of Education's National Center for Education Statistics (2015), the number of charter schools doubled in the decade from 2003–04 to 2013–14 (from 3,181 to 6,465). Nearly 70% of the nation's charter schools were located in eight states: California (1,238), Texas (658), Florida (623), Arizona (600), Ohio (390), Wisconsin (242), New York (233), and Colorado (200). Of the forty-two states with charter school legislation, charters represent an average of 7% of the public schools in those states. The outliers are the District of Columbia and Arizona, in which 48% and 27% of public schools were charter schools, respectively; in the aftermath of Hurricane Katrina, over 60% of public schools in New Orleans became charter schools.

Charter schools are public schools, as defined by federal and state law, so when it comes to issues of religion and education, they are bound by the same laws and legal precedents as public schools. As a result, local developers and state chartering agencies that seek to establish religious or faith-based charter schools are likely to fail in state and federal courts. This subject is best understood in the context of the larger charter school movement.

ORIGINS AND DEVELOPMENTS

To found a charter school, a *developer*—defined as an individual or group of individuals that initiates and implements the charter school project—seeks approval from a chartering agency established or authorized by a state legislature. The developer legally negotiates the contract or "charter" to determine the school's governance (balancing public and private control), the financial formulas (distribution of public and private funds), and the location (public or private property/facilities). The charter also outlines the employment and admissions policies and the scope and purpose of the curriculum. These subjects become legally complicated when a developer affiliates the charter school with a religious organization or when a religious organization serves as the developer.

Although it is not known how many charter schools were established by, with, or for religious groups, there are three notable examples of religiously affiliated or themed charter schools. For instance, from 2010 to 2013, Texas awarded sixteen of the twenty-three charters to schools with religious ties. One of those schools is Beta Academy, which was initially denied a charter in its first application process but later awarded one in 2014. The Beta Academy, which operates from the Houston Christian Temple Assembly of God Church, had previously closed its doors as a private religious school because of its declining enrollment. It reopened in the same facility as a publicly financed charter school. This financially benefited the failing private school, the parents who previously paid private tuition, and the church that now leases its building to the charter school—a now public school founded by the wife of a pastor of this church. Public funds were used to subsidize not only a once-private religious school but the church in which it was located. If challenged, a court would likely define this arrangement as an "excessive entanglement" between a public school and a private church, and thus a violation of the Establishment Clause of the First Amendment to the U.S. Constitution.

The Minnesota chapter of the American Civil Liberties Union (ACLU) filed a lawsuit against the Tarek ibn Ziyad Academy in Inver Grove Heights, Minnesota, for operating "in essence, [as] a private religious school." The ACLU claimed that the school was "holding group prayers during school hours, including a 30-minute prayer session on Fridays, allowing teachers to post religious material on classroom bulletin boards, and enforcing Islamic rules on modesty of dress—including sleeves and skirts or trousers of a certain length, on female but not male students and teachers" (Samuelson, 2009). The school reached a settlement in 2001, the same year the Minnesota Education Department revoked the school's charter.

In Detroit, Michigan, the students at the Marvin L. Winans Academy of Performing Arts sing a "school creed" as a hymn. The lyrics lead students to proclaim, "I am created in the image of a super-intelligent God" (full recording available at winans. spfs.k12.mi.us). If challenged, a court could deem the school creed to be religiously coercive and lack a secular purpose, unless the facts demonstrated that the song was student-written and student-initiated, voluntary, and not endorsed by the school.

These three examples directly relate to case law about religion and public education. A more complicated story is told when, in the absence of religious instruction or coercive religiosity, a charter school is formed to respond to the cultural and linguistic needs of a minority community. Take, for instance, these three additional schools: (1)

the Tsunadeloquasdi Immersion School in Tahlequah, Oklahoma, the first English-Cherokee school in the United States; (2) Ben Gamla School, in Hollywood, Florida, the first English-Hebrew charter school in the United States; and (3) the Hellenic Classical Charter School, in Brooklyn, New York, which is affiliated with the Greek Orthodox Church. All three schools have the mission of teaching about the culture and language associated with their respective religious traditions. The Cherokee school's mission is to "promote the revitalization/usage of the Cherokee language while educating children in a safe and cultural environment" (cherokee.org, 2018). Ben Gamla "provides a safe environment [that] . . . integrates Hebrew instruction giving . . . students a useful tool in our global society" (bengamla-charter.com, 2018). Hellenic Classical provides students with "a rigorous . . . classical study of the Greek and Latin languages" (www.hccs-nys.org, 2018). In all three contexts, the charter school's developers were motivated to preserve their cultural heritage and provide a counterculture for the students who would not have an equivalent immersion in traditional public schools. Immersion is one strategy, and integration is another.

The Adam Adbulle Academy in Rochester, Minnesota, was established to integrate Somali refugees through a dual English-Arabic language curriculum. The director of the school made clear, "We teach language. We don't teach religion" (Mann, 2009). Similarly, the Hmong College Prep Academy in St. Paul and the New Millennium Academy in Minneapolis were founded to integrate the Hmong people, who previously faced religious persecution in China and Vietnam. The purpose was to "develop and nurture pride within the rich heritage of Hmong culture through language literacy, the arts, traditional food and values" (www.hcpak12.org, 2018). Similar to the Cherokee- and Hebrew-language schools mentioned previously, the Hmong school provides a "public school learning environment that is unintimidating, structured and safe" (www.hcpak12.org, 2018).

These examples illustrate the various motivations that religious groups may have in chartering public schools. It is legally impermissible to use public funds to save a failing private-religious school and its house of worship and to explicitly use public funds to endorse, encourage, and regulate religious expression, such as reciting school creeds with theological declarations, mandating prayer times, and issuing religious clothing requirements. The legally permissible examples include cultural-based schools that seek to use language to immerse or integrate students as part of a civic curriculum.

LAWS AND REGULATIONS

What laws and regulations would be used to make distinctions between using public funds to teach religion on one hand and teaching languages that have religious connections on the other? Where are the legal boundaries on this subject when there are so many political landmines in the culture wars surrounding issues of religion and public life?

The National Alliance for Public Charter Schools explicitly states that charter schools must be "nonsectarian" and "[can]not discriminate on any basis" (NAPCS 2014, 2). Here the group referring to the fact that charter schools must comply with judicial tests for interpreting the meaning of the Establishment Clause of the First Amendment to the US Constitution. Charter schools must also comply with education laws outlined in federal regulations, such as Title VII of the Civil Rights Act of 1964 and Title IX of the Education Amendments of 1972, which prohibit discrimination based on religion.

In addition, there are a number of state constitutional clauses that could be used to prohibit the creation of charter schools by or with religious groups. These state laws are far more complex than the federal legal system's. For example:

1. "No aid to religion" and "no establishment" clauses in state constitutions have been used to prohibit the use of public funds to aid religious groups.
2. The "no diversion" clauses in state constitutions have been employed to prohibit public funds from being used for private purposes, including private religious purposes.
3. The "no religious tests for office" and "no religious tests for public teachers" in state constitutions have been used to prohibit publicly funded agencies from making religion a prerequisite for employment.
4. The "no sectarian teaching" clauses in state constitutions have been used to prevent publicly funded teachers from coercing students to take part in devotional practices, such as prayer or worship.
5. The "no preference" clauses in state constitutions have been used to prohibit schools from privileging one religion over another or privileging nonreligion over religion.
6. The "free exercise" of religion, "right to worship," and "right of conscience" clauses in state constitutions have been used to accommodate students' religious practices, including protecting those students who change religions or choose not to identify as religious.

State statutes may also explicitly limit the involvement of religious organizations with charter schools. As of 2008, twenty-six state legislatures require that public charter schools be "nonsectarian" or must conduct "nonsectarian instruction," according to research conducted by the National Resource Center (NRC) on Charter School Finance and Governance (2008). The NRC found that fifteen states prohibited religious organizations from establishing charter schools. New Jersey's Charter School Program Act of 1995 initially prohibited a "parochial school" from being "eligible for charter school status" (§I18A:36A-4); however, this clause was removed via an amendment passed in 2011, with the only restriction in religious affiliation that "the name of the proposed charter school shall not include any religious reference" (§18A:36A-4.1). Five of the eight states previously listed that enroll nearly 70% of students attending the nation's charter schools do not have any statutory restrictions, according to the 2008 NRC report (Arizona, New York, Ohio, Texas, Wisconsin).

In summarizing the legal provisions, charter schools that are established for, with, and by religious groups are likely to fail under either the federal or state constitutions or under federal or state statutes. This does not mean that national and local governments can banish religion from public institutions; on the contrary, there are equally vast protections that require public schools to accommodate religion. Said another way, the Free Exercise and Establishment Clauses of the First Amendment are two principles that make up one freedom: religious liberty (Haynes & Thomas 2008).

PERMISSIBLE ACTIONS

Under the First Amendment, charter schools, like all public schools, may teach *about* religion through the academic study of religion. In *Abington Township School District v. Schempp* (1963), the US Supreme Court declared that state-sponsored religious practices are unconstitutional in public schools. At the same time, however, the Court made clear that study *about* religion is not only constitutionally permissible but also necessary for a "complete education." In writing for eight of the nine Justices, Justice Tom Clark said,

> It might well be said that one's education is not complete without a study of comparative religion or the history of religion and its relationship to the advancement of civilization. It certainly may be said that the Bible is worthy of study for its literary and historic qualities. Nothing we have said here indicates that such study of the Bible or of religion, when presented objectively as part of a secular program of education, may not be effected consistently with the First Amendment.

In helping the public understand how to use this constitutional approach to issues about religion and public schools, Charles C. Haynes of the First Amendment Center (the precursor to the Religious Freedom Center of the Newseum Institute) led a coalition of twenty-one national education, civil liberties, and religious organizations to reach public consensus guidelines on issues of religion and public education. These constitutional principles apply to charter schools. As published in *A Teacher's Guide to Religion in the Public School* (Haynes & Thomas 2011, 98), the coalition clarifies that educators and policymakers must ensure that

> the school's approach to religion is *academic*, not *devotional*; the school strives for student *awareness* of religions, but does not press for student *acceptance* of any

religion; the school sponsors *study* about religion, not the *practice* of religion; the school may *expose* students to a diversity of religious views, but may not *impose* any particular view; the school *educates* about all religions; it does not *promote* or *denigrate* religion; the school *informs* students about various beliefs; it does not seek to *conform* students to any particular belief.

In this way, a charter school, for example, may use an academic approach to teaching about Judaism and/or Islam and offer a language course in Hebrew and/or Arabic; however, it cannot require students to engage in devotional practices, including memorizing and reciting the Tanakh or the Qur'an. The school may offer an *elective* course about religious texts to advance the study of literature, civics, geography, and history, but it may not require students to engage in devotional reading or religious practices.

Religious Accommodations

In this context, it is permissible for a charter school, as with any public school, to make the following accommodations for students' religious beliefs and practices. Public schools may dedicate space for student devotional activities before or after school, such as prayer and worship services; however, these religious expressions must be student-initiated and voluntary and may not involve a teacher. Public schools may create student uniforms or dress codes but must accommodate a student's wearing of religious garb (e.g., Native American hair length, Wiccan pentacle, ashes for Ash Wednesday, Christian cross necklace, Jewish yarmulke, Muslim hijab, Sikh turban). (This is more complicated when it comes to employees—see Chapter 16 in this volume.) A public charter school may implement a dietary policy for school-produced meals (e.g., kosher, halal, vegetarian, no-caffeine); however, it could not prohibit students from bringing food that did not comply with those practices. A public charter school may close on a religious holiday because a critical mass of students and employees observe that holiday (e.g., Hinduism, Diwali; Judaism, Rosh Hashanah, Yom Kippur, and Sukkot; Christianity, Christmas and/or Orthodox Easter; Islam, Eid al-Fitr and Eid al-Adha; Sikhism, the birthday of Guru Nanak Dev Sahib).

In these ways, the First Amendment permits, to some degree, religious accommodations and permits the academic teaching *about* religion. Regardless, traditional public schools and public charter schools are held to the same legal standards.

Defining Religion

Authorities would benefit from defining religion before examining the legality of public schools that are chartered for, with, and by religious groups. This may help them understand the difference between religious establishments that use public funds to coerce students and entangle religion and the state and ethnic groups that seek to preserve their group identities. Under the leadership of Diane L. Moore (2010), the American Academy of Religion published guidelines for teaching about religion in public schools. The guidelines make clear that "religions are internally diverse as opposed to uniform; religions evolve and change over time as opposed to being ahistorical and static," and most important to this discussion, "religious influences are embedded in all dimensions of culture as opposed to the assumption that religions function in discrete, isolated, 'private' contexts" (12–15). This three-pronged definition helps legal authorities recognize that religious groups often divide into subgroups and desire a space to respond to the changing dynamics within and around their religions. Many of these religions' adherents do not separate their private and public lives; at the same time, they often seek autonomy from public services to preserve the essence of their religious identities.

One's religious identity may be constructed in a variety of ways depending on how much value one places on the "3Bs"—belief, behavior, and experiences of belonging (see Chapter 4 in this volume and Saroglou 2011). Religion is not limited to expression of a person or group's beliefs, such as creeds, credos, doctrines, or articles of faith—as often emphasized in Christianity, particularly Protestant Christianity. One's religious identity may also be informed by the behavior of individuals and groups through devotional practices, rituals, rites of passages, holidays, and so on. One's religious identity may also be tightly bound to expressions of belonging related to ethnic and cultural norms that are expressed by individuals or groups. Together these beliefs, behaviors, and acts of belonging may manifest in one's lived experiences. This definition may help authorities determine what is and what is not legally permitted.

The First Amendment does not allow a religious group to use public schools to endorse one religion over another, to compel another to profess beliefs, or to coerce another to engage in particular religious behaviors or to feel pressured to belong to a religious group. The First Amendment does, however, permit a group to use language and culture as the civic foundation for a charter school curriculum, even if the language and culture has a religious connection. The US Supreme Court has made clear that learning about religion from an academic perspective, especially its cultural, literary, and historical influences, is legally permissible in public schools.

CONCLUSION

The rapid growth in charter schools has mistakenly led some religious groups to think that they can use public funds to establish formal or *de facto* religious schools. Some of those groups were motivated by the belief that, as Lawrence Weinberg stated, "Chartering offers a promising and realistic opportunity for leaders of faith-based schools who are considering ways of maintaining the viability of their [religious] institution" (Weinberg 2008). Using public funds to save a private religious institution from bankruptcy is not constitutionally permitted under the Establishment Clause of the US Constitution. Neither is this permitted under the variety of "no aid to religion" clauses in state constitutions. Nor is it constitutionally permissible to use the façade of a public school to charter an institution designed to infringe on the Free Exercise rights of students who hold a variety of beliefs, engage in different behaviors than those of their peers or teachers, belong to different religions than the one associated with the school, or choose to affiliate with no religion at all.

Charter schools, like all public schools, are required to accommodate students' religious beliefs and practices. Charter schools may also use an academic approach to the study of religions and use linguistic and cultural studies approaches to immerse students in a particular cultural heritage. Charter schools may use these approaches to help students integrate from one culture into another. The ultimate question is whether the charter school is truly acting as a public school. The charter fulfills this mission to act as a public school when it provides students with the civic and cultural competencies necessary to participate in a diverse democracy.

FUTURE DIRECTIONS

1. How can community stakeholders better educate the public about the fact that charter schools are public schools, as defined by federal and state law, and thus bound by the same laws and legal precedents as public schools?
2. Legally speaking, why are local developers and state chartering agencies that seek to establish religious or faith-based charter schools likely to fail in state and federal courts?
3. How can the larger charter school movement promote First Amendment education to help founders of charter schools to navigate the complex issues surrounding religion and public education?

REFERENCES

"About HCCS," Hellenic Classical Charter School, accessed January 22, 2018, www.hccs-nys. org.

Haynes, Charles C. and Oliver S. Thomas. 2011. "A Teacher's Guide to Religion in the Public Schools." In *Finding Common Ground: A Guide to Religious Liberty in Public Schools*, edited by Charles C. Haynes and Oliver S. Thomas, 98. Nashville, TN: First Amendment Center.

"Home Page," Ben Gamla Charter School, accessed January 22, 2018, www.bengamla-charter. com.

"Immersion School," Cherokee Nation, accessed January 22, 2018, www.cherokee.org/services/ education/immersion-school.

Mann, Elliot. 2009. "Religion Not in Curriculum at Charter School." *The Post-Bulletin*. Rochester, MN. January 23.

"Mission and Vision," Hmong College Prep Academy District Site, accessed January 22, 2018, www.hcpak12.org/domain/102.

Moore, Diane L., et. al., 2010. *American Academy of Religion Guidelines for Teaching About Religion in K-12 Public Schools in the United States*. Atlanta, GA: American Academy of Religion, May 2010.

National Alliance for Public Charter Schools. August 2014. "Separating Fact & Faction: What You Need to Know About Charter Schools."

National Resource Center on Charter School Finance and Governance. October 2008. "Partnerships Between Charter Schools and Other Organizations: A Guide for State Policymakers."

Saroglou, Vassilis. 2011. "Believing, Bonding, Behaving, and Belonging: The Big Four Religious Dimensions and Cultural Variation." *Journal of Cross-Cultural Psychology* 42, no. 8: 1320–1340.

Samuelson, Charles. 2009. Public statement on lawsuit against Tarek ibn Ziyad Academy, Minnesota ACLUS, January 20, 2009.

US Department of Education, National Center for Education Statistics. 2015. *The Condition of Education 2015* (NCES 2015–144), Charter School Enrollment.

Weinberg, Lawrence D. 2008. "The Potential of Faith-Based Charter Schools: Speech to the White House Summit on Inner-City Children and Faith-Based Schools." April 24, 2008, Washington, DC

FURTHER READING

Cunningham, Josh. December 2011. *Charter School Facilities*, National Conference of State Legislatures.

Miron, Gary, William J. Mathis, and Kevin G. Welner. 2014. *Review of "Separating Fact & Fiction."* National Education Policy Center.

Mulvey, Janet D., Bruce S. Cooper, and Arthur T. Maloney. 2010. *Blurring the Lines: Charter, Public, Private, and Religious Schools Coming Together*. Charlotte, NC: Information Age Publishing, Inc.

National Alliance for Public Charter Schools. 2013. "Public Charter Schools Growing on Native American Reservations." Press Release, August 15, 2013, accessed on January 22, 2018, https://www.publiccharters.org/press/public-charter-schools-growing-native-american-reservations.

Russo, Charles J., and Gerald M. Cattaro. 2009. "Faith-Based Charter Schools: An Idea Whose Time Is Unlikely to Come." *Religion and Education* 36, no. 1: 72–93.

Smith, Morgan. August 11, 2013. "Charter Schools in Churches a Focus of Praise, Concerns." *The Texas Tribune*.

Weinberg, Lawrence D. 2007. *Religious Charter Schools: Legalities & Practicalities*. Charlotte, NC: Information Age Publishing, Inc.

———. 2009. "Religious Charter Schools: Gaining Ground Yet Still Undefined." *Journal of Research on Christian Education* 18: 290–302.

U.S. Code, Title 20—Education, Definitions 20 U.S. Code § 7221i; 20 U.S.C. § 7801.

CHAPTER 15

....

LAW AND RELIGION
IN AMERICAN EDUCATION

....

JOHN WITTE, JR. AND BRIAN KAUFMAN

INTRODUCTION

WHILE American schools are governed by sundry federal, state, and local laws, the most important law on religion and education is the First Amendment guarantee: "Congress shall make no law respecting an establishment of religion, or prohibiting the free exercise thereof." Of the US Supreme Court's two-hundred-plus cases on religious freedom, fully sixty cases have been on issues of religion and education—most of them announced after 1940, the year the Court began to apply the First Amendment to state and local governments alongside "Congress."

These cases address three main questions: (1) What role may religion play in public school education? (2) What role may government play in private religious education? and (3) What religious rights do parents and students have in public and private schools? The Court has worked out a set of rough answers to these questions, which lower courts have continued to refine and extend. While government has the power to mandate education for all children, parents have the right to choose public, private, or homeschool education for their minor children, and government may now facilitate that choice through vouchers and tax relief. While the First Amendment forbids most forms of religion in public schools, it protects most forms of religion in private schools. While the First Amendment forbids government from funding the core religious activities of private schools, it permits delivery of general governmental services and subsidies to public and private schools and students alike. While the First Amendment forbids public school teachers and outsiders from religious instruction and expression in classes and formal school functions, it permits public school students to engage in private religious expression and protects these students from coerced religious activities. It further requires that religious students and other private parties get equal access to public school facilities, forums, and even funds that are open to their nonreligious peers for non-school functions.

Religion and Public Education

Separation of Church and State

In a forty-year series of cases beginning in the 1940s, the Court developed a general argument about the limited place of religion in public schools. The public school is a government entity, the Court argued, one of the most visible and well-known arms of the government in any community. The public school is furthermore a model of constitutional democracy and designed to communicate core democratic norms and constitutional practices to students. The state mandates that all able students attend schools, at least until the age of sixteen. These students are young and impressionable. Given all these factors, the public school must cling closely to core constitutional and democratic values, including the core value of separation of church and state. Some relaxation of constitutional values is possible in other public contexts, where adults can make informed assessments of the values being transmitted, but no such relaxation can occur in public schools, with their impressionable youths who are compelled to be there. In public schools, if nowhere else in public life, strict separation of church and state must be the norm.

The case that opened this series was *McCollum v. Board of Education* (1948). At issue was a "release time" program, adopted by a local public school board for fourth- through ninth-grade students. Once a week, students were released from their regular classes to be able to participate in a religious class taught at the public school. Three religious classes were on offer—Protestant, Catholic, or Jewish—reflecting the religious makeup of the local community. These classes were voluntarily taught by qualified outside teachers, approved by the principal. Students whose parents did not consent continued their "secular studies" during this release time period. A parent challenged the program as a violation of the First Amendment Establishment Clause. The *McCollum* Court agreed, finding that this program constituted the use of "tax-supported property for religious instruction and the close cooperation between school authorities and the religious council in promoting religious education":

> The operation of the State's compulsory education system thus assists and is integrated with the program of religious instruction carried on by separate religious sects. . . . This is beyond all question a utilization of the tax-established and tax-supported public school to aid religious groups to spread their faith. And it falls squarely under the ban of the First Amendment [that] . . . erected a wall of separation between Church and State.

In *Engel v. Vitale* (1962), the Court extended this reasoning to outlaw prayer in public schools. The New York State Board of Regents had adopted a nondenominational prayer to be recited by public school teachers and their students at the commencement of each school day: "Almighty God, we acknowledge our dependence upon Thee, and we beg Thy blessings upon us, our parents, our teachers, and our Country." Students who did not wish to pray could remain silent or be excused from the room during its recitation. Parents challenged the practice as a violation of the Establishment Clause. The *Engel* Court agreed and struck down the practice:

> It is no part of the business of government to compose official prayers for any group of the American people to recite as part of a religious program carried on by government. . . . Neither the fact that the prayer may be denominationally neutral nor the fact that its observance on the part of the students is voluntary can serve to free it from the Establishment Clause. . . . When the power, prestige, and financial support of government [are] placed behind a particular religious belief, the indirect coercive pressure upon religious minorities to conform to the prevailing officially approved religion is plain.

This prohibition on prayer in public schools has remained good law. In the controversial case of *Wallace v. Jaffree* (1985), the Court struck down a state statute that authorized even a moment of silence at the beginning of each school day for "meditation or voluntary prayer," because the legislature had betrayed its "intent to return prayer to the public schools." *Lee v. Weisman* (1992) outlawed a local rabbi's prayer at a one-time public middle school graduation, arguing that such prayers effectively coerced students to participate in religion. And *Santa Fe Independent School District v. Doe* (2000) outlawed elective student-led prayers at the start of each public school football game, arguing that this policy not only coerced students but constituted governmental endorsement of religion.

In *Abington Township School District v. Schempp* (1963), the Court outlawed the reading of ten Bible verses at the beginning of each public school day. Either a teacher or a volunteer student would read a text of their choice, with no commentary or discussion allowed. Students whose parents did not consent could refuse to listen or leave the room. After *Engel*, the *Schempp* Court found this an easy case. The policy in question was an overtly religious exercise, mandated by the state, for impressionable youths required to be in school, with no realistic opportunity for the average young student to forgo participation. "[I]t is no defense that the religious practices here may be relatively minor encroachments on the First Amendment," Justice Clark wrote for the Court. "The breach of neutrality that is today a trickling stream may all too soon become a raging torrent."

In *Stone v. Graham* (1980), the Court further struck down a state statute that allowed a private group to donate and hang the Ten Commandments in public high school classrooms. There was no public reading of the commandments or endorsement of them by teachers or school officials. Each plaque described the Ten Commandments "as the fundamental legal code of Western Civilization and the Common Law of the United States." The *Stone* Court found that the Decalogue was a "clearly religious" text no matter how it was labeled, and that its display improperly commanded students to abide by "religious duties."

Finally, in *Edwards v. Aguillard* (1987), the Court struck down a state law that required public school teachers to give equal time to "evolution-science" and "creation-science" in their science classrooms. The Court held that the statute evinced a "discriminatory preference for the teaching of creation and against the teaching of evolution." It aimed "to advance the religious viewpoint that a supernatural being created humankind" and "to restructure the science curriculum to conform with a particular religious viewpoint." This was not a proper objective teaching of religion but an unconstitutional establishment of religion. Lower courts have used this precedent to outlaw "Intelligent Design" teachings from public school curricula as well.

Liberty of Conscience

While separation of church and state was the major key played in the Court's early orchestrations on religion and public schools, liberty of conscience and freedom of religious exercise was a minor key that periodically sounded as well. *West Virginia State Board of Education v. Barnette* (1943) was a case in point. There Jehovah's Witness children were expelled from a public school because they refused to salute the American flag or recite the Pledge of Allegiance—important patriotic acts in the middle of World War II. The Witnesses regarded such acts as idolatrous and viewed their imposition as a violation of liberty of conscience. The *Barnette* Court agreed. While acknowledging the importance of teaching national loyalty and unity in public schools, the *Barnette* Court held that the Witnesses should be conscientiously exempted from participating:

> If there is any fixed star in our constitutional constellation, it is that no official, high or petty, can prescribe what shall be orthodox in politics, nationalism, religion, or other matters of opinion or force citizens to confess by word or act their faith therein. If there are any circumstances which permit an exception, they do not now occur to us.

In *Zorach v. Clauson* (1952), the Court further allowed students to be released from public school, at their parents' request, to attend important religious functions scheduled during school time. These functions were off school grounds and involved no school officials or expenses. Taxpayers objected that this program violated the Establishment Clause and its principle of strict separation of church and state. The *Zorach* Court disagreed: "We would have to press the concept of separation of Church and State to . . . extremes to condemn the present law on constitutional grounds." But this is neither constitutionally necessary nor desirable: "When the state encourages religious instruction or cooperates with religious authorities by adjusting the schedule of public events to sectarian needs, it follows the best of our traditions."

Modern Equal Access Cases

While official prayers and overt forms of religious expression remain prohibited in public schools, private religious expression by public school students and others, outside of formal school hours, has come to be constitutionally protected. The Supreme Court has reached this conclusion in a series of cases that have often pitted the principles of religious equality and nondiscrimination against that of separation of church and state.

The opening case in this series was *Widmar v. Vincent* (1981). The state University of Missouri had a policy of opening its facilities to voluntary student groups to use outside of formal instructional time. More than 100 student groups organized themselves in the year at issue. A voluntary student group, organized for private religious devotion and charity, sought access to the university facilities. The group was denied access, in application of the university's written policy that the campus could not be used "for purposes of religious worship or religious teaching." The student group appealed, arguing that this policy violated their First Amendment free exercise and free speech rights as well as their Fourteenth Amendment equal protection rights. The university countered that it had a compelling state interest to maintain a "strict separation of church and state."

The *Widmar* Court found for the religious student group. The Court held that where a state university creates a limited public forum open to voluntary student groups, religious groups must be given "equal access" to that forum. Here the university "has discriminated against student groups and speakers based on their desire to use a generally open forum to engage in religious worship and discussion." Religious speech and association are protected by the First Amendment and can be excluded only if the university can demonstrate that its statute serves a "compelling state interest and that it is narrowly drawn to achieve that end." In the Court's view, a general desire to keep a strict separation of church and state was not a sufficiently compelling state interest. The values of "equal treatment and access" outweighed the hypothetical dangers of a religious establishment.

Three years later, Congress extended this equal access right to after-school voluntary meetings of public high school students as well. In *Westside Community Schools v. Mergens* (1990), the Court upheld that law against an Establishment Clause challenge, arguing that Congress had legitimately protected the rights of religious students to "equal treatment" and "equal protection."

In *Lamb's Chapel v. Center Moriches Union Free School District* (1993), the Court extended the "equal access" principle to other religious groups besides students. A local school board opened its public school facilities after hours to local private groups for various "social, civic, recreational, and political uses." A state policy, however, provided that the "school premises shall not be used by any group for religious purposes." Lamb's Chapel, an evangelical group, wanted to use the facilities to show a film series that discussed traditional family values from a Christian perspective. When their application was twice denied, they filed suit, arguing that such exclusion violated their free speech rights. The *Lamb's Chapel* Court agreed. Relying on *Widmar*, the Court found that the school had engaged in religious discrimination, and that its concern to avoid an establishment of religion was not a sufficient reason for denying equal access to this religious group.

In *Rosenberger v. Rector and Visitors of the University of Virginia* (1995), the Court extended this equal access logic to hold that a voluntary group of religious students in a state university was entitled to the same funding made available to nonreligious student groups to publish their materials. The University of Virginia had denied funds to a properly registered religious student group that printed an overtly religious news-paper for circulation on campus. The group appealed, arguing that such discriminatory treatment violated their First Amendment free speech rights. The *Rosenberger* Court agreed. The state university policy, the Court opined, improperly "selects for disfavored treatment those student journalistic efforts with religious editorial viewpoints." This was unconstitutional "viewpoint discrimination."

In its last case in this series, *Good News Club v. Milford Central School* (2001), the Court extended the equal access logic to the public grade school. Authorized by a state statute, a local school board invited qualified local residents to use public school facilities after school hours for "instruction in any branch of education, learning, or the arts" and for "so-cial, civic and recreational meetings." The policy, however, prohibited use of the facilities "for religious purposes." Good News Club, a private Christian organization that instructed six- through twelve-year-old students in Christian morality and practice, sought permis-sion to hold the club's weekly after-school meetings in the public school cafeteria for chil-dren who attended that school. Their lesson plans involved adult-led prayers, religious songs, and student recitation of Bible verses, among other activities. Denied permission, they appealed, arguing that the policy was discriminatory against religion.

The *Good News* Court agreed, arguing that, even in a public grade school, the state "must not discriminate against speech on the basis of viewpoint." The school district was not obliged to create this "limited public forum," but once it did, any restriction had to be viewpoint-neutral and reasonable in light of the forum's purpose. The Good News Club's program clearly included "instruction in any branch of education, learning, or the arts," and it could not be excluded just because the instruction came "from a religious viewpoint."

The upshot of all these Supreme Court cases is that religious teachers, texts, ceremo-nies, and symbols are prohibited from the public school classroom during instructional time, and even at one-time official public school gatherings. But private religious ex-pression by students, parents, community members, and even teachers is permissible on public school grounds before and after classes or on days when school is not in session. Students, however, may not be coerced into participation in any religious activ-ities, whether during or after school. Lower courts and regulations have further insisted that students may not, in turn, be coerced to abandon their religious practices, such as wearing religious apparel or ornamentation, abiding by their religious diet, praying be-fore meals, or observing their Sabbaths and holy days. Lower courts have also made clear that public schools may teach objective facts about religion in appropriate courses: an ancient literature course can include a few Psalms; an American history course can dis-cuss the beliefs of the Mayflower Pilgrims.

Government and Religious Education

In another long series of cases, this one beginning already in the 1920s, the Supreme Court developed a general argument about the role of government in private religious schools. Private schools of all sorts, the Court repeatedly held, are viable and valuable alternatives to public schools. Private religious schools in particular allow parents to educate their students in their own religious tradition, a right they must enjoy without discrimination or prejudice. Given that public education must be secular under the Establishment Clause, private education may be religious under the Free Exercise Clause. To be accredited, all private schools must meet minimum educational standards. They must teach reading, writing, arithmetic, history, geography, social studies, and the like so that their graduates are not culturally or intellectually handicapped. But these private schools may teach these subjects from a religious perspective and add religious instruction and activities beyond them. They may discriminate in favor of hiring teachers that share their faith, and must be free from some of the usual requirements of teachers' unions. And these religious schools are presumptively entitled to the same government services that are made available to their counterparts in public schools—so long as those services are not used for core religious activities. The Supreme Court followed this accommodationist logic from 1925 to 1971, abruptly reversed course in favor of strict separationism from 1971 to 1986, and since then has returned to a new variant of accommodationism, framed in "equal access" terms.

Accommodation of Religious Education

The most important early religious school case was *Pierce v. Society of Sisters* (1925). Oregon had passed a law mandating that all eligible students must attend public schools. The law sought to eliminate Catholic and other private religious schools and to give new impetus to the development of the state's public schools. Local private Catholic schools challenged this as a violation of the educational rights of the parents, children, schools, and schoolteachers alike. The *Pierce* Court agreed and struck down the Oregon law. "The fundamental theory of liberty," the Court opined, "excludes any general power of the state to standardize its children by forcing them to accept instruction from public teachers only." It also forecloses "unwarranted compulsion" of "present and future patrons" of the religious schools. Extending *Pierce, Farrington v. Tokushige* (1927) held that states could not impose unduly intrusive and stringent accreditation and regulatory requirements on religious and other private schools. And *Cochran v. Board of Education* (1930) upheld a state policy of supplying textbooks to all students, including religious school students.

This accommodation of religious schools and students continued into the early 1970s. *Everson v. Board of Education* (1947), though peppered with sweeping dicta on the wall of separation between church and state, still held that states could provide school bus transportation to religious and public school children alike and reimburse the parents of religious and public school children alike for the costs of using school bus transportation. "[C]utting off church schools [and their students] from these services, so separate and indisputably marked off from the religious function, would make it far more difficult for the schools to operate," the Court opined. "But such obviously is not the purpose of the First Amendment. The Amendment requires the State to be neutral in its relations with groups of religious believers and non-believers; it does not require the state to be their adversary."

The Court struck a similar tone in *Board of Education v. Allen* (1968). The State of New York had a policy of lending prescribed textbooks in science, mathematics, and other "secular subjects" to all students in the state, whether attending public or private schools. Many of the private school recipients of the textbooks were religious schools. A taxpayer challenged the policy as a violation of the Establishment Clause. Citing *Cochran*, the *Allen* Court rejected this claim, emphasizing that it was the students and parents, not the religious schools, who directly benefited: "Perhaps free books make it more likely that some children choose to attend a sectarian school, but that was true of the state-paid bus fares in *Everson*, and does not alone demonstrate an unconstitutional degree of support for a religious institution."

The Court opined similarly in *Tilton v. Richardson* (1971), which upheld the use of federal funds for the construction of library, science, and arts buildings at church-related colleges among many other secular colleges and universities. Since these "federally-subsidized facilities would be devoted to the secular and not the religious functions of the recipient institution," and since both religious and secular schools are equally eligible for these funds, there was no violation of the Establishment Clause, the *Tilton* Court concluded.

The Court went even further in accommodating religious education in the 1972 case of *Wisconsin v. Yoder*. Wisconsin, like all states, mandated that able children attend school until the age of sixteen. A community of Old Order Amish, who were dedicated to a simple agrarian lifestyle based on biblical principles, conceded the need to send their children to grade school to teach them the basic fundamentals of reading, writing, and arithmetic that they would need. But the community leaders and parents refused to send their children to higher schools, lest they be tempted by worldly concerns and distracted from learning the values and skills they would need to maintain the Amish lifestyle. After they were fined for disobeying school attendance laws, the parents and community leaders filed suit, arguing that the state had violated their free exercise and parental rights. The *Yoder* Court agreed and ordered that they be exempted from full compliance with these laws. The Court was impressed that the Amish "lifestyle" was centuries old and "not merely a matter of personal preference, but one of deep religious conviction, shared by an organized group, and intimately related to daily living." In the Court's view, compliance with the compulsory school attendance law would pose "a very real threat of undermining the Amish community and religious practice as they exist today; they must either abandon belief and be assimilated into society at large, or be forced to migrate to some other and more tolerant region." To exempt them was not to "establish the Amish religion" but to "accommodate their free exercise rights." This case would later become a *locus classicus* for the homeschooling options, which lower federal and state courts have upheld in a number of states.

Separation of Church and State

In *Lemon v. Kurtzman* (1971), the Supreme Court abruptly reversed course. Drawing on the strict separationist logic of its earlier public school cases, the *Lemon* Court crafted a three-part test to be used in all future cases arising under the First Amendment Establishment Clause, including those dealing with religious schools. To meet constitutional objections, the Court held, any challenged government law must (1) have a secular purpose; (2) have a primary effect that neither advances nor inhibits religion; and (3) not foster an excessive entanglement between church and state.

The *Lemon* Court used this three-part test to strike down a state policy that reimbursed Catholic and religious schools for some of the costs of teaching secular subjects that the state prescribed. The state policy was restricted to religious schools that served students from lower-income families and the reimbursements were limited to 15% of the costs. The *Lemon* Court held that this policy fostered an "excessive entanglement between church and state." The Catholic schools, in question, were notably religious, the Court held: they were closely allied with nearby parish churches, filled with religious symbols, and staffed primarily by nuns who were under "religious control and discipline." "[A] dedicated religious person, teaching at a school affiliated with his or her faith and operated to inculcate its tenets, will inevitably experience great difficulty in remaining religiously neutral." She will be tempted to teach secular subjects with a religious orientation in violation of state policy. "A comprehensive, discriminating, and continuing state surveillance will inevitably be required to ensure that these restrictions are obeyed and the First Amendment otherwise obeyed." This is precisely the kind of excessive entanglement between church and state that the First Amendment Establishment Clause outlaws.

Lemon left open the question whether the state could give aid directly to religious students or to their parents—as the Court had allowed in earlier cases—but two years later, the Court closed this door tightly. In *Committee for Public Education v. Nyquist* (1973) and *Sloan v. Lemon* (1973), the Court struck down state policies that allowed low-income parents to seek reimbursements from the state for some of the costs of religious school tuition. *Nyquist* further struck down a state policy that allowed low-income parents to take tax deductions for the costs of sending their children to private schools. In *Nyquist,* Justice Powell characterized such policies as just another "of the ingenious plans of channeling state aid to sectarian schools." Responding to the state argument that "grants to parents, unlike grants to [religious] institutions, respect the 'wall of separation' required by the Constitution," the Court declared that "the [primary] effect of the aid is unmistakably to provide desired financial support for non-public, sectarian institutions."

Lemon also left open the question of whether the state could give textbooks, educational materials, or other aid to religious schools for the teaching of mandatory secular subjects, or the administration of state-mandated tests and other programs. The Court struck down most such policies in a long series cases from 1973 to 1985. These cases, and their ample extension by lower courts, created a high wall of separation between public and private school facilities, funds, teachers, students, and programs.

Aguilar v. Felton (1985) is a good example of how strict the separation had become. *Aguilar* concerned the remedial educational services that were authorized and funded by Congress in the Elementary and Secondary Education Act (1965), known as the Title I program. The act set detailed standards both for student eligibility and for the nature of the education to be offered eligible students. More than 20,000 religious school students in the city annually availed themselves of these Title I services, alongside tens of thousands of public school students. Lacking sufficient space in existing public buildings, and lacking sufficient land to build new public buildings adjacent to religious schools, the city offered the remedial services on site to eligible religious school students. State-funded public school teachers with materials were sent into the religious schools to teach the eligible religious school students. Field supervisors were sent out monthly to ensure that the Title I funds were directed to remedial, not religious, education in these schools. The program had been in place for nineteen years without challenge.

Local taxpayers, however, then challenged the program as a violation of the Establishment Clause, and the *Aguilar* Court agreed: though "well-intentioned," the Court opined, the program fosters an excessive entanglement of church and state. The religious schools receiving the Title I instructors are "pervasively sectarian," having as a "substantial purpose, the inculcation of religious values." Because of this, "ongoing inspection is required to ensure the absence of a religious message. In short, the scope and duration of New York's Title I program would require a permanent and pervasive State presence in the sectarian schools receiving aid." This is precisely the kind of excessive entanglement between church and state that the disestablishment clause outlaws.

Equal Treatment and Freedom of Choice

This strict separation between public and private schools, however alluring and simple in theory, ultimately proved unworkable in practice, with *Aguilar* an unpopular case in point. Accordingly, in the mid-1980s forward, the Supreme Court moved back toward greater accommodation and government support of religious education, and eventually reversed *Aguilar* and two other strict separationist cases from the 1970s.

The first case in this new series was *Mueller v. Allen* (1983). There the Court upheld a Minnesota law that allowed parents of private school children to claim tax deductions from state income tax for the costs of "tuition, transportation, and textbooks." Ninety-five percent of the private school children in the state attended religious schools, and most of their parents availed themselves of this tax deduction. A taxpayer in the state challenged the law as an establishment of religion, but the *Mueller* Court disagreed: the tax deduction policy had a secular purpose of fostering quality education, fostered no entanglement between church and state, and had the primary effect of enhancing the educational choices of parents and students. The state aid to sectarian schools "becomes available only as a result of numerous, private choices of individual parents of school-age children." This saves it from constitutional infirmity. Several later cases, most recently *Arizona Christian School Tuition Organization v. Winn* (2011), have upheld such state tax deduction, exemption, and credit programs that help parents pay for religious schools, even while they are taxed to support public schools.

In *Witters v. Washington Department of Services for the Blind* (1986), the Court upheld a state program that furnished aid to a student attending a Christian college. The program provided funds "for special education and/or training in the professions, business or trades" for the visually impaired. Money was to be paid directly to eligible recipients, who were entitled to pursue education in the professional schools of their choice. Mr. Witters's condition qualified him for the funds, his profession of choice was the Christian ministry, and he sought funds to attend a Christian college in preparation for the same. The state agency denied funding on grounds that this was direct funding of religious education. The *Witters* Court disagreed. The policy served a secular purpose of fostering educational and professional choice for all, including the handicapped. It involved no entanglement of church and state. Its primary effect was to facilitate this student's professional education, which happened to be religious. This "is not one of 'the ingenious plans for channeling state aid to sectarian schools,'" the Court opined. "It creates no financial incentive for students to undertake sectarian education. It does not provide greater or broader benefits for recipients who apply their aid to religious education. . . . In this case, the fact that aid goes to individuals means that the decision to support religious education is made by the individual not by the State."

In *Zobrest v. Catalina Foothills School District* (1993), the Court extended this logic from a college student to a high school student. Both federal and state disability acts required that a hearing-impaired student be furnished with a sign-language interpreter to accompany him or her to classes. The state paid for the interpreter. Mr. Zobrest's hearing impairment qualified him for an interpreter's services. But after going to a public grade school, he enrolled in a Catholic high school. The state refused to furnish him with an interpreter, on the grounds that this would violate the *Lemon* rule that the state could give no direct aid to a religious school; moreover, the presence of a state-employed interpreter in a Catholic high school would foster an excessive entanglement between church and state. Following *Mueller* and *Witters*, the *Zobrest* Court upheld the act as "a neutral government program dispensing aid not to schools but to handicapped children."

In *Agostini v. Felton* (1997), the Court extended this logic from the high school to the grade school. It reversed *Aguilar v. Felton* and reinstated the Title I services to public and private elementary and high school students alike. Children in religious schools, the Court held, are just as entitled to Title I benefits as children in public schools. They cannot be denied these benefits simply for the sake of upholding "the abstract principle" of separation of church and state.

In *Mitchell v. Helms* (2000), the Court upheld the constitutionality of direct government aid to the secular functions of religious schools. The federal Education

Consolidation and Improvement Act (1981) channeled federal funds to state and local education agencies for the purchase of various educational materials and equipment. The act permitted states to loan such materials directly to public and private elementary and secondary schools, provided that the state retained title to those materials and that the recipient schools used them only for programs that are "secular, neutral, and nonideological." The amount of material aid for each participating school depended on the number of students it matriculated. Using the statutory formula, Louisiana distributed materials and equipment to public and private schools in the state. In one county, some 30% of the federal aid was allocated to private schools, most of which were Catholic. The aid was distributed properly and the materials and equipment were used only for "secular, neutral, and nonideological" programs in each religious school. Local taxpayers brought suit, however, arguing that such "direct aid" to such "pervasively sectarian" schools constituted an establishment of religion.

The *Mitchell* Court disagreed and held that the program was constitutional both on its face and as applied in this case. The federal act did not advance religion, nor did it define its recipients by reference to religion; all accredited public and private schools and students were eligible. And there was no excessive entanglement between religious and governmental officials in the administration of the program. Accordingly, the Court upheld the law, and overruled two earlier cases—*Meek v. Pittenger* (1975) and *Wolman v. Walter* (1977)—that had struck down similar aid programs distributing materials directly to religious schools. The separationist principles at work in these two decisions had become unworkably rigid, the *Mitchell* Court concluded.

In *Zelman v. Simmons-Harris* (2002), the Court further upheld a school voucher program that Ohio had adopted to address a "crisis of magnitude" in its Cleveland public school system. The program gave parents a choice to leave their children in the local Cleveland public school district or to enroll them in another public or private school that participated in the school voucher program. For those parents who chose to send their children to a participating private school, the program provided them with a voucher to help defray tuition costs, though parents had to make copayments according to their means. Some 82% of the private schools participating in the voucher program were religiously affiliated; 96% of the students who used vouchers enrolled in these private religious schools. Taxpayers challenged the program as a violation of the Establishment Clause, but the *Zelman* Court disagreed. For the Court, there was no dispute that the program was enacted for a "valid secular purpose of providing educational assistance to poor children in a demonstrably failing public school system." The primary effect of the program was not to advance religion but to enhance educational choice for poor students and parents:

> Where a government aid program is *neutral* with respect to religion, and provides assistance directly to a *broad class of citizens*, who, in turn, direct government aid to religious schools wholly as a result of their own genuine and independent *private choice*, the program is not readily subject to challenge under the Establishment

Clause. A program that shares these features permits government aid to reach religious institutions only by way of the deliberate choices of numerous individual recipients. The incidental advancement of a religious mission, or the perceived endorsement of a religious message is reasonably attributable to the individual, not the government, whose role ends with the disbursement of the funds.

Several lower courts have used *Zelman* to uphold school voucher programs in other states.

CONCLUSIONS

These First Amendment cases on religion and education have not always followed clean logical lines. The Supreme Court has sometimes digressed and occasionally reversed itself. Several of the Court's religion and education cases have featured brilliant rhetorical and judicial fireworks in majority and dissenting opinions as the Court has occasionally shifted into a new understanding of the demands of the First Amendment. Part of this back-and-forth is typical of any constitutional law in action. "Constitutions work like clocks," American Founder John Adams once put it. To function properly, their pendulums must swing back and forth, and their mechanisms and operators must get "wound up from time to time."

The Court's cases on religion and public education swung from logics of strict separationism to equal access. The controversial 1985 *Wallace v. Jaffree* case, outlawing even private moments of silence in public schools, was the likely tipping point. The 2001 *Good News Club* case, authorizing a public grade school extracurricular program that was heavy on religion, might well become the stopping point to this equal access logic. The Court's cases on government in religious education cases, in turn, swung from accommodation to separation to equal treatment. The controversial 1985 *Aguilar* case that cut 20,000 religious students from remedial education helped catalyze the emergence of equal treatment cases. The controversial 2002 *Zelman* voucher case that allowed state money to be used even for "sectarian education" might well become the stopping point for this new accommodation. Given the centrality of both religion and education in American life, it is inevitable that constitutional litigation will continue apace.

One trend to watch, however, is the current Supreme Court's growing appetite for federalism, and its growing deference to state and local lawmaking on many fronts, including on education. It is unlikely that this Court will follow the call of some originalists to apply the First Amendment religion clauses literally only to "Congress" rather than to all levels of government. But it is likely that the Court will continue to soften the standards of scrutiny in Establishment and Free Exercise cases, leaving local and state governments with more latitude to construct new religion and educational policies without interference from the federal courts.

FUTURE DIRECTIONS

1. In what ways can the law protect the free exercise of religion in public spaces while also ensuring that public schools do not violate the Establishment Clause of the First Amendment?
2. What role can religion constitutionally play in public school education?
3. What is the proper role for government in private religious education? What compelling interests does the state have in regulating private education? When do those interests substantially burden the free exercise of religion, thus constituting government overreach?
4. What religious rights do parents and students have in public and private schools and how might the state train educators and administrators to protect those rights?

REFERENCES

Abington School District v. Schempp, 374 U.S. 203 (1963).
Agostini v. Felton, 521 U.S 203 (1997).
Aguilar v. Felton, 473 U.S 402 (1985).
Arizona Christian School Tuition Organization v. Winn, 563 U.S 125 (2011).
Board of Education v. Allen, 392 U.S 236 (1968).
Cochran v. Louisiana State Board of Education, 281 U.S 370 (1930).
Committee for Public Education v. Nyquist, 413 U.S 756 (1973).
Edwards v. Aguillard, 482 U.S 578 (1987).
Engel v. Vitale, 370 U.S 421 (1962).
Everson v. Board of Education, 330 U.S 1 (1947).
Farrington v. Tokushige, 273 U.S 284 (1927).
Good News Club v. Milford Central School, 533 U.S 98 (2001).
Lamb's Chapel v. Center Moriches Union Free School District, 508 U.S 384 (1993).
Lee v. Weisman, 505 U.S 577 (1992).
Lemon v. Kurtzman, 403 U.S 602 (1971).
McCollum v. Board of Education, 333 U.S 203 (1948).
Meek v. Pittenger, 421 U.S 349 (1975).
Mitchell v. Helms, 530 U.S 793 (2000).
Mueller v. Allen, 463 U.S 388 (1983).
Pierce v. Society of the Sisters, 268 U.S 510 (1925).
Rosenberger v. Rector and Visitors of the University of Virginia, 515 U.S 819 (1995).
Santa Fe Independent School Dist. v. Doe, 530 U.S 290 (2000).
Sloan v. Lemon, 413 U.S 825 (1973).
Stone v. Graham, 449 U.S 39 (1980).
Tilton v. Richardson, 403 U.S 672 (1971).
Wallace v. Jaffree, 472 U.S 38 (1985).
West Virginia State Board of Education v. Barnette, 319 U.S 624 (1943).

Westside Community Board of Education v. Mergens, 496 U.S 226 (1990).

Widmar v. Vincent, 454 U.S 263 (1981).

Wisconsin v. Yoder, 406 U.S 205 (1972).

Witters v. Washington Department of Services for the Blind, 474 U.S 481 (1986).

Wolman v. Walter, 433 U.S 229 (1977).

Zelman v. Simmons-Harris, 536 U.S 639 (2002).

Zobrest v. Catalina Foothills School District, 509 U.S 1 (1993).

Zorach v. Clauson, 343 U.S 306 (1952).

FURTHER READING

Berner, Ashley. 2015. *What Really Matters in Education? The Case for Educational Pluralism*. New York: algrave MacMillan.

Greenawalt, Kent. 2005. *Does God Belong in Public Schools?* Princeton, NJ: Princeton University Press.

Laycock, Douglas. 2010–16. *Religious Liberty*, 4 vols. Grand Rapids, MI: Wm. B. Eerdmans.

McConnell, Michael W., John H. Garvey, and Thomas C. Berg. 2011. *Religion and the Constitution*, 3rd ed. New York: Wolters Kluwer.

Witte, John, Jr. and Joel A. Nichols. 2016. *Religion and the American Constitution*, 4th ed. New York: Oxford University Press.

CHAPTER 16

··

RELIGIOUS EXPRESSION
IN PUBLIC SCHOOLS

··

KEVIN R. PREGENT AND NATHAN C. WALKER

Congress shall make no law respecting an establishment of religion, or prohibiting the free exercise thereof; or abridging the freedom of speech, or of the press; or the right of the people peaceably to assemble, and to petition the Government for a redress of grievances.

The First Amendment to the US Constitution

INTRODUCTION

··

THE Free Exercise Clause of the First Amendment to the US Constitution ensures that students may retain their religious beliefs, practices, identities, and rights when they enter public schools. The free exercise principle also protects government employees; however, the Establishment Clause of the First Amendment prevents teachers and administrators, as agents of the state, from entangling the public school in religious activities or engaging in school speech that advances or endorses religion. These two principles—free exercise of religion and non-establishment of religion—are the basis of the concept of religious freedom.

The constitutional foundation for religious freedom—as it relates to American public education—rests on the idea the school cannot sponsor any religion (or religion over no religion, generally) or prohibit private acts of devotion in public spaces. This means that (1) the federal and state governments, and by extension public and charter schools (see Chapter 14 in this volume), shall not institute, endorse, or sponsor religion or coerce students or employees to engage in religious activities and (2) the state cannot single out religious expression for regulation in the American education system. The US Supreme Court exemplified the spirit of this balance in *Tinker v. Des Moines* (1969) when it stated, "It can hardly be argued that either students or teachers shed their constitutional rights to freedom of speech or expression at the schoolhouse gate."

How, then, does a school respect the rights of those within the building without violating the Constitution? This chapter explores the rights of students and teachers—which for our purposes will include administrators and other school authority figures—to express their religion in the school and how schools can respond, have responded, and should respond to such expression. The chapter is divided into three forms religious expression can take: religious speech, religious garb, and other religiously motivated actions. The following discussion about these forms of expression will cover both students' and teachers' rights.

RELIGIOUS EXPRESSION IN
THE PUBLIC SCHOOLS

Student Religious Speech

Student religious expression can be broken into the dichotomy of voluntary and compelled. It may seem obvious that voluntary religious expression will retain more protection than compelled religious activities—which, as we will see, receive little to no protection at all. Less obvious are the religious expressions that fall in between these two categories.

Compelled student religious expression (e.g., a school's mandatory recitation of prayers) is unconstitutional under the Establishment Clause of the First Amendment. In 1963, the US Supreme Court held that school-sponsored Bible readings and the mandatory recitation of prayers were facially contrary to the US Constitution (*Abington Township v. Schempp*). Currently, there is consensus in the courts and by leading religious liberty advocacy groups that no child should be compelled to engage in religious activity; however, the consensus begins to divide when it comes to students' religious activities during extracurricular activities of graduation ceremonies and sporting events (see Chapter 19 in this volume).

What, then, about compelled student speech involving widely used expressions such as the phrase "One nation, under God" in the Pledge of Allegiance? Congress added this theological rhetoric to the pledge in 1954 in order to show a stark difference with the Soviet Union's embrace of communism. Although the merits of this have never been fully addressed by the US Supreme Court, some federal and state courts have heard the issue. In some jurisdictions, the historical and patriotic nature of the pledge has rendered it constitutional in the face of First Amendment objections. Other jurisdictions have upheld the pledge, refuting the idea that the principle of non-establishment is at odds with policies that permit students and parents to opt out of reciting all or that particular part of the pledge. Any coercive effect on the student is mitigated because of its voluntary nature. There remains, however, a debate over whether peer pressure against conscientious objectors reintroduces a covert coercion.

Voluntary student religious expression is wholly different in its nature than expression the state, school, or teacher invites or compels the student to partake in. Students have First Amendment rights to both free speech and free exercise of religion, both of which cannot be abridged by the school. In fact, school boards and state legislatures have enacted codes and statutes that explicitly permit voluntary student religious speech, such as student-led prayers. However, even this religious activity is not without boundaries. The limit to voluntary student speech of any nature—including religious—is generally that it cannot interfere with the compelling objectives of the school or the rights of other students. A laissez-faire approach to voluntary religious voices in the classroom can actually further public educational objectives of enhancing an individual's choice of how to live, enjoying forms of culture, learning how to participate in democratic society, assisting the moral development of children, and teaching tolerance and respect for one another. Nonetheless, schools still have a need to maintain discipline, control, and bullying, which may be affected by voluntary student religious speech.

Teacher Religious Speech

The courts treat differently two different types of religious expression if engaged in by public school teachers. One type is the teaching of religion in public educational institutions (see Chapter 18 in this volume). In this realm of speech, teachers are encouraged to teach about religion (or religions) using a purely academic approach but not to advance, endorse, or favor any religion (or reject all religions). The second type of teacher religious speech is speech that is not pursuant to a curriculum, such as private acts of devotion in the workplace (e.g., accommodations for private prayer rooms, the wearing of religious garb, or being excused to participate in religious holidays). These types of religious expressions are initially more suspect than the former because they are not explicitly undertaken in pursuit of the educational institution's goals.

In this context, a teacher working in a public school must ensure that any private religious speech in the workplace does not proselytize or coerce students. The teacher cannot engage in religious instruction, or faith-development exercises (see Chapters 7 and 9 in this volume). Any statements about religion must be pursuant to the academic study of religion with the goal of promoting the civic competency of religious literacy (see Chapter 4 in this volume). Therefore, teachers, as agents of the state, must be very careful when communicating their own religious views in front of their students, not only to prevent coercion, but to protect the teacher from the perception of being coercive. Teachers must keep in mind that they are working as agents of the state and therefore, whether accurate or not, may be seen as acting as the state. Teachers must take great precautions to ensure that their own private religious expressions cannot be construed as religious instruction or religious indoctrination of the students.

In equipping schools to navigate these legal parameters, in 2000, twenty-two national organizations joined the US Department of Education to disseminate a document to every public school about the constitutionality of religion in public schools. As republished in *The First Amendment in Schools* (Haynes et al. 2003), the consensus document makes clear that

- The public school's approach to religion is *academic*, not *devotional*.
- The school strives for student *awareness* of religions, but does not press for student *acceptance* of any religion.
- The school sponsors *study* about religion, not the *practice* of religion.
- The school may *expose* students to a diversity of religious views, but may not *impose* any particular view.
- The school *educates* about all religions; it does not *promote* or denigrate religion.
- The school *informs* the students about various beliefs; it does not seek to *conform* students to any particular belief.

Further explanations and examples are provided in *A Teacher's Guide to Religion in the Public Schools* (Haynes 2010) and *Finding Common Ground: A First Amendment Guide to Religion and Public Schools* (Haynes and Thomas 2007).

RELIGIOUS GARB IN PUBLIC SCHOOLS

Both students' and teachers' religious expressions can manifest in the wearing of religious garb, which has a precise legal definition. Over the last twelve decades, state courts have defined religious garb as any dress, mark, emblem, or insignia indicating that a person is a member or adherent of any religious order, sect, or denomination (Walker 2018). To illustrate this definition, courts have seen that religious garb comes in many expressions—to name a few:

- African Hebrew Israelite (headdress),
- Buddhist (dharma wheel insignia),
- Catholic (habit, rosaries, Ash Wednesday marking),
- Church of the Brethren (hair covering and long dress),
- Daoist (*yin yang* symbol),
- Hindu (*bindi* [red dot] or Om symbol),
- Jewish (yarmulke [skullcap], beard, tzitzit [knotted tassel], mezuzah pendant, or *tichel* [headscarf]),
- Mennonite (bonnet [hat tied under chin]),
- Muslim (*hijab* [headscarf]),
- Native American (hair length),
- Nazirite (hair length),
- Protestant Christian (cross necklace, bracelet, or ring),
- Rastafarian (dreadlocks),

- Sikh (turban),
- Shriner (fez [hat]),
- Sikh (*kirpan* [small ceremonial dagger]),
- Wiccan (pentacle), and so on.

This short list of examples of religious garb derive from cases involving students and teachers (as well as military personnel and police officers), who have found themselves petitioning government regulations of religious garb. Generally speaking, schools may not arbitrarily regulate religion or act in hostility toward religion. Schools can, however, accommodate a religious objector to a dress code or use a compelling state interest to decide to uphold their policies.

If a dispute reaches the judicial system, the court will likely apply the *strict scrutiny* judicial standard under the Free Exercise Clause of the First Amendment to the US Constitution (*Cantwell*, 1940; *Sherbert v. Verner*, 1963; *Yoder*, 1972). As the highest form of judicial review, *strict scrutiny* has three prongs. Judges first turn to the plaintiffs to determine whether (1) their constitutional right to free exercise of religion was *substantially burdened*. If so, the court turns to the state to examine whether lawmakers had a (2) *compelling government interest* to justify the burden and then examines whether the legislature (3) *narrowly tailored* the law to achieve that interest through the *least restrictive* means possible. This judicial standard is applicable to the question of religious garb worn by both students and teachers in public schools.

Student Religious Garb

In the United States, the courts have held that students have a right to wear religious garb in public schools, even—as we will see—when it conflicts with a neutral, generally applicable dress code. Students' choice of religious dress can be analogized to their voluntary free speech because they have discretion—perhaps subject to parent or guardian approval—over what they wear to school. The following discussion will explore what the limits to a student's right to wear religious dress in public schools are in the face of opposing school interests.

The case law on students' religious garb is often resolved in three ways: accommodating the garb-wearing student; upholding a schools' decision when students reject the dress code as a whole; or requiring the parties to find a least restrictive alternative and reach a compromise.

First, if students agree to modify their religious garb into an otherwise conforming dress, courts will generally require the school to accommodate the student. To give examples, a Muslim student who agrees to wear a blue hijab to match the school's blue uniforms should be exempted from the dress code. Jewish students who wear a yarmulke in a public school that rejects their plea based on a "no hat" policy should receive a religious accommodation from their school. If they do not, a court will generally mandate such an accommodation. Similarly, Native American students have objected to hair length requirements in some public schools that generally prohibit male student hair length to "reach past the ears" or "go below the collar." Native American hair length is often tied to tribal culture and spirituality in such a way that it has garnered much support in courts when raised in opposition to a dress code.

The second legal trend is found in cases where students failed to convince the court that their religion was substantially burdened when refusing to conform to any form of regulation. A Native American high school student wished to wear a bird feather on her graduation cap, pursuant to her tribe's spiritual heritage (*Griffith* 2016). The school had a neutral policy prohibiting any embellishment to the graduation caps. However, the school did offer the student the option of wearing the feather in her hair, tucked in her ear, or as a necklace. The student refused and a court sided with the school because of its attempts to offer narrowly tailored accommodations. Schools can best situate themselves by crafting content-neutral policies, offering students reasonable accommodations, and reaching reasonable compromises whenever possible.

In other contexts, schools have rejected religious claims in which students stated they could not conform to the dress code as a whole. In one instance, the school required objectors to fill out a questionnaire, asking whether the student had ever worn uniforms in other contexts. If the student answered yes, the school denied his or her religious objection. A court ruled this procedure unconstitutional for allowing schools to be an arbiter of its students' beliefs but left open whether schools could—with other methods—reject religious claims asking for exclusion from an entire dress code. Another example in this vein is when a school's dress code mandated khaki pants and a solid-color top. Two students objected to the dress code, one by wearing a shirt expressing the student's religious views and the other adhering to a religion that prohibits conformity. The school sought to enforce the dress code and a court upheld enforcement of the code. In doing so, the court emphasized that this school—like many others—is not trying to discriminate against religions but is trying to pursue legitimate educational objectives.

In other contexts, courts may require parties to reach a reasonable compromise, even when the question of students' religious liberty rights come up against a school's interest in promoting safety. For example, virtually all schools have some policy prohibiting students from carrying weapons. However, as part of the Sikh tradition, some adherents carry the *kirpan*, a small ceremonial knife. Following precedent such as the yarmulke and hair length examples previously listed, one appellate court exempted Sikh students who carried *kirpans* from a school's weapon ban (*Cheema* 1995). This is the most controversial of the religious garb cases because the courts must weigh the religious expression of the student with the school's compelling interest in ensuring students' safety. The appellate court found that the school did, in fact, have a compelling interest to uphold a no-weapons ban; however, the students prevailed in the court because the school did not *narrowly tailor* the policy to meet the *least restrictive means* possible. For instance, the school could have permitted the student to bring the *kirpan* but require that it be permanently fused to a sheath so that it can never be used as a weapon. The school could have required that the *kirpan* be expressed in the form of an illustration on a belt or piece of cloth, thus allowing the student to express his identity without being perceived as being dangerous. These kinds of compromises are possible only when school leaders effectively mediate conflict before it reaches the courts, a lesson also applicable to the question of public school teachers' religious garb.

Teacher Religious Garb

A particularly complex and unresolved legal question is whether teachers can wear religious garb in the public classroom. This question has been brewing in the US legal system for over twelve decades and continues to be extremely controversial in Europe (Walker 2018). In contrast to students' rights, teachers' right to wear religious garb while teaching in a public school has been more limited, although there are currently more efforts today to accommodate employees in the workplace.

The twelve-decade debate over public school teachers' religious garb in the United States originated when, in 1894, the Pennsylvania Supreme Court ruled in favor of Catholic nuns who were dismissed for wearing habits while teaching at a public school (*Hyson v. Gallitzin*). The state's high court held that religious dress did not disqualify a teacher from employment. The court went on to issue these fateful words, setting this age-old saga into motion: "The legislature may, by statute, enact that all teachers shall wear in the schoolroom a particular style of dress." In contemporary legal terms, the court explained that the legislature could create a *neutral and generally applicable* (*Smith* 1990; *Church of Lukumi Babalu Aye* 1993) dress code that applied equally to all teachers. They did not. Rather, the Pennsylvania General Assembly responded by enacting the first religious garb statute in the United States—a statute that was neither general nor neutral. The Assembly prohibited public school teachers from wearing "any dress, mark, emblem or insignia indicating . . . that such teacher is a member or adherent of any religious order, sect or denomination." This statute explicitly targeted religious garb for government regulation, and remains in effect today. The statute justifies permanently disqualifying any teacher from employment who fails to follow the law and provides criminal penalties for any public school administrator who fails to suspend or terminate the offending teacher after notice of a violation. In 1910, the Pennsylvania Supreme Court, comprised of none of the same members who had heard the previous case in 1894, denied the petition of a Mennonite teacher who was fired for wearing "usual plain dress" in the classroom. This legitimized the state's anti-garb law, the language of which became the legal template for other state statutes and regulatory bans. By the end of World War II, Pennsylvania was one of twenty-two states to ban religious garb worn by public school teachers. The bans came in either the form of state statutes or regulatory policies issued by state superintendents.

In a 1946 study published by the National Education Association, state superintendents in sixteen states confirmed that they employed public school teachers who wear religious garb, and state superintendents in twenty-two states responded that they did not, whereas thirteen states either did not comment or reported that their laws were silent on the matter. Of the states whose superintendents reported that they did not employ public schoolteachers wearing religious garb, only three of the twenty-two states actually had statutory bans on teachers' religious garb:

- Nebraska's statute was enacted in 1919 and repealed through legislative action in 2017;
- Oregon's statute was enacted in 1922, affirmed by the Oregon supreme court in 1986, and repealed by the state legislature in 2010; and
- Pennsylvania's statute was the nation's first anti-religious garb law enacted in 1895, affirmed by the Pennsylvania supreme court in 1910, and is currently the only state remaining with an anti-religious garb law (Walker 2018).

The case law on the question of public school teachers' religious garb falls into two categories: no-aid-to-religion cases and religious-garb cases (Walker 2018). The no-aid-to-religion-cases include the evidence of teachers wearing religious garb in the statement of facts for cases that take up the larger questions of public funding of private religious schools. In these cases, the practice of educators wearing religious garb while teaching was one part of a larger question and, as a result, this precise question was not singled-out and dissected for judicial review. These cases illustrate the complex lineage of court decisions regarding regulations of teachers' religious garb in public schools, controlled and managed by public authorities with the use of public funds.

The second category was comprised of cases that solely took up the question of whether public schoolteachers' can wear religious garb. There is no uniformity in legal reasoning among the religious-garb cases. The only consistent pattern is the fact that public school teachers won their cases in states that did not have an anti-religious garb statute at the time; whereas, they failed when challenging states whose legislatures had enacted anti-religious garb statutes.

The precise question of the constitutionality of teachers First Amendment rights is situated in the larger discussion of regulation of religious garb worn by government employees. For instance, in 1986, the US Supreme Court upheld the military's decision to prevent an Orthodox Jew and ordained rabbi from wearing a yarmulke while on duty and when wearing an Air Force uniform (*Goldman v. Weinberger*). A few months later Congress overrode the US Supreme Court by including a religious apparel accommodation clause in the 1987 defense authorization bill signed into law by President Ronald Reagan. This accommodation was limited to military personnel and did not address public school teachers directly.

In another controversial religious accommodation case, the US Supreme Court ruled against Native Americans for using peyote in *Employment Division v. Smith* (1990), which Congress overrode by passing the federal Religious Freedom Restoration Act of 1993 (RFRA), signed into law by President Clinton. Four years later, the US Supreme Court found Congress to have overstepped its authority by applying federal regulation to state/local ordinances (*City of Boerne v. Flores*, 1997). As a result, twenty state legislatures passed "mini-RFRAs," affirming the federal RFRA's position that generally neutral laws that substantially burden religion must past the most stringent judicial review—*strict scrutiny*. This period between *Goldman* (1986) and the passage of the federal RFRA (1993) is considered to be one of the most confusing periods in church/state law in American history. During this era of uncertainty, public school teachers continued the age-old attempt to legally challenge anti-religious garb regulations in their states. There are three cases, in particular, that explain why the legal question of public school teachers' religious garb remains an unresolved constitutional issue.

First, in *Cooper v. Eugene School District* (July 1986), the Oregon Supreme Court upheld the termination of Janet Cooper, a Sikh teacher who was fired for violating the state's anti-religious garb statute—a law that was enacted by open members of the Ku Klux Klan in 1923. Before examining the court's findings, it is important to note that the *Cooper* decision was issued four months after *Goldman* (March 1986), which may have had an influence and set a tone for justifying banning religious garb in government settings. In *Cooper*, the Oregon Supreme Court found that the Sikh teacher's right to exercise her religion was "reasonably denied" because of the state's interest in preserving religious "neutrality" in public schools. The state's high court found that the interest of preserving the "image of a nonsectarian public school" outweighed the infringements of her free exercise rights under the Oregon constitution's Free Exercise clause. The Oregon Supreme Court did, however, note that it would be permissible for public schools to allow teachers to wear "common decorations" from a religious "heritage," such as a necklace with a small cross or Star of David. No definition of "small" was offered, and neither was a distinction made between "common decorations" and head coverings worn by Catholics, Sikhs, or Muslims. It is also important to note that the Oregon Supreme Court explicitly rejected the use of federal judicial tests under the Free Exercise clause of the US Constitution. Rather, the court focused on the Free Exercise Clause of the Oregon State Constitution and on their own earlier Oregon state court rulings against Native American counselors' use of peyote, which four years later would become the infamous US Supreme Court decision of *Employment Division v. Smith* (1990). In bringing this legal conflict to a close, in 2010, the Oregon state legislature repealed the state's anti-religious garb law of 1923, stating both that the original bill had been proposed by leaders of the Ku Klux Klan to prevent Catholic teachers from being employed by public schools and that the anti-religious garb law violated precedents set by the Oregon Supreme Court and the US Supreme Court.

A second contemporary case was issued three months before the US Supreme Court issued *Smith* in April 1990. In *Mississippi Employment Security v. McGlothin* (January 1990), the Mississippi Supreme Court held that a public schoolteacher's periodic wearing of a head wrap as a religious cultural expression of her identity as an African Hebrew Israelite from Ethiopia was constitutionally protected under both the Free Exercise clause of the US Constitution's First Amendment, as incorporated by the Fourteenth Amendment, and the "no religious tests," "no preference," and "free enjoyment of all religious sentiments" clauses of Mississippi's Constitution (Art. III §18). The Mississippi Supreme Court applied the US Supreme Court's *strict scrutiny* test and did not find applicable the US Supreme Court's decision in *Goldman v. Weinberger*, in part because Congress had overturned it two years earlier. Three months after issuing the *McGlothin* decision, the US Supreme Court issued *Smith*, eclipsing the *McGlothin* case and preempting another emerging garb case in Pennsylvania.

Four months after the April 1990 decision of *Smith*, the Third Circuit issued a negative ruling against a Philadelphia public schoolteacher (*Reardon*, 1990). In this case, decided in August 1990, Alima Delores Reardon was fired for wearing a hijab (Muslim headscarf) and loose dress while teaching in the school district of Philadelphia. Earlier, the District Court for the Eastern District of Pennsylvania had held that the state's anti-religious garb statute violated Title VII of the Civil Rights Act of 1964, which prohibits employment discrimination based on religion. The Third Circuit reversed the lower court, holding the garb statute valid under Title VII because the school district could experience an "undue hardship" to accommodate Reardon's religious expression. The Third Circuit reasoned that requiring the school board to violate a "reasonable" religious garb statute would make the school board vulnerable to a "substantial risk of criminal prosecution, fines, and expulsion from the [education] profession" (*Reardon*, 1990). The federal appellate judges further claimed that the school district would not satisfy its compelling state interest in allowing her to wear religious apparel, failing to uphold the "appearance of a secular public-school system." The court asserted that the "Garb Statute permissibly advanced a compelling interest in maintaining the appearance of religious neutrality in the classroom" and that while, admittedly, the statute "was enacted with a putatively anti-Catholic motivation, the commonwealth was not practicing discrimination in enforcing the statute" (*Reardon*, 1990).

This sampling of contemporary cases are recent episodes of an 123-year legal history in which only one court, the Mississippi state court, applied the Free Exercise Clause standard of judicial review—*strict scrutiny*—to the question of public schoolteachers' religious garb. No federal or state court since the US Supreme Court's *Smith* decision has ruled on the question of whether anti-religious garb statutes are *generally applicable* (*Smith*, 1990), as compared to targeting religion for government regulation, which the constitution prohibits (*Church of Lukumi Babalu Aye*, 1993). As a result, the question of the legality of public schoolteachers' religious garb remains unresolved today.

In summary, the US Supreme Court has not yet determined the constitutionality of teachers' wearing religious garb in the public schoolroom. If given the opportunity, it will likely overturn such a regulation, as it did in two 2015 decisions: the high court held unanimously that the Arkansas Department of Corrections' ban on religious garb was unconstitutional (*Holt v. Hobbs*, 2015), and the Justices ruled in an 8-to-1 decision (*EEOC v. Abercrombie*, 2015) that Abercrombie & Fitch knowingly refused to hire Samantha Elauf because she was a Muslim, as the supervisor interpreted because she wore a *hijab* during the job interview. The latter case focused on the employer's burden to notify applicants and employees of dress policies, at which point the employee can request an exemption based on religious grounds. These recent US Supreme Court cases and the state legislative developments to rescind Nebraska and Oregon's anti-religious garb statutes illustrate the trend of the government, at all levels, to accommodate religious expression in the workplace, including public schools.

RELIGIOUS ACTIONS

Student Religious Action

It is unconstitutional to compel students to engage in religious activity. As examined in Chapter 18, the state may not mandate that students recite prayers or read aloud passages from the Bible (Abington Township v. Schempp 1963) and the state may not mandate a daily moment of silence "for meditation or voluntary prayer" (Wallace v. Jaffree 1985). Both of these scenarios are unconstitutional because the government is giving preference to religion over nonreligion—or a specific religious tradition over other religions. The courts treat forced scripture readings similar to forced vocal prayers, regardless of whether they are denominationally neutral or whether students can remain silent or excused from the classroom where the prayer is taking place (*Engel v. Vitale* 1962; *Abington Township v. Schempp* 1963). As a result of these legal distinctions, moments of silence are increasingly the preferred vehicle to accommodate students who pray without school coercion of mandatory Bible readings or vocal prayers. Additionally, the Supreme Court has upheld mandatory moments of silence to open up the school day (*Wallace v. Jaffree* 1985). Students can use the moment of silence for prayer or not—but they can also use this time for secular purposes such as being still, for calming down, or for quietly thinking. For example, the very nature of a moment for silence allows students to contemplate upcoming school assignments, sporting events, or home life— all without revealing their thoughts or motivations to teachers or peers.

The US Supreme Court has twice ruled that public schools violate the Establishment Clause when government-sponsored speakers engage in nonsectarian prayers, such as at graduation ceremonies (*Lee v. Weisman* 1992), or when a student council elects a chaplain to deliver prayers at football games (*Santa Fe Independent School District v. Doe* 2000). In both contexts, a graduation prayer and an invocation at a football game were considered by the US Supreme Court to be government–sponsored speech, therefore, unconstitutional. On the other hand, students may engage in private acts of devotion in public places, as long as they are not disruptive, such as gathering at the school flag pole for prayer or saying grace over one's meal in the cafeteria. These cases further reinforce the view that students' religious activity must be voluntary and public schools' policies cannot result in the student body being held captive, whether by an adult or their peers.

Teacher Religious Action

A teacher cannot compel devotional reading of religious texts or prayers, whether during the school day or at an extracurricular activity. This does not, however, prohibit teachers from reading the text of their religious viewpoint in their free time in private spaces. Teachers should not engage in such reading in front of their students. Even if the students are occupied with another activity—such as a test, guest speaker, or so forth—teachers should not engage in devotional readings or prayers while in the same room as their students. The students could notice the teacher's action and perceive it as an endorsement of religion. Teachers should feel comfortable reading their religious texts if they are in the teachers' lounge or when their students are outside for recess. In fact, the American Civil Liberties Union explicitly encourages such an accommodation for teachers, and this could serve as a model for school districts across the country. Many of these suggestions, however, may be outdated given technological advances: sacred texts are readily available on a smartphone, making it unlikely that students would know whether teachers were in the back of the room contemplating a biblical verse or reading their emails.

Another issue many public schoolteachers may face is over the use of religious objects or images in the classroom that represent the teacher's devotional practices. A teacher can have a temporary religious object/symbol as a teaching tool in the classroom only if it is a part of a civics education course about the world's religions that displays many symbols without preferential treatment of one symbol over another. Use of religious symbols must be done for academic purposes to advance the students' civic competency or religious literacy (see Chapter 4). Despite the fact that similar objects residing in government buildings or on government land are considered constitutional, the courts would likely consider a classroom location different. Again, this distinction is due to the impressionability of K-12 students and the longstanding conflicts over use of taxpayer dollars for public schools. Therefore, while a teacher may be trying to use a religious object in a classroom with the intent to display its historical significance—the usual justification for including symbols like the Ten Commandments in a courthouse—it could easily be construed as the teacher's, and therefore the government's, endorsement of that particular religion. That said, a major tenet among religion and public education proposals is that religion can be taught about in public schools from an academic perspective (See Chapter 4 in this volume)—it just cannot be proselytizing or coercive or include any form of religious instruction.

CONCLUSION

Both students and teachers retain their First Amendment rights to free exercise and freedom from established religion while in the public school; however, teachers face unique scrutiny because of their status as government officials. As is often the case among the religion clauses of the First Amendment, public schools must strike a balance between non-establishment and supporting the free exercise rights of those within the building. Unfortunately, it is not the easy answer to grant accommodations for all those claiming a religious right. But the school's ability to justifiably reject religious claims of its students and teachers can also cause legal conflicts. If the accommodations that are allowed—whether purposefully or inadvertently—create a pattern of favoring a religion (particularly a majority religion) while denigrating other, minority religions, the school could be violating the Establishment Clause. For these reasons it is critical to view the non-establishment and free exercises as inseparable principles to ensure religious freedom for all.

FUTURE DIRECTIONS

1. How might the increasing religious diversity in America challenge the way public schools view students' and teachers' religious expression?
2. List the various ways that students and teachers may express themselves religiously in a public school. How might the school accommodate those expressions? In which contexts would administrators need to intervene, and for what compelling reasons? If so, how can the school achieve its goals by ensuring that religion is regulated in the least restrictive means possible?
3. Compare the research presented in Chapter 4 with the case law in this chapter. How can education leaders cultivate their own religious literacy so as to serve a diverse public? How can principals and school board members model for the public how to make religious literacy a fundamental civic competency, so as to better promote mutual understanding about issues related to religion and society? How might religiously literate leaders better promote religious liberty for people of all religions and no religion?
4. How might First Amendment education become a fundamental competency in teacher training and principal preparation programs? How can these curricula explicitly address the religious liberty issues facing students and teachers?

ACKNOWLEDGMENT

We offer a special thanks to Professor Kent Greenawalt, University Professor at Columbia Law School, for his thoughtful feedback and collegial support.

REFERENCES

Abington School District v. Schempp, 374 US 203 (1963).
Cantwell v. State of Connecticut, 310 US 296 (1940).
Cheema v. Thompson, 67 F.3d 883 (9th Cir. 1995).
Church of Lukumi Babalu Aye v. City of Hialeah, 508 US 520 (1993).
City of Boerne v. Flores 521 US 507 (1997).
Cooper v. Eugene Sch. Dist. No. 41, 301 Ore. 358 (1986), app. Dismissed, 480 US 942 (1987).
EEOC v. Abercrombie & Fitch Stores, Inc., 135 US 2028 (2015).
Engel v. Vitale, 370 US 421 (1962).
Employment Division v. Smith, 494 US 872 (1990).
Goldman v. Weinberger, 475 US 503 (1986).

Griffith v. Caney Valley Public Schools, 157 F.Supp.3d 1159 (2016).

Haynes, Charles C. 2010. *A Teacher's Guide to Religion in the Public Schools*. Nashville, TN: First Amendment Center.

Haynes, Charles C., Haynes and Oliver Thomas. 2007. *Finding Common Ground: A First Amendment Guide to Religion and Public Schools*. Nashville, TN: First Amendment Center.

Haynes, Charles C., Sam Chaltain, John E. Ferguson, Jr., David L. Hudson, Jr., and Oliver Thomas. 2003. *The First Amendment in Schools: A Guide from the First Amendment Center*. Nashville, TN: First Amendment Center and Alexandria, VA: Association for Supervision and Curriculum Development.

Holt v. Hobbs, 135 US 853 (2015).

Mississippi v. McGlothin, 556 So.2d 324 (MS Sup. Ct. 1990).

National Education Association. 1946. "Practice and Usage in Aid to Sectarian Schools and Sectarianism in Public Schools as Reported by State Superintendents" in *The State and Sectarian Education Research Bulletin*. (Washington, DC: National Education Association of the United States), Vol. XXIV, No. 1, Feb. 1946, p. 24–25, 36. (The NEA report inaccurately reports Arizona enacting an anti-religious-garb law, which it did not. Arizona became a state in 1919. The reported regulation on public schoolteachers' religious garb was a remanence of a federal policy in federal schools that terminated the employment of Catholic nuns when they were hired by the national government to convert indigenous people to Christianity in Federal Indian Schools.)

[Reardon] *United States v. Board of Education*, 911 F.2d 882 (3rd Cir. 1990).

Sherbert v. Verner, 374 US 398 (1963).

Tinker v. Des Moines Independent Community School District, 393 US 503 (1969).

Walker, Nathan C. "An Analysis of Federal and State Law Governing Public Schoolteachers' Religious Garb in Pennsylvania and Nebraska Under the Free Exercise Clause to the First Amendment to the United States Constitution and the Pennsylvania Religious Freedom Protection Act." Doctor of Education diss., Teachers College Columbia University (2018).

Wallace v. Jaffree, 472 US 38 (1985).

Wisconsin v. Yoder, 406 US 205 (1972).

FURTHER READING

Bastian, Holly M. 1992. "Religious Garb Statutes and Title VII: An Uneasy Coexistence," 80 Geo. L.J. 211, 1991–1992.

Blum, Virgil C. 1955. "Religious Liberty and the Religious Garb, and Religious Garb in the Public Schools: A Study in Conflicting Liberties." *University of Chicago Law Review* 22, no. 4: 875–888 and 888–895.

Foehrenbach Brown, Josie. 2009. "Representative Tension: Student Religious Speech and the Public School's Institutional Mission." *Journal of Law and Education* 38: 1–82.

Grathwohl, Linda. 1993. "The North Dakota Anti-religious garb Law: Constitutional Conflict and Religious Strive," *Great Plains Quarterly*, 13: 187–202.

Greenawalt, Kent. 2005. *Does God Belong in Public Schools?* Princeton, NJ: Princeton University Press, 155–159.

———. 2006. *Religion and the Constitution: Free Exercise and Fairness*. Princeton, NJ: Princeton University Press.

———. 2008. *Religion and the Constitution: Establishment and Fairness.* Princeton, NJ: Princeton University Press.

Gunn, T. Jeremy. "Religious Symbols and Religious Expression in the Public Square." In *The Oxford Handbook of Church and State in the United States,* edited by Derek H. Davis, 226–310. Oxford University Press, New York.

Howard, Erica. 2012. *Law and the Wearing of Religious Symbols: European bans on the wearing of religious symbols in education.* New York, NY: Routledge.

Stefkovich, Jacqueline A. 1992. "Religious Garb in the Schools: A Different Time, A Different Place. Religion & Public Education." *Religion & Public Education* 19 no. 1 (Winter): 43–46.

Volokh, Eugene, 2016. *The First Amendment and Related Statutes: Law, Cases, Problems and Policy Arguments.* 6th ed. St. Paul, MN: Foundation Press.

....

CHAPTER 17

RELIGION AND THE PUBLIC SCHOOL CURRICULUM

....

WALTER FEINBERG

INTRODUCTION

IN this chapter I will begin by providing background information on the relationship between religion and public schools and then will describe the different kinds of courses currently offered in some public schools. I will show that different kinds of religion courses command different kinds of justifications, and I will weigh the legal and educational merits of these justifications. I will conclude by presenting a case for teaching religion that is both constitutionally and educationally acceptable. This case rests upon the importance of the development of autonomy to the liberal tradition, and it shows how the teaching of religion as a humanistic study can serve this ideal.

BACKGROUND

Public schools are generally defined as free, state-supported, state-controlled primary and secondary educational institutions. In most Western countries education is now compulsory up to the secondary level, and in many religious and private schools exist alongside public ones serving to satisfy the compulsory education requirement. In some countries religious schools receive considerable state support, and in others public schools may have a particular religious orientation. However, this has not been the case in the United States: the First Amendment to the US Constitution, ratified in 1791, stipulates a strong separation between religious and government institutions. In recent years the Supreme Court has interpreted this to limit public support for officially sponsored religious expression in public schools. The reasoning behind this interpretation is associated with Thomas Jefferson's view that freedom of conscience forbids government from taxing one person to support the religious beliefs of another. Hence the Constitution forbids the federal government from establishing a religion, and it protects the right of individuals to worship as they choose. Yet the question of the role of religion courses in public education continues to be debated.

When the Constitution was enacted, the question of state support for education was moot since most people were unschooled, laws requiring compulsory public education did not yet exist, and most of the schools that did exist were sponsored by religious denominations. In addition, the scope of the First Amendment applied only to the federal government until after the ratification of the Fourteenth Amendment (1868), which required all states to uphold the federal guarantee to due process & equal protection. In the 1940s, the U.S. Supreme Court incorporated the Free Exercise and Establishment clauses of the First Amendment to individual state governments (*Cantwell* 1940 and *Everson* 1947; see Chapters 13 and 15 in this volume).

Compulsory education laws developed gradually through the initiative of individual states. Beginning with Massachusetts in 1852 and ending with Mississippi in 1918, all the states passed compulsory education laws, usually until the age of sixteen years. These laws were established for a number of reasons, including the promotion of literacy and character development, the advancement of industrialization in the service of capitalism, child protection, national cohesion, and citizenship education.

Religion was not absent from these schools. Schools in many states would begin the day with a reading from the Bible as well as the Pledge of Allegiance and would observe major Christian holidays. During the latter part of the nineteenth century, as individual states began to enact compulsory attendance laws, public schools often became the focal point of religious tension between Catholics and Protestants. Catholics often complained that government-supported schools were advancing a form of soft Protestantism, and Protestants feared Catholics were all antidemocratic papists.

In an attempt to blunt the demand of Catholics to support their religious schools, the Blaine Amendment, prohibiting state support to religious schools, was presented to Congress in 1875. It failed to pass the Senate by four votes. Had it passed, and ratified by the states, it would have made it unconstitutional for any government—local, federal, or state—to provide aid to religious schools. While it was narrowly defeated, a number of states did adopt the amendment for their own constitutions. While the Blaine Amendment had the appearance of neutrality, many felt that it was actually aimed at Catholic schools, which represented the only significant alternative to the growing public school system. Anti-Catholic feeling was fueled by the view that Catholicism fostered antidemocratic attitudes, a view that was reinforced by the reactionary turn of Pope Pius IX in the late 1840s, and by the influence of the antirepublican sentiments of the Jesuit order of the time.

Partly as a result of such mutual suspicion, the growth of Catholic parochial schools came to shadow the development of public ones. Church authorities often encouraged parents to send their children to the parish school rather than the public one, while some state authorities tried to force parents to send their children to the public school, questioning the legitimacy of full-time religious schools. This issue was partially settled by the US Supreme Court when it ruled in *Pierce v. Society of Sisters* (1925) that parents had the right to choose to send their children to nonpublic private or religious schools. The decision did not address the First Amendment or the question of whether the state had any obligation to support religious or private education. While *Pierce* then allowed parents to send their children to religious schools, it did not place any financial obligation on the states to support that choice. Although the case was decided on Due Process grounds under the Fourteenth Amendment, and not under the guarantee of free exercise rights under the First Amendment, *Pierce* prepared the way for many later decisions that were.

For the remainder of the century most of the Court's rulings served to protect both religious believers and nonbelievers from undue state coercion in public schools. For example, in 1943, in an unusual reversal of an earlier decision, the Court ruled that the state could not compel Jehovah's Witnesses children to salute the flag. The case was especially poignant, coming as it did at the height of World War II. Justice Jackson wrote, "If there is any fixed star in our constitutional constellation, it is that no official, high or petty, can prescribe what shall be orthodox in politics, nationalism, religion, or other matters of opinion or force citizens to confess by word or act their faith therein."

A short time later, in *McCollum v. Board of Education* (1948), the Court struck down an arrangement between a local school board and a religious association that allowed religious representatives to conduct voluntary religious classes within the schools. In this ruling the Court invoked the Establishment Clause, noting that the arrangement constituted tax support to religion. And again, a decade later, in *Abington Township v. Schempp* (1963), the Court banned compulsory Bible reading for devotional purposes from public schools on the grounds that it violates the Establishment Clause of the Constitution that prohibits the government from making any laws "respecting an establishment of religion."

The Court has continued to refine the relationship between religion and public schools and to address some of the more subtle questions that arise as times change (see Chapters 13 and 15 in this volume). For example, while official school-sponsored prayer is banned as unconstitutional (*Engel v. Vitale* 1962; *Wallace v. Jaffree* 1985; *Lee v. Weisman* 1992), student-initiated prayer may be allowed, but only if it does not utilize school resources such as an intercom system, or if students are not serving to represent the school in some capacity, such as when athletes might pray prior to a game (See US Supreme Court case that found student-initiated, student-led invocations at football games unconstitutional in *Santa Fe v. Doe* 2000).

NONDEVOTIONAL RELIGION COURSES

While the US Supreme Court has now banned compulsory devotional religious exercises, it has not banned the nondevotional academic teaching of religion. As the majority opinion in Schempp (1963) noted: "Nothing we have said here indicates that such study of the Bible or of religion, when presented objectively as part of a secular program of education, may not be effected consistently with the First Amendment." Moreover, recent Court decisions have backtracked on this distinction when it comes to the support of religious schools. In one important case the Court ruled that public funds could be provided to religious schools as long as those schools were a part of a viable choice program where parents had the option of sending their children to a private, religious or public school (*Zelman* 2002). Many groups still question this decision, and many states and localities do not provide support for religious schools.

As mentioned above, the touchstone of the relationship between public education and religion can itself be traced back to the concern to reject tyrannical government policies that favored one religion over others. Hence, the very First Amendment to the US Constitution begins: "Congress shall make no law respecting an establishment of religion or prohibiting the free exercise thereof." The first religion clause is referred to as the Establishment Clause, the second as the Free Exercise Clause, and their enactment was supported by arguments against tyranny, defined loosely as the state imposing belief, abridging freedom of conscience, or forcing one party to finance the beliefs of another.

DEFINING OBJECTIVITY

Debate continues over exactly what constitutes an "objective" treatment of religion. In recent years, for example, lower courts have continued to confront the issue of whether it is constitutional to teach creationist doctrine or Intelligent Design as viable options to Darwinian evolutionary theory in biology classes. While it is clear that presenting these as viable scientific competitors in a biology class is unconstitutional (*Edwards v. Aguillard* 1987), it is less clear how they might be presented in some other subject, say a literature class or a social studies class. While the courts continue to fine-tune these decisions, a minority of schools are finding different ways to familiarize students with religious issues and texts. Still, many school districts remain unconvinced that the constitutional risk is worth the educational benefits. Those that do decide to offer courses in the academic study of religion have a number of different alternatives.

NATIONAL INTEREST GROUPS

Two influential and well-financed national lobbies advocate the inclusion of Bible courses in the public school curriculum. The first of these, the National Council on Bible Curriculum in Public Schools (NCBCPS), advocates Christian-oriented Bible courses. It has been criticized not only by those who are opposed to the teaching of religion in the public schools but also by a competing Bible advocacy group, the Bible Literacy Project (BLP), a group that advances a more ecumenical approach to the teaching of religion. The BLP has produced a well-designed textbook, *The Bible and Its Influence* (Schippe and Stetson 2006), that has been praised by a number of groups, both religious and nonreligious (see Chapter 18 in this volume for a complete discussion of the constitutionality of Bible courses in American Public Schools).

Four Types of Nondevotional Religion Courses

Among schools that do offer a religion option there is little consensus, and at least four different kinds of religion courses vie for limited space in the curriculum. These courses generally go under the labels Bible History, The Bible in History and Culture, The Bible as Literature, and World Religions. Given the large diversity among American teachers and schools, any generalizations about any of these labels would be subject to many qualifications, but there are important similarities and differences between these courses that should be mentioned.

Bible history courses are most common in evangelical, Bible Belt communities. Their official aim is to familiarize students with the Bible and to address what many perceive as troubling Bible illiteracy. Because they are often taught in religiously conservative, Christian communities, they may also serve to add to the standing of the school among devoted Christians. However, these courses can be troubling from a constitutional point of view because of the temptation to teach the Bible as if it were a history textbook. Some of these courses use a chronologically ordered Bible as the sole text, reinforcing the impression that the Bible is a report of events that occurred in real time.

Some teachers believe that they can remain neutral as long as they refrain from providing students with interpretive commentaries on the readings. From their point of view the Bible speaks for itself and any interpretive material must be biased. However, critics see the assumption that the Bible speaks for itself as a Protestant bias. Nevertheless, the courses are popular among many religious fundamentalists and can reduce their suspicion of public schools as "Godless humanistic" institutions, and some administrators believe that offering such courses may help slow the move toward religious homeschooling (see Chapter 12 in this volume).

The price paid is high in terms of the neglect of the development of critical or interpretive skills. One of the interesting features of the NCBCPS curriculum is the strong emphasis that it places on Proverbs, with its emphasis on the need to follow authority—for example, the "fear of the Lord is the beginning of knowledge" and "hear your father's instruction, and do not reject your mother's teaching" (Prov. 1:7–8). As my colleague Richard Layton and I have observed, this

> preserves at least one of the trappings of the pre-*Schempp* devotional use of the Bible, in which readings and recitations of the Psalms and Proverbs figured prominently in mandated school exercises. In this facet of its curriculum, the BHL [Biblia Hebraica Leningradensia] echoes the traditional moral justifications for Bible reading, in a manner that sets this component apart from the historical course of study (Feinberg and Layton 2014, 67).

In contrast, courses labeled The Bible in History and Culture generally avoid the question of the historical accuracy of the Bible and focus on the way in which the Bible has influenced movements from the Crusades to classical and popular music. The focus here is rather open-ended, and it is often up to the teacher to decide just what to emphasize. At this point the most influential text is probably the BLP text mentioned earlier, *The Bible and its Influence* (Schippe and Stetson 2006). The text provides students with a comprehensive sense of the influence the Bible has had on cultural events and identity, and does not discourage discussion. The curriculum has received praise from religious groups, including some evangelical groups, and some nonreligious ones as well. However, it has been criticized by other evangelical Christian groups for undermining faith.

Although the evangelical community is divided, sometimes bitterly, between the two curricula (NCBCPS and BLP), some other groups, such as the American Jewish Congress and the Anti-Defamation League, either enthusiastically endorsed the BLP project or viewed it as a reasonable compromise that they are willing to live with. The BLP curriculum not only has endorsements from a wider spectrum of concerned groups, but it also is less problematic from a constitutional point of view than is the NCBCPS curriculum (for further discussion see Chapter 18 in this volume).

While there are significant differences between Bible history and Bible influence courses, they are both usually placed in the social studies curriculum (as are world religion courses, which I will discuss shortly). In contrast, courses labeled "The Bible as Literature" are likely to be taught in the English or language arts departments and emphasize the Bible's literary qualities. While the question of the literal and historical value of the Bible may remain unaddressed, the emphasis is on the narrative elements of the Bible, and students may be encouraged to develop their interpretive skills.

All three of the above courses focus on the Abrahamic religions and, in practice, frequently privilege Christianity. Even in those classes where the focus is on the Hebrew Bible, a Christian point of view is privileged, as is illustrated by the frequently used label "The Old Testament" and by teachers who advance, either implicitly or explicitly, a supersessionist viewpoint.

The outstanding exceptions to the Abrahamic standpoint are courses in world or comparative religions. World religions courses aim to inform students about the key beliefs and practices of different religious systems and to produce citizens who will function in multireligious societies. In addition to the three Abrahamic religions, these courses often provide students with a basic understanding of Buddhism, Hinduism, and sometimes Confucianism and Indigenous religions. Students are encouraged to ask "What is religion, anyway?," to appreciate diversity ("to make the strange familiar and the familiar strange"), and to gain academic and critical skills (Feinberg and Layton 2014). Teachers may work to help students locate their own beliefs within a field of religious beliefs and to see how their own subjectivity is influenced by religious factors and how that subjectivity influences their own understanding of the world. Unlike the other religion courses, world religions teachers may help students to recognize and develop a critical distance from their own prejudices and stereotypes.

Justifications for Nondevotional Religion Courses

The particular type of religion course chosen by a school district will depend a great deal on the makeup of the community. Bible history classes is most likely to be available in schools with a large evangelical population, and frequently the teachers chosen to teach the course are themselves well-respected members of a church community. In contrast, world religions classes are more likely to be taught in religiously diverse, economically advantaged communities with a strong cosmopolitan ethos.

The push to teach courses in religion is increasing, as indicated by the activity of the BLP and the NCBCPS. The climate has also been aided by a number of scholarly arguments put forth to justify one or another of the different programs. Five arguments are the most common.

The first argument is a *patriotic* one: the United States is a Christian nation, founded on Christian principles, so failing to teach religion threatens the basic fabric of our country. The second argument is a *moral* one: the Bible is an important source for character development and hence should be a critical component of moral education. These two arguments are most common in religiously conservative communities and are clearly reflected in the NCBCPS curriculum. The patriotic argument confuses a demographic fact with a collective value: true, a majority of Americans come from a Christian background, but the sum of individual identities does not always a collective identity make. The American creed of life, liberty, and the pursuit of happiness, was born more from the Enlightenment than from the Bible. The moral argument presents a somewhat different problem. It holds that the Bible presents many moral exemplars that can serve as role models for students. This is true, but the Bible also sanctions models of behavior (e.g., genocide in Samuel I, anti-Semitism in Paul) that must be rejected by any modern society.

The third argument is a *constitutional* one: the absence of religion in the schools advantages nonbelief over belief, creating an antireligious climate that violates the First Amendment of the Constitution. This argument holds that under the First Amendment, schools must not favor one religion over another, religion over nonreligion, or *nonreligion over religion*. Proponents argue that neglecting to treat the religious point of view violates this injunction and is the same as disfavoring religion. Hence, when public schools disregard religion they are promoting an unconstitutional antireligious point of view. The problem with this argument is that it assumes equivalence between nonreligion and antireligion, and it assumes too that not treating a religious point of view is the same as being antireligious. If one were to accept this argument, there would be a number of additional complications. For example, if a school decided to address the Islam and Christianity, would that mean that it were anti-Hindu and anti-Jewish? Or, is the assumption that all religions are essentially the same? Most religious people would reject this assumption. Clearly the problem is with the equation made between *not treating something* and *being opposed to that thing*, an equivalence that is defensible only under certain conditions. For example, to fail to address anti-gay acts in a homophobic environment would rightly be seen as supporting that act. However, the factual premise of the patriotic argument, correctly understood, refutes the constitutional argument. The environment in which schools are embedded is certainly a religious, if not a Christian one, and clearly supports a myriad of religious expressions. Religion is not ignored when, say, biology class does not treat creationism. This is a topic for a Sunday School class, not a science class, and if taught correctly it will represent the consensus of biologists, not theologians.

Warren Nord (1995, 2010) has attempted to address the constitutional concerns, arguing that the Constitution requires equal time for religious and nonreligious perspectives, and that when schools fail to include a religious point of view throughout the curriculum, they are in violation of the First Amendment (see Chapter 5 in this volume). Nord's logic is questionable because he confuses "neglecting to treat something" and "being opposed to that thing." Few legal or educational scholars have been willing to follow him and push the argument for teaching religion in public schools to the constitutional level, and the courts have already taken a stand against this view when addressing the argument that creationism is permissible to teach as an alternative to evolution in biology classes.

The fourth argument is the *religious literacy* one: schools need to teach religion in order to address rampant religious illiteracy, as revealed by the failure of many students to correctly answer the simplest question about the content of the Bible. This is one of the most common justifications for both Bible history and Bible influence courses. Interpreted more broadly, it could also serve as a reasonable justification for teaching about the Bible in literature, world history, and world religions courses, but it is usually restricted to illiteracy about the Old and New Testaments (see Chapter 4 in this volume).

There are two parts to this argument, a factual claim and an ethical conclusion about the public school's responsibility. Assuming the factual claim is correct—a big assumption given the anecdotal nature of the evidence—the moral issue is problematic: Given the long list of subjects about which students are purportedly illiterate (e.g., economics, history, literature), what is so special about religious illiteracy that religion courses should jump in front of the line? Besides, there is a long tradition in the United States of family and church providing religious education; why change that now? Many school districts besieged by claims about falling test scores and low achievement in traditional areas are unlikely to find this argument especially compelling.

Finally, the *academic* argument holds that knowledge of the Bible can help students to understand classical texts such as Shakespeare, so Bible knowledge will offer an advantage to students striving to get into a good college. This argument is often used to support courses in Bible literacy. The problem is not that the argument is false, but that it proposes a very inefficient method to correct it. If students need to be informed about a certain biblical allusion to understand a passage in *Hamlet*, why not just tell them about that particular Bible passage instead of requiring them to take an entire course in Bible knowledge?

The Liberal Case
for Teaching Religion

A compelling reason to teach a course on the Bible may be found in a new twist on the patriotic argument and in the attempt to find a justification rooted in the character of the country. And while this justification will not be satisfied with the problematic claim that this is a Christian country, it will be satisfied by the historical fact that the country is rooted in the liberal philosophy of the Enlightenment. Thus, if a viable case is to be made for teaching religion in the public schools, it will best be advanced as a part of its founding liberal tradition. From the point of view of liberal theory, there are two powerful justifications for introducing academic-based religion courses into the public schools: (1) to help students develop autonomy and (2) to improve the quality of civic participation.

Autonomy can be defined as the capacity to choose and to revise one's own conception of the good. Autonomy does not develop spontaneously; rather, it requires (1) an understanding of the particular traditions from which prevalent conceptions of the good arise, (2) a willingness to select one of these conceptions, and (3) the capacity to recognize and reflect upon one's inherited conception of the good. Educational theorists have traditionally held that a good education must avoid manipulating students' beliefs and indoctrinating them. However, this is a negative injunction, telling schools what they must not do. Schools that aim to *promote* autonomy need to do more: they must provide the logical skills and the information necessary to assess different conceptions of the good.

The second liberal argument for teaching religion involves the requirements of a democratic public in the postmodern age. A democratic public arises when people from different traditions engage with one another in constructing meaning and building a common future, and the unique role of a public school is to create such a public. At a time when different religions are playing such an important role in civic life throughout the world, citizenship and informed public participation require a greater understanding of the role religion plays in people's lives. As part of their unique mission, public schools have a responsibility to provide this understanding.

Despite the many difficulties that academic-based religion courses present, they could serve important civic ends and contribute to the construction of such a democratic public. Public education at its best is a process where citizens learn to recognize strangers as inheriting a shared fate and as co-agents in building a common future. Although often an arena for sectarian interests, academic-based religion courses, taught by well-trained teachers as a part of the public school humanities curriculum, could serve this civic role (but, alas, too often they do not). Given the importance of religion in both American culture and in global connections, given the many misconceptions perpetrated about certain religious traditions, and given the difficulty that many people have in rationally discussing differences of faith and commitment, these courses have the potential to make a unique and positive contribution to the civic role of public education.

RELIGION AND THE ROLE OF THE HUMANITIES

Studying the humanities (which is where religion courses should be firmly situated) should awaken students to the significance of interpretive and analytic skills. In religion courses, students can learn about their own interpretive framework and how it influences their understanding of religious texts and practices. This would require teachers to learn how to promote reflection. Because autonomy must be respected as well as developed, the proper aim of religion courses in public schools is not to change students' beliefs or to encourage them to believe that all religions are of equal worth (although some students may conclude that they are). Rather, the aim of the humanities from a civic standpoint is to promote civic skills by preparing the ground for engaging different points of view in constructive ways.

Nevertheless, the failure to teach the academic-study of religion is not due to a lack of interest on the part of students. As Noddings (1993) has shown, there is certainly intense student concern about religious questions, best left for parents and faith-communities (see Chapters 7 and 9 in this volume). Nor is it likely that most public high school students are not mature enough or intellectual enough to critically engage the academic-study of religion. Yet one of the most telling paradoxes of American education is the reluctance of many public schools to teach the most canonical of all books in the Western traditions, the Bible. Consequently, the Hebrew Bible, the New Testament, to say nothing of the Qur'an, is not a common source material (see Chapter 18 in this volume).

As long as a division of labor between home and school is respected, religion courses should have a role to play in public education. Religion can be taught in the public schools as a part of the human experience and as a way for students to understand their own traditions and those of others. It is the task of the parents, should they choose, to initiate their children into a religion and to teach them to worship in a particular tradition. It is also their right to *not* do this. Public schools have no business in the worship business, and they step over important educational and legal boundaries when they advance one religion over another or religion over nonreligion. Nevertheless, religion is a vital part of the human experience, and while many parents can engage their children in their own religious tradition, few have the knowledge or the interest to place that tradition in a wider context of traditions and interpretations, a context that we see as one of the critical dividing points between teaching religion as a devotional act and teaching it as a humanistic subject.

FUTURE DIRECTIONS

1. Recent court decisions have provided ways for religious schools to receive state funding through vouchers that support parental choice, yet these decisions have

not addressed the issue of state supervision. In the long run, will state funding entail state supervision?

2. If religious schools receive state funding, should there be greater state supervision?

3. If there is to be more state supervision of religious schools, should the religion courses be exempt, and if they are, will this satisfy the First Amendment?

4. What kind of training should teachers in public schools receive if they are to be certified to teach the academic study of religion?

REFERENCES

Abington Township v. Schempp, 374 U.S. 203 (1963).

Edwards v. Aguillard, 482 U.S. 578 (1987).

Everson v. Board of Education, 330 U.S. 1 (1947).

Engel v. Vitale, 370 U.S. 421 (1962).

Lee v. Weisman, 505 U.S. 577 (1992).

Feinberg, Walter, and Richard A. Layton. 2014. *For the Civic Good: The Liberal Case for Teaching Religion in the Public Schools*. Ann Arbor: University of Michigan Press.

McCollum v. Board of Education, 333 U.S. 203 (1948).

Noddings, Nel. 1993. *Educating for Intelligent Belief or Unbelief*. New York: Teachers College Press.

Nord, Warren A. 1995. *Religion and American Education: Rethinking a National Dilemma*. Chapel Hill: University of North Carolina Press.

———. 2010. *Does God Make A Difference: Taking Religion Seriously in Our Schools and Universities*. Oxford: Oxford University Press.

Santa Fe Independent School Dist. v. Doe, 530 U.S. 290 (2000).

Schippe, Cullen, and Chuck Stetson. 2006. *The Bible and Its Influence*. New York: BLP Publishing.

Wallace v. Jaffree, 472 U.S. 38 (1985).

Zelman v. Simmons-Harris 536 U.S. 639 (2002).

FURTHER READING

Brighouse, Harry. 2000. *School Choice and Social Justice*. Oxford: Oxford University Press.

DelFattore, Joan. 2004. *The Fourth R: Conflicts over Religion in America's Public Schools*. New Haven, CT: Yale.

Diamond, Larry, Marc F. Plattner, and Phillip J. Costopoulos, eds. 2005. *World Religions and Democracy*. Baltimore: Johns Hopkins University Press.

Dworkin, Ronald. 1978. *Taking Rights Seriously*. Cambridge, MA: Harvard, 1978.

Dwyer, James G. 1998. *Religious Schools v. Children's Rights*. Ithaca, NY: Cornell University Press.

Feinberg, Walter. 2006. *For Goodness Sake: Religious School and Education for Democratic Citizenry*. New York: Routledge.

Kunzman, R. 2006. *Grappling with the Good: Talking About Religion and Morality in Public School*. Albany: State University of New York Press.

McGreevy, John T. 2003. *Catholicism and American Freedom*. New York: W. W. Norton & Co.

Nash, Robert J. 1999. *Faith, Hype, and Clarity: Teaching About Religion in American Schools and Colleges,* New York: Teachers College Press.

Prothero, Stephen. 2008. *Religious Literacy: What Every American Needs to Know—and Doesn't*. New York: HarperCollins.

———. 2010. *God Is Not One: The Eight Rival Religions that Run the World—and Why Their Differences Matter*. New York: Harper Row.

Witte, John Jr. 2000. *Religion and the American Constitution: Essential Rights and Liberties,* Boulder, CO: Westview.

CHAPTER 18

···

THE BIBLE AND AMERICAN
PUBLIC SCHOOLS

···

MARK A. CHANCEY

INTRODUCTION

···

A 2013 survey by the American Bible Society found that a solid two-thirds of American adults believe it is "important to teach the values found in the Bible in public schools." The fact that the survey itself left "values found in the Bible" undefined did not inhibit many respondents from affirming their crucial importance. Three-quarters of those respondents who favored biblical instruction in schools did so because "the Bible teaches moral principles that are badly needed in society." Intensity of support varied across geographical lines, proving strongest in the South, where 73% of respondents felt it "extremely" or "somewhat" important, but in no region did it dip below 60%. Practicing Protestants and Catholics were most likely to consider it "extremely" or "somewhat" important (97% and 88%), with nonpracticing Christians also overwhelmingly supportive (68%). In contrast, most non-Christians (67%) regarded it as "not too important" or "not at all important." Though many poll respondents agreed that "it is important to be familiar with [the] Bible in order to be a well-educated person," many also acknowledged concern that such teaching "would favor one religion over another." Support for teaching biblical values was lowest among those aged 18 to 28 (49%) and highest among those aged 67 and above (82%) (American Bible Society 2013).

Citizens in the oldest age bracket are precisely those most likely to have personal memories of a time when many public schools ritualistically read the Bible daily, some of them also offering Bible courses for students' spiritual edification. Such practices were once common, but they have never been universal. Just as support for teaching biblical values varied in 2013, so did enthusiasm for Bible reading and Bible courses in the more distant past. Those customs were never without controversy, as many citizens regarded them as governmental promotion of certain religious views and marginalization of others.

In the mid-twentieth century the Supreme Court prohibited school-sponsored religious instruction and devotional Bible reading as unconstitutional establishments of religion. It affirmed, however, the importance of teaching about the Bible and other expressions of religion from nonsectarian and academic perspectives. Hitting the legal benchmark of nonsectarianism has at times proved to be challenging, despite broad support in many quarters for the general project of religious literacy.

This chapter charts the historical development of Bible reading and Bible courses in public schools. It pays particular attention to the ways such practices often favored some religious perspectives over others and to the efforts of courts, educators, and special interest groups to identify constitutional ways to teach about the Bible. Putting contemporary practice into historical perspective demonstrates just how firmly ongoing debates about the Bible and public education are rooted in past controversies.

BIBLE READING IN NINETEENTH-CENTURY AMERICAN SCHOOLS

Modern proponents of increasing the Bible's place in public schools who claim it was once central to American education are correct. In the colonial period and the early Republic, the Bible was used not only for spiritual formation but also to teach reading and morals, and biblical material filled primers and textbooks. Because schooling was squarely in the hands of private groups, particularly religious organizations, it is perhaps unsurprising that the Bible played such a prominent role.

In the mid-nineteenth century, however, the "Common School" system of public education began to emerge. The Common School movement took its name from the idea that schools should teach the "common knowledge" needed by all citizens. For movement proponents, that knowledge included religious training in the nation's majority religious tradition, Protestantism. Common School educators not only incorporated the Bible into their curricula but also emphasized the importance of daily Bible reading to instill character, morals, and piety—reading typically done from the King James translation favored by Protestants. They developed a system designed to avoid offending any particular Protestant church or denomination: reading the Bible without comment, thus leaving interpretation up to the student.

Such an approach ignored the sensibilities of non-Protestants. What about Roman Catholics, whose Old Testament had more books and for whom individualistic, private interpretation of scripture was regarded as disrespectful of the Church's authority? What about Jews, who rejected the New Testament entirely and whose Bible differed in organization from Christian Old Testaments? What about agnostics, atheists, freethinkers, and adherents of other traditions? For them, the Common Schools' promotion of a generic Protestantism was hardly neutral.

The 1840s introduced decades of occasional conflict over such concerns, with particularly intense controversies occurring in New York City; Ellsworth, Maine; Boston; and elsewhere. The most famous and tragic of these episodes were the 1844 Philadelphia Bible Riots. When the local school board there ordered the King James Version to be read in city schools, the Catholic bishop requested that his parishioners instead be allowed to hear the Catholic Douay-Rheims translation or excused from the exercise altogether. Although the board agreed to this compromise, at least some Protestant officials, teachers, and students refused to acquiesce, reportedly bullying Catholic students. Nativists, resentful of Irish Catholic immigrants, interpreted the substitution of the Douay-Rheims Bible for the King James Bible as an insult to American culture and identity. They leveled the erroneous charge that the bishop was trying to ban the Bible from schools. In May and again in July, Nativist protests led to large-scale riots that leveled whole city blocks, damaging or destroying numerous houses and businesses as well as several Catholic churches. Thousands of militia were ultimately required to quell the violence, which claimed several lives and wounded dozens. Grand juries later largely blamed Catholics for the disorder, and use of the King James Version remained the norm.

In contrast, the Cincinnati Bible War of 1869–1873 remained metaphorical, political, and legal. The school board there responded to local diversity by prohibiting school-sponsored Bible reading altogether, a policy intended to show equal respect to all religious groups. Many Protestants did not see things that way, however, interpreting the change as encroachment on their rights. One commentator warned that appeasement of Catholics would lead to unacceptable placation of other groups, arguing, "The attempt to please Mormons, Chinese, Jews, idolaters, atheists and infidels is out of the question" (Peabody 1870). When a lawsuit over the issue made its way to the state supreme court, the school board's attorney emphasized the difficulty of creating a genuinely neutral policy. He reasoned, "The teachers in our public schools, by whom or under whose direction the Bible is read, are not abstract, non-denominational Christians; they are or may be, some or all of them, Lutherans, Presbyterians, Methodists, Baptists, Trinitarians, Unitarians, etc. Each one has his religious bias, of which he will find it difficult to divest himself when he comes to read the Bible." He chided those who asserted a Protestant national identity that would ignore "the rights of Jews, Catholics and freethinkers" (Stallo 1870, 65 and 77). The court ultimately ruled in favor of the school board's prohibition of Bible reading (*Minor*, 1873).

Protestants and Catholics alike were distraught by such controversies, albeit often for different reasons. In the late 1800s, Catholics increasingly devoted resources to developing their own school system. Some Protestants worked diligently to uphold and expand school Bible reading, while others opposed it, whether on separatist grounds or because they viewed its generic Protestant flavor as insufficiently theological and thus too secular. Well into the twentieth century, state legislatures debated and sometimes passed laws regarding Bible reading and state courts heard cases on the matter, with varying outcomes in regard to both legal status and actual practice.

The Birth of Bible Courses in the Early Twentieth Century

As wrangling over Bible reading continued, educators in Protestant circles devised a new approach to strengthening students' religious instruction: academic courses taught in cooperative arrangements between schools and local congregations and religious organizations. Such programs, they believed, would facilitate evangelism, enhance the lackluster teaching provided at churches, check society's accelerating secularization, reverse declining morals, and improve cultural literacy. In the 1910s, states began developing plans to ensure students had access to religious education opportunities, particularly Bible study. North Dakota and Colorado led the way in 1912 and 1913, with other states following so quickly that by 1927, at least thirty-three gave academic credit for Bible study. Plans differed in the degree to which they reflected awareness of different views of the Bible between Protestants, Catholics, and Jews. Many of the early proposals granted credit for work done at Sunday School. In those cases, the state standardized expectations regarding content covered, time spent in instruction, and means of assessment. Congregations provided the teachers.

Over time, however, the Sunday School–based system yielded in popularity to Weekday Religious Education. In this arrangement, courses were taught Monday through Friday in virtually every logistical fashion imaginable: on campus and off, during school hours and afterwards, for academic credit and not, by regular school personnel and by teachers appointed by religious groups. Most programs were Protestant, but in some geographical areas there were also well-developed Jewish, Catholic, and Latter-day Saints versions. Although some focused on theology or character formation, many kept the Bible at the center. By the early 1940s, such programs were thriving.

The Impact of Court Rulings

Legal developments would soon pose new challenges. In 1945, Vashti McCollum protested the plan used by her school district in Champaign, Illinois. That program allowed students to be dismissed from their classes (an arrangement known as "released time") but remain on school premises to take religion courses from representatives of local religious communities. The program reflected some intentionality in respecting religious diversity; the courses were theoretically optional, and students initially could take them from a Protestant, Catholic, or Jewish perspective. Nonetheless, its implementation generated tensions: school authorities excluded Jehovah's Witnesses, Jewish students experienced taunting, and nonparticipants were criticized. McCollum's withdrawal of her fifth-grade son from the class brought ostracism. She filed a lawsuit claiming that the teaching of religious classes by religious organizations as a component of public education on school grounds violated the Establishment Clause.

As the Supreme Court considered the case, many religious educators feared a blow that would dismantle three decades of their work. The North Carolina Council of Churches, for example, warned that a negative decision would be a "staggering tragedy for Protestantism" and asked committees sponsoring Bible courses there to send $5 apiece to Champaign schools to help cover legal expenses (*Church Council Bulletin*, 1947). To the consternation of such groups, in 1948 the Court ruled in favor of McCollum, prohibiting compulsory on-campus religious education programs during the school day. A subsequent case, the 1952 decision *Zorach v. Clauson*, clarified that noncompulsory off-campus released time arrangements were permissible, but confusion persisted in educational and religious circles regarding what could happen on campus during school hours. Some schools abandoned religion classes altogether, others shifted them off grounds, and still others continued whatever arrangements they already had in place, even if they were religious in nature.

For Bible courses, the long-term trajectory was one of decline. A survey sent to schools in 4,000 communities suggests that by 1960 such classes were uncommon. Nationwide, only 4.51% of respondents reported offering "regular formal Bible instruction," a little over half of those for academic credit. Regional variations were noticeable, with the South (9%) and West (8.57%) far more likely to sponsor courses than the Midwest (4.14%) or East (1.32%) (Dierenfield 1962, 49–54).

In the meantime, the practice of school-sponsored Bible reading had continued. The same survey found that 41.74% of respondent schools read the Bible, typically the Protestant favorite, the King James Version. Southern and eastern states were most likely to read scripture (76.84% and 67.56%), and larger communities more likely to do so than smaller ones.

In Pennsylvania, a Unitarian family, the Schempps, filed suit to stop this practice, which a 1949 state law had mandated. When their case reached the US Supreme Court, it was combined with a similar one brought against Baltimore schools by Madalyn Murray (later to become the famous atheist activist Madalyn Murray O'Hair). In 1963, the Supreme Court ruled in *Abington Township School District v. Schempp* that this type of Bible reading was, in effect, a religious exercise that constituted a government establishment of religion. *Schempp* gained notoriety in many quarters for supposedly "banning the Bible," but it in fact explicitly affirmed the academic study of the Bible when done from a nonsectarian perspective. In an oft-quoted passage, the Court specified:

> It might well be said that one's education is not complete without a study of comparative religion or the history of religion and its relationship to the advancement of civilization. It certainly may be said that the Bible is worthy of study for its literary and historic qualities. Nothing we have said here indicates that such study of the Bible or of religion, when presented objectively as part of a secular program of education, may not be effected consistently with the First Amendment (*Schempp* 1963, 225).

This dictum authorized what was effectively a new type of course: one taught for cultural literacy rather than spiritual formation and in ways that treated different religious perspectives (including those of atheists and agnostics) equitably.

As with *McCollum*, the decision's immediate impact was mixed. Some older religious education courses faded away, but others maintained their overtly theological character for years, despite claims by their host districts that they were academically oriented and religiously neutral. Elsewhere, educators revamped courses or created new ones to match the spirit of *Schempp*. They used resources such as *The Bible Reader: An Interfaith Interpretation*, which presented biblical excerpts alongside commentary written by a rabbi, a Catholic priest, and a Protestant minister, and the popular textbook *The Bible As / In Literature*, which focused on biblical themes and allusions in Western literature (Abbott 1969; Ackerman 1971).

Confusion frequently prevailed over what constituted a legal course. Exactly how, to use the Court's terms, does one teach about the Bible objectively as part of a secular program of education? Figuring out constitutional parameters fell to lower federal courts, which have handled multiple cases on the matter, mostly in the Southeast. The 1979 and 1980 rulings in *Wiley v. Franklin*, which addressed Bible teaching in Chattanooga-area elementary schools, articulated a basic benchmark: "If that which is taught seeks either to disparage or to encourage a commitment to a set of religious beliefs, it is constitutionally impermissible in a public school setting" (*Wiley* 1979, 474 F. Supp. 525 at 531). That court emphasized that the constitutional issue "is not the Bible itself, but rather the selectivity, emphasis, objectivity, and interpretive manner, or lack thereof, with which the Bible is taught" (*Wiley* 1979, 468 F. Supp. 133 at 150). Some of the issues it and other courts have noted as problematic include the presentation of miracle stories as accurate historical narratives; inattention to differences between the canons of different religious traditions; the use of overtly religious curricula and classroom resources; the teaching of Bible-based life lessons and Christian theology; compulsory participation; selection of teachers on the basis of religious views; incorporation of worship practices; and, of course, outright evangelism. In general, the courts have spoken with more clarity about what is unacceptable than about what is desirable, though groups like the First Amendment Center (now part of the Newseum Institute) and the Society of Biblical Literature have developed guidelines to assist teachers in this regard.

BIBLE COURSES IN THE EARLY TWENTY-FIRST CENTURY

Bible courses have continued to attract attention and generate controversy in the new century. State legislators have occasionally adopted them as a cause, citing the same sorts of justifications uttered by advocates a century earlier: the importance of religious literacy and the necessity of improving morals. As the sponsor of a 2007 Texas bill put it, "There's a lot of stuff in the Bible that finds its way into our dictionaries, into our art, into all of our literature and into our laws." Bible courses, he suggested, can help young people tell right from wrong: "It is important to every one of us that we have . . . [a] moral society" (Scharrer 2007). Some have emphasized what they see as the Bible's foundational role for the American governmental and legal systems, like the New Hampshire lawmaker whose 2012 bill argued that the Founding Fathers' political ideas were "rooted in the belief in God and the teachings of the Bible" (House Bill 1712). Such claims, drawn primarily from the rhetorical arsenal of Christian Right groups who view America as an inherently Christian nation, unwittingly echo the linkage between the Bible and American identity deployed by Protestants against Catholics in the 1800s.

At least seventeen state legislatures have debated Bible bills in the twenty-first century, with eight (Arizona, Arkansas, Georgia, Kentucky, Oklahoma, South Carolina, Tennessee, and Texas) creating laws encouraging Bible courses. In addition, Ohio and South Carolina have authorized credit for religiously oriented released time courses, and legislators in Louisiana and South Dakota adopted nonbinding supportive resolutions for Bible classes. Most legislative measures explicitly require courses that follow guidelines articulated by federal courts, but they vary widely in how much direction they provide school districts, administrators, and teachers on how to present and engage biblical material appropriately.

State law or not, districts across the country offer the courses. The exact number in any given year is unknown but reaches at least into the hundreds. North Carolina, for example, offered 283 Bible courses with 3,954 students in 2011–2012—a small percentage of the state's total student population, but a higher share than many observers might expect. Texas, in contrast, offered significantly fewer courses in 2011–2012, with only 57 school districts out of over 1,030 teaching Bible, along with three charter schools. A few states have course standards developed by state boards of education or education agencies, but most offer no official guidelines at all (Chancey 2013).

Heightened public interest in Bible courses can be attributed in part to the efforts of two organizations. The older of these is the Greensboro, North Carolina–based National Council on Bible Curriculum in Public Schools (NCBCPS). Founded in 1993, the NCBCPS claims that its curriculum has been "been voted into 1, 280 school districts" in thirty-nine states, but its numbers appear to be inflated (NCBCPS 2018). The council includes individuals associated with the Christian Right, state and national legislators, celebrities such as Chuck Norris and Jane Russell, and a handful of academics (NCBC 2011).

The group claims that its curriculum, a teacher's guide, focuses on historical and literary aspects of the Bible (thus its title, *The Bible in History and Literature*) (NCBC 2011). Although it maintains that the course is academic in nature and has never been legally challenged, the reality is otherwise. In 1998 a federal judge prohibited a Florida school district from teaching the New Testament segment of the course and allowed the Hebrew Bible component to be taught only because local educators had already drastically modified it (*Gibson* 1998). In 2008, a West Texas school district abandoned the curriculum rather than defend it in court.

The curriculum's various editions have typically blended literalistic reading strategies with a strong dose of Christian nationalism. Some have explicitly advocated biblical inspiration, the historical accuracy of miracle stories, and the near-perfect preservation of the original wording of biblical texts. At least one edition presented as fact the urban legend that NASA had discovered a missing day in time corresponding to the biblical story of the sun standing still (Joshua 10). Although more recent versions have omitted many of the more egregious missteps, they still strongly reflect conservative Protestant presuppositions. What has not changed is the curriculum's claim that the Bible was the primary inspiration for the Founding Fathers and is thus the basis of the American political and legal systems. To some readers, its not-so-subtle message appears to be that "real Americans" are socially and theologically conservative Christians.

Dissatisfaction with the NCBCPS contributed to the formation in 2001 of a new organization, the Bible Literacy Project (BLP). The BLP also promotes public school Bible courses, but it has been far more intentional than the NCBCPS in networking across the religious and political spectrums. It textbook (*The Bible and Its Influence*), instructor's manual, teacher workshops, and online teacher training reflect considerable effort to present the material in ways that cohere with First Amendment jurisprudence and respect religious diversity. The BLP is often quite successful in describing different religious groups' interpretations of key biblical passages (for example, Jewish rejection of Christian readings of prophetic books like Isaiah as predictive of Jesus). Beautifully illustrated, its textbook makes good use of literary reading strategies and explores the Bible's reception in literature, music, art, and other media (Schippe and Stetson 2006).

Despite such successes, the BLP materials are not without their own issues. The textbook's treatment of historical-critical and authorship issues and its use of biblical scholarship strike some as uneven. Discussion of the Book of Isaiah, for example, nods to traditional views of authorship as well as alternatives: "Most Orthodox Jews and Evangelical Christians tend to look at [it] . . . as a single book written by the Prophet Isaiah," but "liberal Jews, mainline Protestant Christian and Roman Catholics see [it] . . . in three parts written by three different people at three different times" (Schippe and Stetson 2006, 108–109). The volume often lacks such nuance elsewhere, instead presenting traditional positions as the norm. More significantly, the BLP's overall thrust is that the Bible is primarily a source for positive social and personal transformation; it downplays or disregards altogether the Bible's deployment throughout history to justify oppression or violence. For example, its textbook highlights scripture-citing abolitionists while ignoring scripture-citing slaveholders.

The availability of these two curricula was not enough to discourage Steve Green, president of the Hobby Lobby craft store chain, from exploring the possibility of creating his own. Having amassed one of the largest private collections of Bible-related artifacts in the world, Green announced in 2013 that he would develop a Bible course showcasing that assemblage. He insisted that the course would be constitutional and nonsectarian but also made clear that it would affirm the Bible's historical accuracy and reliability. He pledged to place it in thousands of public schools, but when his organization (Museum of the Bible) provided an Oklahoma school district with portions of a draft in 2014, critics quickly pointed out religious underpinnings and academic flaws. The district ultimately opted not to offer the course, and Green shelved his plan to market it across the United States—at least temporarily.

Teachers who do not use NCBCPS or BLP materials typically cobble together courses from whatever resources are available, whether Sunday School materials, older religious education curricula, classics like *The Bible As / In Literature*, popular books, or scholarly literature. If Texas courses are representative of those elsewhere, classes exhibit considerable variety in content, quality, and legal appropriateness. Surveys of curricular materials used there in 2005–2006 and 2011–2012 found that while some teachers succeeded admirably in crafting academic, nonsectarian courses, others infused their courses with theology, whether intentionally or not. The bias in the latter cases was always toward Christianity, typically in its conservative Protestant forms: classes favored a sixty-six-book canon, read biblical accounts literalistically, and interpreted the Hebrew Bible messianically. A few even explicitly tried to convert students. The functional understanding of *nonsectarian* in those cases seemed to be nondenominational evangelicalism, in ways that resembled nineteenth-century understandings of the term as generic, nondenominational Protestantism. Findings about Texas courses were similar to those for Florida courses in the late 1990s, as documented by People for the American Way. More work is needed on Bible courses in other states to determine how they fare (Chancey 2006; Chancey 2013; People for the American Way 2000).

CONCLUSION

The original purposes of both Bible reading and Bible courses were to promote students' spiritual and moral development. Both practices sometimes proved controversial in religiously diverse communities where some members felt that schools were privileging certain religious perspectives over others. The Supreme Court prohibited school-sponsored religious instruction in 1948 and school-sponsored Bible reading in 1963, but reading and studying the Bible from an academic, nonsectarian perspective "as part of a secular program of education" remains legal. For many who believe that religious literacy is a crucial component of cultural literacy and formation for responsible citizenship, increased study of the Bible in public schools is desirable. Success in reaching the Court's bar of objectivity, however, has proved to be mixed. While some courses neither promote nor disparage particular religious viewpoints, others are undergirded by theological assumptions, usually Protestant in nature. In this regard, the project of public school, academic study of the Bible has yet to fully escape its Protestant origins of a hundred years ago.

FUTURE DIRECTIONS

1. If Bible classes are offered in most states, why have so few states developed official course standards?
2. How does the geographical distribution of contemporary Bible courses reflect variations in population density, religious demographics, and socioeconomic factors?
3. Why do so few state agencies monitor the number and content of Bible courses offered under their purview?
4. What are the best practices for teaching Bible courses that are academically informed, legally sound, and respectful toward diverse religious sensibilities?
5. Why have courses devoted to world religions received less attention and support than those focused solely on the Bible?
6. What types of pre-service and in-service training are needed for Bible teachers, and why are opportunities for such training not more available?
7. What should the civic functions and goals of Bible courses be?
8. How can Bible courses help students better engage the growing diversity of America's religious landscape?
9. To what extent should high school courses make use of the types of insights from biblical scholarship typically encountered in college-level courses?

BIBLIOGRAPHY

Abbott, Walter M., Arthur Gilbert, Rolfe Lanier Hunt, and J. Carter Swaim, (Eds.). 1969. *The Bible Reader: An Interfaith Interpretation.* London: Geoffrey Chapman and New York: Bruce Books.

Abington Township School District v. Schempp, 374 US 203 (1963).

Ackerman, James S. and Thayer S. Warshaw. 1971, 1995. *The Bible As/ In Literature.* Palo Alto: Scott, Foresman. 2nd ed., Glennview, Il.: ScottForesman.

American Bible Society, *State of the Bible, 2013.* New York: American Bible Society, 2013.

Board of Education v. Minor, 23 Ohio St. 211 (1873).

Chancey, Mark A. 2006. *Reading, Writing, & Religion II: Teaching the Bible in Texas Public Schools.* Austin, TX: Texas Freedom Network Education Fund.

———. 2013. *Reading, Writing, & Religion II: Teaching the Bible in Texas Public Schools, 2011–2012.* Austin, TX: Texas Freedom Network Education Fund.

Dierenfield, Richard B. 1962. *Religion in American Public Schools.* Washington, DC: Public Affairs Press.

First Amendment Center. 1999. *The Bible and Public Schools: A First Amendment Guide.* New York, NY: Bible Literacy Project, Nashville, TN: First Amendment Center, Atlanta: Society of Biblical Literature.

Gibson v. Lee County School Board, 1 F. Supp. 2d 1426 (M.D. Fla. 1998).

Hodge, Charles. 1870. "Recent Publications on the School Question." *Biblical Repertory and Princeton Review* 42: 313–325. London: Forgotten Books Press.

McCollum v. Board of Education, 333 US 203 (1948).

Moss, Candida R. and Joel S. Baden. 2017. *Bible Nation: The United States of Hobby Lobby*. Princeton, NJ: Princeton University Press.

National Council on Bible Curriculum in Public Schools. 2018. "Where This Has been Implemented." At http://www.bibleinschools.net/Where-This-Has-Been-Implemented. php.

National Council on Bible Curriculum in Public Schools. 2011. *The Bible in History and Literature*. Greensboro, NC: Ablu Publishing.

New Hampshire House of Representatives. 2012. House Bill 1712. Available at https://legiscan. com/NH/text/HB1712/id/522497.

North Carolina Council of Churches. 1947. "Cooperative Action Imperative to Save Bible in Schools." *Church Council Bulletin* 8, no. 3: 1–2.

North Carolina State Board of Education and Department of Public Instruction. North Carolina Public Schools Statistical Profile.

Peabody, James A. 1870. "Recent Publications on the School Question." *Biblical Repertory and Princeton Review* 42: 313–325.

People for the American Way. 2000. "Bible History Courses Violate Constitution, New Investigation Reveals." Jan. 13 press release.

Scharrer, Gary. 2007. "Texas Lawmaker Seeks Bible Classes at Schools." *Houston Chronicle*, April 4.

Schippe, Cullen and Chuck Stetson, eds. 2006, 2nd ed. *The Bible and its Influence*. Fairfax: BLP Publishing.

Society of Biblical Literature. 2008. *Bible Electives in Public Schools: A Guide*. Atlanta, GA: Society of Biblical Literature.

Stallo, J. B. 1870. "Argument of J. B. Stallo, For the Board of Education." In *Arguments in the Case of John D. Minor et al. Versus the Board of Education of the City of Cincinnati et al*, 59–105. Cincinnati, OH: Robert Clarke.

Wiley v. Franklin, 474 F. Supp. 525 (E.D. Tenn. 1979).

Wiley v. Franklin, 468 F. Supp. 133 (E.D. Tenn. 1979).

Zorach v. Clauson, 343 U.S. 306 (1952).

FURTHER READING

Barr, David L., and Nicholas Piediscalzi, eds. 1982. *The Bible in American Education: From Source Book to Textbook*. Philadelphia: Fortress Press; Chico: Scholars Press.

Chancey, Mark A. 2007. "Sectarian Elements in Public School Bible Courses: Lessons from the Lone Star State." *Journal of Church and State* 49, no. 4: 719–742.

———. 2007. "A Textbook Example of the Christian Right: The National Council on Bible Curriculum in Public Schools." *Journal of the American Academy of Religion* 75, no. 3: 554–581.

———. 2013. "Public School Bible Courses in Historical Perspective: North Carolina as a Case Study." *Religion & Education* 40, no. 3: 253–269.

Davis, Derek H. 2010. "The Interplay of Law, Religion, and Politics in the United States." In *The Oxford Handbook of Church and State in the United States*, edited by Derek H. Davis. New York: Oxford University Press.

Deckman, Melissa, and Joseph Prud'homme, eds. 2014. *Curriculum and the Culture Wars: Debating the Bible's Place in Public Schools*. New York: Peter Lang.

DelFattore, Joan. 2004. *The Fourth R: Conflicts over Religion in America's Public Schools*. New Haven, CT, and London: Yale University Press.

Feinberg, Walter, and Richard A. Layton. 2014. *For the Civic Good: The Liberal Case for Teaching Religion in the Public Schools*. Ann Arbor: University of Michigan Press.

Fessenden, Tracy. 2005. "The Nineteenth-Century Bible Wars and the Separation of Church and State." *Church History* 74, no. 3: 1–28.

Fraser, James W. 2016, 2nd ed. *Between Church and State: Religion and Public Education in Multicultural America*. Baltimore: Johns Hopkins University Press.

Green, Steven K. 2010. "Church and State in Nineteenth-Century America." In *The Oxford Handbook of Church and State in the United States*, edited by Derek H. Davis. New York: Oxford University Press.

———. 2012. *The Bible, the School, and the Constitution: The Clash That Shaped Modern Church-State Doctrine*. New York: Oxford University Press.

Haynes, Charles C. 2014. "Battling over the Bible in Public Schools: Is Common Ground Possible?" In *The Bible in the Public Square: Its Enduring Influence in American Life*, edited by Mark A. Chancey, Carol Meyers, and Eric M. Meyers, 181–192. Atlanta: Society of Biblical Literature.

Michaelsen, Robert. 1970. *Piety in the Public School*. London: MacMillan.

Moore, Diane L. 2007. *Overcoming Religious Illiteracy: A Cultural Studies Approach to the Study of Religion in Secondary Schools*. New York: Palgrave Macmillan.

Moore, R. Laurence. 2000. "Bible Reading and Nonsectarian Schooling: The Failure of Religious Instruction in Nineteenth-Century Public Education." *Journal of American History* 86: 1581–1599.

Prothero, Stephen. 2007. *Religious Literacy: What Every American Needs to Know—and Doesn't*. San Francisco: HarperSanFranciso.

Wilcox, Clyde, and Sam Potolicchio. 2010. "The Christian Right and Church–State Issues." In *The Oxford Handbook of Church and State in the United States*, edited by Derek H. Davis. New York: Oxford University Press.

Zimmerman, Jonathan. 2002. *Whose America? Culture Wars in the Public Schools*. Cambridge, MA: Harvard University Press.

CHAPTER 19

RELIGION, EXTRACURRICULAR ACTIVITIES, AND ACCESS TO PUBLIC SCHOOL FACILITIES

CHARLES J. RUSSO

INTRODUCTION

IN *Board of Education of Westside Community Schools v. Mergens* (1990), the Supreme Court upheld the Equal Access Act (EAA), a federal law enacted to permit organized groups of high school students to meet in public secondary schools during noninstructional time, periods when classes are not scheduled so that non-curriculum-related clubs can gather. Given the importance of *Mergens* and later developments, this chapter is divided into four parts: (1) the situation that existed before the EAA was enacted; (2) the EAA itself; (3) *Mergens* and later judicial developments; and (4) the meaning of *Mergens* and its progeny.

BEFORE THE EAA

The EAA traces its roots, albeit indirectly, to *Widmar v. Vincent* (1980). *Widmar* arose when members of an on-campus religious group at the University of Missouri at Kansas City challenged a campus rule forbidding them from meeting in campus facilities even though over 100 registered student groups were free to do so. On further review of an order in favor of the students, the Supreme Court affirmed in their favor, thereby ushering in a new era for access to public educational facilities.

Relying on the framework of freedom of speech, in an 8-to-1 judgment written by Justice Lewis Powell, the Supreme Court reversed in favor of the students. The Court pointed out that insofar as university officials created a forum that made facilities generally available for the exchange of ideas, but without explicitly using the term viewpoint discrimination, they could not deny a religious group equal access to them solely due to the content of the speech of its members.

The Supreme Court also specified that insofar as university officials created a limited public forum for student speech, the Court determined that they failed to demonstrate that the policy was narrowly drawn to achieve the compelling state interest of not violating the Establishment Clause. The Court went so far as to observe that the rule went further than the First Amendment required. At the same time, the Court distinguished *Widmar* from disputes involving religious activities in public grade schools, conceding both that facilities in those settings are generally not used as open forums and that university students are less impressionable than young children.

At the heart of its analysis, the Supreme Court applied the seemingly ubiquitous tripartite test from *Lemon v. Kurtzman* (1971). According to this test,

> Every analysis in this area must begin with consideration of the cumulative criteria developed by the Court over many years. Three such tests may be gleaned from our cases. First, the statute must have a secular legislative purpose; second, its principal or primary effect must be one that neither advances nor inhibits religion; finally, the statute must not foster "an excessive government entanglement with religion." (612–613)

In *Widmar* the Justices noted that both lower courts agreed that the forum policy created at issue passed the first and third parts of the *Lemon* test because it had a secular purpose and avoided excessive government entanglement with religion. As to the effects part of the *Lemon* test, the Supreme Court agreed that absent evidence demonstrating that religious groups would have dominated the university's open forum, providing equal access to the religious group did not have had the primary effect of advancing religion.

The Supreme Court indicated that given the facts, officials could not have been perceived as endorsing religious speech, because they would only have been providing the same benefit to the religious club that was available to other groups. Rounding out its rationale, the Supreme Court reiterated that once officials created a limited open forum, they could not exclude religious groups from using meeting space.

Justice John Paul Stevens concurred to highlight his concern that the Supreme Court may have threatened academic freedom by requiring officials to open campus facilities as they did. Justice Byron White's dissent rejected the application of the Free Speech claims. He argued that any burdens that campus officials placed on the religious group were minimal insofar as its meetings only would have had to move a short distance off campus.

THE EQUAL ACCESS ACT

Spurred on in part by *Widmar*, Congress passed the EAA and President Ronald W. Reagan signed it into law on August 11, 1984. The Act states that

[i]t shall be unlawful for any public secondary school which . . . has a limited open forum to deny equal access or a fair opportunity to, or discriminate against, any students who wish to conduct a meeting . . . on the basis of the religious, political, philosophical, or other content of the speech at such meetings (20 U.S.C. § 4071(a)).

In addition, the EAA specifies that "[a] public secondary school has a limited open forum whenever such school grants an offering to or opportunity for one or more noncurriculum related student groups to meet on school premises during noninstructional time" (20 U.S.C. § 4071(b)).

The EAA does set limits:

(c) Fair opportunity criteria

Schools shall be deemed to offer a fair opportunity to students who wish to conduct a meeting within its limited open forum if such school uniformly provides that—

(1) the meeting is voluntary and student-initiated;

(2) there is no sponsorship of the meeting by the school, the government, or its agents or employees;

(3) employees or agents of the school or government are present at religious meetings only in a nonparticipatory capacity;

(4) the meeting does not materially and substantially interfere with the orderly conduct of educational activities within the school; and

(5) non-school persons may not direct, conduct, control, or regularly attend activities of student groups (20 U.S.C. § 4071(c)).

THE *MERGENS* CASE

High school students in Nebraska sued their board for refusing to permit them to organize a Christian club under the terms of the EAA. After the federal trial court, in an unpublished opinion, upheld the board's action, the Eighth Circuit (1989) reversed in favor of the students. The court found that the presence of more than thirty noncurriculum-related clubs at the school, including the band, chess club, cheerleaders, choir, future medical assistants, Latin and math clubs, student publications, intramurals, competitive athletics, and the National Honor Society, meant that the board created a limited open forum such that the religion club had to be allowed to form.

On appeal to the Supreme Court in *Mergens*, Justice Sandra Day O'Connor was joined in parts by Chief Justice William Rehnquist and Justices White, Harry Blackmun, Antonin Scalia, and Anthony Kennedy as eight Justices generated four different opinions. Following a review of the EAA's history, the Court deferred to congressional ability to enact such a law. However, as to the Establishment Clause question, a plurality, meaning that the Court lacked a clear majority of five Justices, could not agree on whether the EAA was constitutional.

A majority of the Supreme Court agreed that Congress had the authority to extend the reasoning of *Widmar* to eliminate discrimination against religious speech in public secondary schools. As such, it explained that a "noncurriculum related student group" is "best interpreted broadly to mean any student group that does not *directly* relate to the body of courses offered by the school" (239), thereby making it easier for EAA clubs to form.

Turning to the Establishment Clause question, Justice O'Connor reasoned that in *Widmar* the Supreme Court upheld the principle of equal access under the *Lemon* test that it applies in most cases involving religion. Justice O'Connor then reviewed each of the three prongs of the *Lemon* test (cited above). First, she described the act's legislative purpose, to prevent discrimination against religious speech, as clearly secular. As such, the EAA passed muster on this test. In the second prong of *Lemon*, she rejected the board's argument that the EAA had the primary effect of advancing religion because high school students can distinguish between when officials permit clubs on campus and their being officially endorsed. O'Connor observed that if educators make it clear prayer clubs are on campus because students asked to create them, this would not infer endorsement. Finally, O'Connor pointed out that insofar as the prayer club was only one of a wide variety of student-initiated voluntary organizations, students would have been unlikely to perceive it as an official endorsement. As to the third part of the *Lemon* test, Justice O'Connor rejected the board's argument that the club's presence resulted in excessive entanglement. She observed that while the EAA allows educational officials to assign supervisory personnel to oversee student behavior, it forbids monitoring, participation, or involvement by faculty or non-school personnel, concluding that the EAA also prohibits school sponsorship of clubs.

Justice Kennedy, joined by Justice Scalia, agreed that the act did not violate the Establishment Clause. Instead of the *Lemon* test, though, Kennedy would have upheld the EAA because it did not afford such a direct benefit to religion clubs bordering on establishment or to coerce participation in activities infringing on the right to free exercise of religion. Justice Thurgood Marshall, joined by Justice William J. Brennan, agreed that the EAA could withstand Establishment Clause scrutiny but cautioned educators to take special care to avoid creating even the appearance of endorsing the goals of prayer clubs. Arguing that Congress intended to create a narrower forum for student clubs, in dissent, Justice Stevens would have rejected the EAA as unconstitutional without reaching the Establishment Clause question.

Because only four Justices agreed that the EAA passed Establishment Clause analysis, the Supreme Court left the door open to more litigation over the status of the EAA.

LATER JUDICIAL DEVELOPMENTS

Religious Groups

Later cases extended the scope of the EAA. The first post-*Mergens* EAA case arose in New York when all three members of a panel of the Second Circuit allowed students to create a policy establishing a religious test for its president, vice president, or music coordinator because these key officers were expected to lead Christian prayers and devotions while safeguarding the "spiritual content" of the meetings (*Hsu v. Roslyn Union Free School District* 1996a, b). Only the concurring judge would have extended this to the club's secretary and activities coordinator since their duties had little, if anything, to do with religion. Nothing in board policy prevented students who disagreed with the religious club from creating their own group.

In a case from Pennsylvania, the Third Circuit permitted an EAA club to meet during a school's morning activity period at which attendance was taken (*Donovan ex rel. Donovan v. Punxsutawney Area School Board* 2003).

The Ninth Circuit allowed an EAA club in California to meet during lunchtime (*Ceniceros v. Board of Trustees of the San Diego Unified School District* 1997); it also granted a group in Washington access to public funding, the school yearbook, public address system, bulletin board, school supplies, school vehicles, and audiovisual equipment and allowed it to engage in fundraising activities (*Prince v. Jacoby* 2002, 2003). The federal trial court in Arizona allowed a club to broadcast a video promoting itself during morning announcements (*Krestan v. Deer Valley Unified School District No. 97, of Maricopa County* 2008).

On the other hand, a federal trial court in Mississippi rejected the claim that a board created a limited open forum designed to permit members of a religious club to make announcements involving prayers and Bible readings before classes on a school's public address system (*Herdahl v. Pontotoc County School District* 1996). The court did permit voluntary student prayer before school to continue.

The Ninth Circuit initially upheld a California school board's refusal to recognize a club due to its proposal to require voting members to express their faith in the Bible and in Jesus Christ because officials feared this was a violation of its nondiscrimination policies (*Truth v. Kent School District* 2007). However, an en banc panel reversed in favor of the club because a question of fact remained over whether educators refused to grant the club the exemption due to its Christian character or the religious content of its speech (*Truth v. Kent School District* 2008).

Lesbian, Gay, Bisexual, Transgender (LGBT) Clubs

Unanticipated applications of the EAA arose when LGBT students and their supporters sought to form clubs. These groups relied on EAA language forbidding boards from discriminating "on the basis of the religious, political, philosophical, or other content of the speech at such meetings" (20 U.S.C. § 4071(a)).

The Eighth Circuit, in a case from Minnesota (*Straights and Gays for Equality v. Osseo Area Schools–District No. 279* 2008), plus federal trial courts in California (*Colin ex rel. Colin v. Orange Unified School District* 2004), Florida (*Gay–Straight Alliance of Yulee High School v. School Board of Nassau County* 2009), Indiana (*Franklin Central Gay/ Straight Alliance v. Franklin Township Community School Corp.* 2002a, b), Kentucky (*Boyd County High School Gay Straight Alliance v. Board of Education of Boyd County, Ky.* 2003), and Utah (*East High Gay/Straight Alliance v. Board of Education* 1999a, 1999b; *East High School Prism Club v. Seidel* 2000), agreed that educational officials could not deny LGBT EAA clubs the opportunity to use school facilities. These courts largely agreed that school officials failed to respect the meaning of the EAA and that denying clubs their right to meet would have violated their First Amendment rights.

Insofar as the dispute from Utah had an extensive history, passing through three rounds of litigation, it is worth reviewing in some detail. High school students with a gay-positive perspective challenged a board policy denying them an opportunity to meet at school during noninstructional time and to have access to school facilities. The federal trial court interpreted the policy as violating the group's rights under the EAA because it denied the students the chance to meet when another non-curriculum-related group was permitted to do so (*East High Gay/Straight Alliance v. Board of Educ.* 1999a). Shortly thereafter, the same court decided that insofar as the plaintiffs failed to demonstrate how the policy had a disparate impact on their viewpoint, it did not have to examine the actual motives of board members regarding their allegations (*East High Gay/Straight Alliance v. Board of Educ.* 1999b).

In the third case, the court reviewed the standards governing access to the limited forum that the board created for curriculum-related student clubs at the high school when a club sought to examine the impact, experience, and contributions of gays and lesbians in history and current events (*East High School Prism Club v. Seidel* 2000). The court granted the club's request for a preliminary injunction because there was substantial likelihood that it would succeed on the merits of its First Amendment claim that the school official who was responsible for evaluating their application misapplied the appropriate standards or added a new one.

Three federal trial courts disagreed. When a board in Colorado limited clubs to those that are curriculum-related, the court refused to disturb the judgment of school officials (*Palmer High School Gay/Straight Alliance v. Colorado Springs School District No. 11* 2005). A court in Texas deferred to educators due to their concerns based on sexually explicit content accessible from the group's website (*Caudillo v. Lubbock Independent School District* 2004). More recently, a federal trial court in Florida refused to extend the act to a middle school (*Carver Middle School Gay-Straight Alliance v. School Board of Lake County, Fla.* 2014) because it applies only to secondary, not middle, schools.

Postscript

The status of the EAA may be in doubt in light of the Supreme Court's opinion in *Christian Legal Society v. Martinez* (2010). This case examined whether Christian law students at a public law school in California could apply membership and leadership requirements to individuals who wished to join their organization.

In a 5-to-4 judgment, the Justices affirmed that law school officials could require all on-campus groups to admit all comers from the student body, even for leadership positions, regardless of whether they agree with organizational beliefs. Even though a related issue was unresolved in *Truth*, a case predating *Christian Legal Society*, it remains to be seen how this might impact EAA clubs.

ACCESS TO SCHOOLS BY NON-SCHOOL RELIGIOUS GROUPS

The Supreme Court's judgment in *Lamb's Chapel v. Center Moriches Union Free School District* (1993) is worth addressing briefly because it set the stage for a case involving students. In *Lamb's Chapel* the Court reviewed the policy of a New York school board that, pursuant to a state statute, made its facilities available to an array of social and civic groups. A religious group sued the board when it refused to rent its facilities to show a film series on childrearing based on fears of violating the Establishment Clause.

In a rare unanimous judgment, in *Lamb's Chapel* the Supreme Court again treated religious speech as a form of free speech, essentially extending its rationale from *Mergens*. The Court explained that insofar as the board created a limited open forum, it violated the group's free speech rights by explicitly finding that it engaged in viewpoint discrimination by excluding the religious group based on the content of its speech.

Eight years later, a dispute erupted when officials in another New York district refused to permit a non-school-sponsored club for children aged six to twelve to meet during non-class hours so that members and moderators could discuss childrearing along with character and moral development from a religious perspective. While forbidding the religious club from meeting, officials allowed three other groups, the Boy Scouts, Girl Scouts, and the 4-H Club, to gather because although they addressed related topics, they did so from secular perspectives. All of the sessions, regardless of the club, occurred after the school day was over and children could remain only if their parents had given express written permission for them to do so.

The Supreme Court agreed to hear an appeal in the case from New York in order to resolve a split below because the Eighth Circuit (*Good News/Good Sports Club v. School Dist. of the City of Ladue* 1994 1995) had upheld the right of such a club in Missouri to use school facilities for its meetings. In *Good News Club v. Milford Central School* (2001), the Court reversed in favor of the club.

In a 6-to-3 judgment, the *Milford* Court reasoned that the board violated the club's rights to free speech by engaging in impermissible viewpoint discrimination when it refused to permit it to use school facilities for its meetings while allowing other groups to convene on similar topics. The majority rejected the dissenters' claim that the meetings were impermissible as worship services. In addition, the Court rejected the school board's argument that the meetings should have been prohibited because they might have violated the Establishment Clause. Insofar as the Court's response pointed out, in part, that meetings were held after school and children were present with parental consent, the Justices viewed this concern as unfounded. The dissenters essentially feared that insofar as the meetings were largely devotional, they should not have been allowed in public schools.

A case involving a teacher and a Good News Club arose in South Dakota. The Eighth Circuit affirmed that school officials violated the teacher's free speech rights by refusing to allow her to join after-school meetings of a Good News Club (*Wigg v. Sioux Falls School Dist. 49–5* 2004). The court reversed part of an earlier order allowing the teacher to meet with the club only at schools other than where she taught. Viewing the teacher's after-school activity as private speech, the court explained that her involvement did not put the board at risk of violating the Establishment Clause.

In Minnesota a dispute arose when officials excluded a religious club from the list of organizations qualified to offer after-school enrichment programs. The Eighth Circuit maintained that insofar as the religious group's activities occurred after the end of the school day, officials engaged in impermissible viewpoint discrimination because they lacked a compelling interest in avoiding a purported Establishment Clause violation (*Child Evangelism Fellowship of Minn. v. Minneapolis Special School District* 2012).

REPERCUSSIONS OF THE EAA

In the immediate aftermath of *Mergens*, many school boards adopted policies preventing students from organizing clubs of any type, whether related to the curriculum or not, religious or nonreligious, while others limited activities to curriculum-related groups during noninstructional time. However, this draconian approach of forbidding student organizations risked throwing the proverbial baby out with the bath water because clubs typically enhance the experiences of high school students. Aware that such an approach failed to achieve anything worthwhile at the expense of denying students opportunities to interact, most boards relented and now allow clubs to form even as litigation continued over the parameters of the EAA.

When reviewing the status of prayer and Bible study, LGBT clubs, or other organizations, such as the almost thirty identified in *Mergens*, in schools, it is important to recall why Congress enacted the EAA: to ensure that students could have their own voices in schools where boards and educational officials allowed other groups to meet during noninstructional time. If we recognize the rights of students, while reflecting on the future of the EAA, then, the following reflections offer food for thought.

Some educators fear that allowing EAA clubs to meet in schools will be interpreted as supporting student views, whether about religion or sexuality, possibly in violation of the Establishment Clause (an issue that emerged in *Milford*), even as their presence adds costs for supervision. Accordingly, it is worth reviewing the safeguards contained in the EAA to help to allay such concerns:

1. Student participation must be voluntary (20 U.S.C. § 4071(c)(1)), thereby avoiding any concern over official coercion or endorsement.
2. The EAA prevents educators from serving as moderators or sponsors (20 U.S.C. § 4071 (c)(5)), thereby avoiding Establishment Clause concerns (20 U.S.C. § 4071 (c)(2)).
3. Educators can be present in nonparticipating capacities (20 U.S.C. § 4071(c) (5)), essentially to supervise (20 U.S.C. § 4071(c)(3)), but cannot be present regularly (20 U.S.C. § 4071(c)(5)). As such, the occasional presence of educators is unlikely to raise legitimate Establishment Clause concerns because they are responsible for student safety regardless of what pupils are doing during the school day.
4. The EAA allows educational leaders to prevent clubs from forming if they "materially and substantially" (20 U.S.C. § 4071(c)(4)) interfere with school activities. Even so, educators cannot use this fear to prevent clubs from forming because it has been applied to non-club members who were unhappy with the formation of groups rather than individuals belonging to EAA clubs. Thus, this section cannot be used to deny clubs the opportunity to form absent evidence that their members, rather than others, are likely to be disruptive even if the content of their speech may not be popular in their communities.

Unresolved Questions

At least four issues remain open about the status of EAA clubs and student religious expression in schools in light of *Christian Legal Society*. There can be little doubt that board policies should allow membership to be open to all who wish to join student clubs. Less clear, though, is whether clubs should be required to permit students who do not share their values to become leaders or whether groups can be able to develop their own criteria so as to be able to preserve their identity and missions. While the Supreme Court brushed aside such concerns when the students raised them in *Christian Legal Society*, this is an issue worthy of consideration. After all, would it make sense to permit an atheist to try to become president of a Christian prayer and Bible study club or a homophobe to seek to head up an LGBT group? Further, to the extent that the EAA allows opposing groups to establish their own organizations, policies should consider granting clubs the freedom to apply reasonable membership requirements, especially if they are grounded in long-held, sincere religious or other beliefs or values.

As school officials work to develop policies regulating student clubs, questions emerge about the future of the EAA. First, policies should address the nature of EAA clubs. In other words, policies should state whether clubs can be organized for socialization or extracurricular purposes or if they must be curriculum-related. If EAA clubs are not curriculum-related, then boards probably do not have to recognize them, provide funding, or grant them access to facilities during noninstructional time. However, as discussed earlier, this approach is likely unacceptable because it runs the risk of shortchanging students insofar as they can benefit greatly from clubs.

Second, if policies do allow EAA clubs to form, as in *Hsu*, they need to specify whether they grant organizations exceptions from district antidiscrimination rules so founders can set reasonable criteria for candidates seeking leadership positions. Again, as discussed above, if board officials are going to allow EAA clubs to form, it seems to make sense to allow their organizers to create fair standards designed to allow them to preserve group goals because students who disagree are free to form their own clubs taking on different perspectives. However, in light of *Christian Legal Society*, this is certainly an open question.

The issue here is the extent to which religious or other groups should be able to have a right of self-determination to set qualifications for leadership. As noted, regardless of whether a club is religious, based on LGBT values, political, or oriented toward other areas, does it make sense to mandate that leadership positions be made open to members who do not share a group's values? While there are concerns of discrimination, especially when issues of sexuality arise, the courts have typically granted exceptions to religious groups for their sincere, long-held beliefs. It is thus incumbent upon legislative leaders to define the parameters of what religious clubs, in particular, can do when setting qualifications for leadership so that educational officials can ensure the smooth application of the EAA in their schools.

Third, board policies should be sure to comply with the express terms of the EAA by forbidding adults from being involved in supervisory capacities except to ensure student safety or in occasional, but certainly not regular, visits such as guest speakers. Insofar as the goal of the EAA is to allow student clubs to run, it is important to limit adult activity.

Fourth, it remains to be seen whether Congress or states will expand the parameters of EAA clubs to cover middle schools. Although the court in Florida, in the only case on point, refused to extend the act to cover middle schools, nothing prevents legislatures, whether the Congress or states, from expanding the reach of the law.

CONCLUSION

Insofar as religious speech had been excluded in schools as a form of impermissible viewpoint discrimination, the EAA was designed to remedy such situations. To date, it appears that the EAA has succeeded in achieving its goal of granting equal access to religious speech even as it has been applied in ways beyond what its authors likely intended by including LGBT groups and others. By giving students opportunities to voice their opinions in public schools, the EAA has met its worthwhile goal by opening schools to a greater diversity of perspectives.

FUTURE DIRECTIONS

1. Should EAA clubs be limited to curricular activities or should they broadly encompass all student interests?
2. Should clubs be free to select leaders based on religious (or other criteria) even if it means that not all members are eligible for such positions?
3. To what extent should adults be allowed to participate in the activities of EAA clubs?
4. Should the EAA be expanded to cover middle schools, not just high schools?

REFERENCES

Board of Education of Westside Community Schools v. Mergens, 867 F.2d 1076 (8th Cir. 1989), 496 U.S. 226 (1990).

Boyd County High School Gay Straight Alliance v. Board of Education of Boyd County, Ky., 258 F. Supp.2d 667 (E.D. Ky. 2003)

Carver Middle School Gay-Straight Alliance v. School Board of Lake County, Fla., 2 F. Supp.3d 1277 (M.D. Fla. 2014).

Caudillo v. Lubbock Independent School Dist., 311 F. Supp.2d 550 (N.D. Tex. 2004).

Ceniceros v. Board of Trustees of the San Diego Unified School District, 106 F.3d 878 (9th Cir. 1997).

Child Evangelism Fellowship of Minn. v. Minneapolis Special School Dist., 690 F.3d 996 (8th Cir. 2012).

Christian Legal Society v. Martinez, 561 U.S. 661(2010).

Colin ex rel. Colin v. Orange Unified School District, 83 F. Supp.2d 1135 (C.D. Cal. 2004).

Donovan ex rel. Donovan v. Punxsutawney Area School Board, 336 F.3d 211 (3d Cir. 2003).

East High Gay/Straight Alliance v. Board of Educ., 81 F. Supp.2d 1166 (D. Utah 1999a); 81 F. Supp.2d 1199 (D. Utah 1999b).

East High School Prism Club v. Seidel, 95 F. Supp.2d 1239 (D. Utah 2000).

Equal Access Act, 20 U.S.C. §§ 4071 *et seq.*

Franklin Central Gay/Straight Alliance v. Franklin Township Community School Corp., 2002 WL 32097530 (S.D. Ind. 2002), *reconsideration denied*, 2002 WL 31921332 (S.D. Ind. 2002).

Gay–Straight Alliance of Yulee High School v. School Board of Nassau County, 602 F. Supp.2d 1233 (M.D. Fla. 2009).

Good News Club v. Milford Central School, 533 U.S. 98 (2001).

Good News/Good Sports Club v. School Dist. of the City of Ladue, 28 F.3d 1501 (8th Cir. 1994), *cert. denied*, 515 U.S. 1173 (1995).

Herdahl v. Pontotoc County School District, 933 F. Supp. 582 (N.D. Miss. 1996).

Hsu v. Roslyn Union Free School District, 85 F.3d 839 (2d Cir. 1996a), *cert. denied*, 519 U.S. 1040 (1996b).

Krestan v. Deer Valley Unified School District No. 97, of Maricopa County, 561 F. Supp.2d 1078 (D. Ariz. 2008).

Lamb's Chapel v. Center Moriches Union Free School District, 508 U.S. 384 (1993), *on remand*, 17 F.3d 1425 (2d Cir. 1994).

Lemon v. Kurtzman, 403 U.S. 602 (1971).

Palmer High School Gay/Straight Alliance v. Colorado Springs School District No. 11, 2005 WL 3244049 (D. Colo. 2005).

Prince v. Jacoby, 303 F.3d 1074 (9th Cir. 2002), *cert. denied*, 540 U.S. 813 (2003).

Straights and Gays for Equality v. Osseo Area Schools–Dist. No. 279, 540 F.3d 911 (8th Cir. 2008).

Truth v. Kent School District, 499 F.3d 999 (9th Cir. 2007), 524 F.3d 957 (9th Cir. 2008).

Widmar v. Vincent, 454 U.S. 263 (1981).

Wigg v. Sioux Falls School Dist. 49–5, 382 F.3d 807 (8th Cir. 2004), *reh'g and reh'g en banc denied* (2004).

....

CHAPTER 20

RELIGIOUS FREEDOM, COMMON SCHOOLS, AND THE COMMON GOOD

....

ERIK OWENS

AMERICAN public schools have a complicated legacy that includes the best and the worst of our moral, educational, and political impulses. Since their origins in the mid-nineteenth century, public schools have been sites of racial segregation, religious bigotry, and xenophobia, but also integration, toleration, and inclusion (Cremin 1980; Kaestle 1983). Public schools reflect the broader culture in many ways but are also expected (by differing constituencies) to restore, reinforce, or reform that culture. When we collectively worry about this country's apparently declining morals, shaky economic competitiveness, rising inequality, social fragmentation, or the like, we frequently look to the public school system to correct the problem for future generations. In this way debates over public education are proxies for conversations about the things that matter to us most as a society.

This is a heavy burden for the schools—indeed an impossible one, if schools are expected to solve these problems in isolation from other political, economic, and cultural institutions—and yet it persists because public schools are one of the quintessential civic institutions in the United States. It is hard to imagine another civic institution with comparable reach into the lives of so many Americans. Ninety percent of American schoolchildren are enrolled in public schools of some sort, a number that has increased slightly over the past twenty years despite a robust market for private religious and nonreligious schools (US Department of Education 2013). While only one-quarter of American families have school-aged children, everyone is connected in some way to the public school system: taxpayers finance it, employers hire its graduates, and its effectiveness is widely understood to be a key measure of social and economic justice.

With great reach comes great responsibility (if I may rephrase a moral truism). Public schools are not simply institutions that enhance the intellect of individual students; they are civic institutions that we entrust to inculcate knowledge, skills, and values to those who will contribute to the culture of our common home. We want our schools, in other words, to educate students to contribute to the common good of our diverse society.

In this chapter I sketch the outlines of what may be called "civic education for the common good." The first section examines the concept of the common good and explains why religious freedom is an essential component. The second section distinguishes between civic virtue and the civic virtues, and describes which of the latter must be inculcated in schools to sustain the former. The final section argues that the common good is well served by a form of common education that is, structurally speaking, neither homogeneous nor radically pluralistic.

THE COMMON GOOD

The common good is a concept that eludes easy or precise definition. Conceived within the Greek and Roman traditions of civic republicanism, it was taken up by early Christian Church Fathers and later incorporated into the systematic theology of Thomas Aquinas. Revisited in political terms during occasional revivals of civic republican thought (including the Italian Renaissance, the French Revolution, and the American founding periods), the common good tradition was most thoroughly carried into the contemporary era by the encyclicals and other documents of modern Catholic social teaching. Recent decades in American academic political philosophy have seen a notable return to republican themes in response to the perceived failures of liberalism (Dagger 1997; Pettit 1997; Quill 2005; Sandel 1996), yet the concept remains vague even to many who embrace it, especially in popular discourse.

"Working for the common good" is an expression in contemporary American politics that veers into platitude when it simply means we should work together on something important. A more thoughtful use of the term in public discourse usually suggests attending to the good of all citizens (what the Constitution's preamble calls "the general welfare"), as opposed to that of the "special interests" of factions or individuals. For example, when a recent national survey asked American voters to describe in open terms (not multiple choice) "what the phrase 'the common good' means to you personally," 53% said that it meant a focus on the good of all, not just the few (Center for American Progress 2006). This popular understanding of the common good is vaguely utilitarian in that it is defined as what's best for the greatest number of people, whose interests have somehow been aggregated and counted. This majoritarian impulse fits a democratic sensibility in many ways, but it also shares two of the key downsides of utilitarianism, namely the proclivity to overlook unjust distributions of wealth and power (in favor of average utility), and to resist special protections for minority groups or perspectives (Hollenbach 2002, 3–4).

A related but distinct view of the common good is closely tied to the economic concept of "public goods." Economists describe a public good as something that is present for all members of the community whenever it is present for any of them. As David

Hollenbach has argued, public goods are "non-rivalrous" in that you can enjoy them without diminishing others' enjoyment, and "non-excludable" in that once present, their benefits are difficult to confine (8–9). Sunsets are the paradigmatic example of a natural public good; clean air and water are natural public goods impacted by human action. In this sense, a strong educational system is a public good as well, one created and sustained by human action. Public goods are goods we share in common; they are an important part—but not the whole picture—of the common good as we should apply it in the civic educational context.

If we look to older philosophical and theological traditions of the common good, we can see a clearer and more profound picture for the contemporary context. Two snapshots, from Aristotle and from Catholic social teaching, can serve as starting points.

The common good originated in ancient Greek political thought as a means of framing the relationship between the good of individuals and the good of the community. Aristotle (1996) understood citizenship—the activity of governing and being governed— as an intrinsic good necessary for human flourishing, and something that requires active involvement in public life. Politics in this view is not a means of securing freedom or justice; it is the way of being free or being just. Thus for Aristotle the full range of human virtues can only be developed and exercised in the life of a good polis— and more than that, only by full citizens of that polis. Our conception of membership in political communities is of course very different than Aristotle's—less exclusive, less intense, and much broader—but his insight into the ties that bind together the flourishing of individuals and communities remains crucial in our day.

The Catholic tradition is a bit more specific when describing the common good as "the sum of those conditions of social life which allow social groups and their individual members relatively thorough and ready access to their own fulfillment" (Second Vatican Ecumenical Council 1965, *Gaudium et Spes*, par. 26). Pope Francis described the common good as "a central and unifying principle of social ethics" in his 2015 encyclical *Laudato Si*, which placed responsibility for its realization on individuals, society, and the state alike in a process known as subsidiarity:

> Underlying the principle of the common good is respect for the human person as such, endowed with basic and inalienable rights ordered to his or her integral development. It has also to do with the overall welfare of society and the development of a variety of intermediate groups, applying the principle of subsidiarity. Outstanding among those groups is the family, as the basic cell of society. Finally, the common good calls for social peace, the stability and security provided by a certain order which cannot be achieved without particular concern for distributive justice; whenever this is violated, violence always ensues. Society as a whole, and the state in particular, are obliged to defend and promote the common good (*Laudato Si*, par. 156–157).

This recognition that the flourishing—indeed the fate—of all citizens hinges on the equal and humane treatment of all is something different than a general call to work for the good of all, or even to sacrifice for the poor in times of economic collapse or large-scale war. As such it steps away from forms of liberal individualism that have increasingly dominated American political (and educational) culture for more than a century.

We may say, then, that the common good is an ancient concept that offers a vision of human flourishing rooted in the recognition of human interconnectedness and sociality. It links the good of individuals with the good of the communities to which they belong, without exalting one over the other. As a result, the common good in this sense presents an alternative to political theories and theologies grounded in individualist or collectivist visions of human flourishing. But what does religious freedom have to do with it?

Religious Freedom and the Common Good

Religious freedom is the political principle by which an indeterminate plurality of religions is legitimated in a civil polity (Gamwell 1995, 1–11). In the United States, religious freedom is instantiated in the First Amendment and protected through the broad range of liberties and rights that flow from it by tradition and by jurisprudential interpretation. Whatever else it does, religious freedom promotes the active engagement of religious people and organizations in the public life of our society by guaranteeing the right to participate in politics on one's own terms.

Religious freedom is an integral component of the common good of a pluralistic polity because it protects the full and free discourse *about* the common good. The public domain is the proper place to discuss the nature of the good life, since the good life is lived in community. The public sphere is where the common good is forged, and so it must also be the place where all notions of the good life can be expressed, whether or not they originate in or involve religion. Of course there is no reason to believe that in a diverse society citizens will somehow come to agree upon a single conception of the good life through discussion, regardless of the conditions (or lack thereof) placed upon that discussion. Disagreement and difference are inherent in human relations. Fortunately, the common good does not require consensus, and it may change for different situations.

In fact, one of the key civic virtues in a pluralistic democracy is the respect for others that leads to mutual engagement on issues of common concern. Good citizens not only limit themselves to supporting policies and legislation that they genuinely believe will conduce to the common good (rather than simply advancing their own interests), they also strive to justify their support in ways that diverse others will find persuasive. When the good citizen is motivated by both secular and religious reasons (which is likely to be the case most of the time), both should be articulated. A policy of civic education for the common good would seek to provide the skills and inclination to enable this model of civic engagement, which is more permissive than (though not too distant from) the "wide view of public reason" John Rawls offered in his later work (1999, 129–180) and the "ideal of conscientious engagement" Christopher Eberle presented soon after (2002).

It should be clear, then, why the requirements of "public reason" (when conceived as the only morally permissible form of public speech) are not only onerous to many religious believers but also corrosive of the common good. The full and free participation of citizens in public affairs is intrinsic to the good of a free society, not simply an external condition necessary for realizing this good. Preventing full and free discourse—especially about the nature of the good life and the political implications that would follow from it—cripples the very means by which some understandings of the common good are brought into focus. Religious believers *qua* religious believers contribute to American civic life in numerous ways, and ought to be considered full participants in public life (Smith, et al. 1998; Weithman 2002).

CIVIC VIRTUE AND THE CIVIC VIRTUES

It follows, then, that a program of civic education for the common good has as its primary goal the formation of citizens who recognize the inextricable connection between individual and community, and thereby commit themselves to both self-development (autonomy) and to developing the common good—in part through full and free discussion about the content of the common good. These commitments require certain liberal-republican ideals of character, cultivated through both general and specific virtues.

A virtue is a moral and intellectual disposition to act in a way that conduces to the good life of an individual or community. Put another way, virtue is a form of excellence within a given social practice. Civic virtue and the civic virtues relate to the practice of citizenship; other forms of virtue delineate excellence in other social practices or roles such as parent, spouse, friend, or professor.

Civic virtue in the singular, general sense is best described as the inclination to act on behalf of the common good. The implied alternative is an unpraiseworthy inclination to act on behalf of one's private interests at the expense of the common good. A mistaken belief that individual and common goods are polar opposites has led some critics to charge that civic virtue per se is an illiberal concept at the top of the slippery slope to collectivism. But concepts of civic virtue and the common good need not support the monist, statist, or unitary aims of those who have abused these concepts in the past. Republicanism does not rest upon Robespierre's desire to remake citizens into a single mold. On the contrary, contemporary republican thought along the lines proposed by Michael Sandel and Philip Pettit, among others, explicitly recognizes pluralism as an inescapable and indeed desirable feature of human existence. Conversely, liberalism—the champion of pluralism and diversity—has long claimed civic virtue as integral to the pursuit and protection of individual liberties. Like the freestanding liberal and republican traditions, then, liberal republicanism requires that civic virtue be widespread among the population.

What specific virtues should be inculcated as part of a liberal-republican program of civic education for the common good? Two clusters of virtues hold special prominence from this perspective: one involves the commitment to the democratic process of collective self-government itself, while the other entails meeting the deliberative requirements of this process—fulfillment of which has a much broader effect than simply the tone or content of public speech. In the first case, good citizens of a democratic polity need to be committed to the democratic process that sustains popular sovereignty and collective self-government. This means that citizens must respect the rule of law by evincing what Thomas Spragens calls the virtue of "law-abiding self-restraint" (1999, 219–229). But more than that, they must feel an affinity—whether this virtue be named patriotism, fraternity, or something else—with the polity that includes some sense of shared identity and fellow-feeling. Any form of patriotic civic education congenial to the common good as I understand it would have to encourage *critical* appreciation of the nation's history and future, along the lines of what Jean Bethke Elshtain has called "chastened patriotism" (1987, 252–258). The virtues of respect for the rule of law and of patriotism/fraternity form the boundaries of civic virtue and civic education. If they are breached in the main—if, for example, citizens routinely reject the democratic process and seek resolution of conflict through violent coercion—then there will be no polity in which to deliberate.

The second key cluster of civic virtues corresponds to deliberative requirements of life in a pluralistic, democratic polity: honesty, prudence, tolerance, and mutual respect. Honesty is an important virtue not only because it builds trust within the community, but also because it provides the only means of tracking citizens' interests over time. If citizens fail to truthfully convey their interests or their reasons for supporting or rejecting a particular issue or candidate, their fellow citizens (and thus the political system as a whole) cannot register their views or adapt to their needs. In some cases the virtue of courage may be required to truthfully convey one's views, especially if those views contravene those of the majority. Prudence is a virtue associated with practical wisdom in the Aristotelian tradition; for our purposes it can be understood as the disposition to conscientiously weigh alternatives before acting or speaking on matters of public import, and to integrate civic virtue into the process.

Tolerance is a key civic virtue in that it defines the minimal level of respect for individual liberty required to sustain a free society. Tolerance is not to be confused or conflated with an affirmation of one or more rival views; it is not a form of moral relativism that equates all claims to truth. Being tolerant does not make one a secular humanist. Tolerance can stem from any number of attitudes about pluralism and otherness; Michael Walzer identifies resignation, indifference, stoical acceptance, curiosity, and enthusiasm as the primary options. But whatever the cause, those who manifest the virtue of tolerance simply "make room for men and women whose beliefs they don't adopt, whose practices they decline to imitate; they coexist with an otherness that, however much they approve of its presence in the world, is still something different from what they know, something alien and strange" (1997, 11–12).

Tolerance is closely tied to the last key virtue in this cluster, mutual respect, which entails the recognition of the equal dignity and rights of all fellow citizens. But mutual respect demands more active engagement with others than mere toleration does, and the discursive requirements of civic education for the common good push this further with regard to religious freedom. One of the biggest challenges of life in a deeply diverse society is that we tend to lose the ability to talk to one another about the things that matter to us most, whether out of fear of giving offense or simply because the relevant grammar and vocabulary was lost or never learned. To talk about the things that matter most—which are also often the things that divide us most deeply—citizens need a package of knowledge, skills, and dispositions that bring them into what has been conceived as *imaginative engagement* with rival moral and religious traditions. Genuine respect for the religious freedom of others must be informed by some appreciation of the complex relationships that exist between and among various religious and moral traditions. This requires an active engagement with viewpoints that conflict deeply with our own (Callan 1997; Kunzman 2006).

In general terms, however, this means that citizens should have some exposure to diverse religious, moral, and cultural traditions and they should strive to explore areas of shared belief or concern as well as deep difference, particularly with regard to issues with resonance for civil society and the public sphere. In practice this engagement may be focused on the diverse traditions that intersect in a given community, but it should not exclude imaginative engagement with cultures and traditions that exist outside the community. This sort of civic education is not simply about learning to interact with one's current neighbors—as difficult as that can be—but also about learning to engage one's future fellow citizens, whatever their provenance. This is the civic educational upshot of the political principle of religious freedom as the legitimation of an indeterminate plurality of religions, and it is deeply rooted in the virtue of mutual respect.

To characterize this second cluster as the deliberative virtues—or more colloquially, the virtues that help us to talk to one another—risks calling forth the fierce critiques scholars have lodged against deliberative democracy at large (Bohman and Rehg 1997; Fishkin and Laslett 2003; Macedo 1999). Some of these critiques are well justified, including the charge that Amy Gutmann and Dennis Thompson's original statement of deliberative democracy dealt in such abstruse philosophical terms that only elite academic philosophers seemed able to partake in true deliberation (Gutmann and Thompson 1998). But this does not change the fact that engaged civic discourse is essential to a robust democracy, and that sustaining this deliberation (however it is named) is not a trivial enterprise. I have tried to overcome the threat of idealizing civic discourse or forcing it into procrustean notions of "public" and "private" by taking into account how citizens actually talk about the things that matter to them today. In short, a vast number of citizens reject the concept of public reason, and while they feel free to use "God talk" as a means of justifying their views, they do so with a contextual awareness that signals a recognition that not everyone shares that perspective.

Of course many other virtues would be expressly inculcated in a program of civic education for the common good. These would include the virtues conducive to education itself (e.g., industry, reliability, adaptability, perseverance, and discipline) as well as general social virtues such as courage and loyalty. And it should be said that virtues such as mutual respect, honesty, and tolerance are not simply deliberative virtues; they are also praiseworthy features in almost any context.

Finally, a word about autonomy, which although not itself a virtue, is tied up with many of the virtues I have described here. Autonomy is the capacity for self-development and critical thought, and as such it is a core goal of liberal civic education. I have argued that it is also a core civic educational goal of liberal republicanism, and that it should be inculcated in tandem with civic virtue. Autonomy is not about the individual acting in isolation from the community, but rather the community fostering and enabling autonomous self-development. The autonomous individual, writes Charles Taylor,

> is himself only possible within a certain kind of civilization; [it takes] a long development of certain institutions and practices, of the rule of law, of rules of equal respect, of habits of common deliberation, of common association, of cultural self-development, and so on, to produce the modern individual; [. . .] without these the very sense of oneself as an individual in the modern meaning of the term would atrophy (1985, 309).

Not coincidentally, each of the institutions and practices Taylor cites as formative of autonomy are represented in the virtues I list above.

Civic Educational Institutions

In keeping with the expansive definition of civic education I have employed, I would like to suggest that virtually all education in all forms and forums is civic education to the extent that it enables participation in and enhances commitment to democratic civil society and government. Americans have been (and continue to be) educated by a wide array of institutions, including the family, religious organizations, news, museums, and voluntary associations, not to mention schools and universities (Cremin 1970, 1980, 1988). There are, in other words, a vast number of places where civic education occurs, even if this is not the intended or primary institutional goal.

Each of these institutions offers (or can, in principle, offer) civic benefits to the polity, but schools stand above the fray as especially important sites of civic education. Schools are explicitly designed as spaces for the conscious formation of children's intellect and values, and the intensity and duration of compulsory education in this country mean that this formation is likely to be both substantial and enduring. Debates over education have long served as a proxy for other social conflicts in this society, precisely because citizens know that schools are the place where values are explicitly considered and conveyed. The Pledge of Allegiance, Intelligent Design lessons in biology class, student prayers at football games and graduation ceremonies, Bible study classes—all these have generated controversial litigation in recent years that pitted advocates for rival values against one another (see chapters 13, 15, 18, 19 in this volume). In a sense that is both trite and true, schools represent the future, and so the battle to shape the values of the future is often waged in the halls of the local public school. In the next (and final) section, I will examine what sets public schools apart from private schools and what brings them together from a civic perspective.

COMMON SCHOOLS AND THE COMMON GOOD

What exactly is "public" about public education in the United States today? What distinguishes public schools from secular or religious private schools? Three characteristics are often said to differentiate them: funding, access, and governance. First, public schools are for the most part funded entirely by general taxation rather than tuition or charitable contributions. Second, public schools are grounded upon the principle of universal access, meaning they are obliged to educate every child who chooses to attend them, regardless of race, class, income, religion, or even ability to learn. Third, public schools are set apart by the structure of their governance and oversight, which can be broadly characterized as democratic, whatever variations exist in different school systems. Together, these three characteristics define a public school system that ideally offers equal opportunity for all students through free, universal, and democratically controlled education.

It could be argued, however, that none of these characteristics is unique or necessary to public schools. In the first case, most public schools receive at least some funds from private sources, while many private schools receive some form of support from public sources. Though public schools do not charge tuition, in an era of tightening budgets it is not uncommon for parents to be asked to pay for all sorts of extracurricular activities that once were provided at no cost, and in some communities parent groups and local businesses provide a constant revenue stream of operating funds for the local public schools. More important, though, is the counterexample of private schools receiving taxpayer funds. In a handful of cities and states around the country, vouchers worth a set dollar amount have been issued to a certain number of parents selected by lottery (once they meet eligibility requirements), who are then able to spend the value of that voucher as tuition at eligible public or private schools, including religious schools. School voucher programs are the most controversial expenditure of public funds for private education, but many others exist as well: tax credits are issued in many states for private educational expenses, and state governments in some cases provide transportation, books, technology, and even teachers to private schools at the taxpayers' expense. This complex arrangement challenges the notion that public and private can be defined on the basis of funding sources (see chapter 13 in this volume).

The second characteristically "public" feature of schooling is the obligation to accept all students who meet certain residential requirements. Private schools have no such legal obligation and are able to restrict attendance by religious affiliation or scholastic aptitude, among many other characteristics. But in practice many private schools admit students without regard to race, religion, income, and so forth, and explicitly seek to serve the community's neediest children. The two largest private school systems in the United States are operated by the Catholic and Lutheran Churches, both of which have a long history of educating students from poor and nonwhite families. A general trend toward open-door admission policies among parochial schools still falls short of an obligation to educate all students (as advocates for students with special needs often note), but it nevertheless raises questions about how far universal access sets public schools apart.

Finally, with regard to school governance, the distinction between public and private schools is again more muddled that it might appear at first glance. The vast collection of American public school systems is governed by public officials who are in some manner accountable to the citizens who elected them or the officials who appointed them. But the actual levers of public school governance can be somewhat removed from the voters. Conversely, private schools must follow a host of state regulations related to student safety and health as well as general curricular requirements and achievement standards. In this sense they are "governed" by state regulation, although they are free to pursue these requirements in ways that public schools could not (most notably through pervasively religious forms of education).

Important distinctions remain between public and private schools with regard to funding, access, and governance, but these distinctions are blurred more than most observers recognize. In an era of public-private educational partnerships, a more salient analysis would shift the focus from funding or governance toward institutional ethos: Is education understood to be a common or a separate enterprise, and what features of the school itself reflect this commitment? Thus we can speak of common or separate schools that provide common or separate education. Philosopher Eamonn Callan describes common education as that which "prescribes a range of educational outcomes—virtues, abilities, different kinds of knowledge—as desirable for all members of the society to which the conception applies" (1997, 163). Separate education, by contrast, prescribes different educational outcomes for particular religious, ethnic, racial, linguistic, or other such groups. These divisions among groups are what James Fishkin (1992) calls social "cleavages" that already serve as a basis for conflict or competition among groups. A separate school differentiates students on the basis of one or more cleavages, whereas a common school welcomes all students who meet its age and residential requirements without regard to such cleavages (Fishkin 1992, chap. 7).

It is not enough, however, for common schools to eschew discrimination on the basis of social cleavage; they must actively create an environment that supports the pluralism of the wider culture, in part by encouraging policies that make the student body reflect the demographics of the community at large. Given the persistent segregation along social cleavages in American housing markets, this sort of demographic mirroring is often impossible without massive efforts to bus students across the community. Support for common schools does not require a policy of forced busing, which creates its own important educational and political problems. The important point is that the common school ideal includes a conception of a school population that crosses social cleavages rather than cutting along them. To the extent that public schools do not do so—and few do—they diverge from the common school ideal (Callan 2003).

In related fashion, common education is predicated upon the dialogical task of fostering reciprocity across social cleavages. This is a core civic purpose of common education, one that squarely fits within the model of civic education for religious freedom I have presented here. This sort of education is best accomplished in classrooms that straddle social cleavages, though doing so will require a broader understanding of how students and teachers can and should talk about these deep differences.

Civic education for the common good requires a commitment to some form of common education as a means of generating or sustaining a shared political culture of the sort I described in the previous section. This is not to suggest that a political monoculture is desirable or that education should be homogenized across widely divergent communities. On the contrary, the shared values that civic education for the common good promotes are those that assist in discussing our deepest differences without suggesting that they can be eliminated. At least some kinds of separate education must be accepted as well, out of respect for what Callan nicely describes as "the many different convictions and ways of life that flourish under pluralism and the divergent educational aspirations that flow from these" (1997, 166).

Where does this leave us with regard to the question of public and private schools? Perhaps the question is best put like this: Is it possible that private schools can provide a common education of the sort that civic education for religious freedom encourages? This is often the argument of school voucher supporters who point to evidence that Catholic schools frequently produce graduates who are better educated *and* more civically engaged than their public school counterparts. Christian Smith and David Sikkink, for example, draw upon statistical data from the US government to argue that families with students in religious (but not nonreligious) private schools are "more likely than public schoolers to participate in public life through a broad array of civic activities—even when we statistically remove the possible effects of seven other potentially related social factors" (1999, 18). Anthony Bryk, Peter Holland, and Valerie Lee (1993) have shown how Catholic schools offer a model of success in educating diverse student populations (without regard for students' religious affiliation) that public schools should emulate.

In each of these cases what is being extolled is the common educational endeavor of separate schools. To the extent that Catholic schools admit and educate students without regard to religious affiliation or other social cleavage, they are providing common education. Education in Catholic schools is unlikely to be more than quasi-common, given the religious ethos of the school and theological content of some of its courses, but this may well be preferable to the quasi-common education in public schools if the one is more effective than the other in educating students in the liberal-republican array of knowledge, skills, and dispositions I have sketched here. Civic education for the common good is committed to common education, not to public schools per se. The simple fact, however, is that public schools are more likely to provide a common edu cation than religious schools, since the extent to which a religious school focuses on the religious nature of its education is precisely the extent to which it is no longer common. This point is not lost to supporters of religious schools who believe that a focus on common education prevents schools from fulfilling their mission to produce well-educated Christians, Jews, Muslims, and so forth.

But what of the arguments for separate education? Like Smith and Sikkink, Michael McConnell (2002) argues that religious schools best represent liberal political values because they can provide a coherent moral education that is proscribed in public schools. Since moral coherence, in their view, is the essential ingredient to education and the value most centrally protected by the principle of religious freedom, only a program of universal school vouchers remains true to liberal political values. They condemn the homogenizing effect of public education, especially when public schools are the only ones funded by general taxation. John Stuart Mill (1998) offered similar views in *On Liberty*, where he supported public funding for compulsory education but argued that separate education is more likely to enhance the collective pursuit of truth by producing citizens with differing perspectives. Unlike Mill, however, whose prescriptions are drawn from their perceived social benefits, McConnell is more interested in purity of process, namely the maximization of the parental right to direct a child's education at public expense.

Here I part ways with the argument for publicly funded separate education (as opposed to separate schools). In the first case, while respecting religious diversity is a core obligation of liberal societies, fostering it (by providing separate education) is not. An analogy to religious freedom makes the point: while the First Amendment protects the right to free exercise of one's religious beliefs, it does not mandate—and it arguably prohibits—the construction or support of venues for religious exercise in the event that citizens cannot afford them. The public is not obligated to build Buddhist temples for small communities of believers without access to necessary funds any more than it must fund religious schools for citizens who would otherwise not be able to send their children to such schools (see Chapter 13 in this volume).

Some sort of common education must be provided in the service of fostering a cohesive and stable political order. I have argued that separate (private) schools can provide common education in some circumstances, but it remains the case that public schools are the most obvious place for common education to take place. In part this stems from a recognition of the importance of institutional considerations; liberal-republican civic education should exemplify as well as teach democratic principles (which *ipso facto* support religious freedom), and this cannot occur if the educational system is privatized or fractured into separate educational arenas. Public schools are unique in that their formative intentions are pursued openly, and thus they allow citizens to debate these purposes in local as well as national democratic venues.

FUTURE DIRECTIONS

- Do the principles of civic education and the common good that have been articulated here also apply to the emerging concept of global citizenship?
- How does the widespread religious illiteracy in the United States impact the understanding of religious freedom and the common good? What should be done about it?
- Is common education a plausible goal in a country (the United States) whose social fissures run so deep?

REFERENCES

Aristotle. 1996. *The Politics and Constitution of Athens*, edited by Stephen Everson, translated by Jonathan Barnes. Cambridge, UK: Cambridge University Press.

Bohman, James, and William Rehg, eds. 1997. *Deliberative Democracy: Essays on Reason and Politics*. Cambridge, MA: MIT Press.

Bryk, Anthony S., Peter B. Holland, and Valerie E. Lee. 1993. *Catholic Schools and the Common Good*. Cambridge, MA: Harvard University Press.

Callan, Eamonn. 1997. *Creating Citizens: Political Education and Liberal Democracy*. Oxford: Oxford University Press.

———. 2003. "The Civic Purposes of Public Schools." *Public Affairs Report* 44, no. 1 (Spring): 1, 10–12.

Center for American Progress. 2006. "Faith Values and the Common Good: Overview of Quantitative Findings." June 6.

Cremin, Lawrence A. 1970, 1980, 1988. *American Education*, 3 vols. New York: Harper & Row.

Dagger, Richard. 1997. *Civic Virtues: Rights, Citizenship, and Republican Liberalism*. New York: Oxford University Press.

Eberle, Christopher. 2002. *Religious Convictions in Liberal Politics*. Cambridge, UK: Cambridge University Press.

Elshtain, Jean Bethke. 1987. *Women and War*. New York: Basic Books.

Fishkin, James S. 1992. *The Dialogue of Justice: Toward a Self-Reflective Society*. New Haven, CT: Yale University Press.

Fishkin, James S., and Peter Laslett, eds. 2003. *Debating Deliberative Democracy*. Philosophy, Politics and Society, vol. 7. Malden, MA: Blackwell Publishing.

Gamwell, Franklin. 1995. *The Meaning of Religious Freedom: Modern Politics and the Democratic Resolution*. Albany, NY: SUNY Press.

Gutmann, Amy, and Dennis Thompson. 1998. *Democracy and Disagreement*. Cambridge, MA: Belknap Press.

Hollenbach, David. 2002. *The Common Good and Christian Ethics*. Cambridge, UK: Cambridge University Press.

Kaestle, Carl F. 1983. *Pillars of the Republic: Common Schools and American Society, 1780–1860*. New York: Hill & Wang.

Kunzman, Robert. 2006. *Grappling with the Good: Talking About Religion and Morality in Public Schools*. Albany, NY: SUNY Press.

Macedo, Stephen, ed. 1999. *Deliberative Politics: Essays on Democracy and Disagreement*. New York: Oxford University Press.

McConnell, Michael. 2002. "Education Disestablishment: Why Democratic Values Are Ill-Served by Democratic Control of Schooling." In *Moral and Political Education* (NOMOS XLIII). New York: New York University Press.

Mill, John Stuart. 1998. *On Liberty and Other Writings*, edited by Stefan Collini. Cambridge, UK: Cambridge University Press.

Pettit, Philip. 1997. *Republicanism: A Theory of Freedom and Government*. Clarendon Press.

Pope Francis. *Laudato Si*. Vatican City: 2015.

Quill, Lawrence. 2005. *Liberty After Liberalism: Civic Republicanism in a Global Age*. New York, NY: Palgrave Macmillan.

Rawls, John. 1999. "The Idea of Public Reason Revisited." In *The Law of Peoples*. Cambridge, MA: Harvard University Press, 129–180.

Sandel, Michael. 1996. *Democracy's Discontent: America in Search of a Public Philosophy*. Cambridge, MA: Harvard University Press.

Smith, Christian, with Michael Emerson, Sally Gallagher, Paul Kennedy, and David Sikkink. 1998. *American Evangelicalism: Embattled and Thriving*. Chicago, IL: University of Chicago Press.

Spragens, Thomas. 1999. *Civic Liberalism: Reflections on Our Democratic Ideals*. Lanham, MD: Rowman & Littlefield.

Taylor, Charles. 1985. *Philosophy and the Human Sciences: Philosophical Papers, vol. 2*. Cambridge, UK: Cambridge University Press.

US Department of Education, National Center for Education Statistics, Private School Universe Survey (PSS), 1995–96 through 2011–12. See Digest of Education Statistics 2013, table 205.20.

Walzer, Michael. 1997. *On Toleration*. New Haven, CT: Yale University Press.

Weithman, Paul. 2002. *Religion and the Obligations of Citizenship*. Cambridge, UK: Cambridge University Press.

FURTHER READING

Dill, Jeffrey S. 2013. *The Longings and Limits of Global Citizenship Education: The Moral Pedagogy of Schooling in a Cosmopolitan Age*. New York: Routledge.

Gaudelli, William. 2016. *Global Citizenship Education: Everyday Transcendence*. New York: Routledge.

Hollenbach, David. 2002. *The Common Good and Christian Ethics*. Cambridge, UK: Cambridge University Press.

Mathewes, Charles. 2007. *A Theology of Public Life*. Cambridge, UK: Cambridge University Press.

Second Vatican Ecumenical Council, Pastoral Constitution on the Church in the Modern World—Gaudium et Spes. Promulgated by Pope Paul VI. [Vatican City]: 1965.

Smith, Christian, and David Sikkink. 1999. "Is Private Schooling Privatizing?" *First Things* 92 (April). Accessed on January 24, 2018, www.firstthings.com/article/1999/04/is-private-schooling-privatizing

PART V

RELIGION AND
HIGHER EDUCATION

CHAPTER 21

RELIGION IN MAINLINE AND INDEPENDENT PRIVATE HIGHER EDUCATION

DOUGLAS JACOBSEN AND RHONDA HUSTEDT JACOBSEN

INTRODUCTION

IN June 1630, when the Puritans were about to disembark from the *Arabella* and begin building the Massachusetts Bay Colony, Governor John Winthrop preached a stirring sermon entitled "A Model of Christian Charity." Their new community in America was to be a "City on a Hill," a beacon to the rest of the world, showing how personal success, devotion to God, and caring for others could be seamlessly combined. In those rare instances when someone was required to choose between individual success and the interests of the community, personal gain was to be subservient to the common good. Winthrop's reasoning was both theological and practical: "the care of the publique must oversway all private respects, by which, not only conscience, but meare civill pollicy, dothe binde us. For it is a true rule that particular Estates cannot subsist in the ruin of the publique" (1630, 45).

Winthrop's reasoning was a classic formulation of the concept of vocation as understood by Protestants: using individual gifts and talents to fashion the earthly world so that it more fully approximates the Kingdom of God as described by Jesus. When the Puritans founded Harvard College (now Harvard University) just six years later, in 1636, the institution used that same theology of vocation as its rationale for existence. Harvard's goal was to intellectually and morally shape godly individuals into leaders who would be capable of making wise decisions on behalf of the entire community.

Nearly four centuries later, Harvard and the entire system of American higher education still harbors that same idealistic hope: that educating students for personal growth and enrichment will simultaneously produce students who use their gifts and talents to make the world a better place for everyone. However, the United States now has a far more diverse population than the uniformly Protestant community addressed by Winthrop, and the American system of higher education has become infinitely more complex. This essay will describe how schools like Harvard and hundreds of other "mainline and independent" institutions currently operating in the United States (1) have understood the relationship between personal flourishing and social responsibility and how their understanding was modified over time, (2) have been challenged by contemporary changes in religion and in educational expectations, and (3) continue to educate students for leadership roles in a religiously complex world.

A Brief History of Religion
in American Higher Education

Higher Education to the Late 1800s

During the first three centuries of American higher educational history (from 1636 to the beginning of the twentieth century), America was an overwhelmingly Protestant place. In many ways, "American" culture equated with "Protestant" culture, and Protestantism was a powerful influence that shaped all public educational systems, from primary instruction through college. This was so much the case that the nation's largest minority religious tradition, Roman Catholicism, needed to create its own separate educational system—one independent of the public primary and secondary school system—in order to keep Catholic children from being indoctrinated into Protestant ways of faith and life. The same was true at the tertiary level: Georgetown University, the first Catholic college in the nation, was established in 1789.

The world of higher education in the first centuries of American history was steeped in Protestantism, and it was socially elitist. Until the late 1800s, almost all college students were male, almost all were white, and almost all were Protestant. As decreed by Winthrop and assumed by other authorities, higher education was preparation for those who were already destined for leadership roles in society based on inherited wealth and social standing. Going to college was a kind of finishing school for future Protestant leaders in Protestant America, and the focus accordingly was on morality and character formation. Up until 1900, the American population remained about 80% Protestant, but less than 2% of young adults attended college or university. The ideal was to produce students who understood both the responsibilities of leadership and the moral and religious ideals of Protestant Christianity. The college president, who was often an ordained Protestant clergyman, typically taught a senior seminar that focused specifically on character, moral philosophy, and practical theology. The focus of this course was not on sectarian dogma but on broadly defined Protestant Christian values that were seen as vital to American society as a whole.

Higher Education in the Twentieth Century

A new phase in the history of American higher education began in the late 1800s. The pervasiveness of Protestantism declined and a new vision of higher learning emerged that made the advancement of knowledge and the development of technical skills the primary focus of higher learning (emphases derived from a new model of higher education being championed in Germany). As this new vision of higher education became more influential, the prominence of religion on college and university campuses began to decline.

This development can be described as a form of secularization, but it was rarely driven by antireligious prejudice. More typically it was a byproduct of educational modernization: as the focus of higher learning shifted toward facts, theories, and technical skills, there were fewer hours available for theology and moral education. Religious instruction and character formation were still assumed to be important, and many colleges and universities built impressive chapels on their campuses that were meant to signal the continuing centrality of Christianity. Even at Johns Hopkins University, often described as the first nonreligious, knowledge-focused university in the country, the original plan for the campus included a conspicuous chapel (albeit one that was never actually constructed). Protestant Christianity continued to be respected on almost all campuses, but the faculty and governing boards of those schools, aware of the divisions of labor required by modern society, were concluding that churches had primary responsibility for moral and religious development while colleges and universities did not (Grubiak 2014).

The early Puritans of the Massachusetts Bay Colony could never have imagined the complexity of today's systems of higher education. As colleges and universities added more specialized programs of study, some institutions became four-year undergraduate liberal arts colleges and others provided a technical curriculum focused on agriculture or technology. "Normal schools" were founded to prepare teachers for public schools. Freestanding divinity schools for ministerial training were established, and so were universities offering specialized graduate-level programs alongside undergraduate programs. Each of the states eventually established public institutions of higher education as well. Despite this proliferation of different kinds of institutions of higher learning, most of these schools, including state-funded colleges and universities, continued to be decidedly Protestant in campus ethos and culture well into the twentieth century—and many required some form of chapel attendance. The explicitly religious dimensions of higher learning evaporated very slowly at most colleges and universities, but the overall trajectory was toward an ever-increasing privatization of religion.

Following World War II, when the ideal of America as a social melting pot was at its peak, the privatization of religion became a much broader social trend affecting public life in general. This development obviously had an impact on college and university campuses as well. Protestants still made up two-thirds or more of the national population, but Protestantism no longer defined the religious character of the country. The new term of choice was "Judeo-Christian," which referred to America as a place where Protestants, Catholics, and Jews were all equally welcomed and respected. During this era, religion and partisan politics became topics to avoid in polite conversation both on and off campus. As more non-Protestants applied for admission, many colleges and universities, both private and public, felt compelled by the "Golden Rule" (Jesus' instruction to "do unto others as you would have them do unto you") to moderate the Protestant ethos of their campuses so non-Protestant students would feel more at home.

Over the course of the twentieth century, Protestant institutions of higher education divided into two basic camps, each of them paying homage to one particular element of Winthrop's sermon. Some schools, and especially those associated with more conservative denominations, stressed the need to be holy "Cities on a Hill" where doctrine and pure living trumped modern theories and sensibilities. Other schools, especially campuses associated with the major mainline Protestant denominations, emphasized "care of the public" and opened their doors to everyone—both as faculty and as students—in an effort to advance the common good without regard to sectarian loyalties. Because of this, campuses associated with mainline Protestant churches tended to follow patterns of development that were more similar to independent private institutions of higher learning and public research universities than they were to conservative, sectarian church-related schools.

The Late Twentieth-Century Marginalization of Religion in American Higher Education

In the 1960s, the broad tendency to privatize religion within higher education was magnified on some campuses by a new antireligious dynamic. Scholars in diverse disciplines began to question the value of religion, and some adopted Marxist or other philosophies that viewed religion as an obstacle to social and intellectual progress. Rather than being marginalized for pragmatic and demographic reasons, religion began to be marginalized on some campuses on the basis of being morally suspect and intellectually corrupt. Some critics insisted that higher education needed to be liberated from religion so that moral and intellectual inquiry could move ahead unimpeded by the distorting influence of religion. This view never became the majority opinion on most university campuses, but religious studies departments were recalibrated to study religion "objectively" as a dimension of human cultures and to avoid teaching religion as "theology" that privileged one particular tradition. But it was not just antireligious professors who were pushing religion out of the curriculum: many faculty members who had no antireligious sentiments were concluding that the study of religion was superfluous to the core goals and purposes of higher education. The reigning theory of religion during the last decades of the twentieth century surmised that religion was fading away as a major dimension of human existence. Accordingly, college curricula almost universally assumed that students needed to learn how to think clearly about themselves and the world without recourse to obsolete views of traditional religion.

Many academic observers of higher education in the late twentieth century presumed that this marginalization of religion represented the final chapter in the story of religion's influence on American higher learning—that henceforth all higher education in the nation, apart from a smattering of conservative church-related colleges, would be secular and religion would be irrelevant. The historian George Marsden described the history of religion in American higher education in the subtitle of one of his books as a journey "from Protestant establishment to established nonbelief" (1994). American higher education, he argued, had been forged on the Protestant principle of developing faithful leaders to shape public life, but colleges and universities had become zones of intellectual inquiry where religion had to be checked at the door as a requirement for entry. Almost before the ink was dry on the pages of Marsden's book, however, dramatic changes in the educational and social realities of America made it clear that reports of religion's demise had been premature.

WHY AND HOW RELIGION HAS RETURNED TO AMERICAN HIGHER EDUCATION

Starting in the 1990s and increasingly in the twenty-first century, religion has become much more visible at colleges and universities across the nation. The religion that is returning to these campuses, however, is not the same kind of religion that was there before 1900, and it does not play the same role in educational programs. Religion has changed and higher educational policies have changed, and those changes are ushering in a new era for religion at American universities, whether they are public or private institutions.

The Changing Nature of Religion

A primary reason for religion's return to campus visibility is that religion has surged into visibility globally. The Islamic Revolution that took place in Iran in 1979 was a watershed in this regard. Before that upheaval, many historians and sociologists of religion were operating under the assumption that secularization was an inexorable, one-way process by which religion would be eliminated first from the public domains of society and subsequently from the consciousness of individuals. The reimposition of religion on Iranian public life that took place with the return of Ayatollah Khomeini was simply not supposed to happen. And then similar resurgences of religion began to appear all over the globe. The 1980s saw the demise of communism and a concomitant revival of religion in Russia and Eastern Europe, while the Hindutva movement in India sought to transform India from a secular democracy into a Hindu state. In the United States, the rise of the Religious Right represented a reintroduction of religion into politics. The explosive growth of Christianity in Africa and Asia, and the growth of Islam as well, added more data that called the theory of inevitable secularization into question. Religion was not fading away, and it was becoming clear that colleges and universities committed to preparing students for the future needed to teach their students about the world's different religions.

The religious composition of the United States was also changing at an ever-increasing pace. In 1970, more than 90% of the population was still Christian (65% were Protestant, 25% Catholic, and 2% belonged to other Christian groups). About 4% belonged to "other religions," almost all of them Jewish, and another 4% were nonreligious. Today, about 75% of the population is Christian and 6% belong to "other religions," with Jewish, Muslim, Buddhist, and Hindu communities of roughly equal size (Pew Research Center 2015). The diversity is even greater among young adults. On university campuses, adherents of "other religions" are often present in higher proportions, and many of these individuals refuse to make their religious identity invisible. This is partly a matter of dress—like Muslim women wearing headscarves and Christians wearing crosses—but it also has to do with diet (vegetarian meals for Hindus and halal food for Muslims), differing religious holidays (and excuses from class to participate), the demand for appropriate places for worship, and disparate values being expressed in classrooms and dormitory rooms.

The most significant recent change in America's religious profile is in the category labeled "nonreligious." Roughly 20% of the total population now identifies as nonreligious, and at least one-third of the traditional college-age population falls into this category. Being nonreligious does not equate with being antireligious, however: perhaps one-third of the American nonreligious population self-identifies as atheistic, but many of these "nones" (as they are now frequently designated in sociological studies)—including atheists and agnostics—consider themselves to be spiritual in some sense (Pew Research Center 2015). They do not belong to any organized religious group, but often these nonreligious individuals deem their views to be just as deep and meaningful as those of adherents to traditional religion. What this means is that in addition to being newly diverse in terms of traditional organized religions, faith (or religion or spirituality) in America has become remarkably fuzzy: the boundary line between what is and is not considered to be religion is far less clear than it was previously. This new mixture of diversity and fuzziness has been termed "pluriform religion" (Jacobsen and Jacobsen 2012).

In an era of pluriform religion, it is problematic for colleges and universities to say that some deeply held convictions are allowable in the classroom because they are "secular," while others are not allowed because they are "religious." Deeply held personal convictions fall along a spectrum ranging from traditional religion on one pole to atheistic spirituality on the other, and it is impossible to fence one pole off from the other. In essence, pluriform religion has become so fluid that it can no longer be safely sequestered and kept out of sight on campuses. It seeps into the curriculum and co-curriculum in unexpected ways.

Changing Policies and Practices in American Higher Education

It is not just the changed nature of religion that has altered the higher educational land-scape, however. Higher education itself has changed in ways that make it more difficult to isolate and privatize religion. These alterations in epistemology, educational philos-ophy, and pedagogical practices were not constructed with the intention of resurrecting religion, but they nonetheless created spaces for religion to reemerge into visibility. Five specific educational developments have been especially significant in opening room for religion: (1) feminist, multicultural, and postmodern ways of knowing, (2) student-centered learning, (3) professional studies, (4) globalization, and (5) programs of civic engagement. These five developments are not unique to mainline and independent higher education, but they have been especially influential at these schools.

Feminist, Multicultural, and Postmodern Ways of Knowing

Starting in the 1960s and 1970s, and blossoming in the 1980s and 1990s, feminist, mul-ticultural, and postmodern modes of scholarship have reshaped the epistemological ground on which American higher education is predicated. In the early twentieth cen-tury, the academy held a relatively naïve belief in the difference between facts versus values and interpretations. Today, most scholars recognize that the framing of knowl-edge involves a complex interplay among facts, values, and interpretations. Who a person is affects how that person sees and understands the world, even when that person is attempting to conduct an unbiased scholarly analysis. Religious (and spir-itual and various kinds of secular) convictions, values, and predilections are part of this mix, and any honest, adequate academic grappling with epistemology needs to ac-knowledge those influences. Most feminist, multicultural, and postmodernist thinkers had no intention of making higher education more porous to religion, but religious permeability has been an unintended consequence of the academy's embrace of these perspectives.

Student-Centered Learning

A huge pedagogical transformation has taken place in American higher education in the last thirty years. The "sage on the stage"—the lofty professor who decides what students need to know and how well they have objectively mastered the materials assigned for a course—has been largely replaced by the "guide by the side," the professor who serves as a mentor and catalyst for learning. In this new model, students are actively engaged in setting their own educational goals and life plans, and professors are expected to fa-cilitate students' achievement of their own personalized goals. Good education in this new pedagogical paradigm brings the student as a whole person into the processes of learning and personal development. Since religious or spiritual values and orientations are formative for many students, this new student-centered mode of pedagogy makes it virtually impossible to segregate religion in all of its contemporary pluriform complexity from classroom learning. Instead, good teaching requires engagement with students' deeply held personal commitments and values, including religious ones.

Professional Studies

The tremendous growth of professional studies has also made it more difficult to keep religion invisible. On the surface, the dramatic expansion of professional studies in the academy seems to point away from any kind of engagement with matters of faith, religion, or spirituality. The shift away from liberal arts education and toward professional training in the twentieth century helped push religion out of higher education, but almost all programs of professional studies now include some attention to ethics and morality. Sometimes they deal only with how to avoid getting in trouble professionally; however, many courses in professional ethics probe more deeply, asking students to examine their own value commitments and the way those convictions might affect their work as professionals. For many students, this kind of self-reflection will include religious considerations.

Globalization

Globalization has similarly ushered religion back into higher education. About 85% of the world's people belong to one or another historical religious tradition, and religion plays a huge role in the internal politics of many nations and in international relations. Preparing students to live in a globalized world thus has to include some introduction to the plethora of faiths that flourish across the globe. This would be necessary even if Western culture were thoroughly secular—which is far from the truth. Whether the field of study is literature or music or business or politics or medicine or psychology, globalizing that field of study requires some awareness of how local cultures and religions relate to these concerns.

Programs of Civic Engagement

Finally, higher education's renewed emphasis on civic engagement is providing another mechanism through which religion is returning to visibility in American higher education. Obviously anyone can be civically engaged, and many leaders in the field are themselves personally nonreligious. But recent studies have shown that individuals who are religiously active—people who attend church, synagogue, or temple on a regular basis—are much more likely to be involved in community service and care for the needy (Putnam and Campbell 2010). Two consequences flow from this fact. First, it is likely that religiously active students will be disproportionately represented in campus programs of civic engagement. Second, the community groups and programs with which students work will likely introduce them to religious people. In recent years, many mainline and independent campuses have enlisted the Interfaith Youth Core founded by Eboo Patel (2013) to organize and broker interfaith conversations in conjunction with civic service projects. When civic engagement is a focus of higher learning, religion will almost always be an implicit, and often an explicit, dimension of the experience.

DISTINCTIVE CHARACTERISTICS OF MAINLINE AND INDEPENDENT HIGHER EDUCATION

Mainline and independent colleges and universities have always sought to be civically engaged; social responsibility is the heartbeat of these institutions. In addition, their undergraduate programs have always been designed to enhance the personal flourishing of their students. In other words, they have continued to embody the dualistic ideal first enunciated at the founding of Harvard. These schools are now positioned to continue leading the way as higher education responds to the new visibility of religion in American society and on its college and university campuses.

Which schools are included among the "mainline and independent" colleges and universities? There are currently more than 10.5 million students in the United States who are enrolled in bachelor's degree programs at four-year institutions (as opposed to two-year schools), with roughly two-thirds at public institutions and one-third at private institutions. About 4 million postsecondary (undergraduate and graduate) students are enrolled in private nonprofit postsecondary institutions, almost evenly divided between independent schools (52%) and religiously affiliated institutions (48%). Of the students at religiously affiliated schools, 40% attend Catholic institutions and about 60% attend some other variety of Christian school. (The number of students enrolled at non-Christian religiously affiliated institutions of higher learning is miniscule.) More than half of non-Catholic, church-related colleges and universities are associated with mainline Protestant denominations. This means that mainline and independent schools together annually enroll about 3 million undergraduate students (US Department of Education 2013).

Taken together, the categories of mainline and independent colleges include hundreds of institutions. In 2012, the United States was home to 4,726 degree-granting postsecondary institutions, including 887 religiously affiliated and 765 independent nonprofit institutions. These schools are astonishing in their diversity. They include top-tier research universities like Harvard, the University of Chicago, and Stanford, and they also include tiny liberal arts colleges that enroll fewer than one hundred students. Schools like Reed College and Berea College, which have never been formally related to any church or denomination, fit in this group alongside places like Pacific Lutheran College (which is owned by the Evangelical Lutheran Church in America) and Elon University (which is associated with the United Church of Christ).

Other colleges and universities, like Williams College and Vanderbilt University, began as churchly institutions and later disaffiliated. Disaffiliation can mean many things, however, and some kind of semi-affiliation with the founding denomination often remains in place at many formerly church-related colleges and universities. Being a mainline institution of higher learning is not so much an on/off switch as it is a rheostat, with relationships that can be more or less intense.

Denominational names have changed often over the decades. Currently the eight denominations usually defined as "mainline" include the United Methodist Church, Evangelical Lutheran Church in America, Presbyterian Church USA, Episcopal Church, American Baptist Church, United Church of Christ, Disciples of Christ, and Reformed Church in America.

What is common to almost all of these schools, whether they are mainline or nonreligious independent colleges and universities, is that they have no religious requirements for employment and they impose no religious limits on what can be taught in the classroom. Most mainline and independent colleges and universities now actively seek to recruit a student body that is religiously diverse because they believe such diversity will enhance the education that takes place on campus. Inviting people of differing faiths to campus requires these institutions to be welcoming of all religious traditions, and that requires extending hospitality to all aspects of campus life. Many of these schools now have designated places on campus for Muslim prayer and Buddhist meditation, and they offer kosher, halal, and vegetarian entrees in the dining halls. Professors are encouraged to be aware of multiple religious calendars and to excuse student absences on holy days.

A NEW ENGAGEMENT WITH RELIGION

Mainline and independent campuses have generally adopted one of two primary responses to religion's recent return to visibility on campuses. Some have reacted tactically, accommodating religion and trying to control its place within the university so it does not disturb existing (late twentieth-century, religiously privatized) modes of teaching and learning. Other mainline and private institutions of higher learning have been more proactive in their reengagement, seeking to use religion's new visibility in society and on campuses to deepen and improve learning. Whichever path has been pursued, mainline and independent institutions have become increasingly aware that engaging religion in the contemporary era requires careful and nuanced thinking.

Accommodating Religion

Tactical reactive accommodations of religion have the general purpose of corralling religion on campus so it does not undermine or hijack the institution's core nonreligious educational goals and purposes. Accommodations can take many forms, but one of the most common is to highlight a pedagogical policy of only *teaching about* religion and never teaching religion itself. The goal is to draw a sharp line between objective instruction about religion and subjective indoctrination of students into one particular religious vision of life. This is a helpful distinction, and yet this kind of neat and clear differentiation of pedagogical goals is often impossible to maintain: adequate comprehension of religion usually entails some attempt to understand its attraction, which can call for some level of sympathetic imagination or participatory affectivity. Nonetheless, the distinction between informing and proselytizing in the classroom remains an important curricular rule.

A second general approach is to shift the emphasis away from religion itself and to subsume it under some other supposedly larger and more inclusive umbrella of concern. The three most commonly used rubrics in this regard are culture, spirituality, and "big questions." Harvard University provides an example of a school employing the concept of "culture." In 2006, a faculty committee recommended adding a new category to the school's general education requirements. The originally proposed category was "faith and reason," and those courses were to help students understand the interplay between religion and secularity, become more informed and reflective citizens, and reflect on their own beliefs. The Harvard faculty rejected this proposal, with the last item—student self-reflection—being a key point of contention. When the new general education parameters were finally approved, the proposed "faith and reason" category had been redefined as "culture and belief" courses that would help students develop "understanding of and appreciation for the ways that social, political, religious, economic, and historical conditions shape the production and reception of ideas and works of art, either within or across cultural boundaries" (Harvard University Registrar's Office). The personal dimension, the goal of helping students sort out their own religious or religious-like beliefs, was eliminated.

Other private colleges and universities use the notions of "spirituality" and "big questions" to manage the potentially disruptive presence of religion on their campuses. The notion of spirituality is substituted for religion, with spirituality used to refer to personal sources of meaning and purpose that shape student lives. Traditional religion may be a source for a student's spirituality, but focusing on spirituality limits the discussion to the personal and subjective attitudes of the individual alone—what "I have experienced"—rather than requiring examination of the broader truth claims or social teachings of any particular tradition. Similarly, the "big questions" framework translates religious categories of thought and action into language deemed more neutral: questions about personal meaning and purpose, ethics, civic engagement, or encounters with otherness. Approaches to higher learning that address culture, spirituality, and big questions can be enormously helpful to students, but sometimes they are used to sidestep religion itself, potentially short-circuiting conversations that might enrich the learning experience for everyone.

Proactively Engaging Religion

Instead of taking a reactive posture toward religion's new visibility on campuses, some institutions are engaging religion proactively. Harvard's nearest neighbor, the Massachusetts Institute of Technology, is a case in point. In 2007, MIT appointed its first ever "Chaplain to the Institute." The rationale was simple, straightforward, and interreligious: "keeping [students] talking to each other, so that the stereotypes that have operated for far too long are not allowed to re-impose themselves (Randolph). The assumption is that MIT graduates will soon be global leaders, so having some first-hand familiarity and appreciation of the world's differing faiths will be an enormous aid in negotiating agreements and avoiding conflicts, whether in commerce, professional life, or international politics. At Vassar College, educators have described their desire to move beyond a secular/secularist approach to higher learning that is biased against religion to a more classically secular stance that acknowledges the broad variety of religious and nonreligious perspectives present on campus and allows all of those views to be expressed, debated, and critically examined (Vassar College). At the University of Southern California, the concern for dialogue and understanding has resulted in the creation of several centers—the Institute for Advanced Catholic Studies, the Center for Muslim-Jewish Engagement, and the Center for Religion and Civic Culture, among others—devoted to exploring the positive dimensions of faith as well as potential conflicts between religions.

Institutions whose recent histories have been more closely connected to their mainline church roots are also rethinking the place of religion in their educational programs. Two Lutheran institutions capture a sense of the variety in those recent dynamics. Hartwick College in upstate New York, founded as a Lutheran seminary, became a four-year liberal arts college in 1927 and severed its ties with the Lutheran Church in 1968. Not everyone was happy about disconnecting from the school's ecclesial heritage. In the early 1970s, someone (rumored to be a member of the school's board of trustees) hired carpenters to surreptitiously hang a wooden cross on the front wall of the college's chapel space, and in protest a group of faculty members, also surreptitiously, installed a curtain to cover the cross. Some professors asked for removal of the letters A.D. (*anno domini*, meaning "the year of our Lord") on the cornerstone of the oldest building on campus, saying such words were inappropriate on a secular campus. They wanted Hartwick to model a religiously privatized college. In the mid-1990s, however, the atmosphere on campus began to change. A Muslim student asked why there was no *qibla* in the chapel, a group of Catholic students suggested that images of all the world's religions should be on display, and another group of students proposed adding plants and a fountain to the chapel to make the space feel less spiritually sterile. Students' suggestions were not immediately embraced by faculty and administrators, but students' sensibilities are nudging Hartwick to reengage religion in both the curriculum and co-curriculum (Herion, 2014).

St. Olaf College, a Lutheran institution in Minnesota, has never severed its church ties. As American culture and higher education moved into the new era of pluriform religion, St. Olaf has taken a lead in exploring how a mainline institution can integrate religion into its educational goals and practices. Central to St. Olaf's vision is the notion of vocation or calling understood as a blending together of personal talents and service to others in keeping with one's own deepest values and commitments (Schwehn and Lagerquist 2014). John Winthrop would be delighted by this approach to education, but the setting, context, and content are very different from anything he might have imagined. For Winthrop, there was one right way forward; for the St. Olaf faculty, the way forward is a conversation about meaning making across disciplines that involves the best practices of academic inquiry and welcomes the perspectives of a religiously and secularly diverse cohort of scholars. Their work obliterates neat bipolarities of faith versus learning and of religion versus secularity and reflects the fuzzy realities of thought and life as they exist in contemporary America.

Similar projects are under way at many private institutions, in sufficient number to warrant the establishment of institutional networks. The Project on Purpose and Values in Education (PAVE) promotes the development of co-curricular programs that require reflection on big questions of meaning and purpose at two dozen private schools ranging from large research universities like Harvard, Notre Dame, Stanford, and the University of Southern California to small liberal arts colleges like Bowdoin, Dominican, St. Olaf, and Wabash. Nearly two hundred campuses affiliated with the Council of Independent Colleges—including Catholic and evangelical as well as mainline and unaffiliated campuses—have joined the Network for Vocation in Undergraduate Education (NetVUE) in order to more fully explore the intellectual and theological dimensions of vocational choice.

A New Framework for Understanding Religion's Presence Within Higher Education

As colleges and universities reengage religion, many educators lack an adequate vocabulary for describing the complex realities surrounding contemporary religion. Conceptualizing religion into three distinct expressions—historic, public, and personal—can serve as a helpful starting point (Jacobsen and Jacobsen 2012). Religion in the most common usage of the term refers to "historic religion," the historic traditions and religious institutions that have formal names like Christianity, Islam, Judaism, Buddhism, and Hinduism and that are expressed in a wide variety of local groups, communities, churches, temples, and other associations. Religion is more than this single dimension, however. In a second meaning of the term, religion also refers to "personal religion," how each person individually connects with the transcendent and makes meaning in his or her life. Sometimes this kind of "personal religion" overlaps significantly with "historic religion," but for many contemporary Americans it does not, which is what the phrase "spiritual, but not religious" is meant to signal. Finally, religion has a public dimension. Sometimes called civic or civil religion, "public religion" refers to the differing and often contentious ways in which societies seek to articulate their own highest ideals. Public religion varies in both content and intensity across different societies, but it has always played a major role in the public life of the United States, a nation that has traditionally seen itself as having a unique, and many would say God-given, mission in the world. All three of these expressions—historic, personal, and public—are evident in higher education's new engagement with religion.

CONCLUSION

It is not possible to develop any single normative model of how all mainline and independent colleges and universities should engage or are engaging religion. Campuses vary dramatically in terms of religious/secular composition, flashpoints of interaction, resource availability, and desired outcomes. Institutional missions differ, and institutional histories also deeply shape how religion is perceived or rendered visible or invisible in different campus contexts. But the need to constructively reengage religion in all of its complex historical, personal, and public dimensions is being felt all across the mainline and independent continuum.

Religion will not, at least not in the near future, disappear from either American society or American higher education. Colleges and universities of all stripes will be required to confront its continuing existence in both their curricular and co-curricular programming. Mainline and independent colleges and universities are especially well situated to address these concerns. Unlike public institutions that need to worry about mixing faith and education in ways that transgress the constitutional separation of church and state, private schools are free from such legal restrictions. Unlike many evangelical or conservative church-related colleges and universities, where religious diversity is often significantly limited and where the ability to respond to religious diversity is often hemmed in by religious doctrines and tight ecclesiastical connections, mainline and independent institutions generally have no limitations on who can be admitted or hired. Their position as neither public nor sectarian allows them to explore the interactions between religion and education in ways not possible elsewhere. They can be bold about their own missions, examining, embracing, moderating, rearticulating, and critiquing the messy richness of religion in its entirety. Aware of their own particularity and of the needs of the global community, mainline and independent campuses are uniquely positioned to educate individuals for their own personal flourishing and for responsible engagement with a pluralistic world.

FUTURE DIRECTIONS

1. Should colleges and universities focus primarily on preparing students for the workplace (competencies and skills model)? To what degree is personal

development, maturation, intellectual curiosity, and civic engagement (liberal arts model) legitimately included in higher education? How does the role of religion differ in the two models?

2. Most private colleges and universities assign religious concerns primarily to campus chaplains (or offices of religious and spiritual life), who are typically construed as student life staff rather than as academics. As religion becomes more visible, will chaplains become more central to campus life? Is religion likely to become a larger presence in the curriculum?

3. The modern Western understanding of religion, which developed during the Enlightenment, sees religion as one particular and easily demarcated sector of human existence: the human response to beliefs about God, the gods, or the sacred. Today religion or "the spiritual" is sometimes described as finding or constructing personal meaning, purpose, and values in dialogue with communal norms and morals. What are the educational, social, political, and legal consequences of adopting either of these definitions?

4. Do all colleges and universities have a responsibility to educate students about interfaith etiquette? Do all colleges and universities have a responsibility to educate students about comparative and conflicting religious truth claims?

5. Many mainline Protestant churches have scaled back involvement with their denominationally related colleges and universities almost to the point of total noninvolvement. Since most Americans make long-lasting decisions about the religious/spiritual trajectories of their lives during their young adult years (ages eighteen to thirty), should mainline denominations connect more closely with their affiliated campuses?

REFERENCES

Grubiak, Margaret M. 2014. *White Elephants on Campus: The Decline of the University Chapel in America, 1920–1960*. Notre Dame, IN: University of Notre Dame Press.

Harvard University, Registrar's Office, "Culture and Belief." http://www.registrar.fas.harvard.edu/courses-exams/courses-instruction/culture-and-belief, accessed January 1, 2016.

Herion, Gary. 2014. Personal communication with Professor Gary Herion and authors, October 2, 2014

Jacobsen, Douglas and Rhonda Hustedt Jacobsen. 2012. *No Longer Invisible: Religion in University Education*. New York: Oxford University Press.

Marsden, George, 1994. *The Soul of the American University: From Protestant Establishment to Established Nonbelief*. New York: Oxford University Press.

Patel, Eboo. 2013. *Sacred Ground: Pluralism, Prejudice, and the Promise of America*. Boston: Beacon.

Pew Research Center, 2015. *America's Changing Religious Landscape*. Washington, DC: Pew Research Center.

Putnam, Robert D., and David E. Campbell, 2010. *American Grace: How Religion Divides and Unites Us*. New York: Simon and Schuster.

Randolph, Robert. "Inventing Our Future." http://diversity-stage.mit.edu/people/robert-randolph, accessed March 15, 2015.

Schwehn, Kaethe, and L. DeAne Lagerquist, eds. 2014. *Claiming Our Callings: Toward a New Understanding of Vocation in the Liberal Arts*. New York: Oxford University Press.

US Department of Education. Digest of Education Statistics, 2013. "Table 303.60: Total fall enrollment in degree-granting postsecondary institutions, by level of enrollment, sex of student, and other selected characteristics 2012" and "Table 303.90: Fall enrollment and number of degree-granting institutions, by control and religious affiliation of institution: Selected years, 1980 through 2012."

Vassar College, "Secularity and the Liberal Arts." Vassar College, http://projects.vassar.edu/secularity, accessed January 1, 2016.

Winthrop, John. 1630. *A Modell of Christian Charity*. Collections of the Massachusetts Historical Society. http://history.hanover.edu/texts/winthmod.html, accessed January 1, 2016.

Further Reading

Astin, Alexander W., Helen S. Astin, and Jennifer A. Lindholm. 2011. *Cultivating the Spirit: How College Can Enhance Students' Inner Lives*. San Francisco: Jossey-Bass.

Burtchaell, James Tunstead. 1998. *The Dying of the Light: The Disengagement of Colleges and Universities from Their Christian Churches*. Grand Rapids, MI: Eerdmans.

Cunningham, David, ed. 2016. *At This Time and in This Place: Vocation and Higher Education*. New York: Oxford University Press.

Hart, Daryl G. 1999. *The University Gets Religion: Religious Studies in American Higher Education*. Baltimore: Johns Hopkins University Press.

Edwards, Mark U., Jr. 2006. *Religion on Our Campuses: A Professor's Guide to Communities, Conflicts, and Promising Conversations*. New York: Palgrave Macmillan.

Forster-Smith, Lucy. 2013. *College and University Chaplaincy in the 21st Century: A Multifaith Look at the Practice of Ministry on Campuses Across America*. Woodstock, VT: Skylight.

Freitas, Donna. 2010. *Sex and the Soul: Juggling Sexuality, Spirituality, Romance, and Religion on America's College Campuses*. New York: Oxford University Press.

Jacobsen, Douglas, and Rhonda Hustedt Jacobsen. 2008. *The American University in a Postsecular Age*. New York: Oxford University Press.

Kazanjian, Victor, and Peter L. Laurence. 2000. *Education as Transformation: Religious Pluralism, Spirituality, and a New Vision for Higher Education in America*. New York: Peter Lang.

Lindholm, Jennifer A. 2014. *The Quest for Meaning and Wholeness: Spiritual and Religious Connections in the Lives of College Faculty*. San Francisco: Jossey-Bass.

Nord, Warren. 2010. *Does God Make a Difference?: Taking Religion Seriously in Our Schools and Universities*. New York: Oxford University Press.

Palmer, Parker. 1998. *The Courage to Teach: Exploring the Inner Landscape of a Teacher's Life*. San Francisco: Wiley.

Parks, Sharon Daloz. 2000. *Big Questions, Worthy Dreams: Mentoring Young Adults in Their Search for Meaning, Purpose, and Faith*. San Francisco: Jossey-Bass.

Prothero, Stephen. 2007. *Religious Literacy: What Every American Needs to Know—and Doesn't*. New York: HarperCollins.

Reuben, Julie A. 1996. *The Making of the Modern University: Intellectual Transformation and the Marginalization of Morality*. Chicago: University of Chicago Press.

Roberts, Jon H., and James Turner. 2000. *The Sacred and the Secular University*. Princeton, NJ: Princeton University Press.

Schwehn, Mark R., *Exiles from Eden: Religion and the Academic Vocation in America*. New York: Oxford University Press, 1993.

Shapiro, Harold T. 2005. *A Larger Sense of Purpose: Higher Education and Society*. Princeton, NJ: Princeton University Press.

Sloan, Douglas. 1994. *Faith and Knowledge: Mainline Protestantism and American Higher Education*. Louisville, KY: Westminster John Knox.

Sommerville, John C. 2006. *The Decline of the Secular University*. New York: Oxford University Press.

CHAPTER 22

....

EVANGELICAL HIGHER EDUCATION

....

P. JESSE RINE

INTRODUCTION

THE story of American higher education is one of religious commitment and abandonment. Every one of the early colonial colleges was religious in character, and the overwhelming majority of colleges founded during the period between the American Revolution and the Civil War were established by Protestant denominations (Schuman 2010). As the needs of the emerging nation and the values of its people evolved, so too did the religious ethos of most of these institutions. A handful of these religiously founded colleges, however, have persisted in their original missions, which continue to animate campus life and practice to this day. Along with a group of younger Christian colleges established after the Civil War, these institutions make up what is known today as American evangelical higher education. These colleges and universities are distinguished as much by their commitment to biblical orthodoxy as their culturally engaged, socially responsible, and irenic posture (Carlburg 2002). Although they represent a relatively small segment of the private nonprofit postsecondary sector, evangelical colleges and universities carry on the educational legacy of America's earliest institutions of higher education. This chapter seeks first to provide an overview of the foundations and permutations of evangelical Christian higher education in the United States, and then to consider a number of key challenges these institutions currently face.

FOUNDATIONS OF EVANGELICAL CHRISTIAN HIGHER EDUCATION

Historical Development

Evangelical Christian colleges share a commitment to Christ-centered higher education in the liberal arts and sciences, a commonality distinguishing them from the wider ecology of American higher education. Consequently, many external observers often assume a greater uniformity in character and practice among evangelical colleges than actually exists. The evangelical segment is a rich tapestry woven from multiple dimensions of institutional diversity, not the least of which are the divergent circumstances in which these colleges and universities were founded.

Most of today's evangelical colleges can trace their origins to one of three periods of American history. The first spanned the dawn of the nineteenth century to the eve of the American Civil War and was inspired by the Second Great Awakening (c. 1800–1835), a time of intense spiritual revival in the early American republic. Ringenberg (2006) notes that the newfound evangelistic zeal motivated missionary excursions to the westward frontier, and growing acceptance of higher learning led Protestant denominations to work with local communities to found new colleges (Table 22.1). In addition to training future ministers, these colleges provided institutional support for the societal reforms made by the Protestant missionaries. Two of the fastest-growing Protestant denominations, the Baptists and the Methodists, were especially active in founding new colleges during this period (Ringenberg 2006).

A second period of Christian college growth began near the close of the nineteenth century and extended into the early twentieth century. Protestant denominations continued to create new colleges during this era, with groups such as the Nazarenes establishing their first institutions of higher education. In addition, existing patterns of growth were augmented by a new movement that would make its own unique contribution to evangelical higher education. Arising in part as a reaction to the increasing theological liberalism of Protestant denominations and their colleges, and in part as

Table 22.1 Evangelical Colleges Founded 1800–1861

Name	State	Denominational Affiliation	Year
Union University	TN	Southern Baptist	1823
Mississippi College	MS	Southern Baptist	1826
Judson College	AL	Southern Baptist	1838
Erskine College	SC	Associate Reformed Presbyterian	1839
University of Mary Hardin-Baylor	TX	Southern Baptist	1845
Taylor University	IN	Interdenominational, but founded by the Methodist Episcopal Church	1846
Geneva College	PA	Reformed Presbyterian Church of North America	1848
Waynesburg University	PA	Presbyterian Church U.S.A.	1849
Carson-Newman University	TN	Southern Baptist	1851
Hannibal-LaGrange University	MO	Southern Baptist	1858
Wheaton College	IL	Interdenominational	1860

Source: Institutional websites.

a response to the Third Great Awakening (c. 1875–1915), the Bible college movement produced a number of schools and institutes that would eventually expand into Bible colleges, then Christian liberal arts colleges (Ringenberg 2006; Table 22.2). However, the Bible college legacy remains strong in many of these evangelical colleges, as evidenced by their emphasis on missions and evangelism, intentional efforts to cultivate personal piety among students, and, in some cases, curricular requirements in Bible and theology that exceed standard liberal arts distribution requirements (Ringenberg 2006).

A third wave of expansion in the evangelical college ranks began as World War I concluded and continued through the middle of the twentieth century. Although some institutions were founded by well-established denominations that had entered the higher education market in earlier periods (e.g., the American Baptist Church, which founded Eastern University in 1952 and Judson University in 1963), the majority of evangelical colleges founded during this time were established either by more theologically conservative factions of mainline American Protestantism that formed their own separate denominations or by existing denominations that simply had not yet sponsored an institution of higher education (Ringenberg 2006). Examples of the former include the General Association of Regular Baptists (Cornerstone University, 1941) and the Bible Presbyterian Church (Covenant College, 1955), while examples of the latter include Pentecostal denominations such as the Assemblies of God (Evangel University, 1955) and the Church of God–Cleveland (Lee University, 1918). As the modernist/fundamentalist battles that animated American Protestantism for the early part of the twentieth century eventually settled to a simmer by mid-century, evangelical colleges were able to turn their attention to affirmatively defining their educational task, enhancing their institutional credentials, and developing professional connections through participation

Table 22.2   Select Evangelical Colleges Founded 1875–1915

Name	State	Original Name	Year
Lipscomb University	TN	Nashville Bible School	1891
Malone University	OH	Cleveland Bible College	1892
Nyack College	NY	The Missionary Training Institute	1892
Gordon College	MA	Boston Missionary Training Institute	1889
Azusa Pacific University	CA	Training School for Christian Workers	1899
Trevecca Nazarene University	TN	Literary and Bible Training School for Christian Workers	1901
Point Loma Nazarene University	CA	Pacific Bible College	1902
The Bible Institute of Los Angeles	CA	The Bible Institute	1908
Colorado Christian University	CO	Denver Bible Institute	1914

Source: Institutional websites.

in national associations such as the Council for the Advancement of Small Colleges, known today as the Council of Independent Colleges (Patterson 2001).

Evangelical college leaders also began earnestly exploring possible avenues for formal collaboration in areas of mutual interest in the 1960s. Spurred by concerns over negative enrollment trends, the continued financial health of their institutions, and the growth of an unflattering public perception of theologically conservative colleges, the presidents of eleven evangelical colleges met in December 1970 to discuss the future of the movement of evangelical Christian higher education in the United States (Patterson 2001). Four months later, the Christian College Consortium was born, an organization dedicated to both securing the resources and providing the supports necessary for its member institutions to achieve and maintain educational effectiveness (Patterson 2001). The Christian College Consortium served as a proof of concept for the more robust association that would follow, the Christian College Coalition. Known today as the Council for Christian Colleges and Universities (CCCU), this international membership association of intentionally Christ-centered colleges and universities offers professional development opportunities for evangelical college faculty and administrators, provides semester-long study abroad opportunities for students, and advocates on Capitol Hill in Washington, DC, for the religious liberties of its member institutions.

Philosophical and Religious Commitments

The evangelical Christian college is grounded in the belief that an ultimate reality exists beyond the physical world, one authored by a personal God who has made Himself known through two types of revelation. The created order is a general revelation that testifies to the existence and character of God, while the Holy Scriptures and Incarnation of Christ—the moment in history at which God became man and dwelt among humanity—are direct, special revelations. If the purpose of the Incarnation of Christ was to reconcile a fallen world to God, then the mission of the evangelical Christian college is to explore the implications of the Incarnation for every academic field and discipline. The dominant organizing paradigm employed by evangelical higher education to accomplish this mission is known as "the integration of faith and learning."

Holmes' (1987) influential work on the philosophical foundations of evangelical Christian higher education introduces a number of concepts fundamental to the integration paradigm. Holmes elucidates the unique character of the evangelical college by distinguishing it from other forms of Christian involvement in higher education—such as the Christian professor who serves in a nonsectarian institution, or the Bible institute that exists solely to train Christian workers—and from the secular academy, which tends to treat religion as largely irrelevant and to sequester it from other areas of inquiry. Holmes notes that the evangelical college is the only type of Christian involvement in higher learning that seeks to provide an education that is both Christian and comprehensive. Moreover, in contrast to the secular academy's compartmentalization of religion, Holmes explains that the evangelical college operates from a conviction that

Christianity can generate a worldview large enough to give meaning to all areas of human endeavor and should therefore be integrated across all academic disciplines. This conviction rests on an understanding of truth as unified and noncontradictory—"all truth is God's truth"—as well as the belief that humanity falls under a cultural mandate to explore, develop, and renew the created order.

The integration paradigm gained widespread acceptance across evangelical higher education during the latter half of the twentieth century (Ringenberg 2006), and a great deal of theoretical and practical literature that explores its application has developed over the decades since Holmes' work first appeared. Nevertheless, one oft-cited piece by Hasker (1992) illustrates representative strategies for and dimensions of faith-learning integration. Hasker describes three strategies scholars can employ to achieve integration, each varying according to the level of agreement between Christianity and the scholar's academic discipline. The integrative task is fairly straightforward in cases where natural connections exist, as the scholar can simply take a *compatibilist* tack that seeks to highlight points of intersection. Integration is more challenging, however, when disciplines are incongruent with or even contradictory to Christianity. For disciplines that offer limited points of contact, Hasker recommends a *transformationist* strategy that applies a Christian lens to reform areas of discordance while retaining areas of agreement. In instances where the discipline's dominant methods, assumptions, or content stands in opposition to Christian perspectives, Hasker advocates a *reconstructionist* approach that seeks to rebuild the discipline on Christian foundations.

Just as the strategies for integration of faith and learning will vary depending on the state of a particular discipline, so too will approaches to integration differ according to a discipline's theoretical or applied nature. For theoretical disciplines, Hasker identifies four dimensions of faith-learning integration. *Worldview foundations* and *worldview contributions* bring the theoretical disciplines and the Christian vision into conversation, asking how they relate to one another. *Disciplinary foundations* assess the compatibility of the theoretical discipline's basic tenets of Christianity, while *disciplinary practice* asks which particular aspects of the theoretical discipline might be of special interest to Christians. Hasker also presents four dimensions of faith-learning integration for the applied disciplines. The first, *theory applied to practice*, interrogates common practices in the applied discipline to determine if they achieve ends in harmony with Christian objectives. Two other applied dimensions examine the internal character one brings to the discipline—namely, what *ethics and values* motivate one's professional behavior and what *attitudes* are displayed when practicing one's craft. A final dimension asks what *contribution to the kingdom of God* is made by practicing the applied discipline.

Organizational Structure and Campus Ethos

The CCCU's membership requirements provide a window into the character of evangelical higher education. To join the CCCU, a Christian college must meet a set of expectations relating to institutional quality, organizational structure, and general ethos. First, the college must be not-for-profit, possess nonprobationary regional accreditation, offer a comprehensive undergraduate program grounded in the liberal arts and sciences, demonstrate responsible financial operations, and conduct fundraising in accordance with the standards of the Evangelical Council for Financial Accountability. Next, the college must possess a public, board-approved mission statement that is explicitly Christian, offer curricular and co-curricular programs that integrate scholarship, faith, and service, and employ a policy of hiring only professing Christians as full-time faculty members and salaried administrators. Finally, the college must exhibit a cooperative posture toward other Christian colleges and a willingness to support the wider cause of Christian higher education.

Pointing to the mission statement and hiring requirements, Litfin (2004) argues that CCCU members are *systemic*, rather than *umbrella*, institutions. In the umbrella institution, the Christian worldview provides a general framework, and a critical mass representing the sponsoring tradition occupies a place of privilege within the campus community. However, alternative voices that fall outside the sponsoring tradition are welcome to participate in the life of the institution provided that they support its broad educational mission (Litfin 2004). In contrast, the systemic institution not only employs the Christian worldview as an organizing framework, but its academic and extracurricular program seeks to engage the world of thought and action from the standpoint of the institution's religious tradition (Litfin 2004).

The distinctive philosophical and religious commitments of the evangelical college manifest themselves across multiple dimensions of institutional life. For example, Woodrow's (2006) study of mission statements at CCCU members revealed an institutional intentionality unique among American colleges and universities. Braskamp, Trautvetter, and Ward (2006) conducted case studies of ten religiously affiliated institutions, two of which were evangelical colleges, and found a common holistic approach to student development that sought to foster psychological, social, ethical, and spiritual maturation among undergraduates even as they pursued their intellectual callings. This holistic approach was supported by a campus *culture* that understood and acted upon its institutional mission, a *curriculum* rooted in the liberal arts and emphasizing the integration of faith and learning, a *co-curriculum* that provided mutual reinforcement of in-class and out-of-class learning, and a welcoming *community* that facilitated student–faculty interaction (Braskamp, Trautvetter, and Ward 2006). One final key aspect of campus life at evangelical colleges is its spiritual programming. Rine (2012) found that nearly three-quarters of all CCCU member institutions held chapel services at least two times each week, and a similar proportion required students to attend a certain number of services each semester. Rine also discovered that 96% of CCCU member institutions required students to complete at least six credit-hours in Bible or theology coursework.

CONTEMPORARY FORMS OF EVANGELICAL CHRISTIAN HIGHER EDUCATION

There are multiple ways to divide a postsecondary sector into specific segments; common approaches include regional location, enrollment size, and financial resources. To be sure, these dimensions do shape institutional behavior, yet their development often results from accidents of history, rendering them largely incidental to founding intent. Perhaps more consequential are those characteristics that emanate from institutional mission. Attributes such as denominational status, membership requirements, and curricular orientation constitute distinct forms of evangelical higher education and merit special attention.

Denominational Status: Church-Related Versus Nondenominational

Approximately three-quarters of the current CCCU membership claim a denominational affiliation. The remaining institutions either do not maintain official ties with their founding churches or were originally established as nondenominational or interdenominational colleges. More than two dozen Protestant denominations are represented among the church-related evangelical colleges, and the lineage of each of these denominational traditions can be traced back to one of the four major strands of the Protestant Reformation: Anglican, Lutheran, Reformed, and Anabaptist (Rine 2012).

In a systemic institution that seeks to engage the educational task from the standpoint of its religious mission, the theological tradition of the sponsoring denomination fundamentally shapes institutional structure and practice (Hughes and Adrian 1997). Though many instances of this phenomenon could be cited, the educational implications of the Reformed, Wesleyan/Holiness, and Mennonite traditions are illustrative. Reformed theology stresses the majesty of God and teaches that creation was designed to show forth His glory, but humanity's fall into sin led to the corruption of the entire created order and the need for redemption through Christ (Bratt 1997). Although sin has severely marred the divine handiwork, humanity retains a shadow of the image of God and society remains under the law of God, thus rendering the work of even those outside the church intelligible and potentially meritorious. The Reformed college, then, explores every area of human endeavor, integrates seemingly disparate domains into a cohesive whole, and equips students to be agents of redemption who restore order to a broken world (Bratt 1997). The Wesleyan/Holiness tradition employs a quadrilateral theological method that relies on scripture, tradition, reason, and experience, an inclusive approach suggesting that truth is accessible through multiple avenues (Stanley and Stanley 1997). The notions of personal and social holiness also loom large in the Wesleyan/Holiness tradition, orienting adherents around notions of wholesomeness, integrity, outreach, renewal, and service. Colleges in this tradition tend to evidence vibrant campus worship programs and chapel ministries, campus lifestyle codes that emphasize personal purity, and service through compassionate ministries, such as social outreach to the poor and summer service projects (Stanley and Stanley 1997). The Mennonite tradition views the church as an alternative community separate from the world, one redeemed by Christ and committed to radical discipleship. Obedience to Christ requires nonresistant love, peacemaking, and compassion for all humanity. Mennonite colleges therefore attempt to nurture both a sense of belonging within the church community and an understanding of other peoples and cultures. These institutions tend to offer robust programs in helping professions such as teaching, ministry, and nursing as well as opportunities for service and study abroad (Sawatsky 1997).

In addition to variations by theological heritage, evangelical higher education also differs according to the level of involvement a sponsoring denomination exerts in the operations of its affiliated colleges. Benne (2001) has crafted a typology that presents four distinct forms of church-related higher education on a continuum plotting the relative strength of an institution's connection to its religious heritage: *orthodox, critical-mass, intentionally pluralist,* and *accidentally pluralist.* Benne's typology describes the character of each form across a series of dimensions, such as public relevance of Christian vision, religion/theology required courses, ethos, support by church, and governance. The two forms most relevant to evangelical higher education, the orthodox and critical-mass types, both employ the Christian vision as their organizing paradigm but differ in their membership requirements; whereas the orthodox type expects all adult members of the campus community to belong to the institution's sponsoring tradition, the critical-mass type seeks only to assemble a substantial group of denominational adherents to anchor the institution's ethos. Building on the work of Burtchaell (1998), whose case-study research demonstrated that an institution's abandonment of denominational affiliation regularly preceded a decline in its Christian character and mission, Benne crafted his typology in order to map the stages through which a church-related college would progress on its way from fidelity to founding mission to overt secularism.

Benne acknowledges that typologies, while useful as organizing tools, are also limited in that they often miss important nuances present in particular instances. Evangelical higher education illustrates this limitation, for while all evangelical colleges require a profession of Christian faith from every full-time faculty and salaried administrative staff member, most could not satisfy every dimension of the orthodox type. However, to conclude that a large proportion of evangelical colleges have started down the path to secularization would be a mistake, as current institutional practices are not necessarily indicative of an attempt to create distance from a founding church. Results of the most recent large-scale study of denominational identity among evangelical colleges substantiate this point by demonstrating the relative stasis of institutional policy in the area of governance. Glanzer, Rine, and Davignon (2013) found that at least a portion of the college trustees are appointed by the sponsoring denomination at three-quarters of church-related evangelical institutions, and an even larger proportion of these institutions—87%—require either some or all of their trustees to be members of the college's sponsoring denomination. Moreover, these membership requirements have not changed over the past twenty years at four-fifths of the colleges surveyed. In addition, Glanzer et al. found that the college president is required to belong to the sponsoring denomination at three-quarters of evangelical colleges, and that this policy has remained the same over the past two decades at 92% of the institutions surveyed.

Membership Requirements: Confessional and Behavioral Expectations

A Christian college is by definition a community of the committed. All faculty members and salaried administrators serving in evangelical colleges profess a personal faith in Jesus Christ. Across the landscape of evangelical higher education, however, one finds variation in the existence and extent of further personal requirements for participation in particular campus communities. Additional confessional and behavioral expectations for faculty and students can foster an even more distinctive educational ethos that further differentiates the evangelical college from its private nonprofit peers.

One common example is a confessional requirement for faculty. In addition to affirming personal faith in Christ, many evangelical colleges ask faculty applicants to indicate their agreement with the institution's statement of faith, and, once hired, to reconfirm that agreement annually or upon renewal of their teaching contracts. Moreover, as a measure to protect institutional integrity, some evangelical colleges require faculty members to notify the administration if their personal beliefs fall out of alignment with the institution's statement of faith. In these rare instances, typical procedure is to allow completion of the current teaching contract to facilitate a smooth transition for both the institution and the affected faculty member.

Confessional requirements range from affirmation of a basic set of evangelical theological tenets to in-depth engagement with detailed doctrinal statements. Among institutions that require assent to a particular confession, interdenominational or nondenominational colleges often take the former approach while church-sponsored colleges tend to take the latter. For example, Taylor University in Indiana requires all faculty to indicate their belief in a basic, seven-point evangelical statement of faith that details the doctrines of the Trinity, biblical authority, the incarnation of Christ, the Holy Spirit, human sinfulness, salvation by faith, and the church. Covenant College in Georgia, the official college of the Presbyterian Church in America, requires faculty applicants to respond to the thirty-three-chapter Westminster Confession of Faith by offering a rationale for any areas of disagreement.

In addition to affirmation of the institutional statement of faith, some church-related evangelical colleges expect their faculty members to belong to congregations within the sponsoring denomination. Glanzer, Rine, and Davignon (2013) found that only 8% of denominationally affiliated evangelical colleges require their entire faculty to be members of the sponsoring church. One example of an institution that adheres to this employment policy is Calvin College in Michigan, which not only requires all of its faculty members to affirm a set of confessions of faith and to be active members in good standing at a congregation of the Christian Reformed Church (CRC) or a denomination in ecclesiastical fellowship with the CRC, but also expects that faculty will provide their children with Christian schooling for grades K-12. Another 51% of church-related evangelical colleges require at least some of their faculty to belong to the sponsoring denomination, presumably those persons teaching in the religion or theology department; Glanzer, Rine, and Davignon found that 43% of evangelical colleges require all faculty in this discipline to hold membership in the sponsoring church.

Expectations for students who attend evangelical colleges are often more behavioral than confessional. Rine (2012) found that 39% of CCCU member institutions require a profession of faith to attend, and 62% of this subset require that students sign a lifestyle covenant that governs both on- and off-campus behavior. Every CCCU institution prohibits premarital sex and academic dishonesty, while nearly all prohibit alcohol (98%) and tobacco use (96%), and about a third prohibit dancing and watching R-rated movies (Rine 2012).

Academic Program: Curricular Orientation and Delivery Format

Given the natural connections between the humanities and their unique institutional missions, it is little surprise that evangelical colleges have historically placed the liberal arts at the center of their educational programs. Their foundational position within the Christian college curriculum has been justified by two main arguments: the liberal arts (1) have intrinsic value as formative resources for making students more like Christ and (2) have instrumental value as practical means for teaching students how to serve the world (Mannoia 2000).

Although the liberal arts still occupy a place of prominence within the Christian college curriculum, scholars have perceived that the character of evangelical higher education is changing. In their reexamination of Holmes' (1987) seminal work *The Idea of a Christian College,* Ream and Glanzer (2013) note that evangelical higher education has evolved significantly beyond the largely residential liberal arts colleges of Holmes' time. In particular, they cite the tremendous enrollment growth among CCCU institutions during the 1990s, which was nearly three times greater than that of all private colleges and universities and roughly seven times greater than that of all US institutions of higher education. Curricular expansion has accompanied enrollment growth: Ream and Glanzer observe that many evangelical institutions have changed their names from "college" to "university," and nearly 70% of CCCU members now call themselves universities. In addition to new majors and advanced degrees, many evangelical colleges have adopted new delivery formats, such as online education (one exemplar is Indiana Wesleyan University), and serve a more diverse range of students, such as part-time, commuter, and adult students (Ostrander 2014).

Shifts over time in the Carnegie Classifications of evangelical colleges further illustrate these trends. As many of these institutions expanded their curricular offerings to include graduate programs, they often received new basic classifications to reflect the increases in the number of graduate degrees they awarded annually. For example, from 1994 to 2010, the CCCU membership experienced a 17-percentage-point decrease in its proportion of baccalaureate and associates of arts colleges and a 17-percentage-point increase in its proportion of master's colleges and universities (Table 22.3). Beginning in 2005, the Carnegie Foundation for the Advancement of Teaching issued classifications for the undergraduate instructional program, which provided information regarding the proportion of bachelor's degree majors in the

Table 22.3 Distribution of CCCU Member Institutions by Carnegie Classifications (N = 118)

Basic Classification				
	1994		2010	
	Count	%	Count	%
Special Focus Institutions	5	4%	1	1%
Associates of Arts Colleges	5	4%	0	0%
Baccalaureate Colleges	81	69%	66	56%
Master's Colleges and Universities	26	22%	46	39%
Doctorate-Granting Institutions	1	1%	5	4%
Proportion of Bachelor's Degree Majors				
	2005		2010	
	Count	%	Count	%
Special Focus Institutions	3	3%	1	1%
Majority Arts & Sciences	10	8%	6	5%
Balanced	37	31%	35	30%
Majority Professional	68	58%	76	64%
Prevalence of Graduate Degrees Corresponding to Undergraduate Majors				
	2005		2010	
	Count	%	Count	%
Special Focus Institutions	3	3%	1	1%
No Graduate Coexistence	43	36%	26	22%
Some Graduate Coexistence	71	60%	89	75%
High Graduate Coexistence	1	1%	2	2%

Source: US Department of Education's Integrated Postsecondary Education Data System (IPEDS), Carnegie Classification: Basic, and Carnegie Classification: Undergraduate Instructional Profile.

arts and sciences versus the professional fields as well as the prevalence of graduate degree programs that correspond to undergraduate majors offered by the institution. From 2005 to 2010, there was an ever-so-slight shift within the CCCU membership toward more professional majors. The increase in graduate degree programs during this same period was more pronounced: the proportion of institutions with no graduate coexistence decreased by 14 percentage points, while the proportion of institutions with some graduate coexistence increased by 15 percentage points (Table 22.3).

Present Challenges to Evangelical Christian Higher Education

The evangelical segment of private higher education is uniquely positioned for continued success; market distinctives include a high degree of mission integrity across all facets of the institution and a personalized, holistic approach to student development. To ensure their continued survival and distinctive character, however, evangelical Christian colleges must address a number of significant challenges to their current financial models, strategies for faculty recruitment, and curricular paradigms.

Fiscal Concerns

The primacy of teaching fosters a sense of shared purpose and cohesion within the faculty ranks at evangelical colleges, as most professors devote the majority of their professional effort to classroom practice. Consequently, a relatively high percentage of faculty members serving in evangelical colleges have regular and frequent contact with a wide range of students, which enables them to collectively detect and respond to shifts in student needs and preferences in a timely fashion. Indeed, this instruction-centric orientation cultivates a campus ethos that distinguishes the evangelical college from other institutional types, such as large public universities.

Ironically, however, this near-singular focus on the teaching enterprise provides both a market distinctive and a structural challenge to financial health. For, while the public university's multiple functions may threaten to dilute its focus on the teaching enterprise, they ultimately provide a diversified portfolio of institutional revenue streams that shields the institution from fluctuations in any one area of endeavor. For example, a decline in enrollment can be offset by an increase in sponsored research, government appropriations, or hospital revenue. In contrast, because tuition is by far the largest source of revenue for the evangelical college (57% of total revenue [Fig. 22.1]), it is financially dependent upon steady enrollment from year to year.

Tuition dependence is a form of financial risk all smaller private colleges must manage. For religiously affiliated institutions, however, the risk of tuition dependence

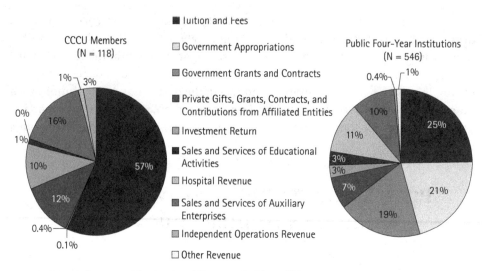

FIGURE 22.1. Sources of Institutional Revenue by Type, FY 2013

Note: Public four-year category includes only institutions using GASB accounting method.

Source: US Department of Education's Integrated Postsecondary Education Data System (IPEDS).

is compounded by potential federal mandates hostile to their core character. Because federal grants and loans finance a significant portion of the cost to attend evangelical colleges, maintaining continued eligibility to participate in the federal student aid program is paramount. When federal agencies tie institutional eligibility to compliance with mandates many evangelical colleges view as violating their religious character—such as the recent Health and Human Services contraceptive mandate requiring college health care plans to cover abortifacients—achieving this objective becomes much more difficult.

Next to tuition and fees and auxiliary enterprises (e.g. residence halls, food services, student health services), the evangelical college's largest sources of revenue are private gifts and investment return. Both of these revenue streams contribute a greater proportion to the overall budget at CCCU member institutions than they do at public universities (Fig. 22.1). Thus, an effective institutional advancement strategy and wise management of financial assets are critical; in years when enrollment declines, these areas often shoulder the burden of offsetting lost tuition revenue.

The goal of financial stability is made more difficult to attain because endowment values for the CCCU membership tend to lag behind benchmarks for the wider private nonprofit nondoctoral sector. Because the average annual operating budget for the CCCU membership is only about three-quarters the size of the average for the private nondoctoral sector ($46.3M vs. $60.0M [Table 22.4]), one would expect the average endowment for the CCCU membership to be smaller but the endowment-to-budget ratio for both groups to be comparable. However, because the average endowment value among CCCU institutions is only about a third of the average for all private nondoctoral colleges ($39.7M vs. $107.7M), the gap between the endowment-to-budget ratio for the

Table 22.4 Endowment Values and Annual Operating Budgets, FY 2013

	25th Percentile	Median	75th Percentile	Average
CCCU Members (N = 118)				
Endowment Value	$9,157,752	$20,852,864	$43,319,941	$39,732,232
Annual Operating Budget	$23,604,645	$37,093,660	$55,670,637	$46,260,769
Endowment-to-Budget Ratio	0.28	0.54	1.08	0.83
Private Nondoctoral Institutions (N = 839)				
Endowment Value	$12,953,988	$36,096,461	$93,754,316	$107,745,180
Annual Operating Budget	$24,213,904	$42,358,698	$74,670,955	$59,999,084
Endowment-to-Budget Ratio	0.41	0.85	1.59	1.41

Source: US Department of Education's Integrated Postsecondary Education Data System (IPEDS).

two groups is substantial (0.83 vs. 1.41). Although the presence of outliers at the top end of the distribution results in a positive skew for the group averages, this gap persists across all quartiles.

Evangelical colleges do not benefit from the government appropriations that public universities enjoy, but many church-related institutions have historically received financial assistance from another key source—their affiliated denominations. One recent study found that nearly three-quarters of denominationally affiliated evangelical colleges were funded by their ecclesiastical patrons, but these appropriations constituted only 4% of the institutions' annual operating budgets, on average (Glanzer, Rine, and Davignon 2013). Moreover, the authors discovered a 46% drop in average denominational funding from 2002 to 2011. This denominational divestment within evangelical higher education is cause for concern, and not just from a financial perspective: religiously affiliated institutions have historically distanced themselves from their founding traditions as a reaction to declines in financial support (Thelin 2006).

Challenges to Faculty Recruitment

A basic hurdle evangelical colleges must cross when recruiting competent faculty members is their noncompetitive compensation relative to other four-year colleges and universities (Table 22.5). Compared to the wider private nondoctoral sector, an assistant professor at a CCCU institution earns nearly 10% less in annual salary on average, and the discrepancy widens as CCCU professors progress through the faculty ranks, with the greatest gap existing for full professors (nearly 18%). Moreover, if one assumes that CCCU members must compete with institutions beyond the private nondoctoral sector, then their ability to attract the best instructors is further called into question.

Table 22.5 Average Faculty Salaries by Rank, FY 2013

	Assistant Professor	Associate Professor	Full Professor	All Ranks
CCCU Members (N = 118)	$49,381	$56,194	$65,072	$55,608
Private Nondoctoral (N = 839)	$54,154	$62,649	$76,618	$61,218
Public Nondoctoral (N = 371)	$59,073	$68,291	$84,291	$65,787
Public Doctoral (N = 175)	$70,279	$81,126	$111,600	$82,739
Private Doctoral (N = 106)	$77,661	$90,478	$129,385	$95,238

Source: US Department of Education's Integrated Postsecondary Education Data System (IPEDS).

Presumably, many faculty members choose to serve in evangelical colleges for nonmonetary reasons, such as a personal sense of calling, and few of these motivations are affected by institutional action. One significant exception, however, is tenure, which provides a sense of job security attractive to many who have chosen an academic career. Harris and Lumsden (2007) found that about one-third of all CCCU members utilized term-appointment systems rather than tenure. Although fixed-term appointments have proliferated across American higher education, at most universities they have been an addition to, rather than a replacement for, the tenure system. Thus, faculty candidates motivated by job security may find a non-tenure-track offer from an institution that utilizes a tenure system to be more attractive than an opportunity to join a CCCU institution with a term-appointment system only; the former offers the possibility, however remote, of future migration onto the tenure track, while the latter does not.

Another challenge in faculty recruitment relates to doctoral student training. As the evangelical Christian higher education movement in America matured, leaders such as Carl Henry and Billy Graham recognized its primarily undergraduate focus and general lack of high-quality graduate programs—with the exception of theological studies—and began exploring the feasibility of establishing a "Christian Johns Hopkins" to provide graduate training from an evangelical viewpoint (Ringenberg 2006). This idea would become one of the founding purposes of the Christian College Consortium (Patterson 2001), though the vision of a comprehensive Christian university was never realized. The misalignment between the doctoral training many newly minted PhDs typically receive and the teaching role they are expected to fill at the evangelical college has remained. An adjustment to the culture and responsibilities at a primarily teaching institution is often required for many recent doctoral graduates of research universities. However, the transition from a secular university to the evangelical college context can be even more stark, as few graduate students have the opportunity to think "Christianly" about their disciplines as part of their formal education.

Although many evangelical colleges offer orientation and mentoring programs designed to acclimate new faculty to the principles of integrating faith and learning, the extent and resourcing of these programs can vary widely from campus to campus. The resulting institutional gaps within the evangelical segment have often been addressed by supplemental programming offered by external organizations. In particular, three organizational types have made notable contributions to the development of the Christian college professoriate:

1. Campus-based research centers devoted to examining the relationship between Christianity and scholarship, such as the Center for Faith and Inquiry at Gordon College, the Kuyers Institute for Christian Teaching and Learning at Calvin College, and the Weyerhaeuser Center for Christian Faith & Learning at Whitworth University
2. National disciplinary associations offering opportunities for presentation of scholarship at annual conferences, publication of peer-reviewed research, and professional networking, such as the Association of Christian Economists, the Society of Christian Philosophers, and the Conference on Christianity & Literature
3. Faculty development programs designed to connect Christian academics and foster a theological consideration of the academic vocation, such as the Lilly Fellows Program in Humanities and the Arts and the Emerging Scholars Network of InterVarsity Christian Fellowship.

A fourth organizational type, the national higher education association, likely holds the greatest promise for developing the Christian college professoriate in a targeted yet comprehensive manner. The CCCU has historically provided professional development programming for faculty members and administrators serving within its member institutions. By leveraging its national profile, the CCCU can continue to set an agenda for faculty development within the evangelical college context, attract resources to support programming, and disseminate supplemental content throughout its membership. Moreover, by extending professional development opportunities to future faculty members as they complete their doctoral training, the CCCU can significantly enhance and enlarge the potential pool of Christian college faculty candidates.

Perhaps most important to the future of Christian higher education is the ability of evangelical colleges to maintain their distinctive character by exercising their legal right to hire only professing Christians as full-time faculty, a concern that has remained central to the advocacy work of the CCCU (Patterson 2006). In a recent landmark case, *Hosanna-Tabor Evangelical Lutheran Church and School v. Equal Employment Opportunity Commission* 565 US 171 2012, the US Supreme Court ruled unanimously that federal discrimination laws do not apply to religious organizations' selection of religious leaders. Although the ruling suggests that this "ministerial exception" can apply both to Christian colleges as religious organizations and to Christian college faculty members as religious leaders, subsequent case law will elucidate the exact scope and application of this legal doctrine.

Curricular Considerations

As noted above, the integration of faith and learning served as the dominant organizing paradigm for evangelical higher education for much of the twentieth century, providing curricular direction and purpose across multiple academic disciplines and Protestant faith traditions. More recently, however, the continued suitability of the integration paradigm has been called into question on various grounds. One line of critique explores the limitations of its theological framework. Jacobsen and Jacobsen (2004) argue that the integration paradigm's Reformed (i.e., Calvinist) vision of Christian scholarship can restrict its applicability to faculty working within other theological traditions, as many core theological concepts of non-Reformed traditions do not translate well to the language of the integration model. Consequently, they contend, admiration for the explanatory power of the integration paradigm must be tempered by the recognition that it is only one of many legitimate ways to frame the task of the Christian scholar.

Others have interrogated the language employed by the integration paradigm. Observing that the human need to integrate faith and learning results from a state of fallenness and lack of omniscience, Glanzer (2008) proposes that the phrase "creation and redemption of scholarship" more closely mirrors the actions of God as described in the Bible. Moreover, he ventures that Christian scholars who engage in this work can more completely fulfill their potential as divine image bearers in their academic vocations. Objecting to its underlying modernist sensibilities, Dowling (2004) argues that the term "integration" is informed by a conception of persons as autonomous beings who blend faith and scholarship into a unified whole. Building on the postmodern insight that the self is informed by multiple and at times differing discourses, she submits instead the "imbrication of faith and learning," a phrase suggesting that the identity of the Christian scholar results from various vocabularies that may not completely reconcile but will always overlap.

A final type of criticism has questioned the appropriateness of the integration paradigm for our present postmodern cultural context. Smith (2012) contends that the integration paradigm is grounded in a modernist anthropology that views persons as principally cognitive beings whose faith is revealed through belief in a set of propositions, rather than affective creatures whose faith is embodied by the practices of worship. In place of the integration paradigm, he advocates for an "unapologetic" Christian scholarship grounded in the social imagery of religious ritual. Rine (2013) highlights the discordance between the pluralism and heterogeneity of postmodernity and the exclusionary tendencies of the integration paradigm, suggesting instead a fallibilist institutional orientation that approaches diversity as a potential source of greater understanding rather than an automatic threat to orthodoxy.

As evangelical higher education reconsiders, revises, or even replaces the integration paradigm, attention must be paid not just to the task of the Christian scholar but also to the educational outcomes of Christian college students. Evangelical colleges must be able to articulate and demonstrate the competencies their graduates obtain beyond the standard outcomes of a liberal arts education, such as broad content knowledge and critical thinking and communication skills. This imperative is amplified by the heightened attention paid throughout American higher education to spirituality in the name of holistic student development (e.g., Love and Talbot 2000). Moreover, recent national studies of the religious and spiritual lives of college students (Astin, Astin, and Lindholm 2011) and faculty members (Lindholm 2014) have created space in the wider academy for investigation and discussion of issues at the heart of evangelical higher education.

This newfound legitimacy is not without its challenges, however. As nonsectarian institutions begin to embrace and attend to the spiritual dimension of college student development, the contrast between evangelical and nonsectarian higher education in the area of spiritual development becomes less pronounced. Add to this the prevalence of para-church campus student groups and the lower tuition charged by public universities, and prospective Christian college students may conclude that the benefit of a Christian college experience does not outweigh its additional cost, given the alternatives. For a heavily tuition-dependent segment, even a minor shift in this direction could spell serious trouble. To flourish in this environment, evangelical higher education must define its desired student outcomes and articulate why the Christian college context is uniquely suited to foster those outcomes.

One important step toward accomplishing this goal is to identify an instrument that translates across various contexts, though this task may prove difficult. Measures of religiosity and spirituality are legion (Hill and Hood 1999), yet instruments that are theoretically grounded in evangelical theology and evidence sound psychometric properties are far less common. One instrument that appears to meet both of these criteria is Hall's Spiritual Transformation Inventory (STI). Based on the earlier Spiritual Assessment Inventory (Hall and Edwards 1996, 2002), the STI seeks to measure a broadly evangelical relational spirituality applicable across multiple differing Protestant faith traditions and has demonstrated both statistical reliability and construct validity (Hall 2013). Whether or not the STI gains wide acceptance among evangelical colleges and universities, it is important that these institutions employ standardized instruments so that they can measure student spiritual growth over time, investigate which aspects of the Christian college experience are most impactful, and use empirical data to inform institutional practice. Moreover, adoption of a common measure across evangelical higher education would empower individual colleges to benchmark their performance against peer and aspirant institutions.

Conclusion

The structural challenges faced by the evangelical segment mirror those encountered by the larger private sector of American higher education. How to finance and resource a largely residential, cost-intensive educational model is the critical question of our day. Evangelical colleges and universities are well positioned to navigate this uncertain terrain, as they possess a market distinctive few of their competitors can claim. For these institutions, religious affiliation is not simply an historical artifact or some vestige of the past that has yet to fall away, but rather a touchstone that centers all aspects of campus life, giving a shared sense of purpose to institutional actors and a clear direction for organizational action. This robust and enduring model of higher education not only provides historical continuity with the earliest American colleges and universities, but it also offers a coherent vision of beauty, truth, and goodness that is comprehensive enough to address contemporary societal concerns. Articulation of this virtue can offer an effective counter to the now-dominant utilitarian justifications for a college education as well as a compelling invitation to prospective students, donors, and faculty.

Unlike many segments of higher education that are organized around structural factors such as enrollment size, Carnegie Classification, or governance structure, evangelical colleges and universities are bound together by their shared mission: advancing the cause of Christ-centered higher education. This shared commitment to a movement greater than any one institution is the great strength of evangelical higher education. Thus, although individual campuses often must compete for the same students and resources, the segment as a whole has a long history of mutual support. Indeed, the diversity of institutional types within the evangelical segment cultivates a fertile ground for rich discussion of institutional identity, positioning, and practice, and it curates a wide range of resources from which individual institutions can draw support and inspiration. As evangelical colleges seek to balance adaptation with constancy, their long-term success will depend largely upon this continued collaboration.

Future Directions

1. How can evangelical colleges and universities reformulate their financial models to increase their likelihood of survival? What theological frameworks might be accessed to reimagine how students pay for a Christian college education and how resources are procured and deployed to support the work of these institutions?
2. What types of professional training and socialization best prepare future evangelical college faculty? What types of programs or resources would equip rising scholars to serve in the Christian college context?
3. Is there an organizing paradigm that is sufficiently biblical, ecumenical, and culturally attuned to provide cohesion among the diverse theological traditions of American evangelicalism? Would this new organizing paradigm replace previous models, such as the integration of faith and learning, or should it serve as an umbrella that accommodates multiple models?

REFERENCES

Astin, A. W., H. S. Astin, and J. A. Lindholm. 2011. *Cultivating the Spirit: How College Can Enhance Students' Inner Lives*. San Francisco: Jossey-Bass.

Benne, R. 2001. *Quality with Soul: How Six Premier Colleges and Universities Keep Faith with Their Religious Traditions*. Grand Rapids, MI: Wm. B. Eerdmans Publishing Co.

Braskamp, L. A., L. C. Trautvetter, and K. Ward. 2006. *Putting Students First: How Colleges Develop Students Purposefully*. Bolton, MA: Anker Publishing Company, Inc.

Bratt, J. D. 1997. "What Can the Reformed Tradition Contribute to Christian Higher Education?" In *Models for Christian Higher Education: Strategies for Survival and Success in the Twenty-First Century*, edited by R. T. Hughes and W. B. Adrian, 125–140. Grand Rapids, MI: Wm. B. Eerdmans Publishing Co.

Burtchaell, J. T. 1998. *The Dying of the Light: The Disengagement of Colleges and Universities from Their Christian Churches*. Grand Rapids, MI: Wm. B. Eerdmans Publishing Co.

Carlburg, R. J. 2002. "The Evangelical Vision: From Fundamentalist Isolation to Respected Voice." In *The Future of Religious Colleges: The Proceedings of the Harvard Conference on the Future of Religious Colleges, October 6–7, 2000*, edited by P. J. Dovre, 224–245. Grand Rapids, MI: Wm. B. Eerdmans Publishing Co.

Dowling, C. L. 2004. "Imbricating Faith and Learning: The Architectonics of Christian Scholarship." In *Scholarship & Christian Faith: Enlarging the Conversation*, edited by D. Jacobsen and R. H. Jacobsen, 33–44. New York: Oxford University Press.

Glanzer, P. L. 2008. "Why We Should Discard the Integration of Faith and Learning: Rearticulating the Mission of the Christian Scholar." *Journal of Education and Christian Belief* 12, no. 1: 41–51.

Glanzer, P. L., P. J. Rine, and P. Davignon. 2013. "Assessing the Denominational Identity of American Evangelical Colleges and Universities, Part I: Denominational Patronage and Institutional Policy." *Christian Higher Education* 12, no. 3: 181–202.

Hall, T. W. 2013. "Spiritual Transformation Inventory Technical Report." http://drtoddhall.com/wp-content/uploads/2015/03/STI-2.0-Technical-Report-REV-3-25-15.pdf

Hall, T. W., and K. J. Edwards. 1996. "The Initial Development and Factor Analysis of the Spiritual Assessment Inventory." *Journal of Psychology and Theology* 24, no. 3: 233–246.

———. 2002. "The Spiritual Assessment Inventory: A Theistic Model and Measure for Assessing Spiritual Development." *Journal for the Scientific Study of Religion* 41, no. 2: 341–357.

Harris, S., and D. B. Lumsden. 2007. "Tenure Policies and Practices of American Evangelical Colleges and Universities: Part 3: Schools Not Granting Tenure." *Christian Higher Education* 6, no. 1: 1–13.

Hasker, W. 1992. "Faith-Learning Integration: An Overview." *Christian Scholar's Review* 21, no. 3: 234–248.

Hill, P. C., and R. W. Hood, Jr., eds. 1999. *Measures of Religiosity*. Birmingham, AL: Religious Education Press.

Holmes, A. F. 1987. *The Idea of a Christian College*, rev. ed. Grand Rapids, MI: Wm. B. Eerdmans Publishing Co.

Hughes, R. T., and W. B. Adrian, eds. 1997. *Models for Christian Higher Education: Strategies for Survival and Success in the Twenty-First Century*. Grand Rapids, MI: Wm. B. Eerdmans Publishing Co.

Jacobsen, D., and R. H. Jacobsen. 2004. *Scholarship & Christian Faith: Enlarging the Conversation*. New York: Oxford University Press.

Lindholm, J. A. 2014. *The Quest for Meaning and Wholeness: Spiritual and Religious Connections in the Lives of College Faculty*. San Francisco: Jossey-Bass.

Litfin, D. 2004. *Conceiving the Christian College*. Grand Rapids, MI: Wm. B. Eerdmans Publishing Co.

Love, P., and D. Talbot. 2000. "Defining Spiritual Development: A Missing Consideration for Student Affairs." *Journal of Student Affairs Research and Practice* 37, no. 1: 21–35.

Mannoia, V. J. Jr. 2000. *Christian Liberal Arts: An Education That Goes Beyond*. Lanham, MD: Rowman & Littlefield Publishers, Inc.

Ostrander, R. 2014. *Reconsidering College: Christian Higher Education for Working Adults*. Abilene, TX: Abilene Christian University Press.

Patterson, J. A. 2001. *Shining Lights: A History of the Council for Christian Colleges & Universities*. Grand Rapids, MI: Baker Academic.

———. 2006. *Shining Lights and Widening Horizons: A History of the Council for Christian Colleges & Universities, 2001–2006*. Washington, DC: CCCU.

Ream, T. C., and P. L. Glanzer. 2013. *The Idea of a Christian College: A Reexamination for Today's University*. Eugene, OR: Cascade Books.

Rine, P. J. 2012. *Charting the Terrain of Christian Higher Education in America: A Profile of the Member Institutions of the Council for Christian Colleges & Universities*. Washington, DC: CCCU.

———. 2013. "Christian College Persistence in the Postmodern Turn." In *Spirituality in College Students' Lives: Translating Research into Practice*, edited by A. B. Rochenbach and M. J. Mayhew, 69–87. New York, NY: Routledge.

Ringenberg, W. C. 2006. *The Christian College: A History of Protestant Higher Education in America*, 2nd ed. Grand Rapids, MI: Baker Academic.

Sawatsky, R. J. 1997. "What Can the Mennonite Tradition Contribute to Christian Higher Education?" In *Models for Christian Higher Education: Strategies for Survival and Success in the Twenty-First Century*, edited by R. T. Hughes and W. B. Adrian, 187–199. Grand Rapids, MI: Wm. B. Eerdmans Publishing Co.

Schuman, S. 2010. *Seeing the Light: Religious Colleges in Twenty-First-Century America*. Baltimore: Johns Hopkins University Press.

Smith, J. K. A. 2012. "Beyond Integration: Re-Narrating Christian Scholarship in Postmodernity." In *Beyond Integration? Inter/Disciplinary Possibilities for the Future of Christian Higher Education*, edited by T. C. Ream, J. Pattengale, and D. L. Riggs, 19–48. Abilene, TX: Abilene Christian University Press.

Stanley, J. E., and S. C. Stanley. 1997. "What Can the Wesleyan/Holiness Tradition Contribute to Christian Higher Education?" In *Models for Christian Higher Education: Strategies for Survival and Success in the Twenty-First Century*, edited by R. T. Hughes and W. B. Adrian, 313–326. Grand Rapids, MI: Wm. B. Eerdmans Publishing Co.

Thelin, J. R. 2006. "Small by Design: Resilience in an Era of Mass Higher Education." In *Meeting the Challenge: America's Independent Colleges and Universities Since 1956*. Washington, DC: Council of Independent Colleges.

Woodrow, J. 2006. "Institutional Mission: The Soul of Christian Higher Education." *Christian Higher Education* 5, no. 4: 313–327.

FURTHER READING

Carpenter, J. A., and K. W. Shipps. 1987. *Making Higher Education Christian: The History and Mission of Evangelical Colleges in America*. Grand Rapids, MI: Christian University Press.

Dockery, D. S. 2008. *Renewing Minds: Serving Church and Society through Christian Higher Education*. Nashville, TN: B&H Academic.

Marsden, G. M. 1994. *The Soul of the American University: From Protestant Establishment to Established Nonbelief*. New York: Oxford University Press.

Ream, T. C., J. Pattengale, and D. L. Riggs (Eds.). *Beyond Integration? Inter/Disciplinary Possibilities for the Future of Christian Higher Education*. Abilene, TX: Abilene Christian University Press.

Smith, D. I., and J. K. A. Smith. 2011. *Teaching and Christian Practices: Reshaping Faith & Learning*. Grand Rapids, MI: Wm. B. Eerdmans Publishing Co.

Wolterstorff, N. 2004. *Educating for Shalom: Essays on Christian Higher Education*, edited by C. W. Joldersma and G. G. Stronks. Grand Rapids, MI: Wm. B. Eerdmans Publishing Co.

CHAPTER 23

....

CATHOLIC HIGHER
EDUCATION

....

MICHAEL GALLIGAN-STIERLE AND PAULA MOORE

INTRODUCTION

THIS chapter provides an overview of Catholic higher education in the United States, primarily the major themes that have developed in the twentieth and twenty-first centuries. "Catholic higher education" is defined as colleges and universities affiliated with the Roman Catholic faith, generally through founding by a Catholic religious order of priests, sisters, or brothers, or through affiliation with a Catholic diocese. Broad issues related to higher education in the United States, such as curricula, student demographics, and financing, are not covered, except as those issues may have distinctive features related to the Catholic faith.

HISTORY

In 1789, John Carroll, Archbishop of Baltimore, secured the deed to sixty acres of land on a hilltop overlooking the Potomac River in Washington, DC. On this parcel, Carroll founded what is now Georgetown University, where classes began in 1792. According to the university's website, "Within the first year, attendance grew to more than 40 students, from as far away as the West Indies. In 1817, the school awarded its first two bachelor's degrees."

Georgetown, the first Catholic college to open in the United States, is now one of approximately 250 such institutions. Most trace their nineteenth- or early twentieth-century origin to a particular founding religious community of men or women—Jesuits, Dominicans, Franciscans, Benedictines, Mercy Sisters, and so forth—often responding to the needs of Catholic ethnic groups that had immigrated to the country. Many of these immigrant groups looked to parochial elementary and secondary schools both to protect their religion and to enhance their culture and language, desires that were gradually extended to their hopes for postsecondary education (Hennesey 1983). This foundation in serving first-generation college students continues to distinguish many Catholic colleges.

Through the 1800s, many other Catholic colleges opened their doors, including such notable institutions as the University of Notre Dame (1842); the College of Notre Dame of Maryland (1895), the first US Catholic college for women to award a four-year baccalaureate degree; and the Catholic University of America (1887), the only university founded by the US bishops. While society at this time generally gave little heed to the higher education of women, Catholic women religious "opened a coterie of Catholic women's colleges" during the late nineteenth century (Mahoney 2002, 25). By the middle of the next century, Catholic women's colleges were educating more women than their non-Catholic counterparts (26).

The majority of Catholic colleges and universities were founded by and continue to be sponsored by particular religious congregations. Examples include twenty-eight universities founded by the Jesuits, sixteen founded by the Sisters of Mercy, six founded in the LaSallian tradition, and four founded by the Ursuline Sisters. Despite differences in origin or geographical location, by the mid-twentieth century, the roughly 250 Catholic colleges and universities in the United States shared certain elements (Gallin 2000). Gallin points out that by the 1960s, these institutions shared similar missions, as well as a common commitment to the liberal arts, character formation, and sense of campus community "openly proclaimed as rooted in their Catholic faith" (1).

Gallin also finds that during the years that followed, Catholic colleges struggled both to assert their distinctiveness within the broader higher education landscape, and to garner respect for the value of their academic and intellectual endeavors. She documents the ongoing struggles related to academic freedom at Catholic colleges during the 1950s and beyond, and how these discussions shaped contemporary Catholic higher education. Shortly thereafter, the Second Vatican Council (1962–1965) would harness an "intellectual ferment" that found voice in the work of the Council and resonated throughout Catholic higher education, particularly with regard to two themes: (1) the necessity for the Church to recognize the autonomy of scientific knowledge in the search for the truth and (2) a conviction that the gift of human freedom demanded respect for individual consciences (Gallin 2000, 22).

During this time, the precise nature of the organizational structure, academic curriculum, and canonical function of Catholic higher education institutions drew a multitude of opinions (Gleason 1995). As a result, it wasn't until the 1960s that the contemporary definition of a "Catholic university" finally began to come into focus.

James J. Conn, SJ, cites various avenues to define Catholic universities and concludes that a Catholic institution of higher education is both a place of higher learning and one that remains faithful to the teachings of the Catholic Church, noting that "a university itself must profess its Catholic identity precisely as a university": "The particular means which a university employs in the pursuit of its purpose are those which are proper to itself, namely, serious scholarship and cooperation among the various branches of academic study" (Conn 1991, 18–19).

A New Era

Conn's definition portends the words of *Ex corde Ecclesiae,* the apostolic constitution for Catholic colleges and universities issued by Pope Saint John Paul II in 1990. *Ex corde* ushered in a new era for American Catholic higher education and remains an essential reference for US Catholic colleges and universities. According to that document, Catholic institutions of higher learning share four characteristics:

- A Christian inspiration not only of individuals, but also of the university community as such
- A continuing reflection in the light of the Catholic faith upon the growing treasury of human knowledge, to which it seeks to contribute by its own research
- Fidelity to the Christian message as it comes to us through the Church
- An institutional commitment to the service of the people of God and of the human family in their pilgrimage to the transcendent goal which gives meaning to life (*Ex corde*, par. 13).

The years since the release of *Ex corde* have been marked by renewed attention to Catholic identity and university mission and its implications for academics, governance, and operation, particularly the indication found within *Ex corde* that "in a Catholic university . . . Catholic ideals, attitudes, and principles penetrate and inform university activities" (*Ex corde*, par. 14).

Similarly, the *Application of Ex corde Ecclesiae for the United* States (US Conference of Catholic Bishops 2012) issued ten years later, sparked the continuation of a national dialogue and a renewed sense of commitment to and clarity about Catholic identity across the sector—a dialogue that continues to the present day. Institutions engage in a continued refinement of what it means to be *Catholic* in their identity and a *university* in their mission, using Catholicism to inform institutional decisions and engaging society in addressing topics that reverberate throughout Catholicism, academia, and the world at large: research, diversity, religious formation, internationalization, the labor market, and so forth.

US Catholic Higher Education Today

The strength of Catholic colleges and universities in the United States derives from several factors, none more apparent than its diversity. Consider a few statistics from the Association of Catholic Colleges and University (ACCU)'s website:

- There are 247 Catholic degree-granting institutions in the United States.
- 210 enroll undergraduate students in programs leading to a bachelor's degree.
- Eleven institutions grant only associate degrees.
- 210 Catholic universities award advanced degrees. This total includes six medical schools, 46 schools of engineering, 28 law schools, 128 schools of nursing, and 184 schools of education.
- Twelve Catholic colleges are women's colleges.
- US Catholic higher education serves nearly 875,000 students.
- More than 70% of US Catholic colleges and universities are led by nonordained presidents.

As noted earlier, the majority of Catholic institutions of higher education are sponsored by their founding religious congregations (although approximately a dozen universities are affiliated with the local diocese and about ten are independent). These religious orders reflect a variety of perspectives on how to live out the Catholic faith. The particular *charism* of the order derives from its founder's lived experience and emphasis on certain characteristics and priorities. For instance, the Dominican order was founded in the early thirteenth century by Saint Dominic, who saw the need for greater education; thus, the order actively engages in teaching "to combat heresy and propagate religious truth" (Religious Vocations, 107). In addition to the Dominicans, among the most prolific orders in establishing institutions of higher education in the United States are the Mercy, Jesuit, Benedictine, and Franciscan orders, as well as the Sisters of Saint Joseph and the Sisters of Charity.

Regardless of their individual perspectives, these charisms are united by their embrace of the Catholic intellectual heritage that makes itself discernible throughout the curricula. Catholic higher education employs this Catholic intellectual tradition to integrate and understand its academic disciplines through three fundamental beliefs: *sacramentality* (seeing God in all things), *mediation* (using the human, the material, the finite), and *communio* (seeking the unity of humankind). As a result, many Catholic institutions base their core curriculum in the humanities, requiring undergraduates to take two theology and two philosophy courses, one of which is a morals course. Similarly, the values of Catholic social teaching—a commitment to the poor and vulnerable founded on the life and words of Jesus Christ—are integrated into both curricular and co-curricular activities.

From an administrative perspective, Catholic universities seek to integrate their Catholic identity and advancement of the common good in an authentic and effective way into not only curricular choices, but also university protocol. The task of the institution is to help students, faculty, and other employees understand and appreciate the value that this brings. On many Catholic campuses, extra effort is made to create initiatives wherein Catholic identity and university mission can be summarized clearly and concisely for those throughout the university. This often helps those throughout the entire university articulate and embrace the distinctive mission of the institution and its founding charism.

Distinctive Qualities of US Catholic Higher Education

One of the hallmarks of Catholic higher education in the United States is its intentional contribution to Catholicism in ways that benefit both the individual and the community. Students, faculty, administrators, and other members of the Catholic campus find a particular environment that supports intellectual development and faith formation.

Students

Enrollment in Catholic institutions of higher education continues to grow. During the 2011–12 academic year, according to the ACCU's website, Catholic higher education educated more than 940,000 students, a figure that represents dramatic growth in overall student enrollment over the previous decade. The percentage of Catholic students at these universities varies; at some institutions, Catholic students represent more than 90% of students, while others serve increasingly non-Catholic populations. In his 2010 speech to the ACCU, Yanikoski noted the decline in recent decades in the proportion of students at Catholic universities who identified themselves as belonging to Catholicism. He cited several contributing factors, in particular the closing of numerous Catholic grade schools and high schools, which traditionally acted as feeders to Catholic higher education, as well as changes among Catholic families. "Their commitment to Catholic education at all levels has diminished over time," he asserted.

While some observers are critical of this reality, others remain firm that Catholic higher education is stronger, broader, and more effective because different institutions tend to different populations and different needs. Indeed, *Ex corde* asks institutions both to embody a Catholic institutional identity and to welcome all to their doors. Catholic health care and Catholic social service agencies provide a useful parallel: they provide care in a Catholic context to all comers, regardless of religious affiliation.

This open-door approach extends to students with financially limited means. Many Catholic campuses exhibit an explicit commitment to educate students seeking to rise above financially constrained backgrounds, often stemming from the principles of their institutional founders. Embrace of that historical mission remains a guiding force for institutional financial aid practices and drives efforts to keep access to Catholic higher education affordable in the United States. This is an especially critical issue at present, as debates about spiraling costs dominate the national conversation about higher education. As of the 2012–13 academic year, according to the ACCU's website, more than two-fifths of US Catholic colleges and universities had at least 40% of full-time, first-time undergraduates receiving Pell Grants (the federal need-based grants program for low-income students). In addition, 96% of all full-time, first-year students at Catholic campuses receive some form of financial aid, with the amount of aid awarded across all

Catholic colleges averaging $16,295. As a portion of this, institutional aid is awarded to 88% of students on US Catholic campuses, averaging about $12,100.

Driving this commitment to openness is the firmly held principle that all people should have the opportunity to grow personally and spiritually within the intellectual environment of a university. To that end, Catholic colleges and universities are uniquely positioned to integrate intellectual progress with spiritual growth. Addressing questions of meaning and supporting students' holistic personal development remain essential to the mission and reflect the core values, beliefs, and commitments of Catholic colleges and universities.

Independent studies have demonstrated that students are eager for this type of attention. Research has shown that 65% of all Catholic college alumni said they "benefited very much from an emphasis on personal values and ethics," compared with the 21% of public university alumni who said the same (Hardwick Day 2011, slide 36). More anecdotal findings have shown that students of all faiths, including (most recently) Muslim students, increasingly find contentment at Catholic universities because these campuses allot space for spiritual formation, whatever a student's particular religious identity. As a community, Catholic universities are noted for their efforts in interfaith and ecumenical dialogue.

Catholic colleges and universities also help students look outward, preparing them to engage with the society and culture around them in an authentically and thoughtfully Catholic way. The concern for social justice, both as an institutional priority and a curriculum hallmark, is among the more readily identifiable characteristics of US Catholic higher education.

Students are invited to view their eventual careers and callings as vocations in service of the common good. Catholic social teaching is applied across disciplines in ways particular to the standards of those disciplines and as a means to foster interdisciplinary dialogue and cooperation. Education from this framework also incorporates a service-learning approach, which helps students experience solidarity with their community while developing the intellectual capabilities to confront social issues. In this way, Catholic colleges and their students address both academic and community needs, thus engaging in an education that intellectually and practically meets the standards of Church teaching. Research has shown that three of every four Catholic institution graduates had volunteered or otherwise participated in community service during college, compared with fewer than six in ten public college graduates or seven in ten graduates of non-Catholic private colleges in the United States (Hardwick Day 2011, slide 25).

Faculty

On any campus—Catholic or secular—faculty are hired for their expertise in a particular discipline, for a promising research agenda, and for their instructional skills. At a Catholic college or university, faculty also lie at the heart of the institution in advancing its Catholic identity. At a Catholic institution of higher education, faculty members have the unique opportunity to seek truth through their teaching and research, whether in the humanities or in the sciences, and elevate a teaching job to the level of vocation, or calling.

Faculty at Catholic colleges and universities are encouraged to embrace this vocational view in service of the institutional mission to change the lives of students, contribute to contemporary culture, and be enriched from and help advance the Catholic intellectual tradition. *Ex corde*, in fact, endorses the value of faculty contributions, whether they practice Catholicism themselves or not, asking only that they respect the institution's Catholic identity: "The university community of many Catholic institutions includes members of other Churches, ecclesial communities and religions, and also those who profess no religious belief. These men and women offer their training and experience in furthering the various academic disciplines or other university tasks" (par. 26).

Helping faculty—few of whom may have a foundation in Catholic education—learn the Catholic intellectual tradition and then integrate it into their work is essential to advancing the institution's aspirations. In writing about the critical role of faculty within Catholic higher education, Heft (2015) notes that contemporary headlines may give faculty a false view of the intellectual life of a Catholic institution: "If most candidates for faculty positions have little exposure to the reality of Catholicism other than what the media provides, they will think that being a Catholic makes it impossible to have an open and robust intellectual life." On the contrary, he adds, it produces a vibrant community wholly conducive to original teaching and research: "While the Catholic Intellectual Tradition has much to offer the modern academy, any serious research, for example on the French Revolution, immunology, reform of the tax code, or in nanotechnology, can make an important contribution to the Catholic mission of a university, for it contributes to the understanding of the truth of things."

Many opportunities exist for faculty to hone their understanding in this area and enhance their own spiritual lives. Most Catholic institutions offer regular opportunities for faculty to deepen their beliefs and integrate faith with reason, often centered around the particular guiding principles of the university's charism. In addition, Collegium, a summer colloquy for faith and intellectual life, engages faculty from all traditions to discover how they can contribute to their institution's Catholic identity, while also respecting and taking advantage of their own religious perspectives and talents.

Faculty within US Catholic higher education also have access to the approximately a thousand scholarly centers and institutes that exist on their campuses. Within these ventures, faculty and other professionals explore topics as varied as ethics, justice, global studies, health sciences, interreligious studies, and many, many more. The ACCU's website houses a national database of these centers and institutes that is fully searchable, revealing the scholarly contributions that Catholic colleges and universities make beyond the classroom.

Catholic University Leadership

A distinctive feature of US higher education is governance by a board of trustees (or board of directors), generally made up of community representatives with a connection and commitment to the institution. Catholic colleges and universities are no different; trustees at these institutions, in fact, hold the primary responsibility for preserving and promoting the institution's Catholic identity and mission. Nowhere else among the multitude of Catholic institutions of higher learning worldwide is this the case to the same scope and degree. This situation is a special embodiment of the results of the Second Vatican Council, Catholic tradition, and American innovation (ACCU 2012).

Critical to fulfilling the board's responsibility is the selection and support of a president who understands, appreciates, and is committed to Catholic identity and mission as the driving force of the institution. At the time of inauguration, many new presidents make a public profession of faith, proclaiming to the community the serious nature of the president's role with regard to the mission.

Nearly two of every three Catholic university campuses are led by lay (i.e., nonordained) presidents. Prior to 2004, about half of these institutions were led by priests, sisters, and brothers. The increase in lay leadership parallels the dwindling number of men and women entering religious orders. As such, the role of Catholic university president is a fairly new phenomenon for laypersons, but one that is clearly a growing trend in the United States.

Some laypeople come to the presidency without formal religious formation and lack access to the network of Church-related resources for clerics and vowed religious serving in higher education leadership. There are numerous formation programs for new and aspiring presidents to help cultivate the knowledge and networks presidents will need, unique to the Catholic mission. For instance, the Catholic Mission Institute for New Presidents, an annual program offered to all ACCU member presidents in their first or second year of office, helps enhance their understanding of the Catholic dimensions of their new leadership role.

Efforts to groom the next generation of Catholic institution leadership are vital given the role that campus presidents can play in the public square. Observers often refer to the *bully pulpit* of the college president—that is, the position's authority and visibility. This prominence imbues campus leaders with a responsibility, at times, to take a public stand on urgent social matters from a position that is aligned with the Church's stance. A good example of this is a July 2013 letter signed by more than 100 Catholic university presidents and sent to every Catholic member of the House of Representatives calling for comprehensive immigration reform, a subject on which bishops have themselves been outspoken. The letter enabled campus leaders to voice their support for the DREAM Act, urging lawmakers to "draw wisdom and moral courage from our shared faith tradition" and recalling the value that Catholics place on human dignity and the worth of all immigrants.

Relationships between Catholic campus presidents and the local bishop are critical, given that *Ex corde* grants bishops the responsibility to

promote and assist in the preservation and strengthening of [universities'] Catholic identity. . . This will be achieved more effectively if close personal and pastoral relationships exist between University and Church authorities, characterized by mutual trust, close and consistent cooperation and continuing dialogue (Part I §3, para. 28).

Conflicts related to differing opinions about visiting speakers or campus policies that appear to run counter to Church teachings sometimes garner media attention (Redden 2009). However, what these stories often overlook is the fact that the vast majority of Catholic colleges and universities in the United States seek active participation by the local bishop and a genuinely open rapport between the bishop and the president. The Committee on Catholic Education of the US Conference of Catholic Bishops noted that

the relationship between bishops and presidents on the local level can be characterized as positive and engaged, demonstrating progress on courtesy and co-operation in the last ten years. Clarity about Catholic identity among college and university leadership has fostered substantive dialogues and cultivated greater mission-driven practices across the university (US Conference of Catholic Bishops 2012).

A working group of bishops and college presidents continues the national dialogue begun by the Committee, with the goal of advancing best practices and bringing creative new approaches to hiring for mission and the formation of trustees, faculty, and staff.

Other Campus Leaders

While trustees are charged with being the keepers of Catholic identity and university mission, it falls to campus staff to implement this reality. The Office of Student Affairs, grounded in the care of the person, is uniquely suited to advance this integrative approach, joined by the mission officer and the university ministry office.

Student Affairs

Learning that takes place within residential life, recreational and sporting activities, student life organizations, and career planning and services represents the important focus of Office of Student Affairs professionals. At a Catholic college or university, the Student Affairs office is especially distinct, charged with offering programs and services that develop students spiritually, emotionally, intellectually, and physically in the context of Catholic values and Christian community.

The Student Affairs office in this setting encourages students to learn about themselves and the world around them by taking into account the spiritual dimension of what it means to be a good and moral citizen, to lead ethically, to care for the common good, and to know and love God (ACCU 2013).

In 2007, a group of Catholic college and university Student Affairs professionals published *The Principles of Good Practice for Student Affairs at Catholic Colleges and Universities*. The publication offers a blueprint for Student Affairs practice in Catholic higher education, citing eight foundational principles that offer the ideals and aspirations of student affairs professionals who work at Catholic institutions. The *Principles of Good Practice* provides a framework for reflection, conversation, planning, staff development, and assessment for these professionals. Though many in this position are laity who receive their training from state universities, those who have appropriated a mature faith grounded in service to others contribute to strong Student Affairs offices that help Catholic college and university students grow as individuals.

Mission Office

Throughout US Catholic higher education, the dwindling number of people entering religious orders is prompting a growing reliance on laity. The trend presents a multifaceted predicament: How does an institution keep the founding charism alive on campus? How does it leverage that charism as a resource in the ongoing formation of individuals on campus? And how does it cultivate future institutional leaders who are committed to the values of the founding order?

On US Catholic campuses, keeping the founding principles alive is a primary responsibility of the mission officer, a position that has seen exponential growth on Catholic campuses since the 1980s (James et al. 2014). A highly collaborative position, the mission officer is charged with maintaining and promoting the religious heritage of the institution while remaining inclusive of people from other religious traditions and diverse backgrounds. The effectiveness of the mission officer on Catholic campuses in promoting Catholic identity has become a model for other faith-based higher education institutions.

One of the most important responsibilities of a mission officer is collaborating with the institution's board of trustees. The mission officer helps orient new board members to the Catholic identity and heritage of the institution, providing the trustees with the formation needed to carry out their roles as stewards of the mission (Galligan-Stierle 2014).

Campus Ministry

Since the late nineteenth century, the Catholic Church has sought ways to keep Catholic students in touch with their faith while in college. On a Catholic campus, this effort finds expression through campus ministry, which gathers students for prayer, worship, and learning in order that they might "bring the light of the Gospel to illumine the concerns and hopes of the academic community" (National Conference of Catholic Bishops 1985, par. 21).

Campus ministers may be laypersons, religious, or ordained and work with faculty and staff, as well as Church officials, to carry out a number of key roles. Campus ministers may, for instance, gather Catholics on campus into a religious community, attend to students' personal development from a Catholic perspective (e.g., helping them form a Christian conscience), and work to develop future leaders of the Church and society (Galligan-Stierle 1996).

No single formula exists for performing the work of campus ministry; to be most effective, it should be tailored to the needs and resources of the particular institution. As noted in *Empowered by the Spirit*, some ministries are carried out by well-organized teams and others by individuals, serving part time. Some are primarily sacramental, while others may influence policymaking on campus (National Conference of Catholic Bishops 1985, par. 9).

Regardless of structure, the personal attention and one-on-one connections between campus ministers and the students with whom they interact are especially important in carrying out the functions of the office. Church officials have praised campus ministry efforts that include focus on developing young people's personal relationship with Catholicism, particularly within a culture that often seems at odds with Church values. In *The Gospel on Campus*, the Rev. George M. Schroeder describes campus ministry as "the place where the Church can enter into dialogue with and foster community among students. Indeed, it is where the Church can assist students in developing wisdom, so vitally needed in an age of cultural challenges for the traditional-age student" (Galligan-Stierle 1996, 13–14).

CHALLENGES

In order for Catholic higher education to continue its vital mission of contributing to the growth of both individuals and the common good, those who are engaged in this enterprise must regularly examine it within the context of contemporary culture. Doing so makes clear certain challenges and issues—for instance, the effect of the declining number of religious on future leadership, as noted above.

In addition, headlines in popular media regularly decry the high cost of postsecondary education: "The Rise in Tuition Is Slowing, But College Still Costs More" (Bidwell 2013), "How the Cost of College Went from Affordable to Sky-High" (Sanchez 2014). Catholic higher education is not immune to these criticisms, nor to the broad economic factors that limit colleges' ability to reduce student costs. Increasing regulatory requirements, declining enrollments, and rising overhead costs effectively reduce colleges' ability to offer institutional aid to students (though, as previously noted, Catholic institutions on the whole offer considerable aid, especially to first-time, first-generation students). Catholic higher education is as complex as any other sector of American higher education, and while embracing its faith tradition still must contend with the realities of education financing that impact all US colleges and universities.

Aside from cost pressures, other prosaic concerns of twenty-first-century higher education include such national issues as a proposed college and university ratings system, campus sexual assaults, reform of teacher education programs, and the success of first-generation students, including those affected by immigration reform. These issues prompt conversations about government regulation and policy—conversations made more complex when the faith-based values and identity of Catholic institutions are considered.

One example concerns the Patient Protection and Affordable Care Act, designed to expand the affordability of health care insurance for Americans. In early 2012, the Obama administration released details related to one of the act's mandates, which required employers to offer coverage of contraceptive and sterilization products and services. Many faith-based institutions, including some Catholic colleges and universities, balked at the mandate, noting that such a provision violated their moral and ethical values. Over the next several years, the administration offered various "conscience protection" clauses that did little to ameliorate some institutions' objections, and a number of religiously affiliated employers filed legal suit to block implementation of the requirement.

The dialogue that developed centered on the concept of "religious liberty"—that is, the ability of a faith-based employer to conduct business in a manner consistent with its religious beliefs, free from government intrusion. The issue also became a rallying cry among Catholic campuses that faced government interference on other fronts as well. For instance, as adjunct faculty—those instructors who teach less than full time and are not eligible for the protections of tenure—on both private and public campuses began to organize into unions, the National Labor Relations Board sought to assert its jurisdiction. While much of the public conversation sought to cast Catholic campuses as dismissing principles of social justice, organizations such as the ACCU—citing numerous case precedents—asserted the right of faith-based institutions to make independent decisions when addressing conditions that affect employees, free of questions about their religious identity from government bodies using unfounded and subjective criteria.

CONCLUSION

Throughout its history, the Church has been instrumental in cultivating the intellectual life (National Conference of Catholic Bishops 1985, par. 13). Contemporary Catholic higher education in the United States remains a uniquely valuable component of the Church's mission. The more than 200 Catholic colleges and universities in the country may trace their foundations to a variety of religious orders, serve varying student profiles, and possess a range of institutional strengths, but what they share is deeper and more meaningful than any of these traits. US Catholic higher education continues to be committed to fulfilling Saint John Paul II's vision that a

> Catholic university is without a doubt one of the best instruments that the Church offers to our age which is searching for certainty and wisdom . . . The mission that the Church . . . entrusts to Catholic universities holds a cultural and religious meaning of vital importance because it concerns the very future of humanity. (*Ex corde*, par. 10, Conclusion)

FUTURE DIRECTIONS

1. How can Catholic colleges and universities in the United States continue to develop their Catholic identity and university mission amid cultural and society challenges?
2. How can Catholic higher education retain its historical commitment to serving first-generation and underserved students while responsibly addressing contemporary financial challenges?
3. How can Catholic higher education guarantee that future generations of leaders are as committed to the Catholic identity of their institutions as current and past leaders?

REFERENCES

Association of Catholic Colleges and Universities. n.d. http://www.accunet.org; accessed March 22, 2014. (See especially the FAQs section [http://www.accunet.org/Catholic-Higher-Ed-FAQs], which describes enrollment trends using data from the US Department of Education's IPEDS system.)

———. 2012. "Boards of Trustees." *Strengthening Catholic Identity* series. Washington, DC: Association of Catholic Colleges and Universities (http://www.accunet.org/Strengthening-Catholic-Identity).

———. 2013. "Student Affairs." *Strengthening Catholic Identity* series, Washington, DC: Association of Catholic Colleges and Universities (http://www.accunet.org/Strengthening-Catholic-Identity).

Association of Catholic Colleges and Universities, the Association for Student Affairs at Catholic Colleges and Universities, and the Jesuit Association of Student Personnel Administrators. 2007. *The Principles of Good Practice for Student Affairs at Catholic Colleges and Universities.*

Bidwell, Allie. 2013. "The Rise in Tuition Is Slowing, But College Still Costs More." *U.S. News and World Report*, October 24.

Conn, James Jerome, SJ. 1991. *Catholic Universities in the United States and Ecclesiastical Authority*. Rome: Pontifical Gregorian University.

Galligan-Stierle, Michael, ed. 1996. *The Gospel on Campus: A Handbook of Campus Ministry Programs and Resources,* 2nd ed. Washington, DC: United States Catholic Conference, 1996.

———, ed. 2014. *A Mission Officer Handbook: Advancing Catholic Identity and University Mission,* vol. 1. Washington, DC: Association of Catholic Colleges and Universities.

———, ed. 2015. *A Mission Officer Handbook: Collaborating with Partners,* vol. 2. Washington, DC: Association of Catholic Colleges and Universities.

Gallin, Alice OSU. 2000. *Negotiating Identity: Catholic Higher Education Since 1960.* Notre Dame, IN: University of Notre Dame Press, 2000.

Georgetown University. 2014. http://www.georgetown.edu/about/history/index.html; accessed April 9.

Gleason, Philip. 1995. *Contending with Modernity.* New York: Oxford University Press.

Hardwick Day. 2011. *A Comparative Advantage Alumni Study,* December (http://www.accunet. org/files/public/Comparative_Advantage_Summary.pdf); accessed May 8, 2014.

Heft, James L., SM. 2015. "Advancing the Mission with or without a Mission Officer: The Role of Faculty." In *A Mission Officer Handbook,* vol. 2, edited by Michael Galligan-Stierle. Washington, DC: Association of Catholic Colleges and Universities.

Hennesey, James J., SJ. 1983. *American Catholics: A History of the Roman Catholic Community in the United States.* Oxford: Oxford University Press.

James, Michael J., Oscar Mayorga, and Joseph J. Lehman, TOR. 2014. "Mission Matters: The Mission Leader—An Innovative Strategy in Catholic Higher Education." In *A Mission Officer Handbook,* vol. 1, edited by Michael Galligan-Stierle. Washington, DC: Association of Catholic Colleges and Universities.

Mahoney, Kathleen A. 2002. "American Catholic Colleges for Women: Historical Origins." In *Catholic Women's Colleges in America,* edited by Tracy Schier and Cynthia Russett. Baltimore: Johns Hopkins University Press.

National Conference of Catholic Bishops. 1985. *Empowered by the Spirit: Campus Ministry Faces the Future.* Washington, DC: National Conference of Catholic Bishops.

Pope Saint John Paul II. 1990. *Ex corde Ecclesiae: On Catholic Universities.* Vatican City: Typis Polyglottis Vaticanis.

Redden, Elizabeth. 2009. "A Special Relationship." *Inside Higher Ed,* April 10 (https://www. insidehighered.com/news/2009/04/10/scranton).

Sanchez, Claudio. 2014. "How the Cost of College Went from Affordable to Sky-High." NPR, March 18.

US Conference of Catholic Bishops. 2012. *Final Report for the 10-Year Review of The Application of Ex Corde Ecclesiae for the United States.*

Yanikoski, Richard A. 2010. "Catholic Higher Education: The Untold Story," address to the Association of Catholic Colleges and Universities, Washington, DC, February 1.

CHAPTER 24

....

RELIGION AND SPIRITUALITY IN PUBLIC HIGHER EDUCATION

....

MICHAEL D. WAGGONER

INTRODUCTION

....

RELIGION has been inextricably entwined with colleges and universities from their founding in Europe early in the second millennium through their rooting in the New World, first by Catholics in sixteenth-century Mexico, the Caribbean, and South America and then by Protestants in seventeenth-century British North America. In addition to the pervasive religious ethos of these early institutions, the early colonial colleges were of a singular identity—neither private nor public. The public–private dichotomy would come into use in US education beginning in the nineteenth century as the courts elaborated their application of the young country's constitution. The distinction between public and private would come to be important in terms of the clientele to be served, the sources of funding sought, and (in the case to be considered in this chapter) the place of religion in public institutions of higher education. Of the more than 1,800 institutions currently listed in the four-year and graduate categories of Carnegie Classification of Institutions of Higher Education—Doctoral Granting, Masters, and Baccalaureate, nearly one-third are identified as public. They constitute a majority of students enrolled, however, representing nearly 60% of the total student population in the above categories.

This chapter traces the origins of religion in public higher education in four stages: (1) from its antecedents in Europe and the British North American colonies, (2) into the first hundred years of the national experience, (3) through the publication of Darwin's *Origin of the Species* to the 1950s, and (4) continuing to the present by way of the themes and trends emerging from the 1960s that fuel the challenges surrounding religion in US public higher education today. Three themes may be seen throughout the history of religion in public institutions in the United States:

1. The accommodation of increasing religious diversity and the concomitant dilution of the exclusive dominance of Protestant Christianity and its associated privilege within public higher education
2. The conscious attention to religion and, more recently, spirituality, and their respective places in the academic and co-curricular life of public higher education
3. The continuing evolution of US law relating to the use of public resources by religious groups.

EUROPEAN ANTECEDENTS
AND COLONIAL AMERICA

The first universities in Europe and North America were suffused with religion primarily because they were creations of the Roman Catholic Church, whose expanding reach required advanced training for its priests, missionaries, and administrators. In line with such a mission where the singular truth of Christianity was assumed, the curriculum was based upon the Bible, the teachings of the Church, and selected texts that needed to be properly interpreted (Axtell 2016). The first English university, Oxford, would initially follow this model, but it and Cambridge, founded shortly thereafter, were established with a royal charter, thereby introducing a secular source of authority that some five centuries later would lead to the now-common entity of the public university.

Oxford and Cambridge (Oxbridge, as the model would become known), along with significant elements from Scottish universities, would serve as referents for the colleges that were established in the seventeenth and eighteenth centuries in British colonial North America. The basis of authority for them was also secular, a charter from the Crown, much as with Oxbridge. However, the curriculum initially followed the format of the medieval European and English universities, with the Protestant reformers now providing the interpretive lens. Just as the Catholic Church established universities to provide advanced education for clerics administering their expanding realm from 1200 forward, so the American colonists founded their colleges to provide similar education for their expanding secular civil and economic infrastructure throughout the growing colonies. The impact on the curriculum would be to dilute its heavily religious character to accommodate these expanding educational demands. As the colonies formed into the United States and these demands increased, colleges would proliferate: many of them retained religious missions and practices, while others opted for a more secular educational focus while still assuming a mostly Protestant Christian ethos.

The founding of the first colonial college illustrates this singular approach to education. In 1636 the Massachusetts General Court voted to allocate £400 to establish a "schoale or colledge" (Schlesinger 2005, 3–4). Two years later, the untimely death to tuberculosis of young Cambridge-trained minister John Harvard resulted in a bequest of £400 and 329 books from his library to this fledgling college. One year later the General Court named the college after him. Money from the public coffers combined with private resources to establish this first college in the colonies. Created by the state, the college was imbued with a Puritan Protestant ethos and was mandated to prepare clergy to carry on the true Christian message in the New World. There was no public–private dichotomy.

Higher education in the British American colonies borrowed its form, function, and curriculum from Old World models, adapting the particulars of the new colleges to the needs of the fledgling society, but the ideas emerging from the Enlightenment altered the course of the development of colleges, especially with respect to religion. French and English intellectuals articulated arguments for the preeminent use of reason to understand nature, cutting through the obfuscation of social and political convention to lay a new foundation for human progress. This new social and intellectual arrangement placed greater emphasis on individual liberty over institutional control, in the process undermining the authority of political and religious hierarchies. The emergent promise of science and the technology made possible by it created a hope that human progress could proceed without the encumbrances of authoritarian political or religious systems.

In colonial colleges Enlightenment thought came to be in tension with some traditional religious ideas. These tensions were worked out in conflict among presidents, boards, and faculty, and often new colleges were formed to either preserve traditional understandings or to incorporate and support new perspectives. In the larger colonial society, Enlightenment ideas reflected in the Declaration of Independence, for example, influenced politics, contributing to the American Revolution and the break from England (Bailyn 1967; 1992). Founders Thomas Jefferson, John Adams, and Benjamin Franklin, serving as diplomats in the French court during the American Revolution, gained further exposure to Enlightenment ideas that would find expression in the US Constitution.

THE NATION'S FIRST CENTURY

The First Amendment to the Constitution, which "prohibits the making of any law respecting an establishment of religion, impeding the free exercise of religion," was the next step in shaping the place of religion in public higher education. Central to understanding the challenges of the modern public university with respect to religion is the evolving interpretation of the religion clauses of this amendment. Among the concerns of the framers of the Constitution were individual rights: protection of such rights against political and religious infringement was a major tenet of Enlightenment ideals reflected in the founding documents of the United States. Yet along with those individual rights, political and religious freedom was guaranteed for all. Making sure that individual rights are adequately protected while not unduly infringing upon the rights of others soon became the work of the courts, continuing to this day as perhaps the most contested aspect of the Constitution.

The first Supreme Court case to take a step toward the public–private dichotomy, however, did not directly relate to the First Amendment. Awarded a charter by King George III in 1769, Dartmouth College functioned as a private corporation. When the board of trustees deposed the president in 1816, the state attempted to take over control of Dartmouth with a new board of trustees and make it a public institution controlled by the legislature. In *Trustees of Dartmouth College v. Woodward* (17 US 518 (1819)), the Supreme Court ruled for the existing Dartmouth trustees, citing the state's challenge as a violation of the contracts clause. The Court elaborated on the public–private dichotomy, circumscribing government intrusion in public settings, in coming years.

The distinction between public and private higher education institutions evolved as states began creating and funding their own colleges and universities. The first four such major universities appeared late in the eighteenth and early in the nineteenth centuries: the University of Georgia, the University of North Carolina, South Carolina College (later the University of South Carolina), and the University of Virginia. They all received financial support from their respective states in one form or another, with religious denominations playing little if any role. Under the increasing influence of Enlightenment ideals and the strictures of the First Amendment, none of these institutions was under church control, although religious toleration enabling "free exercise" was a hallmark of their character. Religious practices ranged widely. Most state colleges and universities conducted religious services; however, in the case of the University of Virginia, there was no required daily chapel attendance and no connections to religious denominations. This distancing of explicit religious control and influence and the *Dartmouth* decision were the first subtle steps in creating the public–private dichotomy that now characterizes US higher education.

These trends were supported through the Morrill Acts of 1862 and 1890. These federal land grants helped to further the proliferation of publicly funded colleges and universities, albeit often indirectly (the land was sold and the funds were in turn used to establish universities). This direct public financing of universities did not, however, require or result in the separation of religion from the institution. Examples were the publicly established and funded historically black colleges and universities that were set up following the Civil War: religious life was an integral part of these institutions from their beginning (Little 1980).

The general pattern of regulation left most control of public institutions to the states. The federal government applied its oversight comparably to public and private institutions in the wake of the 1868 ratification of the Fourteenth Amendment, mandating the application of due process and equal protection under the law to all citizens in every state.

Developments on the intellectual and cultural fronts paralleled this legal evolution, also challenging and altering the place of religion in higher education. Through the colonial period and into the early decades of nationhood, many faculty and, subsequently students encountered the "new" higher criticism developed by European scholars that challenged traditional understandings of biblical texts and, subsequently, some Christian tenets. Early national collegians also became increasingly enamored of the success and promise of modern science and technology. These intellectual, social, and cultural developments triggered challenges to their religiously based worldview, and some became distracted from or disenchanted with religious explanations that seemed less complete or compelling than the new thinking. In public colleges and universities, believers abandoned religion, sought to reconcile their beliefs with ideas emerging from science and philosophy, or compartmentalized their beliefs from their academic work.

The Protestant establishment that obtained through much of the first hundred years of the United States began, by the last quarter of the nineteenth century, to experience a slow erosion of influence that would continue through the twentieth century. This was due, in part, to the continuing waves of immigration that brought more religious diversity, particularly a more vital Catholic presence.

Mid-Nineteenth Century
THROUGH THE 1950S

The erosion and displacement of the influence of religion in US society and higher education is a complex story; however, strands of that story are illustrated in the publication of and the subsequent controversy emanating from (and reverberating down to present day) Charles Darwin's *Origin of the Species* in 1859. Darwin propounded a theory of biological evolution wherein organisms arose and developed by way of a natural selection of small, inherited variations that enhanced the organism's ability to compete for resources and reproduce ("survival of the fittest"). He based his theory on an extensive body of evidence that exemplified the increasing sophistication of modern science using empirical observation. Darwin's work also seemed to directly counter a literal reading of the Christian account of creation in Genesis.

These scientifically based ideas were conceived in the context of the growing influence of Auguste Compte, a French Enlightenment thinker who, building on the work of David Hume and Immanuel Kant, argued that the human mind can only know natural phenomena carefully observed with positive, incrementally accumulated deductions. Divine or supernatural explanation (i.e., religion) should be left behind as an earlier developmental stage of theorizing. British writer Herbert Spencer, also agreeing with Compte's naturalistic phenomenology, popularized Darwinism and extended its application to social institutions. The idea that society could evolve and that humankind could control that evolution, combined with the increasing successes of science and technology, gave rise to the idea of perhaps unlimited progress. This Progressivism captured the imagination of the intellectual elite and, subsequently, much of the general populace for decades to come. Much of this intellectual ferment occurred in colleges and the emerging research universities of the late nineteenth century, with the secondary effect of challenging religious ideas.

The reaction by the religious establishment was mixed, as churches for some time had been trying to reconcile the new findings from science with their own understandings. The challenge to religious authority that seemed to attend these new theories engendered tensions that continue to this day. These tensions stemmed from conflicting stories of the origin of the Earth as understood from a literal reading of the Christian Bible and illustrated in Bishop Ussher's famous seventeenth-century chronology dating the age of the Earth from 4004 BC. In contrast, according to the theories of Darwin and other scientists, evolution would have required millions of years. The controversy spilled immediately into higher education: a Vanderbilt University professor was fired for espousing evolution, but he was welcomed by the University of Michigan (Rudolph 1990).

For centuries the aim of higher education had been to search for the truth, as understood in Christian terms. Now the idea of truth was being more broadly cast, and religion had to compete for standing. This trend was abetted by the increasing professionalization of knowledge as disciplines and emerging academic associations and publications (e.g., American Historical Association, American Sociological Association) formed to adjudicate research and knowledge claims of the emerging fields. These groups convened conferences and created academic peer-reviewed journals to disseminate their findings. Each discipline focused on its own philosophical underpinnings and methodology. John Schmalzbauer and Kathleen Mahoney argue that the influence of Freud, Nietzsche, and Darwin cast doubts on religious understandings; as the disciplines became increasingly specialized, the emphasis came to be "to think small: to ask questions for which there were determinate and publically verifiable answers" (2012, 215). The work of these organizations was conducted primarily within the elite universities. Religious subdisciplines also followed similar paths to forming organizations, though they did not often intersect with the more positivistic philosophical stance of many of the evolving disciplines.

This period saw a continued proliferation of colleges and new universities, with most of the latter touting science and research as their animating ideal. Still other colleges were formed to defend or preserve religious orthodoxy. This differentiation of mission was consistent from the earliest establishment of colleges in colonial America. Beginning in the mid-nineteenth century, however, most state and some private institutions identified themselves as nonsectarian Christian schools. Julie Reuben describes the 1886 debate at the Nineteenth Century Club between Harvard President Charles Eliot and Princeton President James McCosh on "the Place which Religion should have in the College" (1996, 82). Eliot saw three types of higher education institutions relative to religious emphasis: denominational, partially denominational, and undenominational. McCosh's typology was simply religious or irreligious. Eliot saw a place for the denominational college where parents could have their children educated in the beliefs they desired, but he saw the undenominational institution as more openly committed to tolerance of religious difference and freedom of inquiry. The public tended to view this latter type of institution as irreligious despite Eliot and colleagues' protestations to the contrary.

McCosh and his sympathizers, like Yale President Noah Porter, supported a freedom of inquiry, though within the "essential condition" of Christian instruction. All concurred that religion was too important to not be positively supported within the university.

Eliot's position won the day. The establishment of Johns Hopkins (1876), Chicago (1890), and Stanford (1891) all cited similar arguments regarding the superiority of the unsectarian university. The Stanfords and trustees, however, did insist upon language "to prohibit sectarian instruction, but to have taught in the university the immortality of the soul, the existence of an all-wise and benevolent Creator, and that obedience to His laws is the highest duty of man" (Reuben 1996, 84).

The relative degree of freedom of inquiry was especially evident in controversies over religion and science. The "fundamentalist–modernist controversy" drew clearer lines between sectarian colleges and the emerging public universities on issues related to religion. Those seeking to defend Christianity from the perceived attack by so-called modern interpretations of scripture considered certain fundamentals to be basic to orthodoxy: (1) biblical inspiration and infallibility of scriptures, (2) virgin birth of Jesus, (3) Christ's death as atonement for sin, (4) bodily resurrection of Jesus, and (5) historical reality of the miracles of Jesus. These were first enumerated at the Niagara Bible Conferences from 1878 to 1897 and were later formalized in twelve books on five subjects published in 1910.

Colleges and universities, public and private, and seminaries were the locus for academic debate on these issues. But while these discussions were taking place regarding the place of religion in higher education, chapels were being built and services continued to be conducted across the country on campuses, private as well as public, continuing a de facto culturally Protestant Christian ethos.

The religion and science debates spilled over into the early twentieth century, as illustrated in the famous Scopes trial of 1925. In this case, high school science teacher John Scopes was tried for teaching evolution, which was judged to be contrary to the biblical account of creation. He was convicted, though the verdict was overturned on a technicality. The case was seen as a test of whether modern science should be taught in public schools. The issue reverberates into contemporary discussions of what should be taught in public education and is debated at the secondary and university levels.

World War I brought a crisis of confidence in the idea of progress that had been building through the last part of the nineteenth century and the early twentieth century: if the advances of science and technology could not produce a society that could avoid such destruction, then was the idea of perpetual progress truly viable and attainable? The failure of the League of Nations as an international forum to maintain the peace, followed by the Great Depression, World War II, and the lingering tensions of the Cold War seemed to further undercut the idea of progressive improvement of society.

Throughout this period, however, the number and types of higher education institutions continued to grow, particularly following World War II. A college degree was seen as a vehicle to a satisfying middle-class life with a good career with which to support a family. The dominant international status of the United States after the war created a period of stability and peace at home that allowed the latent Protestant ethos of the previous 150 years to solidify as the pervasive social norm of the country.

In the nearly twenty years between the end of World War II and the election of John F. Kennedy, a set of conservative cultural standards formed, "assumptions and aspirations shared by millions of Americans, that came to constitute a 'normative' America" (Hartman 2015, 5). These standards included

> hard work, personal responsibility, individual merit, delayed gratification, social mobility. . . stringent sexual and gender expectations within heterosexual marriage, a consensus around white Judeo-Christian values, and a cohesiveness required in these standards due to a shared perceived threat of Cold War and alien cultural and ideology. (Hartman 2015, 5)

The growing public higher education establishment perpetuated this Protestant norm until the turbulent 1960s set many mores on a new trajectory.

THE 1960S TO THE PRESENT

Several important features of the contemporary US cultural landscape derive from developments in the 1960s. The civil rights movement, the feminist movement, protests over the Vietnam War, and religious activism created a seismic shift in norms governing social conventions—a number of which continue to be contested today. The movement for racial equality quickened during the 1960s under the leadership of Martin Luther King, Jr., Malcolm X, and President Lyndon Johnson, resulting in groundbreaking civil rights legislation and challenging long-established white privilege. Women's rights gained momentum during this time as well, as feminists challenged the male domination of power and influence in society. The assassinations of President John Kennedy and his brother Robert, Martin Luther King, and Malcolm X; the violent protests on college and university campuses; riots in Watts, in Detroit, and at the Democratic Party convention in Chicago; and of course the polarizing Vietnam War challenged democracy's much-vaunted claim to peaceful decision-making. The war not only diverted national resources away from antipoverty programs but further undermined the authority of intellectuals in society by becoming identified as a technocratic war—that is, a war waged by intellectuals who found themselves in power rather than a "general's war" (Lora 1974, 26).

Organized religion faced significant cultural upheaval as well. A Vatican Council convened by Pope John XXIII issued liberalizing reforms in Roman Catholicism that challenged the traditionally conservative church. The "death of God" movement, though originating some 100 years prior in the work of Nietzsche, gained popularity during the 1960s, bringing another challenge to religion's authority. And while the US Supreme Court issued decisions disallowing government-sponsored Bible reading and prayer in public schools, those same decisions opened the way to teaching about religion in a nonsectarian manner in public schools, from elementary schools through higher education (*Abington Township v. Schempp*, 374 US 203 (1963)). This included the creation of an increasing number of religious studies departments in universities, which focused on the academic study of religion as distinguished from theology departments, where the focus was more on formation within religious traditions.

Another more oblique but important development in religion came in the form of the Immigration Act of 1965. The new wave of immigrants coming to the United States differed from earlier immigrants in that they were not European; rather, they were from Asia and the Middle East. While earlier immigrants were predominantly Roman Catholic and Protestant Christians, these newcomers brought primarily non-Western religious traditions. Gradually, mosques and temples appeared across the United States, challenging the architectural and ideological landscape (Eck 1993, 2003). New resources for spiritual development were introduced into the heretofore predominantly Christian culture: Transcendental Meditation, yoga, Eastern mysticism, and other practices that came to be known collectively as New Age. Many of these ideas were introduced on public college and university campuses. Though these traditions remain in the minority, their increasing presence represents another challenge to the dominant Christian influence. These ideas combined in a zeitgeist that seemed to enable an alternative vision for personal meaning and flourishing apart from religion (Waggoner 2011).

Spirituality Joins Religion in Higher Education

The radical changes involving religion in the 1960s also prepared the way for a more open treatment of spirituality in higher education. Parker Palmer introduced the idea of "education as a spiritual journey" in his 1983 book *To Know As We Are Known*. In 1993 the Council of Independent Colleges gave him an Outstanding Service to Higher Education award for his contributions reflected in this book.

The signature event that initiated this new emphasis on spirituality in higher education came in October 1998 with a conference at Wellesley College organized by Victor Kazanjian (new Dean of Religious and Spiritual Life at Wellesley) and Peter Laurence (co-founder with Kazanjian of the Education as Transformation Project). Conference planners anticipated 300 attendees and had to cut off registration at 800, so great was the interest. Parker Palmer, Diana Eck, and many other leaders in thinking about religion and spirituality in higher education spoke. A 2000 book edited by Kazanjian and Laurence collected papers from these speakers and others to reflect the state of thinking at the outset of this movement.

In 1999 the first treatment of spirituality appeared in a major peer-reviewed academic journal in higher education, Patrick Love and Donna Talbot's article in the *NASPA Journal*, "Defining Spiritual Development: A Missing Consideration in Student Affairs." Calling for attention to this neglected dimension of student development theory, they cited the founding documents of the student affairs profession in 1937, where a commitment was made to consider the student as a whole, including moral and religious values (American Council on Education 1937, 1949). Love and Talbot also developed a five-part definition for spirituality: (1) searching for personal authenticity and wholeness, (2) transcending the self, (3) connecting to self and others, (4) finding meaning and purpose, and (5) relating to the transcendent.

Also in 1999 a book appeared by Robert J. Nash, *Faith, Hype and Clarity: Teaching About Religion in America's Schools and Colleges*. Though it received less attention at first than Love and Talbot's article, Nash made a fuller case for the same issue, distinguishing "religion-less" spirituality as a legitimate alternative basis for morality in addition to religion. Nash went on to write several books and articles on spirituality as part of holistic development. During this same period Warren Nord and Charles Haynes were advocating the serious treatment of religion as an academic subject in schools, colleges, and universities (Nord 1995, 2010; Nord and Haynes 1998).

The year 2000 brought the publication of one of the most important books for conceptualizing the spiritual development of emerging adults, Sharon Daloz Parks' *Big Questions, Worthy Dreams: Mentoring Young Adults in their Search for Meaning, Purpose, and Faith*. A student and colleague of James Fowler (author of the seminal 1981 work *Stages of Faith: The Psychology of Human Development and the Quest for Meaning*), Parks extended Fowler's model of faith development with an additional nuanced phase for emerging adults, including college students. From this point forward the literature on spirituality and religion grew rapidly (Waggoner 2016).

UCLA Spirituality and Higher Education Study

It soon became clear to leading higher education scholars Alexander and Helen Astin that this burgeoning field needed better data to understand how college students thought about these issues in relation to their own development. Building on their many years of research on college students through the UCLA Higher Education Research Institute, the Astins led a team through a seven-year study (2003–2009) surveying initially a nationally representative sample of more than 112,000 students to ascertain the extent to which spirituality figures in the life of emerging adults (http://spirituality.ucla.edu/). Their book, *Cultivating the Spirit: How College Can Enhance Students' Inner Lives*, reported their results (Astin, Astin, and Lindholm 2011).

The UCLA research team organized their findings relative to spirituality and college students around five qualities: equanimity, spiritual quest, ethic of caring, charitable involvement, and ecumenical worldview. Data showed that overall, students continue to grow spiritually during college, though their overtly religious activities may decrease.

A major contributor to this spiritual growth is work related to the "inner selves" of students. Self-reflection and meditation are key vehicles to facilitate this attention to the self, and these practices, in combination with exposure to diversity, enhance students' ability to appreciate multiple perspectives. Experience with diversity may come in several forms, including study abroad, interdisciplinary study, and contact with differing people and cultures. This spiritual development contributes to students' self-confidence and academic and leadership skills as well as making them more satisfied with college.

Given that faculty members play a central role in teaching and learning interactions with students, it seemed a natural step to study faculty attitudes in this same area. This process also began with a study by the Astins in 1999. Jennifer Lindholm joined the team as they surveyed faculty in 2004–2005 and then followed in 2012 with the Faculty Beliefs and Values Survey. Significant among their findings was that faculty members at public universities agree that opportunities for religious and spiritual development are important for college students, but they are at best ambivalent about the role of the institution or faculty in facilitating such discussions (Lindholm 2014).

One further major research product came from this UCLA project, an edited volume by Alyssa Rockenbach and Matthew Mayhew (2013) of nine in-depth studies that fell into three categories: student characteristics and group differences, college contexts, and outcomes. Together they provide solid underpinnings supporting the importance and benefits of addressing religion and spirituality in all higher education institutions, including public ones.

Public higher education institutions in the United States continue to respond to the two major themes addressed so far in this chapter: the increasing religious diversity in the country and the concomitant dilution of the Protestant Christian cultural ethos that dominated much of the country's history. This is all taking place within the context of a third theme: the continuing evolution of US law regarding the use of public resources by religious education organizations.

Religion, the Constitution, and Public Higher Education

The First Amendment delineates freedoms guaranteed to its citizens, the first of which are freedom from "establishment of religion" and protection of the "free exercise of religion." The common objective of the combined clauses is to ensure government neutrality in the treatment of religion. In an important twentieth-century explanation of neutrality, Justice Tom Clark, writing the majority opinion in *School District of Abington Township v. Schempp* (374 U.S. 203 (1963)), noted the country's historic entanglements of religion and government and underscored the importance of continuing to safeguard against them. Government must neither allow the tenets of a particular religious tradition to have the force of law, nor constrain individual free exercise of religion.

Adjudicating conflicting views among the public, particularly in the area of free exercise in combination with free speech, is arguably a leading area of contemporary jurisprudence with respect to religion.

Neutrality

How one chooses to interpret neutrality is part of the issue. One may opt for a "total abstinence" perspective that invokes a strict application of separation of church and state: no religion is allowed within public institutions. Or one may opt for a "fairness" perspective of neutrality that, with an eye toward the free exercise and free speech protections, seeks an even hand in accommodating religion in public institutions. Though some believe the former should be the case (per Thomas Jefferson's famous phrase about a "wall of separation between church and state"), the Court has ruled that generally the latter is more constitutionally appropriate.

Two Court decisions underlay evolving law elucidating neutrality in public higher education. The first is *Lee v. Weisman* (505 U.S. 577 (1992)). Though set in a public high school context and reinforcing earlier landmark cases *Engel v. Vital,* 370 U.S. 421 (1962) and *Abington v. Schempp* 374 U.S. 203 (1963) it became applicable to broader contexts. The decision added a "coercion test" to the *Lemon* test to determine the appropriateness of a religious activity in a public school. Still, noncoercive religious activities were permissible without violating neutrality; they were even, in the words of Justice Clark from the *Abington v. Schempp* decision, appropriate and encouraged:

> one's education is not complete without a study of comparative religion or the history of religion and its relationship to the advancement of civilization. It certainly may be said that the Bible is worthy of study for its literary and historic qualities. Nothing we have said here indicates that such study of the Bible or religion, when presented objectively as part of a secular program of education, may not be effected consistently with the First Amendment. (*Abington v. Schempp* 226)

The second case, *Widmar v. Vincent* (454 U.S. 263 (1981)), became even more important in determining the parameters of neutrality for public higher education institutions. The Court ruled that First Amendment free speech guarantees protect student religious activities and that the Establishment Clause was not violated by policies permitting equal access to campus facilities by both religious and nonreligious groups. In *Widmar v. Vincent*, members of Cornerstone, an evangelical Christian student organization, sued the University of Missouri-Kansas City (UMKC) over denial of use of campus facilities. The group claimed this denial abridged their rights of free exercise of religion and freedom of speech. In what they saw as the spirit of the separation of church and state, UMKC had formulated a policy for facilities use prohibiting use for religious purposes. The Court treated the students' activities as religious speech and, in turn, as free speech, thereby meeting the threshold for consideration as a free speech case. Inasmuch as UMKC had created a limited public forum and open forum, the university would have to justify discrimination based on religious content as a compelling state interest. UMKC based its argument upon the Establishment Clause as such an interest, but the Court rejected this argument upon application of the tripartite *Lemon* test. According to *Lemon*, relations between government and religion are subject to three tests:

> Every analysis in this area must begin with consideration of the cumulative criteria developed by the Court over many years. Three such tests may be gleaned from our cases. First, the statute must have a secular legislative purpose; second, its principal or primary effect must be one that neither advances nor inhibits religion; finally, the statute must not foster "an excessive government entanglement with religion. (*Lemon* 403 U.S. at 612–613)

The Court rejected UMKC's argument that greater separation of church and state should override the students' free speech claim, ruling that separation is sufficiently guaranteed by the Establishment Clause and therefore this argument is not adequate to justify content-based discrimination against religious speech.

While *Widmar* is widely applicable, there remain areas where public institutions may exercise authority over student religious groups. The decision prohibits most content-based discrimination, but it does not prohibit time, place, and manner considerations. Institutions may also make discriminatory decisions based upon scarce resource allocation.

Academic Freedom and Nondiscrimination

Evolving law from the *Dartmouth* case forward established public higher education as an environment that is distinct from both private higher education and public schools. Two overarching concepts combine to guide this evolution: academic freedom and the marketplace of ideas, and nondiscrimination deriving from neutrality. The courts have held that public higher education is a unique environment in which competing ideas should be free to be tested, and no person or organization should be discriminated against in the process of this exercise of academic freedom. Religious activities became a major test of the constitutional viability of these ideas.

Academic Freedom and the Marketplace of Ideas

Healy v. James (408 U.S. 169 (1972)) is the premier case establishing the balance between institutional authority and the rights of an organization. The Court ruled that higher education institutions may not withhold recognition of student organizations over concerns about potentially disruptive intentions; rather, the institution bears the burden of justifying prior restraint in light of constitutional freedom of expression and association protections. The majority and concurring opinions of eight justices underscored that higher education institutions are important as sanctuaries of academic freedom, and in this they are distinct from other public forums.

In *Rosenberger v. Rector and Visitors of the University of Virginia* (515 U.S. 819 (1995)), the Court extended *Healy v. James* to campus student religious groups. In *Rosenberger* the University of Virginia withheld funding of a student religious group's publication on the grounds that to do so would violate the Establishment Clause. The group sued the university, arguing that their rights to freedom of speech, press, association, religious exercise, and equal protection under the law had been violated. The district court rejected the claims and the appellate court upheld the district court's holding. The Supreme Court, however, reversed the lower courts' judgments, deciding for the student organization's publication on the basis of free speech and its failure to violate the Establishment Clause. To allow the university to withhold funds from the organization would constitute viewpoint discrimination.

In this decision, the Court drew upon *Lamb's Chapel v. Center Moriches Union Free School District* (508 U.S. 384 (1993)) and *Perry Educational Association v. Perry Local Educators' Association* (460 U.S. 37 (1983)). In *Lamb's Chapel* the Court had allowed Christian groups to use public school buildings after hours (a limited public forum); to disallow such use while allowing use by secular groups would constitute viewpoint discrimination. In *Perry* the Court ruled that government guidelines may not regulate speech when the ideas are the cause for restriction. The University of Virginia had allowed a "limited public forum" in the form of the student magazine, albeit in the realm of ideas rather than facilities; consequently, withholding support was an abridgment of the group's free speech rights.

The Court has, however, recognized a "government speech" that is to be protected on par with individual speech. With its decision in *O'Connor v. Washburn University* (416 F.3d 1216 (10th Cir. 2005)), the Court brought this concept into the public higher education environment. Washburn University, a public institution, approved a public art display that offended a religious group; the group argued that the display violated its establishment rights. The Court noted the public university represents a unique marketplace of ideas, citing the precedents and rationale from *Healy v. James* and *Rosenberger v. University of Virginia*, and such differing opinions and controversies are appropriately debated in the university.

Nondiscrimination

The Fourteenth Amendment to the Constitution, ratified nearly 150 years ago, remains among the most litigated parts of the Constitution, particularly the Due Process and Equal Protection Clauses:

Section 1. All persons born or naturalized in the United States, and subject to the jurisdiction thereof, are citizens of the United States and of the State wherein they reside. No State shall make or enforce any law which shall abridge the privileges or immunities of citizens of the United States; *nor shall any State deprive any person of life, liberty, or property, without due process of law; nor deny to any person within its jurisdiction the equal protection of the laws.* (emphasis added)

Written, passed, and ratified in years immediately following the Civil War, this amendment's initial aim was to ensure citizenship for former slaves and their descendants, overruling *Dred Scott v. Sandford* (1857). Importantly, it extended First Amendment guarantees to all states. It has since seen broad application in such historic cases as *Roe v. Wade* (1973) and *Bush v. Gore* (2000).

The federal Fourteenth Amendment, as well as comparable state constitutional provisions, applies to public higher education institutions; consequently, those colleges and universities must draft policies governing institutional life in ways that do not breach the rights of its students, staff, and faculty. Federal civil rights laws may also pertain, though grounds of sexual orientation and religion are not covered by these statutes.

The initial challenges of discrimination were raised with respect to sex and race. Most recently, however, religious discrimination has generated the most controversy. Two cases in particular mark the leading edge of these discussions: *Christian Legal Society v. Martinez* (130 S. Ct. 2971 (2010)) and *Alpha Delta Chi-Delta Chi Chapter v. Reed* (648 F.3d 790 (9th Cir. 2011)). Both cases dealt with restrictive membership policies of student organizations, though the policies were materially different from each other.

Christian Legal Society involved a challenge by a student group to Hastings College of Law, part of the California state system. The group sought to be a recognized student organization at Hastings, which would afford them access to resources and the imprimatur of the college. The group required prospective members to sign a Statement of Faith stipulating beliefs and behavior, including rejection of "unrepentant homosexual conduct." Hastings refused to grant the group recognized student organization status, arguing that the organization's membership requirements represented a breach of its nondiscrimination policy that allowed anyone to pursue membership in and leadership of a student organization. The Supreme Court, in a 5-to-4 decision, upheld the constitutionality of Hastings' "all-comers policy" using *Rosenberger v. Rector and Visitors of the University of Virginia*'s "limited public forum" as the guiding precedent for the case. The Court concluded that the "all-comers policy" was constitutional but remanded the dispute to the Ninth Circuit for further consideration. The Justices pointed out that insofar as the lower courts failed to address whether Hastings officials selectively enforced the "all-comers policy," the Ninth Circuit had to determine whether the student group's argument remained viable. On remand the Ninth Circuit rejected the group's remaining claims (*Christian Legal Soc'y v. Wu* 2010). The court refused to allow the group's leaders to proceed with their case because they failed to preserve their argument that law school officials selectively applied the policy to their members.

In *Alpha Delta Chi*, a case following *Christian Legal Society v. Martinez*, San Diego State University (SDSU) similarly had a nondiscrimination policy regarding recognized student organizations. A Christian sorority and fraternity had applied for recognized student organization status, and as in the prior case, were denied on grounds that they discriminated based upon sexual orientation. The sorority and fraternity challenged the policy, claiming it violated their First Amendment rights of free speech, free association, and free exercise of religion. The Court determined that since SDSU's nondiscrimination policy was materially different from Hastings' policy, it was not controlling in this case. The Court did find, however, that SDSU's recognized student organization policy resulted in a "limited public forum" as with the *Christian Legal Society* case. Consequently, viewpoint neutrality, a concept central to limited public forum, was at the crux of the case. Restricting the analysis to the limited public forum issue, the Court decided that the SDSU policy did not discriminate on the basis of content of speech but was designed to remove barriers from previously excluded groups. The plaintiff's alternative argument entered territory not covered by the *Christian Legal Society* case—that is, the allegation that SDSU differentially applied its policy to other religious groups, thereby violating their free exercise and equal protection rights. The Court recognized these concerns and remanded the case to the district court for resolution. The Supreme Court later denied the plaintiff's appeal, thereby letting the appeals court decision stand.

Religious Freedom in Public Higher Education

The nature and extent of religious freedom in US public higher education is yet to be fully determined, and further litigation should be expected. Absent the constraints available to private colleges and universities to abridge individual rights in line with their missions, public institutions must operate in full accord with the Constitution as interpreted by the courts. With respect to religious freedom, this means that these institutions must continually seek to find a balance between the free exercise of individual religious freedom and the equal protection of individuals within the larger body. A few considerations should be taken into account here.

First, everyone's religious freedom must be considered. Religious freedom is not the exclusive domain of one particular individual or group along the conservative to progressive spectrum. It is the nature of religious truth claims that one group or another may assert their position as *the* exclusively correct one. We must remember that there are a number of groups—each with its own authority sources, traditions, and practices—who make what they feel is a legitimate claim to their perspective and, consequently, seek religious freedom for their exercise of it. Nevertheless, the Founders established a nation of laws rather than a theocracy; as a result, matters of law, not religious truth, are adjudicated in the courts.

Following from such a basis in law, this means that individuals with values and beliefs that they feel are irreconcilable with legal policy in a public higher education institution where they work must decide if they are able, with accommodation, or willing to work within that policy. One individual or group's religious belief or lack thereof may not have the force of law over those who do not share those beliefs. The United States has an extensive collection of private and public schools, colleges, and universities that can accommodate most all positions on the religious–nonreligious spectrum. Someone who elects to attend a public school or college, then, must expect to operate under the law of the land.

In this public context, nondiscrimination through equal protection must be the governing idea. In many instances this means finding accommodations, if possible, for minority positions. Such has been the consistent theme of the Court decisions discussed above. There remain boundaries to be contested in public institutions, and we should expect to see them challenged. For example, public institutions may now make discriminatory decisions relative to student religious groups with respect to time, place, and manner considerations as well as claims of scarce resources. One could foresee challenges here from both majority and minority religious or nonreligious groups seeking space and financial support for their initiatives.

CONCLUSION

The pursuit of religious liberty was a leading impetus of immigrants to form colonies in British America in the seventeenth century, but no sooner were these colonies established than the inhabitants disagreed, often violently, over whose religious liberty was to be recognized. Four centuries later, the place that religion should play in our institutions continues to evolve in the United States. We must be particularly careful in public higher education, where academic freedom allows for unusually wide-ranging debate, to develop policies and practices that honor the intent of our country's founding documents regarding the individual right to free exercise of religion, but in ways that do not unduly infringe upon the rights of others.

FUTURE DIRECTIONS

1. What successful models exist among public higher education institutions for addressing the religious and spiritual development of students in a constitutional manner?

2. What historical experience can guide policy development regarding religion and spirituality on a public university campus?
3. Where will future legal challenges likely come regarding religion and spirituality in public higher education institutions?

REFERENCES

The Student Personnel Point of View, 1937, 1949. Series VI—Student Personnel Work—Number 13, American Council on Education Studies. Washington, D. C. Volume XIII.

Astin, A., H. Astin, and Lindholm, J. 2011. *Cultivating the Spirit: How College Can Enhance Students' Inner Lives.* San Francisco: Jossey-Bass.

Axtell, J. 2016. *Wisdom's Workshop: The Rise of the Modern University.* Princeton, NJ: Princeton University Press.

Bailyn, B. 1967. *The Ideological Origins of the American Revolution.* Cambridge, MA: Harvard University Press.

Eck, D.L. 1993; 2003. *Encountering God: A Spiritual Journey from Bozeman to Baneras.* Boston, MA: Beacon Press.

Fowler, J. W. 1981. *Stages of Faith: The Psychology of Human Development and the Quest for Meaning.* San Francisco: Harper Collins.

Hartman, A. 2015. *A War for the Soul of America: A History of the Culture Wars.* Chicago: University of Chicago Press.

Kazanjian, V., and P. Laurence. 2000. *Education as Transformation: Religious Pluralism, Spirituality, and a New Vision for Higher Education in America.* New York: Peter Lang Publishers.

Lindholm, J. A. 2014. *The Quest for Meaning and Wholeness: Spiritual and Religious Connections in the Lives of College Faculty.* San Francisco: Jossey-Bass.

Little, M. N. 1980. "The Extracurricular Activities of Black College Students 1868–1940." *Journal of Negro History* 65, no. 2: 136–139.

Lora, R. 1974. *America in the 60s: Cultural Authorities in Transition.* Hoboken, NJ: John Wiley & Sons.

Love, P., and D. Talbot. 1999. "Defining Spiritual Development: A Missing Consideration in Student Affairs." *NASPA Journal* 37, no. 1: 361–376.

Nash, Robert J. 1999. *Faith, Hype and Clarity: Teaching About Religion in America's Schools and Colleges.* New York, NY: Teachers College Press.

Nord, W. A. (1995). *Religion and American Education: Rethinking a National Dilemma.* Chapel Hill: University of North Carolina Press.

———. 2010. *Does God Make a Difference: Taking Religion Seriously in Our Schools and Universities.* New York: Oxford University Press.

Nord, W. A., and C. C. Haynes. 1998. *Taking Religion Seriously Across the Curriculum.* Alexandria, VA: Association for Supervision and Curriculum Development.

Palmer, P.J. 1983; 1993. *To Know As We Are Known.* San Francisco: HarperSanFrancisco.

Parks, S. D. 2010. *Big Questions, Worthy Dreams: Mentoring Young Adults in Their Search for Meaning, Purpose, and Faith.* San Francisco: Jossey-Bass.

Reuben, J. A. 1996. *The Making of the Modern University: Intellectual Transformation and the Marginalization of Morality.* Chicago: University of Chicago Press.

Rockenbach, A., and M. Mayhew, eds. 2013. *Spirituality in College Students' Lives: Translating Research into Practice*. New York: Routledge.

Rudolph, F. 1990. *The American College and University*. Athens: University of Georgia Press.

Schlesinger, A. 2005. *Veritas: Harvard College and the American Experience*. Chicago: Ivan R. Dee.

Schmalzbauer, J.A., and K. Mahoney. 2012. "Religion and Knowledge in the Post-Secular Academy." In *The Post-Secular in Question: Religion in Contemporary Society*, edited by Gorski, P.S., D.J. Kim, J. Torpey, and J. VanAntwerpen. New York, NY: New York University Press.

Waggoner, M. D. 2016. "Spirituality in Contemporary Higher Education." *Journal of College and Character* 17, no. 3: 146–155.

———, ed. 2011. *Sacred and Secular Tensions in Higher Education: Connecting Parallel Universities*. New York: Routledge Books.

FURTHER READING

Eck, D. L. 2001. *A New Religious America: How a "Christian Country" Has Become the World's Most Religiously Diverse Nation*. San Francisco: Harper Collins.

Kaplin, W. A., and B. A. Lee. 2014. *The Law of Higher Education*, 5th ed. San Francisco: Jossey-Bass.

CHAPTER 25

....

THEOLOGICAL EDUCATION

....

DANIEL O. ALESHIRE

INTRODUCTION

EDUCATING ministers was at least part of the reason that many institutions of higher education were founded in the United States—especially during colonial and early nationhood years. Like other forms of higher education that have a long history, theological education has changed over time. The current dominant model, with its origins in the education of Protestant ministers, has been adopted (with some significant variations) as the educational model for Roman Catholic and Orthodox priesthood. Because religion in the United States is a remarkably free-market phenomenon, the dominant pattern is not the only one, and because religion itself is not a static social institution, the dominant model may be different in the future.

The story of the education of ministers in the United States is as old as the nation. It involves the ongoing interaction of education, religious practices, and higher education conventions, and is full of conflict and contest at many points. As is true with much of American higher education at this time, its next chapter is not altogether clear or settled.

THE DEVELOPMENT OF A NORMATIVE PATTERN OF EDUCATION OF MINISTERS

The early history of American higher education is all but indistinguishable from the early history of education for ministry. Schools founded in the seventeenth or eighteenth centuries (Harvard, Yale, Princeton, Brown, William and Mary—or their predecessor institutions) began with ministry education as part of their founding purpose. The nineteenth- and twentieth-century development of theological education, especially for Protestant ministers, involved separating from other higher education institutions while maintaining their conventions and adopting many of their innovations. The result is a current pattern of theological education that is unique and has been widely adopted as a normative model for the education of ministers.

Educating Ministers in Classical Studies

The reason that theological education and American higher education shared a common history in the colonies and early years of nationhood is that they shared a common educational curriculum and goal. Glenn Miller, the premier historian of American Protestant theological education, writes that "clergy and laity were to receive the same education, one that fitted them ideally for service in either of the two public realms, church or commonwealth" (Miller 1990, 48). These colonial schools had adapted the English model of the "learned gentleman," where "learned" meant steeped in classical subjects and languages more than a specialized proficiency in biblical texts and theology. While the education of ministers was at the center of higher education, there was no specialized education for ministry.

In the first decade of the nineteenth century, religious leaders shaped culture as much as they led religion. Joseph Willard, president of Harvard in 1800, came to the university from the pastorate, and his two successors were also clergymen. During the same period, Samuel Smith, a clergyman, was the president of the College of New Jersey, now Princeton University. Benjamin Moore, the president of what is now Columbia University, was the Anglican bishop of New York when he became president. Clergy in colonial America and in the first decades of nationhood contributed significantly to the nation's cultural and intellectual leadership. They were able to do this in part because of religious motivations in the founding of institutions of higher education and in part because a common educational experience equipped graduates for service in both religious and civic contexts.

Development of Institutions for Educating Ministers

As the nineteenth century began to mature, education for Protestant ministers gradually moved from the colleges to specialized theological schools. The first two freestanding Protestant seminaries in the United States were Andover in Massachusetts (now Andover Newton Theological School) and the Theological Seminary of the Presbyterian Church (now Princeton Theological Seminary) in New Jersey. Andover was founded in 1808 by Congregationalists who opposed the appointment of a Unitarian-leaning professor to the Hollis Chair at Harvard (the oldest endowed chair in American higher education). The Theological Seminary was founded in 1811 as a freestanding institution that separated Presbyterian ministerial education from the College of New Jersey, now Princeton University. While Andover was aligned with the religious understandings of Congregationalists, it maintained some distance from churchly structures, while

Princeton Seminary was placed under the direct control of the church. In effect, "Andover defined the academic standards; Princeton set the ecclesiastical standards" (Miller 1990, 113).

Theological education did not leave university settings entirely. Yale and Harvard continued to provide theological education, and several universities founded in the nineteenth and early twentieth centuries included education for ministry in their founding missions (e.g., Howard, Vanderbilt, Chicago, Boston, Duke, Emory, and Southern Methodist). The dominant institution for clerical education, however, became the freestanding seminary or theological school.

Andover and Princeton were not only the first of their kind; they also invented a hybridity that has continued into the present. Theological schools reflect the structures and practices of both religion and higher education. Seminaries are embedded in religion, and while they are not churches, they have practices like churches, such as worship and liturgical celebrations. Theological schools are also embedded in a broader system of higher education, and while they are not colleges or universities, they have practices that resemble higher education in general, like degree programs, faculty rank and promotion, and understandings about the importance of freedom of inquiry. The resulting institutional hybridity has generated conflict and misunderstanding as well as creativity and accomplishment throughout the history of Protestant theological education.

Development of Specialized Curriculum and Scholarly Disciplines

Andover and Princeton, and the scores of other freestanding theological schools that were founded as the nineteenth century progressed, changed the structure of the education of clergy. The move of ministerial education away from colleges and universities was accompanied by a changed curriculum that vacated the liberal arts study of classics and developed several areas of theological studies. The curriculum at Andover would have been typical: natural theology (apologetics, philosophy, and ethics), sacred literature, ecclesiastical history, and Christian theology (Bendroth 2008, 19). Theological education was morphing into something different in both institutional form and curricular content.

Through the nineteenth century, a generalized pattern of study emerged into disciplines, and as disciplines became more defined, scholarship advanced. Old Testament appears to be the first area that developed as its own specialty and New Testament the last, since it belonged to the whole theological faculty (Miller 2007, 45). With the development of disciplines, scholarship expanded and began taking on the forms currently associated with fields of disciplinary inquiry. Academic guilds formed, including what is now the Society of Biblical Literature and the American Society of Church History (1880s) and what is now the American Academy of Religion (1908).

As American scholars attended to new biblical and theological disciplines, controversies ensued in both conservative and liberal schools. Some of the creeds to which faculty were required to subscribe became less affirmable as a result of the scholarly work. Charles Briggs at Union Theological Seminary in New York lost his fight with the Presbyterians over his views on the Bible in the 1890s and was defrocked. He kept his job at Union, but Union lost its ties with the Presbyterians. William Whitsitt resigned as president of Southern Baptist Theological Seminary in Louisville in the same decade because of controversy resulting from claims he made as a historian about Baptist origins. A history of a seminary related to the United Methodist Church characterizes a mid-nineteenth-century Methodist perception about theological schools this way: "We had got along quite well so far without them. Why run the risks of quenching the spirit and opening the floodgates of heresy" (Norwood 1978, 6).

Many American Protestants, especially more theologically conservative ones, developed a combative dualism between fervent faith and piety, on the one hand, and scholarly study of theological disciplines, on the other. The scholarly study of theological disciplines, especially the Bible, threatened traditional religious beliefs and piety. This division was deep and has continued. It has been the basis for denominational battles, including perhaps the two fiercest struggles in American Protestantism in the second half of the twentieth century: the Lutheran Church-Missouri Synod in the 1970s and the Southern Baptist Convention in the 1980s. Theological education both has been and continues to be influenced by the tension between theological scholarship and religious creeds, commitments, and personal faith. The development of theological disciplinary scholarship did not invent the dualism, but it served as an accelerant for the fire. The tension is not just an American invention; John Wesley included this plea in a hymn text in eighteenth-century England: "Unite the pair so long disjoined, knowledge and vital piety" (Gunter 1999, 18).

Ministry Education as Professional Education

With freestanding seminaries, theological disciplines, and more technical forms of theological scholarship, the basic architecture for twentieth-century theological education was taking shape. While theological education in the nineteenth century had been conducted at both the baccalaureate and post-baccalaureate levels, the educational programs of the better theological schools—both freestanding and university-related—were conducted at the post-baccalaureate level by the twentieth century. Theological schools formed an accrediting agency in an effort to enhance educational quality and standardize institutional practices, as did several other patterns of American professional education. The curriculum began to expand to include courses in the work of ministry that had not been present previously, with early twentieth-century names like Church Efficiency and Sunday School Pedagogy.

As the professional model continued to develop in the second half of the twentieth century, theological disciplines related to the practice of ministry expanded. Field education or contextual education was introduced in many schools after World War II. Courses in church and society developed, as did programs in clinical pastoral education and congregational studies, and courses in religious education and church administration became more numerous. The older degree nomenclature of Bachelor of Divinity (a three-year, post-baccalaureate degree) was renamed the Master of Divinity (MDiv), also a three-year, post-baccalaureate degree. Theological education had matured into a form of graduate, professional education.

Understanding ministry as a "profession," however, was more difficult than understanding theological education as professional education. Ministry has been perceived as a "calling," and the language of "profession" proved unacceptable to many. Ministry was a profession in that the minister had knowledge and skills that laypeople did not have and that this knowledge and these skills contributed to effective ministry. Ministry was also a profession in the sense that certain ethical standards were expected of ministers. It was not a profession, however, in the sense that the profession was self-regulating or had public accountability through licensure and laws that governed it. While most mainline Protestant denominations have accountability structures for clergy, many denominations do not. In some, the religious authorizing agent (the entity that ordains) is the local congregation, and no formal accountability exists beyond the congregation that the minister currently serves. The contest over professional status in ministry runs most deeply, perhaps, in the perception that the legitimating resource for ministry is the minister's authentic faith. While other professions are legitimated on the basis of professional knowledge and skills, a crucial qualifying characteristic in ministry is authentic religious faith, which may be nurtured by theological teaching and learning but cannot be construed as an educational outcome of that learning.

Education for the Priesthood of the Roman Catholic and Orthodox Churches

Roman Catholic theological education began quite early in United States with the founding of St. Mary's Seminary in 1791 in Baltimore. With few exceptions, however, Roman Catholic and Orthodox theological schools were not founded until the late nineteenth or early twentieth centuries. Early immigrant churches were often served by immigrant clergy educated in Europe. With the numbers of Catholics and Orthodox Christians increasing as a result of late-nineteenth-century and early twentieth-century immigration, the need for American clergy grew and seminaries were founded. The Catholic seminary system before Vatican II included a six-year minor seminary program (roughly equivalent to high school and the first two years of college), followed by a six-year major seminary program (roughly equivalent to the last two years of college and four years of post-baccalaureate study). These schools awarded ecclesiastical degrees that were recognized by the Church but had no parallel in US higher education degrees. The educational processes were distinctive, and it was not until after the reforms of Vatican II were instituted that much interaction occurred among Catholic and Protestant schools. Those reforms changed the seminary system so that candidates for priesthood were required to earn a baccalaureate degree from either a seminary college or other degree-granting institution and an MDiv from a seminary formally approved by the Church for education for the ministerial priesthood.

Roman Catholic schools became accredited members of the Association of Theological Schools in the United States and Canada (ATS) in the late 1960s and 1970s. In that process, they adopted many though not all of the conventions that Protestant schools had developed. They retained their historical focus on a formational pattern of theological education. The current *Program of Priestly Formation* (2006), adopted by the US Conference of Catholic Bishops as the episcopal expectation for education for priesthood, identifies human, spiritual, pastoral, and intellectual as necessary areas of formation. These four "pillars" form the primary basis for curricular and other requirements in Roman Catholic MDiv programs.

Orthodox theological education began in the United States in the twentieth century. The primary providers are the Orthodox Church in America, which is separate from but historically related to the Russian Orthodox Church, and the Greek Archdiocese of the Americas, a part of the Greek Orthodox Church. Orthodox theological education reflects both the normative patterns of theological education in North America and education related to the unique liturgical life of Orthodox Christians.

THE NORMATIVE PATTERN OF EDUCATING MINISTERS

The normative model of theological education that became dominant in the twentieth century had identifiable educational goals, curricula, and pedagogical practices.

Educational Goal and Curriculum

The model has a coherent educational goal in that the

> overarching goal is the development of theological understanding, that is, aptitude for theological reflection and wisdom pertaining to responsible life in faith. Comprehended in this overarching goal are others such as deepening spiritual awareness, growing in moral sensibility and character, gaining an intellectual grasp of the tradition of the faith community, and acquiring the abilities requisite to the exercise of ministry in that community. (ATS Commission on Accrediting Standards, 3.1.1, http://www.ats.edu/uploads/accrediting/documents/general-institutional-standards.pdf)

The ideas contained in this statement reflect a comprehensive understanding of the aims and purposes of the education of ministers with a focal point on the cultivation of a kind of wisdom, not just professional knowledge and skills. The MDiv is the normative degree program for ordained and other general ministry religious professionals, and requires curricular attention to (1) the text and tradition of the religious community, (2) skills requisite to the exercise of ministry, (3) contextual and community analysis, and (4) personal and spiritual growth (ATS Commission on Accrediting Standards, http://www.ats.edu/uploads/accrediting/documents/degree-program-standards.pdf).

Pedagogical Practices

The Carnegie Foundation for the Advancement of Teaching's comprehensive study of education for the professions in the early years of the twenty-first century included the education of clergy, along with the education of engineers, lawyers, nurses, and physicians, in separate but coordinated studies. In the study of clergy education, researchers observed classes with a wide variety of faculty members in a wide range of theological schools, and on the basis of these observational studies and other research efforts identified "four shared intentions for student learning, originating in clergy practice and embedded in a variety of pedagogies" (Foster et al. 2006, 33). These four intentions were (1) showing a facility for interpreting texts, (2) nurturing dispositions and habits integral to the vocation of religious leadership, (3) raising students' consciousness about historical and contemporary contexts, and (4) cultivating student performance in public clergy roles. These intentions are not identical to the areas of educational effort in the accrediting standard for the MDiv, but they reflect three of those expectations, and the fourth pedagogy reflects the broader curricular goal of the cultivation of wisdom.

Other Forms of Education for Protestant Ministers

This narrative has focused on what has become master's-level education of ministers and religious professionals. The history of the education of ministers since colonial America however, is also a history of the "non-education" of ministers—at least in a formal sense. The kind and level of education depended on the denomination. Congregationalists and Presbyterians tended to have educated clergy in the nineteenth century, while revival movements like Methodists and Baptists had fewer formally educated ministers. A significant number of Hispanic Protestant ministers are currently being educated in a large number of institutes and ministry training programs whose primary language of instruction is Spanish. No accurate count exists of either the number of these programs or their total enrollment, but it is a large number for both. Throughout the history of the education of American ministers, a significant percentage—often a majority—has received no formal theological education.

As the dominant model of ministry education moved to the graduate level in the late nineteenth and early twentieth centuries, a pattern of specialized baccalaureate education for ministry emerged. The Bible college movement began out of a sense of urgency to get ministers and other religious workers in fast-growing urban areas and other settings that were perceived to be in need of Christian ministry. Seven years of education may not be too much for the kind of work ministry would require, but it was too long. Bible colleges developed a baccalaureate degree that focused on the disciplines associated with seminary education: biblical studies, theological studies, courses in pastoral practices, as well as some general education. This movement continues with a focus on education for ministers, religious workers, teachers, laypersons, and others, and the almost two hundred institutions that identify with it are connected through the Association for Biblical Higher Education (http://www.abhe.org/).

Drivers That Will Influence the Future of Education for Ministry

After more than two centuries of development resulting in an educationally robust community of theological schools that serve a wide range of Christian constituencies, with a normative pattern of educating ministers, theological schools in the initial decades of the twenty-first century are facing a complex set of drivers that will cause fundamental changes in patterns of ministry education in future decades. Theological schools tend to change as a function of external forces more than of internal initiatives, and they will be deeply influenced by external factors that are located primarily in the religious constituencies that the schools serve, the conventions of higher education in which the schools participate, and the broader culture in which both religion and higher education are located. These drivers have not just appeared recently, nor are they likely suddenly to disappear. They are strong currents that have a predictable flow over time, although their effects on theological education are less predictable.

Diminishing Cultural Privilege of Religion

While many of the colonies had an official or state religion, such as Puritanism in Massachusetts and the Anglican Church in Virginia, the First Amendment specifically precluded a state church for the nation, which represents a first disestablishment of religion. Nevertheless, religion enjoyed a privileged place in American culture and civic life. In the nineteenth century, this privilege meant "Protestant" because Protestants constituted most of the religious presence in the country for much of the century. Roman Catholics and Jews immigrated in large numbers toward the end of the century, and both they and their faith were met with considerable prejudice by Protestants.

While there was not a state church, there was a culturally established Protestantism that functioned much as a state church, including negative reactions to other forms of religious presence.

By the mid-twentieth century, however, the cultural privilege for religion was redefined to include Catholics and Jews, as well as Protestants. This change has been referred to as the second disestablishment. Protestants continued to be part of a cultural privilege of religion but were no longer the sole beneficiaries of that privilege. The privilege was evident in tax policies; in the inclusion of the minister, priest, and rabbi at civic events; and in the tendency of some public school calendars to allow release time for religious instruction.

Toward the end of the twentieth century, as the presence of other world religions was becoming more visible and the culture in general was becoming more secular, a third disestablishment of religion has occurred, this one involving the diminishing of cultural privilege that had been extended to religion. Phillip Hammond (1992) summarizes the first two disestablishments and argues for the third.

Theological schools developed in the context of a cultural privilege for religion, and it is unclear how changes in this privilege will also change theological education. Theological schools will educate religious leaders who will function in a world where religion exercises its influence through the ministry of congregations, parishes, and the entities they support, but they will not be able to support religion's role in shaping the culture as religious leaders did in the early years of nationhood through much of the nineteenth century. The normative graduate professional model of theological education also reflects a certain cultural privilege, and it is unclear if this model will be sustainable as the culture becomes increasingly secular and religion increasingly privatized.

Fundamental Issues in Higher Education

Religion is not the only social institution with waning cultural privilege; higher education is facing a similar shift in cultural perspective. Higher education may hold more privilege than religion, but it is not nearly as privileged as it was after World War II. The loss of privilege is evident in the questions related to affordability and accountability that are being asked of higher education. These kinds of questions are not asked of institutions with cultural privilege, and today they are being asked, and with considerable intensity, of higher education. Because theological schools are hybrid institutions—part religious and part higher education—they have historically benefited from a double dose of the privilege the culture extended to these two social institutions. With the social location of both religion and higher education changing, the consequences are amplified in these institutions that provide much of the education for ministers in the United States.

Higher education is changing in substantive ways unrelated to cultural privilege. The changing composition of the faculty, the changing demographics of students, the increasingly utilitarian basis for judgments about the value of higher education, and fundamentally shifting patterns of financing higher education are reshaping higher education practices and institutions. These long-term changes will also affect theological schools.

Shifting Religious Structures and Practices

Religious structures and practices have been changing and continue to do so, and these changes will drive future patterns of theological education.

The past fifty years have witnessed the shift from mainline Protestant to evangelical Protestant dominance; in the process, the conventions of mainline Protestantism have been receding while the conventions of evangelical Protestants have become more dominant. The change is a function of both the increase of evangelical Protestants and the decline of mainline Protestants over these decades. If the current rate of decline in mainline Protestantism continues for the next two decades, a significant number of congregations will close, and a considerably larger number will no longer be able to support a full-time pastor. Mainline Protestants historically have been the strongest advocates for ministers educated at the post-baccalaureate level and have the organizational structures to regulate ministerial credentials. These changes will have a significant impact on the seminaries related to these ecclesial constituencies. Evangelical Protestants have been increasing in number and have founded many seminaries since World War II, but they vary from mainline denominations in ways that could affect their future. Many evangelical denominations have limited ability to regulate ministerial credentials because authority over educational credentials for ordination and employment for ministry is vested in individual congregations. Evangelical Protestants have been more likely than mainline Protestants to question the value of advanced theological studies. The future of seminaries related to evangelical Protestantism will be influenced by these questions and denominational structures.

The ability of denominations to function as central organizing structures in Protestantism has declined. Denominations provided patterns of established work for congregations, resources that congregations could use in that work, and effective ways for congregations to work in larger ecclesial contexts on missions, social ministry, education, and public witness. Every Protestant seminary founded in the nineteenth century was a denominational seminary, and its denominational connection was a sign of robust denominational structures. Those denominations historically provided the schools with students and financial resources, and the seminaries supplied the denomination with graduates for ministry positions and advancing its theological beliefs and practices. While mainline and evangelical denominational structures continue to have significance in the landscape of American religion, they no longer have the capacity to organize and resource religious practices in the way they did, and to the extent they did, in the nineteenth century and the first half of the twentieth century. And as denominations have weakened, the mutually beneficial relationship they share with seminaries has begun to change in fundamental ways. Most denominational seminaries now depend on individual donors more than denominational grants and recruit students from a wide variety of denominational backgrounds. Graduates pursue an ever-wider array of ministry positions both within and beyond congregational and church-related positions.

Religious practices are changing. An ever-increasing percentage of church attenders attend churches with larger memberships (Chaves 1998/2006/2012). The fastest-growing religious preference for adults in the United States is "no religious preference." Pew Forum's recent study of "millennials" indicates that these young adults are not only less likely to be religiously affiliated than any other age cohort in the United States but are less religiously active than their parents or grandparents were at the same age (Pew 2010). Multiple indicators suggest that religious practices in the United States are changing in other significant ways (Putnam and Campbell 2010). Changes in religious practices have a direct relationship on the education of ministers; they influence how many positions will be available for graduates and what kinds of work those graduates will be expected to do.

Theological schools are products of religious vision; they are founded as religion is growing and forming a unique or expanding expression but are never founded as the last act of a dying religious community. During the nineteenth century, seminaries were founded as growing denominations drew more adherents. At the end of that century and the beginning of the twentieth, new immigrant communities provided the impetus for the founding of many Roman Catholic and Orthodox theological schools. The growth of the number of evangelical Protestants since World War II contributed to the founding of almost 100 seminaries. Seminaries are sustained over time because an ecclesial community continues to affirm the religious vision that brought them into being. Theological schools typically do well when their constituencies are strong and struggle when their religious constituencies decline. Many of the theological schools that have experienced the most significant financial or enrollment stress in recent years are related to religious communities that are in decline in the United States. As changes continue to mount in the practices and religious commitments of the population at large, the education of ministers will be changed, in either subtle or dramatic ways.

Fundamental Shift in the US Population

By 2040 the American population will have completed a fundamental shift that began in the late nineteenth century. This nation of immigrants largely from Europe and the British Isles will become a nation in which "white" will be the racial minority. By mid-century, if not before, persons of African, Asian, and Hispanic descent will outnumber residents of European descent. The America that was the new world of Europe will become the new world of the world. This is a huge change, and no liberal democracy has ever experienced a similar change in the composition of its population. Religion will be influenced by the fundamental shift in racial/ethnic composition. Religious communities that are unable to become culturally and racially amphibious will decline, and those that master this fundamental cultural capacity will thrive.

The changing racial/ethnic composition of society and the church will challenge assumptions in theological education that influence fundamental questions about what constitutes intellectual excellence, what backgrounds qualify individuals for admission to study, what issues constitute an appropriate intellectual agenda, and which faculty members should be promoted by what criteria.

The Growing Influence of World Christianity

The face of Christianity—what people think of when they think of Christian practices and patterns—is changing. Culture does not create religion, but it influences its expression in significant ways. When the same religion exists in deeply different cultures, it takes on different practices and emphases depending on the culture. North America has functioned as the normative center of Christian practice, and practices of Christianity in the Global South have been considered as new, perhaps eccentric, exceptions to the norm. But increasingly, North American practices will recede as the normative center, and the culturally different practices in the Global South will advance. Theological education in the United States, especially Protestant theological education, has had a dominant influence in world Christianity. That influence grew in the last half of the twentieth century when North America was a dominant center of theological scholarship. The future of theological schools in the United States will be defined, in part, on the basis of their engagement with Christian practices from the Global South.

Plurality of Educational Practice as the Emerging Model

If the past is characterized by change that led to consensus on the current dominant model, the future will be characterized by the development of multiple models and less consensus. The range and magnitude of drivers influencing theological education will contribute to the development of many models—some complementary and others competitive. The current professional model will continue. Another model has been developing, reflecting a Protestant adaptation of Roman Catholic theological education, that is more formational and focused on the religious identity and character of ministry students. These two models may prove to be the most dominant in the future, but neither will likely be normative. Other educational patterns will emerge. Pluralism in theological education and religious life is already present (Miller 2014), and it follows that the future of education for ministry will include a growing plurality of educational models.

CONCLUSION

Theological education in the United States has institutions, faculties, curricular design, endowments, libraries, and pedagogical practices that together advance theological disciplines, serve religious constituencies, and effectively educate ministers. Theological education has been changing since the colonies formed a nation; in fact, it has been changing since the early days of the Christian church (González 2015). It will continue to change. The complexity of change at this time is a function of several strong and diverse drivers that are exerting pressure on theological schools and patterns of education.

The majority of theological schools in the United States have been built for stability. The characteristics that give them strength to achieve their mission both contribute to and require stability. When change is needed, schools first attempt to "change without changing." They layer innovations on top of existing practices, with the result that old conventions are never altogether gone and new ones never fully replace old ones. There comes a time, however, when the layering of change, or accommodation, won't work. The drivers influencing schools at this time will make accommodation impossible. The change that will come over time will be as substantial as it will be unpredictable.

Regardless of its magnitude, this change will be in *form*, not *function*. Because Christian communities will still need educated leaders, ancient texts will still need to be interpreted in the intellectual idiom of a new moment in time, and the practices of Christian ministry will continue to change, ministers will need education. The function served by the current normative model of theological education will continue securely into an indefinite future, even as the forms of ministerial education will surely change.

FUTURE DIRECTIONS

1. If higher education and religion both continue to change in the future, and in the process further distance themselves from their common roots, will theological education remain a specialized form of higher education or will it revert to educational models run by religious bodies unrelated to the conventions of higher education?
2. If the education of ministers moves from a common, normative pattern to a multitude of educational models, what will the effect be on practices of American religion?
3. Given the often troubled history of American religion and race, how will the profound shift in the racial/ethnic composition of the American population influence religion, and how will those influences, in turn, reshape theological education?
4. The leadership of North American theological scholarship will change as the center of gravity in Christianity moves from North America to the rest of the world. How will thoughtful and faithful scholarship respond and adapt to this reality, given the cultural boundedness of scholarly practices and agenda?

REFERENCES

Bendroth, Margaret Lamberts. 2008. *A School of the Church: Andover Newton Across Two Centuries*. Grand Rapids, MI: Eerdmans.

Chaves, Mark. 1998/2006/2012. National Congregations Study. Retrieved May 29, 2018: http://www.soc.duke.edu/natcong/

Foster, Charles R., Lisa E. Dahill, Lawrence A. Golemon, and Barbara Wang Tolentino. 2006. *Educating Clergy: Teaching Practices and Pastoral Imagination*. San Francisco: Jossey-Bass.

González, Justo L. 2015. *The History of Theological Education*. Nashville, TN: Abingdon Press.

Gunter, W. Stephen, ed. 1999. *The Quotable Mr. Wesley*. Atlanta, GA: Candler School of Theology.

Hammond, Phillip E. 1992. *Religion and Personal Autonomy: The Third Disestablishment in America*. Columbia: University of South Carolina Press.

Miller, Glenn T. 1990. *Piety and Intellect: The Aims and Purposes of Ante-Bellum Theological Education*. Atlanta, GA: Scholars Press.

———. 2007. *Piety and Profession: American Protestant Theological Education, 1870–1970*. Grand Rapids, MI: Eerdmans.

———. 2014. *Piety and Plurality: Theological Education Since 1960*. Eugene, OR: Cascade Books.

Norwood, Frederick A. 1978. *From Dawn to Midday at Garrett*. Evanston, IL: Garrett-Evangelical Theological Seminary.

Putnam, Robert D., and David E. Campbell. 2010. *American Grace: How Religion Divides and Unites Us*. New York: Simon & Schuster.

Pew Research Center. 2010. *Religion Among the Millennials*. Washington, DC: Pew Forum on Religion & Public Life.

US Conference of Catholic Bishops. 2006. *Program of Priestly Formation*, 5th ed. Washington, DC.

FURTHER READING

Aleshire, Daniel O. 2008. *Earthen Vessels: Hopeful Reflections on the Work and Future of Theological Schools*. Grand Rapids, MI: Eerdmans.

Carroll, Jackson W., Barbara G. Wheeler, Daniel O. Aleshire, and Penny Long Marler. 1997. *Being There: Culture and Formation in Two Theological Schools*. New York: Oxford University Press.

Klimoski, Victor, Kevin O'Neil, and Katarina Schuth. 2005. *Educating Leaders for Ministry*. Collegeville, MN: Liturgical Press.

Richey, Russell E. 2014. *Formation for Ministry in American Methodism: Twenty-first Century Challenges and Two Centuries of Problem-Solving*. Atlanta, GA: Candler School of Theology.

Schuth, Katarina. 1999. *Seminaries, Theologates, and the Future of Church Ministry: An Analysis of Trends and Transitions*. Collegeville, MN: Liturgical Press.

CHAPTER 26

....

RELIGION, SPIRITUALITY, AND COLLEGE STUDENTS

....

ALYSSA N. ROCKENBACH AND JULIE J. PARK

IN the final decades of the twentieth century, new questions began emerging in higher education's scholarly and professional circles about the significance of religion and spirituality in college students' lives (Patel 2012; see Kazanjian and Laurence 2000). As researchers, educators, leaders, and campus chaplains came together, they inquired: To what extent is spirituality—or the "inner life"—a salient phenomenon among young adults? How are the meanings students assign to notions of "religious" and "spiritual" distinctive? How do college students engage the search for meaning and purpose in life? And, importantly, to what degree are higher education institutions prepared to nurture the spiritual journeys of students? In the midst of posing these questions, a new area of research inquiry and educational practice took shape and flourished as the twenty-first century began.

Our intent in this chapter is to present a synthesis of innovative research and practice that has, by and large, transformed our view of college students and reminded us to treat students as whole individuals (American Council on Education 1949) by giving balanced attention to both intellectual and affective domains in educational settings. These developments have also reinvigorated conversations around the purpose of a college education and challenged tendencies to focus solely on its "exterior" aims (Astin 2004). In so doing, we move beyond the limited perspective of college as merely a utilitarian means to an end (i.e., succeed academically in order to secure a high-paying job) and open the door to richer possibilities for students' development as engaged and compassionate citizens of the world. When the inner life is taken seriously—when we begin to expect higher education to serve as a forum for asking life's "big questions" (Parks 2000) about meaning, purpose, values, and calling—we ensure that students are prepared to face the major challenges of our time (Astin 2004).

We begin the chapter with a general assessment of spirituality and religion in college students' lives and examine the perspectives students have shared in the aggregate that attest to the relevance of these dimensions of experience. Although national data portray trends to help characterize this generation of collegians, overarching patterns are disrupted by the unique experiences and perspectives of diverse populations. Thus, in addition to identifying key findings from research that considers students collectively, we deconstruct the singular narrative to reveal heterogeneous pathways navigated by students of different faiths and worldviews. We also consider how a variety of social identity markers—race, gender identity, and sexual orientation—play a part in spiritual development and campus experiences. Lastly, we turn to questions of college impact to shed light on emerging evidence regarding the connections between educational engagement and multidimensional aspects of spiritual growth.

Throughout the chapter we are mindful of the challenges of language. Love and Talbot (1999) were among the first to comprehensively define "spirituality" in the context of higher education and student affairs. Their five-part definition underscored the centrality of seeking personal authenticity and wholeness; transcending the self; connecting to self and others; finding meaning and purpose; and relating to the transcendent. Astin, Astin, and Lindholm (2011), UCLA scholars who conducted the first national study of college student spirituality, represented the multilayered nature of spirituality in attending to five dimensions: spiritual quest (e.g., searching for meaning and purpose in life and attaining inner harmony); equanimity (e.g., feeling centered and at peace); ethic of caring (e.g., committing to helping others and reducing suffering in the world); charitable involvement (e.g., participating in community service and donating to charity); and ecumenical worldview (e.g., expressing interest in and acceptance of diverse religions and cultures). Importantly, "spirituality" is distinctive from "religion," although the two concepts may overlap to varying degrees within a person's life. Stamm characterizes religion as "beliefs and practices delineated by established denominational institutions and framed through defined doctrines, theology, and historical narratives or myths" (2006, 37). Although religion has both personal and institutional elements, it is often connected to a particular, shared narrative that serves as a foundation for values, beliefs, and ways of life. Beyond distinguishing spirituality and religion, we are sensitive to the fact that these words do not appeal to all college students. Goodman and Mueller (2009) recommend expanding language to be inclusive of nonreligious students for whom "spirituality" may not resonate. Thus, throughout the chapter we use a variety of terms—inner life, meaning, and purpose—in addition to spirituality. Likewise, we use the term "worldview" to signal that existential points of view and personal life philosophies are rooted in both nonreligious and religious perspectives.

Relevance of Spirituality and Religion in College Students' Lives

Until the early 2000s, claims regarding the resurgence of spiritual interest among college students were largely anecdotal. One landmark study of religion on US campuses of four diverse institutional types revealed tendencies toward vibrant religious pluralism and voluntary spiritual seeking on campus, which stood in contrast to the Christian emphases and mandated religious observances of earlier eras (Cherry, DeBerg, and Porterfield 2001). In 2004, researchers at the UCLA Higher Education Research Institute surveyed a nationally representative sample of more than 112,000 first-year college students about their beliefs and values to illuminate the degree to which spirituality, or the inner life, matters to young adults in higher education. The findings confirmed that college students are attuned to the spiritual and religious facets of life. In fact, 80% of students express an interest in spirituality, and 83% believe in the sacredness of life. Approximately three-quarters of respondents report searching for meaning and purpose in life and having discussions about the meaning of life with friends (Astin et al. 2005). With respect to religious indicators, close to 80% of first-year students suggest they believe in God, attend religious services, and discuss religion and spirituality with friends and family; a full 69% of students report they pray (Astin et al. 2005).

Another compelling revelation of the study was the contrast shown in the data between student expectations for their campuses and reality. According to the researchers, about two-thirds of first-year students assert it is "very important" or "essential" for their college to "enhance their self-understanding (69%), prepare them for responsible citizenship (67%), develop their personal values (67%), and provide for their emotional development (63%)" (Astin et al. 2005, 6). Approximately half of students surveyed (48%) assign importance to their college encouraging personal expressions of spirituality (Astin et al. 2005). Yet, upon experiencing several years of college, the majority of students (62%) report their faculty "never" encourage discussion of religious and spiritual matters, and only one in five students say their professors "frequently" invite explorations of meaning and purpose (Astin et al. 2011). Although significant numbers of college faculty across the country express personal religious and spiritual commitments, many are tentative about the appropriate ways to facilitate conversations concerning the inner life with students (Astin et al. 2011; Lindholm 2014).

In 2007, 14,527 students who were part of the 2004 first-year sample were surveyed again to assess spiritual and religious change over the first three years of college, as well as the experiences associated with their development (Astin et al. 2011). On the whole, students exhibited spiritual growth across a variety of dimensions, including spiritual quest (searching for meaning and purpose), equanimity (feeling peaceful and centered even during hardships), ethic of caring (relating compassionately to others), and ecumenical worldview (being open to others of different faiths/life philosophies) (Astin et al. 2011). Although students' religious commitments remain fairly constant over time—resonating with other national studies of young adults showing similar patterns of religious continuity (Smith and Snell 2009)—religious behaviors change appreciably, most notably illustrated by declining participation in religious services (Astin et al. 2011).

Other national studies that characterize the millennial generation illuminate important patterns in religiosity. The Pew Research Center (2010), for example, reports that around one-quarter of the millennial generation is religiously unaffiliated. Reflecting a similar inclination among college students, about one in five students in the UCLA study were identified as religious skeptics (Astin et al. 2011). Although young adults are less likely to affiliate religiously when compared to older generations, beliefs about life after death, as well as the existence of heaven, hell, and miracles, are quite similar to older cohorts. Some of the religious differences between younger and older adults related to prayer and belief in God have more to do with age than generation, as people tend to focus on religion to a greater extent as they grow older (Pew Research Center 2010).

RELIGIOUS AND WORLDVIEW DIVERSITY
AMONG COLLEGE STUDENTS

Colleges and universities are sites of considerable religious and worldview diversity. The vast majority of students in recent years report informally interacting with peers of other worldviews on a fairly regular basis in social settings, during meals, and in daily conversations (Rockenbach et al. 2014). While this contact with other worldviews is nearly ubiquitous, the experiences, beliefs, and perceptions of students vary tremendously across religious and nonreligious identity groups (Mayhew, Bowman, and Rockenbach 2014; Rockenbach et al. 2014). How do students of different faith perspectives experience their personal development as they navigate the college years? According to studies that examine the beliefs, values, practices, and experiences of students by religious affiliation, a number of distinguishing patterns surface.

Religious minority students identify with a rich array of religious traditions that have a smaller number of adherents in the United States relative to Christian-identified denominations. One of the earlier investigations of religious minority students in US higher education stressed the multiplicity apparent when comparing beliefs about God, religious behaviors, perceptions of spiritual quest, opinions on the intersections of science and religion, and political leanings by worldview (i.e., Islam, Hinduism, Buddhism, Judaism, Unitarian Universalism, and nonreligiousness; Bryant 2006). For instance, "Buddhists and Unitarian Universalists quest most often for the purpose of self-discovery, whereas Hindu students desire self-improvement . . . Muslim students identify most with the quest to discover God's plan for their life" (Bryant 2006, 22). Jewish and nonreligious students do not identify as strongly with the notion of "spiritual quest," but their responses are similar to their peers when asked about spiritual concepts using other language (e.g., purpose, meaning-making, and compassion; Bryant 2006).

Beyond variations in beliefs and behaviors, experiences and personal development on campus are also distinctive. Religious minority students attending religiously affiliated institutions—particularly Catholic institutions—experience declining spiritual development over time (Bowman and Small 2010). Likewise, religious minority students may not fare as well on indicators of self-rated confidence, cooperativeness, and understanding of others when attending religiously affiliated institutions rather than secular institutions (Bowman and Small 2012), and they may become more religiously skeptical from the first to third years of college relative to mainline Protestants (Small and Bowman 2011). A number of other studies, many of which are qualitative, focus on particular religious minority groups and add texture and voice to the general evidence about their experiences and development. Small (2011) depicted the stories, meaning-making strategies, and nuanced concerns of students in four "faith frames"—Christianity, Judaism, Islam, and atheism/agnosticism—to provide a basis for cultivating constructive interfaith and intrafaith exchanges. In another burgeoning line of research, scholars are attending to the experiences of Muslim students on campus as they navigate campus norms in relation to their own religious and cultural identities (Cole and Ahmadi 2003, 2010; Mir 2014). Efforts to impart Muslim student narratives and foster campus inclusion are sorely needed in an era when such students regularly face discrimination, silencing, and diminished freedom of religious expression (Gallman and Sayers 2015).

Reflecting on the reasons behind poorer outcomes for religious minority students, Bowman and Small (2012, 502) suggest that "religious minority students may feel socially isolated in institutions that practice and privilege Christianity." Indeed, hallmarks of Christianity—including holidays, symbols, stories, and rituals—are highly visible and often taken for granted as normative in US society at large and within many college and university settings (Fairchild 2009; Seifert 2007; Small 2011). Small (2011) recommends campus audits to identify and address privileges afforded in the academic calendar, access to worship spaces, and curricular and co-curricular offerings.

Research portraying the experiences of religious majority students (e.g., Roman Catholics, mainline Protestants, and evangelical Protestants) reveals some striking contrasts between notions of Christian privilege and students' lived experiences. Small found that the students in her study "exhibited a range of understanding of how their privilege of religion operated in this country, from total lack of awareness to active opposition" (2011, 118). Studies of evangelical Christian students call attention to their encounters with stereotyped impressions of Christians and disregard for their faith on campus (Bryant 2005; Magolda and Gross 2009; Moran 2007; Moran, Lang, and Oliver 2007). Thus, the privileges that religious majority students enjoy may be overshadowed upon hearing critical views from peers and others. Moran et al. (2007) have applied the term "social status ambiguity" to characterize the paradoxical positioning of Christian students who experience dual forces that privilege and marginalize them.

Nonreligious young adults are a growing population in the United States and contribute significantly to pluralism on campus given the sheer variety of identities they adopt as atheists, agnostics, secular humanists, "spiritual but not religious," and simply unaffiliated (Astin et al. 2011; Putnam and Campbell 2010; Smith and Snell 2009). General privileges afforded to religious individuals in society leave nonreligious students in a disadvantaged position. Fearing stigmas, many nonreligious students choose to hide their identities, furthering their sense of invisibility (Goodman and Mueller 2009). Inequalities between religiously affiliated and unaffiliated students come at a cost, according to several empirical studies. For instance, students with no religious affiliation show smaller gains in well-being (Bowman and Small 2012) and less satisfaction with college (Bowman and Toms Smedley 2013) than mainline Christians. In a study of the campus climate for religious diversity, atheist students perceived that the campus climate was less satisfactory for nonreligious individuals compared to their peers. Moreover, attesting to the complex dynamics of religious privilege on campus, committed Christians tended to have more positive perceptions of the nonreligious climate than do students of other worldviews (Rockenbach, Mayhew, and Bowman 2015b).

Identity Intersectionality:
How Spirituality Interfaces
with Multiple Identity Dimensions

As scholarship on college student spirituality has taken shape over the years, researchers have noted myriad intersections of spirituality and religion with other social identities, including race and culture, gender identity, and sexual orientation. Importantly, how students experience the confluence of these identities has implications for their journey through college and personal development.

Race and Culture

Race has played a notable role in religious and spiritual practice since the earliest days of American history, from early missionary attempts to convert Native Americans to the mandated racial segregation of churches both predating and following slavery (Emerson and Smith 2000). While the number of racially diverse religious communities has increased over the last decade, religious practice in the United States continues to be starkly divided along racial/ethnic lines. These patterns have numerous implications for religious and spiritual dynamics on college campuses, as well as the pre-college socialization that students experience in religious communities.

Studies addressing the unique role of race in campus religious communities and religious/spiritual engagement for college students are a relatively recent development. These studies include examining the role of spirituality in the identity development of diverse student populations (Stewart 2002) and the racial/ethnic makeup of campus fellowships within the evangelical population, particularly for Asian-American students (Busto 1996; Kim 2006). These studies, generally qualitative in nature, ask why US-born Asian-American college students often worship in racially and/or ethnically homogeneous religious student communities, raising important questions about the racialization of religious practice, as well as the role that race plays in religious communities. Scholars have also investigated multiracial religious communities, examining the tensions that can come from diversification, or lack thereof (Christerson, Edwards, and Emerson 2005; Park 2013).

National studies of spirituality, religion, and campus diversity indicate varying patterns across race. Both religious and spiritual engagement vary notably by race, with African-American students and faculty having particularly high levels of religious and spiritual engagement (Astin et al. 2011; Lindholm 2014). Religious participation also appears to have an impact on patterns of engagement with racial diversity, although the effects are varied. Studies have found that students participating in campus religious organizations have lower levels of close interracial friendship, but that such participation has no effect on more general cross-racial interaction (Park 2012; Park and Bowman 2015; Park and Kim 2013). Studies have also found that general religiosity and being from a minority religious worldview are associated with significantly higher levels of cross-racial interaction during college (Park and Bowman 2015).

Sexual Orientation and Gender Identity

Some of the earliest work on college students' spirituality in relation to sexual orientation posited that lesbian and gay students experience several possible statuses with regard to their identity development. Some students are successful in reconciling sexuality and spirituality, others remain in an unreconciled state, and still others maintain an undeveloped spirituality (Love et al. 2005). The researchers concluded that discord between religious and sexual identities may inspire spiritual growth because of the "conflict inherent between religious teaching, our study participants' emerging awareness of their sexual orientation, and the dissonance that this awareness generated" (Love et al. 2005, 205). Other scholars confirm the importance of identity integration for well-being among lesbian, gay, and bisexual individuals (Lease, Horne, and Noffsinger-Frazier 2005). Moreover, among transgender individuals, the process of physical transformation yields spiritual rebirth as one's physical and personal gender identities come into alignment, spirituality is redefined, and meaning and purpose are discovered (Reinsmith-Jones 2013). Supporting the notion that LGBT-identified students may benefit developmentally from negotiating multiple identity statuses, there is evidence to suggest that self-authored worldview commitment and pluralism orientation are more pronounced among LGBT students (Rockenbach et al. 2015d).

In addition to developmental milestones unique to LGBT students, perceptions of the campus religious and spiritual climate differ substantially by sexual orientation and gender identity (Rockenbach, Lo, and Mayhew 2015a). Generally speaking, LGBT students do not perceive the climate as favorably as heterosexual and cisgender students. Specifically, LGBT students are more inclined than heterosexual and cisgender students to see the campus as insensitive and coercive and to have negative encounters across worldview diversity. Although LGBT students are more engaged than their peers in interfaith interactions, they are less apt to affirm that the campus provides a diverse and supportive environment for students of varying worldviews (Rockenbach et al. 2015a). Perhaps these differential experiences on campus help to explain the propensities to struggle spiritually among students with minoritized identities (Bryant Rockenbach, Walker, and Luzader 2012).

Comparisons of female- and male-identified students have yielded many noteworthy gender distinctions on measures of spirituality and religion. With respect to primarily religious indicators, Buchko noted that "Women's religious faiths appear to reflect greater daily connection with God through prayer, more assurance of God's presence and activity in their lives, and more emotive connection with God as evidenced by more frequent feelings of reverence or devotion" (2004, 95). Likewise, on most measures of spirituality, with the exception of religious skepticism, women exhibit higher scores than do men (Bryant 2007). Some of these differences may be explained by gendered patterns in spiritual development associated with religious identity (stronger positive effects on spiritual development among men), academic experiences in science (stronger negative effects on spiritual development among men), and peer relationships (stronger positive effects on spiritual development among women; Bryant 2007). Taken together, such research supports the claims of Longwood, Muesse, and Schipper (2004) that neglecting spirituality and uncritically accepting conventional masculinity distorts men's humanity, whereas innovative programming geared toward men on campus can help foster the connectivity necessary for men's spiritual development.

Impact of College on Religious and Spiritual Development

How does college shape students' inner development? Opportunities abound for higher education to serve as a critical intervention in developing students' spiritual qualities, worldview commitments, and openness to others of diverse beliefs. As Patel contends, "all the positive social capital in our broader society—faith-based groups, volunteer programs, educational opportunities, forums for discussion and exchange—exist on campuses in concentrated form" (2012, 123). Given the immense educational potential afforded by colleges and universities, in the next section we explore how environments and experiences are linked to student outcomes.

Environments

Kuh and Gonyea assert that "Institutional mission and campus culture matter more to spirituality and liberal learning outcomes than most other institutional characteristics" (2006, 46). To be sure, recent research on the campus religious and spiritual climate confirms the significance of climate dimensions in shaping student outcomes during college. Applying a framework that accounts for structural diversity (the proportional representation of different religious and nonreligious groups on campus), psychological climate (affective perceptions of intergroup relationships on campus), and behaviors (how groups actually interact with one another on campus), two dimensions of the campus environment consistently surface. The degree to which students feel supported and free to express their worldviews on campus and the degree of challenge they experience in provocative encounters with diverse peers create inspiring conditions for outcomes related to satisfaction, commitment, and pluralism (Bryant Rockenbach and Mayhew 2014; Mayhew, Rockenbach, and Bowman 2016; Rockenbach et al. 2015c).

Experiences

In reflecting on the ways in which higher education might address and engage religious pluriformity—or the sheer expansiveness of religious options in our society—Jacobsen and Jacobsen (2012) articulate several opportunities for practice to support students' religious literacy, knowledge framing, and convictions. These "sites of engagement" involve interfaith etiquette, civic engagement, and character and vocation development, and have the potential to enrich students' educational experiences in college (Jacobsen and Jacobsen 2012). Indeed, when we consider the curricular and co-curricular practices that have the strongest effects on students' spiritual development, many fall into the realms noted by Jacobsen and Jacobsen (2012). Reporting on their national longitudinal study that involved following students over a three-year period, Astin et al. found that multifaceted spiritual qualities (i.e., spiritual quest, equanimity, ecumenical worldview, ethic of caring, charitable involvement) are "enhanced when undergraduates are provided with opportunities to experience multiple perspectives and diverse people and cultures, opportunities such as interdisciplinary studies, service learning, interracial interaction, student organizations, and study abroad" (2011, 137). Faculty also play an important role in spiritual development, as students experience growth when faculty integrate student-centered approaches in the classroom, interact with students outside of class, and encourage students to discuss meaning, purpose, and spirituality (Astin et al. 2011).

Other studies help to illuminate how experiences in college, including religious and spiritual involvement, are associated with a wide range of behavioral and attitudinal outcomes. Based on findings from the National Survey of Student Engagement, we know that spiritually enhancing practices (e.g., worship, meditation, prayer) are positively associated with other influential forms of campus engagement, such as attending cultural events and participating in community service (Kuh and Gonyea 2006). Research focused on "ecumenical worldview" and "pluralism orientation" has revealed the factors in college that help to enhance students' understanding of diverse worldviews and good will toward others with different perspectives. Peer socialization, provocative diversity experiences, formal and informal interfaith engagement, encountering religion and spirituality in academic contexts, and religious/spiritual struggles predict students' development of an ecumenical or pluralistic orientation (Bryant 2011a, 2011b; Bryant Rockenbach and Mayhew 2013; Mayhew 2012; Rockenbach et al. 2015c). Participation in religious student organizations is linked with key patterns in engagement with racial diversity (Park 2012; Park and Bowman 2015). Moreover, reiterating the theme of intersectionality, many of the effects of college on ecumenical/pluralistic worldview are conditional on gender, race, and (especially) religion/worldview (Bryant 2011b; Bryant Rockenbach and Mayhew 2013; Rockenbach et al. 2015c). Resonating with the primarily quantitative research base attending to spiritual development, Small's (2011) qualitative investigation of students' faith frames identified the import of interactions with religiously diverse peers and academic courses on religion for spiritual growth.

Finally, we are learning from longitudinal research that spiritual development introduces further benefits. Astin et al. noted a compelling relationship between spiritual development and "more traditional outcomes of higher education such as academic performance, leadership development, self-esteem, satisfaction with college, and motivation for further education" (2011, 138). In other words, spiritual development is not an end unto itself; growth along these dimensions significantly impacts students' success in college and life.

Conclusion

Overall, our chapter demonstrates that religion and spirituality affect students and campus life in myriad ways. There is incredible diversity in how college students experience spirituality and the inner life. No single narrative exists that can neatly summarize the complex range of experiences, but, on the whole, studies indicate that both religion and spirituality continue to play pivotal roles in the lives of college students. Educators must be cognizant of these trends, and we encourage both faculty and student affairs educators to develop comfort and literacy around the challenging issues that supporting religion and spirituality bring to the table. Conversations around such topics can also help the university be attuned to the needs of the whole student, cultivating holistic development for citizenship in a diverse democracy. Altogether there are no easy answers, but any commitment to supporting religious and spiritual questions on campus inevitably includes a commitment to grappling with challenging questions and difficult dialogues.

Future Directions

1. How do campuses support dialogue between students of diverse religious traditions, including those who may maintain "exclusive" claims to truth?
2. How can universities work to coordinate curricular and co-curricular learning opportunities for student learning around religion and spirituality?

3. As higher education continues to diversify, what are the religious and spiritual experiences of adult learners and other groups that are outside of the traditional 18-to-24-year-old college student population?

REFERENCES

American Council on Education. 1949. *The Student Personnel Point of View*. Washington, DC: American Council on Education.

Astin, A. W. 2004. "Why Spirituality Deserves a Central Place in Liberal Education." *Liberal Education* 90, no. 2 (Spring): 34–41.

Astin, A. W., H. S. Astin, and J. A. Lindholm. 2011. *Cultivating the Spirit: How College Can Enhance Students' Inner Lives*. San Francisco: Jossey-Bass.

Astin, A. W., H. S. Astin, J. A. Lindholm, A. N. Bryant, K. Szelényi, and S. Calderone. 2005. *The Spiritual Life of College Students: A National Study of College Students' Search for Meaning and Purpose*. Los Angeles: Higher Education Research Institute, UCLA.

Bowman, N. A., and J. L. Small. 2010. "Do College Students Who Identify with a Privileged Religion Experience Greater Spiritual Development? Exploring Individual and Institutional Dynamics." *Research in Higher Education* 51: 595–614.

———. 2012. "Exploring a Hidden Form of Minority Status: College Students' Religious Affiliation and Well-Being." *Journal of College Student Development* 53: 491–509.

Bowman, N. A., and C. Toms Smedley. 2013. "The Forgotten Minority: Examining Religious Affiliation and University Satisfaction." *Higher Education* 65: 745–760.

Bryant, A. N. 2005. "Evangelicals on Campus: An Exploration of Culture, Faith, and College Life." *Religion & Education* 32: 1–30.

———. 2006. "Exploring Religious Pluralism in Higher Education: Non-majority Religious Perspectives Among Entering First-Year College Students." *Religion and Education* 33, 1–25.

———. 2007. "Gender Differences in Spiritual Development During the College Years." *Sex Roles* 56: 835–846.

———. 2011a. "The Impact of Campus Context, College Encounters, and Religious/Spiritual Struggle on Ecumenical Worldview Development." *Research in Higher Education* 52: 441–459.

———. 2011b. "Ecumenical Worldview Development by Gender, Race, and Worldview: A Multiple-Group Analysis of Model Invariance." *Research in Higher Education* 52: 460–479.

Bryant Rockenbach, A. N., and M. J. Mayhew. 2013. "How the Collegiate Religious and Spiritual Climate Shapes Students' Ecumenical Orientation." *Research in Higher Education* 54: 461–479.

———. 2014. "The Collegiate Religious and Spiritual Climate: Predictors of Satisfaction Among Students with Diverse Worldviews." *Journal of College Student Development* 55: 41–62.

Rockenbach, A. B., Walker, C. R., and Luzader J. 2012. "A Phenomenological Analysis of College Students' Spiritual Struggles." *Journal of College Student Development* 53: 55–75.

Buchko, K. J. 2004. "Religious Beliefs and Practices of College Women as Compared to College Men." *Journal of College Student Development* 45: 89–98.

Busto, R. V. 1996. "The Gospel According to the Model Minority? Hazarding an Interpretation of Asian American Evangelical College Students." *Amerasia Journal* 22, no. 1: 133–147.

Cherry, C., B. A. DeBerg, and A. Porterfield. 2001. *Religion on Campus*. Chapel Hill: University of North Carolina Press.

Christerson, B., K. L. Edwards, and M. O. Emerson. 2005. *Against All Odds: The Struggle for Racial Integration in Religious Organizations*. New York: New York University Press.

Cole, D., and S. Ahmadi. 2003. "Perspectives and Experiences of Muslim Women Who Veil on College Campuses." *Journal of College Student Development* 44, no.1: 47–66.

———. 2010. "Reconsidering Campus Diversity: An Examination of Muslim Students' Experiences." *Journal of Higher Education* 81, no. 2: 121–139.

Emerson, M., and C. Smith. 2000. *Divided by Faith: Evangelical Religion and the Problem of Race in America*. New York: Oxford University Press.

Fairchild, E. E. 2009. "Christian Privilege, History, and Trends in U.S. Higher Education." In *Intersections of Religious Privilege: Difficult Dialogues and Student Affairs Practice*, edited by S. K. Watt, E. E. Fairchild, and K. M. Goodman (New Directions for Student Services, no. 125), 5–11. San Francisco: Jossey-Bass.

Gallman, S., and D. Sayers. 2015. "Duke Reverses Decision to Allow Muslim Call to Prayer." *CNN*. Retrieved January 26, 2015: http://www.cnn.com/2015/01/15/us/duke-call-to-prayer/.

Goodman, K. M., and J. A. Mueller. 2009. "Invisible, Marginalized, and Stigmatized: Understanding and Addressing the Needs of Atheist Students." *New Directions for Student Services* 125: 55–63.

Jacobsen, D., and R. H. Jacobsen. 2012. *No Longer Invisible: Religion in University Education*. New York: Oxford.

Kazanjian, V. H., Jr., and P. L. Laurence, eds. 2000. *Education as Transformation: Religious Pluralism, Spirituality, and a New Vision of Higher Education in America*. New York: Peter Lang.

Kim, R. 2006. *God's Whiz Kids: Korean American Evangelicals on Campus*. New York, NY: New York University Press.

Kuh, G. D., and R. M. Gonyea. 2006. "Spirituality, Liberal Learning, and College Student Engagement." *Liberal Education* 92, no. 1 (Winter): 40–47.

Lease, S. H., S. G. Horne, and N. Noffsinger-Frazier. 2005. "Affirming Faith Experiences and Psychological Health for Caucasian Lesbian, Gay, and Bisexual Individuals." *Journal of Counseling Psychology* 52, no. 3: 378–388.

Lindholm, J. A. 2014. *The Quest for Meaning and Wholeness: Spiritual and Religious Connections in the Lives of College Faculty*. San Francisco: Jossey-Bass.

Longwood, W. M., M. W. Muesse, and W. Schipper. 2004. "Men, Spirituality, and the Collegiate Experience." *New Directions for Student Services* 107: 87–95.

Love, P., M. Bock, A. Jannarone, and P. Richardson. 2005. "Identity Interaction: Exploring the Spiritual Experiences of Lesbian and Gay College Students." *Journal of College Student Development* 46, no. 2: 193–209.

Love, P. G., and D. Talbot. 1999. "Defining Spiritual Development: A Missing Consideration for Student Affairs." *NASPA Journal* 37: 361–375.

Magolda, P. M., and K. E. Gross. 2009. *It's All About Jesus! Faith as an Oppositional Collegiate Subculture*. Sterling, VA: Stylus.

Mayhew, M. J. 2012. "A Multi-level Examination of College and Its Influence on Ecumenical Worldview Development." *Research in Higher Education* 53: 282–310.

Mayhew, M. J., N. A. Bowman, and A. Bryant Rockenbach. 2014. "Silencing Whom? Linking Campus Climates for Religious, Spiritual, and Worldview Diversity to Student Worldviews." *Journal of Higher Education* 85: 219–245.

Mayhew, M. J., and A. N. Bryant Rockenbach. 2012. "Achievement or Arrest? The Influence of the Collegiate Religious and Spiritual Climate on Students' Worldview Commitment." *Research in Higher Education* 54: 63–84.

Mayhew, M. J., A. N. Rockenbach, and N. Bowman. 2016. "The Connection Between Interfaith Engagement and Self-Authored Worldview Commitment." *Journal of College Student Development* 57, no. 4: 362–379.

Mir, S. 2014. *Muslim American Women on Campus: Undergraduate Social Life and Identity.* Chapel Hill: University of North Carolina Press.

Moran, C. D. 2007. "The Public Identity Work of Evangelical Christian Students." *Journal of College Student Development* 48: 418–434.

Moran, C. D., D. J. Lang, and J. Oliver. 2007. "Cultural Incongruity and Social Status Ambiguity: The Experiences of Evangelical Christian Student Leaders at Two Midwestern Public Universities." *Journal of College Student Development* 48: 23–38.

Park, J. J. 2012. "'Man, This Is Hard': A Case Study of How Race and Religion Affect Cross-Racial Interaction for Black Students." *Review of Higher Education* 35, no. 4: 567–593.

———. 2013. *When Diversity Drops: Race, Religion, and Affirmative Action in Higher Education.* New Brunswick, NJ: Rutgers University Press.

Park, J. J., and N. A. Bowman. 2015. "Religion as Bridging or Bonding Social Capital: Race, Religion, and Cross-Racial Interaction for College Students." *Sociology of Education* 88, no. 1: 20–37.

Park, J. J. and Y. K. Kim. 2013. "Interracial Friendship, Structural Diversity, and Peer Groups: Patterns in Greek, Religious, and Ethnic Student Organizations." *Review of Higher Education* 37, no. 1: 1–24.

Parks, S. D. 2000. *Big Questions, Worthy Dreams: Mentoring Young Adults in Their Search for Meaning, Purpose, and Faith.* San Francisco: Jossey-Bass.

Patel, E. 2012. *Sacred Ground: Pluralism, Prejudice, and the Promise of America.* Boston: Beacon.

Pew Research Center. 2010. *Religion Among the Millennials.* Washington, DC: Pew Forum on Religion & Public Life.

Putnam, R. D., and D. E. Campbell. 2010. *American Grace: How Religion Divides and Unites Us.* New York: Simon & Schuster.

Reinsmith-Jones, K. 2013. "Transsexualism as a Model of Spiritual Transformation: Implications." *Journal of GLBT Family Studies* 9, no. 1: 65–99.

Rockenbach, A. N., M. Lo, and M. Mayhew. 2015a. "How LGBT College Students Experience and Engage the Campus Religious and Spiritual Climate." Unpublished manuscript.

Rockenbach, A. N., M. J. Mayhew, and N. A. Bowman. 2015b. "Perceptions of the Campus Climate for Non-religious Students." *Journal of College Student Development* 56, no. 2, 181–186.

Rockenbach, A. N., M. J. Mayhew, A. Kinarsky, and Interfaith Youth Core 2014. *Engaging Worldview: A Snapshot of Religious and Spiritual Climate. Part I: Dimensions of Climate and Student Engagement.* Chicago: Interfaith Youth Core.

Rockenbach, A. N., M. J. Mayhew, S. Morin, R. Crandall, and B. Selznick. 2015c. "Fostering the Pluralism Orientation of College Students Through Interfaith Action and Informal Peer Engagement." Unpublished manuscript.

Rockenbach, A. N., T. Riggers-Piehl, J. Garvey, M. Lo, and M. Mayhew. 2015d. "The Differential Effects of Campus Climate and Interfaith Engagement on Self-Authored Worldview Commitment and Pluralism Orientation Among LGBT and Heterosexual Students." Unpublished manuscript.

Seifert, T. A. 2007. "Understanding Christian Privilege: Managing the Tensions of Spiritual Plurality." *About Campus* 12, no. 2: 10–17.

Small, J. L. 2011. *Understanding College Students' Spiritual Identities: Different Faith, Varied Worldviews*. Cresskill, NJ: Hampton Press.

Small, J. L., and N. A. Bowman. 2011. "Religious Commitment, Skepticism, and Struggle Among College Students: The Impact of Majority/Minority Religious Affiliation and Institutional Type." *Journal for the Scientific Study of Religion* 50: 154–174.

Smith, C., and P. Snell. 2009. *Souls in Transition: The Religious and Spiritual Lives of Emerging Adults*. New York: Oxford University Press.

Stamm, L. 2006. "The Dynamics of Spirituality and the Religious Experience." In *Encouraging Authenticity and Spirituality in Higher Education*, edited by A. W. Chickering, J. C. Dalton, and L. Stamm, 37–65. San Francisco: Jossey-Bass.

Stewart, D. L. 2002. "The Role of Faith in the Development of an Integrated Identity: A Qualitative Study of Black Students at a White College." *Journal of College Student Development* 43, no. 4: 579–596.

FURTHER READING

Chickering, A. W., J. C. Dalton, and L. Stamm. 2006. *Encouraging Authenticity and Spirituality in Higher Education*. San Francisco: Jossey-Bass.

Eck, D. L. 1993. *Encountering God: A Spiritual Journey from Bozeman to Banaras*. Boston: Beacon Press.

Fowler, J. W. 1981. *Stages of Faith: The Psychology of Human Development and the Quest for Meaning*. San Francisco: Harper & Row.

Joshi, K. 2006. *New Roots in America's Sacred Ground*. New Brunswick, NJ: Rutgers University Press.

Kim, R. 2006. *God's Whiz Kids: Korean American Evangelicals on Campus*. New York: New York University Press.

Nash, R. 2001. *Religious Pluralism in the Academy: Opening the Dialogue*. New York: Peter Lang Publishing.

Pearce, L., and M. L. Denton. 2011. *A Faith of Their Own: Stability and Change in the Religiosity of America's Adolescents*. New York: Oxford University Press.

Seifert, T. A., and N. Holman-Harmon. 2009. "Practical Applications for Student Affairs Professionals' Work in Facilitating Students' Inner Development." *New Directions for Student Services* 125: 13–21.

Tisdell, E. J. 2003. *Exploring Spirituality and Culture in Adult and Higher Education*. San Francisco: Jossey-Bass.

CHAPTER 27

....

RELIGION, SPIRITUALITY, AND COLLEGE FACULTY

....

JENNIFER A. LINDHOLM

INTRODUCTION

THE terms "spiritual" and "religious" both connote a belief in, and desire to relate to, some higher power along with engagement in practice and behavior that nurtures that connection. For those who differentiate between the two terms, spirituality tends to be conceived as a multidimensional construct that is associated with private thought and experience. Spirituality also includes internal processes related to seeking authenticity and wholeness and deriving meaning, purpose, and direction in life as well as developing connected-ness through relationship and community (see, e.g., Hill et al. 2000; Love and Talbot 1999 Zinnbauer, Pargament, and Scott 1999). Religion, on the other hand, can be conceptualized as a more public manifestation of "group activity that involves specific behavioral, social, doctrinal, and denominational characteristics" (Fetzer Institute 2003, 1). Because spirituality encompasses the "values, priorities, overall purposes, and principles that a person may use to live by" (irrespective of whether those orientations are conceptualized by an individual as being connected with religion), Paloutzian and Lowe (2012, 181) maintain that "spiritual" (rather than "religious") is the overarching construct. For many people, as Fuller (2001) has detailed, religious beliefs and traditions compose the core of their spirituality. For others, however, such considerations play little, if any, part in their spiritual lives.

Essentially, spirituality involves an active quest for answers to life's "big questions" (spiritual quest); a global worldview that transcends ethnocentrism and egocentrism (ecumenical worldview); a sense of caring and compassion for others (ethic of caring) coupled with a lifestyle that includes service to others (charitable involvement); and a capacity to maintain one's sense of calm and centeredness, especially in times of stress (equanimity) (Astin, Astin, and Lindholm 2011). Ultimately, it is the spiritual compo-nent of human beings, as Zohar and Marshall (2004) have explained, that urges us to question why we do what we do and to seek better ways of engaging in our life pursuits, and propels us to make a difference in the world.

This chapter provides a synopsis of what we know to date about the spiritual/religious connections in faculty members' lives. It also addresses why this dimension of their lives is important to consider within the context of academic workplaces and undergraduate education. Associated implications for research and institutional practice are also discussed.

THE SPIRITUAL AND RELIGIOUS LIVES
OF COLLEGE FACULTY

With few exceptions (see, e.g., Astin and Astin 1999; Braskamp and Remich 2003; Shahjahan 2010; Tisdell 2003), research within higher education institutions about spiritual and religious dimensions of life has focused primarily on students; the associated experiences, attitudes, expectations, and influences of faculty have been largely overlooked. Faculty who participated in the 2012 Faculty Beliefs and Values Survey (FBVS)[1] shared their perspectives on the meaning that spirituality has in their lives; the intersections they may see between the spiritual dimension of their lives and their work as professors, along with associated tensions they may experience; and their broader views on the roles they and their institutions should play in supporting students' spiritual growth and development.

As reflected in responses provided by those faculty and the earlier replies of their counterparts who completed the Higher Education Research Institute's 2004–2005 Triennial National Survey of College Faculty,[2] roughly 80% of traditionally appointed four-year college and university faculty who teach undergraduates consider themselves spiritual to at least "some" extent. Four in ten embrace a spiritual self-identity to a "great" extent, while just over two in ten say they are "not at all" spiritual. In the aggregate, as illustrated through the responses of 2012 FBVS respondents, today's four-year college and university faculty report relatively high levels of spiritual interest and involvement:

Believe in the sacredness of life	87%
Have an interest in spirituality	77%
Believe we are all spiritual beings	73%
Seek out opportunities to grow spiritually	65%
Feel connected to a Higher Power	64%
Believe that understanding the world requires spiritual self-understanding	54%
Gain spiritual strength by trusting in a Higher Power	54%
Place high priority on integrating spirituality in their lives	47%

Across different types of four-year colleges and universities and disciplinary contexts, 60% of faculty consider themselves religious people to at least "some" extent. Within that group, just under one-third consider themselves religious to a "great" extent, but four in ten say they are "not at all" religious (Lindholm 2014). When asked to rate their level of religiousness relative to others their age, just 22% consider themselves "above average." One in three agree "strongly" that they find religion to be personally helpful. The responses of 2012 FBVS respondents to selected questionnaire items also reflect generally high levels of religious tolerance and acceptance:

Believe that nonreligious people can lead lives that are just as moral as those of religious believers	94%
Disagree that people who don't believe in God will be punished	85%
Believe that most people can grow spiritually without being religious	78%
With respect to spiritual existence, believe that questions are far more central than answers	62%

On the whole, college and university faculty are less likely than other US adults to consider themselves religious. Inclinations to characterize themselves as spiritual, however, tend to parallel the broader US adult population (see, e.g., Pew Forum on Religion & Public Life 2012). Overall, 57% of faculty identify as being both spiritual and religious; 21% consider themselves spiritual but not religious; 2% as religious but not spiritual; and 19% as neither spiritual nor religious (Lindholm 2014).

As elaborated elsewhere (see Lindholm 2014), the personal meaning that spirituality has for faculty, and the extent to which the spiritual/religious dimension of life and associated values, beliefs, and behaviors are centrally important to them, varies tremendously. In part, these variations are based on demographic differences. For some faculty, including many faculty of color—most notably African Americans and Hispanics—spiritual epistemologies play a central role both in their work with students and in navigating their academic lives (see, e.g., Aguirre 1987; Berry and Mizelle 2006; Denton and Ashton 2004; Dillard 2006; Dillard, Abdur-Rashid, and Tyson 2000; Fernandes 2003; Shahjahan 2004a, 2004b, 2005, 2010; Turner 2002; Umbach 2006). Some faculty who consider themselves traditionally religious also have reservations about the term "spirituality." As such, they are reluctant to embrace it fully in characterizing their own identities. Many atheist and agnostic faculty who responded to the 2012 FBVS also have strong opinions about the damaging societal influences of religious adherence and, by extension, generally negative impressions of those who are "believers."

Spiritual quest inclinations also vary widely by academic discipline, with faculty in the humanities and fine arts being much more likely overall to be quest-oriented than their colleagues in other fields, particularly engineering, the physical sciences, biological sciences, and mathematics. The extent to which faculty members' internally focused spiritual inclinations tend to translate to externally focused ethic of caring and ecumenical worldview orientations also varies depending not only on personal characteristics, perspectives, and experiences but also on institutional and disciplinary contexts. Generally speaking, and as detailed elsewhere by Lindholm

(2014), faculty who characterize themselves as both spiritual *and* religious are more likely than other colleagues to experience equanimity, or a sense of calmness and peace, in their lives.

The majority (82%) of respondents to the 2012 FBVS indicated that their spiritual life and professional life are at least "somewhat" integrated. Of these, 30% reported that the two are "tightly" integrated. The rest (18%) view the two as "completely separate." Moreover, 64% disagree that "the spiritual dimension of faculty members' lives has no place in the academy." Within all types of four-year colleges and universities and across academic disciplines/fields, at least half the faculty share that perspective. The most common tensions that faculty experience between their spiritual and professional lives relate to their interactions with colleagues (Lindholm 2014).

Overall, 57% of the faculty who responded to the 2012 FBVS indicate that, to a "great" extent, they feel they are fulfilling a calling through their work. As Dik and Duffy (2012) have described, inherent in that conceptualization is an implied responsibility to fulfill one's duty to society and the common good by working in ways that are useful and helpful to others. "Calling," as Leider and Shapiro have explained, is a concept that "challenges us to see our work in relation to our deepest beliefs" (2001, 17). Ultimately, alignment between one's sense of purpose and meaning in work and one's broader sense of purpose and meaning in life provides people with a sense of stability and coherence (Baumeister and Vohs 2002). People who characterize themselves as having a calling have been found to be more intrinsically motivated and engaged, more confident that they can make good career decisions, more committed to their jobs and organizations, and more satisfied with their work lives. They also tend to cope more effectively with challenges; are more likely to engage in good organizational citizenship behavior, which encompasses altruism, civic virtue, conscientiousness, courtesy, and sportsmanship; and are less likely to suffer from stress and depression (Dik and Duffy 2012).

When it comes to questions of the "appropriateness" of a place for spirituality in undergraduate education, faculty opinion is considerably divided. Three-quarters of the respondents to the 2012 FBVS, for example, tend to agree that "this campus should be as concerned about students' personal development as it is with their intellectual development." However, underscoring the discomfort many faculty feel with the use of the term "spiritual," 56% disagree with the notion that "colleges should be concerned with facilitating students' spiritual development." Among faculty at public universities, that figure rises to 77% disagreement. As Astin, Astin, and Lindholm (2011) have detailed, the concerns that faculty commonly express within this realm include fear of being criticized by colleagues because discussions about spirituality may be perceived as antithetical to academic norms. Also prevalent are concerns about maintaining appropriate separation of church and state, feeling a lack of expertise, and worrying that such discussions might be perceived as a form of indoctrination or proselytizing.

WHY THE SPIRITUAL ORIENTATIONS
OF COLLEGE FACULTY MATTER

Whether religiously grounded or not, spiritual considerations play an important role in the ways that many people make meaning of their lives. Drawing on the work of Emmons (1999) and Lewis and Cruise (2006), Park explains that religious and spiritual aspects of global meaning "can influence individuals' lives through their interpretation of occurrences in their daily lives, the ways they structure their daily pursuits, and their general sense of well-being and life satisfaction" (2012, 27). Helminiak's (1987) work links human development within the spiritual realm with increased capacities for integrating cognitive, social, emotional, and moral aspects of development as well as enhanced capacities for integrity or wholeness, openness, self-responsibility, and authentic self-transcendence.

People's abilities to access, nurture, and give expression to the spiritual dimension of life also have implications for how they engage with the world. More specifically, researchers have found that individuals who are more spiritually grounded tend to exhibit a heightened sense of connectedness that promotes empathy, ethical behavior, civic responsibility, passion, and action for social justice (see, e.g., Allport and Ross 1967; Batson 1976; De Souza 2003; Klaassen and McDonald 2002). Others, such as Ellison and Smith (1991), have found that spiritual well-being tends to be positively associated with self-confidence, general assertiveness, and inclinations toward offering praise, and to be negatively associated with depression, aggressiveness (including passive-aggressiveness), dependency, conflict avoidance, and negatively experienced effects of potentially stressful situations. In its most potentially transformative role, a spiritual orientation to life stresses what Lerner described as "the unity of all human beings and the unity of all being . . . without negating the importance and value of individual difference and individual freedom" (1998, 1). Community development that is spiritually oriented includes what Chile and Simpson (2004) have characterized as recognizing personal values, respecting individual human rights, reducing inequality, enhancing personal security, promoting social justice, facilitating empowerment, and enriching people's essential humanity.

Work, whether academically oriented or otherwise, can be especially meaningful when individuals seek "paths of integration" between their personal and professional lives (Dik and Duffy 2012), focus on the broader purpose(s) of their work, are able to use their personal talents to promote others' well-being, and perceive their work as contributing to society's greater good (see, e.g., Schlegel et al. 2007, 2011; Steger, Dik, and Duffy 2012). Comprehension (i.e., making sense of one's experiences) and purpose (i.e., identifying and intending to pursue highly valued overarching goals) play central roles in people's perceptions that their work is meaningful (Steger 2010). As Dik, Duffy, and Tix (2012) have explained, comprehension and purpose are also important in that they provide potential pathways for helping people align and integrate the personal and professional aspects of their lives.

Those who pursue professorial careers in the current era must be prepared to contend with complex challenges. Shifting financial support and increasing budgetary constraints, increasing enrollments, expanding diversity in student demographics and levels of academic preparedness, and intensifying pressures for providing direct evidence of student learning, workforce readiness, and "success" are increasingly prevalent (see, e.g., Gappa, Austin, and Trice 2007). Emphasis on credentialing and outcomes that prioritize individual achievement, competitiveness, materialism, and objective knowing comes too often at the expense of investing in the development of self-awareness and understanding and establishing and nurturing a sense of connectedness (see Astin, Astin, and Lindholm 2011). Under such conditions, as Astin (2004) has described, academic work can become disconnected from the core values that compelled faculty to pursue professorial careers. The resulting sense of fragmentation may increase faculty members' hesitancy to discuss issues of meaning, purpose, authenticity, and wholeness with their colleagues. Inadvertently or otherwise, they may likewise discourage their students from engaging these issues among themselves or with their professors.

For traditionally aged undergraduates, the predominating orientation within higher education today is especially problematic. As these students refine their identities, formulate adult life goals and career paths, and test their emerging senses of independence and interdependence, they often grapple for the first time with issues of meaning, including questions such as: Who am I? What are my values? Do I have a mission or purpose in life? (If so, what is it?) Why am I in college? What kind of person do I want to become? What sort of world do I want to help create? How students deal with these questions has important implications for other critical decisions they will make, including their choices of courses, majors, and careers; whether they opt to stay in college or drop out; and whether they decide to pursue post-baccalaureate study.

The process of seeking answers to life's "big questions" and developing greater self-awareness and understanding is also directly relevant to developing other inner qualities such as empathy, caring, equanimity, and social responsibility. The broad formative roles that colleges and universities play in society position us well to support students in developing inner qualities that can enrich their capacities to live meaningful lives; cope with life's inherent uncertainties and discontinuities; and serve their communities, our society, and the world at large. Toward achieving these goals, we must be open to reconsidering our traditional ways of being and doing. As we endeavor to provide evidence of student success with respect to federally mandated "core competencies" (e.g., critical thinking, information literacy, quantitative reasoning, oral communication, and writing), we must also remain mindful of how our institutional principles, priorities, and practices impact the development of inner competencies that are essential for enabling students to contribute effectively and to thrive in an increasingly complex world.

Palmer (1983, 1999) has written eloquently about the emotional and spiritual dimensions of life and the unique potential that educators have to help students develop their capacity for connectedness, responsiveness, and accountability. Similarly,

Laurence and Kazanjian (2000) maintain that colleges and universities have tremendous potential to shape society positively. These avenues include examining issues of purpose and meaning within the context of the campus environment, acknowledging the multiple aspects of self that operate simultaneously within individuals, and celebrating the diverse experience that people bring to their encounters with one another. Student affairs professionals have an especially rich legacy of concern for holistic education and personal development. Certainly, the significance of their contributions to the "softer" aspects of undergraduate student development should not be underestimated or overlooked. However, for spirituality to have a truly "authentic" place in campus life, its fundamental components must also be reflected in the values, beliefs, and commitments of academic affairs personnel. Faculty members are the heart of the academic community. As such, their views on spirituality, its expressions in their personal and professional lives, and the challenges they encounter in the quest for meaningfully integrated lives and a sense of wholeness are critical to understand.

When faculty directly encourage students to explore questions of meaning and purpose, students are more likely to show positive growth in spiritual quest, equanimity, ethic of caring, and ecumenical worldview (see Astin, Astin, and Lindholm 2011). Additionally, Astin, Astin, and Lindholm (2011) found students show considerably greater growth in the same four spiritual qualities, as well as in charitable involvement, if faculty encourage discussion of religious and spiritual matters, support students' expressions of spirituality, and act as spiritual role models. Faculty interactions with students, both inside and outside the classroom, also affect undergraduate students' propensity to embrace an ethic of caring, or what Rhoads described as "a sense of self firmly rooted in concern for the well-being of others" (2000, 37). Specifically, students who experience more mentoring interactions with faculty, especially (but not exclusively) when those interactions relate to discussion of ethical and spiritual issues, tend to place higher value on the "caring self" (Fleming, Purnell, and Wang 2013). Rockenbach and Mayhew's research (2013) on undergraduate students' ecumenical development also reaffirms the value of faculty members' efforts (along with broader institutional efforts) to "challenge and support" (Sanford 1968) students' spiritual explorations and struggles. As academic role models for students and interpreters of institutional missions, faculty also play a potentially influential role in helping students make connections between academic knowledge and skills, social issues, and civic life (see, e.g., Stanton 1994).

Largely independent of institutional and disciplinary contexts, college and university faculty who themselves are spiritually oriented are more likely to emphasize the importance of students' personal development (in addition to, not in lieu of, students' intellectual development). Such orientation is reflected by the personal priorities faculty place on goals for undergraduate education that include enhancing self-understanding, preparing for responsible citizenship, developing moral character and personal values, facilitating the search for meaning and purpose, and providing for emotional development (Lindholm 2014). Not unexpectedly, faculty who are highly spiritual (whether or not they exercise those inclinations within the context of a particular religion) are also more inclined to endorse the value of explicitly supporting undergraduate students' spiritual development. For example, among 2012 FBVS respondents, 36% of faculty who self-identified as highly spiritual see "promoting students' spiritual development" as a "very important" goal for undergraduate education; 29% feel that such a focus is "essential" (Lindholm 2014).

Faculty members' use of developmental classroom teaching methods is also predictive of enhanced spiritual outcomes related to meaning-making, spirituality as quest, and moral care for others (Piehl 2013). Piehl (2013) also found that when faculty display personal interest in students' inner lives, especially as related to helping them "navigate questions of meaning and purpose," students tend to report greater gains across spiritual development measures. This latter finding also reaffirms the important mediating role that students' perception of faculty support for fostering spiritual development has on students' openness to actively exploring issues of meaning and purpose in their lives (see, e.g., Bowman and Small 2013).

Looking Forward

The ways in which higher education institutions are evolving compel us to reconsider longstanding expectations and deeply held assumptions about many aspects of undergraduate education. As part of that process, we must reflect on our work as educators, especially with respect to the effects that our values, beliefs, and behaviors have on our own and others' lives, both within and beyond the academy. To enhance the capacity of colleges and universities to support the personal and professional growth of faculty themselves and, by extension, to facilitate students' growth and development, we must understand what educators think, what they believe, what they do, and why. It is also important that we go beyond those pursuits to listen to the heart of who they are and what they feel. This is especially true in the case of faculty, whose behaviors shape (and are shaped by) the personal inclinations and orientations of those who pursue professorial careers as well as by the structural and cultural characteristics of their disciplinary and institutional affiliations. As central figures in determining the culture and the climate of their institutions, faculty are also at the heart of higher education's capacity to change. Efforts to increase understanding of faculty values and beliefs provide an essential foundation for creating educational environments that maximize the personal and professional potential of students and faculty alike.

In reconnecting higher education with human wholeness, reinvigorating the integrative capacity of college and university campuses, and making valued space for the spirit within the academy, we are challenged to consider how our ways of being ultimately extend to our ways of doing and relating. Within campus communities, this process necessarily begins with self-reflection and group dialogue. Writing about the "disconnected" life of educators, Palmer (1999) explained how our cultural habits within the academy—namely our competitiveness and our tendencies to think oppositionally, question others' perspectives aggressively, and respond dismissively or with quick fixes for whatever might seem to be wrong—tend to result in environments where it feels threatening to listen openly or to speak genuinely (see also Twale and DeLuca 2008). Within academic work environments, one essential consideration is finding ways to create time and space for more open exchanges among colleagues.

Engaging in new conversations, such as how we make meaning of our work, how we experience our work environments, and what connections (if any) we may see between our spiritual/religious lives and our work, makes all of us vulnerable. In terms of opening the conversation, the direct similarity of experiences is likely to matter far less than the openness to share one's own journey as well as an expressed interest in learning what others' experiences might be. Indeed, in revealing our individual experiences, we often come to see more clearly not only the ways in which we are unique but also how our perceptions and experience are like those of some others and how they are like those of all others. Toward facilitating such dialogue, effective leadership from department heads is especially important, as is the engagement of well-respected senior faculty, who, by all accounts, are in the "safest" position career-wise to share the joys, trials, and tribulations of their own academic careers and to offer perspective on how they— whether spiritually oriented or otherwise—have made meaning of their academic careers and life experiences (Lindholm and Szelényi 2003; Miller and Scott 2000).

Dialogue and reflection centered around what Chickering (2006) refers to as "institutional formation" are foundational for developing academic units and broader work environments that excel in maintaining a place for individuality while also promoting community (see also Cooperrider and Whitney 1999; Manning 2000). Wilcox's volume (2013) on "revisioning mission" within Catholic higher education provides a wealth of additional insight into options and approaches for engaging colleagues in discussion and action around issues of spirituality, meaning, and purpose. As illustrated by Felten et al. (2013), mentoring communities can also play a powerful role in supporting faculty members' personal and professional growth interests and, by extension, laying the foundation for transformative institutional change. Included within each chapter are questions for reflection and growth that can facilitate purposeful dialogue. Braskamp, Trautvetter, and Ward (2006) and Nash and Murray (2010) have also provided valuable perspectives on engaging campus communities in meaning-making that are useful for considerations related to both institutional practice and future empirical research. Finally, Palmer and Zajonc's (2010) call to renew higher education through collegial conversations includes promising examples of how colleges and universities can help faculty, staff, and students realize their deepest potential.

Conclusion

Ultimately, it takes an engaged and committed community of faculty, staff, administrators, and students to nurture the development of campus cultures and climates that contribute to cultivating a sense of meaning and wholeness within and among institutional members and, through that process, honor the spiritual and religious connections in many of our lives. Through the continued process of empirical, theoretical, and practical discovery, we can provide additional insights to promote the development of spiritually enriching academic workplaces, teaching and learning environments, and campus communities.

FUTURE DIRECTIONS

1. What are ways in which faculty are preparing themselves to address questions of religion and spirituality in their disciplines and classrooms?
2. What are some examples of institutional initiatives involving faculty and staff in addressing student concerns about religion and spirituality on public higher education campuses?
3. How, if at all, are professional academic associations developing initiatives to equip faculty for dealing with religious and spiritual questions that arise within their disciplines?
4. Are there examples of interdisciplinary collaborations to address questions of religion and spirituality college teaching?

NOTES

1. Building on the UCLA Higher Education Research Institute's 2004–2005 Triennial National Survey of College Faculty and the 2004 and 2007 College Students' Beliefs and Values Surveys, the 2012 Faculty Beliefs and Values Survey was designed to learn more about the values and beliefs of college faculty and to understand how faculty members construct a sense of meaning and purpose in their lives, including their professional pursuits. The institutional sample was designed to ensure diversity with respect to type (colleges and universities), control (public, private nonsectarian, Roman Catholic, Protestant, evangelical), and selectivity level (high, medium, and low, based on the average SAT/ACT scores of entering students). The web survey, administered in summer and fall 2012, was completed by 8,447 full-time, traditionally appointed (i.e., tenured or tenure-track, if institution had such a system) faculty members who teach undergraduates and are employed at one of 264 colleges and universities within the United States.
2. Supported by supplementary grant funding from the John Templeton Foundation, the 2004–2005 HERI Triennial National Survey of College Faculty included approximately two dozen items that queried faculty members' own spiritual inclinations as well as their attitudes about the potential role that colleges and universities might play in facilitating students' spiritual development. Aggregated normative findings related to those spirituality-oriented items were featured in a brief monograph (see Lindholm, Astin, and Astin 2005).

REFERENCES

Aguirre, A. J. 1987. "An Interpretive Analysis of Chicano Faculty in Academe." *The Social Science Journal* 24, no. 1: 71–81.

Allport, G. W., and J. M. Ross. 1967. "Personal Religious Orientation and Prejudice." *Journal of Personality and Social Psychology* 5, no. 4: 432–443.

Astin, A. W. 2004. "Why Spirituality Deserves a Central Place in Liberal Education." *Liberal Education* 90, no. 2: 34–41.

Astin, A. W., and H. S. Astin, with the assistance of A. L. Antoniao, J. S. Astin, and C. M. Cress. 1999. "Meaning and Spirituality in the Lives of College Faculty: A Study of Values, Authenticity, and Stress." Higher Education Research Institute, UCLA.

Astin, A. W., H. S. Astin, and J. A. Lindholm. 2011. *Cultivating the Spirit.* San Francisco: Jossey-Bass.

Batson, C. D. 1976. "Religion as Prosocial Agent or Double Agent?" *Journal for the Scientific Study of Religion* 15, no. 1: 29–45.

Baumeister, R. F., and K. D. Vohs. 2002. "The Pursuit of Meaningfulness in Life." In *The Handbook of Positive Psychology,* edited by C. R. Snyder and S. Lopez, 608–618. New York: Oxford University Press.

Berry, T. R., and N. Mizelle. 2006. *From Oppression to Grace: Women of Color and Their Dilemmas Within the Academy.* Sterling, VA: Stylus.

Braskamp, L. A., L. C. Trautvetter and K. W. Ward. 2006. *Putting Students First: How Colleges Develop Students Purposefully.* Boston: Anker Publishing Company.

Braskamp, L.A. and R.G. Remich 2003. "The Centrality of Student Development in the Life of Faculty at Church and Faith Related Colleges and Universities." *Journal of College and Character,* 4: 4, 1–13.

Bowman, N.A. and Small, J. L. 2013. "The Experiences and Spiritual Growth of Religiously Privileged and Religiously Marginalized College Students. In *Spirituality in College Students' Lives: Translating Research Into Practice,* Bryant Rockenbach, A., Mayhew, M. J (Ed.). New York, NY: Routledge, 19–34.

Chickering, A. W. 2006. "Planned Change and Professional Development." In *Encouraging Authenticity and Spirituality in Higher Education,* edited by A. W. Chickering, J. C. Dalton, and L. Stamm, 189–219. San Francisco: Jossey-Bass.

Chile, L. M., and G. Simpson. 2004. "Spirituality and Community Development: Exploring the Links between the Individual and the Collective." *Community Development Journal* 39, no. 4: 318–331.

Cooperrider, D., and D. Whitney. 1999. *Appreciative Inquiry.* San Francisco: Berrett-Koehler.

De Souza, M. 2003. "Contemporary Influences on the Spirituality of Young People: Implications for Education." *International Journal of Childhood Spirituality* 8, no. 3: 269–279.

Denton, D., and W. Ashton, eds. 2004. *Spirituality, Action, and Pedagogy: Teaching from the Heart.* New York: Peter Lang.

Dik, B. J., and R. D. Duffy. 2012. *Make Your Job a Calling: How the Psychology of Vocation Can Change Your Life at Work.* West Conshohocken, PA: Templeton Press.

Dik, B. J., R. D. Duffy, and A. P. Tix. 2012. "Religion, Spirituality, and a Sense of Calling in the Workplace." In *Psychology of Religion and Workplace Spirituality: A Volume in Advances in Workplace Spirituality: Theory, Research, and Application,* edited by P. C. Hill and B. J. Dik, 113–133. L. W. Fry, Series Ed. Charlotte, NC: Information Age Publishing.

Dillard, C. B. 2006. *On Spiritual Strivings: Transforming an African American Woman's Academic Life*. New York: SUNY Press.

Dillard, C. B., D. Abdur-Rashid, and C. A. Tyson. 2000. "My Soul is a Witness: Affirming Pedagogies of the Spirit." *International Journal of Qualitative Studies in Education* 13, no. 5: 447–462.

Ellison, C. W. and J. Smith. 1991. "Toward an Integrative Measure of Health and Well-being." *Journal of Psychology and Theology* 19, no. 1: 35–48.

Emmons, R. A. 1999. *The Psychology of Ultimate Concerns: Motivation and Spirituality in Personality*. New York: Guilford.

Felton, P., H. L. Bauman, A. Kheriaty, and E. Taylor. 2013. *Transformative Conversations: A Guide to Mentoring Communities Among Colleagues in Higher Education*. San Francisco: Jossey-Bass.

Fernandes, L. 2003. *Transforming Feminist Practice: Non-violence, Social Justice, and the Possibilities of a Spiritualized Feminism*. San Francisco: Aunt Lute Books.

Fetzer Institute. 2003. *Multidimensional Measurement of Religiousness/Spirituality for Use in Health Research*. Kalamazoo, MI: Fetzer Institute.

Fleming, J. J., J. Purnell, and Y. Wang. 2013. "Student-Faculty Interaction and the Development of an Ethic of Care." In *Spirituality in College Students' Lives: Translating Research into Practice*, edited by A. N. Rockenbach and M. J. Mayhew, 153–169. New York: Routledge.

Fuller, R. C. 2001. *Spiritual But Not Religious: Understanding Unchurched America*. New York: Oxford University Press.

Gappa, J. M., A. E. Austin, and A. G. Trice. 2007. *Rethinking Faculty Work: Higher Education's Strategic Imperative*. San Francisco: John Wiley & Sons, Inc.

Helminiak, D. A. 1987. *Spiritual Development: An Interdisciplinary Study*. Chicago: Loyola University Press.

Hill, P. C., K. I. Pargament, R. W. Hood Jr., M. E. McCullough, J. P., Swyers, D. B. Lawson, and B. J. Zinnbauer 2000. "Conceptualizing Religion and Spirituality: Points of Commonality, Points of Departure." *Journal for the Theory of Social Behavior* 30, no. 1: 51–77.

Klaassen, D. W., and M. J. McDonald. 2002. "Quest and Identity Development: Reexamining Pathways for Existential Search." *International Journal for the Psychology of Religion* 12, no. 3: 189–200.

Laurence, P., and V. Kazanjian. 2000. *Education as Transformation: Religious Pluralism, Spirituality, and a New Vision for Higher Education in America*. New York: Peter Lang.

Leider, R. J., and D. A. Shapiro. 2001. *Whistle While You Work: Heeding Your Life's Calling*. San Francisco: Barrett-Koehler.

Lerner, M. 1998. "Spirituality in America." *Tikkun* X: 1.

Lewis, C.A. and Cruise, S. M. 2006. "Religion and happiness: Consensus, contradictions, comments and concerns." *Mental Health, Religion & Culture* 9, no. 3: 213–225.

Lindholm, J. A. 2014. *The Quest for Meaning and Wholeness: Spiritual and Religious Connections in the Lives of College Faculty*. San Francisco: Jossey-Bass.

Lindholm, J. A., H. S. Astin, and A. W. Astin. 2005. *Spirituality and the Professoriate: A National Study of Faculty Beliefs, Attitudes, and Behaviors*. Los Angeles: UCLA Higher Education Research Institute.

Lindholm, J. A., and K. Szelényi. 2003. "Becoming One of 'Us': Promoting a Sense of Institutional Fit Among Faculty." *The Department Chair* 14, no. 1 (Summer): 7–9.

Love, P. G., and D. Talbot. 1999. "Defining Spiritual Development: A Missing Consideration for Student Affairs." *NASPA Journal* 37, no. 1: 361–375.

Manning, K. 2000. *Rituals, Ceremonies, and Cultural Meaning in Higher Education*. Westport, CT: Bergin & Garvey.

Miller, V. W., and D. K. Scott. 2000. "Making Space for Spirit in the Department." Available at www.umass.edu/pastchancellors/scott/papers/spirit.html.

Nash, R. J., and M. S. Murray. 2010. *Helping College Students Find Purpose: The Campus Guide to Meaning Making*. San Francisco: Jossey-Bass.

Palmer, P. J. 1983. *To Know as We Are Known: Education as a Spiritual Journey*. San Francisco: Jossey-Bass.

———. 1999. *The Courage to Teach: A Guide for Reflection and Renewal*. San Francisco: Jossey-Bass.

Palmer, P. J., and A. Zajonc. 2010. *The Heart of Higher Education: A Call to Renewal*. San Francisco: Jossey-Bass.

Paloutzian, R. F., and D. A. Lowe. 2012. "Spiritual Transformation and Engagement in Workplace Culture." In *Psychology of Religion and Workplace Spirituality: A Volume in Advances in Workplace Spirituality: Theory, Research, and Application*, edited by P. C. Hill and B. J. Dik, 179–199. L.W. Fry, Series Ed. Charlotte, NC: Information Age Publishing.

Park, C. L. 2012. "Religious and Spiritual Aspects of Meaning in the Context of Work Life." In *Psychology of Religion and Workplace Spirituality: A Volume in Advances in Workplace Spirituality: Theory, Research, and Application*, edited by P. C. Hill and B. J. Dik, 25–42. L.W. Fry, Series Ed. Charlotte, NC: Information Age Publishing.

Pew Forum on Religion & Public Life. 2012. "'Nones' on the Rise: One-in-Five Adults Have No Religious Affiliation." Washington, DC.

Piehl, T. A. 2013. *Enhancing Classrooms and Conversations: How Interactions with Faculty Predict Change in Students' Spirituality in College*. Los Angeles: University of California.

Rhoads, R. A. 2000. "Democratic Citizenship and Service Learning: Advancing the Caring Self." *New Directions in Teaching and Learning* 2000: 37–44.

Rockenbach, A. N., and M. J. Mayhew. 2013. "How Institutional Contexts and College Experiences Shape Ecumenical Worldview Development." In *Spirituality in College Students' Lives: Translating Research into Practice*, edited by A. N. Rockenbach and M. J. Mayhew, 88–104. New York: Routledge.

Sanford, N. 1968. *Where Colleges Fail: A Study of Student as Person*. San Francisco: Jossey-Bass.

Schlegel, R. J., J. A. Hicks, L. A. King, and J. Arndt. 2011. "Feeling Like You Know Who You Are: Perceived True Knowledge and the Meaning of Life." *Personality and Social Psychology Bulletin* 37, no. 6: 745–756.

Shahjahan, R. A. 2004a. "Centering Spirituality in the Academy: Toward a Transformative Way of Teaching and Learning." *Journal of Transformative Education* 2, no. 4: 294–312.

———. 2004b. "Reclaiming and Reconnecting to our Spirituality in the Academy." *International Journal of Children's Spirituality* 9, no. 1: 81–95.

———. 2005. "Spirituality in the Academy: Reclaiming from the Margins and Evoking a Transformative Way of Knowing the World." *International Journal of Qualitative Education* 18, no. 6: 685–711.

———. 2010. "Toward a Spiritual Practice: The Role of Spirituality Among Faculty of Color Teaching for Social Justice." *Review of Higher Education* 33, no. 4: 473–512.

Stanton, T. K. 1994. "The Experience of Faculty Participants in an Instructional Development Seminar on Service-Learning." *Michigan Journal of Community Service Learning* 1, no. 1: 7–20.

Steger, M. F. 2010. "Work as Meaning." In *Oxford Handbook of Positive Psychology and Work*, edited by P. A. Linley, S. Harrington, and N. Page, 131–142. Oxford: Oxford University Press.

Steger, M. F., B. J. Dik, and R. D. Duffy. 2012. "Measuring Meaningful Work: The Work and Meaning Inventory (WAMI)." *Journal of Career Assessment* 20, no. 3: 322–337.

Steger, M. F., B. M. Hicks, T. B. Kashdan, R. F. Krueger, and T. J. Bouchard Jr. 2007. "Genetic and Environmental Influences on the Positive Traits of the Values in Action Classification, and Biometric Covariance with Normal Personality." *Journal of Research in Personality* 41, no. 3: 524–539.

Tisdell, E. J. 2003. *Exploring Spirituality and Culture in Adult and Higher Education*. San Francisco: Jossey-Bass.

Turner, C. S. 2002. "Women of Color in Academe: Living with Multiple Marginality." *Journal of Higher Education* 73, no. 1: 74–93.

Twale, D. J., and B. M. DeLuca. 2008. *Faculty Incivility: The Rise of the Academic Bully Culture and What to Do About It*. San Francisco: Jossey-Bass.

Umbach, P. 2006. "The Contribution of Faculty of Color to Undergraduate Education." *Research in Higher Education* 47, no. 3: 317–345.

Wilcox, J. R., with J. A. Lindholm and S. D. Wilcox. 2013. *Revisioning Mission: The Future of Catholic Higher Education*. CreateSpace.

Zinnbauer, B. J., K. I. Pargament, and A. B. Scott. 1999. "The Emerging Meanings of Religiousness and Spirituality: Problems and Prospects." *Journal of Personality* 67, no. 6: 889–919.

CHAPTER 28

....

TEACHING RELIGIOUS STUDIES

....

EUGENE V. GALLAGHER

INTRODUCTION

TEACHING about religion in American higher education has always been shaped by multiple contexts, including the personal, departmental, institutional, national, and international. In particular, religious commitments on the parts of both individuals and institutions have played a prominent role in influencing how and why religion is taught. Colonial era colleges forthrightly put Christian moral instruction and character formation at the forefront of their missions. For example, an advertisement in 1754 for King's College, which would become Columbia University, described its goals as "to teach and engage the children to know God in Jesus Christ, and to love and serve him in all sobriety, godliness, and righteousness of life" (Thelin 2004, 18). That understanding of the goal of teaching about religion was echoed nearly two centuries later in an essay that confidently declared that "We do not teach the Bible as an end but as a means to the end of Christian character and experience" (Domm 1945, 155). Some teachers also put the goal of character formation into a much broader national and civilizational context. As Mary Lakenan of Mary Baldwin College urged in 1933, "If the future leadership of the country is to be prepared to meet spiritual needs and stay the tide of utter materialism, opportunity must be afforded in the college curriculum for a grounding in religion" (Lakenan 1933, 16). In a survey of the field in 1970, John Wilson correctly emphasized that up to World War II, the primary purpose of teaching about religion in colleges and universities was "religious nurture" (Wilson 1970, 6).

In the late nineteenth and twentieth centuries, however, several factors combined to unsettle that view of the purposes of teaching about religion in American higher education. The rise of the modern research university with its focus on the application of scientific reason to all fields of study, the greater awareness of various Asian civilizations and the economic and ideological challenges they posed to the United States, and the 1963

Supreme Court decision in *Abington Township School District v. Schempp*, which paved the way for teaching about religion in public schools, were some of the most prominent factors prompting a reconsideration of how and why religion could and should be taught (see Hart 1999; Houf 1948; Welch 1972). The impact of those developments on religiously affiliated colleges and universities, nonsectarian liberal arts colleges, and state universities has been uneven, gradual, and ongoing. Today, there remain marked differences from institution to institution, department to department, and even professor to professor about the appropriate goals and processes for teaching about religion. There is no consensus. Some commentators lament that in too many courses "students will encounter religions only in historical contexts, rather than as live options (in their intellectually, morally, and spiritually most compelling forms for understanding the world here and now)" (Nord 2008). But others note with approval the continuing efforts of the academic study of religion to free itself from "submission to transcendental authority" (Sharpe 1988, 249).

The post–World War II expansion of American higher education also saw a substantial increase in the number of departments of religion. In that context, which contrasts with the situation in the early decades of the twenty-first century, multiple questions came to the fore for wide discussion, even though some of them had already been the topics of vigorous exchanges for some time. Among them were questions about the proper goals for teaching about religion at the collegiate level, appropriate curricula for undergraduate instruction, the role of the religion professor, the readiness of students to undertake serious study, and the ideal staffing of departments. This chapter will focus on how those questions were taken up with particular reference to undergraduate teaching about religion under the headings of goals, curriculum, and teacher.

GOALS

In 1937, David E. Adams of Mount Holyoke College reported to the National Association of Bible Instructors, the professional association that in the 1960s would mutate into the American Academy of Religion, on the results of a survey of thirteen colleges and universities that were not church-related. Adams quoted at length from one response to the survey. It captures succinctly the dilemma of the religion teacher who could no longer be certain that the single purpose of instruction was the cultivation of Christian morality and the formation of educated Christians. In response to the question of whether the institutional curriculum provided "a satisfactory approach to life," itself a revealing statement about the purposes of collegiate instruction about religion, the respondent expressed a quandary about the goals of such teaching:

> I hardly see how this admits of answer. Satisfactory to whom? I think that there might possibly be fruitful discussion of the meaning of "satisfactory" approach. For instance, do we want to make theists? Social reformers? Mystics? People who

understand the nature of religion and its relation to other cultural expressions? Fundamentalists? Humanists? . . . Is it possible that in a liberal college nothing is proper beyond an attempt to get the student to understand, and that such maturity of attitude which only understanding can bring is the "spiritual value" at which we should aim? (Adams 1937, 179)

That statement vividly expresses the diversity of understandings of the purpose of teaching about religion. The respondent clearly accepts the notion that undergraduate teaching is supposed to be somehow transformative, but also poses the pointed question: Transformative to what end? That question continues to be taken up by teachers in all sorts of institutions, although institutional context is no trustworthy predictor of how an individual will respond.

The crucial, and divisive, question continues to be whether, and if so how, teaching about religion should contribute to the religious formation or growth of the individual student. Efforts to separate teaching about religion from Christian moral instruction and character formation began early in the twentieth century, and despite many robust attempts, the dilemma remains unresolved for the field at large. In 1935, a special committee of the faculty of Princeton University insisted on the distinction between "the study of religion and the practice of it" and also on the distinctiveness of religion as a separate field of investigation (Michaelson 1965, 137). Also arguing for the autonomy of the academic study of religion, Bernard Meland, of Pomona College, stressed that "The liberal arts objective and the narrowly defined evangelical interest are simply two mutually exclusive projections" (Meland 1937, 68). He also emphasized that a department of religion shares, but only shares, with other departments the responsibility to expose students to "ideals of living" (Meland 1937, 67).

Efforts to distinguish clearly the study of religion from its practice, however, were not unanimously endorsed. In 1950 A. Roy Eckhardt, of Lawrence College, asserted that the goal of the introductory course in religion is "to aid in the promotion of intelligent Christian faith and life" (Eckhardt 1950, 173). Eckhardt also disparaged many courses in comparative religion because, he asserted, "the enrollee is spared the discomfiture of ever having to make a religious *decision*" (174). In 1964, Lawrence DeBoer observed critically that "there are still considerable numbers of colleges and universities as well as theologians and churchmen who are operating under the illusion that the study of religion does and should produce Christian character and commitment" (DeBoer 1964, 346).

Although the distinction between the study of religion and its practice, as articulated in the 1935 Princeton report, appeared to have progressively won the day in the period from the 1960s onward, in recent years several new challenges to that understanding of the purpose of the academic study of religion have surfaced. In a substantial survey of college introductory courses on religion, Barbara Walvoord noticed what she called a "great divide" between the goals of teachers and those of students. Teachers overwhelmingly identified the development of critical thinking capabilities as their primary goal, but students saw such courses as an opportunity to develop their own "spiritual" or religious sensibilities (Walvoord 2008, 13–18). Walvoord's perception of student interests was echoed by an extensive longitudinal study of college students conducted by the Higher Education Research Institute at UCLA between 2003 and 2010. That study emphasized the positive contributions that attention to student "spiritual development" can have on students' performance in college. It argued that "Educational experiences and practices that promote spiritual development . . . have uniformly positive effects on traditional college outcomes" (Astin, Astin, and Lindholm 2010).

The Higher Education Research Institute's work on students' "spirituality," a term with a very broad definition at best, has been taken up by a loose coalition of academic administrators, teachers, and others who see themselves as a part of the "Spirituality in Higher Education" movement. Their broad goal is to infuse attention to students' spirituality throughout the college experience, including the curriculum. In many ways, they see themselves returning to the model of the early colonial colleges, which "honored both the intellect and the spirit" (Hoppe 2007, 117). They decry the influence of the German research university model and its quest for objective, scientific knowledge at the expense of ignoring character development. Although the major voices in the Spirituality in Higher Education movement have not been teachers of religious studies, its prescriptions for what ails American higher education have been endorsed by some in the field (see Grace 2009).

An overlapping development is the growing interest in various forms of "contemplative pedagogy," which frequently introduce into the classroom actual religious practices as ways of linking academic study to personal experience. According to one practitioner, contemplative pedagogy can include, among other practices, "silent sitting meditation, compassion practices, walking meditation, deep listening, mindfulness, yoga, calligraphy, chant, guided meditations, nature observation, [and] self-inquiry" (Grace 2011, 99). Advocates of contemplative pedagogies tend to be more modest about their claims for such practices than the participants in the Spirituality in Higher Education movement. One acknowledges, for example, that "contemplative courses are not helpful to all students, just as contemplative pedagogy is not appealing to all professors. However, contemplative methods do provide, for those so inclined, a demonstrably effective means for fulfilling the key purposes of liberal arts education" (Grace 2011, 105). That author is referring to the goals articulated by the American Association of Colleges and Universities (2007, 23) in *College Learning for the New Century*, especially those concerning the cultivation of inner resources like moral courage, the ability to engage moral and social dilemmas with a clear sense of one's own values, and the development of character and conscience (Grace 2011). In some ways, advocates of contemplative pedagogies are embracing the mission of character formation and moral instruction for which the partisans of Spirituality in Higher Education movement are so nostalgic, but they are bringing to the classroom an array of practices that is far broader than the resources offered by either an explicit or implicit Protestantism. Nonetheless, they are endorsing a model of the goals of education about religion that has much in common not only with that other contemporary movement but also with the focus on "religious nurture" that dominated instruction about religion from the colonial period through at least World War II.

Another recent current of thinking approaches the topic of the purposes of teaching about religion in colleges and universities from a different angle. Stephen Prothero (2007) has articulated the fullest argument in favor of cultivating "religious literacy" through instruction about religion in higher education. Arguing that "high school and college graduates who have not taken a single course about religion cannot be said to be truly educated," Prothero asserts that "at least one course in religious studies should also be required of all college graduates" (Prothero 2007, 17, 139). Beyond that general exhortation, Prothero focuses on the types of factual knowledge about religion that he thinks every American should know. He stops short, however, of offering fuller guidance about how to design a course that will provide such knowledge (Gallagher 2009).

Although Prothero's prescriptions are tailored to acknowledge the contemporary religious diversity of the United States and to promote the specific types of knowledge he believes necessary for participation in American civic life, concerns about the religious literacy of college students actually have a longer pedigree. More than sixty-five years before the publication of Prothero's *Religious Literacy*, Herman Brautigam noted that the establishment of courses in religion at Colgate University in 1911 stemmed from the conviction that "Literacy in the field of religion was considered just as central in a program of general education as for example, literacy in the history of political institutions, in the sciences or in secular literature" (Brautigam 1941, 162). Also, some sixty years before Prothero's book Dwight Beck, of Syracuse University, issued a broadly condemnatory, but prescient, assessment of college students' knowledge about religion, stating flatly that "The average American undergraduate is a religious illiterate" (Beck 1947, 50). Some saw students' religious illiteracy and their general lack of "a vital religious commitment" as related to broad civilizational concerns. Noting that many who fought in World War II thought they were acting "to preserve values of justice, freedom, decency, and honesty," William F. Quillian, of Ohio Wesleyan University, argued that teaching about religion necessarily entailed "helping the student to understand and to interpret rightly those religiously significant experiences which are part of the fabric of his own life" and subsequently "enriching . . . the student's religious experiences" (Quillian 1950, 113). The concern for increasing students' religious literacy could take on a variety of forms. It could refer to providing them with the factual information that would equip them with at least a minimal understanding of their fellow citizens and a variety of public issues, but it could also refer to training them to identify and understand their own experiences as religious even if they did not initially think that they were. On the topic of religious literacy, as with other characterizations of the purposes of instruction about religion, there remains a divide between those who see teaching about religion as a purely intellectual process and those who emphasize its contribution to character formation.

While institutional sites for the study of religion in American higher education proliferated in the latter half of the twentieth century, the field has continued to wrestle with issues that, despite appearing decisively settled to some, receive contrasting answers in the field at large. The history of teaching about religion in colleges and universities represents more a dynamic ebb and flow than a progressive development. The idea that collegiate instruction about religion should provide character formation and moral guidance remains alive and well, both in something like its original form (and not only in religiously affiliated institutions) and in the more innovative forms espoused by the Spirituality in Higher Education and Contemplative Pedagogy movements. Teachers still lament the lack of knowledge displayed by their students and strive to raise the level of their religious literacy, though why they are concerned and what they propose to do about it vary widely. The goals of teaching about religion remain as diverse as the people who teach and the institutional locations they occupy.

CURRICULUM

Where the focus of undergraduate instruction about religion has been Christian character formation and moral instruction, courses about the Bible and ethics have dominated departmental curricula. Reporting on a survey of sixty-two institutions offering courses in religion in 1942, Paul Johnson noted that nearly half of the courses offered were on the New Testament, Old Testament, and Ethics, in decreasing order of frequency (Johnson 1942, 148). He also noted that the majority of institutions "seem to regard Bible courses as the best introduction to religion" (149). Writing at the same time about a similar survey, Robert McEwen detected no significant evidence that "departments of Bible and religion are moving away from a Biblically-centered curriculum" in which the Bible provided material for understanding the nature of religion and for "the solving of pressing human problems" (McEwen 1942, 153). One teacher of New Testament provided a rationale for such a focus, contending that the teacher's goal "should not be primarily to study the religion of the New Testament as a social phenomenon of a specific period of history, but rather to present it as a vital and revolutionary factor in the life of man in every age. Nor is it to be taught solely as generic religion" (Brewer 1947, 211). Teachers of the Old Testament made similar claims (see Hazzard 1947, 207).

When the American Academy of Religion undertook a survey of 897 undergraduate programs in 2000, the results showed that teaching about the Bible was still a focal interest of undergraduate instruction about religion. Courses on Introduction to the Bible, Introduction to the New Testament, and Introduction to the Old Testament were three of the five most frequently offered, and together they constituted 29.5% of the total courses offered. When ethics was added, the total came either 35% to 38.4%, depending on whether a course was specifically identified as being devoted to Christian ethics (American Academy of Religion n.d., 66). Those results show substantial continuity from the 1930s to the 1990s, despite the growth in courses on Asian religions, among other topics.

Despite the heavy focus on the Bible and ethics, there were already signs in the 1930s that American colleges were "somewhat awake to their obligation of acquainting the student with Asia" (Matthews 1936, 90). The growth in course offerings in Asian religions posed distinctive challenges to Bible instructors who had been drafted to offer courses on "Comparative Religion" or "World Religions." While leaving no doubt about where her own investments were lodged, Mary Frances Thelen, of Randolph-Macon College, suggested that "The great questions concerning nature, man, and God which are raised in Judaism and Christianity are asked in the other religions as well, and there may be a methodological gain in having the students and the teacher come to the New Testament answers after having wrestled together with a number of solutions" (Thelen 1952, 71). As Americans became more familiar with the diversity of religions in the world after World War II and increasingly aware of the diversity of religions within the United States, questions about how to apportion the courses in a departmental curriculum became more acute. In the eyes of some professors the existing and, likely, growing interactions between Christianity and other religions made it imperative to offer courses on various religious traditions (see Buck 1957). Some even argued that the task of the historian of religions or professor of comparative religion "is not simply to dispense information about ancient systems but to open up avenues of creative interchange in the contemporary world as well" (Altizer and Buck 1964, 25). Others argued that the task of comparative religions was "to appraise all the religions equally so that, when it is all over, the student can make his own religious choice" (Walhout 1961, 49). In those constructions, the introduction of courses on Buddhism, Hinduism, Islam, and other religions besides Judaism and Christianity was still meant to serve either outright apologetic purposes, by strengthening the "New Testament answers" to perennial questions, or purposes of formation, by enabling students to make informed choices among the religions about which they learned. Even as the curriculum broadened, in many contexts teaching about religion retained a fundamentally religious purpose.

With the broadening of curricular offerings about religion also came questions of who would teach those courses. In keeping with the fundamentally religious orientation toward teaching about religions other than Judaism and Christianity, many departments subscribed to a "zoo theory" in making staffing decisions. Winston King, of Grinnell College, succinctly laid out the animating assumptions, asking, "how can one who himself knows nothing of religious experience in his own life feel any resonances, either sympathetic or intolerant, aroused by the religious experience of another." More pointedly, he asked, "Who better than a Muslim should be able to present the meaning of Islam?" (W. King 1964, 16). But that conception of populating a department with persons who taught only about "their own" religions also received sharp criticisms, not least for its undertones of advocacy. One critic wryly noted that "Universities do not customarily insist that only a Platonist can teach Platonism, or only a Marxist about Communism. Demonstrated learning in an area, and an imaginative openness to the import of its data, are what we look for in a university teacher" (Battenhouse 1967, 33).

The argument that religions must be taught by their partisans again brings to the surface two different conceptions of what teaching about religion in American higher education should be. Advocates of a fundamentally religious understanding of the task of teaching about religion, in this case frequently the promotion of interreligious understanding and dialogue, endorse the proposition that religiously committed individuals are best able to teach about their own traditions. Advocates of a nonreligious, scientific, or "objective" study of religion focus instead on the research and teaching credentials of a candidate no matter what personal commitments that person might have.

A 2008 report from the American Academy of Religion described the religion major as being "in flux" (American Academy of Religion 2008, 4). It noted that even at some religiously affiliated institutions the religion major was moving from being based on a "seminary model . . . in which courses in Bible, Christian history, and Christian doctrine are seen as primary and courses on other religions and aspects of religion are deemed secondary or even unnecessary" to a "comparative model . . . in which the focus is on promoting student understanding of the beliefs, practices, and histories of multiple religious traditions in a comparative context" (6). Despite its acknowledgment that "the tasks of defining the major and then assessing it represent continuing challenges across the discipline," the report nonetheless identifies a "strong and growing consensus" about the nature of the major in religious studies (6, 11). It lists the following emphases as characteristic of the religious studies major:

> It is intercultural and comparative, multidisciplinary, critical in both its analysis of the other and the self.
> It is integrative in its application of theoretical knowledge to concrete instances of lived religion.
> It is creative and constructive in using knowledge and skills from the study of religion to address multiple and social issues (11–12).

In their broadness, however, those characteristics admit of different, even contradictory, understandings of the purposes of teaching about religion.

One aspect of collegiate teaching about religion that has not received sufficient attention is the role it plays in various programs of general education. D. G. Hart has stressed that in the 1920s "The emergence of undergraduate courses in general education and western civilization was a remarkable blessing for the scholars who taught religion" (Hart 1999, 94). But that influx of students into religion courses also created a pedagogical challenge. Horace T. Houf, of Ohio University, acknowledged in 1938 that "The majority of our students will take one course only in religion or Bible" (Houf 1938, 16). Claude Welch affirmed in his survey of undergraduate teaching about religion in 1972 that "in all types of institutions, religion departments tend to be service departments, with the bulk of their enrollments coming in a few courses from students who take an elective or two out of general interest" (Welch 1972, 71). It is in such courses that fulfill general education or distribution requirements that the academic study of religion actually finds its largest audience. Far more people than read the typical monograph or refereed article populate introductory courses about religion term after term and year after year. The preponderance of students who will most likely be "one and done" raises acute questions about what such courses should be designed to accomplish.

The challenge is often depicted as constituting a choice between coverage and depth, but the goal of coverage can never really be accomplished. When the field of religion is conceived as including all religious traditions throughout history and across cultures, the futility of the notion of coverage becomes evident. For introductory courses, then, consequential choices must be made (Smith 2013a, 13). Intentionally or not, those choices will necessarily reflect a teacher's fundamental understandings of the nature and purpose of the academic study of religion, which, in turn, are communicated to students through the design and execution of the course. Consequently, introductory courses in the study of religion should be the objects of sustained and serious reflection, particularly as concrete instantiations of the scholarly enterprise of studying about religion. The extraordinary diversity of introductory courses about religion taught today suggests that the field remains divided about its first principles and thus about what constitutes an appropriate introduction to the study of religion (see Wabash Center 2015).

Directly related to that lack of consensus is the absence of agreement on what the structure of the major should be. In Claude Welch's 1972 report on the undergraduate major, Peter Slater contrasted his conception of the ideal structure of a major in religion to the actual disarray that he observed in the departments surveyed (Slater 1972, 34). Jonathan Z. Smith has extended that observation by contending that "most majors are incoherent," which at least puts the study of religion in the company of other disciplines (Smith 2013b, 114). In fact, curricular disarray appears at the introductory, intermediate, and advanced levels of course offerings about religion in American higher education. Just as there are typically multiple points of entry, there is a diverse array of intermediate courses that can be counted toward the major, and capstone experiences vary substantially from one department to another (see Upson-Saia 2013). While the American Academy of Religion's white paper saw signs of convergence on the "comparative model" for a religion curriculum, diversity remains the most significant factor.

TEACHER

Those who see teaching about religion as including character formation and moral instruction have often put the person of the professor to the forefront. Earl Cranston, of the University of Southern California, argued in 1949 that "the best teacher of religion is one who reveals personal convictions" (Cranston 1949, 112). Dwight Marion Beck, of Syracuse University, gave the adage "good teaching comes from good teachers" a very specific meaning when he argued that "Teaching ability does not depend on ordination though without holiness can no man see true success in our work" (Beck 1949, 91, 93). That perspective resurfaces in the work of the widely influential Parker Palmer, who asserts that "we teach who we are" and urges teachers not only to cultivate but to share their interior lives with their students (Palmer 2007, 1). Palmer's writings about teaching have found a receptive audience in the Spirituality in Higher Education movement.

But other professors have offered distinctively different understandings of their roles in the classroom. In 1954 C. Milo Connick, of Whittier College, proposed the metaphor of the guide as a way of thinking about the role of the teacher. In a description that anticipates contemporary discussions of replacing the "sage on the stage" with the "guide on the side," Connick recommended that the teacher "along with the other students, becomes a co-seeker, a co-worker, a co-learner, and a co-finder" (Connick 1954, 111; see A. King 1993). Connick still adheres to the goal of character formation, including as one of his five objectives for the collegiate study of religion that students "should develop a lively concern for the well-being of their fellowmen," but he portrays himself as a co-investigator with his students rather than as a moral exemplar (Connick 1954, 110).

The idea that the teacher of religion should both declare his or her own religious sympathies and guide students to develop their own religious commitments has been contested at least since the Princeton University attempt to distinguish the study of religion from the practice of it. Amanda Porterfield cites some of the difficulties she perceives in teaching students to *be* religious. She contends that "When instructors make religious self-development part of academic work, the pedagogical logistics and problems of religious authority can create intellectual confusion" and "the instructor faces the problem of having to grade students on the basis of their religious performance" (Porterfield 2008, 190). As with other topics, there is currently a diverse and clashing array of opinions on what the proper role of the teacher is in college and university courses about religion.

CONCLUSION

From the outset, teaching about religion in American higher education has served fundamentally religious purposes, along with the allied goals of character formation and moral instruction. That emphasis continues today, and not only in religiously affiliated institutions. The institutional and curricular structures that direct students toward the study of religion sometimes explicitly and often more dimly reflect the conception that learning about religion is, somehow, good for college students. Some professors, too, believe that the nurturing of religious sensibilities is within their purview. On the other hand, for nearly a century there has been a vigorous attempt to establish the study and teaching of religion on a firm and equal footing among the humanities and social sciences in the contemporary university and to banish from its precincts any taint of advocacy. The position one takes on the fundamental purpose of teaching about religion has multiple consequences for conceiving the role of the professor; course and curriculum design; assessment; the roles which self-disclosure, both by teachers and students, can play in the classroom; and many other pedagogical topics. The diversity of institutions offering instruction about religion in American higher education itself guarantees that consensus on any of those topics is unlikely to be reached. But the factors are not just institutional: individual teachers, even within departments, can, and often do, have very different conceptions of what teaching about religion entails. While there may be some signs of convergence on a comparative model for the religion department curriculum, that model will continue to be adapted to diverse purposes.

FUTURE DIRECTIONS

1. What is the proper role of the study of religion in an undergraduate education, particularly in a program of general education?
2. What is the ideal structure of an undergraduate major in the study of religion?
3. What would be the ideal structure and content of an introductory course in the study of religion?
4. What are the appropriate roles of a teacher's own religious convictions, or lack thereof, in teaching about religion in colleges and universities?
5. Similarly, what are the appropriate roles of students' religious convictions, or lack thereof, in the religious studies classroom?
6. What ideally constitutes religious literacy?

REFERENCES

Adams, David E. 1937. "Notes on Curriculum." *Journal of Bible and Religion* 5, no. 4 (October–December): 178–180.

Altizer, Thomas J. J., & Harry M. Buck 1964. "Two Comments on Professor King's Article." *Journal of Bible and Religion* 32, no. 1 (January): 23–25.

American Academy of Religion. n.d. "Survey of Undergraduate Religion and Theology Programs in the U.S. and Canada: Further Data Analysis, Summary of Results." Available at https://www.aarweb.org/sites/default/files/pdfs/Programs_Services/Survey_Data/Undergraduate/dataanalysis-20040309.pdf; accessed December 23, 2014.

———. 2008. "The Religious Studies Major in a Post-9/11 World: New Challenges, New Opportunities." Available at https://www.aarweb.org/sites/default/files/pdfs/About/Committees/AcademicRelations/Teagle_WhitePaper.pdf; accessed December 23, 2014.

American Association of Colleges and Universities. 2007. *College Learning for the New Global Century*. Available at http://www.aacu.org/sites/default/files/files/LEAP/GlobalCentury_final.pdf; accessed December 23, 2014.

Astin, Alexander W., Helen S. Astin, and Jennifer Lindholm 2010. "Overall Findings: A National Study of Spirituality in Higher Education: Students' Search for Meaning and Purpose." Available at http://spirituality.ucla.edu/findings/; accessed December 23, 2014.

Battenhouse, Roy W. 1967. "A Strategy and Some Tactics for Teaching in Religion." In *Religious Studies in Public Universities*, edited by Milton D. McLean, 29–34. Carbondale: Southern Illinois University Press.

Beck, Dwight M. 1947. "A Freshman Course in Religion." *Journal of Bible and Religion* 15, no. 1 (January): 50–52.

———. 1949. "The Teacher of Religion in Higher Education." *Journal of Bible and Religion* 17, no. 2 (April): 91–97.

Brautigam, Herman A. 1941. "The Curriculum of Religion at Colgate." *Journal of Bible and Religion* 9, no. 3 (August): 162–166.

Brewer, Raymond R. 1947. "Conduct Objectives in Teaching the New Testament." *Journal of Bible and Religion* 15, no. 4 (October): 210–214.

Buck, Harry M. Jr., 1957. "Teaching the History of Religions." *Journal of Bible and Religion* 25, no. 4 (October): 279–286.

Connick, C. Milo. 1954. "Achieving Religious Objectives." *Journal of Bible and Religion* 22, no. 2 (April): 110–112.

Cranston, Earl. 1949. "And Gladly Teach Religion." *Journal of Bible and Religion* 17, no. 2 (April): 112–115.

DeBoer, Lawrence. 1964. "Seminary and University: Two Approaches to Theology and Religion." *Journal of Bible and Religion* 32, no. 4 (October): 342–349.

Domm, Edward E. 1945. "Teaching Undergraduates." *Journal of Bible and Religion* 13, no. 3 (August): 155–157, 176.

Eckhardt, A. Roy. 1950. "Theological Presuppositions for an Introductory Course in Religion." *Journal of Bible and Religion* 18, no. 3 (July): 172–177.

Gallagher, Eugene V. 2009. "Teaching for Religious Literacy." *Teaching Theology and Religion* 12: 208–221.

Grace, Fran, ed. 2009. *Spirituality in Higher Education: Problems, Practices, and Programs.* Special issue of *Religion and Education.*

———. 2011. "Learning as a Path, Not a Goal: Contemplative Pedagogy—Its Principles and Practices." *Teaching Theology and Religion* 14, no. 2 (April): 99–124.

Hart, D. G. 1999. *The University Gets Religion: Religious Studies in American Higher Education.* Baltimore: Johns Hopkins University Press.

Hazzard, Lowell B. 1947. "Conduct Objectives in Teaching the Old Testament." *Journal of Bible and Religion* 15, no. 4 (August): 206–209.

Hoppe, Sherry L. 2007. "Spirituality and Higher Education Leadership." In *Searching for Spirituality in Higher Education*, edited by Bruce W. Speck and Sherry L. Hoppe, 111–136. New York: Peter Lang.

Houf, Horace T. 1938. "A First Course in the Study of Religion." *Journal of Bible and Religion* 6, no. 1 (Winter): 16–17.

———. 1948. "A College Course in Life's Meaning." *Journal of Bible and Religion* 16, no. 3 (July): 147–150.

Johnson, Paul E. 1942. "College Courses in Religion." *Journal of Bible and Religion* 10, no. 3 (August): 147–150, 183–184.

King, Allison. 1993. "From Sage on the Stage to Guide on the Side." *College Teaching* 41, no. 1: 30–35.

King, Winston L. 1964. "Problems and Prospects in Teaching World Religions." *Journal of Bible and Religion* 32, no. 1 (January): 15–22.

Lakenan, Mary E. 1933. "Some Principles Governing the Formulation of a College Bible Curriculum." *Journal of the National Association of Biblical Instructors* 1, no. 1: 15–17.

Matthews, Charles D. 1936. "A Curriculum for a Department of Religion." *Journal of the National Association of Bible Instructors* 4, no. 2: 89–92.

McEwen, Robert W. 1942. "A Study of Objectives Published in College Catalogs." *Journal of Bible and Religion* 10, no. 3 (August): 152–153.

Meland, Bernard Eugene. 1937. "The Study of Religion in a Liberal Arts College." *Journal of Bible and Religion* 5, no. 2 (April–June 1937): 62–69.

Michaelson, Robert. 1965. *The Study of Religion in American Universities: Ten Case Studies with Special Reference to State Universities*. New Haven, CT: The Society for Religion in Higher Education.

Nord, Warren A. 2008. "Taking Religion Seriously in Public Universities." In *The American University in a Postsecular Age*, edited by Douglas Jacobsen and Rhonda Hustedt Jacobsen, 167–185. New York: Oxford University Press.

Palmer, Parker J. 2007. *The Courage to Teach: Exploring the Inner Landscape of a Teacher's Life.* San Francisco: Jossey-Bass.

Porterfield, Amanda. 2008. "Religious Pluralism, the Study of Religion, and 'Postsecular' Culture." In *The American University in a Postsecular Age*, edited by Douglas Jacobsen and Rhonda Hustedt Jacobsen, 187–201. New York, NY: Oxford University Press.

Prothero, Stephen. 2007. *Religious Literacy: What Every American Needs to Know—and Doesn't.* San Francisco: HarperCollins.

Quillian, William F. 1950. "Teaching the Religiously Indifferent." *Journal of Bible and Religion* 18, no. 2 (April): 110–114.

Sharpe, Eric J. 1988. "Religious Studies, the Humanities, and the History of Ideas." *Soundings: An Interdisciplinary Journal* 7, no. 2/3: 245–258.

Slater, Peter. 1972. "Religion as an Academic Discipline." In Claude Welch, *Religion in the Undergraduate Curriculum: An Analysis and Interpretation*, 26–36. Washington, DC: Association of American Colleges.

Smith, Jonathan Z. 2013a. "The Introductory Course: Less is Better." In *On Teaching Religion: Essays by Jonathan Z. Smith*, edited by Christopher I. Lehrich, 11–19. New York: Oxford University Press.

———. 2013b. "Why the College Major." In *On Teaching Religion: Essays by Jonathan Z. Smith*, edited by Christopher I. Lehrich, 111–118. New York, NY: Oxford University Press.

Thelen, Mary Frances. 1952. "The Biblical Instructor and Comparative Religion." *Journal of Bible and Religion* 20, no. 2 (April): 71–76.

Thelin, John R. 2004. *A History of American Higher Education*. Baltimore: Johns Hopkins Press.

Upson-Saia, Kristi 2013. "The Capstone Experience for the Religious Studies Major." *Teaching Theology and Religion* 16, no. 1, 3–17.

Wabash Center for Teaching and Learning in Theology and Religion. 2015. Syllabus Collection. Available at http://www.wabashcenter.wabash.edu/resources/guide-syllabi.aspx; accessed January 1, 2015.

Walhout, Donald. 1961. "Ought the Teacher Judge Other Religions?" *Journal of Bible and Religion* 29, no. 1 (January): 48–51.

Walvoord, Barbara. 2008. *Teaching and Learning in College Introductory Religion Courses*. Oxford: Blackwell.

Welch, Claude. 1972. *Religion in the Undergraduate Curriculum: An Analysis and Interpretation*. Washington, DC: Association of American Colleges.

Wilson, John F. 1970. "Introduction: The Background and Present Context of the Study of Religion in Colleges and Universities." In *The Study of Religion in Colleges and Universities*, 3–21. Princeton, NJ: Princeton University Press.

CHAPTER 29

....

TEACHING ABOUT RELIGION OUTSIDE OF RELIGIOUS STUDIES

....

ROBERT J. NASH

INTRODUCTION

....

> How are we as a community, dedicated to pluralism, to find room for the different values and moral perspectives of different people and different groups? How, that is, are we to respect *particularism*? . . . How can we as a community, made up of diverse individuals and groups, find a way to transcend those differences in order to reach consensus on some matters of common human welfare? How, that is, are we to respect *universalism*?
>
> —Daniel Callahan (2000, 44)

As a nonreligious studies professor in a career-focused professional college—a college of education and social services—I have long held that the undergraduate and graduate students who come to my classes need to understand, and embrace, pluralism of every type in the work that they will do in both the public and private sectors. Like Daniel Callahan, whose epigraph leads off this section, I maintain that, in the end, what we are about as educators, regardless of our specializations, is to help our constituencies to understand, and to respect, both particularism and universalism. In today's complex world of difference, there is simply no other way for all of us to coexist without destroying one another.

What all of my pre-professional and professional students have in common is that whether they are public school teachers or public school administrators, social workers, health care professionals, higher education administrators, law enforcement officials, or a variety of other helping professionals who provide service, they all see themselves as *educators* in some way. And because they are educators in a number of venues, they serve diverse audiences of every race, ethnic group, social class, and worldview. So, too, my students have to confront the reality and the inevitable conflicts that are the result of religio-spiritual difference in all these venues. And, yet, when I first started teaching at the college level, I did not find a single course on religious pluralism anywhere in the United States that existed outside of a religious studies department or a school of divinity. I have been an interdisciplinary professor of educational studies for almost fifty years, and I have frequently wondered why educators take the challenges of cultural, social class, gender, and racial identity difference more seriously than religio-spiritual difference.

And, so, three decades ago, I decided to create an applied course for professional educators called "Religion, Spirituality, and Education." It is still going strong, and it is one of the most popular elective courses in my professional college. Few of my students through the years have been religious studies majors or, for that matter, have ever taken a course in religious studies. I, myself, only after a quarter of a century teaching foundations courses in education went back to earn a graduate degree in religious studies. Ironically, in trying to construct my new course, I had no model for such an experiment anywhere in the country to guide me. In fact, my course, which has now served thousands of students through the decades, was the very first offering of its kind in the United States. Since the origins of this course, I have written, spoken, and taught for decades to professional audiences throughout the country on the importance of understanding, and encouraging, religious pluralism (Nash 1997, 2001, 2002; Nash and Bishop 2005, 2010).

WHY AN UNDERSTANDING OF RELIGIOUS PLURALISM IS NECESSARY FOR EVERYONE

My disciplinary background is in applied philosophy, cultural anthropology, and educational theory, but philosophy of religion has always been a primary intellectual interest of mine. I am also a postmodern pluralist in all matters philosophical, political, and religious. In this chapter, I want to propose that before college and university administrators, as well as educators in every human service setting, can do anything worthwhile about dealing with the conflicts all too frequently ignited by cultural differences, they need to understand the complex nature of religious pluralism. My contention is that *religious pluralism, if left unattended, is a phenomenon that in the future will threaten to divide students, faculty, and administrators in a way that makes all the other campus, and off-campus, divisions look tame by comparison. In fact, unattended religious illiteracy throughout the world is worsening, and in its wake are the violent atrocities that make daily headlines in all the media.*

Even now, on many US campuses, members of minority religious groups are asserting their rights to autonomy, and, in some cases, complete separation. Many Eastern religious groups demand their own faith centers instead of having to worship in formerly Christian chapels. Muslim students are angry because they do not have a prayer space of their own. They are tired of sharing space with Christians or Jews. They want prayer rugs, not pews. So, too, Buddhists want a separate location for a meditation room. Jews want their own chapel sites complete with Torah scrolls. On some Catholic campuses, representatives of non-Christian religions are insisting on autonomous spaces for the full expression of their own devotions. In fact, several groups of evangelical Christians in secular universities are feeling ghettoized because their own worship areas are contracting in size, given the escalating demands for space by other religious groups (Kazanjian and Lawrence 2000).

My assumption is that unless these separate groups are able to come together to communicate openly in designated, multifaith spaces, then religious balkanization, and the triumphalism and suspicion of others that are its inevitable byproducts, will sooner or later threaten to fragment entire campuses. Since the immigration boom of the 1960s, for example, there are at present 5 to 6 million Muslims, 3 to 5 million Buddhists, and 1.5 to 2 million Hindus in the United States (see the Pluralism Project at Harvard University 1997–2018 [pluralism.org] for the latest statistics). Their numbers are continuing to grow dramatically, and their children have reached college age. Also, the number of evangelical Christians has increased almost exponentially, not just in the United States but throughout the world, constituting in some parts of the globe one-fourth of the adult population (Smith 1995). The real pluralism on college campuses today, and increasingly in every organization throughout the world, is religious, and this phenomenon presents us with an educational opportunity that is unique. Left untapped and misunderstood, the phenomenon can only bring us unmitigated grief.

I make the following pluralistic assumptions about the need to foster an understanding of spiritual self-awareness and religious difference in schools, colleges, and secular organizations beyond the more conventional, highly specialized, religious courses of study.

First, most Americans know very little about the topics of religion and spirituality, even though they might have lots of uninformed opinions that they present as fact. This type of illiteracy is unacceptable in a twenty-first-century, multifaith, multireligious, global community (Prothero 2008).

Second, educators in all settings need to reexamine their own, latent biases both for and against organized religion and private spirituality, because, often, these invisible biases can come across in harmful ways to many believers, nonbelievers, and seekers. These three groups tend to take religion and spirituality very seriously. This self-examination process, although difficult and time-consuming, is key to working with, and understanding, others. Its importance cannot be underestimated. I often refer to this content more holistically as *religio-spiritual*, because it is intellectually unfeasible to separate out religion from spirituality and vice versa.

Third, I believe it is crucial, particularly in higher education, for all of us to think about the role that the study of religion and spirituality plays in the education of college and university students in secular and sectarian venues. Educators in both public and private schools at all levels must think seriously and systematically about the risks and benefits, the disadvantages and advantages, of dealing with such sensitive material. To ignore issues of religion and spirituality in the twenty-first century is to miss what is vitally important to educators everywhere, given all of their diverse clienteles (Nash and Eugenio 2012).

The very popular dichotomy that I hear often on and off campus is one that my students make between religion and spirituality. Unfortunately, this dichotomy represents an unstated bias against organized religion and a bias in favor of private spirituality. I have heard the following clichéd refrain from my students for several years: "I'm spiritual, not religious," as if the former is intrinsically superior to the latter. Throughout most of human history, this type of assertion would simply be unintelligible, because, absent the formal beliefs and practices of a variety of organized religions, spirituality would have had no intrinsic (or extrinsic) meaning for billions of believers. Billions of believers would have considered spirituality alone to be both ephemeral and groundless, because it would have been cut off at its roots.

Fourth, it is important for all of us in higher education, and in all other public service settings, to learn how to talk respectfully and compassionately with one another about a topic that, throughout history, has caused as much pain, suffering, and division as it has comfort, joy, and reconciliation (Nash and Bishop 2005).

Fifth, if faculty members truly want to diversify their formal and informal curricula in academia, regardless of students' major or minor choices of study, then we must respect all kinds of difference, including religious and spiritual difference. This will necessitate a radical revisioning of the nature and content of diversity education. Multiculturalism, diversity, and pluralism represent incomplete ideals unless they include religio-spiritual diversity (and nonbelief diversity as well), along with all of the other worthwhile types of cultural differences. In the twenty-first century, religio-spiritual identity is the core identity of billions of people on this planet.

The Need for Unbounded Versus Bounded Discourse

It is important to state an important pedagogical and professional premise that underlies my teaching about religious difference. Because I do not teach religious studies majors or minors, and because almost all of my students have never taken a single course in religious studies, I need to emphasize in my one-semester course what I call "process knowledge" even more than "content knowledge." *How* I and my students *process* religious material is at least as important as the *content* being processed. My students need to understand the basics of religious content to be sure, but, professionally, they must know how to facilitate unbounded dialogue about a very controversial topic between and among disparate groups and individuals. Helping them learn to do this in one semester can be a very challenging endeavor, but it is an extremely worthwhile one.

Before the pluralistic dialogue can begin in earnest, however, it must become "un-bounded." Stephen Carter introduces a concept he calls "bounded discourse." Bounded discourse—"[deliberately constructing] an arena in which some ideas can be debated and others cannot"—systematically excludes religious ideas from so many disciplines, sites, and practices both on and off campus (Carter 1998, 134). On campus, for example, too many benevolent, liberal academicians and professional practitioners believe that students' religious and spiritual inclinations are best left to the private sphere of life. This automatically rules out of bounds any public conversation about these issues that makes students feel uncomfortable.

While I certainly concur with Carter's insights regarding "bounded discourse," I my-self prefer the term *dialogue* to *discourse*. Dialogue, according to *Webster's New World College Dictionary*, third edition, means having a conversation that is open and frank with the goal of seeking mutual understanding. Dialogue, like Socrates' dialectic, though not as formal, suggests a going back and forth in frank discussion and inter-change, asking questions and searching for the nugget of truth in each other's ideas. It connotes a genuine conversational encounter. Discourse, on the other hand, according to *Webster's*, is less to and fro, and more of a straightforward presentation of ideas in a discussion. Most of the humanities and social science disciplines are taught in the spirit of discourse rather than dialogue, and this is entirely appropriate most of the time. This is what happens in courses that emphasize content knowledge. Discourse in the disciplines still connotes a long, formal treatment of an issue, mainly in the form of a lec-ture, treatise, or dissertation. In principle, I have nothing against this usage, but, for my purposes in trying to encourage open and honest, dialectical conversations about reli-gion on a college campus, I like the notion of dialogue as opposed to discourse.

Thus, what Carter is charging is that whether in the classroom, counseling center, campus coffeehouse, advising office, or residence hall, we consciously or unconsciously "take off the table" what truly matters to many students: *their heartfelt search for religious and spiritual meaning*. The unintended, but no less tragic, result is that in academicians' calculated efforts to "bound discourse" about religion, we severely narrow our mission, along with our effectiveness, as dialogue exponents. Worse, we relegate religion to the nether regions of the private realm where it is not allowed to enter the public arena in any full, rich way. Consequently, the religious voices of our students disappear from public view. Furthermore, Callahan's concerns in the excerpt at the beginning of this chapter notwithstanding, the prospects for "harmonization" of what is *particular* and what is *universal* in religious experience grows more and more unlikely. The robust, plu-ralistic dialogue necessary to examine and understand religious difference and com-monality never gets off the ground.

Callahan wonders how a community can respect genuine differences in values and moral perspectives and still find a way to transcend those differences in order to reach consensus on "some matters of common human welfare." The dilemma for any com-munity, in his view, is to find a way to resolve the conflict between "particularism" and "universalism," a "fight" he wants, at the very worst, to end in a "draw." So do I. This has been the pivotal challenge for college and university communities, of course, in matters of race, class, gender, and sexual orientation. However, the religious implications of this challenge have gone largely unexplored at the present time.

In my own professorial experience, I cannot begin to recount the number of orthodox Christian students—fundamentalists, Pentecostalists, evangelicals, and charismatics—who have complained to me over the years of the derision and sarcasm they experience both in the classroom and in the residence hall. For them, there is neither intellectual nor religious freedom at their universities; there is only the open disdain aimed at their religiosity that forces them to retreat even further into their sectarian groups. It is mainly there that they are able to seek the consolation and strength they need to sustain them in the battles ahead.

Unhappily, I have heard a plethora of such horror stories from undergraduates and graduate students in my own university and throughout the country. Many have seriously considered leaving higher education due to the searing religious ridicule they believe they have received. Even sadder, few have had the courage to take their complaints to a higher university authority, for fear that they would not be taken seriously. One woman on my own campus, a born-again Baptist, who did manage to graduate *summa cum laude*, tearfully recounted to me that in a large science lecture hall during her first year on campus, a professor, who imperiously introduced himself to the class as a "scientist" and an "evolutionist," proceeded throughout the semester to make snide comments about "dumb-amentalist [sic] Christians." Frequently in his lectures, this professor stereotyped all fundamentalists as "Creationists," "zealots," and "intellectual imposters." When in private she confronted him with these cruel and mistaken epithets, he told her he was only "teasing" and said to "lighten up" because he was not referring to her.

CREATING AN ETHIC OF RELIGIOUS DIALOGUE

By way of summary, how then should college and university administrators and educators respond to what is a long-overdue need for us to learn how to talk openly and honestly about religion and spirituality in the academy? How do we begin to participate in "unbounded" religious dialogue? Or is it more desirable for us to relinquish any responsibility by asserting that these "sectarian" matters be contained strictly within the provinces of the human wellness center, the counseling center, campus ministry, the religious studies department, or InterVarsity Christian Fellowship, Hillel, and the Newman Center?

For starters, I assiduously reject the suggestion that we ought to relegate religious dialogue to any number of isolated sectarian enclaves. I believe it is precisely during those times when students pursue meaning outside of religiously designated safety zones that they experience the most compelling learnings, as do others who might initially have been critics or skeptics. We must be willing and able to let students know that whenever and wherever issues of religious and spiritual meaning arise for them, we are ready to respond thoughtfully and knowledgeably, just as we would when racial, gender, and sexual orientation issues arise. We will never arbitrarily rule these questions out of bounds just because they make us nervous, or because we claim to know little about them, or because we ourselves might be harboring stubborn, anti-religious stereotypes that embarrass us.

Moreover, fearless, open-ended, intellectually stimulating, cross-campus dialogue about religio-spirituality is what liberal education ought to be about. Religion has been such a fundamental component of life in all cultures and times that students cannot understand the history, politics, or art of most societies, including the United States, without examining religion's central role in producing both good and evil during the last three millennia. Also, a genuine liberal education requires an in-depth study of religious influences on all the major university disciplines, including the humanities, social sciences, and sciences. Absent this study, students get only half the story of human knowledge, thereby rendering their education as decidedly illiberal.

Finally, because the study of religion is one of the primary tools for making meaning, perforce it must play a key role in any examination of morality, ethics, and the formation of character. Despite claims to the contrary, certain traditional religious virtues (e.g., faith, hope, love, piety, compassion, sacrifice, forgiveness, obedience, self-respect) still have considerable value in secular pluralist societies. Many students consider a purely secularized morality to be foundationless and arbitrary, hence relativistic. Thus, to confine the dialogue on religio-spirituality either to the religious studies department or to designated safety zones is not only to favor (and to protect) secular moral standpoints in the university; in fact, in the words of Warren Nord, it is to prevent all students from coming to terms with the tensions in their lives between "tradition and modernity, community and individualism, consensus and pluralism, faith and reason, and religion and secularity" (Nord 1995, 380).

The *first step* in opening the dialogue is for us to listen intently and nondefensively and to respond in a spirit of active engagement whenever the topic of religion comes up. This approach conveys the unmistakable message to the entire campus that students, faculty, and staff have a right to be heard on religious matters. They do not need to restrict the pursuit of meaning to the goings-on in churches, synagogues, mosques, shrines, temples, or meditation rooms. Free speech on a college campus should be alive and well in all areas of human interest and conviction, including the religious. We should encourage and respond to it, anywhere and everywhere.

The *second step*, in Diana Eck's view, and in my own as well, is that all of us have a mutual obligation, in the interests of academic integrity, to listen critically and, whenever appropriate, to change or modify our own, previous positions on these topics, given the intellectual and emotional force of what we hear (Eck 1993). We expect this outcome, for example, in political, economic, philosophical, and educational conversations in the seminar and lecture hall; why not in religio-spiritual conversations? Anything less than this potentially self-transforming response on our part trivializes, and, worse, consigns to the outer regions of academic dialogue the deepest convictions that indelibly shape the lives of millions of students everywhere.

It goes without saying that this kind of unbounded religious dialogue throughout the academy will be very difficult to achieve. I offer no simplistic answers. In fact, I readily acknowledge that such a dialogue might finally be unachievable, although I will not stop my efforts to encourage it. While, at times, the subject matter may indeed be too hot to handle, given the long history in this culture of maintaining an unbridgeable wall of separation between church and state, I am optimistic. Furthermore, even though my own pedagogical failures in mastering this kind of unbounded religious dialogue both in and outside the classroom are legion, I am continuing to learn how to do it better. I am working hard to locate the religio-spiritual common ground that we all share in class, without being reluctant also to identify the irreconcilable differences that separate us.

I am striving diligently to encourage open, candid, considerate, and critical dialogue among the believers and disbelievers in my classroom and throughout the campus. I am struggling to do this in a way that recognizes the irreducible diversity of each of these, at times cacophonous, religious voices. In addition, I am trying to do this without inadvertently imposing an intellectual uniformity or, worse, a religiously correct blandness on my students. This imposition only guarantees the mind-numbing, soul-killing repression that I find intellectually unacceptable in so many politically correct universities and colleges. I am convinced that consideration for others and passionate conviction are not mutually exclusive. In fact, the former makes it safe to express the latter. I think of myself as both a particularist and a universalist, and, like Daniel Callahan, I want all sides in the religious conversation to get their due, with none being privileged as the *a priori* victor.

The *third step* is to construct what Nicholas Wolterstorff calls an "ethics" of dialogue:

> Thou must not take cheap shots. Thou must not sit in judgment until thou hast done thy best to understand. Thou must earn thy right to disagree. Thou must conduct thyself as if [Moses, Buddha, Confucius, Jesus, Mohammed, Pope John Paul II, Bishop John Shelby Spong, or Pat Robertson (brackets added)] were sitting across the table—the point being that it is much more difficult (I don't say impossible) to dishonor someone to his face. (1988, 150)

If Wolterstorff is right, then ethical dialogue on religion needs to be grounded in the virtues of compassion, generosity, candor, and intellectual integrity. An ethic of religious dialogue ought to begin with the principle that, at all times, one needs to refrain from going on the attack. It must proceed to the principle that a genuine attempt to understand another's religious views must always be a prerequisite for critique and judgment of those views. Honest disagreement is a right to be earned, rather than an entitlement to be expected; and one earns this right by demonstrating the capacity to honor, rather than dishonor, a competing point of view, even while challenging it.

The hardest task for me as a teacher is to enlarge the conversational space—to construct an unbounded-dialogue region—about religion in and out of the classroom without asking adherents of the various religious and nonreligious narratives to bracket their own strong beliefs. The most devastating criticism from students that I sometimes hear is the one that accuses me of enticing them to engage in a "postmodern" dialogue about religion that (wittingly or unwittingly) forces them to voluntarily annihilate a significant piece of themselves in the search for common religious ground—absent all the sectarian particulars.

These students resent what they consider to be my transparent attempts to smuggle my own postmodern preferences for plurality, tolerance, religious equivalence, and what one student called my "narrative-reductionism" into my teaching. They want me to be more honest and upfront about my biases. They demand that I include a personal truth-in-packaging statement in my syllabus at the beginning of my course. They want this in the interests of candor and fairness, so that they are better able to give full, informed consent to taking my course at the very outset. I am only too happy to oblige them.

The *fourth step*, therefore, in encouraging unbounded religious dialogue on college campuses is to start the conversation with candid, personal disclosures on everybody's part concerning where they currently stand on their religio-spiritual journeys and where they would like to end up. Putting our religio-spiritual cards on the table early is a good way to set the stage for enlarging the conversational space for everyone.

Implications for a Cross-Campus Pedagogy of Spiritual Meaning-Making

I begin these final two sections with a series of personal questions for readers to consider:

Why do you think students attend college? Is it only to earn a career credential? Why did we, as faculty or staff, want, or, indeed, complete, the college journey ourselves? How many of us can remember filling out those personal essay questions and reading intently the individual requirements and university goals and mission statements for our respective campuses? What drew us in? What did we choose to include, and exclude, in our personal statement of purpose?

How did we make meaning in our lives then and now? Did the self-narrative we composed in that application, and the mission our alma mater stood for, hold true for us throughout the years? Did we seem to find a new sense of self, and were any of our most challenging life questions approached in the classroom or even referenced in the readings or in the interactions we had with faculty and staff? Were there times when we hoped that the classroom, and the college setting as a whole, might help us to strengthen our self-confidence by allowing us to explore, and create, our own narratives of spiritual meaning?

What concerns us most today about creating, and delivering, a cross-campus pedagogy of spirituality in the educational work that we do?

(These questions were originally asked by Monique Swaby, a former student of mine as
well as a co-teacher of the religion course and a co-author.)

It is safe to say that conversations around students' spirituality in secular universities
and colleges are mostly experienced outside the classroom—in the dorms, in student
advocacy services and departments, in the dining halls, in campus ministry offices, or,
sadly, nowhere at all. This is not good enough. We must begin to expand our minds
around what it means for students to be in meaning-making classrooms and, conversely,
what it means for our students to live and learn in an environment that suffocates and
kills the soul's development. This spiritual abandonment is symptomatic of a long, lonely
journey already compounded by many other roadblocks that students must face during
one of the most crucial foundational periods in their lives. We want our students to be
able to define what their spirituality means by creating a free and open space for them to
inhale, and exhale, the breath of meaning across campus.

I believe strongly that the deepest places where one's spirituality comes from are rooted in
love, compassion, service to others, forgiveness, understanding, social activism, patience,
making deeper, emotional contact with one another, and learning how to live peacefully
and harmoniously in pluralistic communities of difference. If we are willing to focus on
the relevance of our students' spiritual quests in discussions both inside and outside the
classroom, then perhaps we can begin to open a deep-learning dialogue with them before
it is too late. On a college campus, there are so many faith-based, or faith-absent, identities,
whether openly disclosed or not, that characterize members of all groups on a campus. We
believe that it is in the best interest of our universities and colleges to make room not only
for the more conventional, and approved, multicultural conversations among a diverse student body, but also for the open expression of spiritual and religious beliefs. This, for us, is a
genuine, multi-identitied approach to discussions of social justice, pluralism, and diversity.

RECOMMENDATIONS FOR COLLEGE EDUCATORS

I am guided throughout this last section by the wise words of the author, educator, and
activist Parker J. Palmer:

> By this understanding, the spirituality of education is not about dictating ends. It is
> about examining and clarifying the inner sources of teaching and learning, ridding
> us of the toxins that poison our hearts and minds. For example, an authentic spiritu-
> ality of education will address the fear that so often permeates and destroys teaching
> and learning. It will understand that fear, not ignorance, is the enemy of learning,

and fear is what gives ignorance its power. It will try to root out our fear of having our ignorance exposed and our orthodoxies challenged—whether those orthodoxies are religious or secular. A spirituality of education will ground us in the confidence that our search for truth, and truth's search for us, can lead to a new life beyond the death of our half-truths and narrow concepts. (Palmer 2007, xi)

In the spirit of Palmer's sage wisdom, here are some tools that I have employed in my own pedagogy in order to create, and foster, a spirituality of teaching and learning in my college classroom that I hope with transfer to other professional venues for my non-religious studies colleagues as well as for my undergraduate and graduate students who are studying to become human service professionals. Thus, I present a series of general recommendations that I hope all faculty and staff will consider.[1]

Examine the Subtext

Take a pedagogical risk and undertake a closer, subtextual examination of the subject matter you are teaching. What exactly are your goals for selecting, and teaching, the subject matter? What message are you trying to send to your students that may not be implicit in the subject matter itself? How can you reconfigure your subject matter to get beyond the mere presentation, and testing, of information and the cultivation of specific career skillsets? How can you present your subject matter so that students can deepen, enlarge, and expand their multilayered search for truth?

Form a Conversation Circle

If you can, form a circle of conversation with yourself and your students. Talk *with* your students, not *at* them, as often as possible. Everyone in the spirituality learning circle needs to be equally seen and heard. As a teacher, you cannot arbitrarily separate yourself from your conversation circle's process and content. In fact, at times you must be at the forefront of self-disclosure in order to gain your students' trust. You need to learn how to *disclose* rather than *impose* and *depose*. You must be open to mistakes, and misunderstandings, both for yourself and for your students. There are no definitive, right or wrong answers in the process of teaching, and learning, about spirituality; there are only questions. No conversation ever ends; it only stops for a while, to be continued at another time. No religio-spiritual narrative is ever finally and fully formed; instead, it keeps on developing throughout a person's lifetime.

Create a Safe Space

Begin to create a safe space for your students to ask the deeper questions and to make the soulful connections between the subject matter, career preparation, and their personal pursuit of meaning and purpose. Allow for facilitated moral conversation by building trust—by ensuring the confidentiality of names and stories in students' spiritual disclosures that may be directly linked to someone known, and by fostering genuine honesty and respect for varied opinions. A pedagogy of spirituality cannot take the form of a debate. You need to be an advocate (*advocare, L.* someone who *calls to* others, not someone who *calls out* others) for each and every student regardless of his or her religio-spiritual orthodoxies or unorthodoxies.

Exemplify Openness and Flexibility

You will need to *exemplify* a pedagogy of openness and flexibility in your practice all the while you are attempting to *explicate* your subject matter. Draw out your students' belief stories in reference to spirituality. Find out what gives their lives meaning. Be generous in your willingness to help them see the connections between the subject matter you are teaching and their pursuit of spiritual meaning. If you begin to get stuck, evoke ideas and suggestions from students about what they would like to happen in classroom conversations, and how and why studying this subject might bring more meaning into their lives. If given the opportunity, students can be incredibly insightful about what they need from their teachers.

For example, if a student is studying, or majoring in, business, education, psychology, astronomy, or chemistry, you could ask what draws them into these courses of study. Do they have a personal story—such as having lived through a relative's risky venture into creating a small business, or tutored children in a local school or day-care center, or witnessed first-hand a death, or serious illness, in the family, or dealt with a mental disability in the life of someone they love, or marveled at observing a shooting star as a child, or been captivated by the way the body works. Too often we give our students important technical subject matter and vocabulary, relevant facts and data, and significant statistical knowledge, without asking them to think more deeply about how the information in a particular course will touch their lives long after they have finished taking the tests, have earned their diplomas, and have entered long-awaited careers and professions.

Help Students to Reflect

Experiment with helping students to reflect on the deeper meanings, and origins, of the subject matter you are teaching them. This can happen most naturally in the humanities, of course, because so many of these disciplines are grounded in a variety of reflective responses to the perennial enigmas of the human condition. It is more difficult, but not impossible, to do deep meaning analysis if you are a scientist, for example, teaching such *natural sciences* as evolutionary biology or cellular biology within the framework of a so-called *objective* scientific method.

As a scientist, give yourself permission to do some pedagogical experimentation. Step outside the objectivist worldview at least occasionally. Encourage students to reflect on the sheer wonder, and pleasure, of knowing the human body—how it works, its home-ostatic flow, the creation and recreation of cellular elements from old to new, what the possible genesis, and ultimate goals, of such elements might be, and what philosophical or religio-spiritual connections these might have to the more data-based content of the disciplines that students are studying. In some profound sense, as Einstein himself pointed out, every scientific discipline, no matter how objective and rational, contains confounding mysteries that can be approached only by imagining, and creating, meta-scientific hypotheses to explain them. For example, get students to formulate their own imaginative, leap-of-faith hypotheses of origins and destinies that might transcend the conventional, methodological mandates and assumptions of each of the scientific disciplines.

In another cognate area—the *social sciences*—encourage students to explore how a wide range of social scientists differ in their understanding of a topic like human consciousness. Help them to reflect on why there seems to be a universal human need to enlarge consciousness by looking for something larger than the self, in order to explain the unknown. Take time to help them delve deeply into the ontological and metaphysical questions that have remained unanswerable throughout human history. Why, despite our sophisticated social science research methodologies, epistemologies, and our advanced technological prowess, do our metaphysical questions persist? Why do they continue to *haunt*, at times even *taunt*, us? To what extent do our various tribes of social influence condition us to affirm, or deny, the religio-spiritual basis of our existence?

Similar issues can be raised in teaching the *arts* by exploring not only how artists depict their worlds through multiple mediums and styles, but also by examining what serves as the spark of inspiration in their own narratives of meaning—whether these be religio-spiritual, philosophical, literary, or even political. What are those unprovable, nonempirical background assumptions that inevitably influence their artistic expressions?

The subject matter of the *humanities* comes closest to getting at the deeper existential questions. We believe that one way to save the humanities in our career-driven higher education curricula is to convert humanistic study into a journey of spiritual meaning-making for our students. In the end, there is nothing more practical for helping our students to live the good, happy, and fulfilled life. In fact, we are convinced that all subject matter, no matter how diverse its methodologies, content, and goals, is a potential resource for making spiritual meaning in the teaching–learning venture.

FUTURE DIRECTIONS

1. How may disciplines outside religious studies prepare future faculty to address issues of religion and spirituality in their higher education classrooms?
2. What new tools and strategies need to be developed to facilitate classroom discussion relating to religious and spiritual dimensions of disciplinary issues?

3. How might faculty from disciplines other than religious studies or theology collaborate with religious studies faculty to develop a deep religious literacy in their respective disciplines?

NOTE

1. A version of these tools appeared in Nash and Swaby (2011). I develop at length all of these teaching tools in Nash, Bradley and Chickering (2008), Nash and Murray (2009), Nash and Swaby (2011), and Nash and Jang (2015).

REFERENCES

Callahan, Daniel. 2000. "Universalism & Particularism: Fighting to a Draw." *Hastings Center Report* 30, no. 1: 37–44.

Carter, Stephen L. 1998. *Civility: Manners, Morals, and the Etiquette of Democracy*. New York: Basic Books.

Eck, Diana. 1993. *Encountering God: A Spiritual Journey from Bozeman to Banaras*. Boston: Beacon Press.

Kazanjian, Victor H., and Laurence, Peter L., eds. 2000. *Education As Transformation: Religious Pluralism, Spirituality, and a New Vision for Higher Education in America*. New York: Peter Lang.

Nash, Robert J. 1997. *Faith, Hype and Clarity: Teaching About Religion in American Schools and Colleges*. New York: Teachers College Press, Columbia University.

———. 2001. *Religious Pluralism in the Academy: Opening the Dialogue*. New York: Peter Lang Publishing.

———. 2002. *Spirituality, Ethics, Religion, and Teaching: A Professor's Journey*. New York: Peter Lang Publishing.

Nash, Robert J., and Bishop, Penny A. 2005. "Teaching Adolescents about Religious Pluralism in a Post-9/11 World." *Religion & Education* 33, no. 1: 31–53.

———. 2010. *Teaching Adolescents Religious Literacy in a Post-9/11 World*. Charlotte, NC: Information Age Publications.

Nash, Robert J., DeMethra L. Bradley, and Arthur W. Chickering. 2008. *How To Talk about Hot Topics on Campus: From Polarization to Moral Conversation*. San Francisco: Jossey-Bass.

Nash, Robert J., and Vanessa Santos Eugenio. 2012. "Teaching about Religious and Spiritual Difference in a Global Society." In *Transforming Learning Environments Strategies to Shape the Next Generation*, edited by Fayneese Miller, 47–64. New York: Emerald Group Publishing.

Nash, Robert J., and Jennifer J. J. Jang. 2015. *Preparing Students for Life Beyond College: A Meaning-Centered Vision for Holistic Teaching and Learning*. New York: Routledge.

Nash, Robert J., and Michele C. Murray. 2009. *Helping College Students Find Purpose: The Campus Guide to Meaning-Making*. San Francisco: Jossey-Bass.

Nash, Robert J., and Monique Swaby. 2011. "Helping College Students Discover Meaning through Spirituality." In *Spirituality in Higher Education,* edited by Heewon Chang and Darrell Boyd., 111–126. San Francisco: Left Coast Press.

Nord, Warren A. 1995. *Religion and American Education: Rethinking a National Dilemma.* Chapel Hill: University of North Carolina Press.

Palmer, Parker J. 2007. *The Courage To Teach: Exploring the Inner Landscape of a Teacher's Life.* San Francisco: Jossey-Bass.

Pluralism Project at Harvard University 1997–2018. pluralism.org.

Prothero, Stephen. 2008. *Religious Literacy: What Every American Needs To Know—And Doesn't.* New York: HarperOne.

Smith, Jonathan Z., ed. 1995. *The HarperCollins Dictionary of Religion.* San Francisco: HarperCollins.

Wolterstorff, Nicholas. 1988. *Reason Within the Bounds of Religion.* New York: Wm. B. Eerdmans Publishing Co.

CHAPTER 30

....

CAMPUS MINISTRY

....

JOHN A. SCHMALZBAUER

INTRODUCTION

....

WHEN the Reverend William Sloane Coffin, Jr. died in 2006, he was celebrated as one of the last great prophets of postwar mainline Protestantism. During his tenure at Yale University, Coffin was also the best-known chaplain in the United States. Though raised an establishment WASP, he was a passionate advocate for civil rights and an out-spoken critic of the Vietnam War. Educated at Union Theological Seminary and Yale Divinity School, Coffin received the best theological training possible in his era. Joining the Freedom Riders for a trip through the South in 1961, he was later convicted for promoting draft evasion among Yale's students. Through his highly public fights for social justice and peace, Coffin popularized the image of the chaplain as social activist. The model for the Rev. W. S. Sloan, Jr. in Garry Trudeau's *Doonesbury*, he epitomized chaplaincy in the 1960s (Goldstein 2004).

We live in a different era. Reflecting larger shifts in American culture and religion, today's campus ministers are beginning to look less like Coffin and more like Carolyn Cruz (a pseudonym). The daughter of immigrants, Cruz is assistant director of campus ministry at a large Jesuit university. She is also a layperson. Trained at a Jesuit seminary, Cruz has mastered the rubrics and rituals of the liturgical calendar. In fact, she may know them better than the Jesuit priests at her institution—an old joke among liturgists speaks of being as lost as a Jesuit during Holy Week. Reflecting her theological training and liturgical duties, her office contains such books as *Feminist Theology and the Body* and *Penitential Services*. It also includes a quote from Pedro Arrupe, the Superior General of the Jesuits from 1965 to 1983: "Nothing is more practical than finding God . . . Fall in love, stay in love, and it will decide everything." Cruz is clearly in love with Jesuit spirituality. As she puts it, "I believe I have the Jesuit charism," adding, "if I were a man, I would be a Jesuit." In her words, "I had a moment in which Jesus told me to follow him and take nothing."

The National Study
of Campus Ministries

How has campus ministry changed since Coffin's era? Who are Christian campus ministers today? Not since the late 1960s has there been a large national survey of campus ministers. Reflecting dramatic shifts in American culture, they differ markedly from their counterparts in previous generations.

Drawing on the National Study of Campus Ministries (NSCM), this chapter discusses the life and work of campus ministers, incorporating material from earlier stages of the project (DeBerg, Schmalzbauer, and Ehlinger 2007; DeBerg, Schmalzbauer, and Ehlinger 2008; Schmalzbauer 2014). For practical reasons, the NSCM focused exclusively on Christian campus ministries. Conducted between 2002 and 2008 by Betty DeBerg and John Schmalzbauer, it surveyed staff in six denominations, two parachurch groups, and eighty-eight private colleges. The survey portion of the study achieved a response rate of 44 percent, with 1,659 out of 3,788 individuals responding. The denominational campus ministries selected for inclusion in the survey were the Assemblies of God, Evangelical Lutheran Church in America, Presbyterian Church (USA), Roman Catholic Church, Southern Baptist Convention (SBC), and the United Methodist Church. The two parachurch organizations were the Fellowship of Christian Athletes and InterVarsity Christian Fellowship. The study also employed in-depth interviews with eighty private college chaplains and one-week site visits to a dozen campus ministries (college chaplains were not included in this chapter's comparisons of Catholic, Mainline Protestant, and Conservative Protestant campus ministers).

The literature on religion and higher education contains few large-scale studies of campus ministers. The most recent works focus on students more than religious workers (Astin, Astin, and Lindholm 2011), utilize qualitative rather than quantitative methodologies (Dutton 2008; Kim 2006), or look at a single religious tradition rather than a cross-section of campus groups (Bramadat 2000; *Ministry on Campus* 1977). While books like *Religion on Campus* (Cherry, DeBerg, and Porterfield 2001) explore the texture of undergraduate religious life, they do not offer a quantitative portrait of campus ministers. Published during the mid-century campus revival, the most comprehensive studies were conducted between 1930 and 1970, including Clarence Shedd's *The Church Follows Its Students* (1938), Seymour Smith's *The American College Chaplaincy* (1954), Phillip Hammond's *The Campus Clergyman* (1966), and Kenneth Underwood's *The Church, The University, and Social Policy* (1969). For the purposes of comparison, this chapter will contrast the NSCM with these earlier works. It will also draw on recent scholarship on Catholic and Protestant clergy (perhaps the best-developed literature on religious professionals), especially the Pulpit and Pew survey of 1,231 solo and senior pastors (Carroll 2006). The goal is to describe how campus ministry has changed and to compare campus ministers with their counterparts in the parish.

SHIFTING DEMOGRAPHICS: FEMINIZATION, DIVERSIFICATION, AND LAICIZATION

When Coffin served as Yale University chaplain, campus ministry was an overwhelmingly white, male, and clerical occupation. In the midst of Coffin's tenure, Phillip Hammond published *The Campus Clergyman* (1966), a book whose very title assumed this demographic profile. In the 1960s, few laypersons, women, or people of color worked as Protestant campus ministers. Out of Hammond's 997 respondents, 87% were ordained, 92% were male, 94% were white, and 75% were married with children (Hammond n.d.). This picture was virtually unchanged from Shedd's (1938) study of denominational campus ministers and Smith's (1954) study of college and university chaplains. While a Methodist university pastor told Shedd (1938, 271) it was important for campus pastors to have "the right kind of a wife," Smith (1954, 105, 121) unreflectively titled one chapter, "The Chaplain: His Other Responsibilities," noting that "[i]f one dared draw a picture of the average chaplain he would be a man less than 40 years of age, married, with two children probably under 10 years of age." As recently as 1977, a denominational report noted that the "typical United Methodist campus minister . . . is a white married male, in his forties" (*Ministry on Campus* 1977, 27).

In sharp contrast to the "campus clergyman" of 1966, the NSCM revealed a profession that is 44% female, 14% nonwhite, and 60% lay. Of all of these demographic changes, the increased presence of women constitutes one of the most striking shifts. In large measure, it reflects the growing number of women seminarians and a surge in lay ministry. Currently, women constitute 43% of the enrollment in American seminaries and divinity schools (*Student Information Project* 2014). More egalitarian than the local parish, campus ministry has a higher proportion of women in leadership than do American congregations. In the Pulpit and Pew survey of Christian clergy, women made up just 11% of senior and solo pastors (Carroll 2006, 274). By contrast, 37% of the campus program directors surveyed by the NSCM were female. In all three traditions (Roman Catholic, mainline Protestant, and conservative Protestant), the representation of women in leadership was larger on campus than in the local congregations surveyed by Pulpit and Pew (congregational figures in Table 30.1 originally reported in Carroll 2006, 67).

The women in the sample spoke eloquently about their experiences in a field where men continue to enjoy a majority. Reflecting on her status in an all-male organization, a Catholic college chaplain noted that her campus was still "a great place to be in spite of the difficulties of being the lone lay woman on a campus that expects me to be the 'voice' of Catholic identity." A staff worker for InterVarsity Christian Fellowship said she gets to "do a lot of things with IVCF that other campus groups and evangelical churches wouldn't let me do because I am a woman." As the first woman to head her institution's chapel, another respondent remembered "struggling with the role of women in the

Table 30.1 Senior Women as Congregation Ministers vs. Campus Ministry
Directors

	Catholic	Mainline Protestant	Conservative Protestant
Campus Ministry Directors	42%	39%	28%
Congregation Ministers	0%	20%	1%

Catholic church." While employed in a tradition that ordains women, a mainline Protestant expressed similar concerns, noting that "there's still a gender bias."

Other respondents lamented the persistence of racial tensions, acknowledging that "the challenges of multi-ethnicity are very difficult." While diversity is on the rise, campus ministers remain relatively homogeneous. In his 1963 survey, Hammond (n.d.) found that 94% of campus ministers were white, with only 4% identifying as African-American and 1% as other. Today whites make up 86% of the profession, with 4% identifying as black or African-American, 4% as Asian or Pacific Islanders, and 3% as Hispanic or Latino. The most diverse campus ministers can be found in the evangelical parachurch groups and the United Methodist Church. In the words of a parachurch staff worker, "I've never learned so much about justice and diversity as I have with InterVarsity." In the NSCM, 21% of parachurch and 17% of Methodist respondents identified as nonwhite.

Along with feminization and diversification, the profession has undergone a process of laicization. In the NSCM, 60% of respondents identified as laypersons, a substantial increase from previous generations. In 1963 lay campus ministers represented just 13% of the profession (Hammond n.d.). Though nonordained secretaries played a central role in the early twentieth-century YMCA, the "Y" had all but disappeared from campus ministry by the time of Hammond's study (Setran 2007). That year InterVarsity employed just fifty-eight field staff and fifty support personnel (Hunt and Hunt 1991, 398), while Campus Crusade for Christ (now known as Cru) was equally insignificant (Quebedeaux 1979). Fifty years later, lay-led evangelical groups are some of the largest student religious organizations in America. Today's evangelical parachurch ministry is a radically lay endeavor: at the time of the survey, only 9% of parachurch respondents were ordained clergy.

Roman Catholic campus ministry has experienced a similar shift in the ratio of clergy to laypersons. While the field has been dominated by priests, women religious (who are laypersons) have a long history in campus ministry. Published in 1970, *The Sister as Campus Minister* noted that "a new role for women has not only taken root but is enjoying rapid growth" (Davis 1970, 1). At the time, 124 sisters worked in campus ministry (29), making up about 6% of the 1,450 chaplains affiliated with the Newman Movement (Newman statistic taken from Evans 1980, 167). In the National Study of Campus Ministries, approximately one-fifth of Catholic campus ministers were lay members of religious orders. Reflecting further laicization, over half of Catholic respondents came from outside the ranks of priests, nuns, or brothers. Even among campus program directors, just 36% were priests. This trend parallels a shift in the parish, where women have taken on more responsibility. In *They Call Her Pastor*, Ruth Wallace (1992) documented the growth of female lay pastoral administrators, a trend that can also be seen on campus: in 2006 laywomen (including women religious) made up 42% of Catholic campus ministry program directors and 51% of head chaplains at Catholic colleges (for more on church-related college chaplains, see Schmalzbauer, 2014).

Mainline Protestant campus ministry is the only sector of the profession that continues to be dominated by clergy. In the NSCM, 78% of mainline Protestant campus ministers were ordained clergy. Though mainline Protestant campus ministry has incorporated more women, it has not been laicized.

EDUCATION AND TRAINING: POPULISTS AND PROFESSIONALS ON CAMPUS

Closely related to the question of clergy and lay status is the issue of education and training. As E. Brooks Holifield (2007, 103) documents in *God's Ambassadors*, the history of clergy in America reveals a tension between *professional* and *populist* models of ministry. While some traditions stress the value of an educated ministry, others eschew academic training. Well into the twentieth century, many Protestant clergy lacked a theological education: as recently as 1968, only 52% of fully ordained Methodists and 36% of Southern Baptists had earned seminary degrees (Holifield 2007, 245). Historically, campus ministers have been more educated than parish clergy. In 1938 58% reported holding a theological degree (Shedd 1938, 246–247). In 1963 Hammond (n.d.) found that 67% had earned a degree in religion or theology. Four decades later, the NSCM revealed a highly educated profession: of the total sample, 76% had at least some graduate or professional education. In particular, directors of campus ministry programs compared favorably with the senior and solo congregational ministers surveyed by Pulpit and Pew. While 73% of campus ministry program directors had earned a graduate or professional degree, only 60% of congregational ministers had done so (Carroll 2006, 274–275). While most campus ministers reported having a graduate or professional degree, a significant minority (29%) had no academic training in religion. By far the lowest levels of theological education could be found among respondents from parachurch ministries, 68% of whom reported no background in theology.

Over 70% of the sample had some specialized training in campus ministry. Despite this statistic, many felt unprepared for their jobs. According to one respondent, "There is a great need for formal training for directors of campus ministry." Some ministries reported less training than others. While 49% of college chaplains and 64% of denominational campus ministers had received training in campus ministry, 91% of parachurch staff reported some kind of preparation.

To a large extent, campus ministers have reproduced two different models of ministerial education, the seminary and the Bible training school. While mainline Protestants and Catholics have relied on the academic and spiritual formation found in denominational seminaries, evangelical Protestants have a long tradition of ministry training programs (see Foster et al. 2006). Instead of attending a theological seminary, most parachurch workers attend workshops and learn on the job. A minority participate in seminary extension programs or seated classes.

MISSION AND GOALS: ALL THINGS TO ALL PEOPLE

In his history of the American clergy, Holifield (2007, 328) notes that "ministerial duties were not as well defined as those of other professions." As one pastor put it, "You don't know the meaning of variety until you've been a pastor" (quoted in Holifield 2007, 333). The same has been true for campus ministers. Paraphrasing St. Paul, the Methodist theologian Albert Outler declared that the college chaplain "must be all things to all men in order that by one means or another he might save some" (quoted in Smith 1954, 46). Since its origins in the late nineteenth century, the profession of campus ministry has embraced a wide variety of goals. Founded in 1913, the first Wesley Foundation served as a "shrine for worship," "home away from home," and "recruiting station for the ministry" (Wesley Foundation quoted in Shedd 1938, 125). Four decades later, Smith (1954, 46–47) wrote that there are "few professional people on the academic or religious scene who are called upon to perform as many different roles as the chaplain," adding that "[h]e is a preacher, teacher, counselor, and pastor; a leader of group activities, both religious and secular; a public relations agent; and a conference speaker. He is a member of the faculty and an adviser in administrative circles, yet he is a confidant and intimate friend of students." In *The Campus Clergyman*, Hammond (1966, 20) noted that "expectations of what the campus minister shall do are not shared to any great degree." If anything, these goals have multiplied since 1966.

Probing the priorities of twenty-first-century campus ministers, the NSCM asked respondents to indicate their top three goals on a rather long list (Table 30.2). Their most common choices were to facilitate the spiritual formation of students; bring students to Christ; equip students to minister to their peers; help students to integrate faith and learning; provide worship and sacraments; and foster a commitment to social justice. Only the first goal was selected by at least half of the sample, indicating there is no agreement on the goals of campus ministry; instead, there are clusters of 20% to 45% who endorse each goal. These relatively low percentages do not indicate a lack of importance for a particular goal; rather, they indicate that campus ministers have adopted different conceptions of their profession. Like hospital chaplains, some have been religious "jack-of-all-trades." This lack of a clear jurisdiction has made it more difficult to professionalize campus ministry (DeVries, Berlinger, and Cadge 2008, 25).

Table 30.2 Top Three Goals of Campus Ministers

Facilitate the spiritual formation of students	50%
Bring students to Christ	46%
Equip students to minister to their peers	32%
Help students integrate faith and learning	25%
Provide worship or sacraments	23%
Foster a commitment to social justice	22%
Create a community that respects and appreciates diversity	20%
Identify and nurture tomorrow's church leaders	13%
Encourage student involvement in missionary work and outreach	12%
Help students discern their vocations	11%
Make Christianity relevant to postmodern culture	11%
Provide Bible study or religious education	10%
Give students a home away from home	8%
Provide pastoral care or psychological counselling	5%
Serve as pastor to the entire campus	5%
Engage in interfaith dialogue with religions outside Christianity	3%
Articulate the religious identity of your college or university	1%
Encourage ecumenical fellowship with other Christian denominations	1%
Provide crisis intervention on campus	<1%
Protect students from atheistic or secular influences on campus	<1%
Acquaint students with local church opportunities	<1%
Maintain the denominational loyalties of students	<1%
Participate in university or college decision-making	<1%

Reflecting the closest thing campus ministers have to a consensus, 50% of respondents selected spiritual formation as a top three goal. This focus could be found across theological traditions. What explains this strong emphasis on personal spirituality? Although the words "spiritual" and "spirituality" did not appear in Hammond's *The Campus Clergyman* (1966), changes in American religion have influenced the priorities of college chaplains. In *After Heaven*, Robert Wuthnow (1998, 16) charts the rise of "practice-oriented spirituality" in American society. While Leigh Schmidt (2005) has traced the influence of Quaker spirituality on mainline Protestants, Robert Webber (1999) has chronicled the retrieval of Roman Catholic and Eastern Orthodox practices among evangelicals. Anticipating the spiritual turn on campus, Howard Thurman's *Disciplines of the Spirit* (1963) drew on his experiences as an African-American chaplain at Boston and Howard universities. A protégé of the Quaker mystic Rufus Jones, Thurman (1963, 9) emphasized the "raw materials of daily experience." In the 1970s, the Episcopal campus minister Myron Bloy (1972) celebrated the "new spiritual quest." During the early 1980s, "spiritual formation became the new in-word" at InterVarsity (Hunt and Hunt 1991, 368). Likewise, a 1980 report on Catholic campus ministries noted that a "spiritual journey hallmarks the lives of many persons" (*National Survey of Campus Ministries* 1980, 17). A quarter-century later, the NSCM has uncovered a strong focus on student spirituality.

Along with spiritual formation, three other student-centered goals were near the top of the list: bring students to Christ (46%), equip students to minister to their peers (32%), and help students to integrate faith and learning (25%). The first two were especially popular among evangelicals. While 83% of conservative Protestant campus ministers ranked bringing students to Christ as a top three goal, 61% prioritized peer ministry. In the words of an evangelical respondent, "[E]vangelism and discipleship are important."

Connecting religion and social change, many have embraced a prophetic view of their profession. According to one campus minister, "We try to live as members of the 'Beloved Community' taking inspiration from Dr. Martin Luther King, Jr." Such religious activism has a long history on campus. In the early twentieth century, the collegiate YMCA practiced "personal evangelism plus social evangelism" (Super 1922, 53; see Setran 2007). In the 1960s, college chaplains lent their support to the civil rights and antiwar movements. While Coffin modeled an activist style of chaplaincy, the landmark Danforth Study of Campus Ministry focused on "the church, the university, and social policy" (Underwood 1969). In the NSCM survey, 22% of all respondents listed fostering a commitment to social justice among their top goals. Not surprisingly, there were significant differences across religious traditions, with 39% of Roman Catholic, 18% of mainline Protestant, and 12% of conservative Protestant respondents putting it in the top three. Despite these differences, two-thirds of the total sample said that fostering social justice was a very important goal, including 58% of conservative Protestants.

Still others have emphasized the importance of cultural diversity. From the increased presence of ethnic minorities to the growth of religious pluralism, differences matter on college campuses. Reflecting on these concerns, Lucy Forster-Smith (2013, xvii) argues that "the rapidly evolving, multicultural, multifaith context" has changed the chaplain's role. Recognizing this reality, 20% of NSCM respondents ranked creating a community that respects and appreciates diversity among their top goals. On a Lutheran campus, the chaplain's office invites "students of non-Christian backgrounds to speak about their faith." At a Presbyterian institution, the Baha'i Students Association coexists with similar groups for Jewish and Muslim students. Embracing the new diversity, campus ministers have engaged in interfaith dialogue.

WHAT DO CAMPUS MINISTERS DO ALL WEEK? CORE MINISTRY TASKS AND JOB SATISFACTION

Even more than expressed goals, core job activities reveal what really matters in a profession. Studies of American clergy have identified several key tasks. Exploring "What do clergy do all week?" the Pulpit and Pew survey (McMillan n.d.) found that sermon and worship preparation, pastoral care, administration, and teaching occupied the vast majority of working hours. While one-third of clergy time was devoted to preaching and worship, pastoral care consumed one-fifth of the typical work week (McMillan, n.d.). And what do campus ministers do all week? The survey asked respondents to rate each in a list of twenty-five specific tasks on a scale from 1 ("not part of my job") to 4 ("a large part"). At the top of the list was socializing with students, followed by individual mentoring and spiritual direction, participating in a Bible study or small groups, and personal reflection and study (Table 30.3). Preaching ranked eleventh on the list, administration and staff supervision ranked eighth, and committee and staff meetings ranked fifth.

Historically, campus ministry has been a student-centered profession. A 1980 report from the US Catholic Conference noted that "[c]ounseling is the most prominent activity, followed by liturgy planning and visiting students" (*National Survey of Campus Ministries* 1980, 12). Along the same lines, a Methodist study found that 80% of chaplains spent more than 60% of their time with students (*Ministry on Campus* 1977, 51). Like their counterparts in the 1970s and 1980s, today's campus ministers spend a lot of time with undergraduates, devoting an average of 42% of their working hours to students.

Some in the sample reported a tension between helping students and attending to their other duties. Others said they felt overwhelmed. As one respondent put it, "Campus ministry is wonderful, but it can be draining because of the enormous needs students have, especially for someone to listen to them and to walk with them through their various life issues and crises." Commenting on the demands of the job, another said that "students need pastors/campus ministry staff to have time to sit and listen to them."

Despite these pressures, working with students is often the most rewarding part of the job. In the survey, campus ministers indicated which tasks they found most satisfying and dissatisfying (see Table 30.3). Not surprisingly, individual mentoring, coaching, or spiritual direction topped the list of most satisfying tasks, followed by participating in Bible studies or small groups, socializing with students, and going on student trips. Janitorial work, fundraising, and committee meetings ranked near the bottom. Asked what keeps them going in the ministry, respondents repeatedly cited their students. Describing the "energy and life from working with college students," one respondent said, "I enjoy watching them develop and grow into thoughtful adults who practice their faith." Another noted the "joy of learning with young adults."

Overall job satisfaction was quite high, with 82% describing themselves as satisfied. At the same time, only 34% were highly satisfied. Given the large number of solo campus ministers in the sample, it is not surprising that 31% felt lonely and isolated fairly or very often. This compares with just 17% of the solo and senior pastors surveyed by Pulpit and Pew (Carroll 2006, 268). In the words of one chaplain, "It's a tough job to do alone."

Table 30.3 Campus Ministry Tasks as Portion of Job and Satisfaction Ratings

Overall Portion of Job	Task as Portion of Job	Satisfaction with Task	Overall Satisfaction Rank of Task
1. Socializing with students	3.23	4.54	3
2. Individual mentoring/coaching/ spiritual direction	3.22	4.63	1
3. Participation in Bible study or small groups	3.04	4.57	2
4. Personal reflection and study	2.96	4.42	5
5. Committee or staff meetings	2.86	3.44	21
6. Pastoral care or psychological counseling	2.85	4.27	10
7. Worship or sacraments	2.76	4.36	8
8. Administration and staff supervision	2.73	3.51	20
9. Trips with students	2.71	4.52	4
10. Community outreach and involvement	2.61	4.06	12
11. Preaching	2.46	4.39	6
12. Public relations	2.44	3.57	18
13. Continuing education or training	2.33	4.09	11
14. Spending time with faculty and staff	2.24	4.02	13
15. Hospitality and food preparation	2.20	3.70	15
16. Campus-wide ceremonies or rituals	2.16	3.81	14
17. Fundraising for my own salary	2.16	2.90	24
18. Teaching in any other context [than for college credit]	2.16	4.34	9
19. Fundraising for programs	2.13	3.04	23
20. Denominational activities and relations	2.09	3.60	16
21. Participating in professional organizations	1.87	3.56	19
22. Consultation with college or university officers	1.83	3.57	17
23. Local board management and meetings	1.72	3.30	22
24. Building maintenance or janitorial work	1.38	2.72	25
25. Teaching college course for academic credit	1.33	4.38	7

CONCLUSION

What is the state of Christian campus ministry in the United States? Like many American congregations, it has experienced the processes of feminization, diversification, and laicization, though to an even greater extent than in the parish. A sharp contrast from the days of *The Campus Clergyman*, the profession employs a large number of women and laypersons.

In the 1960s, campus ministers emphasized a prophetic conception of their callings. While most remain committed to social justice, they are paying more attention to the inward journey. Such commitments parallel a rediscovery of spiritual practices in American culture. Missing from postwar studies of campus ministry, spiritual formation has become a central focus of today's collegiate ministers.

The greatest difference between campus ministers and their counterparts in the parish may be in the rhythms and routines of a typical day. Though preaching remains the most visible role for American clergy, it is less important on campus. Instead, socializing with students and personal mentoring constitute the work of campus ministry. Though committee meetings and administration demand many hours, more time is spent with students. In its emphasis on personal spirituality, face-to-face encounters, and religious diversity, campus ministry resembles hospital chaplaincy more than ordinary parish life (Cadge 2012).

Like hospital chaplains, campus ministers work in a challenging field with an ambiguous job description. Such ambiguity can make it harder for a profession to garner respect (DeVries, Berlinger, and Cadge 2008). This can lead to low morale. Although most are satisfied with their careers, some are not. Despite such complaints, the vast majority have found campus ministry to be a deeply rewarding profession. As one respondent put it, "My presence makes a difference in the lives of many students, as they live these years of tremendous growth and transformation." Focusing on personal mentoring, they remain deeply invested in the lives of American undergraduates. Accompanying them through their college years, campus ministers are also pilgrims on the way.

FUTURE DIRECTIONS

1. How do campus ministers deal with the challenges of a multireligious campus?
2. How did the Great Recession affect the finances of campus ministries in the United States?
3. How will campus nondiscrimination policies influence the future of campus ministry?
4. What do campus ministers mean by "spiritual formation" and "spirituality"?

References

Astin, A., H. Astin, and J. Lindholm. 2011. *Cultivating the Spirit: How College Can Enhance Students' Inner Lives*. San Francisco: Jossey-Bass.

Bloy, M., ed. 1972. *Search for the Sacred: The New Spiritual Quest*. New York: Seabury Press.

Bramadat, P. 2000. *The Church on the World's Turf: An Evangelical Christian Group at a Secular University*. New York: Oxford University Press.

Cadge, W. 2012. *Paging God: Religion in the Halls of Medicine*. Chicago: University of Chicago Press.

Carroll, J. 2006. *God's Potters: Pastoral Leadership and the Shaping of Congregation*. Grand Rapids, MI: Eerdmans.

Cherry, C., B. DeBerg, and A. Porterfield. 2001. *Religion on Campus*. Chapel Hill: University of North Carolina Press.

Davis, M. W. 1970. *The Sister as Campus Minister: A Survey-Study of the Religious Sister's Role and Status in the Campus Ministry*. Washington, DC: Center for Applied Research in the Apostolate.

DeBerg, B., with J. Schmalzbauer and S. Ehlinger. 2007. "Chaplains and Their Professional Lives: Survey Results." Presentation, Programs for the Theological Exploration of Vocation Final Conference, Indianapolis.

———. 2008. *National Study of Campus Ministries: A Report to Lilly Endowment*. Cedar Falls, IA: University of Northern Iowa, unpublished report.

DeVries, R., N. Berlinger, and W. Cadge. 2008. "Lost in Translation: Sociological Reflections on the Practice of Hospital Chaplaincy." *Hastings Center Report* 38, no. 6: 23–27.

Dutton, E. 2008. *Meeting Jesus at University: Rites of Passage and Student Evangelicals*. Hampshire, UK: Ashgate.

Evans, J. W. 1980. *The Newman Movement: Roman Catholics in American Higher Education, 1883–1971*. Notre Dame, IN: University of Notre Dame Press.

Forster-Smith, L., ed. 2013. *College & University Chaplaincy in the 21st Century: A Multifaith Look at the Practice of Ministry on Campuses Across America*. Woodstock, VT: SkyLight Paths Publishing.

Foster, C. R., L. Dahill, L. Golemon, and B. W. Tolentino. 2006. *Educating Clergy: Teaching Practices and Pastoral Imagination*. San Francisco: Jossey-Bass.

Goldstein, W. 2004. *William Sloane Coffin, Jr.: A Holy Impatience*. New Haven, CT: Yale University Press.

Hammond, P. 1966. *The Campus Clergyman*. New York: Basic Books.

———. n.d. *Code Book for Campus Ministry Project*. New Haven, CT: Unpublished manuscript, Yale University.

Holifield, E. B. 2007. *God's Ambassadors: A History of the Christian Clergy in America*. Grand Rapids, MI: Eerdmans.

Hunt, K., and G. Hunt. 1991. *The Story of InterVarsity Christian Fellowship, 1940–1990*. Downers Grove, IL: InterVarsity Press.

Kim, R. Y. 2006. *God's New Whiz Kids? Korean-American Evangelicals on Campus*. New York: New York University Press.

McMillan, B. n.d. "What Do Clergy Do All Week?" Durham, NC: Duke University, unpublished report.

Ministry on Campus: A United Methodist Mission Statement and Survey Report. 1977. Nashville, TN: National Commission on United Methodist Higher Education.

National Survey of Campus Ministries. 1980. Washington, DC: US Catholic Conference.

Quebedeaux, R. 1979. *I Found It! The Story of Bill Bright and Campus Crusade.* New York: Harper & Row.

Schmalzbauer, J. 2014. "The Evolving Role of the College and University Chaplaincy: Findings from a National Survey." Unpublished paper, NetVUE Chaplaincy Conference, Atlanta, GA.

Schmidt, L. 2005. *Restless Souls: The Making of American Spirituality.* New York: HarperCollins.

Setran, D. P. 2007. *The College "Y": Student Religion in the Era of Secularization.* New York: Palgrave Macmillan.

Shedd, C. 1938. *The Church Follows Its Students.* New Haven: CT: Yale University Press.

Smith, S. 1954. *The American College Chaplaincy.* New York: Association Press.

Student Information Project: Entering Student Questionnaire. 2014. Pittsburgh, PA: Association of Theological Schools.

Super, P. 1922. *What is the YMCA? A Study of the Essential Nature of the Young Men's Christian Association.* New York: Association Press.

Thurman, H. 1963. *Disciplines of the Spirit.* Richmond, IN: Friends United Press.

Underwood, K. 1969. *The Church, the University, and Social Policy: The Danforth Study of Campus Ministries.* Middletown, CT: Wesleyan University Press.

Wallace, R. 1992. *They Call Her Pastor: A New Role for Catholic Women.* Albany: SUNY Press.

Webber, R. 1999. *Ancient-Future Faith: Rethinking Evangelicalism for a Postmodern World.* Grand Rapids, MI: Baker Academic.

Wuthnow, R. 1998. *After Heaven: Spirituality in America Since the 1950s.* Berkeley: University of California Press.

FURTHER READING

Allen B., ed. 2014. *Campus Ministry Memoirs: The Way It Was, 1964–2014.* National Campus Ministry Association.

Mir, S. 2014. *Muslim American Women on Campus: Undergraduate Social Life and Identity.* Chapel Hill: University of North Carolina Press.

Portaro, S., and G. Peluso. 1993. *Inquiring and Discerning Hearts: Vocation and Ministry with Young Adults on Campus.* Atlanta: Scholars Press.

Rosen, M. I., and A. L. Sales. 2006. *The Remaking of Hillel: A Case Study on Leadership and Organizational Transformation.* Waltham, MA: Fisher-Bernstein Institute at Brandeis University.

Schmalzbauer, J. 2013. "Campus Religious Life in America: Revitalization and Renewal." *Society* 50, no. 2: 115–131.

Turner, J. G. 2008. *Bill Bright & Campus Crusade for Christ: The Renewal of Evangelicalism in Postwar America.* Chapel Hill: University of North Carolina Press.

INDEX

....

Page numbers followed by *f* and *t* indicate figures and tables. Numbers followed by n indicate notes.